Reading

Grade 2, Unit 6

Traditions

Scott
Foresman

scottforesman.com

Editorial Offices: Glenview, Illinois • Parsippany, New Jersey • New York, New York
Sales Offices: Boston, Massachusetts • Duluth, Georgia • Glenview, Illinois
Coppell, Texas • Sacramento, California • Mesa, Arizona

We dedicate Reading Street to

Peter Jovanovich.

His wisdom, courage,

and pass   *on*

are

Cover Scott Gustafson

About the Cover Artist

When Scott Gustafson was in grade school, he spent most of his spare time drawing pictures. Now he gets to make pictures for a living. Before he starts a painting, he photographs his family, pets, or friends posing as characters that will appear in the illustration. He then uses the photos to inspire the finished picture.

ISBN-13: 978-0-328-24372-3
ISBN-10:   0-328-24372-8

Copyright © 2008 Pearson Education, Inc.

All Rights Reserved. Printed in the United States of America. This publication is protected by Copyright, and permission should be obtained from the publisher prior to any prohibited reproduction, storage in a retrieval system, or transmission in any form by any means, electronic, mechanical, photocopying, recording, or likewise. For information regarding permission(s), write to: Permissions Department, Scott Foresman, 1900 East Lake Avenue, Glenview, Illinois 60025.

Many of the designations used by manufacturers and sellers to distinguish their products are claimed as trademarks. Where those designations appear in this book, and Scott Foresman was aware of a trademark claim, the designations have been printed with initial capitals and in cases of multiple usage have also been marked with either ® or ™ where they first appear.

2 3 4 5 6 7 8 9 10 V064 16 15 14 13 12 11 10 09 08 07
CC:N1

Reading STREET

Where the Love of Reading Begins

Reading Street Program Authors

Peter Afflerbach, Ph.D.
Professor, Department of
Curriculum and Instruction
University of Maryland at
College Park

Camille L.Z. Blachowicz, Ph.D.
Professor of Education
National-Louis University

Candy Dawson Boyd, Ph.D.
Professor, School of Education
Saint Mary's College of California

Wendy Cheyney, Ed.D.
Professor of Special Education
and Literacy, Florida
International University

Connie Juel, Ph.D.
Professor of Education, School of
Education, Stanford University

Edward J. Kame'enui, Ph.D.
Professor and Director, Institute for
the Development of Educational
Achievement, University of Oregon

Donald J. Leu, Ph.D.
John and Maria Neag Endowed
Chair in Literacy and Technology
University of Connecticut

Jeanne R. Paratore, Ed.D.
Associate Professor of Education
Department of Literacy
and Language Development
Boston University

P. David Pearson, Ph.D.
Professor and Dean,
Graduate School of Education
University of California, Berkeley

Sam L. Sebesta, Ed.D.
Professor Emeritus,
College of Education,
University of Washington, Seattle

Deborah Simmons, Ph.D.
Professor, College of Education
and Human Development
Texas A&M University
(Not pictured)

Sharon Vaughn, Ph.D.
H.E. Hartfelder/Southland
Corporation Regents Professor
University of Texas

Susan Watts-Taffe, Ph.D.
Independent Literacy Researcher
Cincinnati, Ohio

Karen Kring Wixson, Ph.D.
Professor of Education
University of Michigan

Components

Student Editions (1–6)

Teacher's Editions (PreK–6)

Assessment
Assessment Handbook (K–6)

Baseline Group Tests (K–6)

DIBELS™ Assessments (K–6)

ExamView® Test Generator CD-ROM (2–6)

Fresh Reads for Differentiated
Test Practice (1–6)

Online Success Tracker™ (K–6)*

Selection Tests Teacher's Manual (1–6)

Unit and End-of-Year
Benchmark Tests (K–6)

Leveled Readers
Concept Literacy Leveled Readers (K–1)

Independent Leveled Readers (K)

Kindergarten Student Readers (K)

Leveled Reader Teaching Guides (K–6)

Leveled Readers (1–6)

Listen to Me Readers (K)

Online Leveled Reader Database (K–6)*

Take-Home Leveled Readers (K–6)

Trade Books and Big Books
Big Books (PreK–2)

Read Aloud Trade Books (PreK–K)

Sing with Me Big Book (1–2)

Trade Book Library (1–6)

Decodable Readers
Decodable Readers (K–3)

Strategic Intervention
Decodable Readers (1–2)

Take-Home Decodable Readers (K–3)

Phonics and Word Study
Alphabet Cards in English and Spanish
(PreK–K)

Alphabet Chart in English and Spanish
(PreK–K)

Animal ABCs Activity Guide (K)

Finger Tracing Cards (PreK–K)

Patterns Book (PreK–K)

Phonics Activities CD-ROM (PreK–2)*

Phonics Activities Mats (K)

Phonics and Spelling Practice Book (1–3)

Phonics and Word-Building Board and Letters
(PreK–3)

Phonics Songs and Rhymes Audio CD (K–2)

Phonics Songs and Rhymes Flip Chart (K–2)

Picture Word Cards (PreK–K)

Plastic Letter Tiles (K)

Sound-Spelling Cards and Wall Charts (1–2)

Strategies for Word Analysis (4–6)

Word Study and Spelling Practice Book (4–6)

Language Arts
Daily Fix-It Transparencies (K–6)

Grammar & Writing Book and
Teacher's Annotated Edition, The (1–6)

Grammar and Writing Practice Book
and Teacher's Manual (1–6)

Grammar Transparencies (1–6)

Six-Trait Writing Posters (1–6)

Writing Kit (1–6)

Writing Rubrics and Anchor Papers (1–6)

Writing Transparencies (1–6)

Practice and
Additional Resources
AlphaBuddy Bear Puppet (K)

Alphasaurus Annie Puppet (PreK)

Amazing Words Posters (K–2)

Centers Survival Kit (PreK–6)

Graphic Organizer Book (2–6)

Graphic Organizer Flip Chart (K–1)

High-Frequency Word Cards (K)

Kindergarten Review (1)

Practice Book and Teacher's Manual (K–6)

Read Aloud Anthology (PreK–2)

Readers' Theater Anthology (K–6)

Research into Practice (K–6)

Retelling Cards (K–6)

Scott Foresman Research Base (K–6)

Skill Transparencies (2–6)

Songs and Rhymes Flip Chart (PreK)

Talk with Me, Sing with Me Chart (PreK–K)

Tested Vocabulary Cards (1–6)

Vocabulary Transparencies (1–2)

Welcome to Reading Street (PreK–1)

ELL
ELL and Transition Handbook (PreK–6)

ELL Comprehensive Kit (1–6)

ELL Posters (K–6)

ELL Readers (1–6)

ELL Teaching Guides (1–6)

Ten Important Sentences (1–6)

Digital Components
AudioText CDs (PreK–6)

Background Building Audio CDs (3–6)

ExamView® Test Generator
CD-ROM (2–6)

Online Lesson Planner (K–6)

Online New Literacies Activities (1–6)*

Online Professional Development (1–6)

Online Story Sort (K–6)*

Online Student Editions (1–6)*

Online Success Tracker™ (K–6)*

Online Teacher's Editions (PreK–6)

Phonics Activities CD-ROM (PreK–2)*

Phonics Songs and Rhymes
Audio CD (K–2)

Sing with Me/Background Building
Audio CDs (PreK–2)

Songs and Rhymes Audio CD (PreK)

My Sidewalks Early Reading
Intervention (K)

My Sidewalks Intensive Reading
Intervention (Levels A–E)

Reading Street for the Guided
Reading Teacher (1–6)

v

Grade 2
Priority Skills

Priority skills are the critical elements of reading—phonemic awareness, phonics, fluency, vocabulary, and text comprehension—as they are developed across and within grades to assure that instructional emphasis is placed on the right skills at the right time and to maintain a systematic sequence of skill instruction.

Key
- ● = Taught/Unit priority
- ◑ = Reviewed and practiced
- ○ = Integrated practice

	UNIT 1		UNIT 2	
	Weeks		Weeks	
	1–2	3–5	1–2	3–5
Phonemic Awareness	Appears in Strategic Intervention lessons (pp. DI•14–DI•64)			
Phonics				
Know letter-sound relationships	●	●	●	●
Blend sounds of letters to decode				
Consonants	●	◑	○	◑
Consonant blends and digraphs	●	●	◑	◑
Short Vowels	●	○	◑	◑
Long Vowels	●		◑	◑
r-Controlled Vowels			●	●
Vowel Digraphs				●
Diphthongs				
Other vowel patterns	●	◑	◑	○
Phonograms/word families	●	●	○	○
Decode words with common word parts				
Base words and inflected endings		●	◑	●
Contractions			●	◑
Compounds				
Suffixes and prefixes				
Blend syllables to decode multisyllabic words	○	○	●	●
Fluency				
Read aloud with accuracy, comprehension, and appropriate rate	●	●	●	○
Read aloud with expression		●	●	●
Attend to punctuation and use appropriate phrasing		●	●	●
Practice fluency in a variety of ways, including choral reading, paired reading, and repeated oral reading	●	●	●	●
Work toward appropriate fluency goals	50–60 WCPM	50–60 WCPM	58–68 WCPM	58–68 WCPM
Vocabulary				
Read high-frequency words and lesson vocabulary automatically	●	●	●	●
Develop vocabulary through direct instruction, concrete experiences, reading, and listening to text read aloud	●	●	●	●
Use word structure to figure out word meaning				
Use context clues to determine word meaning of unfamiliar words, multiple-meaning words, homonyms, homographs				●
Use grade-appropriate references sources to learn word meanings			●	○
Use new words in a variety of contexts	○	○	○	◑
Use graphic organizers to group, study, and retain vocabulary	●	●	●	●
Classify and categorize words				
Understand antonyms and synonyms		●		●
Examine word usage and effectiveness	●	●	●	●

	UNIT 3		UNIT 4		UNIT 5		UNIT 6	
	Weeks		**Weeks**		**Weeks**		**Weeks**	
	1–2	**3–5**	**1–2**	**3–5**	**1–2**	**3–5**	**1–2**	**3–5**
	●	●	●	●	◐	●	◐	○
	○	○	○	◑	○	●	○	○
	○	◑	○	◐	○	●	◐	◐
	◐	◐	◐	◑	○	○	○	◑
	◑	◑	◑	◑	◑	◐	○	◑
	◐	◐	○	○	○	○	○	○
	●	●	○	○	○	○	◑	○
				●	◐		○	○
	●	●	●	●	◐	●	◐	◑
	○	○	○	○	○	○	○	○
	◐	●	◑	○	◐	◐	●	◑
	○	○	○	○	○	○	●	◑
		◑	◑	○			◑	○
					●		◐	●
	●	●	●	◐	●	◑	●	●
	●	○	●	○	●	○	●	●
	●	●	○	●	●	●	○	○
	○	●	○	●	○	●	○	○
	●	●	●	●	●	●	●	●
	66–76 WCPM	**66–76** WCPM	**74–84** WCPM	**74–84** WCPM	**82–92** WCPM	**82–92** WCPM	**90–100** WCPM	**90–100** WCPM
	●	●	●	●	●	●	●	●
	●	●	●	●	●	●	●	●
				●	●	●	●	●
	○	○	●	●	●	○	●	●
	●	○	●	●	●	●	●	●
	○	○	○	○	○	●	○	○
	●	●	●	●	●	●	●	●
					●	●	◑	◑
	●	●	●	◑	○	○	◑	○
	●	○	○	○	○	○	○	●

Grade 2
Priority Skills

Key
- ● = Taught/Unit priority
- ◐ = Reviewed and practiced
- ○ = Integrated practice

Text Comprehension	UNIT 1 Weeks		UNIT 2 Weeks	
	1–2	3–5	1–2	3–5
Strategies				
Preview the text	○	○	○	○
Set and monitor purpose for reading	○	○	○	○
Activate and use prior knowledge			●	○
Make and confirm predictions	●	○	●	○
Monitor comprehension and use fix-up strategies		●	○	○
Use graphic organizers to focus on text structure, to represent relationships in text, or to summarize text	○	○	○	○
Answer questions	○	○	○	○
Generate questions				
Recognize text structure: story and informational	●	●	○	●
Summarize text by retelling stories or identifying main ideas	○	○	○	●
Visualize; use mental imagery				●
Make connections: text to self, text to text, text to world	○	○	○	○
Use parts of a book to locate information		●	●	○
Skills				
Author's purpose	◐	○	○	●
Cause and effect				
Compare and contrast		◐	○	○
Draw conclusions				●
Fact and opinion				
Graphic sources (charts, diagrams, graphs, maps, tables)			●	○
Main idea and supporting details	●	●	○	○
Realism/fantasy		●	●	◐
Sequence of events			●	●
Literary Elements				
Character (Recognize characters' traits, actions, feelings, and motives)	●	●	◐	○
Plot and plot structure				
Setting	●	●	◐	○
Theme				

UNIT 3		UNIT 4		UNIT 5		UNIT 6	
Weeks		Weeks		Weeks		Weeks	
1–2	3–5	1–2	3–5	1–2	3–5	1–2	3–5
○	○	○	○	○	○	○	○
○	○	○	○	○	○	○	○
○	○	○	○	○	●	○	●
○	●	○	○	○	○	○	○
○	●	○	○	○	●	●	○
○	○	○	●	●	○	○	●
○	○	○	○	○	●	○	○
		●	●	○	●	○	●
●	○	●	○	●	○	○	○
○	○	○	●	○	○	○	●
●	○	○	○	○	○	●	○
○	○	○	○	○	○	○	○
●	○	○	○	○	○	○	○
●	○	○	○	●	●	○	●
○	●	○	○	○	○	○	○
○	◐	○	◐	○	○	●	○
●	○	●	●	○	●	○	●
●	●	●	●	○	●	●	●
○	○	●	◐	●	○	◐	○
○	○	○	○	●	●	○	○
◐	○	○	○	●	◐	○	○
○	○	◐	◐	○	○	○	●
○	●	○	●	◐	●	○	●
○	○	◐	○	○	○	○	●
	●	○	●	◐	●	○	◐

You
Are
Here

Unit 6

Traditions

Unit 1

Exploration

Traditions

How are traditions and celebrations important to our lives?

Just Like Josh Gibson

Grandmama shares the tradition of American baseball.

REALISTIC FICTION

connect to SOCIAL STUDIES

Paired Selection

How Baseball Began

EXPOSITORY NONFICTION

Red, White, and Blue: The Story of the American Flag

Our nation's flag is a traditional symbol.

NARRATIVE NONFICTION

connect to SOCIAL STUDIES

Paired Selection

You're a Grand Old Flag

SONG

A Birthday Basket for Tía

Birthdays are an important family tradition.

REALISTIC FICTION

connect to SOCIAL STUDIES

Paired Selection

Family Traditions: Birthdays

ONLINE DIRECTORY

Cowboys

Cowboys are an American tradition.

NARRATIVE NONFICTION

connect to SOCIAL STUDIES

Paired Selection

Cowboy Gear

PICTURE ENCYCLOPEDIA

Jingle Dancer

Jenna participates in a Native American tradition.

REALISTIC FICTION

connect to SOCIAL STUDIES

Paired Selection

Celebrating the Buffalo Days

PHOTO ESSAY

Unit 6
Skills Overview

	Week 1	Week 2
	300–319 **Just Like Josh Gibson/** **How Baseball Began** REALISTIC FICTION	326–347 **Red, White, and Blue:** **The Story of the** **American Flag/** **You're a Grand Old Flag** NARRATIVE NONFICTION
Oral Language	*Why are sports important in our country?*	*What does our flag mean?*
Word Work — Phonics	T ⊙ Contractions T REVIEW Vowels *aw, au, augh, al*	T ⊙ Inflected Endings T REVIEW Contractions
Spelling	T Words with Contractions	T Words with Inflected Endings
Lesson Vocabulary	T *field, cheers, threw, sailed, plate, bases*	T *freedom, flag, stripes, stars, nick-names, birthday, America*
Reading — Comprehension	T ⊙ **Skill** Compare and Contrast ⊙ **Strategy** Visualize REVIEW **Skill** Fact and Opinion	T ⊙ **Skill** Fact and Opinion ⊙ **Strategy** Monitor and Fix Up: Reread REVIEW **Skill** Main Idea and Details
Vocabulary	**Skill** Multiple-Meaning Words; Homophones T **Strategy** Context Clues	**Skill** Compound Words T **Strategy** Word Structure
Fluency	Accuracy and Appropriate Pace	Read Silently with Fluency and Accuracy
Language Arts — Writing	**Weekly Writing** Research Report **Unit Process Writing**	**Weekly Writing** Research Report **Unit Process Writing**
Grammar	T Capital Letters	T Quotation Marks
Speaking, Listening, Viewing	Speak to Your Audience	Understand Nonverbal Cues
Research/Study Skills	Use People as Resources	Take Notes/Outline
Integrate Science and Social Studies Standards	*Time for* SOCIAL STUDIES American Heroes, History of Baseball, Cultural Traditions, Geography: Maps	*Time for* SOCIAL STUDIES American Heroes, American Revolution, Thirteen Colonies/States, U.S. Symbols, Holidays, Geography: Maps

⊙ Target Skill   T Tested Skill

How are traditions and celebrations important to our lives?

WEEK 3	WEEK 4	WEEK 5
354–373 **A Birthday Basket for Tía/ Family Traditions: Birthdays** — REALISTIC FICTION	380–405 **Cowboys/Cowboy Gear** — NARRATIVE NONFICTION	412–431 **Jingle Dancer/ Celebrating the Buffalo Days** — REALISTIC FICTION
Why are family celebrations special?	*Why should we learn about cowboys?*	*How do different people celebrate?*
T Syllables *-tion, -ture* **T** REVIEW Inflected Endings	**T** Suffixes *-ness, -less* **T** REVIEW Syllables *-tion, -ture*	**T** Prefixes *mis-, mid-* **T** REVIEW Suffixes *-ness, -less*
T Words with Syllables *-tion* and *-ture*	**T** Words with Suffixes *-ness* and *-less*	**T** Words with Prefixes *mis-* and *mid-*
T *present, aunt, basket, collects, bank, favorite*	**T** *cattle, trails, cowboy, herd, campfire, railroad, galloped*	**T** *clattering, jingles, drum, voice, borrow, silver*
T **Skill** Draw Conclusions **Strategy** Summarize REVIEW **Skill** Cause and Effect	**T** **Skill** Cause and Effect **Strategy** Graphic Organizer REVIEW **Skill** Fact and Opinion	**T** **Skill** Character, Setting, Plot **Strategy** Prior Knowledge REVIEW **Skill** Cause and Effect
Skill Homonyms; Words from Other Languages **T Strategy** Context Clues	**Skill** Compound Words; Time Words **T Strategy** Word Structure	**Skill** Unfamiliar Words; Homonyms **T Strategy** Context Clues
Appropriate Phrasing	Accuracy and Appropriate Pace	Appropriate Phrasing
Weekly Writing Research Report **Unit Process Writing**	**Weekly Writing** Research Report **Unit Process Writing**	**Weekly Writing** Research Report **Unit Process Writing**
T Commas	Commas in Compound Sentences	Indenting Paragraphs
Understand Other Cultures	Listen to a Description	Listen for Speaker's Purpose
Technology: Online Directories	Thesaurus	Time Line
Time for SOCIAL STUDIES — Cultural Traditions, Celebrations	*Time for* SOCIAL STUDIES — American West, Cowboys, U.S. Growth, Transportation, Geography	*Time for* SOCIAL STUDIES — Native American Culture, Family History

Unit 6
Monitor Progress

Predictors of Reading Success		WEEK 1	WEEK 2	WEEK 3	WEEK 4
Word Reading	**Phonics**	🔵 Contractions	🔵 Inflected Endings	🔵 Syllables *-tion, -ture*	🔵 Suffixes *-ness, -less*
WCPM	**Fluency**	Read with Accuracy and Appropriate Pace/Rate 90–100 WCPM	Read Silently with Fluency and Accuracy 90–100 WCPM	Read with Appropriate Phrasing 90–100 WCPM	Read with Accuracy and Appropriate Pace/Rate 90–100 WCPM
Vocabulary	**Lesson Vocabulary**	🔵 field 🔵 cheers 🔵 threw 🔵 sailed 🔵 plate 🔵 bases	🔵 freedom 🔵 flag 🔵 stripes 🔵 stars 🔵 nicknames 🔵 birthday 🔵 America	🔵 present 🔵 aunt 🔵 basket 🔵 collects 🔵 bank 🔵 favorite	🔵 cattle 🔵 trails 🔵 cowboy 🔵 herd 🔵 campfire 🔵 railroad 🔵 galloped
Oral Vocabulary	**Vocabulary/ Concept Development** (assessed informally)	athlete challenge champion dainty disguise effort professional shortstop	allegiance frayed history independence indivisible patriotic symbol unfurl	angle brilliant celebration create custom inspect snapshot tradition	buckaroo climate drover lariat legend livestock occupation rawhide
Retelling	**Text Comprehension**	🔵 **Skill** Compare and Contrast 🔵 **Strategy** Visualize	🔵 **Skill** Fact and Opinion 🔵 **Strategy** Monitor and Fix Up	🔵 **Skill** Draw Conclusions 🔵 **Strategy** Summarize	🔵 **Skill** Cause and Effect 🔵 **Strategy** Graphic Organizer

🔵 Target Skill   🔵 SuccessTracker/Unit 6 Benchmark Tested Skills

Make Data-Driven Decisions

Data Management
- Assess
- Diagnose
- Prescribe
- Disaggregate

Classroom Management
- Monitor Progress
- Group
- Differentiate Instruction
- Inform Parents

Reading STREET

Success Tracker™

ONLINE CLASSROOM

WEEK 5

Prefixes *mis-*, *mid-*

Read with Appropriate Phrasing

90–100 WCPM

- clattering
- jingles
- drum
- voice
- borrow
- silver

ceremony
compliment
culture
evergreen
festival
fidget
multicolored
sash

Skill Character, Setting, and Plot

Strategy Prior Knowledge

Manage Data

- Assign the Unit 6 Benchmark Test for students to take online.
- SuccessTracker records results and generates reports by school, grade, classroom, or student.
- Use reports to disaggregate and aggregate Unit 6 skills and standards data to monitor progress.

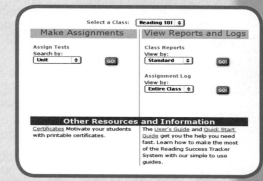

- Based on class lists created to support the categories important for adequate yearly progress (AYP, i.e., gender, ethnicity, migrant education, English proficiency, disabilities, economic status), reports let you track AYP every six weeks.

Group

- Use results from Unit 6 Benchmark Tests taken online through SuccessTracker to regroup students.
- Reports in SuccessTracker suggest appropriate groups for students based on test results.

Individualize Instruction

- Tests are correlated to Unit 6 tested skills and standards so that prescriptions for individual teaching and learning plans can be created.
- Individualized prescriptions target instruction and accelerate student progress toward learning outcome goals.
- Prescriptions include resources to reteach Unit 6 skills and standards.

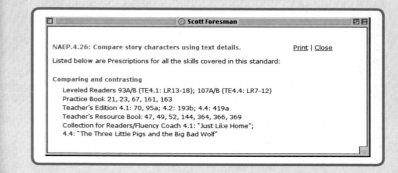

Unit 6
Grouping for AYP

Diagnose and Differentiate

Diagnose
To make initial grouping decisions, use the Baseline Group Test or another initial placement test. Depending on children's ability levels, you may have more than one of each group.

Differentiate

If... a child's performance is	**Below-Level**	then... use the regular instruction and the daily Strategic Intervention, pp. DI·14–DI·62.
If... a child's performance is	**On-Level**	then... use the regular instruction for On-Level learners throughout each week.
If... a child's performance is	**Advanced**	then... use the regular instruction and the daily instruction for Advanced learners, pp. DI·9–DI·63.

Group Time

On-Level	Strategic Intervention	Advanced
• Explicit instructional routines teach core skills and strategies.	• Daily Strategic Intervention provides more intensive instruction, more scaffolding, more practice with critical skills, and more opportunities to respond.	• Daily Advanced lessons provide compacted instruction for accelerated learning, options for independent investigative work, and challenging reading content.
• Ample practice for core skills.		
• Independent activities provide practice for core skills.	• Decodable readers practice word reading skills.	• Leveled readers (LR1–48) provide additional reading tied to lesson concepts.
• Leveled readers (LR1–48) and decodable readers provide additional reading and practice with core skills and vocabulary.	• Reteach lessons (DI·64–DI·68) provide additional instructional opportunities with target skills.	
	• Leveled readers (LR1–48) build background for the selections and practice target skills and vocabulary.	

Additional opportunities to differentiate instruction:
- Reteach Lessons, pp. DI·64–DI·68
- Leveled Reader Instruction and Leveled Practice, LR1–48
- My Sidewalks on Scott Foresman Reading Street Intensive Reading Intervention Program

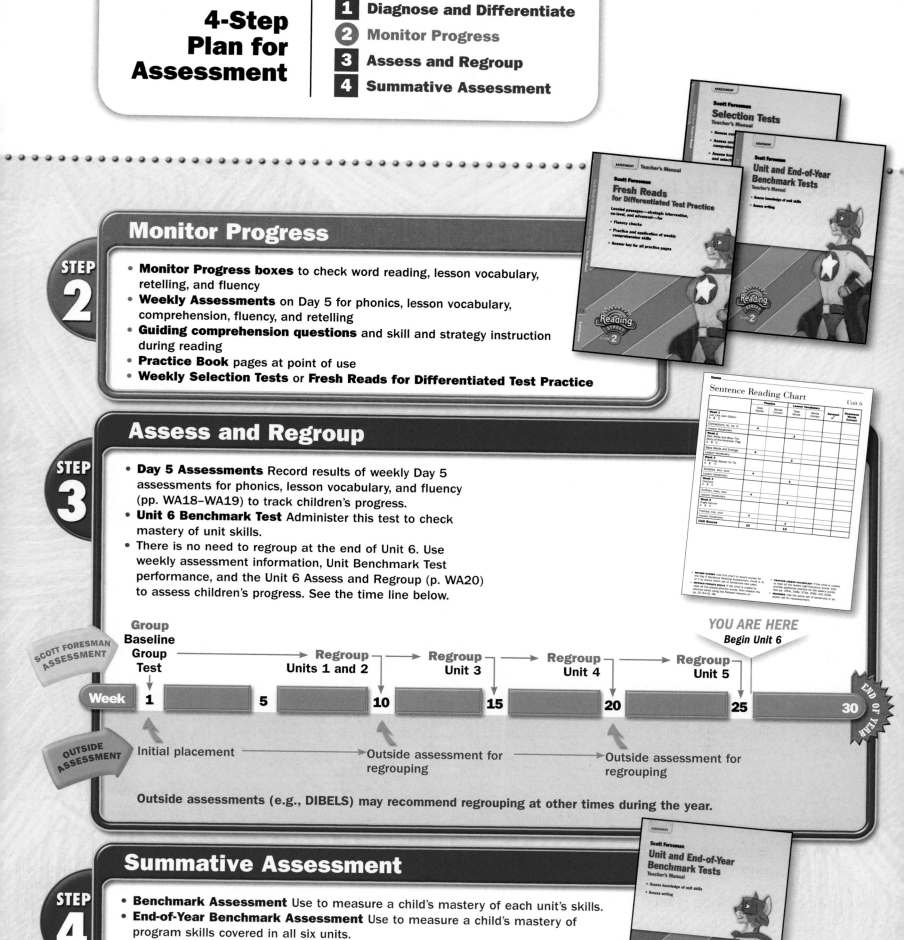

4-Step Plan for Assessment

1. **Diagnose and Differentiate**
2. **Monitor Progress**
3. **Assess and Regroup**
4. **Summative Assessment**

Monitor Progress

STEP 2

- **Monitor Progress boxes** to check word reading, lesson vocabulary, retelling, and fluency
- **Weekly Assessments** on Day 5 for phonics, lesson vocabulary, comprehension, fluency, and retelling
- **Guiding comprehension questions** and skill and strategy instruction during reading
- **Practice Book** pages at point of use
- **Weekly Selection Tests** or **Fresh Reads for Differentiated Test Practice**

Assess and Regroup

STEP 3

- **Day 5 Assessments** Record results of weekly Day 5 assessments for phonics, lesson vocabulary, and fluency (pp. WA18–WA19) to track children's progress.
- **Unit 6 Benchmark Test** Administer this test to check mastery of unit skills.
- There is no need to regroup at the end of Unit 6. Use weekly assessment information, Unit Benchmark Test performance, and the Unit 6 Assess and Regroup (p. WA20) to assess children's progress. See the time line below.

Outside assessments (e.g., DIBELS) may recommend regrouping at other times during the year.

Summative Assessment

STEP 4

- **Benchmark Assessment** Use to measure a child's mastery of each unit's skills.
- **End-of-Year Benchmark Assessment** Use to measure a child's mastery of program skills covered in all six units.

Unit 6
Theme Launch

Discuss the Big Idea

Read and discuss the theme question. Explain

- people have different traditions and celebrations all over the world (Thanksgiving dinner, Kwanzaa, Cinco de Mayo, May Day, Diwali, going to a ballgame)

- celebrations are special (families get together, good food is eaten, games are played)

- traditions are predictable (they are a way of doing things the same each time, people enjoy them and look forward to them)

Have children use the pictures along the side of the page to preview the selections in this unit. Read the titles and captions together. Ask children how each selection might be about a tradition.

Read Aloud

Read the big book *Magda's Tortillas.*

- What tradition did Magda look forward to in this story?

- Was making tortillas like Magda expected it to be?

- Why do you think Magda's family has the tradition of making tortillas when a girl turns seven?

- What tradition will Magda begin when she turns eight?

For more read alouds related to the theme, see the *Read Aloud Anthology.*

UNIT **6**

Read It Online
PearsonSuccessNet.com

Traditions

How are traditions and celebrations important to our lives?

Connecting Cultures

You can use the following selection to help children learn about their own and other cultures and explore common elements of culture.

Just Like Josh Gibson Point out that baseball is a favorite sport in the United States, but other countries have other sports as their favorites. Have children discuss other countries they know that have other favorite sports, such as cricket in India and Great Britain, soccer in most parts of Europe, and baseball in Santa Domingo and Colombia.

Just Like Josh Gibson

Grandmama shares the tradition of American baseball.

REALISTIC FICTION

connect to SOCIAL STUDIES

Paired Selection

How Baseball Began

EXPOSITORY NONFICTION

Red, White, and Blue: The Story of the American Flag

Our nation's flag is a traditional symbol.

NARRATIVE NONFICTION

connect to SOCIAL STUDIES

Paired Selection

You're a Grand Old Flag

SONG

A Birthday Basket for Tía

Birthdays are an important family tradition.

REALISTIC FICTION

connect to SOCIAL STUDIES

Paired Selection

Family Traditions: Birthdays

ONLINE DIRECTORY

Cowboys

Cowboys are an American tradition.

NARRATIVE NONFICTION

connect to SOCIAL STUDIES

Paired Selection

Cowboy Gear

PICTURE ENCYCLOPEDIA

Jingle Dancer

Jenna participates in a Native American tradition.

REALISTIC FICTION

connect to SOCIAL STUDIES

Paired Selection

Celebrating the Buffalo Days

PHOTO ESSAY

Unit Inquiry Project
Research Traditions

Children can work individually or in groups to research traditions of various cultures and use the information to make plans and materials for a new family or school tradition.

PROJECT TIMETABLE

WEEK	ACTIVITY/SKILL CONNECTION
1	**INTERVIEW AND LIST** Children list traditions and interview family members and teachers for ideas to add to the lists.
2	**GATHER INFORMATION** Children choose one tradition and read about it. They research and gather information about what the tradition is like.
3	**MAKE PLANS** Children make plans to celebrate their new tradition at home or at school.
4	**PREPARE MATERIALS** Children prepare materials they need for the tradition.
5	**PRESENT** Children present their traditions and plans to the class.

An assessment rubric can be found on p. 434a. Rubric 4 3 2 1

CONCEPT DEVELOPMENT

Unit 6
Traditions

CONCEPT QUESTION

How are traditions and celebrations important to our lives?

Week 5

Expand the Concept

What are some different ways that people celebrate?

Connect the Concept

Develop Language
ceremony, compliment, culture, evergreen, festival, fidget, multicolored, sash

Teach Content
Native American Culture: Powwow Ceremony
Family History

Writing
A Story

Literature

Time for SOCIAL STUDIES

Week 4

Expand the Concept

Why should we learn about cowboys?

Connect the Concept

Develop Language
buckaroo, climate, drover, lariat, legend, livestock, occupation, rawhide

Teach Content
American West
Cowboys
U.S. Growth
Transportation
Geography

Writing
An Advertisement

Literature

Time for SOCIAL STUDIES

Week 3

Expand the Concept

Why are family celebrations special?

Connect the Concept

Develop Language
angle, brilliant, celebration, create, custom, inspect, snapshot, tradition

Teach Content
Cultural Traditions
Celebrations

Writing
A Report

Literature

Family Traditions: Birthdays

Time for SOCIAL STUDIES

Week 1

Expand the Concept

Why are sports important in our country?

Connect the Concept

Develop Language
athlete, challenge, champion, dainty, disguise, effort, professional, shortstop

Teach Content
American Heroes
Cultural Traditions
History of Baseball
Geography: Maps

Writing
Facts

Literature

JOSH GIBSON

Time for SOCIAL STUDIES

Week 2

Expand the Concept

What does our flag mean?

Connect the Concept

Develop Language
allegiance, frayed, history, independence, indivisible, patriotic, symbol, unfurl

Teach Content
American Heroes
American Revolution
Thirteen Colonies/States
U.S. Symbols
U.S. Holidays
Geography: Maps

Writing
Answers

Literature

Red, White, and Blue

You're a Grand Old Flag

Time for SOCIAL STUDIES

Illinois

Planning Guide for Performance Descriptors

Just Like Josh Gibson

Reading Street Teacher's Edition pages	Grade 2 English Language Arts Performance Descriptors
Oral Language Build Concepts: 296l, 298a, 314a, 316a, 320a Share Literature: 296m, 298b, 314b, 316b, 320b	**1A.Stage B.4.** Use a variety of decoding strategies (e.g., phonics, word patterns, structural analysis, context clues) to recognize new words when reading age-appropriate material. **1B.Stage B.1.** Read fiction and non-fiction materials for specific purposes.
Word Work **Phonics** Contractions *'re, 've, 'd*: 296n–296q, 298c–298d, 314c–314d, 316c–316d, 320c–320f **Spelling:** 296p, 298d, 314d, 316d, 320d	**1A.Stage B.1.** Use phonics to decode simple words in age-appropriate material. **1A.Stage B.4.** Use a variety of decoding strategies (e.g., phonics, word patterns, structural analysis, context clues) to recognize new words when reading age-appropriate material. **3A.Stage B.5.** Use correct spelling of high frequency words.
Reading **Comprehension** Compare and Contrast: 296r–297, 300–313a, 314g, 320e Visualize: 296r–297, 300–313, 314g **Vocabulary** Context Clues: 298–299 Homophones: 314e Multiple-Meaning Words: 298–299, 316–317, 320b **Fluency** Paired Reading: 296q, 313a Choral Reading: 314f, 319a **Self-Selected Reading:** LR1–9, TR16–17 **Literature** Genre—Realistic Fiction: 300–301 Reader Response: 314g–314h	**1A.Stage B.7.** Use a variety of resources (e.g., context, previous experiences, dictionaries, glossaries, computer resources, ask others) to determine and clarify meanings of unfamiliar words. **1B.Stage B.1.** Read fiction and non-fiction materials for specific purposes. **1C.Stage B.7.** Compare an author's information with the student's knowledge of self, world, and other texts in non-fiction text. **1C.Stage B.8.** Compare a broad range of books that have the same theme and topic. **2B.Stage B.1.** Investigate self-selected/teacher-selected literature (e.g., picture books, nursery rhymes, fairy tales, poems, legends) from a variety of cultures.
Language Arts **Writing** Facts, Letter, Respond to Literature, Diagram: 297a, 313b, 314g, 319b, 320–321 **Six-Trait Writing** Sentences: 315a, 320–321 **Grammar, Usage, and Mechanics** Capital Letters: 297d, 313c, 315b, 319c, 320–321 **Speaking/Listening** Speak to Your Audience: 319d **Research/Study** People as Resources: 321a	**1C.Stage B.1.** Respond to analytical and interpretive questions based on information in text. **3A.Stage B.3.** Use appropriate capitalization (e.g., beginning capitalization, proper nouns). **4B.Stage B.2.** Use presentation techniques appropriate for the situation (e.g., eye contact with audience, volume, rate, tone, avoid distracting behaviors). **5A.Stage B.3.** Generate questions gained from experiences (e.g., field trip, visitors, stories, discussions) to gather information.
Unit Skills **Writing** Research Report: WA2–9 **Project/Wrap-Up:** 434–435	**3C.Stage B.4.** Experiment with different forms of writing (e.g., song, poetry, short fiction, recipes, diary, journal, directions). **5C.Stage B.5.** Create a report of ideas (e.g., drawing, using available technology, writing a story, letter, report).

This Week's Leveled Readers

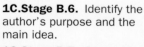

Below-Level

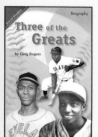

1C.Stage B.3. Ask questions to seek clarification of meaning.

1C.Stage B.7. Compare an author's information with the student's knowledge of self, world, and other texts in non-fiction text.

Nonfiction

On-Level

1C.Stage B.6. Identify the author's purpose and the main idea.

1C.Stage B.7. Compare an author's information with the student's knowledge of self, world, and other texts in non-fiction text.

Nonfiction

Advanced

1C.Stage B.7. Compare an author's information with the student's knowledge of self, world, and other texts in non-fiction text.

1C.Stage B.8. Compare a broad range of books that have the same theme and topic.

Nonfiction

Content-Area Illinois Performance Descriptors in This Lesson

Social Studies

16D.Stage B.5. List examples of past traditions found within the local community.

16D.Stage B.6. Interpret stories and folktales from the past to show various customs from groups of people in the past and the influence these customs had on their society.

18A.Stage B.2. Identify cultural traits.

18A.Stage B.3. Identify symbols of local culture.

18B.Stage B.1. Define social group.

18B.Stage B.2. Explain how contact with others shapes peoples' lives.

18B.Stage B.3. Give examples of personality differences.

18B.Stage B.4. Tell about the role of families in the community.

Math

6A.Stage B.4. Use cardinal and ordinal numbers appropriately.

7B.Stage B.2. Estimate standard measurements of length, weight, and capacity.

Science

12D.Stage B.2. Apply scientific inquiries or technological designs to make connections between the basic concepts of motion to real world applications: describing how gravity affects motion; demonstrating the rate, time and distance factors and units for speed; describing examples of inertia and momentum in the classroom, playground and at home.

A FAMOUS ILLINOISAN
Don Marquis

Don Marquis (MAHR-kwis) (1878–1937) was born in Walnut. He studied at Knox College in Galesburg and then worked as a journalist. Marquis created the characters of Archy the cockroach and Mehitabel the cat, who appeared in his column in 1916. The two characters' stories were "written" by Archy, using Marquis's typewriter. Because Archy was so small he could not push the shift key, he typed only in lowercase letters, which gave Marquis's column a unique appearance.

Children can . . .
Learn more about Don Marquis's work. Have them draw pictures of Archy the cockroach and Mehitabel the cat. Children can draw Archy typing on a typewriter.

A SPECIAL ILLINOIS PLACE
Waukegan

Waukegan is in the northeastern part of the state. The name comes from the Potawatomi word for "little fort." Waukegan was first known as Little Fort and was renamed in 1849 when the settlement became a village. Comedian Jack Benny (1894–1974) and author Ray Bradbury (1920–) are two of Waukegan's most famous former residents.

Children can . . .
Discuss what forts look like and create a welcome banner for Waukegan that includes an image of a fort.

ILLINOIS FUN FACTS
Did You Know?

- In 1809 President James Madison appointed Ninian Edwards, from Kentucky, as the first governor of the Illinois Territory.

- The first commercial television station in Illinois, WBKB, started broadcasting in Chicago in 1940. That station is still broadcasting today as WBBM.

- Between 1820 and 1830, the population of Illinois grew from 55,000 to 157,000.

Children can . . .
Find out what the current population of their community is and compare it with the population of the community ten years ago.

Unit 6
Traditions

Week 1

CONCEPT QUESTION

How are traditions and celebrations important to our lives?

Week 1

Why are sports important in our country?

Week 2

What does our flag mean?

Week 3

Why are family celebrations special?

Week 4

Why should we learn about cowboys?

Week 5

What are some different ways that people celebrate?

EXPAND THE CONCEPT
Why are sports important in our country?

Time for **SOCIAL STUDIES**

CONNECT THE CONCEPT

▶ **Build Background**

athlete	dainty	professional
challenge	disguise	shortstop
champion	effort	

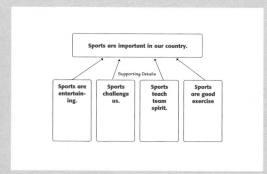

▶ **Social Studies Content**
American Heroes, Cultural Traditions, History of Baseball, Geography: Maps

▶ **Writing**
Facts

Preview Your Week

Why are sports important in our country?

Just Like JOSH GIBSON

by Angela Johnson
illustrated by Beth Peck

Genre **Realistic fiction** is made up but could really happen. Look for things that really could have happened to a little girl.

Can a girl really hit a baseball just like Josh Gibson?

300

301

Audio CD

Student Edition pages 300–315

Genre	Realistic fiction
Phonics	Contractions
Vocabulary Strategy	Context Clues
Comprehension Skill	Compare and Contrast
Comprehension Strategy	Visualize

Paired Selection

Time for **SOCIAL STUDIES**

Reading Across Texts

Baseball Time Line

Genre

Expository nonfiction

Text Features

Headings
Captions
Diagrams
Charts

Social Studies in Reading

Expository nonfiction

- Expository nonfiction explains an object or an idea.
- Expository nonfiction gives facts.

Text Features
- Headings, diagrams, captions, and charts or graphs are often used in nonfiction to help the reader better understand the text.
- This article includes picture graphs to show information about numbers of teams.

Link to Social Studies
Use the library to find information about another game you want to learn about.

How Baseball Began

by Tammy Terry
illustrated by Clint Hansen

Baseball is called the national pastime of the United States. Hundreds of games are played and watched every spring and summer. But have you ever wondered how baseball began?

Who Invented it?
Well, no one knows for sure who invented the game. Many people believe that a man named Abner Doubleday invented baseball in 1839 in Cooperstown, New York.

Abner Doubleday

Baseball probably developed from the English game of the 1600s called "rounders."

Settlers living in America played rounders in the 1700s. They also called the game "town ball" and "base ball." Rules of the game varied from place to place. Over the years, the game of rounders became the game we now call baseball. One of the biggest differences between the two games is in how the batter is put out.

In rounders, players threw the ball at runners. If a runner got hit, he was out.

In baseball, players tag runners to put them out.

Compare and Contrast What two games are being compared?

316

Student Edition pages 316–319

Audio CD

Read It
ONLINE
PearsonSuccessNet.com

- **Student Edition**
- **Leveled Readers**
- **Decodable Reader**

Leveled Readers

◉ **Skill** Compare and Contrast

◉ **Strategy** Visualize

Lesson Vocabulary

Below-Level

On-Level

Advanced

ELL Reader
- Concept Vocabulary
- Text Support
- Language Enrichment

Play Ball!

Decodable Reader

Apply Phonics

- *Hide and Seek!*

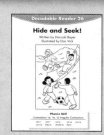

Decodable Reader 26
Hide and Seek!

Integrate Social Studies Standards

- **American Heroes**
- **Cultural Traditions**
- **Geography: Maps**
- **History of Baseball**

✓  **Read**

Just Like Josh Gibson
pp. 300–315

"How Baseball Began"
pp. 316–319

✓  **Read**

Leveled Readers

Below-Level · On-Level · Advanced

- **Support Concepts**
- **Develop Concepts**
- **Extend Concepts**
- **Social Studies Extension Activity**

✓  **Read**

ELL Reader

Play Ball!

✓ **Build Concept Vocabulary**
Traditions, p. 296m

✓ **Teach Social Studies Concepts**
Josh Gibson, p. 310–311
Opportunities, p. 312–313

✓ **Explore Social Studies Center**
Compare Sports, p. 296k

Weekly Plan

READING

90-120 minutes

TARGET SKILLS OF THE WEEK

Phonics
Contractions *'re, 've, 'd*

Comprehension Skill
Compare and Contrast

Comprehension Strategy
Visualize

DAY 1 PAGES 296l–297b

Oral Language

QUESTION OF THE WEEK, 296l
Why are sports important in our country?

Oral Vocabulary/Share Literature, 296m
Sing with Me Big Book, Song 26
Amazing Words *athlete, challenge, effort*

Word Work

Phonics, 296n–296o
Introduce Contractions *'re, 've, 'd* **T**

Spelling, 296p
Pretest

Comprehension/Vocabulary/Fluency

Read Decodable Reader 26

Grouping Options 296f–296g

Review High-Frequency Words
Check Comprehension
Reread for Fluency

Comprehension Skill/Strategy Lesson, 296r–297
Compare and Contrast **T**
Visualize

DAY 2 PAGES 298a–313c

Oral Language

QUESTION OF THE DAY, 298a
Do you know any girls who are good baseball players?

Oral Vocabulary/Share Literature, 298b
Read Aloud Anthology "The Princesses Have a Ball"
Amazing Word *dainty*

Word Work

Phonics, 298c–298d
Review Contractions *'re, 've, 'd* **T**

Spelling, 298d
Dictation

Comprehension/Vocabulary/Fluency

Build Background, 298e
Women's Baseball Leagues

Lesson Vocabulary, 298f
Introduce *bases, cheers, field, plate, sailed, threw* **T**

Vocabulary Strategy Lesson, 298–299a
Context Clues **T**

Read *Just Like Josh Gibson,* 300–313a

Grouping Options 296f–296g

Compare and Contrast **T**
Visualize
REVIEW Fact and Opinion **T**
Reread for Fluency

LANGUAGE ARTS

20-30 minutes

Trait of the Week

Sentences

Shared Writing, 297a
Facts

Grammar, 297b
Introduce Using Capital Letters **T**

Interactive Writing, 313b
Letter

Grammar, 313c
Practice Using Capital Letters **T**

DAILY JOURNAL WRITING

Day 1 *Write a paragraph about a time you played or watched baseball.*

Day 2 *Write about a time you got a chance to play something you'd always wanted to play.*

DAILY SOCIAL STUDIES CONNECTIONS

Day 1 Sports Are Important in Our Country Concept Chart, 296m

Day 2 Time for Social Studies: Josh Gibson, 310–311; Opportunities, 312–313

DAILY SUCCESS PREDICTORS
for Adequate Yearly Progress

Monitor Progress and Corrective Feedback

Phonics
Check Word Reading, *296o*
Spiral **REVIEW** Phonics

Fluency
Check Lesson Vocabulary, *298f*
Spiral **REVIEW** High-Frequency Words

RESOURCES FOR THE WEEK

- Practice Book 2.2, *pp. 101–110*
- Phonics and Spelling Practice Book, *pp. 101–104*
- Grammar and Writing Practice Book, *pp. 101–104*
- Selection Test, *pp. 101–104*

- Fresh Reads for Differentiated Test Practice, *pp. 151–156*
- Phonics Songs and Rhymes Chart 26
- The Grammar and Writing Book, *pp. 200–205*

Grouping Options for Differentiated Instruction

Turn the page for the small group lesson plan.

DAY 3 PAGES 314a–315b

Oral Language

QUESTION OF THE DAY, 314a
What do you think the ball will be like?

Oral Vocabulary/Share Literature, 314b
Read Aloud Anthology "The Princesses Have a Ball"
Amazing Word *disguise*

Word Work

Phonics, 314c
REVIEW Vowels *aw, au, augh, al* **T**

Lesson Vocabulary, 314d
Practice *bases, cheers, field, plate, sailed, threw* **T**

Spelling, 314d
Practice

Comprehension/Vocabulary/Fluency

Vocabulary, 314e
Homophones

Read *Just Like Josh Gibson,* 300–315

Grouping Options
296f–296g

Fluency, 314f
Read with Accuracy and
Appropriate Pace

Reader Response, 314g

Trait of the Week, 315a
Introduce Sentences

Grammar, 315b
Write with Capital Letters **T**

Day 3 *Write about a baseball game you played or attended.*

Day 3 Sports Are Important in Our Country Concept Chart, 315b

DAY 4 PAGES 316a–319d

Oral Language

QUESTION OF THE DAY, 316a
What else do team sports teach us?

Oral Vocabulary/Share Literature, 316b
Read Aloud Anthology "Yankee Doodle Shortstop"
Amazing Words *champion, professional, shortstop*

Word Work

Phonics, 316c
REVIEW Sentence Reading **T**

Spelling, 316d
Partner Review

Comprehension/Vocabulary/Fluency

Read "How Baseball Began," 316–319
Leveled Readers

Grouping Options
296f–296g

Multiple-Meaning Words
Reading Across Texts

Fluency, 319a
Read with Accuracy and
Appropriate Pace

Writing Across the Curriculum, 319b
Diagram

Grammar, 319c
Review Using Capital Letters **T**

Speaking and Listening, 319d
Speak to Your Audience

Day 4 *Write about becoming a better athlete.*

Day 4 Social Studies Center: Compare Sports, 296k

DAY 5 PAGES 320a–321b

Oral Language

QUESTION OF THE DAY, 320a
Why are sports important in our country?

Oral Vocabulary/Share Literature, 320b
Read Aloud Anthology "Yankee Doodle Shortstop"
Amazing Words Review

Word Work

Phonics, 320c
Review Contractions *'re, 've, 'd* **T**

Lesson Vocabulary, 320c
Review *bases, cheers, field, plate, sailed, threw* **T**

Spelling, 320d
Test

Comprehension/Vocabulary/Fluency

Read Leveled Readers

Grouping Options 296f–296g

Monitor Progress, 320e–320g
Read the Sentences
Read the Story

Writing and Grammar, 320–321
Develop Sentences
Use Capital Letters **T**

Research/Study Skills, 321a
Use People as Resources

Day 5 *Write about an athlete who meets a challenge.*

Day 5 Revisit the Sports Are Important in Our Country Concept Chart, 321b

KEY 🎯 = Target Skill **T** = Tested Skill

Comprehension Check Retelling, *314g*

Fluency Check Fluency WCPM, *319a*
Spiral REVIEW Phonics,
High-Frequency Words

Oral Vocabulary Check Oral Vocabulary, *320b*
Assess Phonics,
Lesson Vocabulary, Fluency,
Comprehension, *320e*

SUCCESS PREDICTOR

Small Group Plan *for Differentiated Instruction*

Daily Plan
AT A GLANCE

Reading
Whole Group
- Oral Language
- Word Work
- Comprehension/Vocabulary

Group Time

Meet with small groups to provide:
- Skill Support
- Reading Support
- Fluency Practice

Read

This week's lessons for daily group time can be found behind the Differentiated Instruction (DI) tab on pp. DI·14–DI·23.

Whole Group
- Comprehension/Vocabulary
- Fluency

Language Arts
- Writing
- Grammar
- Speaking/Listening/Viewing
- Research/Study Skills

Use *My Sidewalks on Reading Street* for Tier III intensive reading intervention.

DAY 1

On-Level
Teacher-Led
Page 296q
- **Read** Decodable Reader 26
- **Reread** for Fluency

Strategic Intervention
Teacher-Led
Page DI·14
- Blend Words with Contractions
- **Read** Decodable Reader 26
- **Reread** for Fluency

Advanced
Teacher-Led
Page DI·15
- Extend Word Reading
- **Read** Advanced Selection 2
- Introduce Concept Inquiry

(i) Independent Activities
While you meet with small groups, have the rest of the class...
- Reread for fluency
- Write in their journals
- Read self-selected reading
- Visit the Word Work Center
- Complete Practice Book 2.2, pp. 103–104

DAY 2

On-Level
Teacher-Led
Pages 300–313
- **Read** *Just Like Josh Gibson*
- **Reread** for Fluency

Strategic Intervention
Teacher-Led
Page DI·16
- Blend Words with Contractions
- **Read** SI Decodable Reader 26
- **Read** or Listen to *Just Like Josh Gibson*

Advanced
Teacher-Led
Page DI·17
- **Read** *Just Like Josh Gibson*
- Continue Concept Inquiry

(i) Independent Activities
While you meet with small groups, have the rest of the class...
- Read self-selected reading
- Write in their journals
- Visit the Listening Center
- Complete Practice Book 2.2, pp. 105–107

DAY 3

On-Level
Teacher-Led
Pages 300–315
- **Reread** *Just Like Josh Gibson*

Strategic Intervention
Teacher-Led
Page DI·18
- **Reread** *Just Like Josh Gibson*
- Read Words and Sentences
- Review Compare and Contrast and Visualize
- **Reread** for Fluency

Advanced
Teacher-Led
Page DI·19
- Self-Selected Reading
- Continue Concept Inquiry

(i) Independent Activities
While you meet with small groups, have the rest of the class...
- Read self-selected reading
- Write in their journals
- Visit the Writing Center
- Complete Practice Book 2.2, pp. 108–109

① Begin with whole class skill and strategy instruction.

② Meet with small groups to provide differentiated instruction.

③ Gather the whole class back together for fluency and language arts.

On-Level

Teacher-Led
Pages 316–319, LR4–LR6

- **Read** "How Baseball Began"
- Practice with On-Level Reader *Women in Baseball*

Strategic Intervention

Teacher-Led
Pages DI • 20, LR1–LR3

- **Read** or Listen to "How Baseball Began"
- **Reread** for Fluency
- Build Concepts
- Practice with Below-Level Reader *Three of the Greats*

Advanced

Teacher-Led
Pages DI • 21, LR7–LR9

- **Read** "How Baseball Began"
- Extend Vocabulary
- Continue Concept Inquiry
- Practice with Advanced Reader *Baseball Heroes*

DAY 4

ⓘ Independent Activities

While you meet with small groups, have the rest of the class...

- Reread for fluency
- Write in their journals
- Read self-selected reading
- Review spelling words with a partner
- Visit the Listening and Social Studies Centers

On-Level

Teacher-Led
Pages 320e–320g, LR4–LR6

- Sentence Reading, Set B
- Monitor Comprehension
- Practice with On-Level Reader *Women in Baseball*

Strategic Intervention

Teacher-Led
Pages DI • 22, LR1–LR3

- Practice Word Reading
- Sentence Reading, Set A
- Monitor Comprehension
- Practice with Below-Level Reader *Three of the Greats*

Advanced

Teacher-Led
Pages DI • 23, LR7–LR9

- Sentence Reading, Set C
- Monitor Fluency and Comprehension
- Share Concept Inquiry
- Practice with Advanced Reader *Baseball Heroes*

DAY 5

ⓘ Independent Activities

While you meet with small groups, have the rest of the class...

- Reread for fluency
- Write in their journals
- Read self-selected reading
- Visit the Technology Center
- Complete Practice Book 2.2, p. 110

Grouping Place English language learners in the groups that correspond to their reading abilities in English.

Use the appropriate Leveled Reader or other text at children's instructional level.

TIP Send home the appropriate Multilingual Summary of the main selection on Day 1.

Take It to the NET
ONLINE
PearsonSuccessNet.com

Sharon Vaughn
For ideas on professional development, see the article "The Role of Mentoring . . ." by Scott Foresman author S. Vaughn along with M. Coleman.

TEACHER TALK

Modeling is demonstrating for others to imitate. Modeling reading skills often involves **thinking aloud** as one reads.

Be sure to schedule time for children to work on the unit inquiry project "Research Traditions." This week children should list traditions and interview family members and teachers for ideas to add to the list.

Looking Ahead

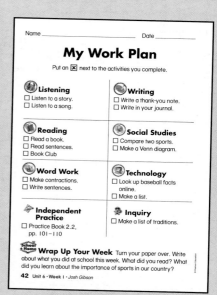

▲ **Group-Time Survival Guide**
p. 42, Weekly Contract

Josh Gibson — **296g**

☑ Customize Your Plan *by Stran*

ORAL LANGUAGE

Concept Development

Why are sports important in our country?

 to build oral vocabulary

athlete	challenge	champion
effort	dainty	disguise
professional	shortstop	

BUILD

☐ **Question of the Week** Use the Morning Warm-Up! to introduce and discuss the question of the week. This week children will talk, sing, read, and write about the importance of sports in America. **DAY 1** *296l*

☐ **Sing with Me Big Book** Sing a song about being an athlete. Ask children to listen for the concept-related Amazing Words *athlete, challenge, effort.* **DAY 1** *296m*

☐ **Build Background** Remind children of the question of the week. Then create a concept chart for children to add to throughout the week. **DAY 1** *296m*

Sing with Me Big Book

DEVELOP

☐ **Question of the Day** Use the questions in the Morning Warm-Ups! to discuss lesson concepts and how they relate to the unit theme, Traditions. **DAY 2** *298a*, **DAY 3** *314a*, **DAY 4** *316a*, **DAY 5** *320a*

☐ **Share Literature** Read big books and read aloud selections that develop concepts, language, and vocabulary related to the lesson concept and the unit theme. Continue to develop this week's Amazing Words. **DAY 2** *298b*, **DAY 3** *314b*, **DAY 4** *316b*, **DAY 5** *320b*

CONNECT

☐ **Wrap Up Your Week!** Revisit the Question of the Week. Then connect concepts and vocabulary to next week's lesson. **DAY 5** *321b*

CHECK

☐ **Check Oral Vocabulary** To informally assess children's oral vocabulary, ask individuals to use some of this week's Amazing Words to tell you about the concept of the week—Traditions. **DAY 5** *320b*

PHONICS

🔊 **CONTRACTIONS 'RE, 'VE, 'D** A *contraction* is a shortened form of two words. An apostrophe appears where letters have been dropped from the original words.

TEACH

☐ **Contractions 're, 've, 'd** Introduce the blending strategy for words with contractions 're, 've, 'd. Then have children blend and build words by naming the contraction and identifying which letter or letters were left out. **DAY 1** *296n-296o*

☐ **Fluent Word Reading** Use the Fluent Word Reading Routine to develop children's word reading fluency. Use the Phonics Songs and Rhymes Chart for additional word reading practice. **DAY 2** *298c-298d*

Phonics Songs and Rhymes Chart 26

PRACTICE/APPLY

☐ **Decodable Reader 26** Practice reading words with contractions 're, 've, 'd in context. **DAY 1** *296q*

☐ *Just Like Josh Gibson* Practice decoding words in context. **DAY 2** *300-313*

☐ **Homework** Practice Book 2.2 p. 103. **DAY 1** *296o*

☐ **Word Work Center** Practice contractions 're, 've, 'd. **ANY DAY** *296j*

Decodable Reader 26

Main Selection—Fiction

RETEACH/REVIEW

☐ **Review** Review words with this week's phonics skills. **DAY 5** *320c*

☐ **Reteach Lessons** If necessary, reteach contractions 're, 've, 'd. **DAY 5** *DI-64*

☐ **Spiral REVIEW** Review previously taught phonics skills. **DAY 1** *296o*, **DAY 3** *314c*, **DAY 4** *316c*

ASSESS

☐ **Sentence Reading** Assess children's ability to read words with contractions 're, 've, 'd. **DAY 5** *320e-320f*

SPELLING

CONTRACTIONS 'RE, 'VE, 'D　A contraction is a shortened form of two words. An apostrophe appears where letters have been dropped from the original words.

TEACH

❑ **Pretest** Before administering the pretest, model how to segment contractions to spell them. Dictate the spelling words, segmenting them if necessary. Then have children check their pretests and correct misspelled words. **DAY 1** *296p*

PRACTICE/APPLY

❑ **Dictation** Have children write dictation sentences to practice spelling words. **DAY 2** *298d*

❑ **Write Words** Have children practice writing the spelling words by writing sentences about things that happen at a baseball game. **DAY 3** *314d*

❑ **Homework** Phonics and Spelling Practice Book pp. 101–104. **DAY 1** *296p*, **DAY 2** *298d*, **DAY 3** *314d*, **DAY 4** *316d*

RETEACH/REVIEW

❑ **Partner Review** Have pairs work together to read and write the spelling words. **DAY 4** *316d*

ASSESS

❑ **Posttest** Use dictation sentences to give the posttest for words with contractions 're, 've, 'd. **DAY 5** *320d*

Spelling Words

Contractions

1. we're	7. won't
2. I've	8. they're
3. don't	9. I'd
4. can't	10. they'd*
5. he'd	11. she'd
6. you're*	12. we've

Challenge Words

13. could've	15. should've
14. would've	

* Words from the Selection

VOCABULARY

STRATEGY CONTEXT CLUES　Context clues are the words and sentences around an unfamiliar word. Use context clues to help you figure out a word's meaning.

LESSON VOCABULARY

bases　　cheers　　field　　plate　　sailed　　threw

TEACH

❑ **Words to Know** Introduce and discuss this week's lesson vocabulary. **DAY 2** *298f*

❑ **Vocabulary Strategy Lesson** Use the lesson in the Student Edition to introduce/model *context clues*. **DAY 2** *298-299a*

Vocabulary Strategy Lesson

PRACTICE/APPLY

❑ **Words in Context** Read the lesson vocabulary in context. **DAY 2** *300-313*, **DAY 3** *300-315*

Main Selection—Fiction

❑ **Lesson Vocabulary** Have children use vocabulary words. **DAY 3** *314d*

❑ **Leveled Text** Read lesson vocabulary in leveled text. **DAY 4** *LR1-LR9*, **DAY 5** *LR1-LR9*

❑ **Homework** Practice Book 2.2 pp. 106, 109. **DAY 2** *298f*, **DAY 3** *314d*

Leveled Readers

RETEACH/REVIEW

❑ **Homophones** Discuss homophones. Give examples. Have partners write sentences for *soar* and *sore*. **DAY 3** *314e*

❑ **Review** Review this week's lesson vocabulary words. **DAY 5** *320c*

ASSESS

❑ **Selection Test** Use the Selection Test to determine children's understanding of the lesson vocabulary words. **DAY 3**

❑ **Sentence Reading** Assess children's ability to read this week's lesson vocabulary words. **DAY 5** *320e-320f*

HIGH-FREQUENCY WORDS

RETEACH/REVIEW

❑ **Spiral REVIEW** Review previously taught high-frequency words. **DAY 2** *298f*, **DAY 4** *316c*

☑ Customize Your Plan *by Stran*

<table>
<tr><th>COMPREHENSION</th><th>FLUENCY</th></tr>
</table>

COMPREHENSION

SKILL COMPARE AND CONTRAST To compare is to describe how two ideas or things are alike. To contrast is to describe how ideas or things are different.

STRATEGY VISUALIZE Active readers make pictures in their minds as they read a story. As you read, picture in your mind the characters and what is happening.

TEACH

☐ **Skill/Strategy Lesson** Use the Skill/Strategy Lesson in the Student Edition to introduce *compare and contrast* and *visualize*. **DAY 1** *296r–297*

Skill/Strategy Lesson

PRACTICE/APPLY

☐ **Skills and Strategies in Context** Read *Just Like Josh Gibson*, using the Guiding Comprehension questions to apply *compare and contrast* and *visualize*. **DAY 2** *300–313a*

Main Selection—Fiction

☐ **Reader Response** Use the questions on Student Edition p. 314 to discuss the selection. **DAY 3** *314g–315*

☐ **Skills and Strategies in Context** Read "How Baseball Began," guiding children as they apply skills and strategies. **DAY 4** *316–319*

Paired Selection—Nonfiction

☐ **Leveled Text** Apply *compare and contrast* and *visualize* to read leveled text. **DAY 4** *LR1–LR9*, **DAY 5** *LR1–LR9*

☐ **Homework** Practice Book 2.2 pp. 104, 105. **DAY 1** *296–297*, **DAY 2** *298e*

Leveled Readers

ASSESS

☐ **Selection Test** Determine children's understanding of the main selection and assess their ability to *compare and contrast*. **DAY 3**

☐ **Story Reading** Have children read the passage "Luke and Carlos." Ask questions that require them to *compare and contrast*. Then have them retell. **DAY 5** *320e–320g*

RETEACH/REVIEW

☐ **Reteach Lesson** If necessary, reteach *compare and contrast*. **DAY 5** *DI·64*

FLUENCY

SKILL READ WITH ACCURACY AND APPROPRIATE PACE Accuracy is identifying words correctly as you read and reading without omitting or substituting any words. Appropriate pace means that you don't read too fast or too slow.

REREAD FOR FLUENCY

☐ **Oral Rereading** Have children read orally from Decodable Reader 26 or another text at their independent reading level. Listen to children read and provide corrective feedback regarding their oral reading and their use of the blending strategy. **DAY 1** *296q*

☐ **Paired Reading** Have pairs of children read orally from the main selection or another text at their independent reading level. Listen to children read and provide corrective feedback regarding their oral reading and their use of the blending strategy. **DAY 2** *313a*

TEACH

☐ **Model** Use passages from *Just Like Josh Gibson* to model reading aloud with accuracy and appropriate pace. **DAY 3** *314f*, **DAY 4** *319a*

PRACTICE/APPLY

☐ **Choral Reading** Choral read passages from *Just Like Josh Gibson*. Monitor progress and provide feedback regarding children's accuracy and pace. **DAY 3** *314f*, **DAY 4** *319a*

☐ **Listening Center** Have children follow along with the AudioText for this week's selections. **ANY DAY** *296j*

☐ **Reading/Library Center** Have children build fluency by rereading Leveled Readers, Decodable Readers, or other text at their independent level. **ANY DAY** *296j*

☐ **Fluency Coach** Have children use Fluency Coach to listen to fluent reading or to practice reading on their own. **ANY DAY**

ASSESS

☐ **Story Reading** Take a one-minute timed sample of children's oral reading. Use the passage "Luke and Carlos." **DAY 5** *320e–320g*

WRITING

Trait of the Week

SENTENCES Good writers use different kinds of sentences. A mix of short and longer sentences gives writing rhythm and style.

TEACH

☐ **Write Together** Engage children in writing activities that develop language, grammar, and writing skills. Include independent writing as an extension of group writing activities.

> **Shared Writing** DAY 1 *297a*
> **Interactive Writing** DAY 2 *313b*
> **Writing Across the Curriculum** DAY 4 *319b*

☐ **Trait of the Week** Introduce and model the Trait of the Week, *sentences.* DAY 3 *315a*

PRACTICE/APPLY

☐ **Write Now** Examine the model on Student Edition pp. 320–321. Then have children write facts. DAY 5 *320-321*

> **Prompt** *Just Like Josh Gibson* describes a baseball player's skills. Think about someone you know who has special skills or abilities. Now write facts that tell about that person's skills.

Write Now

☐ **Daily Journal Writing** Have children write about concepts and literature in their journals. **EVERY DAY** *296d-296e*

☐ **Writing Center** Have children write a thank-you note to the team, pretending to be Grandmama. **ANY DAY** *296k*

ASSESS

☐ **Scoring Rubric** Use a rubric to evaluate children's facts. DAY 5 *320-321*

RETEACH/REVIEW

☐ **The Grammar and Writing Book** Use pp. 200–205 of The Grammar and Writing Book to extend instruction. **ANY DAY**

The Grammar and Writing Book

SPEAKING AND LISTENING

TEACH

☐ **Speak to Your Audience** Speakers should always think of their audience. Conduct a class survey on their favorite baseball team and discuss the results. DAY 4 *319d*

GRAMMAR

SKILL USING CAPITAL LETTERS Sentences always begin with a capital letter. Days of the week, months of the year, holidays, and titles for people begin with capital letters.

TEACH

☐ **Grammar Transparency 26** Use Grammar Transparency 26 to teach *using capital letters.* DAY 1 *297b*

Grammar Transparency 26

PRACTICE/APPLY

☐ **Develop the Concept** Review the concept of *using capital letters* and provide guided practice. DAY 2 *313c*

☐ **Apply to Writing** Have children use capital letters in writing. DAY 3 *315b*

☐ **Define/Practice** Review the definition of *capital letters.* Then have children identify words that need capital letters. DAY 4 *319c*

☐ **Write Now** Discuss the grammar lesson on Student Edition p. 321. Have children use capital letters in their own factual sentences. DAY 5 *320-321*

Write Now

☐ **Daily Fix-It** Have children find and correct errors in grammar, spelling, and punctuation. DAY 1 *297b*, DAY 2 *313c*, DAY 3 *315b*, DAY 4 *319c*, DAY 5 *320-321*

☐ **Homework** The Grammar and Writing Practice Book pp. 101–104. DAY 2 *313c*, DAY 3 *315b*, DAY 4 *319c*, DAY 5 *320-321*

RETEACH/REVIEW

☐ **The Grammar and Writing Book** Use pp. 200–203 of The Grammar and Writing Book to extend instruction. **ANY DAY**

The Grammar and Writing Book

RESEARCH/INQUIRY

TEACH

☐ **People as Resources** Model using people as resources. Have children use their family members to create a simple family tree. DAY 5 *321a*

☐ **Unit Inquiry Project** Allow time for children to list traditions and interview family members and teachers for ideas. **ANY DAY** *295*

Resources for Differentiated Instruction

LEVELED READERS

▶ **Comprehension**
  - 🎯 **Skill** Compare/Contrast
  - 🎯 **Strategy** Visualize

▶ **Lesson Vocabulary**
  - 🎯 Context Clues

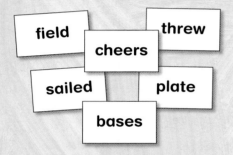

field threw cheers sailed plate bases

▶ **Social Studies Standards**
  - American Heroes
  - Cultural Traditions
  - History of Baseball

Leveled Reader Database ONLINE
PearsonSuccessNet.com

Use the Online Database of over 600 books to
- Download and print additional copies of this week's leveled readers
- Listen to the readers being read online
- Search for more titles focused on this week's skills, topic, and content

---

On-Level

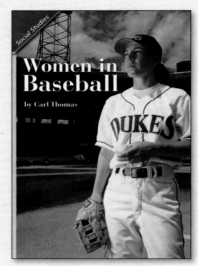

On-Level Reader

Compare and Contrast
Use the chart below to compare and contrast baseball with another sport, like basketball, soccer, or football. Write the name of the sport you choose on the line provided.   Possible answer given.

Baseball	Both	Soccer
hit ball with bat	women play.	kick ball
run around the bases		run up and down the field

On-Level Practice TE p. LR5

Vocabulary
Pretend that you are playing baseball. Write a short story using each of the words in the word box once. The story has been started for you.

Words to Know
athlete bases cheers field plate sailed threw

When I first got to the game, I heard all of the loud
_____cheers_____ from the crowd.
Stories will vary.

On-Level Practice TE p. LR6

Strategic Intervention

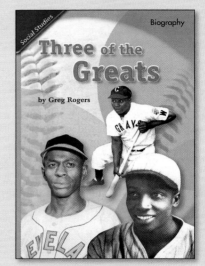

Below-Level Reader

Compare and Contrast
In the book *Three of the Greats*, you learned about Satchel Paige and Josh Gibson. Compare and contrast these baseball players. Use the chart below to organize the facts. Write two facts for each player. Then, write one fact that they share. Possible answer given.

Satchel Paige	Both	Josh Gibson
great pitcher	African American	great hitter
over 20 yrs.		17 yrs.

Below-Level Practice TE p. LR2

Vocabulary
Choose a word from the box to complete the following story about baseball. Write the word on the line. The first one has been done for you.

Words to Know
bases   cheers   field   plate   sailed   threw

Playing baseball is a lot of fun, but I was nervous when
I got up to the _____plate_____. The pitcher
_____threw_____ the ball. I hit it as hard as I could.
The ball _____sailed_____ high through the air. It
landed far out in the _____field_____. I ran around
the _____bases_____ as fast as I could. I heard loud
_____cheers_____ from the crowd. I scored a home run!

Below-Level Practice TE p. LR3

Advanced

Advanced Reader

Compare and Contrast

In the book *Baseball Heroes*, you learned about Jackie Robinson and Hank Aaron. Compare and contrast these two baseball players. Use the chart below to organize the facts. Write two facts for each player. Then list one fact that they share.

Possible answer given.

Jackie Robinson	Both	Hank Aaron
played for the Dodgers	faced many challenges	played for the Braves and the Brewers
great hitter		set many records

Advanced Practice TE p. LR8

Vocabulary

Write the word from the box next to its meaning.

Words to Know			
athletes	banned	challenges	effort
prejudice	record	rookie	talented

1. rookie — *n.* player in his or her first year of professional athletics; beginner
2. challenges — *n.* difficulties
3. talented — *adj.* skillful; able to do something very well
4. effort — *n.* a hard try
5. banned — *v.* forbidden by law
6. record — *n.* the best number, rate, or speed yet reached
7. athletes — *n.* people trained in sports
8. prejudice — *n.* an unreasonable dislike of a group of people

Advanced Practice TE p. LR9

ELL Reader

ELL Poster 26

Teacher's Edition Notes

ELL notes throughout this lesson support instruction and reference additional resources at point of use.

ELL Teaching Guide pp. 176–182, 262–263

- Multilingual summaries of the main selection
- Comprehension lesson
- Vocabulary strategies and word cards
- ELL Reader 26 lesson

ELL and Transition Handbook

Ten Important Sentences

- Key ideas from every selection in the Student Edition
- Activities to build sentence power

More Reading

Readers' Theater Anthology

- Fluency practice
- Five scripts to build fluency
- Poetry for oral interpretation

Leveled Trade Books

Below-Level

On-Level

Advanced

- Extend reading tied to the unit concept
- Lessons in Trade Book Library Teaching Guide

Homework

- Family Times Newsletter
- ELL Multilingual Selection Summaries

Take-Home Books

- Decodable Readers
- Leveled Readers

Literacy Centers

 Listening

Let's Read Along

MATERIALS | SINGLES
CD player, headphones, print copies of recorded pieces

LISTEN TO LITERATURE As children listen to the following recordings, have them follow along or read along in the print version.

AudioText
Just Like Josh Gibson
"How Baseball Began"

Sing with Me/Background Building Audio
"An Athlete's Challenge"

Phonics Songs and Rhymes Audio
"A Great Tradition"

A Great Tradition

I've been playing lots of baseball,
Just like Grandpa always did.
Grandpa learned it from his father
Years ago as a small kid.

He'd play baseball with his friends too.
Now he plays all day with me.
We've been having a great time and
We're as happy as can be.

Baseball is a great tradition.
Don't you hope it stays the same?
Oh, today we still love baseball.
We won't miss a single game.

Audio CD **Phonics Songs and Rhymes Chart 26**

 Reading/Library

Read It Again!

MATERIALS | SINGLES PAIRS GROUPS
collection of books for self-selected reading, books about sports figures, reading logs

REREAD BOOKS Have children select previously read books from the appropriate book box and record titles of books they read in their logs. Use these previously read books:

- Decodable Readers
- Leveled Readers
- ELL Readers
- Stories written by classmates
- Books from the library

TEN IMPORTANT SENTENCES Have children read the Ten Important Sentences for *Just Like Josh Gibson* and locate the sentences in the Student Edition.

BOOK CLUB Have children work in groups to read about two sports figures and then use a Venn diagram or Graphic Organizer 17 to compare and contrast them.

 Word Work

Contraction Action

MATERIALS | SINGLES
index cards with word sets, blank index cards, pencils

CONTRACTIONS Children combine words to make contractions.

1. Make word cards with word pairs such as *you are, we have, I would, will not, do not, he is*.
2. Have children use blank index cards to write the contraction that can be made from each word pair along with a sentence using the contraction.
3. Then have children share their cards with others.

 This interactive CD provides additional practice.

I would

he is

I'd
I'd like to ride my bike.

he's
He's going to win the race.

 296j Traditions • Week 1

Scott Foresman Reading Street Centers Survival Kit

Use the *Just Like Josh Gibson* materials
from the Reading Street Centers Survival Kit
to organize this week's centers.

Writing

Grandmama Says Thanks

MATERIALS `SINGLES`
card stock or any heavy paper, pencils, crayons or markers

THANK-YOU NOTES Ask children to think about how happy Grandmama felt when playing with the boys' team in *Just Like Josh Gibson*.

1. Have children pretend they are Grandmama and write a thank-you note to the team for letting her play.
2. Have them decorate their notes and display them in the classroom.

LEVELED WRITING Encourage children to write at their own ability level. Some may write with little attention to purpose or audience. Others will write with some attention to purpose and audience. Your best writers will write with a clear focus on purpose and audience.

Dear Maple Grove All-Stars,
    I have always wanted to play with your boys' team. Thank you for letting me play in the game today. It was fun!

Yours truly,
Danny's cousin

Social Studies

What a Sport!

MATERIALS `PAIRS`
copies of Venn diagram or Graphic Organizer 17, pencils

COMPARE SPORTS Children compare and contrast baseball and another sport.

1. Ask pairs to pick a sport besides baseball.
2. Have children work together to complete a Venn diagram comparing their chosen sport with baseball.
3. Display the completed diagrams in the classroom.

Baseball
9 players
9 innings
You hit the ball.

played with a ball
played on a team

11 players
2 halves
You kick the ball.
Soccer

Technology

Let's Play Baseball

MATERIALS `GROUPS`
computer with Internet access, paper, pencil, list of suggested Web sites

LEARN ABOUT BASEBALL Have children look up facts about the game of baseball online.

1. Have groups look at Web sites that you have suggested to learn about the game of baseball.
2. Ask groups to work together to make a list of five things they found out about baseball.
3. Display the finished lists in the classroom.

Search Engine

1. There are nine players on each team.
2. The game is nine innings long.
3. Each team bats and plays the field in each inning.
4. Gloves, baseballs, bats, and bases are needed to play.
5. Balls, hits, and strikes are part of the game.

ALL CENTERS

Day 1
AT A GLANCE

Oral Vocabulary
"An Athlete's Challenge" 26

Phonics and Spelling
Contractions
Spelling Pretest:
    Contractions

Read Apply Phonics
Group Time < Differentiated Instruction

Listening Comprehension
Skill Compare and Contrast
Strategy Visualize

Shared Writing
Compare and Contrast

Grammar
Using Capital Letters

Materials

- *Sing with Me Big Book*
- Decodable Reader 26
- Student Edition 296–297
- Graphic Organizer 16
- Skill Transparency 26
- Writing Transparency 26
- Grammar Transparency 26

Take It to the NET™
ONLINE

Professional Development
To learn more about building comprehension skills, go to PearsonSuccessNet.com and read the article "Reading Aloud to Build Comprehension" by J. Gold and A. Gibson.

Morning Warm-Up!

This week we will read about a girl who played baseball long ago.

She liked running toward first base.

She enjoyed playing baseball.

Why are sports important in our country?

QUESTION OF THE WEEK Tell children they will talk, sing, read, and write about the importance of sports in America. Write and read the message and discuss the question.

CONNECT CONCEPTS Ask questions to connect to Unit 5 selections.

- The characters in *Horace and Morris but mostly Dolores* join boys-only and girls-only clubs. Can girls and boys enjoy doing the same things?

- Dodger in *Bad Dog, Dodger!* became an honorary member of Sam's team. Do you belong to any sports teams? What sport would you like to play?

REVIEW HIGH-FREQUENCY WORDS

- Circle the high-frequency words *ago* and *toward* in the message.

- Circle the *-ed* and *-ing* endings in the message.

- Have children say and spell each word as they write it in the air.

Build Background Use the Day 1 instruction on ELL Poster 26 to assess knowledge and develop concepts.

ELL Poster 26

Oral Vocabulary

SHARE LITERATURE Display p. 26 of the *Sing with Me Big Book.* Tell children that the class is going to sing a song about being an athlete. Read the title. Ask children to listen for the Amazing Words **athlete, challenge,** and **effort** as you sing. Then sing the song again and encourage children to sing. Ask: What challenges might an athlete face? How might they use effort to overcome these challenges?

Sing with Me/ Background Building Audio

An Athlete's Challenge

When you're an athlete
And part of a team,
Each game is a challenge;
Each win is a dream.

You make your best effort.
You love to hear cheers.
It's what other athletes
Have done through the years.

Sing with Me Big Book

BUILD BACKGROUND Remind children of the question of the week.

- Why are sports important in our country?

Use Graphic Organizer 16. In the Main Idea box write *Sports are important in our country.* Help children identify reasons to support this idea. Add supporting details boxes as necessary. Display the graphic organizer for use throughout the week.

- Why do people like watching sports? (It's entertaining.)
- Why do people like playing sports? (It's good exercise, and people like being part of a team.)

Main Idea

Sports are important in our country.

Supporting Details

| **Sports are entertaining.** | **Sports challenge us.** | **Sports teach team spirit.** | **Sports are good exercise.** |

▲ **Graphic Organizer 16**

 **to build oral vocabulary**

MONITOR PROGRESS

athlete	**If...** children lack oral vocabulary experiences about the concept Traditions,
challenge	
effort	
dainty	**then...** use the Oral Vocabulary Routine below to teach *athlete.*
disguise	
champion	
professional	
shortstop	

Oral Vocabulary ROUTINE

1. **Introduce the Word** Relate the word *athlete* to the song. Supply a child-friendly definition. Have children say the word. Example: An *athlete* is somebody who uses skills and abilities to compete in sports.

2. **Demonstrate** Provide an example to show meaning. The basketball players were skilled *athletes.*

3. **Apply** Have children demonstrate their understanding. Who is your favorite *athlete* and why?

4. **Display the Word/Letter-Sounds** Write the word on a card. Display it. Children can decode the word *athlete.* See p. DI·3 to teach *challenge* and *effort.*

ELL

Access Content Help children recognize the meanings of the English words *athlete* and *team* in "An Athlete's Challenge" by showing them photos of individual athletes, and then ask them to find that athlete within the team photo.

Josh Gibson **296m**

1

OBJECTIVES

- Use structural cues to decode contractions.
- Blend, read, and build contractions.

Skills Trace

Contractions

Introduce/Teach	TE: 2.6 296n-o, 298c-d
Practice	TE: 2.6 296q; PB: 2.2 103; DR26
Reteach/Review	TE: 2.6 320c, 344c, DI-64; PB: 2.2 118
Assess/Test	TE: 2.6 320e-g; Benchmark Test: Unit 6

Generalization

Contractions A contraction is a shortened form of two words. An apostrophe appears where letters have been dropped from the original words.

Strategic Intervention

Use **Monitor Progress,** p. 296o, during Group Time after children have had more practice with contractions.

Advanced

Use **Monitor Progress,** p. 296o, as a preassessment to determine whether or not this group of children would benefit from this instruction on contractions.

ELL

Support Phonics Romance languages, such as Spanish, include contractions but without an apostrophe. For example, in Spanish, *a + el = al* and *d + el = del*. Explain that in English, an apostrophe is used to replace the missing letters. English language learners may need practice changing contractions back to uncontracted forms of the words.

See the Phonics Transition Lessons in the ELL and Transition Handbook.

Contractions

TEACH/MODEL

Blending Strategy

ROUTINE

1 Connect Write *didn't*. What do you know about reading this word? (*Didn't* is a contraction of the words *did* and *not*. An apostrophe takes the place of the letter *o* in *not*.) Today we'll learn about contractions made from other words.

2 Model Write *we're*. This word is a contraction, a short way of saying and writing two words. An apostrophe takes the place of letters that are left out. You can read this word because you know the two words that make this contraction. Write *we are* under *we're*. The apostrophe in *we're* takes the place of the letter *a* in *are*. What two words make the contraction *we're*? (*we* and *are*) To read contractions, I first read the word before the apostrophe and then blend it with what comes after the apostrophe. Model blending *we're*.

3 Group Practice First, look at the word before the apostrophe. Then blend it with what comes after the apostrophe. Continue with *I've, don't, can't, he'd, you're, she'd*. Point out to children that *'d* can mean *had* or *would*. (*She'd* go with us if we ask. *He'd* found the address.)

4 Review What do you know about reading contractions? A contraction is a short way to say or write two words. An apostrophe appears where letters have been dropped from the original words.

BLEND WORDS

INDIVIDUALS BLEND WORDS Call on individuals to read *won't, they're, I'd, they'd, we've, could've*. Have them tell which two words make up each contraction and what letters were left out. For feedback, refer to step four of the Blending Strategy Routine.

BUILD WORDS

READ LONGER WORDS Write the word pairs shown below in the left column. Call on children to read the words and name the contraction they can form. Write the contraction and have them identify which letter or letters were left out to form the contraction. Have all the word pairs and contractions reread.

you are	you're
I have	I've
she had	she'd
you had	you'd
we are	we're
will not	won't

Pick the contraction that is formed from each pair of words.
Write the contraction on the line.

You are cute.
You're cute.

can't	don't	I'd	I've	she'd
they'd	they're	we're	we've	won't

1. we + have	2. I + would
we've	I'd
3. will + not	**4.** they + are
won't	they're
5. I + have	**6.** can + not
I've	can't
7. we + are	**8.** they + would
we're	they'd
9. do + not	**10.** she + would
don't	she'd

Home Activity Your child wrote contractions with 're (we're), 've (I've), 'd (I'd), and 't (won't). Work with your child to make a set of flashcards with a word pair (such as we are) on one side and the matching contraction (such as we're) on the other. Help your child practice contractions using the flashcards.

▲ **Practice Book 2.2** p. 103, Contractions

Monitor Progress | Check Word Reading Contractions

Write the following words and have individuals read them.

he'd	don't	they're	won't	we've
I'll	can't	I'd	we'll	she's
shouldn't	they've	where's	there's	what'll

If... children cannot blend contractions at this point,

then... continue to monitor their progress using other instructional opportunities during the week so that they can be successful with the Day 5 Assessment. See the Skills Trace on p. 296n.

SUCCESS PREDICTOR

Spiral REVIEW

● Row 2 contrasts contractions.
● Row 3 reviews consonant digraphs and high-frequency words.

▶ **Day 1 Check** Word Reading
Day 2 Check Lesson Vocabulary/High-Frequency Words
Day 3 Check Retelling
Day 4 Check Fluency
Day 5 Assess Progress

Word Reading
SUCCESS PREDICTOR

DAY
1

OBJECTIVES

- Segment word parts to spell words.
- Spell contractions.

Spelling Words

Contractions

1. **we're**	7. **won't**
2. **I've**	8. **they're**
3. **don't**	9. **I'd**
4. **can't**	10. **they'd***
5. **he'd**	11. **she'd**
6. **you're***	12. **we've**

Challenge Words

13. **could've**	15. **should've**
14. **would've**	

* **Words from the Selection**

Contractions

Generalization In contractions, an apostrophe (') takes the place of letters that are left out: **we are** becomes **we're**.

Sort the list words by the type of contraction.

are	not	**Spelling Words**
1. we're	6. don't	1. we're
2. you're	7. can't	2. I've
3. they're	8. won't	3. don't
have	**had/would**	4. can't
4. I've	9. he'd	5. he'd
5. we've	10. I'd	6. you're
	11. they'd	7. won't
	12. she'd	8. they're
		9. I'd
		10. they'd
		11. she'd
Challenge Words		12. we've
have		**Challenge Words**
13. could've	14. would've	13. could've
15. should've		14. would've
		15. should've

Home Activity Your child is learning to spell contractions. To practice at home, ask your child to read each word. Help your child make a sentence using each list word. Then make the same sentence using the two words used to make the contraction.

▲ **Spelling Practice Book** p. 101

ELL

Support Spelling Before giving the spelling pretest, clarify the meaning of each spelling word with examples, such as saying *I've got* (a pencil) while holding a pencil, and gesturing no to illustrate *won't*.

Spelling

PRETEST Contractions

MODEL WRITING FOR WORD PARTS Each spelling word is a contraction. Before administering the spelling pretest, model how to segment contractions to spell them.

- You can spell contractions by thinking about the two words that make up the contraction. What words make up *they're?* (*they* and *are*)
- How do you spell *they*? Write *they* or have children spell it.
- What comes next? (**the apostrophe**) The apostrophe takes the place of *a* in *are*.
- After the apostrophe, add the rest of the letters in *are*. What are the letters? (re) Write *re* after the apostrophe.
- When you spell contractions, make sure to put the apostrophe in the right place.
- Repeat with *don't.*

PRETEST Dictate the spelling words. Segment the words for children if necessary. Have children check their pretests and correct misspelled words.

HOMEWORK Spelling Practice Book, p. 101

Group Time

On-Level	Strategic Intervention	Advanced
Read Decodable Reader 26. • Use p. 296q.	**Read** Decodable Reader 26. • Use the **Routine** on p. DI·14.	**Read** Advanced Selection 26. • Use the **Routine** on p. DI·15.

ELL Place English language learners in the groups that correspond to their reading abilities in English.

ⓘ Independent Activities

Fluency Reading Pair children to read the text at children's independent level.

Journal Writing Write a paragraph about a time you played or watched baseball. Share writing.

Independent Reading See p. 296j for Reading/Library activities and suggestions.

Literacy Centers To practice contractions, you may use Word Work, p. 296j.

Practice Book 2.2 Contractions, p. 103; Compare and Contrast, p. 104

Break into small groups after Spelling and before the Comprehension lesson.

Decodable Reader 26

Hide and Seek!
Written by Hannah Bayer
Illustrated by Dan Vick

Phonics Skill
Contractions 're, 've, 'd Irregular Contractions
don't   we're   we've   you're
you've   they're should've she'd

Apply Phonics

⟳ PRACTICE Contractions

HIGH-FREQUENCY WORDS Review *answered, should've,* and *they've.*

READ DECODABLE READER 26

- Pages 82–83 Read aloud quietly with the group.
- Pages 84–85 Have the group read aloud without you.
- Pages 86–88 Select individuals to read aloud.

CHECK COMPREHENSION AND DECODING Have children retell the story to include characters, setting, and plot. Then have children locate contractions in the story. Review contraction spelling patterns. Have children list contractions in the story and write the two words the contraction stands for.

contraction	first word	second word
don't	do	not
she'd	she	had, would
should've	should	have
they've	they	have
we're	we	are
we've	we	have
won't	will	not
you've	you	have

HOMEWORK Take-Home Decodable Reader 26

REREAD FOR FLUENCY

Oral Rereading

ROUTINE

1 Read Have children read the entire story orally.

2 Reread To achieve optimal fluency, children should reread the text three or four times.

3 Provide Feedback Listen as children read and provide feedback regarding their oral reading and their use of the Blending Strategy Routine.

Monitor Progress

Decoding

If... children have difficulty decoding a word,	then... prompt them to blend the word. • What is the new word? • Is the new word a word you know? • Does it make sense in the story?

Access Content

Beginning Preview the story *Hide and Seek!* identifying *hid* and *slide* in the pictures and print. Have children repeat the words and use gestures to act out the meanings.

Intermediate Preview *Hide and Seek!* and point out and explain contractions, such as *don't, should've,* and *you've.* Facilitate a discussion, using these words to build conversational fluency.

Advanced After reading *Hide and Seek!* have partners take turns retelling the story.

Pepper Davis, Play Ball!

Pepper Davis loved to play baseball with her brother, Joe. Pepper had a good arm. In fact, she played better than Joe.

It was wartime. Many men were away fighting the war. That's when the All American Girls Baseball League began. Pepper worked hard to make a team. She became a catcher.

The girl baseball players played games almost every day during the summer. They rode a bus from town to town. They threw, hit, and ran well. The best players made 85 dollars a week.

The girls played in short skirts. They also had to act like young ladies. They took beauty lessons to learn proper behavior.

Pepper loved to win. She played baseball for ten years. Today she is in the Baseball Hall of Fame.

> **Skill** This is a good place to compare these facts with what you know about baseball players today.

> **Strategy** Try visualizing how the girl baseball players looked.

Unit 6 Just Like Josh Gibson   Skill Transparency 26

▲ Skill Transparency 26

Access Content

Beginning/Intermediate For a Picture It! lesson on compare and contrast, see the ELL Teaching Guide, pp. 176–177.

Advanced Before children read "Pepper Davis, Play Ball!" make sure they know the meanings of *wartime, league,* and *catcher.*

●Compare and Contrast
●Visualize

TEACH/MODEL

INTRODUCE Recall *Horace and Morris but mostly Dolores.* Have students compare the boys' club and the girls' club. (Possible response: The pictures show the boys playing games and the girls making projects for their moms.)

- How would the story have been different if the boys had not decided to make their own club?

Read p. 296 with children. Explain the following:

- Good readers compare and contrast what they read with what they already know. Sometimes there are helpful clue words that help us compare and contrast, such as *like, however,* and *but.* Sometimes there aren't.

- Good readers picture what is happening in a story in their minds. Then we compare what we are reading with what we already know.

Use Skill Transparency 26 to teach compare and contrast.

SKILL Use paragraph 1 to model using clue words for compare and contrast.

Think Aloud

MODEL It is important to compare and contrast characters as I read. Thinking about how people are the same and different helps me understand the story. When I read about Pepper and her brother, Joe, I learn that Pepper played better than Joe. I'll remember that as I continue to read.

STRATEGY Continue with paragraph 4 to model how to visualize.

Think Aloud

MODEL I know I can picture in my mind what people look like or what is happening. When I read that the girl players wore short skirts, I can imagine what they looked like as they played baseball.

Comprehension

Skill
Compare
and Contrast

Strategy
Visualize

Compare and Contrast

- When you compare and contrast, you see how things are alike and different.

- You can compare and contrast things you read about with things you already know.

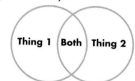

Thing 1 | Both | Thing 2

Strategy: Visualize

As good readers read, they picture in their minds how something looks, sounds, feels, tastes, or smells. Picturing can help you compare what you are reading with what you already know.

Write to Read

1. Read "Pepper Davis, Play Ball!" Make a diagram like the one above. Fill in the diagram to compare and contrast baseball today and long ago.

2. Then use your diagram to write a paragraph that compares and contrasts a player like Pepper Davis with a baseball player today.

296

Pepper Davis, Play Ball!

Pepper Davis loved to play baseball with her brother, Joe. Pepper had a good arm. In fact, she played better than Joe.

It was wartime. Many men were away fighting the war. That's when the All-American Girls Baseball League began. Pepper worked hard to make a team. She became a catcher.

The girl baseball players played games almost every day during the summer. They rode a bus from town to town. They threw, hit, and ran well. The best players made 85 dollars a week. ●

The girls played in short skirts. They also had to act like young ladies. They took beauty lessons to learn proper behavior. ●

Pepper loved to win. She played baseball for ten years. Today she is in the Baseball Hall of Fame.

Skill This is a good place to compare these facts with what you know about baseball players today.

Strategy Try visualizing how the girl baseball players looked.

297

PRACTICE

WRITE Work with children to complete the steps in the Write activity. Have children use the completed diagram to write a paragraph that compares and contrasts a player like Pepper Davis with a baseball player today.

Monitor Progress	Compare and Contrast
If... children are unable to complete Write on p. 296,	**then...** use Practice Book 2.2, p. 104, for additional practice.

CONNECT TO READING Encourage children to ask themselves these questions when they read.

- Am I picturing how the events of the story look?

- Am I imagining how the characters are alike and different?

Read the story.
Follow the directions.

Rita and Will both love to play sports, but they do not like the same ones. Rita plays soccer. She enjoys the game because she likes to run. Will likes baseball. Unlike Rita, Will doesn't like to run much. He likes to hit the ball.

1. **Underline** the part of the story that tells how Rita and Will are alike.

2. **Write** the name of the person who likes soccer. _____ Rita

3. **Write** the name of the person who likes baseball. _____ Will

4. **Write** a sentence to compare and contrast how Rita and Will feel about running.

_____ Rita likes to run, but Will does not. _____

Use what you know about sports. **Think** about what you read.
List another sport that Rita and Will might like.

5. Rita _Children should suggest a sport that involves running, such as basketball or track._

6. Will _Children should suggest a sport that involves hitting a ball, such as golf or tennis._

School + Home Home Activity Your child read a story and answered questions to compare and contrast two characters and their favorite sports. Ask your child to think about two games or activities he or she enjoys. Discuss what your child likes about them. Ask your child to tell how the activities are alike and different.

▲ **Practice Book 2.2** p. 104, Compare and Contrast

OBJECTIVE

● Write facts.

DAILY FIX-IT

1. i want to be an atlete.
   I want to be an at<u>h</u>lete.

2. they're watching ken play
   <u>T</u>hey're watching <u>K</u>en play<u>.</u>

This week's practice sentences appear on Daily Fix-It Transparency 26.

Strategic Intervention

Children who are not able to write independently may copy the facts for one of the sports from the transparency and add an illustration.

Advanced

Have children write facts about their own favorite sport and compare that sport to one of the sports from the Shared Writing.

ELL

Support Writing Have beginning English speakers dictate words or phrases about a sport to the teacher or another more proficient English speaker.

▲ **The Grammar and Writing Book**
For more instruction and practice, use pp. 200–205.

Shared Writing

WRITE Facts

GENERATE IDEAS Ask children to choose two games or sports and briefly explain how many people play, what equipment is used, how the games or sports are played, and what determines who wins.

WRITE FACTS Explain that the class will write facts about two games or sports that they choose and then compare and contrast the facts.

COMPREHENSION SKILL Have children suggest things that are similar and different about the chosen sports.

- Display Writing Transparency 26 and read the title.

- Have children work together as a class to choose the two sports they wish to write about.

- Record children's responses as they describe the number of players, equipment, how to play, and how to win each of the two games or sports.

HANDWRITING While writing, model the letter forms as shown on pp. TR14–TR17.

READ THE FACTS Have children read the completed facts aloud as you track the print.

Facts for Two
Possible answers:

Game or Sport 1 <u>Baseball</u>

Number of players <u>nine</u>
Equipment <u>bat, ball, glove, or mitt</u>
How to play <u>The pitcher on one team throws the ball. The batter on the other team hits the ball. The batter runs around the bases and scores a run.</u>
How to win
<u>Get more runs than the other team does.</u>

Game or Sport 2 <u>Basketball</u>

Number of players <u>five</u>
Equipment <u>ball, two hoops with nets</u>
How to play <u>A player on one team tries to throw the ball through the other team's hoop and make a basket.</u>
How to win
<u>Get more baskets than the other team does.</u>

Unit 6 Just Like Josh Gibson   Writing Model **26**

▲ **Writing Transparency 26**

INDEPENDENT WRITING

WRITE FACTS Have children choose a sport or game and write their own facts. Encourage them to use words from the Word Wall and the Amazing Words board. Let children illustrate their writing. You may gather children's work and save it in their portfolios.

ADDITIONAL PRACTICE For additional practice, use pp. 200–205 in the Grammar and Writing Book.

Grammar

TEACH/MODEL Using Capital Letters

REVIEW USING CAPITAL LETTERS Remind children that sentences should always begin with a capital letter.

USING CAPITAL LETTERS Display Grammar Transparency 26. Read the instruction at the top of the page. Then review it with the class.

- *January* is the first month of the year. *New Year's Day* is a holiday. Months of the year and holidays always begin with capital letters.

- *Mr.* is a title for a person so it begins with a capital letter. *Ms.* and *Mrs.* also begin with capital letters.

Have children work in small groups to write the remaining words from the transparency with correct capitalization.

PRACTICE

IDENTIFY WORDS USING CAPITAL LETTERS Write the following sentence on the board.

tim's birthday is on Tuesday, the fourth of july.

Work with children to identify the words that should be capitalized and why. Invite children to make up one sentence of their own and leave the words to be capitalized lowercase. Have partners switch papers and rewrite the sentence with correct capitalization.

OBJECTIVE
- Identify when to use capital letters.

Using Capital Letters

Days of the week, months of the year, and holidays begin with capital letters.

The first day of January is New Year's Day.

Titles for people begin with capital letters.

Every year Mr. Lewis has a big party.

Find the words that need capital letters. **Write** the words correctly on the line.

1. The last monday in may is memorial day.
Monday, May, Memorial Day

2. Every year coach Scalia and mrs. Kurtz march in the parade.
Coach, Mrs.

3. This year the fourth of july is on a friday.
Fourth of July, Friday

4. We always go to the barbecue at mr. Garcia's house.
Mr.

5. What holiday is on the fourth thursday in november?
Thursday, November

6. I saw dr. Martin and ms. Chang at the thanksgiving party.
Dr., Ms., Thanksgiving

Unit 6 Just Like Josh Gibson — Grammar **26**

▲ **Grammar Transparency 26**

Wrap Up Your Day!

✓ **CONTRACTIONS *'re, 've, 'd, don't* AND *won't*** Write *we're* and *he'd* and ask children to tell what two words make up each contraction and which letters are missing.

✓ **SPELLING WORDS WITH CONTRACTIONS** Have children write contractions: *I have, you are, could have, will not*, and *she would*.

✓ **COMPARE AND CONTRAST** To help children identify comparisons and contrasts, ask: How are football and soccer alike and different?

LET'S TALK ABOUT IT Recall the athletes in "An Athlete's Challenge." Ask children: What would you like to ask one of these athletes?"

School Home HOMEWORK Send home this week's Family Times newsletter.

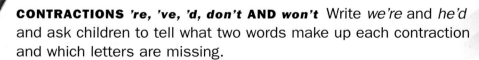

PREVIEW Day 2

Tell children that tomorrow the class will read about a girl that liked to play baseball.

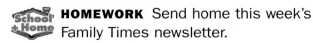

Day 2
AT A GLANCE

Share Literature
The Princesses Have a Ball

Phonics and Spelling
Contractions 're, 've, 'd
Spelling: Contractions

Build Background
Women's Baseball Leagues

Lesson Vocabulary
field	cheers	threw
sailed	plate	bases

Read

Group Time < Differentiated Instruction

Just Like Josh Gibson

Vocabulary
Multiple-Meaning Words
Context Clues

Interactive Writing
Letter

Grammar
Use Capital Letters

Materials

- *Sing with Me Big Book*
- *Read Aloud Anthology*
- Background Building Audio
- Student Edition 298–313
- Tested Word Cards
- Graphic Organizers 2, 15

Morning Warm-Up!

Today we will read about a girl who liked to play baseball.

She wanted to compete with the boys.

She played baseball for recreation.

Do you know any girls who are good baseball players?

QUESTION OF THE DAY Encourage children to sing "An Athlete's Challenge" from the *Sing with Me Big Book* as you gather. Write and read the message and discuss the question.

REVIEW ORAL VOCABULARY

- Read the second and third sentences of the message.
- Have children raise their hands when they hear the Amazing Words *compete* and *recreation* from Unit 2.

Build Background Use the Day 2 instruction on ELL Poster 26 to preview lesson vocabulary words.

ELL Poster 26

Share Literature

BUILD CONCEPTS

POETIC ELEMENTS Read the title. Identify the author. Tell children that this story uses the poetic element called rhyming. The story is written with rhyming words that offer a rhythm and cadence to the story.

BUILD ORAL VOCABULARY Ask children what they know about princesses. They are sometimes described as **dainty**, or delicate, and beautiful. Ask children if they think a dainty person could play sports well. Suggest that as you read, children listen for this word.

Read Aloud Anthology
The Princesses Have a Ball

• What word would you use to describe someone who is delicate and beautiful? (dainty)

• Besides princesses, what else might you use the word dainty to describe? (Possible responses: a doll, sandwiches, china dishes)

MONITOR LISTENING COMPREHENSION

• Who first discovered that the princesses were playing basketball? (Jack, the cobbler)

• Why do you think the princesses were secretive about playing basketball? (Possible response: They were afraid the king would not approve.)

• What special ball did the princesses plan? (a basketball game)

• Why do you think the king is proud of the princesses? (Possible response: They played a great game!)

Amazing Words to build oral vocabulary

	MONITOR PROGRESS
athlete **challenge** **effort** **dainty** **disguise** **champion** **professional** **shortstop**	**If...** children lack oral vocabulary experiences about the concept Traditions, **then...** use the Oral Vocabulary Routine. See p. DI·3 to teach *dainty*.

Build Concepts The princesses enjoy playing basketball in *The Princesses Have a Ball.* Have children demonstrate their athletic ability by role-playing a basketball game (dribbling, passing, defending, shooting the ball).

Josh Gibson   **298b**

Strategic Intervention

Strategic Intervention Decodable Reader 26 This Reader provides more practice with contractions.

ELL

Support Phonics Invite children to act out what happens in "A Great Tradition" as you replay the Phonics Songs and Rhymes Audio.

⟳ Contractions

TEACH/MODEL

ROUTINE

Fluent Word Reading

1 **Connect** Write *I've.* You can read this word because you know how to read contractions. What two words form *I've? (I* and *have)*

2 **Model** When you come to a contraction, read the word before the apostrophe and then blend it with what follows the apostrophe. **Model reading** *she's, they've, they'd, won't, don't, they'll.* When you come to a new contraction, what are you going to do?

3 **Group Practice** Write *they're, we'd, we've, he'll, she'll.* Read these words. Look at the word; say the word to yourself, and then read the word aloud. Allow 1–2 seconds previewing time.

WORD READING

PHONICS SONGS AND RHYMES CHART 26 Frame each of the following words on Phonics Songs and Rhymes Chart 26. Call on individuals to read them. Guide children in previewing.

I've	he'd	we've
we're	don't	won't

Sing "A Great Tradition" to the tune of "My Darling Clementine," or play the CD. Have children follow along on the chart as they sing. Then have individuals take turns locating contractions on the chart.

 **Phonics Songs and Rhymes Audio**

A Great Tradition

I've been playing lots of baseball,
Just like Grandpa always did.
Grandpa learned it from his father
Years ago as a small kid.

He'd play baseball with his friends too.
Now he plays all day with me.
We've been having a great time and
We're as happy as can be.

Baseball is a great tradition.
Don't you hope it stays the same?
Oh, today we still love baseball.
We won't miss a single game.

Phonics Songs and Rhymes Chart 26

BUILD WORDS

INDIVIDUALS MAKE CONTRACTIONS List the word pairs shown below at the left. Have children name the contraction from the Phonics Songs and Rhymes chart that is made from *we have*. Have children complete the activity on paper by writing the contractions made from the word pairs. Ask individuals to read the contractions. Provide feedback as necessary.

we have	we've
he had	he'd
I have	I've
we are	we're
do not	don't
will not	won't

Spelling

PRACTICE Contractions

WRITE DICTATION SENTENCES Have children write these sentences. Repeat words slowly, allowing children to hear each sound. Children may use the Word Wall to help with spelling high-frequency words. [Word Wall]

I'd ask him to come, but I don't think he will.

You're a good friend, and I've always said so!

We've seen that show before!

Won't you walk home with me today?

HOMEWORK Spelling Practice Book, p. 102

Spelling Words

Contractions

1. we're	7. won't
2. I've	8. they're
3. don't	9. I'd
4. can't	10. they'd*
5. he'd	11. she'd
6. you're*	12. we've

Challenge Words

13. could've	15. should've
14. would've	

* Words from the Selection

Contractions

Spelling Words					
we're	I've	don't	can't	he'd	you're
won't	they're	I'd	they'd	she'd	we've

Combine the two words into a contraction.

1. we + are — **we're**   2. they + had — **they'd**

3. do + not — **don't**   4. she + would — **she'd**

5. they + are — **they're**   6. you + are — **you're**

7. we + have — **we've**   8. will + not — **won't**

Write a contraction that could be used instead of the underlined words.

9. I have been riding the roller coaster. — **I've**

10. We cannot go on the bumper cars. — **can't**

11. I know I would like some popcorn. — **I'd**

12. Before today, he had never won a prize. — **he'd**

Home Activity Your child spelled words with contractions. Point to a spelling word. Ask your child to name the words that were combined to make the contraction.

▲ **Spelling Practice Book** p. 102

OBJECTIVES

● Build background.
● Learn lesson vocabulary.

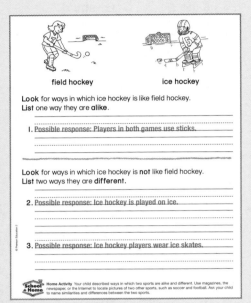

field hockey   ice hockey

Look for ways in which ice hockey is like field hockey.
List one way they are **alike**.

1. Possible response: Players in both games use sticks.

Look for ways in which ice hockey is **not** like field hockey.
List two ways they are **different**.

2. Possible response: Ice hockey is played on ice.

3. Possible response: Ice hockey players wear ice skates.

School + Home Home Activity Your child described ways in which two sports are alike and different. Use magazines, the newspaper, or the Internet to locate pictures of two other sports, such as soccer and football. Ask your child to name similarities and differences between the two sports.

▲ **Practice Book 2.2** p. 105,
Compare and Contrast

Activate Prior Knowledge Display
a picture of a baseball, a baseball bat,
and a baseball field. Ask children to tell
you about a sport that is popular in their
home country.

Build Background

DISCUSS WOMEN'S BASEBALL LEAGUES Display pictures of early baseball games in America, including pictures of women playing the game. Initiate discussion by asking children what they know about women's baseball leagues.

● Have you ever watched women play baseball?

● Where might you see women playing baseball?

● Why do you think it took so long for women to be able to play?

BACKGROUND BUILDING AUDIO Have children listen to the audio and share the new information they learned about challenges people face.

 **Sing with Me/ Background Building Audio**

COMPLETE A WEB Draw a web or display Graphic Organizer 15. Write *Challenges You Have Faced* in the center circle. Ask children to suggest ideas about challenges they have faced.

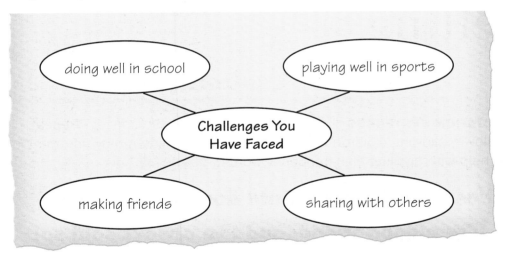

doing well in school   playing well in sports

Challenges You Have Faced

making friends   sharing with others

▲ **Graphic Organizer 15**

CONNECT TO SELECTION Connect background information to *Just Like Josh Gibson.*

Long ago, girls did not play baseball. The story we are about to read is about a girl who loved baseball. She wanted to play baseball just like her hero Josh Gibson. We'll find out what happens one day when she is given a chance to play in a game.

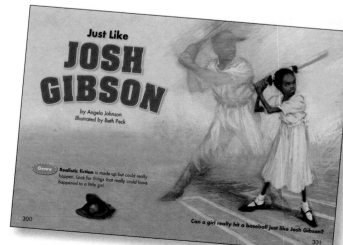

Just Like
JOSH GIBSON
by Angela Johnson
illustrated by Beth Peck

Genre **Realistic Fiction** is made up but could really happen. Look for things that really could have happened to a little girl.

Can a girl really hit a baseball just like Josh Gibson?

Vocabulary

LESSON VOCABULARY

STORY PREDICTION CHART Create a story prediction chart or use Graphic Organizer 2. Write the story title and the vocabulary words in a box at the top. Write the sentence *I think this story might be about* and include a write-on line. Have a box at the bottom where children can draw a picture that shows what the story is about after they have read it.

WORDS TO KNOW

T **field** a piece of land used for some special purpose
T **cheers** calls out or yells loudly to show that you like something
T **threw** sent something through the air by force of your arm
T **sailed** moved smoothly like a ship with sails
T **plate** a hard rubber slab that a baseball player stands beside to bat
T **bases** places that are stations or goals in certain games, such as baseball

MORE WORDS TO KNOW

soar to fly upward
forties the years between 1940 and 1949
Louisville slugger a popular kind of baseball bat

T = Tested Word

- Children should be able to decode all words except *field*. To read *field*, explain that *ie* can stand for /ē/.

- Discuss how children can use the story title and vocabulary words to decide what this story might be about.

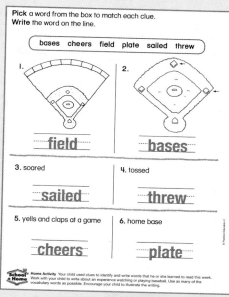

▲ **Practice Book 2.2** p. 106, Lesson Vocabulary

Monitor Progress | Check High-Frequency Words

Write the following words and have individuals read them.

field	cheers	threw	sailed	plate	bases
you're	gone	watch	guess	early	once

If ... children cannot read these words,

then ... have them find each word on the Word Wall, spell it aloud, and then write it. Monitor their fluency with these words during reading, and provide additional practice opportunities before the Day 5 Assessment.

SUCCESS PREDICTOR

Spiral REVIEW

● Reviews previously taught high-frequency words and lesson vocabulary.

Day 1 Check Word Reading

▶**Day 2** Check Lesson Vocabulary/High-Frequency Words

Day 3 Check Retelling

Day 4 Check Fluency

Day 5 Assess Progress

Word Reading

SUCCESS PREDICTOR

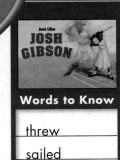

Words to Know

threw

sailed

field

bases

plate

cheers

Remember

Try the strategy. Then, if you need more help, use your glossary or a dictionary.

Vocabulary Strategy
for Multiple-Meaning Words

Context Clues What do you do when you come to a word you know, but the meaning of the word doesn't fit in the sentence? You should think to yourself that the word may have more than one meaning. For example, *bat* means "a stick used to hit a ball." *Bat* also means "a flying animal."

1. Try the meaning you know. Does it make sense in the sentence?

2. If it doesn't, the word may have another meaning. Read on and look at the nearby words. Can you figure out another meaning?

3. Try the new meaning in the sentence. Does it make sense?

Read "Tigers Over Lions." Look for words that can have more than one meaning. Remember to use nearby words to figure out a new meaning.

 Tigers Over Lions

The fifth-place Terryville Tigers played the sixth-place Lincoln Lions last night. The game promised to be an even contest. Tiger pitcher Mike Petrov has won nine games so far. Lion pitcher Kurt Geiger has won 10. Both teams have good hitters. But Petrov had a great night. He threw a perfect game. Geiger was perfect too. Well . . . almost. For eight and one-half innings, Petrov and Geiger did not give up a hit. Batter after batter went down swinging, popped up, or flied out.

In the bottom of the ninth, the Tigers' last batter was Darrell Swann. He looked at a ball and took two strikes. Then Geiger threw a ball hard and outside, and Swann hit it. The ball sailed into the far corner of right field. Swann raced around the bases. He slid across home plate just before the tag. The umpire yelled, "Safe!" The cheers of the crowd said it all. The Tigers won the game 1–0.

Words to Write

Write about an exciting game you have played. Use as many words from the Words to Know list as you can.

298

299

- Use context clues to understand multiple-meaning words.

ELL

Access Content Use ELL Poster 26 to preteach the lesson vocabulary. Reinforce the words with the Vocabulary Activities and Word Cards in the ELL Teaching Guide, pp. 178–179. Choose from the following to meet children's language proficiency levels.

Beginning Use the Multilingual Lesson Vocabulary in the ELL Teaching Guide and other home-language resources to provide translations of the tested words.

Intermediate After reading, children can create a graphic organizer word web to show words related to baseball.

Advanced Teach the lesson on pp. 298–299. Have children add additional vocabulary words and ideas to the graphic organizer word web.

Vocabulary Strategy

TEACH/MODEL Context Clues

CONNECT Remind children of strategies to use when they come across words they don't understand.

- Sometimes we can get the meaning from word parts. We may understand the base word and suffix *(beautiful, full of beauty),* or the two shorter words in a compound *(wildcat, a cat that's wild).*

- We can look in a dictionary or glossary.

- We can look for context clues in the words and sentences around the unknown word. Today we will learn more about using context clues.

INTRODUCE THE STRATEGY

Read and discuss the steps for using context clues on p. 298.

- Have children read "Tigers Over Lions," paying attention to context clues to determine the meaning of highlighted words.

Model using context clues to determine the meaning of *sailed.*

MODEL The word *sailed* describes what the ball did. I know there is no water on a baseball field, so *sailed* must have a different meaning in this sentence. The rest of the sentence tells me that it sailed into the far corner of right field. *Sailed* must mean, "glided through the air."

PRACTICE

- Have children determine the meanings of highlighted words in "Tigers Over Lions" and explain the context clues they used.

Point out that context doesn't work with every word, and that children may wish to use the glossary or a dictionary to find the meaning of some words.

WRITE Children's writing should include lesson vocabulary in a description of an exciting game they have played.

CONNECT TO READING Encourage children to use these strategies to determine the meaning of an unknown word.

- Look for context clues in nearby words or sentences.
- Consider that the word you know may have more than one meaning.
- Use the glossary or a dictionary.

Group Time

On-Level	Strategic Intervention	Advanced
Read *Just Like Josh Gibson.*	**Read** SI Decodable Reader 26.	**Read** *Just Like Josh Gibson.*
• Use pp. 300–313.	• Read or listen to *Just Like Josh Gibson.*	• Use the **Routine** on p. DI·17.
	• Use the **Routine** on p. DI·16	

 Place English language learners in the groups that correspond to their reading abilities in English.

(i) Independent Activities

Independent Reading See p. 296j for Reading/Library activities and suggestions.

Journal Writing Write about a time you got a chance to play something you always wanted to play.

Literacy Centers To provide experiences with *Just Like Josh Gibson,* you may use the Listening and Writing Centers on pp. 296j and 296k.

Practice Book 2.2 Compare and Contrast, p. 105; Lesson Vocabulary, p. 106; Fact and Opinion, p. 107

DAY 2

Break into small groups after Vocabulary and before Writing.

Just Like
JOSH GIBSON

by Angela Johnson
illustrated by Beth Peck

 Genre **Realistic fiction** is made up but could really happen. Look for things that really could have happened to a little girl.

300

Can a girl really hit a baseball just like Josh Gibson?

301

 **AudioText**

Read
Prereading Strategies

PREVIEW AND PREDICT Have children read the title. Identify Josh Gibson and the girl in the picture. Identify the author and illustrator. Do a picture walk of pp. 302–305. Ask children what they think this story will be about.

DISCUSS REALISTIC FICTION Ask children if the characters and setting look as if they could be real. Help children understand that since the pictures look realistic, the story is likely to be realistic too. Remind children that a story that is made up but could really happen is called realistic fiction. Read the definition of realistic fiction on p. 300 of the Student Edition.

SET PURPOSE Read the question on p. 301. Ask children to use their own experiences with playing or watching baseball to answer the question. Ask children what they would like to learn about baseball from reading the story.

Access Content Before reading, review the story summary in English and/or the home language. See the ELL Teaching Guide, pp. 180–182.

_____ Contractions 're, 've, 'd   lesson/tested vocabulary

Grandmama says there's nothing like baseball. The story goes. . . .

Josh Gibson once hit a baseball in Pittsburgh so hard that it didn't come down.

302

The next day he was playing in Philadelphia, and the ball dropped out of the sky, right into a fielder's glove. The umpire pointed at Josh and said, "You're out yesterday in Pittsburgh!"

303

Guiding Comprehension

Draw Conclusions • Critical
- **Do you think people thought Josh Gibson was a good baseball player?**
  Possible response: Yes, because people told stories about how well he played.

Sequence • Inferential
- **Tell the story of Josh Gibson's hit in the order it happened.**
  First, he hit a ball so hard it did not come down. Next, the team traveled to Philadelphia. During the game the next day, the ball came down in Philadelphia.

Graphic Sources • Inferential
- **Look at the illustration. Do you think Gibson just made a good hit? How can you tell?**
  Yes, everyone is looking up and into the distance. The catcher looks amazed.

▲ **Pages 302–303**
Have children read to find out how hard Josh Gibson once hit a baseball.

EXTEND SKILLS

Author's Style/Word Choice
For instruction in word choice, discuss the following:
- This story begins with an impossible tale about Josh Gibson.
- What do you think Gibson really did? What is exaggerated, or goes beyond the truth?
- People who talk and write about sports sometimes exaggerate to make their stories more interesting.

Assess Have children find another example of exaggeration in the story.

Grandmama says her papa showed up on that same day, the day she was born, with a Louisville slugger and a smile. He said his new baby would make baseballs fly, just like Josh Gibson.

So Grandmama's papa threw balls to his baby girl in the early morning dew. Those summer days were like magic as the balls sailed away, sailed away, gone.

But girls in the forties didn't play baseball. They weren't supposed to take the field with the boys or have batting dreams.

So even when Grandmama got bigger, she still had to stand outside the fence and watch her cousin Danny and the Maple Grove All-Stars batting away.

304

305

▲ **Pages 304–305**
Have children read to find out how life was different for girls in the forties.

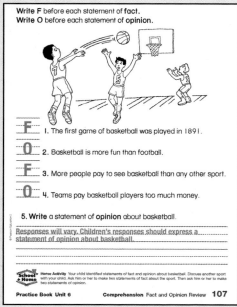

Write **F** before each statement of **fact**.
Write **O** before each statement of **opinion**.

F 1. The first game of basketball was played in 1891.

O 2. Basketball is more fun than football.

F 3. More people pay to see basketball than any other sport.

O 4. Teams pay basketball players too much money.

5. **Write** a statement of **opinion** about basketball.

Responses will vary. Children's responses should express a statement of opinion about basketball.

School + Home **Home Activity** Your child identified statements of fact and opinion about basketball. Discuss another sport with your child. Ask him or her to make two statements of fact about the sport. Then ask him or her to make two statements of opinion.

Practice Book Unit 6 **Comprehension** Fact and Opinion Review **107**

▲ **Practice Book 2.2** p. 107, Fact and Opinion

Strategies in Context

REVIEW FACT AND OPINION

- **Is the sentence "But girls in the forties didn't play baseball" a statement of fact or a statement of opinion?**

  It is a statement of fact because it can be proven true or false.

Monitor Progress	**Fact and Opinion**
If... children are unable to distinguish fact and opinion,	**then...** model how to determine if something is a fact or an opinion.

Think Aloud **MODEL** I know I can look in a book to find information that proves whether this sentence is true. Because it can be shown to be true or false, it must be a fact.

ASSESS Have children find a statement of opinion on these pages.

____ Contractions 're, 've, 'd   ☐ lesson/tested vocabular

But every now and again, when the team was just practicing, they'd let Grandmama play too. Then Grandmama would step up to the plate, hit the ball, and watch it soar.

Grandmama says Danny would imagine he was playing with the Dodgers. But she was always Josh Gibson, playing for the Grays, wearing the team colors and hitting away.

Grandmama says she would play all day, with everybody saying she could do it all, hit, throw, and fly round the bases. "But too bad she's a girl. . . ." Too bad she's a girl. . . .

306

307

Guiding Comprehension

Character • Critical

- **How do you think Grandmama felt when she heard the boys say that it's too bad she's a girl?**
Children may say that she felt bad, she thought it was unfair that she was not allowed to join the team, or that she did not let it bother her.

Make Judgments • Critical

- *Text to Self* **Grandmama's hero was Josh Gibson. Who is your hero? Why?**
Children may name sports figures, celebrities, or family members.

Summarize • Inferential

- **What has happened so far in the story?**
Grandmama has become a really good baseball player. She can hit, throw, and run. She is allowed to practice with the boys, but she cannot join the team because in the forties, girls did not play on boys' baseball teams.

▲ **Pages 306–307**
Have children read to find out how having a role model like Josh Gibson helped Grandmama play better.

Strategy Self-Check

Have children ask themselves these questions to check their reading.

Vocabulary Strategy

- Do I look for context clues?
- Do I remember that a word I know may have more than one meaning?
- Do I use the glossary or a dictionary?

Visualize

- Do I picture in my mind how the events of the story look?
- Do I imagine how the characters are alike and different?

Until . . . two days, hot days after the Fourth of July, Danny hurt his arm sliding into second, and there were only eight All-Stars.

That afternoon the team looked to Grandmama— pink dress with a white bow, and Danny's baseball shoes.

And Grandmama says as she went to the plate she remembered . . .

baseball has always been early morning dew and sunlight, hitting balls with her papa, and standing behind the fence, watching the boys play.

308

309

▲ **Pages 308–309**
Have children picture in their minds how Grandmama looked as she played in the game.

Monitor Progress

Lesson Vocabulary

If...children have a problem reading a new lesson vocabulary word,	**then**...use the Lesson Vocabulary Routine on p. 298f to reteach the problematic word.

Strategies in Context

⟳ VISUALIZE

- **Imagine that you were a spectator at Grandmama's big game. What might you see, hear, feel, and smell?**
  Children may describe sights such as Grandmama in her pink dress and baseball shoes, sounds such as the crack of a bat hitting a ball, feelings such as heat from the sun, and smells such as freshly-cut grass.

Monitor Progress | Visualize

If... children have difficulty visualizing the scene,	**then**... model how to use story details and your own experiences to make a picture in your mind.

Think Aloud **MODEL** Some details make me think of things I have seen or done before. The dew reminds me of my yard in the morning. I've stood behind a fence watching people play baseball, so I can picture that.

ASSESS Have children brainstorm phrases that describe the scene.

 _____ Contractions 're, 've, 'd   lesson/tested vocabulary

The story goes . . . Grandmama hit the ball a mile that day, caught anything that was thrown, and did everything else—just like Josh Gibson.

310

311

Skills in Context

☉ COMPARE AND CONTRAST

- **How is Grandmama just like Josh Gibson? How is she different?**
  They are alike because they are both good at baseball. They are different because Josh Gibson was famous, but Grandmama was not.

Monitor Progress	Compare and Contrast
If... children have difficulty answering the questions,	**then...** model how to use story details to compare and contrast.

Think Aloud

MODEL As I read, I find that Grandmama hit, caught, and "did everything else just like Josh Gibson." So I know they are alike in some ways. Then I remember that Josh Gibson was famous, but Grandmama is not.

ASSESS Have children recall a difference between Grandmama and her cousin Danny. (Danny was on the All-Stars team, while Grandmama was not allowed to join.)

▲ **Pages 310–311**
Have children read to find out what Grandmama did in the baseball game.

Josh Gibson

Time for **SOCIAL STUDIES**

Although the major leagues did not let African American players play until 1947, Josh Gibson had a successful career playing in the Negro National League. He was one of the greatest baseball players of his time, playing catcher on several different teams from 1927–1946. He was elected to the Baseball Hall of Fame in 1972.

Josh Gibson **310–311**

As she hands the ball to me she says, "There's nothing like baseball, baby, and I couldn't help but love it, especially that one time I got to hear the cheers, hear all the cheers, while stealing home."

312

313

▲ **Pages 312–313**
Have children read to find out how Grandmama feels about baseball today.

Opportunities

Time for **SOCIAL STUDIES**

Today there are many more opportunities for women to play sports. Young girls can easily play on soccer, basketball, and baseball teams. In 1997 a professional basketball association was set up just for women's teams. At the 2004 Olympics in Athens, women's teams from the United States won gold medals in softball, basketball, and soccer.

___ Contractions 're, 've, 'd ▢ lesson/tested vocabular

Guiding Comprehension

Draw Conclusions • Inferential

• **How do you think Grandmama feels about baseball today? How do you know?**
Children will probably say that Grandmama still loves baseball because she says, "There's nothing like baseball," and she kept the baseball from her special day.

⊚ **Compare and Contrast • Inferential**

• *Text to World* **How are baseball teams now different from when Grandmama was a little girl?**
Possible responses: Girls can play on teams now. Sometimes girls and boys play together on the same team.

Cause and Effect • Inferential

• *Text to Self* **What is a sport or other activity that means a lot to you? How does it make you feel?**
Possible response: I like kickball because it makes me feel good when I can score a run.

Fluency

REREAD FOR FLUENCY

Paired Reading

ROUTINE

Reader 1 Begins Children read the entire book, switching readers at the end of each page.

Reader 2 Begins Have partners reread; now the other partner begins.

Reread For optimal fluency, children should reread three or four times.

Provide Feedback Listen to children read and provide corrective feedback regarding their oral reading and their use of the blending strategy.

EXTEND SKILLS

Comparing Media

For instruction in comparing ideas from a wide variety of media, discuss the following:

• There are many ways to share ideas, such as TV, music, books and magazines, film, art, and the Internet.

• Some people compare ideas from a variety of sources. For example, if you wanted to learn more about what it was like to be an African American woman in the 1940s, you could read books and magazines about it, listen to music and look at artwork from that time period, search online, and watch movies.

• Once you have found information from a variety of sources, then you can compare the ideas you learn about and draw your own conclusions.

Assess Have children think of a topic or an idea of interest to them. Have them write it on a sheet of paper, and then list the different forms of media they could use to learn about that topic or idea. Finally, have them share with the class what they think the similarities and differences might be, based on the different media sources they use.

Strategic Intervention

Have children copy one sentence from the letter and illustrate their writing.

Advanced

Have children who are able to write complete sentences independently write their own letter to a specific ball player. Encourage children to mail the letter.

Writing Support Before writing, children might share ideas in their home languages.

Beginning Pair children with more proficient English speakers. A more proficient speaker can help the partner choose or write a letter.

Intermediate Help children orally practice the sentence form found in letters before they write.

Advanced Encourage children to write and read aloud their letter.

Support Grammar In languages such as Spanish, French, and Portuguese, the days and months are not usually capitalized. Provide additional practice with this English spelling convention. See the Grammar Transition lessons in the ELL and Transition Handbook.

Interactive Writing

WRITE Letter

DISCUSS Use *Just Like Josh Gibson* to encourage a discussion about baseball players. Picture walk through the story and ask children to discuss Grandmama's baseball experiences.

SHARE THE PEN Have children participate in writing a letter to a ball player. To begin, write *Dear Ball Player* and a comma. Invite children to suggest an opening sentence. Write the first sentence, inviting individuals to write familiar letter-sounds, word parts, and high-frequency words. Ask questions such as:

- What is the first sound you hear in the word *Dear*? (/d/)
- What letter stands for that sound? *(d)* Have a volunteer write *D.*
- What is the vowel sound in the word *Dear*? (/i/)
- What letters stand for that sound? *(ea)* Have a volunteer write *ea.*

Continue to have individuals contribute sentences to the letter. Frequently reread what has been written while tracking the print.

READ THE LETTER Read the completed letter aloud, having children echo you.

Dear Ball Player,

How did you get started playing ball?

Did you play other sports? Do you like

hearing the crowd cheer?

          Sincerely,

          Our Second Grade Class

INDEPENDENT WRITING

WRITE A LETTER TO A BASEBALL PLAYER Have children write their own letters to ball players. Let children illustrate their writing.

Grammar

DEVELOP THE CONCEPT Capital Letters

IDENTIFY COUNTRY NAMES Write *family, Mexico,* and *Italy* on the board. Point to each word as you read it. Ask children to identify the words that are country names. *(Mexico, Italy)*

Special names for people, places, animals, and things are called proper nouns. Names of countries are proper nouns. How do the names of countries begin? (with capital letters)

PRACTICE

NAME COUNTRIES Display a map of North America, or locate the continent on a globe. Model, pointing to the country of Canada.

 Think Aloud

MODEL This is Canada. Write *Canada. Canada* is the name of a country, so it begins with a capital letter.

Have children name other countries on the map or globe and identify the first letter in each name. Write the country names that the children provide.

DAILY FIX-IT

3. The croud chears for me.
   The cro**w**d ch**ee**rs for me.
4. I raned Around the basis.
   I <u>ran</u> <u>a</u>round the <u>bases</u>.

Using Capital Letters

Days of the week, months of the year, and holidays begin with capital letters.
   This year the **Fourth of July** is on **Wednesday**.
Titles for people begin with capital letters.
   Mrs. Davis invited us to a picnic.

Find the words that need capital letters. **Write** the words correctly on the line.

I. On monday, we went to mr. Jung's grocery store.
   Monday; Mr.

2. Mom and ms. Jones made potato salad on tuesday.
   Ms.; Tuesday

3. dr. Webb marched in the parade on independence day.
   Dr.; Independence Day

4. The fourth of july is another name for independence day.
   Fourth of July; Independence Day

5. I wish there were parades in june and august too.
   June; August

Home Activity Your child learned about using capital letters. Find a calendar. Ask your child to write the names of the days of the week. Remind him or her to use capital letters.

▲ **Grammar and Writing Practice Book** p. 101

Wrap Up Your Day!

 LESSON VOCABULARY Write the following sentences. *I step onto the field and the crowd cheers. I threw the ball to home plate.* Ask children to read the sentences and identify the vocabulary words *cheers, threw,* and *field.*

 VISUALIZE Visualize what the crowd looked like as they watched Grandmama hit the ball. Dramatize the expressions on their faces.

LET'S TALK ABOUT IT Recall *Just Like Josh Gibson.* Ask: Why do you think Grandmama is telling this story to her granddaughter? (to tell her that girls can play baseball too) Encourage children to tell about an exciting game they played.

 **PREVIEW Day 3**

Tell children that tomorrow they will hear about some princesses and their secret pastime.

Day 3
AT A GLANCE

Share Literature
The Princesses Have a Ball

Phonics and Spelling
REVIEW Vowels *aw, au, augh, al*
Spelling: Contractions

Vocabulary
Skill Homophones

Fluency
Read with Accuracy and
Appropriate Pace

Writing Trait
Sentences

Grammar
Capital Letters

Materials

• *Sing with Me Big Book*
• *Read Aloud Anthology*
• Student Edition 314–315

Morning Warm~Up!

Once upon a time, there were twelve
princesses.
These girls liked to play basketball
every night.
They wore special high-top shoes.
Today we will read about
a special ball they had.
What do you think the ball will be like?

QUESTION OF THE DAY Encourage children to sing "An Athlete's Challenge" from the *Sing with Me Big Book* as you gather. Write and read the message and discuss the question.

REVIEW LONG *i* PATTERNS Have children find words in the message that have the long *i* pattern

• **found in *bike*** (time, liked, like)

• **found in *high*** (night)

ELL

Build Background Use the Day 3 instruction on ELL Poster 26 to support children's use of English to communicate about lesson concepts.

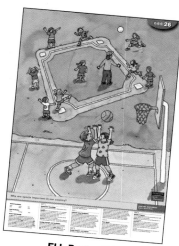

ELL Poster 26

Share Literature

LISTEN AND RESPOND

BUILD ORAL VOCABULARY Remind children that yesterday the class listened for the word *dainty*. Today they will listen for **disguise**. When someone is disguised, they change how they look so that people don't know who they are. Ask children to listen to find out who and what is disguised in this story.

MONITOR LISTENING COMPREHENSION

- What and who were disguised in this story? (Someone used a disguise to spy on the princesses, and the princesses' beds were disguised to look as if the princesses were sleeping in them.)

- Why does the king suspect the girls? What does he do to find out more about them? (The princesses are tired every morning, and they keep getting holes in their shoes. He hires detectives.)

- Who recommends that the girls tell the king and play basketball? (Jack, the cobbler)

- What do the guests wear to the ball? Why? (They wear fancy clothes because they thought they were going to a fancy dance ball, not a ball game.)

Read Aloud Anthology
The Princesses Have a Ball!

OBJECTIVES

- Set purpose for listening.
- Build oral vocabulary.

Amazing Words

to build oral vocabulary

	MONITOR PROGRESS
athlete challenge effort dainty disguise champion professional shortstop	**If...** children lack oral vocabulary experiences about the concept Traditions, **then...** use the Oral Vocabulary Routine. See p. DI·3 to teach *disguise*.

Listen and Respond Help children describe and demonstrate the actions conveyed by the words *dribbling, spun,* and *passed* in "The Princesses Have a Ball."

Josh Gibson **314b**

- Review vowels *aw, au, augh, al.*
- Blend, read, and sort *aw, au, augh, al* words.
- Recognize lesson vocabulary.
- Spell words with contractions.

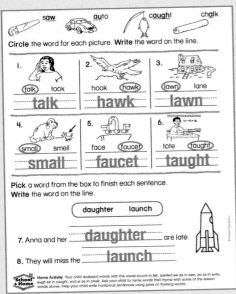

Practice Book 2.2 p. 108, Vowels *aw, au, augh, al*

Review Phonics

REVIEW VOWELS *aw, au, augh, al*

READ *aw, au, augh, al* WORDS Write *awful.* You can read this word because you know that *aw* can stand for the sound /o̊/. What sound do the letters *aw* in this word stand for? (/o̊/) What's the word? (*awful*) Do the same with *auto, caught,* and *walk.*

BUILD WORDS List the words below in random order. Then write *aw, au, augh,* and *al* as headings on a four-column chart or use Graphic Organizer 27. Have children read each word and write it under the appropriate heading.

aw	au	augh	al
draw	August	taught	talk
saw	fault	caught	chalk
thaw	launch		stalk

Lesson Vocabulary

PRACTICE

DISCUSS SITUATIONS Write the lesson vocabulary words on the board and point to each one as children read it. Ask children to use these words to discuss situations relating to them.

- If you went to spend the day in a *field,* what might you do there?
- If you heard *cheers* coming from the park, what might you find when you went to see what was happening?
- If you *threw* a ball, what might your dog do next?
- If you ran to home *plate* and were safe, how would you feel?
- If a wind blew your papers and they *sailed* away, what would you do?
- If you wanted to play baseball, what could you use to make *bases?*

Spelling

PRACTICE Contractions

WRITE SENTENCES Have children practice the spelling words by writing sentences about things that happen at a baseball game.

- Ask children to think about what they would see and do if they were at a baseball game.
- Have them write sentences using each spelling word that describes the experience of being at a baseball game.

HOMEWORK Spelling Practice Book, p. 103

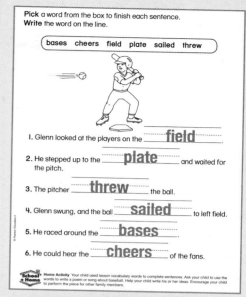

Pick a word from the box to finish each sentence. **Write** the word on the line.

| bases | cheers | field | plate | sailed | threw |

1. Glenn looked at the players on the ___**field**___
2. He stepped up to the ___**plate**___ and waited for the pitch.
3. The pitcher ___**threw**___ the ball.
4. Glenn swung, and the ball ___**sailed**___ to left field.
5. He raced around the ___**bases**___
6. He could hear the ___**cheers**___ of the fans.

Home Activity Your child used lesson vocabulary words to complete sentences. Ask your child to use the words to write a poem or song about baseball. Help your child write his or her ideas. Encourage your child to perform the piece for other family members.

▲ **Practice Book 2.2** p. 109, Lesson Vocabulary

Spelling Words

Contractions

1. **we're**	7. **won't**
2. **I've**	8. **they're**
3. **don't**	9. **I'd**
4. **can't**	10. **they'd***
5. **he'd**	11. **she'd**
6. **you're***	12. **we've**

Challenge Words

13. **could've**
14. **would've**
15. **should've**

* Words from the Selection

Contractions

Spelling Words

| we're | I've | don't | can't | he'd | you're |
| won't | they're | I'd | they'd | she'd | we've |

Read the directions. **Circle** three spelling mistakes. **Write** the words correctly. **Cross out** the extra word in the first sentence.

Frequently Misspelled Words

don't
they're
there's

Go to the the cave. There's a bear inside. It won't hurt you.
Walk northeast until your at the river. Remember, dont cross into the woods!
Dig under the big rock.
Good luck!

1. ___**won't**___ 2. ___**you're**___ 3. ___**don't**___

Fill in the circle next to the word that is spelled correctly.

4. ● she'd ○ sheed ○ shee'd
5. ○ the'yre ○ theyr'e ● they're
6. ○ cann't ● can't ○ can't
7. ○ wer'e ○ wu're ● we're
8. ○ Ive ● I've ○ Iv'e

Home Activity Your child has been learning to spell words with contractions. Your child may enjoy creating a treasure map. Use colored pencils on crumpled paper. Include some contractions in the map directions.

▲ **Spelling Practice Book** p. 103

Strategic Intervention

Have children illustrate the two meanings of *threw* and *through*. Then help them write a caption using the words for each picture.

Advanced

Have children suggest other words that are homophones, such as *sum/some* or *won/one*.

Extend Language Help children practice telling which spelling of *threw/through* should be used in the sentence by paying attention to the words around it.

Vocabulary

HOMOPHONES

DISCUSS HOMOPHONES Explain to children that some words sound the same but are spelled differently and have different meanings. Write the following sentence pair and discuss the spellings and meanings of *threw*—"tossed"—and *through*—"in one side and out the other side of."

Nick threw the ball.

Edna ran through the door.

EXPAND LESSON VOCABULARY Discuss with children the spellings and meanings of each word listed below. Provide an example for each meaning. Have children work with partners to write sentences for each word and meaning. Invite volunteers to share their sentences.

soar   **sore**

Group Time

On-Level	Strategic Intervention	Advanced
Read *Just Like Josh Gibson.* • Use pp. 300–315.	**Read** or listen to *Just Like Josh Gibson.* • Use the **Routine** on p. DI·18.	**Read** Self-Selected Reading. • Use the **Routine** on p. DI·19.

DAY 3

ELL Place English language learners in the groups that correspond to their reading abilities in English.

ⓘ Independent Activities

Independent Reading See p. 296j for Reading/Library activities and suggestions.

Journal Writing Write about a baseball game you have played or been to. Share your writing.

Literacy Centers To provide experiences with *Just Like Josh Gibson,* you may use the Writing Center on p. 296k.

Practice Book 2.2 Vowels *aw, au, augh, al,* p. 108; Lesson Vocabulary, p. 109

Break into small groups after Vocabulary and before Writing.

Fluency

READ WITH ACCURACY AND APPROPRIATE PACE

MODEL READING WITH ACCURACY AND APPROPRIATE PACE Use *Just Like Josh Gibson.*

- Point to the first sentence on p. 305. A good reader reads fluently. I'll try to read this sentence without making any mistakes. I'll read at a good speed, not too fast or slow.

- Ask children to follow along as you read the page with accuracy and appropriate pace.

- Have children read the page after you. Encourage them to read at the same pace, not too fast or slow. Continue in the same way with pp. 306–307.

REREAD FOR FLUENCY

Choral Reading

ROUTINE

Select a Passage For *Just Like Josh Gibson,* use pp. 302–306.

Divide into Groups Assign each group a part to read. The first group reads one page, then the other group reads the next page.

Model Have children track the print as you read.

Read Together Have children read along with you.

Independent Readings Have the groups read aloud without you. Monitor progress and provide feedback. For optimal fluency, children should reread three to four times.

Monitor Progress	Fluency
If... children have difficulty reading at a good pace,	**then...** prompt: • Are you reading too fast? • Are you reading too slow? • Try to read the sentences at a rate so people can follow along.
If... the class cannot read fluently without you,	**then...** continue to have them read along with you.

OBJECTIVE

- Read aloud fluently with accuracy and appropriate pace.

Options for Oral Reading

Use *Just Like Josh Gibson* or one of the following Leveled Readers.

On-Level

Women in Baseball

Strategic Intervention

Three of the Greats

Advanced

Baseball Heroes

Fluency Model the reading of phrases in the story, such as "too bad she's a girl" and "just like Josh Gibson," so that beginning English language learners can practice reading with an appropriate pace.

Retelling Plan

☑ **This week assess Strategic Intervention students.**

☐ Week 2 assess Advanced students.

☐ Week 3 assess Strategic Intervention students.

☐ Week 4 assess On-Level students.

☐ Week 5 assess any students you have not yet checked during this unit.

Look Back and Write
Point out information from the text that answers the question. Then have children write a response to the question. For test practice, assign a 10–15 minute time limit. For assessment, see the Scoring Rubric at the bottom of this page.

Assessment Before retelling, help children name items shown. For more ideas on assessing comprehension, see the ELL and Transition Handbook.

Reader Response

TALK ABOUT IT Model a response. I am excited to finally get to play on the boys' team. I know I will play well because I have practiced so much. I am glad that I can help the team do well.

1. RETELL Have children use the retelling strip in the Student Edition to retell the selection.

Monitor Progress **Check Retelling**

Have children retell *Just Like Josh Gibson.*

If... children have difficulty retelling the story,

then... use the Retelling Cards and the Scoring Rubric for Retelling on pp. 314–315 to help them move toward fluent retelling.

SUCCESS PREDICTOR

| **Day 1** Check Word Reading | **Day 2** Check Lesson Vocabulary/High-Frequency Words | ▶**Day 3 Check Retelling** | **Day 4** Check Fluency | **Day 5** Assess Progress |

---

2. ◉ **COMPARE AND CONTRAST** Model a response. Today girls can play many sports, including baseball.

3. ◉ **VISUALIZE** Model a response. I pictured an early morning with dew and sunlight. That helped me feel what it was like for Grandmama when she thought of playing baseball.

LOOK BACK AND WRITE Read the writing prompt on p. 314 and model your thinking. I'll look back at pages 302 and 303 and reread that part of the story. I'll look for details about what happened to the baseball. Then I'll write my response. Have children write their responses.

Scoring Rubric **Look Back and Write**

Top-Score Response A top-score response will use details from pp. 302–303 of the selection to tell about the baseball Josh Gibson hit in Pittsburgh.
Example of a Top-Score Response Josh Gibson hit a baseball in Pittsburgh so hard that it didn't come down. The next day he was playing baseball in Philadelphia, and the ball landed in a fielder's glove.

For additional rubrics, see p. WA10.

Reader Response

Open for Discussion A little girl puts on her cousin Danny's shoes and plays baseball. Pretend you are there. Tell about that game.

1. Use the pictures below to retell the story.
Retell

2. Grandmama could not play baseball on the Maple Grove All-Stars because she was a girl. How is that different from girls' sports today?
Compare/Contrast

3. Look back at page 309 and reread it. What picture did you have in your mind as you read this part? How did visualizing get you more involved in the story? Visualize

Look Back and Write Look back at pages 302 and 303. Josh Gibson hit a baseball in Pittsburgh. What happened to it? Use details from the story in your answer.

Meet the Author
Angela Johnson

Read two more books by Angela Johnson.

Angela Johnson has written many great stories. Childhood memories of her father's baseball games inspired *Just Like Josh Gibson*. She says, "I remember the smell of the glove oil, the sound the bats made as the players tapped them on home plate, and the hot dogs I couldn't get enough of. Baseball is a wonderful memory for me. I wanted to write a book about it being a memory for another little girl."

Ms. Johnson recently won an important award to help her continue to write her wonderful stories.

Violet's Music

Do Like Kyla

Scoring Rubric Narrative Retelling

Rubric 4 3 2 1	4	3	2	1
Connections	Makes connections and generalizes beyond the text	Makes connections to other events, stories, or experiences	Makes a limited connection to another event, story, or experience	Makes no connection to another event, story, or experience
Author's Purpose	Elaborates on author's purpose	Tells author's purpose with some clarity	Makes some connection to author's purpose	Makes no connection to author's purpose
Characters	Describes the main character(s) and any character development	Identifies the main character(s) and gives some information about them	Inaccurately identifies some characters or gives little information about them	Inaccurately identifies the characters or gives no information about them
Setting	Describes the time and location	Identifies the time and location	Omits details of time or location	Is unable to identify time or location
Plot	Describes the events in sequence, using rich detail	Tells the plot with some errors in sequence that do not affect meaning	Tells parts of plot with gaps that affect meaning	Retelling has no sense of story

Use the Retelling Chart on p. TR20 to record retelling.

Selection Test To assess with *Just Like Josh Gibson,* use Selection Tests, pp. 101–104.

Fresh Reads for Differentiated Test Practice For weekly leveled practice, use pp. 151–156.

Retelling

SUCCESS PREDICTOR

OBJECTIVE

● Recognize and use sentences in writing.

DAILY FIX-IT

5. I thruw the ball to left feild.
   I thr<u>e</u>w the ball to left f<u>ie</u>ld.

6. the crowd cheerd for him.
   <u>T</u>he crowd cheer<u>e</u>d for him.

Connect to Unit Writing

Writing Trait

Have children use strategies for developing **sentences** when they write a research report in the Unit Writing Workshop, pp. WA2–WA9.

Sentences Have language learners read their sentences aloud to check rhythm, completeness, and sense. Point out opportunities to change a declarative sentence to another type or to vary sentence beginnings.

Writing Trait of the Week

INTRODUCE Sentences

TALK ABOUT SENTENCES Explain to children that good writers use different kinds of sentences. Sentences can be statements, exclamations, commands, or questions. Varying types of sentences gives the writing rhythm and style. Write the following sentences, which are about *Just Like Josh Gibson*. Read the sentences aloud. Then model your thinking.

> **Do you know who Josh Gibson is? He was one of the greatest baseball players ever! In 1972, he was elected to the Baseball Hall of Fame. Read more about him in this book.**

Think Aloud

MODEL This paragraph is interesting because it has different kinds of sentences. The first is a question that speaks directly to readers and gets them involved. Sentence two is an exclamation that adds life to the paragraph. Sentence three is declarative and presents a fact. The final sentence is a command. When you write, try to use different types of sentences, rather than all statements.

STRATEGY FOR DEVELOPING SENTENCES On the board, write these sentence pairs. Have children choose the livelier sentence in each pair. Work with them to explain what makes that sentence lively.

> **I am going to tell you about an athlete.**
> **Who is considered the greatest baseball pitcher of all time?** *(The writer asks readers a question and gets them involved.)*
> **Whales have blowholes.**
> **Think about how whales are like teakettles.** *(The writer uses a command. Readers are challenged to think about why these different things are being compared.)*

PRACTICE

APPLY THE STRATEGY Ask children to think about a sport they enjoy. Have them write a paragraph about the sport. Tell them to include at least one question, command, or exclamation.

Grammar

APPLY TO WRITING Capital Letters

IMPROVE WRITING WITH CAPITAL LETTERS Explain to children that using capital letters helps readers identify proper nouns. Add that writing with capital letters lets readers know days, months, holidays, and titles. Remind children to use capital letters in their own writing.

Write *miss brady visited our school on the first friday in may.* Have children identify which letters should be capitalized.

> **miss brady visited our school on the first friday in may.**

> **Miss Brady visited our school on the first Friday in May.**

PRACTICE

WRITE WITH CAPITAL LETTERS Call on individuals to say a sentence aloud that contains a word that should be capitalized. Write the sentence on the board using small letters. Invite children to identify the word(s) to be capitalized and to change the letters on the board. Continue until four or five words have been capitalized.

Using Capital Letters

Underline the word that needs a capital letter. Write the word you underlined.

1. My favorite holiday is <u>christmas</u>.   <u>Christmas</u>

2. I like the month of <u>may</u> best.   <u>May</u>

3. <u>saturday</u> is the best day of the week.   <u>Saturday</u>

4. Is <u>mrs.</u> Garcia coming?   <u>Mrs.</u>

Tell about your favorite holiday. **Explain** why it is your favorite.
Possible answer:

<u>I like Thanksgiving. Everyone</u>
<u>in the family eats together. We</u>
<u>have pie. We tell what we are</u>
<u>grateful for.</u>

Home Activity Your child learned how to use capital letters in writing. Have your child read his or her paragraph about a favorite holiday on this page. Ask your child to circle capital letters.

▲ **Grammar and Writing Practice Book** p. 102

Wrap Up Your Day!

✓ **COMPARE AND CONTRAST** Have children recall Grandmama in *Just Like Josh Gibson.* (a determined, athletic girl playing baseball when girls didn't play baseball) How is the grandma in *Just Like Josh Gibson* similar to the princesses in *The Princesses Have a Ball*? (All play sports, all are athletic, and all are determined.)

✓ **READ WITH ACCURACY AND APPROPRIATE PACE** Remind children that fluent readers avoid making mistakes when reading. They read at a good pace—not too fast and not too slow.

LET'S TALK ABOUT IT Display the "Sports are important in our country" Graphic Organizer 16 from Day 1. Help children identify additional reasons that support this idea. Did the guests who attended the ball in *The Princesses Have a Ball* enjoy the game? Were the princesses in good physical condition?

PREVIEW Day 4

Tell children that tomorrow they will read about how baseball began.

Share Literature
"Yankee Doodle Shortstop"

Phonics and Spelling
REVIEW Words in Context
Spelling: Contractions

Read Apply Phonics
Group Time < Differentiated Instruction
"How Baseball Began"

Fluency
Read with Accuracy and Appropriate Pace

Writing Across the Curriculum
Diagram

Grammar
Capital Letters

Speaking and Listening
Speak to Your Audience

Materials

- *Sing with Me Big Book*
- *Read Aloud Anthology*
- Student Edition 316–319

Morning Warm~Up!

Today we will read to find out how baseball began. Baseball gives us an opportunity to compete and participate in recreation. What else do team sports teach us?

QUESTION OF THE DAY Encourage children to sing "The Athlete's Challenge" from the *Sing with Me Big Book* as you gather. Write and read the message and discuss the question.

REVIEW ORAL VOCABULARY

- Ask children to read the message aloud, snapping when they get to the following words: *opportunity, compete, participate.*
- Ask children the meanings of the words.

ELL

Extend Language Use the Day 4 instruction on ELL Poster 26 to extend and enrich language.

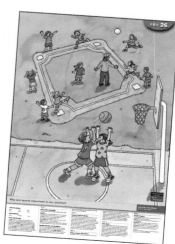

ELL Poster 26

Share Literature

CONNECT CONCEPTS

ACTIVATE PRIOR KNOWLEDGE Recall Grandmama in *Just Like Josh Gibson* and the time she was able to play with the boys in the big game. Explain that you will read another story about a girl athlete. This story is about Meg, a girl baseball player who plays on a team of boys—"Yankee Doodle Shortstop" by Helen Hinterberg.

Read Aloud Anthology
Yankee Doodle Shortstop

BUILD ORAL VOCABULARY Read the first part of the story. Explain that Meg made the boys' baseball team, but she doesn't think she is a good player. Meg knows she will never play **professional** baseball. Professional players are paid for playing. She doesn't feel like a **champion.** This is because she doesn't think of herself as a winner. Meg plays **shortstop,** the infield position between second and third bases. Ask children to listen to find out if Meg sticks it out on the team.

REVIEW ORAL VOCABULARY After reading, review all the Amazing Words for the week. Have children take turns using them in sentences that tell about the concept for the week. Then talk about Amazing Words they learned in other weeks and connect them to the concept, as well. For example, ask:

- Do you ever **daydream** about becoming a professional athlete? Explain.
- What sports or other types of **recreation** do you **appreciate** and enjoy?

MONITOR LISTENING COMPREHENSION

- Why did Coach tell Meg he picked her for the team? (She has good skills and natural talent. She's a hard worker and knows the game. She will pave the way for when his daughters want to play ball with the boys.)

- Do you think Meg will ever play professional baseball? (Possible response: No, because there is no professional baseball for women.)

- How does "Yankee Doodle" help Meg deal with playing shortstop? (She knows it so well, she doesn't have to think about it. It helps her forget the pressure of making a mistake.)

- Coach Russell told Meg there were two kinds of champions. Which kind of champion are you? Explain. (Possible response: I'm the kind who figures out how to deal with the pressure because I get really nervous when I play baseball. I don't want to let my team down.)

OBJECTIVES

- Set purpose for listening.
- Build oral vocabulary.

Amazing Words
to build oral vocabulary

MONITOR PROGRESS

athlete challenge effort dainty disguise **champion** **professional** **shortstop**	**If...** children lack oral vocabulary experiences about the concept Traditions, **then...** use the Oral Vocabulary Routine. See p. DI·3 to teach *champion, professional,* and *shortstop.*

Connect Concepts To show their understanding of *shortstop* in "Yankee Doodle Shortstop," children can use a picture of a baseball diamond and point to where the *shortstop* generally stands. Show children *professional* baseball players by bringing in baseball cards. To illustrate the meaning of *champions,* show children championship celebratory team photos from a newspaper or sports magazine.

Spiral **REVIEW**

● Reviews /f/ *ph, gh*
● Reviews consonant digraphs.
● Reviews high-frequency words *guess, pretty, science, shoe, village, watch, won.*

Sentence Reading

REVIEW WORDS IN CONTEXT

READ DECODABLE AND HIGH-FREQUENCY WORDS IN CONTEXT Write these sentences. Call on individuals to read a sentence. Then randomly point to words and have children read them. To help you monitor word reading, high-frequency words are underlined and decodable words are circled.

I guess you saw the pretty whale.

Did you see them laugh in math and science?

We watch those dolphins and wish they were pets.

That photo of a bunch of shrimp won the contest.

The garden patch near the village has enough flowers.

My shoe is rough, and my foot starts to itch when I wear it.

Monitor Progress	Word Reading
If... children are unable to read an underlined word,	**then...** read the word for them and spell it, having them echo you.
If... children are unable to read a circled word,	**then...** have them use the blending strategy they have learned for that word type.

Support Phonics For additional review, see the phonics activities in the ELL and Transition Handbook.

Spelling

PARTNER REVIEW Contractions

READ AND WRITE Supply pairs of children with index cards on which the spelling words have been written. Have one child read a word while the other writes it. Then have children switch roles. Have them use the cards to check their spelling.

HOMEWORK Spelling Practice Book, p. 104

OBJECTIVE

● Spell contractions.

Spelling Words

Contractions

1. **we're**	7. **won't**
2. **I've**	8. **they're**
3. **don't**	9. **I'd**
4. **can't**	10. **they'd***
5. **he'd**	11. **she'd**
6. **you're***	12. **we've**

Challenge Words

13. **could've**	15. **should've**
14. **would've**	

* Words from the Selection

Group Time

On-Level

Read "How Baseball Began."

• Use pp. 316–319.

Strategic Intervention

Read or listen to "How Baseball Began."

• Use the **Routine** on p. DI·20.

Advanced

Read "How Baseball Began."

• Use the **Routine** on p. DI·21.

ELL Place English language learners in the groups that correspond to their reading abilities in English.

Contractions

Spelling Words					
we're	I've	don't	can't	he'd	you're
won't	they're	I'd	they'd	she'd	we've

Cross out all of these letters: **j, p, m, b. Write** a list word by copying the letters that are left.

1. **we've**
2. **I'd**
3. **he'd**
4. **you're**
5. **they'd**
6. **don't**
7. **we're**
8. **I've**
9. **they're**

Write the missing list word. It will rhyme with the underlined word.

10. We'd like to sit in the sun, but **she'd** rather run.

11. If you <u>don't</u> want to run very far, we **won't**

12. The dog **can't** run any longer. She can only <u>pant</u>.

School + Home Home Activity Your child has been learning to spell words with contractions. Remind your child that the apostrophe (') in the contraction should always be placed in the spot where the letters are missing.

▲ **Spelling Practice Book** p. 104

(i) Independent Activities

Fluency Reading Pair children to reread *Just Like Josh Gibson*.

Journal Writing Write a paragraph telling someone how to become a better athlete.

Spelling Partner Review

Independent Reading See p. 296j for Reading/Library activities and suggestions.

Literacy Centers To provide listening opportunities, you may use the Listening Center on p. 296j. To extend social studies concepts, you may use the Social Studies Center on p. 296k.

Break into small groups after Spelling and before Fluency.

Social Studies in Reading

Expository Nonfiction

Genre
- Expository nonfiction explains an object or an idea.
- Expository nonfiction gives facts.

Text Features
- Headings, diagrams, captions, and graphs help the reader better understand the text.
- This article includes picture graphs to show information about numbers of teams.

Link to Social Studies
Use the library to find information about another game you want to learn about.

How Baseball Began

by Tammy Terry

illustrated by Clint Hansen

Baseball is called the national pastime of the United States. Hundreds of games are played and watched every spring and summer. But have you ever wondered how baseball began?

Who Invented It?

Well, no one knows for sure who invented the game. Many people believe that a man named Abner Doubleday invented baseball in 1839 in Cooperstown, New York.

316

Abner Doubleday

In rounders, players threw the ball at runners. If a runner got hit, he was out.

Baseball probably developed from the English game of the 1600s called "rounders."

Settlers living in America played rounders in the 1700s. They also called the game "town ball" and "base ball." Rules of the game varied from place to place. Over the years, the game of rounders became the game we now call baseball. One of the biggest differences between the two games is in how the batter is put out.

In baseball, players tag runners to put them out.

Compare and Contrast | What two games are being compared?

317

Audio CD AudioText

OBJECTIVE
- Recognize text structure: expository nonfiction.

Read
Social Studies in Reading

PREVIEW AND PREDICT Read the title and author's name. Have children preview the article and tell what they see in the illustrations. (people playing baseball, graphs, globes) Then ask children to predict whether "How Baseball Began" tells a story or provides information. Have children read to learn how baseball began and who is credited for inventing the game.

INFORMATIONAL TEXT Review that selections about real people doing real things are called nonfiction. This informational article uses headings, diagrams, captions, and charts to explain how baseball began. Point out that the sentences, or captions, near each picture provide information about what is pictured.

VOCABULARY/MULTIPLE-MEANING WORDS Review that some words have more than one meaning. Have children locate *play* and *watch* on p. 319. What does *play* mean in this sentence—"a story acted out" or "take part in a game"? What does *watch* mean—"to look at something" or "a device for telling time"?

Players and Teams

The first official baseball game was played in Hoboken, New Jersey, on June 19, 1846. The New York Nine beat the Knickerbockers 23–1. More people became fans of the sport as more games were played.

In 1869, the Cincinnati Red Stockings became the first baseball team to get paid to play baseball. They won every game they played that year. Support for baseball continued to grow. More professional teams were formed. In 1876, eight teams joined to form the National League. The American League began in 1900 with eight teams.

YEAR	LEAGUE	TEAMS
1876	National	⚾⚾⚾⚾⚾⚾⚾⚾
1900	American	⚾⚾⚾⚾⚾⚾⚾⚾

Today, sixteen teams play in the National League. There are fourteen teams in the American League.

YEAR	LEAGUE	TEAMS
2005	National	⚾⚾⚾⚾⚾⚾⚾⚾
		⚾⚾⚾⚾⚾⚾⚾⚾
2005	American	⚾⚾⚾⚾⚾⚾⚾
		⚾⚾⚾⚾⚾⚾⚾

They play in cities across the United States **(1)** and Canada **(2)**. Each year, millions of people go to baseball games, watch the games on TV, and read about the teams in newspapers. The sport has spread throughout the world, and baseball is now played in countries such as Japan **(3)**, Italy **(4)**, and South Africa **(5)**.

Reading Across Texts
The story *Just Like Josh Gibson* tells that Grandmama played baseball in the 1940s. Use what you read in this article to figure out how long after the "invention" of baseball by Abner Doubleday that was.

Writing Across Texts Make a timeline to show the important dates in baseball history. Be sure to include the time when Grandmama played.

(C) **Compare and Contrast** Use the charts to compare the number of teams in each league.

318 / 319

BUILD CONCEPTS

Graphic Sources • Inferential

• **How many more teams were in the National League than the American League in 2005?**

two

Recall and Retell • Literal

• **Where and when was the first official baseball game played?**

Hoboken, New Jersey, on June 19, 1846

CONNECT TEXT TO TEXT

Have children locate the sentence in "How Baseball Began" that tells the year baseball was "invented" by Abner Doubleday. (1839) **Then help children compare that date to the 1940s, when Grandmama played, and tell how long after the invention of baseball Grandmama played.** (more than 100 years)

Tell children to make a time line with the dates 1600, 1700, 1800, 1900, and 2000. Help children fill in important events.

Forces

When we push or pull, we can make things start moving, stop moving, change speed, or change direction. Demonstrate throwing and catching a ball to make it start and stop moving. Demonstrate bouncing a ball to make the ball change speed and direction.

 TIME FOR Science

E L L

Activate Prior Knowledge Ask: Do you have a favorite major league baseball team? Which is it? Supply the names and logos of MLB teams if children do not know them.

- Read aloud fluently with accuracy and appropriate pace.

Options for Oral Reading

Use *Just Like Josh Gibson* or one of the following Leveled Readers.

On-Level

Women in Baseball

Strategic Intervention

Three of the Greats

Advanced

Baseball Heroes

Assess Fluency Provide opportunities for children to echo read, repeating a passage phrase-by-phrase as each phrase is read aloud by the teacher, aide, or another skilled reader such as a proficient student.

Fluency

READ WITH ACCURACY AND APPROPRIATE PACE

MODEL READING WITH ACCURACY/APPROPRIATE PACE Use *Just Like Josh Gibson.*

- Point to the last two sentences on p. 307. When I see the three dots together (…), I know I should slow down and pause.
- Ask children to follow along as you read the page with accuracy and at an appropriate pace.
- Have children read the page after you. Encourage them to read without skipping any words. Continue in the same way with pp. 308–309.

REREAD FOR FLUENCY

Choral Reading

ROUTINE

1 **Select a Passage** For *Just Like Josh Gibson,* use pp. 306–313.

2 **Divide into Groups** Assign each group a part to read. For this story, alternate pages. The first group reads one page. Then the other group reads the next page and so on.

3 **Model** Have children track the print as you read.

4 **Read Together** Have children read along with you.

5 **Independent Readings** Have groups read aloud without you. Monitor progress and provide feedback. For optimal fluency, children should reread three to four times.

Monitor Progress | Check Fluency WCPM

As children reread, monitor their progress toward their individual fluency goals. Current Goal: 90–100 words correct per minute. End-of-Year Goal: 90 words correct per minute.

If… children cannot read fluently at a rate of 90 words correct per minute,

then… make sure children practice with text at their independent level. Provide additional fluency practice, pairing nonfluent readers with fluent readers.

If… children already read at 90 words correct per minute,

then… they do not need to reread three to four times.

SUCCESS PREDICTOR

Day 1 Check Word Reading

Day 2 Check Lesson Vocabulary/High-Frequency Words

Day 3 Check Retelling

▶ **Day 4 Check Fluency**

Day 5 Assess Progress

Writing Across the Curriculum

WRITE Diagram

BRAINSTORM Ask children to name the parts of a baseball field. Encourage them to use selection vocabulary, such as *bases* and *plate*.

SHARE THE PEN Have children participate in creating a diagram. To begin, draw a simple picture of a diamond and explain that the class will work together to write labels for a baseball field. Explain that a diagram is a way to show information using a drawing or a photograph. Call on an individual to name one part of a baseball field and have the class repeat it. Write the label, inviting individuals to help spell the word by writing familiar letter-sounds and lesson vocabulary words. Ask questions, such as the following:

- What is the beginning blend you hear in the word *plate*? (/pl/)
- What letters stand for that blend? *(p and l)* Have a volunteer write *pl.*
- What letter is at the end of *base*? (e)
- How is *field* spelled? (field)

Continue having individuals contribute to writing labels. Frequently reread the labels.

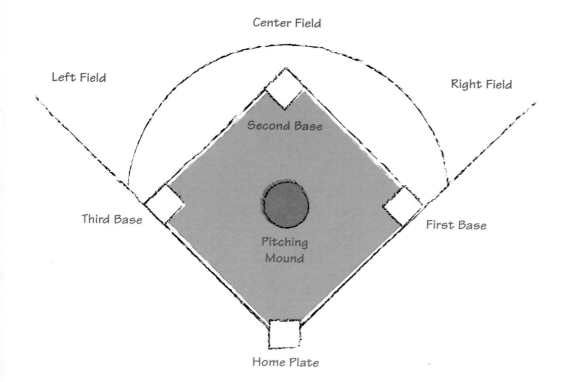

OBJECTIVE

● Identify capital letters.

DAILY FIX-IT

7. We shou'ldve wun the game.
   We should've won the game.

8. We wouldv'e, if w'ed scored!
   We would've, if we'd scored!

Using Capital Letters

Mark the letter of the word or words that complete each sentence and show the correct use of capital letters.

1. On ____, our teacher had a surprise for us.
   ○ A monday
   ⊗ B Monday
   ○ C january

2. ____ brought in many small trees.
   ○ A mr. fisk
   ○ B mr. Fisk
   ⊗ C Mr. Fisk

3. People plant trees on the last Friday in ____ .
   ⊗ A April
   ○ B april
   ○ C Wednesday

4. He told us it was ____ .
   ○ A arbor Day
   ⊗ B Arbor Day
   ○ C Arbor day

5. ____ and other parents helped us plant the trees.
   ⊗ A Mrs. Sloan
   ○ B mrs. sloan
   ○ C mrs. Sloan

6. On ____ , I showed Grandma the trees.
   ○ A september
   ○ B saturday
   ⊗ C Saturday

 Home Activity Your child prepared for taking tests on using capital letters. Look through a newspaper article together. Ask your child to circle days of the week, months, holidays, or titles of people.

▲ **Grammar and Writing Practice Book** p. 103

Grammar

REVIEW Capital Letters

DEFINE CAPITAL LETTERS

● How do names of days, months, and holidays begin? (with a capital letter)
● How do proper nouns and titles of people begin? (with a capital letter)

PRACTICE

IDENTIFY WORDS THAT NEED CAPITAL LETTERS Write *mr. glennon, memorial day, tomorrow, today, april, yesterday, dr. b. regnier, italy, thanksgiving* on the board. Have individuals identify which of these words should be capitalized. Have children make the changes on the board.

Point out that some people use their first and/or middle initials in place of their first or middle names. For instance, the *B* in Dr. B. Regnier is the first letter of the doctor's first name. Remind children that initials and abbreviations are capitalized and end with a period.

Mr. Glennon	**Memorial Day**	**tomorrow**
today	**April**	**yesterday**
Dr. B. Regnier	**Italy**	**Thanksgiving**

Speaking and Listening

SPEAK TO YOUR AUDIENCE

DEMONSTRATE SPEAKING AND LISTENING Review appropriate listening and speaking behaviors. Speakers should first think of their audience. They should consider whether they are speaking informally to family and friends or making a formal class report. Then they should plan what to say and how to say it.

Speakers	Listeners
• **Think about the audience.** • **Decide whether to use formal or informal language.**	• **Sit quietly.** • **Face the speaker.** • **Listen to what the speaker says.** • **Watch for nonverbal cues, such as hand gestures and head movements.**

TAKE A SURVEY Ask children to name their favorite baseball team. Have each child respond in a complete sentence as if they are making a formal presentation. Then record the results.

Cubs	Red Sox	Yankees	Cardinals
6	8	4	3

ADDITIONAL PRACTICE Have children deliver an informal presentation that demonstrates their understanding of a topic. Ask children to choose their favorite book, magazine, or activity and tell the class, or a group, about their choice and why it is their favorite. Remind children to speak informally as they would to family or friends.

Wrap Up Your Day!

✓ **MAKE CONNECTIONS: TEXT TO WORLD** Discuss how baseball has become a part of American culture. What are some ways baseball has become a part of people's lives? (People go to games, watch it on TV, listen to games on the radio, read about baseball in the newspaper, wear team clothes.)

LET'S TALK ABOUT IT Discuss why sports are important in our country and how women play an important role in sports today. Encourage children to add additional items to their list of challenges created earlier in the week.

PREVIEW Day 5

Remind children that they heard about how baseball began and why sports are important in our country. Tell them that tomorrow they will hear about a baseball player.

Day 5
AT A GLANCE

Share Literature
"Yankee Doodle Shortstop"

Phonics and Spelling
 REVIEW Contractions *'re, 've, 'd*

Lesson Vocabulary
field	cheers	threw
sailed	plate	bases

Monitor Progress
Spelling Test: Words with Contractions *'re, 've, 'd*

Group Time < Differentiated Assessment

Writing and Grammar
Trait: Sentences
Capital Letters

Research and Study Skills
People as Resources

Materials

- *Sing with Me Big Book*
- *Read Aloud Anthology*
- Reproducible Pages TE 320f–320g
- Student Edition 320–321

Morning Warm~Up!

This week we read about sports.
Would you like to be an athlete?
Athletes give an extra effort
in every challenge they face.
Why are sports important in our country?

QUESTION OF THE DAY Encourage children to sing "An Athlete's Challenge" from the *Sing with Me Big Book* as you gather. Write and read the message and discuss the question.

REVIEW ORAL VOCABULARY Have children find words in the message that describe

- what we read about this week
- what athletes give
- what athletes face

Assess Vocabulary Use the Day 5 instruction on ELL Poster 26 to monitor children's progress with oral vocabulary.

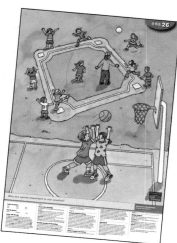

ELL Poster 26

Share Literature

LISTEN AND RESPOND

USE PRIOR KNOWLEDGE Review that yesterday the class listened to find out if Meg stayed on the boys' baseball team. Suggest that today the class listen to find out how the coach feels about her playing ability.

MONITOR LISTENING COMPREHENSION

- When Meg sings "Yankee Doodle," how well does she play? How does she show this? (Most children will say she plays great; she catches the ball, throws it to first base, and gets the runner out. Encourage children to support answers with details from the story.)

- How does Jamie feel about Meg being on his team? (He wants her to play well.) What does he do to show Meg how he feels? (He glances her way and gives her a thumbs-up.)

Read Aloud Anthology
Yankee Doodle Shortstop

BUILD ORAL VOCABULARY

GENERATE DISCUSSION Recall from the Read Aloud how much Meg loves baseball. Have children discuss sports or other activities they love to participate in. Have them use some of this week's Amazing Words as they talk about their hobbies and sports.

| **Day 1** Check Word Reading | **Day 2** Check Lesson Vocabulary/High-Frequency Words | **Day 3** Check Retelling | **Day 4** Check Fluency | ▶ **Day 5 Check Oral Vocabulary Assess Progress** |

OBJECTIVES

- Set purpose for listening.
- Build oral vocabulary.

Amazing Words to build oral vocabulary

athlete	disguise
challenge	champion
effort	professional
dainty	shortstop

Extend Language Tell children that multiple–meaning words look the same but have different meanings. For example, *pitcher* means "ball player who throws the ball to the batter" and *pitcher* can mean "container used to hold and pour out liquids."

Oral Vocabulary

SUCCESS PREDICTOR

Contractions

REVIEW

IDENTIFY CONTRACTIONS Write these sentences. Have children read each one aloud. Call on individuals to name and underline the contractions and identify the word parts.

> **Don't you know if they're here yet?**
> **I don't see it—I should've found it by now.**
> **Don't ask them if they'd been there.**
> **I would've called you but you'd just left the house.**

Lesson Vocabulary

REVIEW

SAY AND SPELL WORDS Read the rhyme. Ask children to complete each line with one of the words from p. 298. Have children say, spell, and locate the word on the Word Wall. Then reread the rhyme. **Word Wall**

I hit the ball and watched as it _____ (sailed)

over the green, grassy _____. (field)

Everyone shouted and gave three _____! (cheers)

I ran the _____ as fast as anyone has seen! (bases)

Just as the pitcher _____ the ball, (threw)

I crossed home _____. "Safe!" was the call! (plate)

Vocabulary For additional practice with lesson vocabulary, use the vocabulary strategies and word cards in the ELL Teaching Guide, pp. 178–179.

SPELLING TEST Contractions

DICTATION SENTENCES Use these sentences to assess this week's spelling words.

1. <u>We're</u> going to see a performance called *The Nutcracker.*
2. <u>I've</u> washed the dishes for you, Mom.
3. We <u>don't</u> want the rain to ruin our baseball game.
4. I <u>can't</u> see the owl, but I can hear it!
5. <u>He'd</u> like to come to our party on Saturday.
6. <u>You're</u> very good at setting up that tent!
7. We <u>won't</u> go to the store until you get here.
8. <u>They're</u> going to make sure everyone has something to eat.
9. <u>I'd</u> love to hear you read that book again!
10. I think <u>they'd</u> like to meet us at the park.
11. Do you think <u>she'd</u> like to go to the circus with us?
12. Each summer <u>we've</u> flown to California to see my grandparents.

CHALLENGE WORDS

13. Who do you think <u>could've</u> painted that beautiful mural?
14. I <u>would've</u> joined the chess club, but it meets when I have piano lessons.
15. Mom said I <u>should've</u> done my homework before dinner instead of after!

ASSESS

● Spell contractions.

Spelling Words

Contractions

1. **we're**	7. **won't**
2. **I've**	8. **they're**
3. **don't**	9. **I'd**
4. **can't**	10. **they'd**＊
5. **he'd**	11. **she'd**
6. **you're**＊	12. **we've**

Challenge Words

13. **could've**	15. **should've**
14. **would've**	

＊ Words from the Selection

Group Time

On-Level	Strategic Intervention	Advanced
Read Set B Sentences.	**Read** Set A Sentences.	**Read** Set C Sentences and the Story.
• Use pp. 320e–320g.	• Use pp. 320e–320g.	• Use pp. 320e–320g.
	• Use the **Routine** on p. DI·22.	• Use the **Routine** on p. DI·23.

ELL Place English language learners in the groups that correspond to their reading abilities in English.

DAY 5

(i) Independent Activities

Fluency Reading Children reread selections at their independent level.

Journal Writing Write a story about an athlete who puts in extra effort to meet a special challenge. Share writing.

Independent Reading See p. 296j for Reading/Library activities and suggestions.

Literacy Centers You may use the Technology Center on p. 296k to support this week's concepts and reading.

Practice Book 2.2 Use People as Resources, p. 110

Break into small groups after Spelling and before Grammar and Writing.

Josh Gibson

ASSESS

- Decode contractions *'re, 've, 'd.*
- Read lesson vocabulary words.
- Read aloud with appropriate speed and accuracy.
- Compare and contrast.
- Retell a story.

Differentiated Assessment

On-Level
Set B

Strategic Intervention
Set A

Advanced
Set C

Fluency Assessment Plan

☑ **This week assess Advanced students.**

☐ Week 2 assess Strategic Intervention students.

☐ Week 3 assess On-Level students.

☐ Week 4 assess Strategic Intervention students.

☐ Week 5 assess any students you have not yet checked during this unit.

Set individual fluency goals for children to enable them to reach the end-of-year goal.

- Current Goal: 90–100 wcpm
- End-of-Year Goal: 90 wcpm
- **ELL** An informal method of assessing oral reading fluency is to simply listen to a child reading orally and judge how clear the reading is.

SENTENCE READING

ASSESS CONTRACTIONS *'re, 've, 'd* AND LESSON VOCABULARY WORDS Use one of the reproducible lists on p. 320f to assess children's ability to read words with contractions *'re, 've, 'd* and lesson vocabulary words. Call on individuals to read two sentences aloud. Have each child in the group read different sentences. Start over with sentence one if necessary.

RECORD SCORES Use the Sentence Reading Chart for this unit on p. WA19.

Monitor Progress	Contractions *'re, 've, 'd*
If... children have trouble reading contractions *'re, 've, 'd,*	**then...** use the Reteach Lessons on p. DI·64.
Lesson Vocabulary Words	
If... children cannot read a lesson vocabulary word,	**then...** mark the missed words on a lesson vocabulary word list and send the list home with the child for additional word reading practice, or have the child practice with a fluent reader.

FLUENCY AND COMPREHENSION

ASSESS FLUENCY Take a one-minute sample of children's oral reading. See Monitoring Fluency, p. WA17. Have children read "Luke and Carlos," the on-level fluency passage on p. 320g.

RECORD SCORES Record the number of words read correctly in one minute on the child's Fluency Progress Chart.

ASSESS COMPREHENSION Have the child read to the end of the passage. (If the child had difficulty with the passage, you may read it aloud.) Ask how the characters are the same and different and have the child retell the passage. Use the Retelling Rubric on p. 314–315 to evaluate the child's retelling.

Monitor Progress	Fluency
If... a child does not achieve the fluency goal on the timed reading,	**then...** copy the passage and send it home with the child for additional fluency practice, or have the child practice with a fluent reader.
Compare and Contrast	
If... a child cannot compare and contrast the characters,	**then...** use the Reteach Lesson on p. DI·64.

READ THE SENTENCES

Set A

1. We'd rather she'd play in right field.
2. They don't know if they've heard cheers.
3. I'd like to catch the ball Bill threw, but I won't.
4. I've seen that you've made it to the plate.
5. They're happy the ball sailed to where we're sitting.
6. They'd like it if we've got runners on all the bases.

Set B

1. I don't know if you're going to play in left field.
2. He'd like the new cheers that you've written.
3. She won't notice if you're running to home plate.
4. We'd be happy if she threw it, but she didn't.
5. Who'd like to clean the bases after they're done?
6. We've sailed once, but they'd like to see it again.

Set C

1. Were the cheers the ones they'd hoped we'd perform?
2. They've wanted to play football on this field since we've been a team.
3. I've never caught a ball he threw, but I know you've done it twice.
4. I don't know if she'd be afraid to run to the plate.
5. You should've seen how the ball sailed over the fence and now it won't be caught.
6. You'd think he'd be proud to make a hit with the bases loaded.

Monitor Progress | Contractions 're, 've, 'd
Lesson Vocabulary Words

SUCCESS PREDICTOR

Luke and Carlos

Luke and Carlos are best friends. They're the   8
same in many ways but different in other ways.   17

They've always lived on the same street.   24
They're both in the second grade. You'd be   32
surprised to know that they each have an older   41
sister and a younger brother. You've probably   48
seen them ride their bikes together. I've seen them   57
play video games together too.   62

They'd like to think that they're the same all the   72
time, but they're not. Luke belongs to a soccer   81
team. He'd rather play soccer than any other   89
sport. Carlos is on a baseball team. I'd guess that   99
he's the best player on the team. Carlos says he   109
won't ever play soccer. Luke says he won't ever   118
play baseball.   120

The boys admit they'd like to play a sport   129
together. But they don't know if they would both   138
like the same sport.   142

Luke says, "We'd like to try playing basketball   150
on the same team. We're both ready to try it this   161
year. I hope it works out."   167

See also Assessment Handbook, p. 357 • REPRODUCIBLE PAGE

SUCCESS
PREDICTOR

Write Now
Writing and Grammar

Facts

Prompt

Just Like Josh Gibson describes a baseball player's skills. Think about someone you know who has special skills or abilities. Now write facts that tell about that person's skills.

Writing Trait

Different kinds of **sentences** make writing smoother.

Student Model

Question grabs reader's attention.

Writer gives facts about person's skills.

Writer uses different kinds of <u>sentences</u>.

> Have you ever had a teacher who juggled in class? I have! Ms. Moody also skipped rope and stood on her head. On Fridays she dressed up as a person from history. You never knew what Ms. Moody would do. She wanted to keep our attention. She did!

Writer's Checklist

- **Focus** Do all sentences tell about a person's skills or abilities?
- **Organization** Does writing build to an ending?
- **Support** Are details clear and interesting?
- **Conventions** Are proper nouns capitalized?

Grammar

Using Capital Letters
Days of the week, months of the year, and **holidays** begin with capital letters. **Titles** for people begin with capital letters.

> I played baseball with **Mr. Gibson** on the **Fourth of July.**

Look at the facts about Ms. Moody. Write your own sentence about what she might do in class on Valentine's Day. Use capital letters correctly.

320

321

Writing and Grammar

LOOK AT THE PROMPT Read p. 320 aloud. Have children select and discuss key words or phrases in the prompt. *(someone you know who has special skills or abilities, facts about that person's skill)*

STRATEGIES TO DEVELOP SENTENCES Have children

write their facts as statements and then try to include at least one question and one exclamation either before or after the facts.

combine two or more short related sentences into one longer sentence. *(Ms. Moody also skipped rope. Ms. Moody stood on her head. Ms. Moody also skipped rope and stood on her head.)*

check the beginning words in their sentences to be sure they do not use the same words more than once or twice.

See Scoring Rubric on p. WA11. **Rubric 4 3 2 1**

HINTS FOR BETTER WRITING Read p. 321 aloud. Use the checklist to help children revise their facts. Discuss the grammar lesson. (Answers will vary. Example sentence: *On Valentine's Day, Ms. Moody taught us a song about Cupid.* Be sure children begin the person's title and the holiday with capital letters.) Have children capitalize the appropriate words in their facts.

DAILY FIX-IT

9. We chear as Joe runs the baises. (ch<u>ee</u>r, b<u>a</u>ses)

10. Center feald is not home playte. (f<u>ie</u>ld, pl<u>a</u>te)

Using Capital Letters

Find the words that need capital letters. **Write** the words correctly. **Circle** the reason why a capital letter is needed.

1. Baseball practice begins on a wednesday in April.
   Wednesday ——— (day of the week) / month / holiday / title

2. I was practicing every day in march.
   March ——— day of the week / (month) / holiday / title

3. I even missed the parade on st. patrick's day.
   St. Patrick's Day ——— day of the week / month / (holiday) / title

Underline the words that need capital letters. **Write** the words.

4. Our baseball coach will be <u>mr.</u> Gibson.
   Mr. ———

5. I will be ready for the first <u>monday</u> game.
   Monday ———

6. The game will be on <u>memorial day.</u>
   Memorial Day ———

Home Activity Your child reviewed using capital letters. Look at a calendar together. Ask your child to select three months and write their names. Remind your child to use capital letters.

▲ **Grammar and Writing Practice Book** p. 104

Josh Gibson **320–321**

OBJECTIVE

● Use people as resources.

Liz is doing a report about girls' baseball. **Look** at the pictures.
Write the answer to each item below.

1. Who could Liz talk to if she wants to find out about girls'
baseball today? **the coach**

2. Write one good question Liz could ask to find out about girls'
baseball today.
Possible response: Do girls today get the same chances to play
baseball as boys do?

3. Who could Liz talk to if she wants to find out about girls'
baseball long ago? **her grandma**

4. Write one good question Liz could ask to find out about girls'
baseball long ago.
Possible response: Were you able to play baseball as much as
you wanted when you were a young girl?

5. Who could Liz talk to if she needs help finding books to use for
her report? **the librarian**

Home Activity Your child learned about using people as resources for information. Talk with your child about the people you turn to when you need answers. Ask your child to write two questions to someone in your family or community.

▲ **Practice Book 2.2** p. 110, People as Resources

Access Content Discuss using teachers and librarians as resources. Have children ask the librarian for help in selecting a book about a particular topic. The librarian can show the child how to locate and select a book.

Research/Study Skills

TEACH/MODEL People as Resources

MODEL USING PEOPLE AS RESOURCES Remind children that people are excellent resources. People have knowledge and expertise in many areas. If children want information about something, they could ask an expert in that area.

Model how to select the appropriate resource person.

Think Aloud **MODEL** I want to find out information about the drop third strike rule in baseball. Who do I know that could answer this question? I could ask an umpire, but I don't know any umpires personally. A baseball player could answer my question, but I also know the coach of our local high school baseball team. He's my neighbor, so I could ask him.

PICK THE RIGHT EXPERT Call on individuals to identify who they would ask if they wanted to find out information about meat (a butcher), growing corn (farmer), what giraffes eat (zookeeper), how to use a computer (computer teacher, electronics store employee).

PRACTICE

USE PEOPLE AS RESOURCES Have children use their families as a resource. Ask children to create a simple family tree with the help of their families, labeling siblings, parents, and grandparents.

Wrap Up Your Week!

LET'S TALK ABOUT Traditions

QUESTION OF THE WEEK Recall this week's question.

- Why are sports important in our country?

Display the Graphic Organizer started on Day 1. Review the main idea (Sports are important in our country.) and the supporting details.

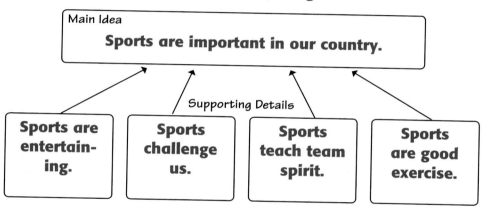

Main Idea

Sports are important in our country.

Supporting Details

| Sports are entertain-ing. | Sports challenge us. | Sports teach team spirit. | Sports are good exercise. |

CONNECT Use questions such as these to prompt a discussion.

- Many athletes are role models for children. What does it take to be a good athlete?

- Playing a sport teaches teamwork. Have you ever been part of a team? Why is it important that all members of a team work together?

- Grandmama, the character in *Just Like Josh Gibson,* was a girl who loved baseball. Most girls did not play baseball in the 1940s when this story took place. Do you think women athletes are important to sports today? Why?

 **ELL**

Build Background Use ELL Poster 27 to support the Preview activity.

| You've learned **008** Amazing Words **this week!** | You've learned **209** Amazing Words **so far this year!** |

PREVIEW Tell children that next week they will read about more traditions and the American flag.

 **PREVIEW** Next Week

Assessment Checkpoints *for the Week*

Selection Assessment

Use pp. 101–104 of Selection Tests to check:

 Selection Understanding

  Comprehension Skill *Compare and Contrast*

 Selection Vocabulary
bases
cheers
filed
plate
sailed
threw

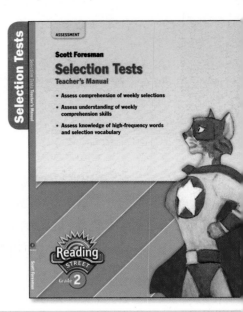

Leveled Assessment

(On-Level)

(Strategic Intervention)

(Advanced)

Use pp. 151–156 of Fresh Reads for Differentiated Test Practice to check:

  Comprehension Skill *Compare and Contrast*

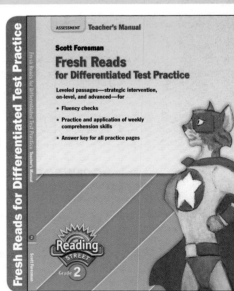 **REVIEW Comprehension Skill** *Fact and Opinion*

Fluency *Words Correct Per Minute*

Managing Assessment

Use Assessment Handbook for:

  Weekly Assessment Blackline Masters for Monitoring Progress

 Observation Checklists

 Record-Keeping Forms

Portfolio Assessment

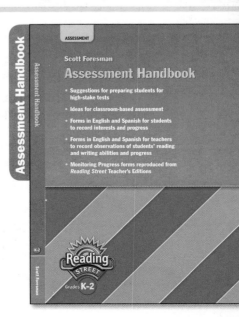

Illinois

Planning Guide for Performance Descriptors

Red, White, and Blue: The Story of the American Flag

Reading Street Teacher's Edition pages | **Grade 2 English Language Arts Performance Descriptors**

Oral Language

Build Concepts: 322l, 324a, 344a, 346a, 348a
Share Literature: 322m, 324b, 344b, 346b, 348b

1B.Stage B.1. Read fiction and non-fiction materials for specific purposes.
2A.Stage B.3. Define unfamiliar vocabulary.
3A.Stage B.5. Use correct spelling of high frequency words.

Word Work

Phonics Inflected Endings: 322n–322q, 324c–324d, 344c–344d, 346c–346d, 348c–348f

Spelling: 322p, 324d, 344d, 346d, 348d

1A.Stage B.1. Use phonics to decode simple words in age-appropriate material.
3A.Stage B.5. Use correct spelling of high frequency words.
3A.Stage B.6. Use phonemic clues, phonetic and/or developmental spelling to spell unfamiliar words.

Reading

Comprehension Fact and Opinion: 322r–323, 326–343a, 344g, 348e
Monitor and Fix Up 322r–323, 326–343, 344g
Vocabulary
Compound Words:324–325, 344e, 346e, 348b
Fluency Paired Reading: 322q, 343a
Silent Reading: 344f
Choral Reading: 347a
Self-Selected Reading: LR10–18, TR16–17
Literature Genre—Narrative Nonfiction: 326–327
Reader Response: 344g–344h

1A.Stage B.5. Use letter-sound knowledge and sight vocabulary to read orally and silently/whisper read age-appropriate material.
1B.Stage B.1. Read fiction and non-fiction materials for specific purposes.
1B.Stage B.6. State facts and details of text during and after reading.
1C.Stage B.5. Use self-monitoring (e.g., re-read question, confirm) to solve problems in meaning to achieve understanding of a broad range of reading materials.
1C.Stage B.7. Compare an author's information with the student's knowledge of self, world, and other texts in non-fiction text.
2B.Stage B.1. Investigate self-selected/teacher-selected literature (e.g., picture books, nursery rhymes, fairy tales, poems, legends) from a variety of cultures.

Language Arts

Writing Answers, Poem, Respond to Literature, Venn Diagram: 323a, 343b, 344g, 347b, 348–349

Six-Trait Writing Conventions: 345a, 348–349
Grammar, Usage, and Mechanics
Quotation Marks: 323b, 343c, 345b, 347c, 348–349

Speaking/Viewing Speak to Your Audience: 347d

Research/Study Take Notes/Outline: 349a

1C.Stage B.1. Respond to analytical and interpretive questions based on information in text.
3A.Stage B.4. Use end marks (e.g., period, question mark, exclamation mark).
3C.Stage B.4. Experiment with different forms of writing (e.g., song, poetry, short fiction, recipes, diary, journal, directions).
5A.Stage B.1. Begin guided brainstorming to generate questions to gather information.
5A.Stage B.7. Begin to include facts and details.

Unit Skills

Writing Research Report: WA2–9
Project/Wrap-Up: 434–435

3C.Stage B.4. Experiment with different forms of writing (e.g., song, poetry, short fiction, recipes, diary, journal, directions).
5A.Stage B.7. Begin to include facts and details.

This Week's Leveled Readers

Below-Level

1B.Stage B.6. State facts and details of text during and after reading.
2A.Stage B.4. Identify the topic or main idea (theme)

Happy Birthday, America! by Vita Richman

Nonfiction

On-Level

1B.Stage B.6. State facts and details of text during and after reading.
2B.Stage B.4. Make a reasonable judgment with support from the text.

Nonfiction

Advanced

1B.Stage B.6. State facts and details of text during and after reading.
1C.Stage B.12. Recognize how specific authors and illustrators express their ideas in text and graphics (e.g., dialogue, characters, color).

Home of the Brave by Barbara Wood

Nonfiction

Content-Area Illinois Performance Descriptors in This Lesson

Social Studies

14A.Stage B.6. Give an example of how governments help people live safely and fairly.

14A.Stage B.7. Identify why people need governments to help organize or protect people.

14F.Stage B.3. Describe how a holiday such as the Fourth of July represents the idea of freedom.

16A.Stage B.3. Use a story or an image about the past to describe what life was like for people who lived during that period.

16B.Stage B.4. Identify significant political figures or groups from the past.

16B.Stage B.6. Tell about a political event featured in a folk tale, story, or legend (e.g., King Arthur, King Midas).

18A.Stage B.3. Identify symbols of local culture.

Math

6A.Stage B.4. Use cardinal and ordinal numbers appropriately.

6B.Stage B.3. Explore multiplication and division through equal grouping and equal sharing of objects.

7A.Stage B.1. Identify the type of measure (e.g., weight, height, volume, temperature) for each measurable attribute.

7A.Stage B.2. Measure objects using standard units.

7A.Stage B.3. Order events chronologically.

7B.Stage B.2. Estimate standard measurements of length, weight, and capacity.

Illinois!

A FAMOUS ILLINOISAN
Gustavus Swift

As a boy, Gustavus Franklin Swift (1839–1903) worked as a butcher's helper. In 1875 he moved to Chicago. Ten years later he formed Swift & Company to process and sell meat. Swift was the first to promote shipping meat in a railway refrigerator car to keep it fresh. He was also one of the first businesspeople to support the idea of employees owning company stock in their business. Swift's company is still in business today.

Children can . . .
Choose a type of factory or other business that they would like to open. Have children draw a picture of their business and give it a name.

A SPECIAL ILLINOIS PLACE
Lisle

Located in Du Page County in the northeastern part of the state, Lisle was first settled in 1830. One of Lisle's most notable attractions is the Morton Arboretum, which is an outdoor park with more than 4,800 varieties of trees and shrubs. Lisle is also home to Benedictine University and Benet Academy.

Children can . . .
Look at pictures of different types of Illinois trees and their leaves. Have children choose their favorite tree and make a fact card with information about the tree on one side and its leaf on the other.

ILLINOIS FUN FACTS
Did You Know?

- All of Illinois except Kaskaskia Island is east of the Mississippi River.

- The state's only national forest is Shawnee National Forest in southern Illinois.

- In 1839 the state offices were moved to Springfield, which became the new state capital.

Children can . . .
Look at Illinois state government buildings. Ask them to work in groups to sketch rooms and halls of a government building of their own design.

Unit 6
Traditions

CONCEPT QUESTION

How are traditions and celebrations important to our lives?

EXPAND THE CONCEPT
What does our flag mean?

Time for SOCIAL STUDIES

Red, White, and Blue
The Story of THE AMERICAN FLAG
BY John Herman
ILLUSTRATED BY Shannan Stirnweiss

Genre
Narrative nonfiction gives facts in the form of a story. Look for

Poetry

Song
Genre
• A song is a poem set to music.
• Songs often use rhyme. In each verse of this song, the first two lines rhyme, and the third and fifth lines rhyme.
• Songs often express the songwriter's feelings. As you read, think about how the songwriter feels about the flag.

Link to Writing
Write words to a song about something you feel is important. It could be a poem set to a familiar tune. Share your song with your classmates.

You're a Grand Old Flag
by George M. Cohan

You're a grand old flag,
You're a high flying flag
And forever in peace may you wave.
You're the emblem of the land I love.
The home of the free and the brave.

Ev'ry heart beats true
'Neath the red, white, and blue,
Where there's never a boast or brag.
Should auld acquaintance be forgot,
Keep your eye on the grand old flag.

Reading Across Texts
"You're a Grand Old Flag" is one song about the flag of the United States. What other song about the flag did you read about in *Red, White, and Blue?*

Writing Across Texts Make a list of other patriotic songs that you know.

Monitor and Fix Up If you are confused, remember to go back and reread.

346   347

CONNECT THE CONCEPT

▶ **Build Background**

allegiance	independence	symbol
frayed	indivisible	unfurl
history	patriotic	

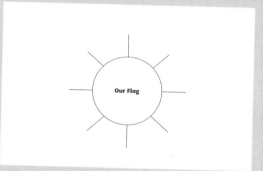

Our Flag

▶ **Social Studies Content**
American Heroes, American Revolution, Thirteen Colonies/States, U.S. Symbols, U.S. Holidays, Geography: Maps

▶ **Writing**
Answers

Preview Your Week

What does our flag mean?

Red, White, and Blue
The Story of THE AMERICAN FLAG
BY John Herman
ILLUSTRATED BY Shannan Stirnweiss

Genre
Narrative nonfiction gives facts in the form of a story. Look for facts as you read.

How did the American flag change over the years?

326 327

Student Edition pages 326–345

Audio CD

Genre	Narrative Nonfiction
Phonics	Inflected Endings
Vocabulary Strategy	Word Structure
Comprehension Skill	Fact and Opinion
Comprehension Strategy	Monitor and Fix Up

Paired Selection

Time for SOCIAL STUDIES

Reading Across Texts
Compare Songs

Genre
Song

Text Features
Song Lyrics

Poetry

Song

Genre
• A song is a poem set to music.
• Songs often use rhyme. In each verse of this song, the first two lines rhyme, and the third and fifth lines rhyme.
• Songs often express the songwriter's feelings. As you read, think about how the songwriter feels about the flag.

Link to Writing
Write words to a song about something you feel is important. It could be a poem set to a familiar tune. Share your song with your classmates.

You're a Grand Old Flag

by George M. Cohan

You're a grand old flag,
You're a high flying flag
And forever in peace may you wave.
You're the emblem of the land I love.
The home of the free and the brave.

Ev'ry heart beats true
'Neath the red, white, and blue,
Where there's never a boast or brag.
Should auld acquaintance be forgot,
Keep your eye on the grand old flag.

Reading Across Texts
"You're a Grand Old Flag" is one song about the flag of the United States. What other song about the flag did you read about in *Red, White, and Blue?*

Writing Across Texts Make a list of other patriotic songs that you know.

Monitor and Fix Up If you are confused, remember to go back and reread.

346

Student Edition pages 346–347

Audio CD

Read It
ONLINE
PearsonSuccessNet.com
• Student Edition
• Leveled Readers
• Decodable Reader

Leveled Readers

⊙ **Skill** Fact and Opinion
⊙ **Strategy** Monitor and Fix Up
Lesson Vocabulary

Below-Level

On-Level

Advanced

ELL Reader
• Concept Vocabulary
• Text Support
• Language Enrichment

Decodable Readers

Apply Phonics
• *Mom's Surprise*

Integrate Social Studies Standards

• **American Revolution**
• **American Heroes**
• **Thirteen Colonies/States**
• **U.S. Symbols, Holidays**
• **Geography**

✓ **Read**

Red, White, and Blue
pp. 326–345

"You're a Grand Old Flag"
pp. 346–347

✓ **Read**

Leveled Readers

Below-Level   **On-Level**   **Advanced**

• Support Concepts   • Develop Concepts   • Extend Concepts
• Social Studies Extension Activity

✓ **Read**

ELL Reader

✓ **Build Concept Vocabulary**
Traditions, p. 322m

✓ **Teach Social Studies Concepts**
Map of U.S., p. 328–329
American Heroes, p. 346e

✓ **Explore Social Studies Center**
Design a Class Flag, p. 322k

Red, White, and Blue **322c**

Weekly Plan

READING

90–120 minutes

TARGET SKILLS OF THE WEEK

- **Phonics**
  Inflected Endings

- **Comprehension Skill**
  Fact and Opinion

- **Comprehension Strategy**
  Monitor and Fix Up

DAY 1 — PAGES 322l–323b

Oral Language

QUESTION OF THE WEEK, 322l
What does our flag mean?

Oral Vocabulary/Share Literature, 322m
Sing with Me Big Book, Song 27
Amazing Words *history, independence, symbol*

Word Work

Phonics, 322n–322o
Introduce Inflected Endings **T**

Spelling, 322p
Pretest

Comprehension/Vocabulary/Fluency

Read Decodable Reader 27

Grouping Options 322f–322g

Review High-Frequency Words
Check Comprehension
Reread for Fluency

Comprehension Skill/Strategy Lesson, 322r–323
Fact and Opinion **T**
Monitor and Fix Up

Shared Writing, 323a
Answers

Grammar, 323b
Introduce Quotation Marks **T**

DAY 2 — PAGES 324a–343c

Oral Language

QUESTION OF THE DAY, 324a
How would you feel if you were told you couldn't fly our flag?

Oral Vocabulary/Share Literature, 324b
Read Aloud Anthology "Great-Grandmother's Secret"
Amazing Words *patriotic, unfurl*

Word Work

Phonics, 324c–324d
Review Inflected Endings **T**

Spelling, 324d
Dictation

Comprehension/Vocabulary/Fluency

Build Background, 324e
American Flag

Lesson Vocabulary, 324f
Introduce *America, birthday, flag, freedom, nicknames, stars, stripes* **T**

Vocabulary Strategy Lesson, 324–325a
Word Structure **T**

Read *Red, White, and Blue: The Story of the American Flag,* 326–343a

Grouping Options 322f–322g

Fact and Opinion **T**
Monitor and Fix Up
REVIEW Main Idea and Supporting Details **T**
Reread for Fluency

Interactive Writing, 343b
Poem

Grammar, 343c
Practice Using Quotation Marks **T**

LANGUAGE ARTS

20–30 minutes

Trait of the Week

Conventions

DAILY JOURNAL WRITING

Day 1 *List important people in history that you have read or heard about.*

Day 2 *Write about a time you saw a flag flying.*

DAILY SOCIAL STUDIES CONNECTIONS

Day 1 Our Flag Concept Web, 322m

Day 2 Time for Social Studies: Map, 328–329

DAILY SUCCESS PREDICTORS
for Adequate Yearly Progress

Monitor Progress and Corrective Feedback

Phonics
Check Word Reading, *322o*
Spiral **REVIEW** Phonics

Fluency
Check Lesson Vocabulary, *324f*
Spiral **REVIEW** High-Frequency Words

RESOURCES FOR THE WEEK

- Practice Book 2.2, *pp. 111–120*
- Phonics and Spelling Practice Book, *pp. 105–108*
- Grammar and Writing Practice Book, *pp. 105–108*
- Selection Test, *pp. 105–108*

- Fresh Reads for Differentiated Test Practice, *pp. 157–162*
- Phonics Songs and Rhymes Chart 27
- The Grammar and Writing Book, *pp. 206–211*

Grouping Options for Differentiated Instruction

Turn the page for the small group lesson plan.

DAY 3 — PAGES 344a–345b

Oral Language

QUESTION OF THE DAY, 344a
Why is the flag so special?

Oral Vocabulary/Share Literature, 344b
Read Aloud Anthology "Great-Grandmother's Secret"
Amazing Word *frayed*

Word Work

Phonics, 344c
REVIEW Contractions *'re, 've, 'd* **T**

Lesson Vocabulary, 344d
Practice *America, birthday, flag, freedom, nicknames, stars, stripes* **T**

Spelling, 344d
Practice

Comprehension/Vocabulary/Fluency

Vocabulary, 344e
Compound Words

Read *Red, White, and Blue: The Story of the American Flag,* 326–345

Grouping Options
322f–322g

Fluency, 344f
Read Silently with Fluency and Accuracy

Reader Response, 344g

Trait of the Week, 345a
Introduce Conventions

Grammar, 345b
Write with Quotation Marks **T**

Day 3 *Write about the colors in the flag.*

Day 3 Our Flag Concept Web, 345b

DAY 4 — PAGES 346a–347d

Oral Language

QUESTION OF THE DAY, 346a
What does our flag mean to you?

Oral Vocabulary/Share Literature, 346b
Read Aloud Anthology "Uncle Sam and Old Glory"
Amazing Words *allegiance, indivisible*

Word Work

Phonics, 346c
REVIEW Sentence Reading **T**

Spelling, 346d
Partner Review

Comprehension/Vocabulary/Fluency

Read "You're a Grand Old Flag," 346–347
Leveled Readers

Grouping Options
322f–322g

Compound Words
Reading Across Texts

Fluency, 347a
Read with Fluency and Accuracy

Writing Across the Curriculum, 347b
Venn Diagram

Grammar, 347c
Review Quotation Marks **T**

Speaking and Viewing, 347d
Understanding Nonverbal Cues

Day 4 *Write about why independence is important.*

Day 4 Time for Social Studies: American Heroes, 346e

DAY 5 — PAGES 348a–349b

Oral Language

QUESTION OF THE DAY, 348a
What does our flag mean?

Oral Vocabulary/Share Literature, 348b
Read Aloud Anthology "Uncle Sam and Old Glory"
Amazing Words Review

Word Work

Phonics, 348c
Review Inflected Endings **T**

Lesson Vocabulary, 348c
Review *America, birthday, flag, freedom, nicknames, stars, stripes* **T**

Spelling, 348d
Test

Comprehension/Vocabulary/Fluency

Read Leveled Readers

Grouping Options 322f–322g

Monitor Progress, 348e–348g
Read the Sentences
Read the Story

Writing and Grammar, 348–349
Develop Conventions
Use Quotation Marks **T**

Research/Study Skills, 349a
Take Notes and Outline

Day 5 *Write about a class that makes a symbol.*

Day 5 Revisit Our Flag Concept Web, 349b

KEY = Target Skill **T** = Tested Skill

Comprehension — Check Retelling, *344g*

Fluency — Check Fluency WCPM, *347a*
Spiral REVIEW Phonics, High-Frequency Words

Oral Vocabulary — Check Oral Vocabulary, *348b*
Assess Phonics, Lesson Vocabulary, Fluency, Comprehension, *348e*

SUCCESS PREDICTOR

Small Group Plan *for Differentiated Instruction*

Daily Plan AT A GLANCE

Reading
Whole Group
- Oral Language
- Word Work
- Comprehension/Vocabulary

Group Time

Meet with small groups to provide:
- Skill Support
- Reading Support
- Fluency Practice

Read

This week's lessons for daily group time can be found behind the Differentiated Instruction (DI) tab on pp. DI·24–DI·33.

Whole Group
- Comprehension/Vocabulary
- Fluency

Language Arts
- Writing
- Grammar
- Speaking/Listening/Viewing
- Research/Study Skills

Use *My Sidewalks on Reading Street* for Tier III intensive reading intervention.

DAY 1

On-Level	Strategic Intervention	Advanced
Teacher-Led *Page 322q*	**Teacher-Led** *Page DI·24*	**Teacher-Led** *Page DI·25*
• **Read** Decodable Reader 27 • **Reread** for Fluency	• Blend Words with Inflected Endings • **Read** Decodable Reader 27 • **Reread** for Fluency	• Extend Word Reading • **Read** Advanced Selection 27 • Introduce Concept Inquiry

ⓘ Independent Activities

While you meet with small groups, have the rest of the class...

- Reread for fluency
- Write in their journals
- Read self-selected reading
- Visit the Word Work Center
- Complete Practice Book 2.2, pp. 113–114

DAY 2

On-Level	Strategic Intervention	Advanced
Teacher-Led *Pages 326–343*	**Teacher-Led** *Page DI·26*	**Teacher-Led** *Page DI·27*
• **Read** *Red, White, and Blue* • **Reread** for Fluency	• Blend Words with Inflected Endings • **Read** SI Decodable Reader 27 • **Read** or Listen to *Red, White, and Blue*	• **Read** *Red, White, and Blue* • Continue Concept Inquiry

ⓘ Independent Activities

While you meet with small groups, have the rest of the class...

- Read self-selected reading
- Write in their journals
- Visit the Listening Center
- Complete Practice Book 2.2, pp. 115–117

DAY 3

On-Level	Strategic Intervention	Advanced
Teacher-Led *Pages 326–345*	**Teacher-Led** *Page DI·28*	**Teacher-Led** *Page DI·29*
• **Reread** *Red, White, and Blue*	• **Reread** *Red, White, and Blue* • Read Words and Sentences • Review Fact and Opinion and Monitor and Fix Up • **Reread** for Fluency	• Self-Selected Reading • Continue Concept Inquiry

ⓘ Independent Activities

While you meet with small groups, have the rest of the class...

- Read self-selected reading
- Write in their journals
- Visit the Writing Center
- Complete Practice Book 2.2, pp. 118–119

① Begin with whole class skill and strategy instruction.

② Meet with small groups to provide differentiated instruction.

③ Gather the whole class back together for fluency and language arts.

On-Level

Teacher-Led
Pages 346–347, LR13–LR15

- **Read** "You're a Grand Old Flag"
- **Practice** with On-Level Reader *Heroes of the American Revolution*

Strategic Intervention

Teacher-Led
Pages DI·30, LR10–LR12

- **Read** or Listen to "You're a Grand Old Flag"
- **Reread** for Fluency
- Build Concepts
- Practice with Below-Level Reader *Happy Birthday, America!*

Advanced

Teacher-Led
Pages DI·31, LR16–LR18

- **Read** "You're a Grand Old Flag"
- Extend Vocabulary
- Continue Concept Inquiry
- Practice with Advanced Reader *Home of the Brave*

DAY 4

ⓘ Independent Activities

While you meet with small groups, have the rest of the class...

- Reread for fluency
- Write in their journals
- Read self-selected reading
- Review spelling words with a partner
- Visit the Listening and Social Studies Centers

On-Level

Teacher-Led
Pages 348e–348g, LR13–LR15

- Sentence Reading, Set B
- Monitor Comprehension
- Practice with On-Level Reader *Heroes of the American Revolution*

Strategic Intervention

Teacher-Led
Pages DI·32, LR10–LR12

- Practice Word Reading
- Sentence Reading, Set A
- Monitor Fluency and Comprehension
- Practice with Below-Level Reader *Happy Birthday, America!*

Advanced

Teacher-Led
Pages DI·33, LR16–LR18

- Sentence Reading, Set C
- Monitor Comprehension
- Share Concept Inquiry
- Practice with Advanced Reader *Home of the Brave*

DAY 5

ⓘ Independent Activities

While you meet with small groups, have the rest of the class...

- Reread for fluency
- Write in their journals
- Read self-selected reading
- Visit the Technology Center
- Complete Practice Book 2.2, p. 120

ELL

Grouping Place English language learners in the groups that correspond to their reading abilities in English.

Use the appropriate Leveled Reader or other text at children's instructional level.

TIP Send home the appropriate Multilingual Summary of the main selection on Day 1.

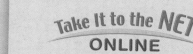

Take It to the NET™ ONLINE

PearsonSuccessNet.com

P. David Pearson
For ideas on effective reading instruction, see the article "Effective Schools/Accomplished Teachers" by Scott Foresman author P. David Pearson, as well as B. Taylor and others.

TEACHER TALK

Leveled text is text that has been assigned a level for instructional use based on its structure, subject, illustrations, words, sentences, punctuation, and so on.

Looking Ahead

Be sure to schedule time for children to work on the unit project "Research Traditions." This week children should choose one tradition and do research to gather information about what the tradition is like.

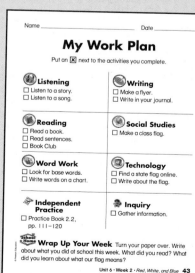

Name _____ Date _____

My Work Plan

Put an ☒ next to the activities you complete.

Listening
- ☐ Listen to a story.
- ☐ Listen to a song.

Writing
- ☐ Make a flyer.
- ☐ Write in your journal.

Reading
- ☐ Read a book.
- ☐ Read sentences.
- ☐ Book Club

Social Studies
- ☐ Make a class flag.

Word Work
- ☐ Look for base words.
- ☐ Write words on a chart.

Technology
- ☐ Find a state flag online.
- ☐ Write about the flag.

Independent Practice
- ☐ Practice Book 2.2, pp. 111–120

Inquiry
- ☐ Gather information.

Wrap Up Your Week Turn your paper over. Write about what you did at school this week. What did you read? What did you learn about what our flag means?

Unit 6 · Week 2 · *Red, White, and Blue* **43**

▲ **Group-Time Survival Guide**
p. 43, Weekly Contract

ORAL LANGUAGE

Concept Development

SOCIAL STUDIES

What does our flag mean?

Amazing Words to build oral vocabulary

allegiance	frayed	history
independence	indivisible	patriotic
symbol	unfurl	

BUILD

☐ **Question of the Week** Use the Morning Warm-Up! to introduce and discuss the question of the week. This week children will talk, sing, read, and write about what our flag means. DAY 1 *322l*

☐ **Sing with Me Big Book** Sing a song about the United States flag. Ask children to listen for the concept-related Amazing Words *history, independence, symbol*. DAY 1 *322m*

Sing with Me Big Book

☐ **Build Background** Remind children of the question of the week. Then create a concept chart for children to add to throughout the week. DAY 1 *322m*

DEVELOP

☐ **Question of the Day** Use the questions in the Morning Warm-Ups! to discuss lesson concepts and how they relate to the unit theme, Traditions. DAY 2 *324a*, DAY 3 *344a*, DAY 4 *346a*, DAY 5 *348a*

☐ **Share Literature** Read big books and read aloud selections that develop concepts, language, and vocabulary related to the lesson concept and the unit theme. Continue to develop this week's Amazing Words. DAY 2 *324b*, DAY 3 *344b*, DAY 4 *346b*, DAY 5 *348b*

CONNECT

☐ **Wrap Up Your Week!** Revisit the Question of the Week. Then connect concepts and vocabulary to next week's lesson. DAY 5 *349b*

CHECK

☐ **Check Oral Vocabulary** To informally assess children's oral vocabulary, ask individuals to use some of this week's Amazing Words to tell you about the concept of the week—Traditions. DAY 5 *348b*

PHONICS

⟳ **INFLECTED ENDINGS** When adding the inflected endings *-er, -est, -s, -es, -ing,* or *-ed* to a word, you may need to double the final consonant, drop the *e* before adding the ending, or change the *y* to *i* before adding the ending.

TEACH

☐ **Inflected Endings** Introduce the blending strategy for words with inflected endings *-er, -est, -s, -es, -ing,* or *-ed*. Then have children blend and build words by adding inflected endings to base words and tell how the spellings change when the endings are added. DAY 1 *322n-322o*

☐ **Fluent Word Reading** Use the Fluent Word Reading Routine to develop children's word reading fluency. Use the Phonics Songs and Rhymes Chart for additional word reading practice. DAY 2 *324c-324d*

Phonics Songs and Rhymes Chart 27

PRACTICE/APPLY

☐ **Decodable Reader 27** Practice reading words with inflected endings in context. DAY 1 *322q*

☐ *Red, White, and Blue* Practice decoding words in context. DAY 2 *326-343*

Decodable Reader 27

☐ **Homework** Practice Book 2.2 p. 113. DAY 1 *322o*

☐ **Word Work Center** Practice inflected endings. **ANY DAY** *322j*

Main Selection—Nonfiction

RETEACH/REVIEW

☐ **Review** Review words with this week's phonics skills. DAY 5 *348c*

☐ **Reteach Lessons** If necessary, reteach inflected endings. DAY 5 *DI·65*

☐ **Spiral REVIEW** Review previously taught phonics skills. DAY 1 *322o*, DAY 3 *344c*, DAY 4 *346c*

ASSESS

☐ **Sentence Reading** Assess children's ability to read words with inflected endings. DAY 5 *348e-348f*

① Use assessment data to determine your instructional focus.

② Preview this week's instruction by strand.

③ Choose instructional activities that meet the needs of your classroom.

SPELLING

INFLECTED ENDINGS   When adding the inflected endings to a word, you may need to double the final consonant, drop the *e* before adding the ending, or change the *y* to *i* before adding the ending.

TEACH

☐ **Pretest** Before administering the pretest, model how to segment base words and endings to spell them. Dictate the spelling words, segmenting them if necessary. Then have children check their pretests and correct misspelled words. **DAY 1** *322p*

PRACTICE/APPLY

☐ **Dictation** Have children write dictation sentences to practice spelling words. **DAY 2** *324d*

☐ **Write Words** Have children practice writing the spelling words by writing down and finishing sentence starters that use spelling words. **DAY 3** *344d*

☐ **Homework** Phonics and Spelling Practice Book pp. 105–108. **DAY 1** *322p*, **DAY 2** *324d*, **DAY 3** *344d*, **DAY 4** *346d*

RETEACH/REVIEW

☐ **Partner Review** Have pairs work together to read and write the spelling words. **DAY 4** *346d*

ASSESS

☐ **Posttest** Use dictation sentences to give the posttest for words with inflected endings. **DAY 5** *348d*

Spelling Words

Inflected Endings

1. tried
2. trying
3. planned
4. planning
5. liked*
6. liking*
7. hiked
8. hiking
9. cried
10. crying
11. skipped
12. skipping

Challenge Words

13. danced
14. dancing
15. replied
16. replying

* Words from the Selection

VOCABULARY

↻ **STRATEGY COMPOUND WORDS**   A compound word is made from two smaller words. Use the two words to figure out the compound word.

LESSON VOCABULARY

America	birthday	flag	freedom
nicknames	stars	stripes	

TEACH

☐ **Words to Know** Introduce and discuss this week's lesson vocabulary. **DAY 2** *324f*

☐ **Vocabulary Strategy** Use the vocabulary strategy in the Student Edition to introduce and model *compound words*. **DAY 2** *324–325a*

Vocabulary Strategy Lesson

PRACTICE/APPLY

☐ **Words in Context** Read the lesson vocabulary in context **DAY 2** *326–343*, **DAY 3** *326–345*

☐ **Lesson Vocabulary** Have children discuss lesson vocabulary questions in groups. **DAY 3** *344d*

☐ **Leveled Text** Read the vocabulary in leveled text. **DAY 4** *LR10–LR18*, **DAY 5** *LR10–LR18*

Main Selection—Nonfiction

☐ **Homework** Practice Book 2.2 pp. 116, 119. **DAY 2** *324f*, **DAY 3** *344d*

Leveled Readers

RETEACH/REVIEW

☐ **Compound Words** Discuss meanings of compound words. Then have partners write sentences using compound words. **DAY 3** *344e*

☐ **Review** Review this week's lesson vocabulary words. **DAY 5** *348c*

ASSESS

☐ **Selection Test** Use the Selection Test to determine children's understanding of the lesson vocabulary words. **DAY 3**

☐ **Sentence Reading** Assess children's ability to read this week's lesson vocabulary words. **DAY 5** *348e–348f*

HIGH-FREQUENCY WORDS

RETEACH/REVIEW

☐ **Spiral REVIEW** Review previously taught high-frequency words. **DAY 2** *324f*, **DAY 4** *346c*

COMPREHENSION

🎯 **SKILL FACT AND OPINION** A statement of fact can be proven true or false. An opinion cannot be proven true or false.

🎯 **STRATEGY MONITOR AND FIX UP** To monitor means to stop occasionally and check to be sure you understand what you are reading. Fix up means to do something if you do not understand or are confused about what you are reading. For example, ask yourself *who, what, where* questions while reading to make sure you understand.

TEACH

☐ **Skill/Strategy Lesson** Use the Skill/Strategy Lesson in the Student Edition to introduce *fact and opinion* and *monitor and fix up*. **DAY 1** *322r–323*

Skill/Strategy Lesson

PRACTICE/APPLY

☐ **Skills and Strategies in Context** Read *Red, White, and Blue*, using the Guiding Comprehension questions to apply *fact and opinion* and *monitor and fix up*. **DAY 2** *326–343a*

Main Selection—Nonfiction

☐ **Reader Response** Use the questions on Student Edition p. 344 to discuss the selection. **DAY 3** *344g–345*

☐ **Skills and Strategies in Context** Read "You're a Grand Old Flag," guiding children as they apply skills and strategies. **DAY 4** *346–347*

Paired Selection— Poetry

☐ **Leveled Text** Apply *fact and opinion* and *monitor and fix up* to read leveled text. **DAY 4** *LR10–LR18*, **DAY 5** *LR10–LR18*

☐ **Homework** Practice Book 2.2 pp. 114, 115. **DAY 1** *322–323*, **DAY 2** *324e*

Leveled Readers

ASSESS

☐ **Selection Test** Determine children's understanding of the main selection and assess their ability to differentiate *fact and opinion*. **DAY 3**

☐ **Story Reading** Have children read the passage "The Grand Canyon." Ask questions that require them to recognize statements of *fact and opinion*. Then have them retell. **DAY 5** *348e–348g*

RETEACH/REVIEW

☐ **Reteach Lesson** If necessary, reteach *fact and opinion*. **DAY 5** *DI·65*

FLUENCY

SKILL READ SILENTLY WITH FLUENCY AND ACCURACY Reading silently means reading only to yourself. When you read silently, you correct yourself when you make a mistake or reread if something does not make sense.

REREAD FOR FLUENCY

☐ **Paired Reading** Have pairs of children read orally from Decodable Reader 27, the main selection, or another text at their independent reading level. Listen to children read and provide corrective feedback regarding their oral reading and their use of the blending strategy. **DAY 1** *322q*, **DAY 2** *343a*

TEACH

☐ **Model** Use passages from *Red, White, and Blue* and "You're a Grand Old Flag" to model reading with fluency and accuracy. **DAY 3** *344f*, **DAY 4** *347a*

PRACTICE/APPLY

☐ **Silent Reading** Have children practice reading short passages from *Red, White, and Blue*, silently then aloud to you. Monitor progress and provide feedback regarding children's fluency and accuracy. **DAY 3** *344f*

☐ **Choral Reading** Have two groups of children sing parts from "You're a Grand Old Flag" with you, alternating lines. Then have groups sing without you. Monitor progress and provide feedback regarding children's fluency and accuracy. **DAY 4** *347a*

☐ **Listening Center** Have children follow along with the AudioText for this week's selections. **ANY DAY** *322j*

☐ **Reading/Library Center** Have children build fluency by rereading Leveled Readers, Decodable Readers, or other text at their independent level. **ANY DAY** *322j*

☐ **Fluency Coach** Have children use Fluency Coach to listen to fluent reading or to practice reading on their own. **ANY DAY**

ASSESS

☐ **Story Reading** Take a one-minute timed sample of children's oral reading. Use the passage "The Grand Canyon." **DAY 5** *348e–348g*

WRITING

Trait of the Week

CONVENTIONS *Conventions are the rules for writing.*

TEACH

❏ **Write Together** Engage children in writing activities that develop language, grammar, and writing skills. Include independent writing as an extension of group writing activities.

   Shared Writing DAY 1 *323a*
   Interactive Writing DAY 2 *343b*
   Writing Across the Curriculum DAY 4 *347b*

❏ **Trait of the Week** Introduce and model the Trait of the Week, *conventions*. DAY 3 *345a*

PRACTICE/APPLY

❏ **Write Now** Examine the model on Student Edition pp. 348–349. Then have children write answers. DAY 5 *348–349*

> **Prompt** *Red, White, and Blue* tells about the history of the American flag. Think about this question: *What do I think about when I see the American flag?* Now write the question and your answer.

Write Now

❏ **Daily Journal Writing** Have children write about concepts and literature in their journals. **EVERY DAY** *322d–322e*

❏ **Writing Center** Have pairs of children make flyers for a flag contest. **ANY DAY** *322k*

ASSESS

❏ **Scoring Rubric** Use a rubric to evaluate children's answers. DAY 5 *348–349*

RETEACH/REVIEW

❏ **The Grammar and Writing Book** Use pp. 206–211 of The Grammar and Writing

The Grammar and Writing Book

SPEAKING AND VIEWING

TEACH

❏ **Nonverbal Cues** Tell children how speakers use nonverbal cues. Have children role play situations. DAY 4 *347d*

GRAMMAR

SKILL QUOTATION MARKS Quotation marks (" ") show the beginning and ending of the words someone says. The speaker's name and words such as *said* or *asked* are not inside the quotation marks.

TEACH

❏ **Grammar Transparency 27** Use Grammar Transparency 27 to teach *quotation marks*. DAY 1 *323b*

Grammar Transparency 27

PRACTICE/APPLY

❏ **Develop the Concept** Review the concept of *quotation marks* and provide guided practice. DAY 2 *343c*

❏ **Apply to Writing** Have children use quotation marks in writing. DAY 3 *345b*

❏ **Define/Practice** Review the definition of *quotation marks*. Then have children add quotation marks to sentences. DAY 4 *347c*

❏ **Write Now** Discuss the grammar lesson on Student Edition p. 349. Have children use quotation marks in their answers to the question, "What do I think about when I see the American Flag?" DAY 5 *348–349*

Write Now

❏ **Daily Fix-It** Have children find and correct errors in grammar, spelling, and punctuation. DAY 1 *323b*, DAY 2 *343c*, DAY 3 *345b*, DAY 4 *347c*, DAY 5 *348–349*

❏ **Homework** The Grammar and Writing Practice Book pp. 105–108. DAY 2 *343c*, DAY 3 *345b*, DAY 4 *347c*, DAY 5 *348–349*

RETEACH/REVIEW

❏ **The Grammar and Writing Book** Use pp. 206–209 of The Grammar and Writing Book to extend instruction. **ANY DAY**

The Grammar and Writing Book

RESEARCH/INQUIRY

TEACH

❏ **Take Notes/Outline** Model taking notes and making an outline. Have partners practice these skills. DAY 5 *349a*

❏ **Unit Inquiry Project** Have children choose a tradition and research it. **ANY DAY** *295*

Resources for
Differentiated Instruction

LEVELED READERS

▶ **Comprehension**

🎯 **Skill** Fact and Opinion

🎯 **Strategy** Monitor/Fix Up

▶ **Lesson Vocabulary**

🎯 **Word Structure**

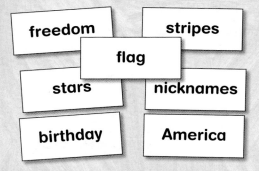

freedom	stripes
flag	
stars	nicknames
birthday	America

▶ **Social Studies Standards**

- **American Heroes**
- **American Revolution**
- **Thirteen Colonies/States**
- **U.S. Symbols**
- **U.S. Holidays**
- **Geography: Maps**

Leveled Reader Database ONLINE

PearsonSuccessNet.com

Use the Online Database of over 600 books to

- Download and print additional copies of this week's leveled readers
- Listen to the readers being read online
- Search for more titles focused on this week's skills, topic, and content

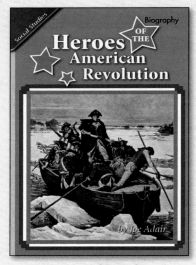

Social Studies · Biography

Heroes OF THE American Revolution

by Joe Adair

On-Level Reader

Fact and Opinion

Read each sentence. Decide if it is a statement of fact or a statement of opinion.
Write the letter **F** on the line if the sentence is a statement of fact.
Write the letter **O** on the line if the sentence is a statement of opinion.

F 1. Benjamin Franklin was born in Boston in 1706.

O 2. Benjamin Franklin was an interesting man with many talents.

O 3. George Washington was a terrific leader of the American Revolution.

F 4. George Washington would become the first President of the United States.

F 5. Deborah Sampson dressed as a soldier during the American Revolution.

O 6. She was an amazing woman and admired by all.

O 7. Dicey Langston was the bravest person of the American Revolution.

F 8. Sybil Ludington was a hero at the age of 16.

🎯 **On-Level Practice** TE p. LR14

Vocabulary

Read each sentence. Choose a word from the box that best fits the sentence. Write one letter on each line.

Words to Know			
America	birthday	flag	freedom
nickname	stars	stripes	

1. The **s t a r s** on the flag stand for the states.

2. The flag also has thirteen **s t r i p e s**

3. The American Revolution was fought for America's **f r e e d o m** from English rule.

4. The new country became known as the United States of **A m e r i c a**

5. Daring Dicey was the **n i c k n a m e** for Dicey Langston.

🎯 **On-Level Practice** TE p. LR15

Social Studies

Happy Birthday, ★★ ★★★ America!

by Vita Richman

Below-Level Reader

Fact and Opinion

Each sentence below is a statement of opinion. **Rewrite** them so it is a statement of fact. The first one has been done for you.

1. **Opinion:** The American flag is a terrific symbol.
   Fact:
   The American flag is a symbol.

2. **Opinion:** The Fourth of July is the most important holiday.
   Fact:
   The Fourth of July is a holiday.

3. **Opinion:** Uncle Sam is a funny American symbol.
   Fact:
   Uncle Sam is an American symbol.

4. **Opinion:** The Liberty Bell rang loudly on July 4, 1776.
   Fact:
   The Liberty Bell rang on July 4, 1776.

5. **Opinion:** After a parade, some people should have a barbecue.
   Fact:
   After a parade, some people have a barbecue.

🎯 **Below-Level Practice** TE p. LR11

Vocabulary

Read each word.
Draw a line to the picture that best shows the meaning of the word.

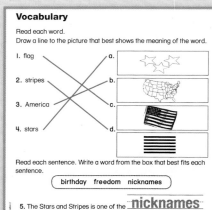

1. flag   a.
2. stripes   b.
3. America   c.
4. stars   d.

Read each sentence. Write a word from the box that best fits each sentence.

birthday	freedom	nicknames

5. The Stars and Stripes is one of the **nicknames** for the American flag.

6. July 4 is America's **birthday**

7. America gained its **freedom** from England many years ago.

🎯 **Below-Level Practice** TE p. LR12

Advanced

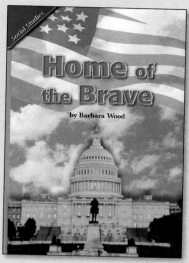

Advanced Reader

Fact and Opinion

Each sentence below is a statement of fact about the United States. On the line below each sentence, write a statement of opinion about this information.
Hint: start your sentence with "I think . . ."

1. **Fact:** The United States was once thirteen colonies ruled by Britain.
   My Opinion: Answers will vary.
   ....

2. **Fact:** Colonists fought against Britain in the American Revolution.
   My Opinion:
   ....

3. **Fact:** The United States formed a type of democratic government.
   My Opinion:
   ....

4. **Fact:** People's rights in the United States are protected by law.
   My Opinion:
   ....

Advanced Practice TE p. LR17

Vocabulary

Read each definition on the right.
Draw a line to match the words with their meanings.

1. democracy   a. a group of settlers ruled by another country
2. continent   b. one of the seven large areas of land on earth
3. symbol   c. a type of government
4. colony   d. an image that reminds us of an idea
5. history   e. how a country is ruled
6. independence   f. a record of events from the past
7. government   g. freedom from control of another person or country

Advanced Practice TE p. LR18

ELL

ELL Reader   **ELL Poster 27**

Teacher's Edition Notes

ELL notes throughout this lesson support instruction and reference additional resources at point of use.

ELL Teaching Guide pp. 183–189, 264–265
- Multilingual summaries of the main selection
- Comprehension lesson
- Vocabulary strategies and word cards
- ELL Reader 1.4.5 lesson

ELL and Transition Handbook

Ten Important Sentences
- Key ideas from every selection in the Student Edition
- Activities to build sentence power

More Reading

Readers' Theater Anthology
- Fluency practice
- Five scripts to build fluency
- Poetry for oral interpretation

Leveled Trade Books

- Extend reading tied to the unit concept
- Lessons in Trade Book Library Teaching Guide

Homework
- Family Times Newsletter
- ELL Multilingual Selection Summaries

Take-Home Books
- Decodable Readers
- Leveled Readers

Literacy Centers

Listening

Let's Read
Along

MATERIALS | SINGLES
CD player, headphones, print copies of recorded pieces

LISTEN TO LITERATURE As children listen to the following recordings, have them follow along or read along in the print version.

AudioText
Red, White, and Blue: The Story of the American Flag
"You're a Grand Old Flag"

Sing with Me/Background Building Audio
"Our Flag, Our Symbol"

Phonics Songs and Rhymes Audio
"Flag Day Parade"

Flag Day Parade

Bunches of high, waving flags.
Folks hurried and made way.
Our town was having a parade
To celebrate Flag Day.

We spotted floats with
the funniest clowns,
And the bands continued to play.
You never saw a happier town!
Best wishes on Flag Day.

Audio CD — **Phonics Songs and Rhymes Chart 27**

Reading/Library

Read It
Again!

MATERIALS | SINGLES / PAIRS / GROUPS
collection of books for self-selected reading, reading logs

REREAD BOOKS Have children select previously read books from the appropriate book box and record titles of books they read in their logs. Use these previously read books:

- Decodable Readers
- Leveled Readers
- ELL Readers
- Stories written by classmates
- Books from the library

TEN IMPORTANT SENTENCES Have children read *Red, White, and Blue* and locate the sentences in the Student Edition.

BOOK CLUB Encourage children to read other books about the early history of the United States. Ask them to look for things that early Americans wanted to provide for all Americans, such as freedom and peace.

Word Work

Take It
Apart

MATERIALS | SINGLES / PAIRS
copies of a T-chart or Graphic Organizer 25, index cards, pencils

BASE WORDS AND ENDINGS -s, -es, -ed, -ing, -er, -est Have children identify base words.

1. Make word cards with words from *Red, White, and Blue* that have the endings listed above, such as *picked, bigger, added, hoping, decided, fighting, flies, knows.*
2. Have children choose a card and use a T-chart to record each word and its base.

 This interactive CD provides additional practice.

word	base
picked	pick
bigger	big
added	add
hoping	hope
deciding	decide
fighting	fight
flies	fly
knows	know

picked   flies   knows

bigger   added   hoping

Scott Foresman Reading Street Centers Survival Kit

Use the *Red, White, and Blue: The Story of the American Flag* materials from the Reading Street Centers Survival Kit to organize this week's centers.

Writing

Win a CONTEST

MATERIALS — **PAIRS**
paper, pencils, crayons or markers

MAKE A FLYER Pairs make flyers for a flag contest.

1. Have children discuss the information they want to include in a flyer announcing a flag contest.
2. Have partners write and illustrate their flyers.
3. Display the flyers in the classroom.

LEVELED WRITING Encourage children to write at their own ability level. Some will write a poorly organized flyer. Others will better organize their flyer but still have lapses. Your best writers' work will be logically ordered.

Make a Flag!

Make a new flag for our country!
- Flags can be made of cloth, paper, or cardboard.
- Flags should be 4 feet by 6 feet.
- Send your flag in by May 28th.
- Winners will be announced on July 4th.

Social Studies

Design a Class Flag

MATERIALS — **GROUPS**
construction paper, art supplies, crayons or markers

MAKE A CLASS FLAG Have groups design a flag for your class.

1. Groups talk about what they would include on a flag for the class.
2. Then they create a class flag.
3. Invite groups to share their flags with the class and explain the reasons for their design.
4. Display the flags in the classroom.

Technology

Flag Search

MATERIALS — **PAIRS**
computer with Internet access, printer, paper, pencils

EXPLORE A WEB SITE Have individuals or pairs of children use the Internet to find a flag for any state in the country.

1. Have pairs choose a state and locate the flag for that state on the Internet.
2. Have them print out a copy of the flag and write a short description of the items on the flag.

The Kansas flag shows a sunflower. The picture shows pioneers moving into Kansas.

ALL CENTERS

Day 1

Oral Vocabulary
"Our Flag, Our Symbol" 27

Phonics and Spelling
Inflected Endings

Spelling Pretest: Words with Inflected Endings

Read Apply Phonics

Group Time < Differentiated Instruction

Comprehension
Skill Fact and Opinion

Strategy Monitor and Fix Up

Shared Writing
Answers

Grammar
Quotation Marks

Materials

- *Sing with Me Big Book*
- Letter Tiles
- Decodable Reader 27
- Student Edition 322–323
- Graphic Organizer 14
- Skill Transparency 27
- Writing Transparency 27
- Grammar Transparency 27

Take It to the NET
ONLINE

Professional Development
To learn more about vocabulary, go to PearsonSuccessNet.com and read the article "Conditions of Vocabulary Acquisition" by I. Beck and M. McKeown.

Morning Warm-Up!

Today we will learn about flags.

**Every country has a flag.
Flags bring cheers.**

**They tell a country's story.
What does our flag mean?**

QUESTION OF THE WEEK Tell children they will talk, sing, read, and write about what our flag means. Write and read the message and discuss the question.

CONNECT CONCEPTS Ask questions to connect to another Unit 6 selection.

- How are flags displayed and used at baseball games?
- The story "How Baseball Began" tells us how the game of baseball began. How do you think our flag began?

REVIEW HIGH-FREQUENCY WORDS

- Circle the high-frequency words *today* and *country* in the message.
- Have children say and spell each word as they write it in the air.

ELL

Build Background Use the Day 1 instruction on ELL Poster 27 to assess knowledge and develop concepts.

ELL Poster 27

Share Literature

BUILD ORAL VOCABULARY Display p. 27 of the *Sing with Me Big Book.* Tell children that the class is going to sing a song about the United States flag. Read the title. Ask children to listen for the Amazing Words **history, symbol,** and **independence** as you sing. Then sing the song again and encourage children to sing and do the motions along with you, demonstrating their understanding of *history, symbol,* and *independence.*

Sing with Me/ Background Building Audio

BUILD BACKGROUND Remind children of the question of the week.

- What does our flag mean?

Draw a web or use Graphic Organizer 14. Label the center circle Our Flag. Draw circles at the end of the spokes around the web. Help children identify words that describe the United States flag. Write these words in the circles. Display the web for use throughout the week.

- What does the U.S. flag look like?

- How do you feel when you see the U.S. flag?

Our Flag, Our Symbol

Our flag, our symbol
Of a great country.
It stands for independence,
And it says that we are free.

Everyone of us
Shares its history.
We love our flag,
Its stars and stripes.
It stands for you and me.

*Sing to the tune of
Row, Row, Row Your Boat*

Unit 6
Traditions
Week 2
Red, White, and Blue

Oral Vocabulary
symbol
independence
history

Sing with Me Big Book

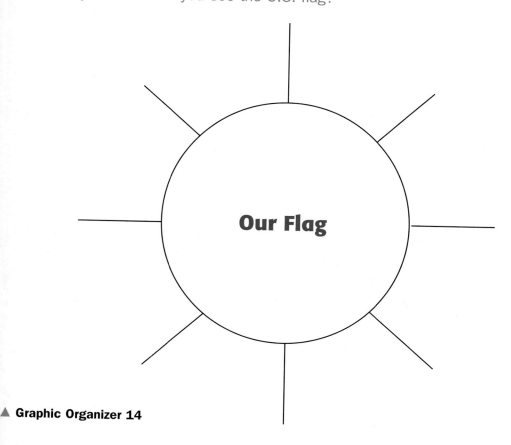

Our Flag

▲ **Graphic Organizer 14**

to build oral vocabulary

Amazing Words	MONITOR PROGRESS
history **independence** **symbol** **patriotic** **unfurl** **frayed** **allegiance** **indivisible**	**If...** children lack oral vocabulary experiences about the concept Traditions, **then...** use the Oral Vocabulary Routine below to teach *history.*

Oral Vocabulary ROUTINE

1 **Introduce the Word** Relate the word *history* to the song. Supply a child-friendly definition. Have children say the word. Example: *History* is all that has happened in the life of a people.

2 **Demonstrate** Provide an example to show meaning. In school we will study U.S. *history.*

3 **Apply** Have children demonstrate their understanding. Which is an example of *history,* when people first walked on the moon or what you plan to have for lunch?

4 **Display the Word/Word Parts** Write the word on a card. Display it. Run your hand under the word parts *his-tor-y* as you read the word. See p. DI·4 to teach *independence* and *symbol.*

Access Content Help children recognize the meanings of the English words *stars* and *stripes* by asking them to point to the stars when "stars" is sung and the stripes when "stripes" is sung.

1

OBJECTIVES

- Use structural cues to decode base words with endings *-s, -es, -ed, -ing, -er, -est.*
- Blend, read, and build base words with endings *-s, -es, -ed, -ing, -er, -est.*

Skills Trace

⊙ Inflected Endings	
Introduce/Teach	TE: 2.6 322n–o
Practice	TE: 2.6 322q, 324c–d; PB: 2.2 113, 128; DR27
Reteach/Review	TE: 2.6 348c, 368c, DI·65
Assess/Test	TE: 2.6 348e–g Benchmark Test: Unit 6

Strategic Intervention

Use **Monitor Progress,** p. 322o, during Group Time after children have had more practice with base words and endings.

Advanced

Use **Monitor Progress,** p. 322o, as a preassessment to determine whether this group of children would benefit from this instruction on base words and endings.

Support Phonics Languages such as Chinese, Hmong, and Vietnamese do not use inflected endings to form verb tenses. Help children understand that adding *-ed* to a verb indicates that the action happened in the past.

Children of various language backgrounds may not hear the difference between *-ing* and *-in,* so they may say *readin* and *sleepin* instead of *reading* and *sleeping.* Help children practice saying words that end with *-ing; walk/walking, eat/eating, plan/planning.*

See the Phonics Transition Lessons in the ELL and Transition Handbook.

⊙ Inflected Endings

TEACH/MODEL

Blending Strategy ROUTINE

1 **Connect** Write *smaller* and *smallest.* What do you know about reading these words? **(They are base words with endings *-er* and *-est.*)** What are the words? Was there a spelling change when *-er* or *-est* were added? **(No)** Today we'll review spelling changes that may be needed when endings are added to base words. Review these types of spelling changes:

- double the final consonant
- drop *e* before adding the ending
- change *y* to *i* before adding the ending

2 **Model** Write *dropped.* How did the base word *drop* change when the *-ed* ending was added? (The consonant *p* was doubled.) You can cover the ending, read the base word, and then blend the base word and ending to read the whole word. Let's blend this word: /drop/ /t/ *(dropped)* Repeat with *joking.*

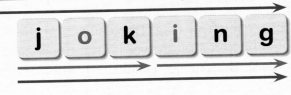

3 **Model Reading Longer Words** Write *spiciest.* Sometimes I have to chunk the base word into smaller parts. Then I blend all the chunks together to read the word: *spi, ci, est—spiciest.*

4 **Group Practice** First, chunk the word into its parts. Read the base word and the ending. Then blend the two to read the whole word. Remember there may be a spelling change. Continue with *smarter, scared, judging, cries, happiest.*

5 **Review** What do you know about reading base words with endings? Read the base word—it may have a spelling change—and then blend the word and ending to read the whole word.

BLEND WORDS

INDIVIDUALS BLEND WORDS Call on children to chunk and blend *plans, crutches, rubbed, beginning, braver, funniest.* Have them tell what they know about each word before reading it. For feedback, refer to step five of the Blending Strategy Routine.

BUILD WORDS

READ LONGER WORDS Write *base word, -s or -es, -ed, -ing, -er,* and *-est* as headings for a six-column chart. Make word cards for the words shown in the chart below. Have children choose a card, read the word, and write it under the appropriate heading. Have children tell how the spelling changed when the ending was added.

base word	-s or -es	-ed	-ing	-er	-est
step	steps	stepped	stepping	X	X
funny	X	X	X	funnier	funniest
bounce	bounces	bounced	bouncing	X	X
cry	cries	cried	crying	X	X
happy	X	X	X	happier	happiest
clear	clears	cleared	clearing	clearer	clearest

Vocabulary TiP

You may wish to explain the meanings of these words.

pouncing	jumping or leaping
reapplied	put on again
discovered	found out about

▲ **Practice Book 2.2** p. 113, Inflected Endings

Monitor Progress — Check Word Reading Inflected Endings

Write the following words and have individuals read them.

tried	pouncing	jogging	funnier	chokes
unhappier	reapplied	prepays	discovered	unluckiest
friendlier	winner	happily	peaceful	writer

If... children cannot blend base words and inflected endings at this point,

then... continue to monitor their progress using other instructional opportunities during the week so that they can be successful with the Day 5 Assessment. See the Skills Trace on p. 322n.

SUCCESS PREDICTOR

Spiral REVIEW

● Rows 2 and 3 review prefixes and suffixes

▶**Day 1 Check Word Reading**

Day 2 Check Lesson Vocabulary/High-Frequency Words

Day 3 Check Retelling

Day 4 Check Fluency

Day 5 Assess Progress

Word Reading

SUCCESS PREDICTOR

- Segment sounds and word parts to spell words.
- Spell base words with endings -ed, -ing.

Spelling Words

Inflected Endings

1.	**tried**	7.	**hiked**
2.	**trying**	8.	**hiking**
3.	**planned**	9.	**cried**
4.	**planning**	10.	**crying**
5.	**liked***	11.	**skipped**
6.	**liking***	12.	**skipping**

Challenge Words

13.	**danced**	15.	**replied**
14.	**dancing**	16.	**replying**

* Words from the Selection

More Adding -ed and -ing

Generalization The spelling of the base word is often changed when adding -ed but kept when adding -ing: tried, trying.

Sort the list words by -ed or -ing.

-ed	-ing	Spelling Words
1. tried	7. trying	1. tried
2. planned	8. planning	2. trying
3. liked	9. liking	3. planned
4. hiked	10. hiking	4. planning
5. cried	11. crying	5. liked
6. skipped	12. skipping	6. liking
		7. hiked
		8. hiking
		9. cried
		10. crying
		11. skipped
		12. skipping

Challenge Words		Challenge Words
-ed	-ing	13. danced
13. danced	15. dancing	14. dancing
14. replied	16. replying	15. replied
		16. replying

Home Activity Your child is learning to spell words that end with -ed or -ing. To practice at home, have your child say the word, study the word ending, and then spell the word aloud.

▲ **Spelling Practice Book** p. 105

Support Spelling Before giving the spelling pretest, clarify the meaning of each spelling word with examples, such as saying *skipping* while skipping across the room and drawing a mountain and stick figures hiking up the side to illustrate *hiking*.

Spelling

PRETEST Inflected Endings

MODEL WRITING FOR WORD PARTS Each spelling word has the ending -ed or -ing. Before administering the spelling pretest, model how to segment base words and endings to spell them.

- You can spell these words by thinking about the base words and endings. What base word and ending make up *hopping*? (*hop* and -*ing*)
- Start with the sounds in the base word *hop*. What letters spell hop? Write *hop*.
- Is there a spelling change before the ending? What is it? (Yes, double the consonant and add -*ing*.) Add *ping*.
- Now spell *hopping*.
- Repeat with *fried* and *baking*.

PRETEST Dictate the spelling words. Segment the words for children if necessary. Have children check their pretests and correct misspelled words.

HOMEWORK Spelling Practice Book, p. 105

A Gift from France

The Statue of Liberty was opened to the people on October 28, 1886. Thousands came to watch. It was an important day in American history.

Since then, it has welcomed millions of people to New York harbor and America. It is a symbol of America. However, it was made in France. The Statue of Liberty was a gift from the people of France to the people of America.

Decodable Reader 27

Mom's Surprise

Group Time

DAY 1

On-Level	Strategic Intervention	Advanced
Read Decodable Reader 27.	**Read** Decodable Reader 27.	**Read** Advanced Selection 27.
• Use p. 322q.	• Use the **Routine** on p. DI·24.	• Use the **Routine** on p. DI·25.

ELL Place English language learners in the groups that correspond to their reading abilities in English.

(i) Independent Activities

Fluency Reading Pair children to reread Leveled Readers or the ELL Reader from the previous week or other text at children's independent level.

Journal Writing List important people in history that you have read or heard about. Share writing.

Independent Reading See p. 322j for Reading/Library activities and suggestions.

Literacy Centers To practice Base Words and Endings, you may use Word Work, p. 322j.

Practice Book 2.2 Inflected Endings, p. 113; Fact and Opinion, p. 114

Break into small groups after Spelling and before the Comprehension lesson.

Decodable Reader 27

Mom's Surprise
Written by Renee McLean
Illustrated by Gill Ross

Phonics Skill

Adding Endings -s, -ed, -ing, -er, -est

longest	planning	biggest	returns	tried
excited	helped	prettiest	tied	nicer
pointed	thinking	cleaned	cooking	making
likes	hopped	going	waved	faster
cried	rushed	peeking	called	closed
opened	nicest	hugged		

Apply Phonics

○PRACTICE Inflected Endings

HIGH-FREQUENCY WORDS Review *always, coming,* and *surprise.*

READ DECODABLE READER 27

- Pages 90–91 Read aloud quietly with the group.
- Pages 92–93 Have the group read aloud without you.
- Pages 94–96 Select individuals to read aloud.

CHECK COMPREHENSION AND DECODING Ask children the following questions about *Mom's Surprise:*

- Who are the characters in the story? (Ben, Jake, Dad, Mom)
- Why is the family planning a surprise for Mom? (She has been gone for a very long time on a trip.)
- What surprises has the family planned for Mom? (flowers, nice soaps, a clean house, a cooked meal, a sign that reads "We love you, Mom!")

Then have children locate words with endings *-ed, -ing, -est, -er,* and *-s* in the story. Review *-ed, -ing, -est, -er,* and *-s* spelling patterns. Sort words according to their spelling patterns.

-ed: called, cleaned, closed, cried, excited, helped, hopped, hugged, liked, nodded, opened, pointed, rushed, tied, waved

-ing: coming, cooking, going, making, peeking, planning, thinking, trying

-est: biggest, longest, prettiest

-er: faster, nicer, wider

-s: likes

HOMEWORK Take-Home Decodable Reader 27

REREAD FOR FLUENCY

Paired Reading

ROUTINE

1. **Reader 1 Begins** Children read the entire story, switching readers at the end of each page.

2. **Reader 2 Begins** Have partners reread; now the other partner begins.

3. **Reread** For optimal fluency, children should reread three or four times.

4. **Provide Feedback** Listen to children read and provide corrective feedback regarding their oral reading and their use of the blending strategy.

OBJECTIVES

- Apply knowledge of letter-sounds and word parts to decode unknown words when reading.
- Use context with letter-sounds and word parts to confirm the identification of unknown words.
- Practice fluency in paired reading.

Monitor Progress

Decoding

If... children have difficulty decoding a word,	**then...** prompt them to blend the word.
	• What is the new word?
	• Is the new word a word you know?
	• Does it make sense in the story?

Access Content

Beginning Preview the story *Mom's Surprise,* identifying people, places, and things in the pictures and print.

Intermediate Preview *Mom's Surprise,* pointing out action verbs, such as *cleaned, hopped, hugged, cooking,* and *peeking.* Have children repeat each word and use gestures to act out the meanings.

Advanced After reading *Mom's Surprise,* page through the story and have children locate words in which the spelling has changed when the ending has been added, such as *biggest, prettiest, tied,* and *nodded.*

OBJECTIVES

- Identify facts and opinions.
- Monitor and fix-up when reading.

Skills Trace

Fact and Opinion

Introduce/Teach	TE: 2.4 42r, 42–43, 124r, 124–125; 2.6 322r, 322–323
Practice	TE: 2.4 48–49, 130–131; 2.6 330–331; PB: 2.2 14–15, 27, 44–45, 107, 114, 115, 137
Reteach/Review	TE: 2.4 74–75, DI-65, DI-68; 2.6 304–305, 392–393, DI-65
Test	TE: 2.4, 64e–g, 148e–g; 2.6 348e–g; Selection Tests 2.4 65–68; 77–80; 2.6 105–108; 109–112; Benchmark Test: Units 4, 6

Flags

A flag is a piece of cloth. But it is also much more. A flag is a symbol. It can stand for a country. It is the best feeling to see your nation's flag flying.

A flag sends a message. Each picture and color on a flag tells something. A circle might mean the sun or life. Blue might stand for the sea or sky.

The first flags were metal or wooden poles. Later, pieces of cloth were added. Long ago, knights in armor carried flags. The flags helped them tell friends from enemies.

Today every country has a flag. Our country's flag is one of the most beautiful. Every state in our country has a flag too. Even some towns have flags.

Skill The clue word—*best*—signals an opinion. It tells only one person's feeling about seeing the flag flying.

Strategy If you are confused, go back and reread. If you're unsure, you can find out whether these facts are true. Where can you go to check?

Unit 6 Red, White, and Blue: The Story of the American Flag   **Skill Transparency 27**

▲ **Skill Transparency 27**

Access Content

Beginning/Intermediate For a Picture It! lesson on fact and opinion, see the ELL Teaching Guide, pp. 183–184.

Advanced Before children read "Flags," make sure they know the meanings of *nation, armor,* and *symbol.*

◉ Fact and Opinion
◉ Monitor and Fix Up

TEACH/MODEL

INTRODUCE Recall *Just Like Josh Gibson.* Have students make a statement of fact about baseball. Then ask students to make a statement of opinion about baseball. (Possible response: fact—Girls in the forties did not play baseball; opinion—Nothing is as good as baseball.)

- How can you tell if a statement of fact is true?

Read p. 322 with children. Explain the following:

- Good readers can identify statements of fact and opinion in a story. Sometimes there are helpful clue words, such as *best* or *great,* to help identify a statement of opinion. Sometimes there aren't.
- We can keep track of statements of fact and statements of opinion by stopping during reading and rereading what we don't understand. Look for clue words to recognize statements of opinion.

Use Skill Transparency 27 to teach fact and opinion and fix-up strategies.

SKILL Use paragraph 1 to model using clue words to identify statements of fact and statements of opinion.

Think Aloud **MODEL** I know that statements of fact can be proved true or false. I also know that words that express a person's feelings or beliefs are often clues to statements of opinion. When I see the word *best* in the last sentence, I know that that sentence is most likely a statement of opinion.

STRATEGY Continue with paragraph 4 to model the monitor and fix-up strategy.

Think Aloud **MODEL** After I read the paragraph, I think about whether the statements I just read are fact or opinion. I go back and read each statement again and ask myself questions: Can I find flags for every country? Can I prove that our country's flag is one of the most beautiful? Can I find state flags? If I can prove something is true or false, I know it is a fact. The words *most beautiful,* however, usually signal an opinion. This fix-up strategy of rereading and asking questions helps me identify statements of fact and opinion.

Comprehension

Skill
Fact and Opinion

Strategy
Monitor
and Fix Up

Fact and Opinion

- A statement of fact can be proved true or false. You can look in a book, ask someone who knows, or see for yourself.

- A statement of opinion tells only someone's feelings or beliefs. It may have a clue word like *best* or *great*.

Fact	→	How Can I Check?
Opinion	→	How Can I Tell?

Strategy: Monitor and Fix Up

Active readers stop and fix up during reading. If you are not sure you are reading facts or opinions, you can go back and read again. See if a statement can be proved true or false. Look for a clue word to an opinion.

Write to Read

1. Read "Flags." Make charts like those above. Write down two facts and two opinions that you read.

2. Write two facts you know about the U.S. flag or another flag. Then write two of your opinions about it.

322

Flags

A flag is a piece of cloth. But it is also much more. A flag is a symbol. It can stand for a country. It is the best feeling to see your nation's flag flying.

A flag sends a message. Each picture and color on a flag tells something. A circle might mean the sun or life. Blue might stand for the sea or sky.

The first flags were metal or wooden poles. Later, pieces of cloth were added. Long ago, knights in armor carried flags. The flags helped them tell friends from enemies.

Today every country has a flag. Our country's flag is one of the most beautiful. Every state in our country has a flag too. Even some towns have flags.

Skill The clue word—*best*—signals an opinion. It tells only one person's feeling about seeing the flag flying.

Strategy If you are confused, go back and reread. If you're unsure, you can find out whether these facts are true. Where can you go to check?

323

PRACTICE

WRITE Work with children to complete the steps in the Write activity. Have children use the completed statements to retell the facts and opinions found in "Flags."

Monitor Progress	Fact and Opinion
If... children are unable to complete **Write** on p. 322,	then... use Practice Book 2.2, p. 114, for additional practice.

CONNECT TO READING Encourage children to ask themselves these questions when they read.

- Do I reread if I forget some details from the selection?
- Do I reread if a part of a selection does not make sense?
- Do I identify statements of fact and opinion as I read?

Read the passage.
Follow the directions.

Everyone should fly the flag. It even flies at the moon. People placed the flag there during the first moon landing. Many schools fly the flag. Helping to raise the school flag is the greatest thrill a student can have.

1. **Underline two** statements of **opinion** in the passage.

2. **Circle three** statements of **fact** in the passage.

3. **Think** about what you know. **Write** one statement of **fact** about the flag.

Children's responses should contain a statement of fact about the U. S. flag.

4. **Think** about how you feel. **Write** one statement of **opinion** about the flag.

Children's responses should contain a statement of opinion about the U. S. flag.

School + Home **Home Activity** Your child read a passage about the U.S. flag and identified statements of fact and opinion. Talk with your child about the flag or other important national symbols. Work together to write one statement of fact and one statement of opinion about the topic you discussed.

▲ **Practice Book 2.2** p. 114, Fact and Opinion

OBJECTIVE
● Write answers to questions.

DAILY FIX-IT

1. Hour flag has stars and strips.
   <u>Our</u> flag has stars and strip<u>e</u>s.

2. We will cook diner for
   thanksgiving.
   We will cook din<u>n</u>er for
   <u>T</u>hanksgiving.

This week's practice sentences appear on Daily Fix-It Transparency 27.

Strategic Intervention

Children who are not able to write independently may copy one or more of the sentences about the importance of the flag and add an illustration.

Advanced

Have children write a description of a time they felt proud to be an American—for example, when seeing military personnel in a parade.

Support Writing Before writing the answers to this question, have children work in pairs to tell each other what they are planning to write about.

▲ **The Grammar and Writing Book**
For more instruction and practice, use pp. 206–211.

Shared Writing

WRITE Answers

GENERATE IDEAS Read aloud the question on the page. Ask children to think of answers to the question.

WRITE ANSWERS Explain that the class will write answers to a question. Point out which answers state facts and which state opinions.

COMPREHENSION SKILL Have children think of an opinion people might have about the American flag.

- Display Writing Transparency 27 and read the title.
- Ask children to describe how they feel when they say the Pledge of Allegiance.
- Read the question at the top of the page.
- As children describe reasons for the flag's importance, record their responses.

HANDWRITING While writing, model the letter forms as shown on pp. TR14–TR17.

READ THE ANSWER Have children read the completed answer aloud as you track the print.

Ask and Answer

Why is the American flag important to Americans?

- It stands for our country, the United States.

Possible answers:
- **It reminds us of our freedom.**

- **It reminds us of the people who fought and died for the United States.**
- **It is part of America's history.**

- **Every country has a flag, so America should have one too.**

Unit 6 Red, White, and Blue   Writing Model **27**

▲ **Writing Transparency 27**

INDEPENDENT WRITING

WRITE ANSWERS Have children write their own answers to the question. Encourage them to use words from the Word Wall and the Amazing Words board. Let children illustrate their writing. You may gather children's work to save in their portfolios.

Grammar

TEACH/MODEL Quotation Marks

IDENTIFY QUOTATION MARKS Display Grammar Transparency 27. Read the definition aloud.

- Emma is the girl who is doing the speaking in the first sentence. What did she say? Is there a clue word to help us figure out what she said?

- Quotation marks let us know what someone said. Quotation marks should be at the beginning and ending of what Emma said.

Continue modeling with items 2–6.

PRACTICE

ADD QUOTATION MARKS Invite a child to stand and say a sentence aloud. Write this sentence on the board with the child's name and the word *said* or *asked*. Encourage children to identify where quotation marks should be placed. Write the quotation marks. Continue with other children's sentences or questions.

ADDITIONAL PRACTICE For additional practice, see pp. 206–211 of the Grammar and Writing Book.

Quotation Marks

Quotation marks (" ") show the beginning and ending of the words someone says. The speaker's name and words such as **said** or **asked** are not inside the quotation marks.

"What is a symbol?" asked Kim.
"A symbol is something that stands for something else," Jerome said.

Add quotation marks to each sentence.

1. "What is a symbol of our country?" asked Emma.

2. David said, "Our flag is a symbol."

3. "The bald eagle is a symbol too," said Liam.

4. Miki asked, "Why is the bald eagle a symbol?"

5. Sasha said, "The bald eagle is strong and free, and so is the United States."

6. "Let's find out more about the bald eagle," Alan said.

Unit 6 Red, White, and Blue: The Story of the American Flag   Grammar **27**

▲ **Grammar Transparency 27**

Wrap Up Your Day!

✓ **INFLECTED ENDINGS** Write *smile* and ask children what needs to be done to add *-ed* to the word. (drop the *e*, and add *-ed*) Now ask children what needs to be done to the word *smile* if you want to add *-ing*. (drop the *e*, and add *-ing*) Write the words with the endings.

✓ **SPELLING WORDS WITH -ed AND -ing** Have children add *-ed* and *-ing* to the base word *jump*. Continue with *hop* and *play*.

✓ **FACT AND OPINION** To help children identify statements of fact and opinion, ask whether this is a statement of fact or opinion: "Our country's flag is one of the most beautiful."

LET'S TALK ABOUT IT Recall what we read about flags. Are there any other words we can add to our web to describe the flag?

School + Home **HOMEWORK** Send home this week's Family Times newsletter.

PREVIEW Day 2

Tell children that tomorrow the class will read about celebrating the American flag.

Share Literature
Great-Grandmother's Secret

Phonics and Spelling
Inflected Endings

Spelling: Words with Inflected Endings

Build Background
American Flag

Lesson Vocabulary
freedom   flag   stripes
stars   nicknames   birthday
America
More Words to Know
Congress   colonies
American Revolution

Vocabulary
Skill Compound Words

Strategy Word Structure

Read

Group Time < Differentiated Instruction

Red, White, and Blue

Interactive Writing
Poem

Grammar
Quotation Marks

Materials
- Sing with Me Big Book
- Read Aloud Anthology
- Phonics Songs and Rhymes Chart 27
- Background Building Audio
- Graphic Organizer 15
- Tested Word Cards
- Student Edition 324–343

Morning Warm-Up!

Today we will read about the American flag. We're going to learn nicknames for our flag. We'll talk about how our flag was made. How would you feel if you were told you couldn't fly our flag?

QUESTION OF THE DAY Encourage children to sing "Our Flag, Our Symbol" from the *Sing with Me Big Book* as you gather. Write and read the message and discuss the question.

REVIEW CONTRACTIONS

- Read the second, third, and fourth sentences of the message.
- Have children raise their hands when they hear a contraction. *(we're, we'll, couldn't)*
- Identify the two words that make up each contraction.

Build Background Use the Day 2 instruction on ELL Poster 27 to preview high-frequency words.

ELL Poster 27

Share Literature

BUILD CONCEPTS

REALISTIC FICTION Read the title. Identify the author. Review that realistic fiction stories have characters that seem real and do things that you could imagine real people doing.

BUILD ORAL VOCABULARY Ask children what they know about the history of our flag. Explain that many people fly the American flag to show that they are **patriotic.** *Patriotic* means "showing love and support for your country." When the American flag is not flying, it is folded in a special way. It is **unfurled** when it is flown again. When you unfurl a flag, you open it up. Listen to the story to find out what flag William unfurls.

Read Aloud Anthology
Great-Grandmother's Secret

- Name some patriotic symbols of our country. (Possible answers: eagle, flag, Statue of Liberty, Liberty Bell)

- Are you patriotic? What are some ways you show your patriotism? (Possible responses: fly flag, say the Pledge of Allegiance, stand and remove hat when flag goes by in a parade, stand quietly when Star Spangled Banner is sung)

MONITOR LISTENING COMPREHENSION

- What special flag did William fly in the story? Why was it so special? (William flew his great-grandfather's flag. It was special because this was the flag that was on his great-grandfather's casket during his funeral.)

- How did Great-Grandmother communicate? (by tapping her cane)

- Why did she use her cane to talk? (It was her way of talking since she had her stroke.)

- Why do you think William's great-grandmother wanted William to fly this flag? (Possible response: It would remind her of her husband, and it would remind William of his great-grandfather.)

OBJECTIVES
- Discuss characteristics of realistic fiction.
- Set purpose for listening.
- Build oral vocabulary.

Amazing Words — to build oral vocabulary

	MONITOR PROGRESS
history independence symbol **patriotic** **unfurl** frayed allegiance indivisible	**If…** children lack oral vocabulary experiences about the concept Traditions, **then…** use the Oral Vocabulary Routine. See p. DI·4 to teach *patriotic* and *unfurl*.

ELL

Build Concepts *Red, White, and Blue* is the story of the American Flag. Have children color an American flag to demonstrate their understanding.

- Review base words with endings -s, -es, -ed, -ing, -er, -est.
- Build base words with endings -s, -es, -ed, -ing, -er, -est.
- Preview words before reading them.
- Spell base words with endings -ed, -ing.

Inflected Endings

TEACH/MODEL

Fluent Word Reading

ROUTINE

1 **Connect** Write *dancing.* You can read this word because you know how to read base words with endings. What base word and ending form *dancing?* (*dance* and *ing*) Do the same with *danced, trips, tripped, larger,* and *largest.*

2 **Model** When you come to a base word with an ending, look at the base word and the ending. Is there a spelling change? Then read them together. Model reading *raked, raking, fished, fishes, blurrier, blurriest.* When you come to a new base word and ending, what are you going to do?

3 **Group Practice** Write *continues, continuing, stops, stopped, funnier, funniest.* Read these words. Look at the word, say the word to yourself, and then read the word aloud. Allow 2–3 seconds previewing time.

WORD READING

PHONICS SONGS AND RHYMES CHART 27 Frame each of the following words on Phonics Songs and Rhymes Chart 27. Call on individuals to read them. Guide children in previewing.

floats	clowns	bands	flags	folks
wishes	bunches	hurried	spotted	continued
waving	having	happier	funniest	

Sing "Flag Day Parade" to the tune of "Auld Lang Syne," or play the CD. Have children follow along on the chart as they sing. Then have individuals take turns underlining and reading words with *-ed* and *-ing* endings on the chart.

 **Phonics Songs and Rhymes Audio**

Flag Day Parade

Bunches of high, waving flags.
Folks hurried and made way.
Our town was having a parade
To celebrate Flag Day.

We spotted floats with
the funniest clowns,
And the bands continued to play.
You never saw a happier town!
Best wishes on Flag Day.

Phonics Songs and Rhymes Chart 27

Support Phonics Invite children to name the items pictured in the art for "Flag Day Parade" as you replay the Phonics Songs and Rhymes Audio CD.

BUILD WORDS

INDIVIDUALS MAKE INFLECTED ENDINGS Write *base word, -s or -es, -ed, -ing, -er,* and *-est* as headings for a six-column chart. Make word cards for the words shown in the chart below. Have children read and sort the words according to their endings, and tell how the spelling changed when the endings were added.

base word	-s or -es	-ed	-ing	-er	-est
clap	claps	clapped	clapping	X	X
dry	dries	dried	drying	drier	driest
scorch	scorches	scorched	scorching	X	X
try	tries	tried	trying	X	X
silly	X	X	X	sillier	silliest
fog	fogs	fogged	fogging	foggier	foggiest

Spelling

PRACTICE Inflected Endings

WRITE DICTATION SENTENCES Have children write these sentences. Repeat words slowly, allowing children to hear each sound. Children may use the Word Wall to help with spelling high-frequency words. **Word Wall**

He liked that we planned to go hiking.

I was skipping and dancing all the way home.

"Dad tried to get the baby to stop crying," I replied.

HOMEWORK Spelling Practice Book, p. 106

Spelling Words

Inflected Endings

1. tried
2. trying
3. planned
4. planning
5. liked*
6. liking*
7. hiked
8. hiking
9. cried
10. crying
11. skipped
12. skipping

Challenge Words

13. danced
14. dancing
15. replied
16. replying

* Words from the Selection

More Adding -ed and -ing

Spelling Words

tried trying planned planning liked liking
hiked hiking cried crying skipped skipping

Write the missing list word. It rhymes with the underlined word.

1. They biked and **hiked** in the park.
2. We would have **liked** to have biked this afternoon.
3. Chris **cried** when her fish died.
4. I kept tripping as I was **skipping** rope.
5. Have you **tried** this fried chicken?
6. Mom is **planning** on canning some tomatoes.

Find two list words that follow each rule. Write the words.

Drop the final e before adding -ing to the base word.	Double the final consonant before adding -ed to the base word.	Just add -ing to the base word.
7. liking	9. planned	11. trying
8. hiking	10. skipped	12. crying

Home Activity Your child spelled words that end with *-ed* and *-ing*. Point to a spelling word. Have your child pronounce and spell the base word and tell whether the base word changed when the ending was added.

▲ **Spelling Practice Book** p. 106

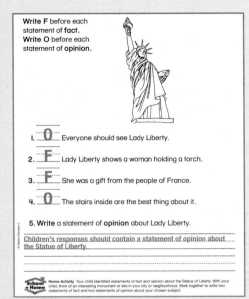
▲ **Practice Book 2.2** p. 115,
Fact and Opinion

Activate Prior Knowledge
Display a U.S. flag. Ask children to name the colors of the flag in their home language and in English.

OBJECTIVES

● Build background.
● Learn lesson vocabulary.

Build Background

DISCUSS FLAGS Display a picture of the American flag. Initiate discussion by asking children what they know about the history of our flag. Have children name the colors of the flag. Ask children what the stars and stripes represent.

● What colors are on the American flag?

● What do the stars stand for? What do the stripes stand for?

● Has our flag always looked the same?

BACKGROUND BUILDING AUDIO Have children listen to the CD and share the new information they learned about the origins of Independence Day and how Americans celebrate.

 **Background Building Audio**

COMPLETE A WEB Draw a web or display Graphic Organizer 15. Write *U.S. Flag* in the center. Ask children to suggest words to describe how the flag looks or how the flag makes people feel.

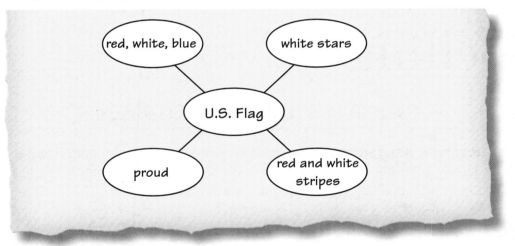

▲ **Graphic Organizer 15**

CONNECT TO SELECTION Connect background information to *Red, White, and Blue.*

The U.S. flag is an important symbol of independence, but it has not always looked as it does today. At one time it had thirteen stars in a circle. The flag changed as our country changed. We'll learn about our flag's history and find out how it became the stars and stripes today.

Vocabulary

LESSON VOCABULARY

VOCABULARY FRAME Display Graphic Organizer 5 or create vocabulary frame pages with two boxes at the top. One box is for the vocabulary word and the other is to draw a picture. Children predict the definition of the word and write a sentence using it. Then children verify the definition and write another good sentence.

WORDS TO KNOW

freedom being able to do, say, and think as you please

flag A *flag* is a piece of colored cloth with stars or other symbols on it. Every country and state has its own *flag*.

stripes A *stripe* is a long, narrow band of color.

stars A *star* is a shape that has five or six points.

nicknames names used instead of real names

birthday Your *birthday* is the day that you were born. Most people celebrate their *birthdays* every year.

America *America* is another name for North America and South America. Some people use the name *America* to mean the United States.

MORE WORDS TO KNOW

Congress the national lawmaking group of the United States

American Revolution war in which the thirteen American colonies gained their freedom from England

colonies groups of people who left their own land to settle in another land

= Tested Word

Children should break apart *nicknames, freedom, birthday*, and *America* into syllables.

Have children share where they may have seen or heard some of these words.

Children should verify their predicted definitions.

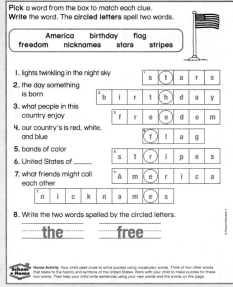

Pick a word from the box to match each clue.
Write the word. The circled letters spell two words.

America	birthday	flag
freedom	nicknames	stars	stripes

1. lights twinkling in the night sky — s **t** a r s
2. the day something is born — b i r t **h** d a y
3. what people in this country enjoy — f r e **e** d o m
4. our country's is red, white, and blue — f l a g
5. bands of color — s t **r** i p e s
6. United States of _____ — A m **e** r i c a
7. what friends might call each other — n i c k n a m **e** s

8. Write the two words spelled by the circled letters.

_____the_____   _____free_____

Home Activity Your child used clues to solve puzzles using vocabulary words. Think of two other words that relate to the history and symbols of the United States. Work with your child to make puzzles for these two words. Then help your child write sentences using your new words and the words on this page.

▲ **Practice Book 2.2** p. 116, Lesson Vocabulary

Monitor Progress | Check Lesson Vocabulary

Write these words and have individuals read them.

freedom	flag	stripes	stars	nicknames	birthday
America	won	very	people	early	together

If... children cannot read these words,

then... have them practice in pairs with word cards before reading the selection. Monitor their fluency with these words during reading, and provide additional practice opportunities before the Day 5 Assessment.

SUCCESS PREDICTOR

Spiral REVIEW

● Reviews previously taught high-frequency words and lesson vocabulary.

Day 1 Check Word Reading	▶**Day 2** Check Lesson Vocabulary/High-Frequency Words	**Day 3** Check Retelling	**Day 4** Check Fluency	**Day 5** Assess Progress

Word Reading

SUCCESS PREDICTOR

Words to Know

nicknames
flag
stars
stripes
birthday
freedom
America

Remember

Try the strategy. Then, if you need more help, use your glossary or a dictionary.

Vocabulary Strategy
for Compound Words

Word Structure When you are reading, you may come to a long word. Do you see two small words in the long word? Then it is probably a compound word. You may be able to use the two small words to help you figure out the meaning of the compound word.

1. Divide the long word into its two small words.

2. Think of the meaning of each small word. Put the two meanings together. Does this help you understand the meaning of the compound word?

3. Try the meaning in the sentence. Does it make sense?

Read "America's Flag." Use the meanings of the small words to help you understand the meanings of the compound words.

324

AMERICA'S FLAG

The Red, White, and Blue. The Stars and Stripes. These are nicknames for the American flag. You can probably guess why people call the flag by those names. Look at the picture of the flag. What colors do you see? You see red, white, and blue. What patterns do you see? You see stars and stripes.

People hang the flag outside their homes on special holidays like the Fourth of July. That is our country's birthday.

On that day long ago, the American colonies declared their freedom from England. But you don't have to wait for a holiday. You can fly your flag anytime you want. When you look at it, think about what it stands for—America and freedom.

Words to Write

Write about what the flag means to you. Use words from the Words to Know list.

325

ELL

Access Content Use ELL Poster 27 to preteach the lesson vocabulary. Reinforce the words with the vocabulary activities and word cards in the ELL Teaching Guide, pp. 185–186. Choose from the following to meet children's language proficiency levels.

Beginning Use the list of Multilingual Lesson Vocabulary in the ELL Teaching Guide, pp. 276–283, and other home-language resources to provide translations.

Intermediate Create a flag web. Have children suggest words that describe the flag.

Advanced Teach the lesson on pp. 324–325. Have children find home-language terms for *flag, stars, stripes.*

Resources for home-language words may include parents, bilingual staff members and bilingual dictionaries.

Vocabulary Strategy

TEACH/MODEL Compound Words

CONNECT Remind children of strategies to use when they come across words they don't understand.

• We can look for context clues in the words and sentences around the unknown word.

• We can look in a dictionary or glossary.

• Sometimes we can get the meaning from word parts. We may understand the two shorter words in a compound (*wildcat, a cat that's wild*). Today we will learn more about compound words.

TRODUCE THE STRATEGY

Read and discuss the steps for understanding compound words on p. 324.

Have children read "America's Flag," paying attention to compound words to determine the meaning of highlighted words.

Model using compound words to determine the meaning of *birthday*.

MODEL The word *birthday* is made up of two smaller words — *birth* and *day*. The previous sentence tells about the Fourth of July. I know this is the day our country was born — its *birth day*, *birthday*.

PRACTICE

Have children determine the meanings of highlighted words in "America's Flag" and identify the smaller words they used.

Point out that knowing the two smaller words in a compound word doesn't always help with word meaning, and they may still have to use the glossary or a dictionary to find the meaning of some words

RITE Children should write how they feel about the flag. This writing should include lesson vocabulary.

ONNECT TO READING Encourage children to use these strategies to determine the meaning of an unknown word.

Say the word aloud. Listen for the two smaller words.

Look for context clues in nearby words or sentences.

Use the glossary or a dictionary.

Group Time

On-Level	Strategic Intervention	Advanced
Read *Red, White, and Blue.* Use pp. 326–345.	**Read** SI Decodable Reader 27. • Read or listen to *Red, White, and Blue.* • Use the **Routine** on p. DI·26.	**Read** *Red, White, and Blue.* • Use the **Routine** on p. DI·27.

DAY 2

 Place English language learners in the groups that correspond to their reading abilities in English.

(i) Independent Activities

ndependent Reading See p. 322j for eading/Library activities and suggestions.

ournal Writing Write about a time you saw a ag flying, maybe in a parade or at a sporting vent. Share your writing.

Literacy Centers To provide experiences with *Red, White, and Blue,* you may use the Writing Center on p. 322k.

Practice Book 2.2 Fact and Opinion, p. 115; Lesson Vocabulary, p. 116; Compare and Contrast, p. 117

Break into small groups after Vocabulary and before Writing.

Red, White, and Blue

★ ★ ★ ★ ★ The Story of ★ ★ ★ ★ ★
THE AMERICAN FLAG

★ ★ ★ ★ ★ ★ BY ★ ★ ★ ★ ★ ★
John Herman

ILLUSTRATED BY
Shannan Stirnweiss

Genre

Narrative nonfiction gives facts in the form of a story. Look for facts as you read.

How did the American flag change over the years?

326

327

AudioText

Read
Prereading Strategies

PREVIEW AND PREDICT Have children read the title. Identify the flags in the picture. Identify the author and illustrator. Do a picture walk of pp. 328–333. Ask children what they think this story will be about.

DISCUSS NARRATIVE NONFICTION Ask children if they think this is a true story. Read the definition of narrative nonfiction on p. 326 of the Student Edition. Guide children to use what they have learned from previewing the text to understand why this selection is narrative nonfiction. (The subtitle tells that the selection is about true events and the graphics give clues that the events are told in time, or chronological, order.)

SET PURPOSE Call on volunteers to tell what they know about the American flag. Then read aloud the question on p. 327. Ask what children expect to learn from reading the selection.

Access Content Before reading, review the story summary in English and/or the home language. See the ELL Teaching Guide, pp. 187–189.

____ Inflected Endings

☐ lesson/tested vocabula

We all know the American flag. Its bright colors fly at baseball games. It flies at Fourth of July parades. We even see it on clothes!

Our flag has lots of nicknames—like Old Glory and the Red, White, and Blue. Sometimes it's called the Stars and Stripes. But where did our flag come from? Who decided what it would look like? The truth is that no one knows for sure.

Back in the 1700s, America didn't have a flag. It didn't need one. It wasn't even a country yet.

It was just thirteen colonies. The colonies belonged to England. The English flag flew in towns from New Hampshire to Georgia.

But as time went on, the thirteen colonies didn't want to belong to England anymore. Americans decided to fight for their freedom.

A war began. It was the American Revolution. Now a new flag was needed—an American flag.

The original 13 American colonies

New Hampshire
Massachusetts
Rhode Island
Connecticut
New York
New Jersey
Pennsylvania
Delaware
Maryland
Virginia
North Carolina
South Carolina
Georgia

328

329

Guiding Comprehension

Author's Purpose • Inferential

- **Why did the author write this selection?**
  The author wrote the selection to tell us where our flag came from and how it has changed.

Cause and Effect • Inferential

- **Why did Americans need a new flag?**
  They were fighting for their freedom from England, and the people wanted their own flag.

Make Judgments • Critical

- **In your opinion, which of the flag's nicknames is the best? Why?**
  Children should choose one of the nicknames from p. 328 and support their opinion.

▲ **Pages 328–329**
Have children read to find out why Americans needed a new flag.

Map

Time for SOCIAL STUDIES

Have children study the map on pp. 338–339. Have them trace the country's border with their finger. Have them identify which areas are states—smaller divisions that are part of the United States — and which are territories, or places where people lived and had laws but had not formed into states yet.

Who made our first flag? Some people say it was a woman <u>named</u> Betsy Ross. Maybe you've <u>heard</u> of her. Betsy Ross <u>owned</u> a <u>sewing</u> shop in Philadelphia. She was famous for her <u>sewing</u>.

The story is that one day a general came to see her. The general was George Washington. He was the head of the American army.

General Washington <u>wanted</u> a new flag. It would make his soldiers feel like a real army <u>fighting</u> for a real country.

He wanted Betsy Ross to make this flag. He drew a picture of what he <u>wanted</u>.

Betsy Ross

George Washington

First American flag

Betsy Ross made some <u>changes</u>. Then she <u>showed</u> the picture to General Washington. He liked it!

Betsy Ross <u>sewed</u> the flag. And that <u>was</u> the very first <u>Stars</u> and <u>Stripes</u>.

That is the story—and it's a good one. But is it true? Betsy Ross's grandson said it was. He said that Betsy told him the story when he was a little boy and she was an old woman of eighty-four. But there is no proof for this story. So what do we know *for sure*?

We know that during the Revolution the <u>colonists</u> <u>used lots</u> of different <u>flags</u>.

Flags from the Revolutionary War

330

331

▲ **Pages 330–331**
Have children read to find out who wanted a new flag.

Monitor Progress

Read New Words

If...	then... remind them to:
children come to a word they don't know,	1. Blend the word. 2. Decide if the word makes sense. 3. Look in a dictionary for more help.

Skills in Context

🎯 FACT AND OPINION

- **In the third paragraph on p. 330, which sentence is a fact and which is an opinion?**
  The first sentence is a fact, while the second is an opinion.

Monitor Progress	**Fact and Opinion**
If... children are unable to identify facts and opinions,	**then...** model how to distinguish fact and opinion.

Think Aloud

MODEL I know that statements of opinion are about feelings, beliefs, or judgments, and statements of fact can be proven to be true or false. I can prove that Washington wanted a new flag, but I can't prove how the flag would make the soldiers feel.

ASSESS Have children search for other facts and opinions as they read.

____ Inflected Endings

▇ lesson/tested vocabula

But once the colonies became the United States of America, the country needed *one* flag—the same flag for everybody.

So on June 14, 1777, a decision was made. The flag was going to have thirteen red and white stripes. The flag was also going to have thirteen white stars on a blue background, one for each of the thirteen colonies. Now the United States had a flag.

Congress had picked the colors and the stars and stripes. But Congress did not say where the stars and stripes had to go. So the flag still did not always look the same!

People could put them any way they liked. Sometimes the stripes were up and down, like this.

Sometimes the stars were in a circle, like this.

But nobody minded. Up and down or side to side, the stars and stripes still stood for the United States.

332

Over the years, the flag became more and more important to people.

In 1812, the United States was at war with England again. British soldiers came to America. They sailed up our rivers. They marched down our streets. They even burned down the White House—the home of the President.

333

Strategies in Context

MONITOR AND FIX UP

- **Why does one flag have stripes that go up and down instead of across?**
Congress decided the flag should have thirteen red and white stripes but did not tell how they should be arranged. So, people made up their own designs.

Monitor Progress	Monitor and Fix Up
If... children have difficulty recalling details that answer the question,	**then...** model rereading the text to find the answers.

Think Aloud **MODEL** If I reread, I find that the fourth paragraph on p. 332 tells about stripes going up and down, but it doesn't tell why. I reread the paragraph before it to find the answer.

ASSESS Have children reread to find out about the colors and the numbers of stars each flag had to have.

▲ **Pages 332–333**
Have children read to find out why the first American flags did not all look alike.

Monitor Progress	
Lesson Vocabulary	
If... children have a problem reading a new lesson vocabulary word,	**then...** use the Lesson Vocabulary Routine on p. 324f to reteach the problematic word.

Red, White, and Blue **332–333**

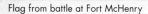

Flag from battle at Fort McHenry

But in the early morning light, he saw the Stars and Stripes. It was still flying above the fort! He knew American soldiers had won the battle.

Key felt very proud. He wrote a poem about the flag on the fort. The poem was "The Star-Spangled Banner." Later the poem was put to music. This song about our flag became a song for our whole country.

Francis Scott Key

On the night of September 13, 1814, British soldiers bombed a fort in Maryland. All that night a man watched the fighting. His name was Francis Scott Key. He was afraid. What if the American soldiers in the fort gave up?

334

335

▲ **Pages 334–335**
Have children read to find out why "The Star-Spangled Banner" was written.

Strategy Self-Check

Have children ask themselves these questions to check their reading.

Vocabulary Strategy
- Do I look for the two smaller words in a compound word?
- Do I look for context clues?
  Do I use the glossary or a dictionary?

Monitor and Fix Up
- Do I reread if I forget some details from the selection?
- Do I reread if a part of a selection does not make sense?

Guiding Comprehension

Cause and Effect • Inferential
- **Why did Francis Scott Key write "The Star-Spangled Banner"?**
  Francis Scott Key wrote "The Star-Spangled Banner" because he was proud that the American soldiers won the battle against the British soldiers.

Summarize • Inferential
- **What has happened so far in the selection?**
  After winning independence from England, the new country needed a flag. Betsy Ross may have made the first American flag. In the beginning, the country had many different flags, but they were all red, white, and blue, and they all had stars and stripes. The citizens began to love their flag. One man, Francis Scott Key, even wrote a poem about it, which became our country's special song.

____ Inflected Endings   lesson/tested vocabular

The flag that Francis Scott Key saw had fifteen stripes and fifteen stars.

Why? Because by then there were two more states–Vermont and Kentucky.

American flag in 1814

First Fifteen American States

Vermont

Kentucky

New Hampshire
Massachusetts
Rhode Island
Connecticut
New York
New Jersey
Pennsylvania
Delaware
Maryland
Virginia
North Carolina
South Carolina
Georgia

Our country was getting bigger. People were heading out west. In time, more places were going to want to be states. Soon there would be too many stripes to fit on the flag!

Congress had to do something. So in 1818 this is what was decided: The flag would go back to thirteen red and white stripes. And in the blue box would be one white star for each state. Every time there was a new state, a new star would be added.

336

337

Guiding Comprehension

Details and Facts • Literal

- **What do the stars on the flag stand for?**
  Each star stands for a state.

Draw Conclusions • Inferential

- **How would the flag change if Puerto Rico became a state?**
  It would have one more star.

▲ **Pages 336–337**
Have children read to find out what the stars on the flag stand for.

EXTEND SKILLS

Graphic Sources

For instruction on graphic sources, discuss the following:

- Graphic sources are features such as pictures and captions, maps, charts, and diagrams.

- Graphic sources such as maps and captions can be used as fix-up strategies. They expand on information from the text and help us understand what we are reading.

- What graphic sources do you see on pp. 336–337?

Assess Have children identify other graphic sources in the selection and tell what they learn from each one.

Red, White, and Blue 336–337

At last the Stars and Stripes looked the same everywhere it flew. And Americans were proud of their flag. They took the flag with them as they moved west. The flag crossed the Mississippi River and the great grassy plains and the Rocky Mountains. It made it all the way to California.

More and more states were added to the country. And more and more stars were added to the flag. By 1837, there were twenty-six stars on the flag. By 1850, there were thirty-one.

American flag in 1850

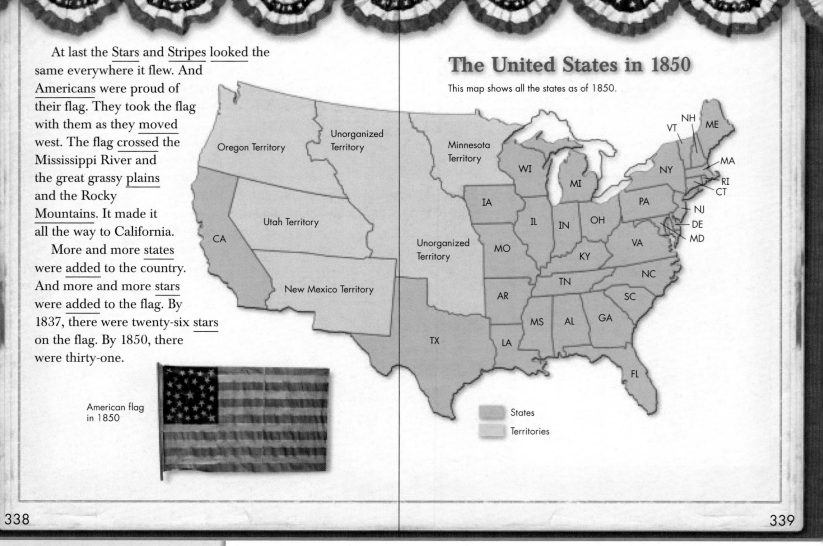

The United States in 1850
This map shows all the states as of 1850.

- Oregon Territory
- Unorganized Territory
- Minnesota Territory
- Utah Territory
- New Mexico Territory
- Unorganized Territory
- CA
- WI
- MI
- IA
- IL
- IN
- OH
- MO
- KY
- AR
- TN
- TX
- LA
- MS
- AL
- GA
- NH
- VT
- ME
- NY
- MA
- RI
- CT
- PA
- NJ
- DE
- MD
- VA
- NC
- SC
- FL

☐ States
☐ Territories

338

339

▲ **Pages 338–339**
Have children read to find out where the flag traveled.

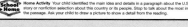

Read the text.
Follow the directions.

Where can you see our country's flag? You can see it on flagpoles. You can see it in parades. Many people wear flag pins. Some firefighters wear flag patches on their shirts. People feel proud of our flag.

1. **Circle** the answer below that tells what the text is all about.
   (the flag)   parades   firefighters

2. **Circle** the answer below that tells the main idea.
   People fly the flag from flagpoles.
   People carry the flag in parades.
   (People are proud of our flag.)

3. **Draw** a picture to show a detail about the main idea.
   Children's artwork should show a detail from the passage, such as a flag hanging from a flagpole, a person carrying a flag in a parade, a flag pin worn on a lapel, or a flag patch worn by a firefighter.

School + Home Home Activity Your child identified the main idea and details in a paragraph about the U.S. flag. Read a story or nonfiction selection about this country or its people. Stop to talk about the most important ideas in the passage. Ask your child to draw a picture to show a detail from the reading.

▲ **Practice Book 2.2** p. 117, Main Idea

Skills in Context

REVIEW MAIN IDEA

- **What is the main idea, or the most important idea, on this page?**
  Americans were proud of their flag and took it with them as they moved west.

Monitor Progress	**Main Idea and Supporting Details**
If... children are unable to identify the main idea,	**then...** model how to distinguish the main idea from the details.

Think Aloud **MODEL** As I read the page, I think the main idea is that Americans were proud of their flag. I also read that Americans took the flag across the Mississippi River, the plains, and the Rocky Mountains. These are details that tell me more about how proud they were of their flag and how patriotic they were.

ASSESS Have children identify other details that support the main idea.

____ Inflected Endings   ☐ lesson/tested vocabulary

One country. One flag. But then in 1861, something happened. Our country split in two. Eleven states in the South broke away from the United States of America. They started their own country. It was called the Confederate States of America.

Abraham Lincoln was President of the United States. He said *all* the states had to stay together.

President Abraham Lincoln

340

War broke out—the Civil War. It was a very sad time in the history of our country.

The eleven southern states stopped flying the Stars and Stripes. They had their own flag.

In the North, some people wanted eleven stars taken off the Stars and Stripes. But Abraham Lincoln would not do that. He said the states would get back together. He was right. The Civil War ended in 1865. The North won. And the United States was one country under one flag again.

341

Guiding Comprehension

Cause and Effect • Inferential

- **Why did our country have two very different flags at one time?**
Our country had two different flags because it was divided by the Civil War.

Cause and Effect • Inferential

- **Why did some people want eleven stars removed from the American flag at this time?**
Some people in the North wanted to remove eleven stars from the flag because eleven states in the South broke away from the United States of America.

▲ **Pages 340–341**
Have children read to find out when and why our country had two different flags.

Understanding Idioms Point out the phrase "War broke out" on p. 341. Explain to children that this is another way of saying "War started."

On June 14, 1877, the flag had a birthday—a big one. It was 100 years old. All across the country, people had picnics and parties and parades. June 14 became a holiday—Flag Day.

Today our flag has fifty stars for the fifty United States of America. Some flags are huge. One weighs 500 pounds! It is flown every Fourth of July from the George Washington Bridge.

The American flag flies in towns and cities from coast to coast.

And that's not all. In 1969, two American astronauts were the first people ever to land on the moon. The astronauts took lots of moon rocks back to Earth. They also left something on the moon . . . the Stars and Stripes.

And do you know what? Our flag is still flying there!

342

343

▲ **Pages 342–343**
Have children read to find out how Americans honor the flag.

Activate Prior Knowledge Have children share their experience and knowledge about the U.S. or another national flag.

_____ Inflected Endings

lesson/tested vocabulary

Guiding Comprehension

Analyze • Inferential

• **What are some ways U.S. citizens show respect for the flag?**
Americans created Flag Day, a special holiday to celebrate the flag. They had picnics, parties, and parades. U.S. astronauts placed a U.S. flag on the moon.

Draw Conclusions • Critical

• *Text to Self* **What activities and decorations would you plan for a Flag Day party?**
Children may mention activities such as wearing clothing or jewelry that shows the flag, saluting the flag, and saying the Pledge of Allegiance. Decorations might include anything that is red, white, and blue.

Fluency

REREAD FOR FLUENCY

Paired Reading

ROUTINE

Reader 1 Begins Children read the entire story, switching readers at the end of each page.

Reader 2 Begins Have partners reread; now the other partner begins.

Reread For optimal fluency, children should reread three or four times.

Provide Feedback Listen to children read and provide corrective feedback regarding their oral reading and their use of the blending strategy.

OBJECTIVES

- Write a poem.
- Identify quotation marks.

Strategic Intervention

Have children copy the poem and illustrate their writing.

Advanced

Have children who are able to write complete sentences independently write their own poem about the flag. Challenge them to write a four-line poem.

Writing Support Before writing, children might share a poem in their home languages.

Beginning Allow children to look at books for sources of visual support as they write their poem.

Intermediate Help children orally practice the rhymes they choose to use in their poems before they write.

Advanced Have children do a 'think-aloud' with a partner and discuss what they plan to write. Encourage children to read their poems aloud.

Support Grammar Children may have difficulty distinguishing dialogue from the rest of a sentence. Point out that words such as *said, shouted,* and *replied* usually are found just before or after the dialogue. See the Grammar Transition lessons in the ELL and Transition Handbook.

Interactive Writing

WRITE Poem

BRAINSTORM Use *Red, White, and Blue* to encourage a discussion about pride in our flag. Picture walk through the book and ask children to identify the ways our flag has changed.

SHARE THE PEN Have children participate in writing a poem about our flag. To begin, children can brainstorm words that rhyme with *me*. Write the phrase *you and me*. Model thinking of other phrases to write in the poem. Invite individuals to write familiar letter-sounds, word parts, and high-frequency words. Ask questions such as:

- How do you spell *me*? *(m-e)*
- How do you spell *see?* *(s-e-e)* Have a volunteer write *see.*
- What is the blend you hear at the beginning of the word *flag*? (/fl/)
- Which letters make that sound? (*f* and *l*)

Continue to have individuals make contributions. Frequently reread what has been written while tracking the print.

READ THE POEM Read the completed poem aloud, having children echo you.

Our Flag
**The colors of our flag make me see
Our land is free for you and me.**

INDEPENDENT WRITING

WRITE A POEM ABOUT OUR FLAG Have children write their own poem about the flag. Remind them to create a rhythm as they write their poems. They can clap each line to see whether they are repeating the rhythm throughout their poem. Let children illustrate their writing.

Grammar

DEVELOP THE CONCEPT Quotation Marks

IDENTIFY QUOTATION MARKS Write *"I'm coming," said Maria.* Point to each word as you read it. Ask children to identify who is speaking in this sentence. *(Maria)* What did Maria say? *(I'm coming.)*

Quotation marks show the beginning and ending of the words someone says. What shows the beginning and ending of the words someone says? (quotation marks)

PRACTICE

WRITE QUOTATIONS Brainstorm a list of five names. Have children suggest sentences these people might say about the flag. Model writing a quotation, using the person's name and words.

MODEL Let's use Sam. Write *Sam said* followed by a comma. Now I need to write what Sam said: Our flag is red, white, and blue. Write *Our flag is red, white, and blue.* Now I need to put quotation marks around what Sam said. Add quotation marks.

Have children suggest names of people and what they might say about the flag. Write the sentences children suggest. Let children add the quotation marks.

DAILY FIX-IT

3. the flag stands for freedum.
   The flag stands for freedom.

4. Our fleg has stars and sripes.
   Our flag has stars and stripes.

Quotation Marks

Quotation marks (" ") show the beginning and ending of the words someone says. The speaker's name and words such as **said** or **asked** are not inside the quotation marks.

"Let's have a parade," said Betsy.
Ross asked, "What kind of parade should we have?"

Add quotation marks to each sentence.

1. "I don't know what kind of parade to have," said Betsy.

2. Abe said, "We could have a flag parade."

3. "What is a flag parade?" asked Francis Scott.

4. "We could all wear red, white, and blue," George said.

5. Lincoln asked, "Could we all carry flags?"

6. Betsy said, "That's a great idea."

Home Activity Your child learned about quotation marks. Look through a newspaper article with your child. Have him or her circle places where quotation marks are used. Ask your child why quotation marks were needed.

▲ **Grammar and Writing Practice Book** p. 105

Wrap Up Your Day!

LESSON VOCABULARY Write: *Stars and Stripes is one of our flag's nicknames.* Ask children to read the sentence and identify the lesson vocabulary words *stars, stripes, flag,* and *nicknames.*

MONITOR AND FIX-UP Write: *Flags help soldiers tell friends from enemies.* Remind children that good readers stop and fix-up during reading. Encourage children to monitor and fix-up if they are not sure what they are reading.

LET'S TALK ABOUT IT Recall *Red, White, and Blue.* Ask: What does our flag mean to you? (Answers will vary.) Encourage children to add to the Our Flag web created on Day 1.

PREVIEW Day 3

Tell children that tomorrow they will hear about Great-Grandmother's secret.

Day 3
AT A GLANCE

Share Literature
Great-Grandmother's Secret

Phonics and Spelling
REVIEW Contractions *'re, 've, 'd*
Spelling: Words with Inflected Endings

Vocabulary
Skill Compound Words

Fluency
Read Silently with Fluency and Accuracy

Writing Trait
Conventions

Grammar
Quotation Marks

Materials

- *Sing with Me Big Book*
- *Read Aloud Anthology*
- Student Edition 344–345

Morning Warm~Up!

Today we will listen again to the story of William and his flag. William wants to be patriotic and fly a flag outside his house. His great-grandmother directs him to a suitcase that has his great-grandfather's special flag in it. Why is the flag so special?

QUESTION OF THE DAY Encourage children to sing "Our Flag, Our Symbol" from the *Sing with Me Big Book* as you gather. Write and read the message and discuss the question.

REVIEW COMPOUND WORDS

- Ask children to raise their hands when you point to a compound word.
- Review that *outside* is made up of the two smaller words *out* and *side*.
- Have children identify the two smaller words that make up other compound words in the morning message.

Build Background Use the Day 3 instruction on ELL Poster 27 to support children's use of English to communicate about lesson concepts.

ELL Poster 27

Share Literature

LISTEN AND RESPOND

BUILD ORAL VOCABULARY Review that yesterday the class listened to the story to find out what special flag William flew. Discuss why William's mother got rid of their old flag. It was **frayed** and worn. *Frayed* means "falling apart at the ends." Frayed flags needed to be disposed of properly. Ask that children listen today to find out what William's mother did with the frayed and worn flag.

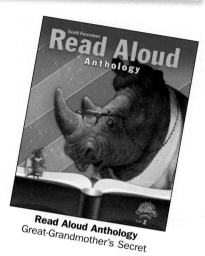

Read Aloud Anthology
Great-Grandmother's Secret

MONITOR LISTENING COMPREHENSION

- What did William's mother do with their frayed and worn flag? Why? (She took it to the American Legion. They collect old flags and dispose of them properly.)

- Why couldn't they buy a new flag at the store? (The stores were all out of flags.)

- What does William use to try to make a flag? (He uses paper and markers.)

- How do you think William felt when he shattered the glass in the picture frame? How do you know? (He felt terrible. He had tears in his eyes as he said "sorry" to his Gram.)

 **to build oral vocabulary**

Amazing Words	**MONITOR PROGRESS**
history independence symbol patriotic unfurl frayed allegiance indivisible	**If...** children lack oral vocabulary experiences about the concept Traditions, **then...** use the Oral Vocabulary Routine. See p. DI·4 to teach *frayed*.

Listen and Respond Help children demonstrate the meaning of the word *frayed* in "Great-Grandmother's Secret." Give children a piece of fabric and begin fraying one end. Allow time for children to fray the edge of the fabric.

Review Phonics

REVIEW CONTRACTIONS

READ CONTRACTIONS Write *you're.* This word is a contraction, a short way of saying and writing two words. You can read this word because you know that an apostrophe takes the place of letters that are left out. Write *you are* under *you're.* If we compare these words, we see that the apostrophe takes the place of the letter *a.* What's the contraction? (*you're*)

Write *I've.* The contraction *I've* is short for *I have.* Write *I have* under *I've.* Which letter or letters have been left out of *I've?* (*h* and *a*) Have children read *I've.* Repeat with *she'd (she had, she would),* and *won't (will not).* Point out that *won't* is a special contraction because the word *will* doesn't appear in it.

BUILD WORDS List the word pairs shown below at the left. Have individuals write a contraction that can be made from the two words.

Two Words	*Contractions*
they are	they're
we have	we've
he had	he'd
will not	won't
do not	don't
we are	we're

OBJECTIVES

- Review contractions 're, 've, 'd.
- Build, blend, and read contractions.
- Recognize lesson vocabulary.
- Spell base words and endings *-ed, -ing.*

Write the contraction on the line.

You are cute.
You're cute.

1. they would	2. we have
they'd	we've

3. you are	4. do not
you're	don't

5. he would	6. we are
he'd	we're

7. will not	8. can not
won't	can't

Find the contraction for each pair of words.
Mark the space to show your answer.

9. they are	10. I have
⌷ there	⌷ I'd
▬ they're	⌷ I'm
⌷ they've	▬ I've

Home Activity Your child reviewed contractions with 're (we're), 've (I've), 'd (I'd), and 't (won't). Work with your child to write sentences using the contractions on this page. Then have your child circle each contraction and tell what pair of words the contraction represents.

▲ **Practice Book 2.2** p. 118, Contractions

Lesson Vocabulary

PRACTICE

USE WORDS Write questions using lesson vocabulary words on the board. Have children read the questions and discuss them in groups.

- What is a kind of *freedom* you have had?
- What are some places in *America?*
- Which is easier to draw—*stars* or *stripes?*
- What are some *nicknames* people have?
- Would you want to get a *flag* on your *birthday?*

Spelling

PRACTICE Inflected Endings

FINISH THE SENTENCE Have children practice spelling words by writing down and finishing sentence starters that use spelling words.

- We *tried* to visit . . .
- She was *trying* to learn . . .
- He *planned* to . . .
- They were *planning* to make . . .
- The dog *liked* the . . .
- She is *liking* . . .
- The club *hiked* . . .
- He was *hiking* in the woods when . . .
- The baby *cried* after . . .
- The little girl was *crying* because . . .
- We *skipped* across . . .
- He was *skipping* when . . .

HOMEWORK Spelling Practice Book, p. 107

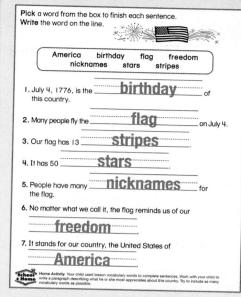

▲ **Practice Book 2.2** p. 119,
Lesson Vocabulary

Spelling Words

Inflected Endings

1. **tried**	7. **hiked**
2. **trying**	8. **hiking**
3. **planned**	9. **cried**
4. **planning**	10. **crying**
5. **liked***	11. **skipped**
6. **liking***	12. **skipping**

Challenge Words

13. **danced**	15. **dancing**
14. **replied**	16. **replying**

* **Words from the Selection**

More Adding -ed and -ing

Read the word puzzle. **Circle** two words that are spelled wrong and a word that is missing its -ing ending. **Write** the words correctly.

Everyone (tryed) to be first in line.
A girl who (skiped) rope was first. She is smiling.
A girl who liked wearing bows in her hair is behind a girl who is (cry).
Who is last in line?
(Answer: The girl wearing bows in her hair)

Spelling Words	
tried	hiked
trying	hiking
planned	cried
planning	crying
liked	skipped
liking	skipping

1. **tried**   2. **skipped**
3. **crying**

Frequently Misspelled Words
thought
caught

Circle the word that is spelled correctly.

4. planing	(planning)	plainning
5. cryed	cryied	(cried)
6. (skipping)	skiping	skipng
7. (liked)	likeed	likd
8. planed	(planned)	pland
9. hikking	hikeing	(hiking)
10. tring	(trying)	tryeing

Home Activity Pronounce a base word. Ask your child to spell the corresponding -ed and -ing words.

▲ **Spelling Practice Book** p. 107

Red, White, and Blue   **344d**

Strategic Intervention

Have children illustrate the compound word *baseball*. Then help them write a caption using the word *baseball*.

Advanced

Have children use a dictionary to look up the definitions of other compound words.

Extend Language Help children identify the meanings of compound words by breaking the word into two smaller words.

Vocabulary

COMPOUND WORDS

DISCUSS COMPOUND WORDS Have children recall that a compound word is made up of two or more smaller words. Explain that sometimes you can figure out the meaning of the compound word if you know the meanings of the smaller words. Write the following sentence and have children identify the compound words. Then have children identify the smaller words and discuss the meaning of the compound word.

At lunchtime I watch my favorite baseball team.

EXPAND SELECTION VOCABULARY Discuss with children the meaning of each compound word listed below. Have children work with partners to write sentences for each compound word. Invite volunteers to share their sentences.

grandson   **nickname**   **birthday**

Group Time

DAY **3**

On-Level

Read *Red, White, and Blue.*
- Use pp. 324–345.

Strategic Intervention

Read or listen to *Red, White, and Blue.*
- Use the **Routine** on p. DI·28.

Advanced

Read *Self-Selected Reading*
- Use the **Routine** on p. DI·29.

 Place English language learners in the groups that correspond to their reading abilities in English.

(i) Independent Activities

Independent Reading See p. 322j for Reading/Library activities and suggestions.

Journal Writing If you could change the colors in the flag, what would they be and why? Write your answers.

Literacy Centers To provide experiences with *Red, White, and Blue*, you may use the Writing Center on p. 322k.

Practice Book 2.2 Vowels *aw, au, augh, al*, p. 118; Lesson Vocabulary, p. 119

Break into small groups after Vocabulary and before Writing.

Fluency

READ SILENTLY WITH FLUENCY AND ACCURACY

MODEL READING WITH FLUENCY AND ACCURACY Use *Red, White, and Blue.*

• Point to the second sentence on p. 328. When I see a word I don't know, I try to sound it out. When I come to the word *bright*, I break it down into chunks I know, *br-igh-t.* I know the *igh* sounds like long *i* from other words I know.

• Ask children to follow along as you read the page with fluency.

• Have children read the page after you. Encourage them to self-correct when reading. Continue in the same way with pp. 329–330.

REREAD FOR FLUENCY

Silent Reading

ROUTINE

1 **Select a Passage** For *Red, White, and Blue,* use pp. 340–343.

2 **Assign** Assign each child a short passage of text.

3 **Practice** Have children read their assigned passage 3–5 times silently.

4 **Independent Readings** Have children read aloud to you. Monitor progress and provide feedback. For optimal fluency, children should read at an appropriate pace.

Monitor Progress	Fluency
If... children have difficulty reading silently with fluency,	**then...** prompt: • Do you read groups of words, not word-by-word? • Where did you get stuck? • Should you try sounding out a word by syllables?
If... the class cannot read fluently without you,	**then...** continue to have them read along with you.

Options for Oral Reading
Use *Red, White, and Blue* or one of the following Leveled Readers.

On-Level

Heroes of the American-Revolution

Strategic Intervention

Happy Birthday, America!

Advanced

Home of the Brave

Model the reading of phrases in the story, such as "one country under one flag" and "cities from coast to coast," so that beginning English language learners can practice reading meaningfully.

Retelling Plan

☑ Week 1 assess Strategic Intervention students.

☑ **This week assess Advanced students.**

☐ Week 3 assess Strategic Intervention students.

☐ Week 4 assess On-Level students.

☐ Week 5 assess any students you have not yet checked during this unit.

Look Back and Write

Point out information from the text that answers the question. Then have children write a response to the question. For test practice, assign a 10–15 minute time limit. For assessment, see the Scoring Rubric at the bottom of this page.

Assessment Focus on comprehension and whether each child can provide good information about the selection, rather than mistakes in English. For more ideas on assessing comprehension, see the ELL and Transition Handbook.

Reader Response

TALK ABOUT IT Model a response. I didn't know that the first American flag only had thirteen stars.

1. **RETELL** Have children use the retelling strip in the Student Edition to retell the selection.

Monitor Progress | **Check Retelling** [Rubric 4 3 2 1]

Have children retell *Red, White,* and *Blue.*

If... children have difficulty retelling the selection,

then... use the Retelling Cards and the Scoring Rubric for Retelling on p. 344–345 to help them move toward fluent retelling.

SUCCESS PREDICTOR

Day 1 Check Word Reading

Day 2 Check Lesson Vocabulary/High-Frequency Words

▶ **Day 3** Check Retelling

Day 4 Check Fluency

Day 5 Assess Progress

---

2. **FACT AND OPINION** Model a response. Fact: There is a star on the flag for each of the states. Opinion: Everyone should fly the flag in front of his or her house.

3. **MONITOR AND FIX UP** Model a response. I had a problem understanding why some people in the North wanted eleven stars taken off. I went back and reread to figure out why this happened.

LOOK BACK AND WRITE Read the writing prompt on p. 344 and model your thinking. I'll look back at pages 334 and 335 and reread that part of the selection. I'll look for the name of the poem and why Francis Scott Key wrote it. Then I'll write my response. Have children write their responses.

Scoring Rubric | **Look Back and Write**

Top-Score Response A top-score response will use details from pp. 334–335 of the selection to tell why Francis Scott Key wrote a poem called "The Star-Spangled Banner."

Example of a Top-Score Response The name of the poem Francis Scott Key wrote was "The Star-Spangled Banner." He wrote it because he felt proud of the American soldiers.

For additional rubrics, see p. WA10.

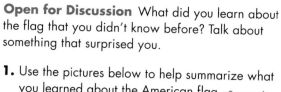

Reader Response

Open for Discussion What did you learn about the flag that you didn't know before? Talk about something that surprised you.

1. Use the pictures below to help summarize what you learned about the American flag. **Summarize**

2. Look for some facts and some opinions in the selection. Then write a fact and an opinion of your own about the flag. **Fact/Opinion**

3. Did anything in this selection confuse you? Where did you have a problem while reading? What did you do about it? **Monitor/Fix Up**

Look Back and Write Francis Scott Key wrote a poem. What is the name of the poem, and why did he write it? Look back at pages 334 and 335. Use details from the selection in your answer.

Meet the Author

John Herman

Read more books about the American flag.

John Herman grew up near New York City. He knew he wanted to be a writer when he was 12 years old. Now he writes books for adults, teenagers, and children.

Mr. Herman likes to make up stories. *Red, White, and Blue* gave him a chance to write about real events. He loves reading about American history, so this was a new thing for him to try. He hopes to write more books like this in the future!

The Flag We Love by Pam Muñoz Ryan

Betsy Ross by Alexandra Wallner

Retelling Strip

344

345

Scoring Rubric | Expository Retelling

Rubric 4 3 2 1	4	3	2	1
Connections	Makes connections and generalizes beyond the text	Makes connections to other events, texts, or experiences	Makes a limited connection to another event, text, or experience	Makes no connection to another event, text, or experience
Author's Purpose	Elaborates on author's purpose	Tells author's purpose with some clarity	Makes some connection to author's purpose	Makes no connection to author's purpose
Topic	Describes the main topic	Identifies the main topic with some details early in retelling	Identifies the main topic	Retelling has no sense of topic
Important Ideas	Gives accurate information about ideas using key vocabulary	Gives accurate information about ideas with some key vocabulary	Gives limited or inaccurate information about ideas	Gives no information about ideas
Conclusions	Draws conclusions and makes inferences to generalize beyond the text	Draws conclusions about the text	Is able to tell some learnings about the text	Is unable to draw conclusions or make inferences about the text

Use the Retelling Chart on p. TR21 to record retelling.

Selection Test To assess with *Red, White, and Blue,* use Selection Tests, pp. 105–108.

Fresh Reads for Differentiated Test Practice For weekly leveled practice, use pp. 157–162.

Retelling

SUCCESS
PREDICTOR

Writing Trait of the Week

INTRODUCE Conventions

TALK ABOUT CONVENTIONS Explain to children that conventions are the rules for writing, including capitalization, spelling, punctuation, and verb forms. Ask them to think about how the author's use of conventions helps readers understand *Red, White, and Blue.* Then model your thinking.

 Think Aloud

MODEL The article *Red, White, and Blue* contains many proper nouns: names of specific people, places, and things. Proper nouns begin with capital letters. This is a convention that makes proper nouns easy to recognize. The article also uses correct verb forms. Let's look at a sentence on page 333 as I read it aloud.

In 1812, the United States was at war with England again.

DAILY FIX-IT

5. some of the strippes are white.
   <u>S</u>ome of the stri<u>p</u>es are white.

6. People move to america
   People move to <u>A</u>merica<u>.</u>

Connect to Unit Writing

Writing Trait

Have children use strategies for developing **conventions** when they write a research report in the Unit Writing Workshop, pp. WA2–WA9.

The first word of the sentence begins with a capital letter. There are other words that begin with capital letters too. These are proper nouns. Capital letters help me understand that the words *United States* and *England* name specific places. The correct use of capital letters is a convention. Another convention is the use of correct verb forms. The word *was* in the sentence I just read is a past-tense verb. Unlike many past-tense verbs, such as *walked* and *liked,* it does not end in *-ed.* It is an irregular verb.

STRATEGY FOR DEVELOPING CONVENTIONS On the board, write the following sentences without capital letters. Ask children to correct the capitalization, choose the correct verb form, and write the sentences.

betsy ross (maked, made) the first flag. *(Betsy Ross made the first flag.)*

Francis scott key (saw, seed) a battle in maryland. *(Francis Scott Key saw a battle in Maryland.)*

many battles of the american revolution (took, taked) place in virginia. *(Many battles of the American Revolution took place in Virginia.)*

PRACTICE

APPLY THE STRATEGY Ask children to brainstorm famous Americans they know about. Have them choose one person and write about what he or she has done. Remind them to use correct capitalization and verb forms.

Grammar

APPLY TO WRITING Quotation Marks

IMPROVE WRITING WITH QUOTATION MARKS Have children recall that quotation marks show the beginning and ending of the words someone says. Add that writing with quotation marks lets readers know someone is talking. Remind children to use quotation marks in their own writing.

Write *Where did you go? asked Mom. I went to the library, said Mark.* Have children supply the quotations marks at the beginning and ending of the words that were said.

> **"Where did you go?" asked Mom.**
> **"I went to the library," said Mark.**

PRACTICE

WRITE WITH QUOTATION MARKS Call on individuals to supply quotation marks in sentences. Select a child. Have him or her stand and say a short sentence. Write the child's name and what he or she said. Continue until three or four examples have been written. Invite children to place quotation marks around what each child said.

▲ **Grammar and Writing Practice Book** p. 106

 # Wrap Up Your Day!

 FACT AND OPINION Have children identify facts and opinions in the story "Great Grandmother's Secret." "Gram, I made a flag, but it looks terrible." Fact or opinion? He finished the remaining red stripes with a crayon. Fact or opinion?

✓ **SILENT READING ROUTINE** Remind children that fluent readers read at a good pace, decode words quickly, and group words as they read.

LET'S TALK ABOUT IT Display the Our Flag web from Day 1. Have children read the words that describe the U.S. flag and add any additional descriptive words.

 **PREVIEW Day 4**

Tell children that tomorrow they will listen to a story about the American flag and what it stands for.

Day 4
AT A GLANCE

Share Literature
Uncle Sam and Old Glory

Phonics and Spelling

Inflected Endings

Spelling: Words with
   Inflected Endings

Read

Group Time < Differentiated
          Instruction

"You're a Grand Old Flag"

Fluency
Read with Fluency and Accuracy

Writing Across
the Curriculum
Venn Diagram

Grammar
Quotation Marks

Speaking and Listening
Understand Nonverbal Cues

Materials

- *Sing with Me Big Book*
- *Read Aloud Anthology*
- Student Edition 346–347
- Graphic Organizer 17

Morning Warm~Up!

Today we will learn another
song about our flag.
Our flag is red, white, and blue.
Our flag is a symbol for our country.
What does our flag mean to you?

QUESTION OF THE DAY Encourage children to sing "Our Flag, Our Symbol"
from the *Sing with Me Big Book* as you gather. Write and read the
message and discuss the question.

REVIEW MULTIPLE-MEANING WORDS

- Ask children to identify words that have more than one meaning in the
  message. *(blue, mean)*

- Discuss the different meanings of the words *blue* and *mean*.

Extend Language Use the Day 4
instruction on ELL Poster 27 to extend
and enrich language.

ELL Poster 27

Share Literature

CONNECT CONCEPTS

ACTIVATE PRIOR KNOWLEDGE Recall the many nicknames for the flag in *Red, White, and Blue.* Explain that you will listen to another story about the U.S. flag—*Uncle Sam and Old Glory* by Delno and Jean West.

Read Aloud Anthology
Uncle Sam and Old Glory

BUILD ORAL VOCABULARY Read the first paragraph. Explain that when people say the Pledge of **Allegiance,** they are promising to be loyal, or faithful, to our country. Reread "one nation under God, **indivisible.**" Tell children that *indivisible* means that our nation is impossible to separate; we cannot be divided. Ask children to listen for these words in the story and find out what the colors of the flag stand for.

REVIEW ORAL VOCABULARY After reading, review all the Amazing Words for the week. Have children take turns using them in sentences that tell about the concept for the week. Then talk about Amazing Words they learned in other weeks and connect them to the concept, as well. For example, ask:

- How do U.S. **citizens** show **respect** for their flag?

- In what ways can we **preserve** the flag as a **valuable** symbol?

- How do some people use the flag to **protest** or to **challenge** the U.S. government?

MONITOR LISTENING COMPREHENSION

- What do the colors of the flag stand for? (White stands for liberty, red for courage, and blue for loyalty.)

- When you pledge allegiance to your country, what does that mean? (It means I promise to be faithful, or loyal, to my country.)

- Which word in the story means "impossible to separate?" (indivisible)

OBJECTIVES

- Set purpose for listening.
- Build oral vocabulary.

Amazing Words to build oral vocabulary

	MONITOR PROGRESS
history independence symbol patriotic unfurl frayed allegiance indivisible	**If...** children lack oral vocabulary experiences about the concept Traditions, **then...** use the Oral Vocabulary Routine. See p. DI·4 to teach *allegiance* and *indivisible.*

Connect Concepts To demonstrate the meaning of *indivisible,* have children take one craft stick and break it in half. Now take many sticks. Explain that these many sticks represent the many people in our country. Together we are *indivisible.* Now ask children to try to break this bundle of craft sticks. The bundle is *indivisible.*

Sentence Reading

REVIEW WORDS IN CONTEXT

READ DECODABLE AND HIGH-FREQUENCY WORDS IN CONTEXT Write these sentences. Call on individuals to read a sentence. Then randomly point to words and have children read them. To help you monitor word reading, high-frequency words are underlined and decodable words are circled.

(Today) I will (draw) the (biggest) (chalk) picture of (sailing) (ships.)

I (saw) (Paul) as I (walked) to school last (Monday.)

Did you <u>wash</u> the (bait) (pails) that we (used) when we (caught) fish?

My <u>parents</u> (always) (say) it is (okay) to be (afraid) or (scared.)

The teacher (taught) us to (raise) our (hands) before (giving) an <u>answer</u>.

In (August) <u>company</u> came from <u>faraway</u> to (stay) with us.

Monitor Progress	Word Reading
If... children are unable to read an underlined word,	**then...** read the word for them and spell it, having them echo you.
If... children are unable to read a circled word,	**then...** have them use the blending strategy they have learned for that word type.

Support Phonics For additional review, see the phonics activities in the ELL and Transition Handbook.

Spelling

PARTNER REVIEW Inflected Endings

READ AND WRITE Supply pairs of children with index cards on which the spelling words have been written. Have one child read a word while the other writes it. Then have children switch roles. Have them use the cards to check their spelling.

HOMEWORK Spelling Practice Book, p. 108

OBJECTIVE

● Spell words with inflected endings.

Spelling Words

Inflected Endings

1. tried	7. hiked
2. trying	8. hiking
3. planned	9. cried
4. planning	10. crying
5. liked*	11. skipped
6. liking*	12. skipping

Challenge Words

13. danced	15. replied
14. dancing	16. replying

* Words from the Selection

Group Time

On-Level	Strategic Intervention	Advanced
Read "You're a Grand Old Flag." • Use pp. 346–347.	**Read** or listen to "You're a Grand Old Flag." • Use the **Routine** on p. DI·30.	**Read** "You're a Grand Old Flag." • Use the **Routine** on p. DI·31.

ELL Place English language learners in the groups that correspond to their reading abilities in English.

 Independent Activities

Fluency Reading Pair children to reread *Red, White, and Blue.*

Journal Writing Write a paragraph telling why independence is important.

Spelling Partner Review

Independent Reading See p. 322j for Reading/Library activities and suggestions.

Literacy Centers To provide listening opportunities, you may use the Listening Center on p. 322j. To extend social studies concepts, you may use the Social Studies Center on p. 322k.

Break into small groups after Spelling and before Fluency.

More Adding -ed and -ing

Spelling Words					
tried	trying	planned	planning	liked	liking
hiked	hiking	cried	crying	skipped	skipping

Unscramble the letters to make a list word.

1. k l d e i — **liked** 2. i c n r y g — **crying**

3. e p s i p k d — **skipped** 4. k n i i l g — **liking**

5. e t d r i — **tried** 6. n i k i h g — **hiking**

Write the missing words. Then use the numbered letters to write the missing word in the sentence.

7. He is ___ to learn chess. **t r y i n g**

8. I ___ my report. **p l a n n e d**

9. He ___ when he got hurt. **c r i e d**

10. She is good at ___ rope. **s k i p p i n g**

If he makes one more **s t r i k e**, he is out.

School + Home **Home Activity** Your child has been spelling words that end with -ed and -ing. Have your child identify and spell the four words that are most difficult for him or her.

108 Unit 6 Week 2 **Day 4** **Spelling Practice Book**

▲ **Spelling Practice Book** p. 108

Audio CD AudioText

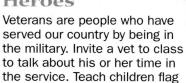

American Heroes

Veterans are people who have served our country by being in the military. Invite a vet to class to talk about his or her time in the service. Teach children flag etiquette and the proper way to fold a flag. Allow children time to practice.

Read Poetry

PREVIEW AND PREDICT Read the title and author's name. Have children preview the poem/song and name the object shown. (flag) Have children read the poem and predict how the writer of this poem must have felt when he was writing it.

POETRY Review that song lyrics have many traits of poetry. Tell children that a song "is a short poem set to music." In this song, "You're a Grand Old Flag," the first two lines rhyme and the third and fifth lines rhyme.

VOCABULARY/COMPOUND WORDS Review that compound words contain two smaller words. Have children locate *forever* on p. 346. What two smaller words are in the compound word *forever?* (for, ever)

Poetry

Song

Genre

- A song is a poem set to music.
- Songs often use rhyme. In each verse of this song, the first two lines rhyme, and the third and fifth lines rhyme.
- Songs often express the songwriter's feelings. As you read, think about how the songwriter feels about the flag.

Link to Writing

Write words to a song about something you feel is important. It could be a poem set to a familiar tune. Share your song with your classmates.

You're a Grand Old Flag

by George M. Cohan

You're a grand old flag,
You're a high flying flag
And forever in peace may you wave.
You're the emblem of the land I love.
The home of the free and the brave.

Ev'ry heart beats true
'Neath the red, white, and blue,
Where there's never a boast or brag.
Should auld acquaintance be forgot,
Keep your eye on the grand old flag.

Reading Across Texts

"You're a Grand Old Flag" is one song about the flag of the United States. What other song about the flag did you read about in *Red, White, and Blue?*

Writing Across Texts Make a list of other patriotic songs that you know.

Monitor and Fix Up If you are confused, remember to go back and reread.

346

347

BUILD CONCEPTS

Draw Conclusions • Inferential

- **What does "forever in peace may you wave" mean?**
  May the country always be in peace times, not war.

Context Clues • Inferential

- **In the line "you're the emblem of the land I love," what does *emblem* mean?**
  symbol

CONNECT TEXT TO TEXT

Have children look through *Red, White, and Blue* to find the name of the poem written by Francis Scott Key and made into a song.

Have children brainstorm and list patriotic songs, such as "America the Beautiful" and "Yankee Doodle." If possible, write the words and identify the words that rhyme.

Activate Prior Knowledge Ask: Have you ever been anywhere when the "Star Spangled Banner" is played? Have children share the experience with the class.

Options for Oral Reading

Use *Red, White, and Blue* or one of the following Leveled Readers.

On-Level

Heroes of the American Revolution

Strategic Intervention

Happy Birthday, America!

Advanced

Home of the Brave

Assess Fluency For English language learners, reading aloud song lyrics, poems, and very short, engaging stories provides good opportunities to increase oral reading fluency.

Fluency

READ WITH FLUENCY AND ACCURACY

MODEL READING Use "You're a Grand Old Flag."

- Point to the title on p. 346. Review that *"You're a Grand Old Flag"* was a poem that became a song. When I come to the end of each line, I emphasize the last word—the words that rhyme. I try to keep a rhythm as I sing the song. I correct myself if I misread a word.

- Ask children to follow along as you sing. Keep a steady rhythm.

- Have children sing the song after you. You may wish to tap the beat with your foot. Encourage children to sing loudly and clearly.

REREAD FOR FLUENCY

Choral Reading

ROUTINE

1 **Select a Passage** Use "You're a Grand Old Flag" on p. 346.

2 **Divide into Groups** Assign each group a part to sing. For this song, alternate lines. The first group sings one line. Then the other group sings the next line and so on.

3 **Model** Have children track the print as you sing.

4 **Read Together** Have children sing along with you.

5 **Independent Readings** Have the groups sing aloud without you. Monitor progress and provide feedback. For optimal fluency, children should reread three to four times.

Monitor Progress | **Check Fluency** WCPM

As children reread, monitor their progress toward their individual fluency goals. Current Goal: 90–100 words correct per minute. End-of-Year Goal: 90 words correct per minute.

If... children cannot read fluently at a rate of 90 words correct per minute,

then... make sure children practice with text at their independent level. Provide additional fluency practice, pairing nonfluent readers with fluent readers.

If... children already read at 90 words correct per minute,

then... they do not need to reread three to four times.

SUCCESS PREDICTOR

Day 1 Check Word Reading : Day 2 Check Lesson Vocabulary/High-Frequency Words : Day 3 Check Retelling : ▶ Day 4 Check Fluency : Day 5 Assess Progress

Writing Across the Curriculum

WRITE Venn Diagram

BRAINSTORM Have children look at the flag on p. 330. Encourage them to describe this flag using selection vocabulary, such as *stars* and *stripes*.

SHARE THE PEN Have children participate in creating a Venn diagram. To begin, draw a Venn diagram or display Graphic Organizer 17. Explain that the class will work together to compare the first American flag with our current flag. Explain that a Venn diagram is a way to compare two objects. Call on an individual to describe a part of the first American flag. Write this in the Venn diagram, inviting individuals to help spell the words by writing familiar letter-sounds. Ask questions, such as the following:

- What is the beginning blend you hear in the word stars? (/st/)
- What letters stand for that sound? *(st)* Have a volunteer write *st*.
- What is the beginning blend you hear in the word *stripes*? (/str/)
- What letters stand for that sound? *(str)* Have a volunteer write *str*.

Continue having individuals contribute. Frequently reread the words in the Venn diagram.

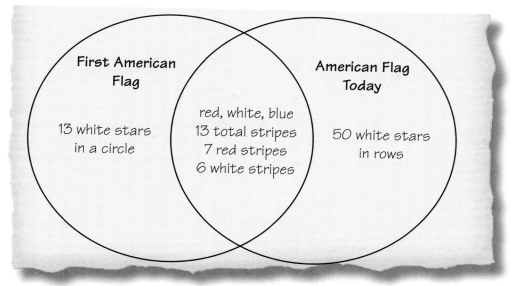

▲ **Graphic Organizer 17**

OBJECTIVE

- Create a Venn diagram.

Advanced

Encourage children to choose flags from two countries and make a Venn diagram to compare the flags.

Support Writing If children suggest phrases or sentences that do not reflect conventional English, respond positively and restate the sentence without the errors. Record the phrase as it is restated.

SUCCESS
PREDICTOR

OBJECTIVE

• Identify quotation marks.

DAILY FIX-IT

7. america's birthdaiy is July 4th.
   <u>A</u>merica's <u>birthday</u> is July 4th.

8. i painted sturs and stripes.
   <u>I</u> painted st<u>a</u>rs and stripes.

Quotation Marks

Mark the correct sentence.

1. ○ A "Our flag has many nicknames, said Martha.
   ⊗ B "Our flag has many nicknames," said Martha.
   ○ C "Our flag has many nicknames, said Martha."

2. ○ A Is the Stars and Stripes one of the names?" asked John.
   ○ B "Is the Stars and Stripes one of the names? asked John."
   ⊗ C "Is the Stars and Stripes one of the names?" asked John.

3. ○ A "George said, Old Glory is another name for the flag."
   ○ B George said, "Old Glory is another name for the flag.
   ⊗ C George said, "Old Glory is another name for the flag."

4. ○ A I like the Red, White, and Blue best," Sally said."
   ⊗ B "I like the Red, White, and Blue best," Sally said.
   ○ C "I like the Red, White, and Blue best, Sally said."

5. ⊗ A Thomas asked, "Why are there 50 stars?"
   ○ B "Thomas asked, Why are there 50 stars?"
   ○ C Thomas asked, "Why are there 50 stars?

6. ○ A "There is one star for each state in the United States,
      Sally said."
   ⊗ B "There is one star for each state in the United States,"
      Sally said.
   ○ C "There is one star for each state in the United States,
      Sally said.

Home Activity Your child prepared for taking tests on quotation marks. Ask your child to write a sentence about the flag. Tell him or her to use quotation marks and the name of a person mentioned on this page in the sentence.

▲ **Grammar and Writing**
   Practice Book p. 107

Grammar

REVIEW Quotation Marks

DEFINE QUOTATION MARKS

• What punctuation shows the beginning and end of the words someone says? (quotation marks)

• Is the speaker's name written inside or outside the quotation marks? (outside)

PRACTICE

USE QUOTATION MARKS Write the following sentences on the board. *Please stand for The Star Spangled Banner, said the principal. The mayor said, Fly your flag on the Fourth of July. Sarita said, I display the flag proudly.* Have individuals supply quotation marks for each sentence.

"Please stand for the The Star Spangled Banner," said the principal.

The mayor said, "Fly your flag on the Fourth of July."

Sarita said, "I display the flag proudly."

Speaking and Viewing

UNDERSTANDING NONVERBAL CUES

DEMONSTRATE SPEAKING AND VIEWING Remind children of nonverbal cues a speaker can use. Discuss body language and the messages you can send without even speaking. Role play various body language positions and how these cues may look to a viewer.

Speakers	Listeners
• **Stand up straight.**	• **Focus on the speaker.**
• **Make eye contact.**	• **Make eye contact.**
• **Use gestures.**	• **Pay attention to the speaker's body language.**
• **Use body language to convey a feeling.**	• **Look for speaker's gestures.**

ROLE PLAY Write several speaking situations on slips of paper (e.g., President speaking to the country; friends talking on the playground; singing the "Star Spangled Banner"; child reciting a poem; saying the "Pledge of Allegiance"; adult talking to preschool child). Ask children to use nonverbal cues as they role play these situations.

Wrap Up Your Day!

MAKE CONNECTIONS: TEXT TO TEXT Discuss "The Star Spangled Banner" talked about in *Red, White, and Blue* and the song "You're a Grand Old Flag." How are these two songs similar? (They are both written by authors who are proud of their flag.)

LET'S TALK ABOUT IT Discuss patriotism and the American flag. Have children add additional information to the American Flag web created earlier in the week.

PREVIEW Day 5

Remind children that they sang a song about the American flag today. Tell them that tomorrow they will hear about the flag's history.

Day 5
AT A GLANCE

Materials

- *Sing with Me Big Book*
- *Read Aloud Anthology*
- Reproducible Pages TE 348f–348g
- Student Edition 348–349
- Graphic Organizer 30

Morning Warm~Up!

This week we read about the history of the American flag. The flag is a symbol of our country's independence. What does our flag mean?

QUESTION OF THE DAY Encourage children to sing "Our Flag, Our Symbol" from the *Sing with Me Big Book* as you gather. Write and read the message and discuss the question.

REVIEW ORAL VOCABULARY Have children identify words in the message that

- describe the American flag
- tell what our flag is a symbol of
- name a subject we study
- describe a citizen of this country

Assess Vocabulary Use the Day 5 instruction on ELL Poster 27 to monitor children's progress with oral vocabulary.

ELL Poster 27

Share Literature

LISTEN AND RESPOND

USE PRIOR KNOWLEDGE Review that yesterday the class listened to find out the meaning of the flag's colors. Suggest that today the class listen to find out how many stars and stripes the real "Star Spangled Banner" had on it.

MONITOR LISTENING COMPREHENSION

Read Aloud Anthology
Uncle Sam and Old Glory

- How many stars and stripes were on the real "Star Spangled Banner?" (fifteen)

- What do the stars and stripes on the flag stand for? (states)

BUILD ORAL VOCABULARY

GENERATE DISCUSSION Recall the nicknames used to describe the U.S. flag. *(Stars and Stripes, Old Glory, Star-Spangled Banner)* Mention how important the flag was to our founding fathers. Display a flag and have children talk about what the U.S. flag means to them. Have children use some of this week's Amazing Words as they talk about the flag.

Monitor Progress | Check Oral Vocabulary

Remind children of the unit concept—Traditions. Ask them to tell you about the concept using some of this week's Amazing Words: *history, independence, symbol, patriotic, unfurl, frayed, allegiance,* and *indivisible.*

If... children have difficulty using the Amazing Words,

then... ask more questions about the Read Aloud selection or the concept using the Amazing Words. Note which questions children can respond to. Reteach unknown words using the Oral Vocabulary routine on p. DI·1.

SUCCESS PREDICTOR

| **Day 1** Check Word Reading | **Day 2** Check Lesson Vocabulary/High-Frequency Words | **Day 3** Check Retelling | **Day 4** Check Fluency | ▶ **Day 5** Check **Oral Vocabulary Assess Progress** |

Amazing Words to build oral vocabulary

history	unfurl
independence	frayed
symbol	allegiance
patriotic	indivisible

ELL

Extend Language Review that compound words are made up of two smaller words. Ask children to create as many compound words as they can using *snow* as one of the smaller words.

Oral Vocabulary

SUCCESS PREDICTOR

OBJECTIVES

- Review words with inflected endings.
- Review lesson vocabulary.

Inflected Endings

REVIEW

INFLECTED ENDINGS Write these sentences. Have children read each one aloud. Call on individuals to name and underline the base words with *-s, -es, -ed, -ing, -er,* and *-est* endings.

We are <u>hoping</u> that Mom will let us help with <u>baking</u> and <u>tasting</u> the <u>cookies</u>!

I <u>walked</u> into the room and <u>hugged</u> Grandma for the <u>longest</u> time.

Pam <u>relies</u> on her <u>studying</u> to keep her from <u>missing</u> any math <u>problems</u>.

I <u>grabbed</u> a sandwich, <u>chatted</u> with my dad, and <u>trotted</u> out the door.

Lesson Vocabulary

REVIEW

MEANING CLUES Write the following clues for children. Have children write a word from Words to Know, p. 324, for each clue. Then read clues and answers together.

This is what a zebra has on its body. **(stripes)**

Everyone has one once a year. **(birthday)**

This is the country we live in. **(America)**

You can see this wave from the top of some poles. **(flag)**

These twinkle in the sky at night. **(stars)**

Teddy, J.R., and P.J. are examples of these. **(nicknames)**

We have this when we are free. **(freedom)**

Access Content For additional practice with lesson vocabulary, use the vocabulary strategies and word cards in the ELL Teaching Guide, pp. 185–186.

SPELLING TEST Inflected Endings

DICTATION SENTENCES Use these sentences to assess this week's spelling words.

1. I <u>liked</u> the meatloaf we ate last night.
2. The kittens were <u>crying</u> for their mother.
3. Dad <u>planned</u> a summer trip for us.
4. I <u>tried</u> to do that math problem.
5. The baby seems to be <u>liking</u> the peas.
6. I <u>cried</u> when I scraped my knee.
7. We <u>skipped</u> all the way to school.
8. We <u>hiked</u> to the top of the cliff.
9. I had fun <u>planning</u> the party!
10. Mom and I went <u>hiking</u> in the woods.
11. Eve and I were <u>skipping</u> and tumbling.
12. Josh was <u>trying</u> to give the cat a bath.

CHALLENGE WORDS

13. "<u>Replying</u> to a letter is good manners," said Dad.
14. Mom and Dad <u>danced</u> to the music.
15. "The answer is twenty," Uncle Bob <u>replied</u>.
16. They love <u>dancing</u> together.

ASSESS

● Spell words with inflected endings.

Spelling Words

Inflected Endings

1.	tried	7.	hiked
2.	trying	8.	hiking
3.	planned	9.	cried
4.	planning	10.	crying
5.	liked*	11.	skipped
6.	liking*	12.	skipping

Challenge Words

13.	danced	15.	replied
14.	dancing	16.	replying

* Words from the Selection

Group Time

On-Level	Strategic Intervention	Advanced
Read Set B Sentences. • Use pp. 348e–348g.	**Read** Set A Sentences and Story. • Use pp. 348e–348g. • Use the **Routine** on p. DI·32.	**Read** Set C Sentences. • Use pp. 348e–348g. • Use the **Routine** on p. DI·33.

DAY 5

ELL Place English language learners in the groups that correspond to their reading abilities in English.

(i) Independent Activities

Fluency Reading Children reread selections at their independent level.

Journal Writing Write about a class that makes a special symbol and tell what it stands for.

Independent Reading See p. 322j for Reading/Library activities and suggestions.

Literacy Centers You may use the Technology Center on p. 322k to support this week's concepts and reading.

Practice Book 2.2 Take Notes/Outline, p. 120

ASSESS

- Decode inflected endings.
- Read lesson vocabulary words.
- Read aloud with appropriate speed and accuracy.
- Recognize statements of fact and opinion.
- Retell a story.

Differentiated Assessment

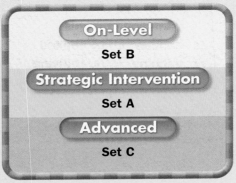

On-Level
Set B

Strategic Intervention
Set A

Advanced
Set C

Fluency Assessment Plan

☑ Week 1 assess Advanced students.

☑ **This week assess Strategic Intervention students.**

☐ Week 3 assess On-Level students.

☐ Week 4 assess Strategic Intervention students.

☐ Week 5 assess any students you have not yet checked during this unit.

Set individual fluency goals for children to enable them to reach the end-of-year goal.

- Current Goal: 90–100 wcpm
- End-of-Year Goal: 90 wcpm
- **ELL** Oral fluency depends not only on reading without halting but also on word recognition. After children read passages aloud for assessment, help them recognize unfamiliar English words and their meanings. Focus on each child's progress.

SENTENCE READING

ASSESS INFLECTED ENDINGS AND LESSON VOCABULARY WORDS Use one of the reproducible lists on p. 348f to assess children's ability to read words with inflected endings and lesson vocabulary words. Call on individuals to read two sentences aloud. Have each child in the group read different sentences. Start over with sentence one if necessary.

RECORD SCORES Use the Sentence Reading Chart for this unit on p. WA19.

Monitor Progress	Inflected Endings
If... children have trouble reading inflected endings,	**then...** use the Reteach Lessons on p. DI·65.
Lesson Vocabulary Words	
If... children cannot read a lesson vocabulary word,	**then...** mark the missed words on a lesson vocabulary word list and send the list home for additional word reading practice, or have the child practice with a fluent reader.

FLUENCY AND COMPREHENSION

ASSESS FLUENCY Take a one-minute sample of children's oral reading. See Monitoring Fluency, p. WA17. Have children read "The Grand Canyon," the on-level fluency passage on p. 348g.

RECORD SCORES Record the number of words read correctly in a minute on the child's Fluency Progress Chart.

ASSESS COMPREHENSION Have the child read to the end of the passage. (If the child had difficulty with the passage, you may read it aloud.) Choose statements and ask if they are facts or opinions, and have the child retell the passage. Use the Retelling Rubric on p. 344–345 to evaluate the child's retelling.

Monitor Progress	Fluency
If... a child does not achieve the fluency goal on the timed reading,	**then...** copy the passage and send it home with the child for additional fluency practice, or have the child practice with a fluent reader.
Fact and Opinion	
If... a child cannot recognize statements of facts or opinions,	**then...** use the Reteach Lesson on p. DI·65.

READ THE SENTENCES

Set A

1. We shopped and baked for her birthday.
2. The raised flag of America waves in the breezes.
3. Justin likes making up nicknames for friends.
4. The people hoped for and tried to win freedom.
5. The stars are brighter and the moon is shinier.
6. Your stripes are redder and thinner than mine.

Set B

1. Mark traced stripes on the wall before painting it.
2. Hang the largest stars higher than the tinier ones.
3. When Jen flies the flag it reminds her of freedom.
4. Rachel liked funnier, cuter nicknames for her cat.
5. Al baked a cake with sprinkles for Mom's birthday.
6. People like swimming and diving in America.

Set C

1. America has some of the rockiest mountains and greenest valleys you will ever see.
2. Those who have freedom are luckier and happier than those who don't.
3. My older brothers have the shortest and easiest nicknames to remember.
4. The racing car had a flag and stripes glued on it.
5. The stars were twinkling and shining like diamonds.
6. My birthday was the snowiest, coldest day of the year.

Monitor Progress | **Inflected Endings**
Lesson Vocabulary Words

SUCCESS PREDICTOR

The Grand Canyon

The Grand Canyon is located in Arizona. It is   9
277 miles long and one mile deep. A river flows   19
through the bottom of the canyon. Many, many   27
years ago the river cut through the rock and   36
formed the canyon. Today, everyone enjoys   42
rafting on the river.   46

The Grand Canyon contains different kinds of   53
plants and animals. There are willow trees as well   62
as cactus plants. You can find foxes, deer,   70
bobcats, chipmunks, and rabbits. We enjoyed   76
watching chipmunks running and rabbits hopping   82
near the canyon trails. In the summer, it is hot. I   93
think it gets hotter than any other place.   101

People like hiking into the Grand Canyon. The   109
trail is slightly sloping as you go down. I think it's   120
easier to take the mule-pack trip. By riding a mule   130
you will not have any worries about tripping. The   139
rock colors are amazing. I think it's the prettiest   148
place you will ever see. Everyone should see this   157
canyon at least one time.   162

See also Assessment Handbook, p. 359 • REPRODUCIBLE PAGE

Monitor Progress | Fluency Passage

SUCCESS PREDICTOR

Write Now
Writing and Grammar

Answer

Prompt

Red, White, and Blue tells about the history of the American flag. Think about this question: *What do I think about when I see the American flag?* Now write the question and your answer.

Writing Trait

Conventions include rules for writing sentences.

Student Model

Capital letters and end marks are sentence <u>conventions</u>.

Writer gives two reasons in the answer.

Last sentence sums up ideas.

What do I think about when I see the American flag? I think about saying, "I pledge allegiance to the flag." That means I promise to be a loyal citizen of the United States. I think about living in a free country. The flag reminds me of my country and my freedom.

348

Writer's Checklist

- **Focus** Do all sentences answer the question?
- **Organization** Are sentences in a logical order?
- **Support** Are reasons clearly explained?
- **Conventions** Does every sentence begin with a capital letter and end with the correct punctuation mark?

Grammar

Quotation Marks
Quotation marks (" ") show the beginning and the end of the words someone says. The speaker's name and words such as **said** and **asked** are not inside the quotation marks.

"Can you make a flag?" **asked** General Washington.
"I will try," Betsy Ross **said.**

Look at the writing model. Find and write the sentence with quotation marks.

349

Writing and Grammar

LOOK AT THE PROMPT Read p. 348 aloud. Have children select and discuss key words or phrases in the prompt. (*What do I think about when I see the American flag?, question, your answer*)

STRATEGIES TO DEVELOP CONVENTIONS Have children

- look at the beginning and end of each of their sentences to make sure that it begins with a capital letter and ends with the appropriate punctuation mark.
- make sure they do not begin common nouns with capital letters. (*American flag*, not *American Flag*)
- check their spelling using a class Word Wall, a dictionary, or other reference tools.

See Scoring Rubric on p. WA11.

HINTS FOR BETTER WRITING Read p. 349 aloud. Use the checklist to help children revise their answers. Discuss the grammar lesson. (Answer: *I think about saying, "I pledge allegiance to the flag."*) Have children use quotation marks correctly in their answers.

DAILY FIX-IT

9. Our flagg has fifty stars?
   Our fla**g** has fifty stars**.**

10. this is my eighth Birthday.
    This is my eighth **b**irthday.

Quotation Marks

Circle the quotation marks. **Write** *Yes* if a sentence uses quotation marks correctly. **Write** *No* if quotation marks are not used correctly.

1. "Did Betsy Ross make the first flag?" asked James.

   Yes

2. Her grandson said she did, "Hillary said."

   No

3. Laura said, "I think Betsy Ross did make the first flag."

   Yes

Add quotation marks to each sentence.

4. "How many stars were on the flag Betsy Ross made?" asked Barbara.

5. Bill asked, "Do you know how many stripes there were?"

6. "There were thirteen stars and thirteen stripes," George said.

 **Home Activity** Your child reviewed quotation marks. Ask your child to rewrite sentence 2 on this page so that the quotation marks are used correctly.

▲ **Grammar and Writing Practice Book** p. 108

Read the paragraph. **Fill** in the notes below.

How to Fly the Flag

We have many customs that tell how to fly our country's flag. The flag should be put up each morning and taken down each night. Some fly the flag 24 hours a day. When they do, a light should shine on the flag at night. The flag should not fly in bad weather unless a special flag is used. When the flag hangs on the same pole as a state or city flag, it should be the highest. These customs help people show respect for the flag.

1. up in morning, down _____ at night _____

2. if up 24 hours, _____ light it at night _____

3. if bad weather,
_____ don't fly or else use special flag _____

4. if with state or city flag,
_____ hang U.S. flag highest _____

5. flag customs show
_____ respect for flag _____

Home Activity Your child practiced taking notes about a reading passage. Ask your child to read a paragraph from a textbook or other nonfiction book. Talk about the most important information. Have your child use his or her own words to make brief notes about the reading.

▲ **Practice Book 2.2** p. 120, Take Notes/Outline

Access Content As you write the information on the outline, discuss each fact. Explain that you do not need to write the entire sentence, just the important words.

Research/Study Skills

TEACH/MODEL Take Notes/Outline

MODEL TAKING NOTES/OUTLINE Draw a simple outline frame on the board or use Graphic Organizer 30. Explain that an outline is a way to organize information. Tell children that when they read something they want to remember, they should take notes. Direct children to *America's Flag* on p. 325.

Model how to take notes and write information in outline form.

 MODEL I can outline the important facts by taking notes. In *America's Flag*, the first paragraph is about nicknames for the American Flag. I'll write *Nicknames for the American Flag* on Line A of my outline. Next, I'll write two nicknames for the flag—*The Red, White, and Blue* and *The Stars and Stripes*—on lines 1 and 2. Now I'll read the second paragraph and take notes on the important information of that paragraph.

TAKE NOTES Call on an individual to identify the main idea of paragraph 2 and the supporting details. Add this information to your outline.

Title _America's Flag_

A. _Nicknames for the American Flag_

   1. _Red, White, and Blue_

   2. _The Stars and Stripes_

B. _Hang flag outside home_

   1. _Fourth of July_

   2. _Anytime_

▲ **Graphic Organizer 30**

PRACTICE

TAKE NOTES/OUTLINE Have childreen work with a partner to take notes and arrange in an outline the important information from *Flags* found on p. 323. Use Graphic Organizer 30 or have children create their own outline.

Wrap Up Your Week!

LET'S TALK ABOUT Traditions

QUESTION OF THE WEEK Recall this week's question.

- What does our flag mean?

Display the Our Flag web created on Day 1. Review words and phrases that describe our flag.

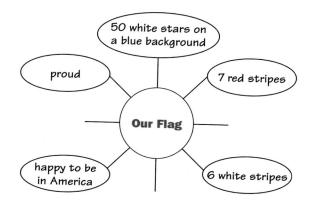

CONNECT Use questions such as these to prompt a discussion.

- There are thirteen stripes on the flag. What do these thirteen stripes stand for?

- The flag is a symbol of independence. Can you think of other American symbols?

- Francis Scott Key and George Cohan each wrote about the flag. Compare their thoughts and feelings about the flag. How do you feel about the American flag?

Build Background Use ELL Poster 28 to support the Preview activity.

You've learned 008 Amazing Words **this week!**

You've learned 217 Amazing Words **so far this year!**

PREVIEW Tell children that next week they will read about more traditions and family celebrations.

PREVIEW Next Week

Assessment Checkpoints *for the Week*

Selection Assessment

Use pp. 105–108 of Selection Tests to check:

 Selection Understanding

  Comprehension Skill *Fact and Opinion*

 Selection Vocabulary
America
birthday
flag
freedom
nicknames
stars
stripes

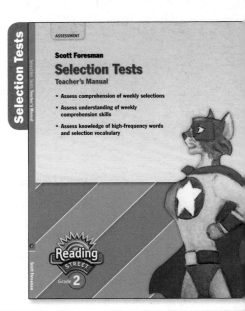

Leveled Assessment

- On-Level
- Strategic Intervention
- Advanced

Use pp. 157–162 of Fresh Reads for Differentiated Test Practice to check:

 Comprehension Skill *Fact and Opinion*

 REVIEW Comprehension Skill *Main Idea and Details*

Fluency *Words Correct Per Minute*

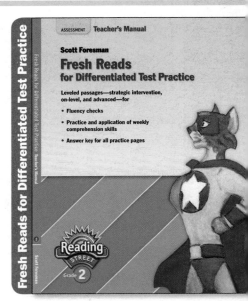

Managing Assessment

Use Assessment Handbook for:

 Weekly Assessment Blackline Masters for Monitoring Progress

 Observation Checklists

 Record-Keeping Forms

 Portfolio Assessment

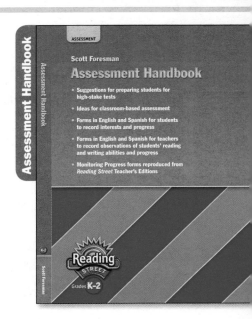

Illinois

Planning Guide for Performance Descriptors

A Birthday Basket for Tía

Reading Street Teacher's Edition pages	Grade 2 English Language Arts Performance Descriptors
Oral Language Build Concepts: 350l, 352a, 368a, 370a, 374a Share Literature: 350m, 352b, 368b, 370b, 374b	**1A.Stage B.5.** Use letter-sound knowledge and sight vocabulary to read orally and silently/whisper read age-appropriate material. **2A.Stage B.3.** Define unfamiliar vocabulary.
Word Work **Phonics** Syllables *-tion, -ture:* 350n–350q, 352c–352d, 368c–368d, 370c–370d, 374c–374f **Spelling:** 350p, 352d, 368d, 370d, 374d	**1A.Stage B.2.** Use phonological awareness knowledge (e.g., isolate, blend, substitute, manipulate letter sounds) to identify phonetically regular one and two syllable words. **3A.Stage B.5.** Use correct spelling of high frequency words. **3A.Stage B.6.** Use phonemic clues, phonetic and/or developmental spelling to spell unfamiliar words.
Reading **Comprehension** Draw Conclusions: 350r–351, 354–367a, 368g, 374e Summarize: 350r–351, 354–367, 368g **Vocabulary** Context Clues: 352–353, 374b Words from an Other Languages: 368e Homonyms: 352–353, 370–371 **Fluency** Oral Reading: 350q, 367a Choral Reading: 368f, 373a **Self-Selected Reading:** LR19–27, TR16–17 **Literature** Genre—Realistic Fiction: 354–355 Reader Response: 368g–368h	**1A.Stage B.7.** Use a variety of resources (e.g., context, previous experiences, dictionaries, glossaries, computer resources, ask others) to determine and clarify meanings of unfamiliar words. **1B.Stage B.1.** Read fiction and non-fiction materials for specific purposes. **1C.Stage B.9.** Summarize and retell text read or heard. **2A.Stage B.3.** Define unfamiliar vocabulary. **2B.Stage B.1.** Investigate self-selected/teacher-selected literature (e.g., picture books, nursery rhymes, fairy tales, poems, legends) from a variety of cultures. **2B.Stage B.4.** Make a reasonable judgment with support from the text. **5C.Stage B.7.** Summarize information.
Language Arts **Writing** Report Card, Respond to Literature, Math Story: 351a, 367b, 368g, 373b, 374–375 **Six-Trait Writing** Organization/Paragraphs: 369a, 374–375 **Grammar, Usage, and Mechanics** Commas: 351b, 367c, 369b, 373c, 374–375 **Speaking/Listening** Understand Other Cultures: 373d **Research/Study** Online Directories: 375a	**1C.Stage B.1.** Respond to analytical and interpretive questions based on information in text. **2A.Stage B.6.** Compare different versions of the same story from different cultures and eras. **2B.Stage B.1.** Investigate self-selected/teacher-selected literature (e.g., picture books, nursery rhymes, fairy tales, poems, legends) from a variety of cultures. **3B.Stage B.2.** Compose a focused story using picture(s) and/or basic text. **5C.Stage B.5.** Create a report of ideas (e.g., drawing, using available technology, writing a story, letter, report).
Unit Skills **Writing** Research Report: WA2–9 **Project/Wrap-Up:** 434–435	**3C.Stage B.4.** Experiment with different forms of writing (e.g., song, poetry, short fiction, recipes, diary, journal, directions). **5C.Stage B.3.** Use life experiences as sources of information for written reports, letters, and stories.

This Week's Leveled Readers

Below-Level	On-Level	Advanced
Very Special Birthdays by Jessica Quilty illustrated by Nicole Wong	Birthdays Around the World by Marilyn Greco	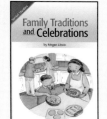Family Traditions and Celebrations by Megan Litwin illustrated by Nicole Wong
1C.Stage B.3. Ask questions to seek clarification of meaning. **2B.Stage B.4.** Make a reasonable judgment with support from the text.	**1B.Stage B.6.** State facts and details of text during and after reading. **2B.Stage B.4.** Make a reasonable judgment with support from the text.	**1B.Stage B.3.** Recognize informational text structure (e.g., sequence, list/example) before and during reading. **2B.Stage B.4.** Make a reasonable judgment with support from the text.
Nonfiction	**Nonfiction**	**Nonfiction**

Content-Area Illinois Performance Descriptors in This Lesson

Social Studies

17C.Stage B.2. Locate pictures showing ways that humans use the natural environment.

18A.Stage B.1. Describe how communities within a culture are similar.

18A.Stage B.2. Identify cultural traits.

18A.Stage B.3. Identify symbols of local culture.

18B.Stage B.2. Explain how contact with others shapes peoples' lives.

18B.Stage B.4. Tell about the role of families in the community.

Math

6A.Stage B.1. Count with understanding, including skip counting from any number by 2's and 10's.

6A.Stage B.2. Extend initial understanding of place value and the base-ten number system using multiple models.

6A.Stage B.4. Use cardinal and ordinal numbers appropriately.

Illinois!

A FAMOUS ILLINOISAN
Carol Moseley Braun

Carol Moseley Braun (1947–) was the first African American woman elected to the U.S. Senate. Born in Chicago, she attended the University of Illinois at Chicago and the University of Chicago. Braun was an assistant U.S. attorney from 1973 to 1977, and she served in the Illinois House of Representatives from 1979 to 1989. Braun also held the position of Cook County recorder of deeds from 1988 to 1992.

Children can . . .
Discuss what it means to be a good leader. As a class, have them create a list of words that describe a leader. Ask children to identify a leader in their community.

A SPECIAL ILLINOIS PLACE
John G. Shedd Aquarium

The John G. Shedd Aquarium in Chicago is one of the largest indoor aquariums in the world. The aquarium opened in 1929, using funds donated by Chicago businessperson John Graves Shedd. It features more than two hundred exhibition tanks, the Coral Reef Exhibit, and the Shedd Oceanarium. The oceanarium is the world's largest indoor marine mammal pavilion.

Children can . . .
Create a poster that shows the kinds of fish and marine mammals that people might see at the Shedd Aquarium.

ILLINOIS FUN FACTS
Did You Know?

- Taste of Chicago is an outdoor festival that takes place in Chicago every summer. Visitors sample food items from dozens of local restaurants.

- In 1818 Illinoisans elected Shadrach Bond to be the first governor of Illinois.

- The Illinois court system is made up of three kinds of courts: supreme, appellate, and circuit. Of these, the supreme court is the highest.

Children can . . .
Find out what the different kinds of courts do. Write a few sentences telling two ways the courts are alike and two ways they are different.

Unit 6
Traditions

CONCEPT QUESTION

How are traditions and celebrations important to our lives?

Week 1
Why are sports important in our country?

Week 2
What does our flag mean?

Week 3
Why are family celebrations special?

Week 4
Why should we learn about cowboys?

Week 5
What are some different ways that people celebrate?

EXPAND THE CONCEPT
Why are family celebrations special?

CONNECT THE CONCEPT

▶ **Build Background**

angle	create	snapshot
brilliant	custom	tradition
celebration	inspect	

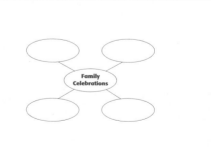

▶ **Social Studies Content**
Cultural Traditions, Celebrations

▶ **Writing**
A Report

Preview Your Week

Why are family celebrations special?

A Birthday Basket for Tía

by Pat Mora
illustrated by Cecily Lang

Genre **Realistic fiction** is a story with characters and events that are like people and events in real life.

354

What will be in the birthday basket for Tía?

355

Student Edition pages 354–369

Audio CD

Genre	Realistic Fiction
Phonics	Syllables *-tion, -ture*
Vocabulary Strategy	Context Clues
Comprehension Skill	Draw Conclusions
Comprehension Strategy	Summarize

Paired Selection

Reading Across Texts
Compare Birthday Celebrations

Genre
Online Directories

Text Features
Links
Keywords

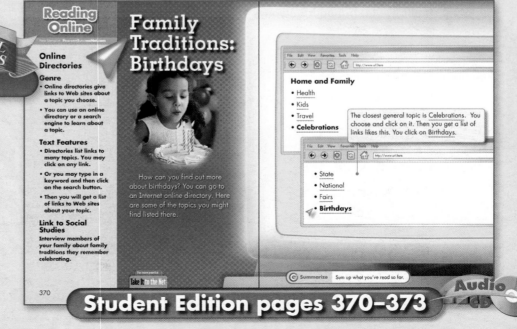

Time for SOCIAL STUDIES

Reading Online

Online Directories

Genre
- Online directories give links to Web sites about a topic you choose.
- You can use an online directory or a search engine to learn about a topic.

Text Features
- Directories list links to many topics. You may click on any link.
- Or you may type in a keyword and then click on the search button.
- Then you will get a list of links to Web sites about your topic.

Link to Social Studies
Interview members of your family about family traditions they remember celebrating.

Take It to the Net

370

Family Traditions: Birthdays

How can you find out more about birthdays? You can go to an Internet online directory. Here are some of the topics you might find listed there.

Home and Family
- Health
- Kids
- Travel
- **Celebrations**

The closest general topic is Celebrations. You choose and click on it. Then you get a list of links likes this. You click on Birthdays.

- State
- National
- Fairs
- **Birthdays**

Summarize Sum up what you've read so far.

Student Edition pages 370–373

Audio CD

Read It
ONLINE
PearsonSuccessNet.com

- **Student Edition**
- **Leveled Readers**
- **Decodable Reader**

Leveled Readers

 **Skill** Draw Conclusions

 **Strategy** Summarize

Lesson Vocabulary

Very Special Birthdays
by Jessica Quilty
illustrated by Nicole Wong

Below-Level

Birthdays Around the World
by Marilyn Greco

On-Level

Family Traditions and Celebrations
by Megan Litwin

Advanced

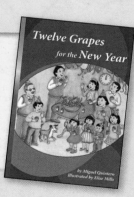

Twelve Grapes for the New Year
by Miguel Quintero
Illustrated by Elise Mills

ELL Reader

- Concept Vocabulary
- Text Support
- Language Enrichment

Decodable Reader

Apply Phonics

- *I Might Be*

Decodable Reader 28

I Might Be
Written by Greg Morton
Illustrated by Brad Williams

Phonics Skill
Common Syllables -tion, -ture

Integrate Social Studies Standards

- Cultural Traditions
- Celebrations

✓ Read

A Birthday Basket for Tía
pp. 354–369

"Family Traditions: Birthdays" pp. 370–373

✓ Read

Leveled Readers

Below-Level   **On-Level**   **Advanced**

- Support Concepts
- Develop Concepts
- Extend Concepts
- Social Studies Extension Activity

✓ Read

ELL Reader

Twelve Grapes for the New Year

✓ **Build Concept Vocabulary**
Traditions, p. 350m

✓ **Teach Science Concepts**
Healthy Foods, p. 356–357
Piñatas, p. 362–363

✓ **Explore Social Studies Center**
Make a Birthday Basket, p. 350k

Weekly Plan

READING

90–120 minutes

TARGET SKILLS OF THE WEEK

- **Phonics**
  Syllables *-tion, -ture*
- **Comprehension Skill**
  Draw Conclusions
- **Comprehension Strategy**
  Summarize

LANGUAGE ARTS

20–30 minutes

Trait of the Week

Organization/Paragraphs

DAILY JOURNAL WRITING

DAILY SOCIAL STUDIES CONNECTIONS

DAILY SUCCESS PREDICTORS
for Adequate Yearly Progress

DAY 1   PAGES 350l–351b

Oral Language

QUESTION OF THE WEEK, 350l
Why are family celebrations special?

Oral Vocabulary/Share Literature, 350m
Sing with Me Big Book, Song 28
Amazing Words *celebration, custom, tradition*

Word Work

Phonics, 350n–350o
Introduce Syllables *-tion, -ture* **T**

Spelling, 350p
Pretest

Comprehension/Vocabulary/Fluency

Read Decodable Reader 28

Grouping Options 350f–350g

Review High-Frequency Words
Check Comprehension
Reread for Fluency

Comprehension Skill/Strategy Lesson, 350r–351
Draw Conclusions **T**
Summarize

Shared Writing, 351a
Report

Grammar, 351b
Introduce Using Commas **T**

Day 1 *List fun celebrations.*

Day 1 Family Celebrations Concept Web, 350m

DAY 2   PAGES 352a–367c

Oral Language

QUESTION OF THE DAY, 352a
Have you ever been to a surprise party?

Oral Vocabulary/Share Literature, 352b
Big Book *Magda's Tortillas*
Amazing Word *create*

Word Work

Phonics, 352c–352d
Review Syllables *-tion, -ture* **T**

Spelling, 352d
Dictation

Comprehension/Vocabulary/Fluency

Build Background, 352e
Birthday Parties

Lesson Vocabulary, 352f
Introduce *aunt, bank, basket, collects, favorite, present* **T**

Vocabulary Strategy Lesson, 352–353a
Context Clues **T**

Read *A Birthday Basket for Tía,* 354–367a

Grouping Options
350f–350g

Draw Conclusions **T**
Summarize
REVIEW Cause and Effect **T**
Reread for Fluency

Interactive Writing, 367b
Card

Grammar, 367c
Practice Using Commas **T**

Day 2 *Write about a special birthday.*

Day 2 Time for Social Studies: Piñatas, 362–363

Monitor Progress and Corrective Feedback

Phonics
Check Word Reading, *350o*
Spiral REVIEW Phonics

Fluency
Check Lesson Vocabulary, *352f*
Spiral REVIEW High-Frequency Words

RESOURCES FOR THE WEEK

- Practice Book 2.2, *pp. 121–130*
- Phonics and Spelling Practice Book, *pp. 109–112*
- Grammar and Writing Practice Book, *pp. 109–112*
- Selection Test, *pp. 109–112*

- Fresh Reads for Differentiated Test Practice, *pp. 163–168*
- Phonics Songs and Rhymes Chart 28
- The Grammar and Writing Book, *pp. 212–217*

Grouping Options for Differentiated Instruction

Turn the page for the small group lesson plan.

DAY 3 — PAGES 368a–369b

Oral Language

QUESTION OF THE DAY, 368a
What would you like to learn how to make?

Oral Vocabulary/Share Literature, 368b
Big Book *Magda's Tortillas*
Amazing Word *inspect*

Word Work

Phonics, 368c
REVIEW Inflected Endings **T**

Lesson Vocabulary, 368d
Practice *aunt, bank, basket, collects, favorite, present* **T**

Spelling, 368d
Practice

Comprehension/Vocabulary/Fluency

Vocabulary, 368e
Words from Other Languages

Read *A Birthday Basket for Tía,* 354–369

Grouping Options
350f–350g

Fluency, 368f
Read with Appropriate Phrasing

Reader Response, 368g

Trait of the Week, 369a
Introduce Organization/Paragraphs

Grammar, 369b
Write with Commas **T**

Day 3 *Write about a special birthday gift.*

Day 3 Family Celebrations Concept Web, 369b

DAY 4 — PAGES 370a–373d

Oral Language

QUESTION OF THE DAY, 370a
Does your family have special birthday traditions?

Oral Vocabulary/Share Literature, 370b
Read Aloud Anthology "Poetry Selections"
Amazing Words *angle, brilliant, snapshot*

Word Work

Phonics, 370c
REVIEW Sentence Reading **T**

Spelling, 370d
Partner Review

Comprehension/Vocabulary/Fluency

Read "Family Traditions: Birthdays," 370–373
Leveled Readers

Grouping Options
350f–350g

Homonyms
Reading Across Texts

Fluency, 373a
Read with Appropriate Phrasing

Writing Across the Curriculum, 373b
Math Story

Grammar, 373c
Review Using Commas **T**

Speaking and Listening, 373d
Understand Other Cultures

Day 4 *Write about your favorite birthday.*

Day 4 Social Studies Center: Make a Basket, 350k

DAY 5 — PAGES 374a–375b

Oral Language

QUESTION OF THE DAY, 374a
Why are family celebrations special?

Oral Vocabulary/Share Literature, 374b
Read Aloud Anthology "Poetry Selections"
Amazing Words Review

Word Work

Phonics, 374c
⟳ Review Syllables *-tion, -ture* **T**

Lesson Vocabulary, 374c
Review *aunt, bank, basket, collects, favorite, present* **T**

Spelling, 374d
Test

Comprehension/Vocabulary/Fluency

Read Leveled Readers

Grouping Options 350f–350g

Monitor Progress, 374e–374g
Read the Sentences
Read the Story

Writing and Grammar, 374–375
Develop Organization/Paragraphs
Use Commas **T**

Research/Study Skills, 375a
Online Directories

Day 5 *Write about a tradition in your family.*

Day 5 Revisit the Family Celebrations Concept Web, 375b

KEY ⟳ = Target Skill **T** = Tested Skill

Comprehension
Check Retelling, *368g*

Fluency
Check Fluency WCPM, *373a*
Spiral REVIEW Phonics,
High-Frequency Words

Oral Vocabulary
Check Oral Vocabulary, *374b*
Assess Phonics,
Lesson Vocabulary, Fluency,
Comprehension, *374e*

SUCCESS PREDICTOR

Small Group Plan *for Differentiated Instruction*

Daily Plan AT A GLANCE

Reading
Whole Group
- Oral Language
- Word Work
- Comprehension/Vocabulary

Group Time

Meet with small groups to provide:
- Skill Support
- Reading Support
- Fluency Practice

Read

This week's lessons for daily group time can be found behind the Differentiated Instruction (DI) tab on pp. DI·34–DI·43.

Whole Group
- Comprehension/Vocabulary
- Fluency

Language Arts
- Writing
- Grammar
- Speaking/Listening/Viewing
- Research/Study Skills

Use *My Sidewalks on Reading Street* for Tier III intensive reading intervention.

DAY 1

On-Level	Strategic Intervention	Advanced
Teacher-Led *Page 350q*	**Teacher-Led** *Page DI·34*	**Teacher-Led** *Page DI·35*
• **Read** Decodable Reader 28 • **Reread** for Fluency	• Blend Words with Syllables *tion, ture* • **Read** Decodable Reader 28 • **Reread** for Fluency	• Extend Word Reading • **Read** Advanced Selection • Introduce Concept Inquiry

(i) Independent Activities

While you meet with small groups, have the rest of the class...

- Reread for fluency
- Write in their journals
- Read self-selected reading
- Visit the Word Work Center
- Complete Practice Book 2.2, pp. 123–124

DAY 2

On-Level	Strategic Intervention	Advanced
Teacher-Led *Pages 354–367*	**Teacher-Led** *Page DI·36*	**Teacher-Led** *Page DI·37*
• **Read** *A Birthday Basket for Tía* • **Reread** for Fluency	• Blend Words with Syllables *tion, ture* • **Read** SI Decodable Reader 28 • **Read** or Listen to *A Birthday Basket for Tía*	• **Read** *A Birthday Basket for Tía* • Continue Concept Inquiry

(i) Independent Activities

While you meet with small groups, have the rest of the class...

- Read self-selected reading
- Write in their journals
- Visit the Listening Center
- Complete Practice Book 2.2, pp. 125–127

DAY 3

On-Level	Strategic Intervention	Advanced
Teacher-Led *Pages 354–369*	**Teacher-Led** *Page DI·38*	**Teacher-Led** *Page DI·39*
• **Reread** *A Birthday Basket for Tía*	• **Reread** *A Birthday Basket for Tía* • Read Words and Sentences • Review Draw Conclusions and Summarize • **Reread** for Fluency	• Self-Selected Reading • Continue Concept Inquiry

(i) Independent Activities

While you meet with small groups, have the rest of the class...

- Read self-selected reading
- Write in their journals
- Visit the Writing Center
- Complete Practice Book 2.2, pp. 128–129

① Begin with whole class skill and strategy instruction.

② Meet with small groups to provide differentiated instruction.

③ Gather the whole class back together for fluency and language arts.

DAY 4

On-Level
Teacher-Led
Pages 370–371, LR22–LR24

- **Read** "Family Traditions: Birthdays"
- Practice with On-Level Reader *Birthdays Around the World*

Strategic Intervention
Teacher-Led
Pages DI · 40, LR19–LR21

- **Read** or Listen to "Family Traditions: Birthdays"
- **Reread** for Fluency
- Build Concepts
- Practice with Below-Level Reader *Very Special Birthdays*

Advanced
Teacher-Led
Pages DI · 41, LR25–LR27

- **Read** "Family Traditions: Birthdays"
- Extend Vocabulary
- Continue Concept Inquiry
- Practice with Advanced Reader *Family Traditions and Celebrations*

ⓘ Independent Activities

While you meet with small groups, have the rest of the class...

- Reread for fluency
- Write in their journals
- Read self-selected reading
- Review spelling words with a partner
- Visit the Listening and Social Studies Centers

DAY 5

On-Level
Teacher-Led
Pages 374e–374g, LR22–LR24

- Sentence Reading, Set B
- Assess On-Level
- Monitor Fluency and Comprehension
- Practice with On-Level Reader *Birthdays Around the World*

Strategic Intervention
Teacher-Led
Pages DI · 42, LR19–LR21

- Practice Word Reading
- Sentence Reading, Set A
- Monitor Comprehension
- Practice with Below-Level Reader *Very Special Birthdays*

Advanced
Teacher-Led
Pages DI · 43, LR25–LR27

- Sentence Reading, Set C
- Monitor Comprehension
- Share Concept Inquiry
- Practice with Advanced Reader *Family Traditions and Celebrations*

ⓘ Independent Activities

While you meet with small groups, have the rest of the class...

- Reread for fluency
- Write in their journals
- Read self-selected reading
- Visit the Technology Center
- Complete Practice Book 2.2, p. 130

Grouping Place English language learners in the groups that correspond to their reading abilities in English.

Use the appropriate Leveled Reader or other text at children's instructional level.

TiP Send home the appropriate Multilingual Summary of the main selection on Day 1.

Take It to the NET™ ONLINE
PearsonSuccessNet.com

P. David Pearson
For research on comprehension, see the article "Comprehension Instruction" by Scott Foresman author P. David Pearson along with L. Fielding.

TEACHER TALK

Miscues are mistakes a child makes when reading. Miscues may include mispronouncing a word, omitting a word, substituting a different word, hesitating, and so on.

Be sure to schedule time for children to work on the unit inquiry project "Research Traditions." This week children should make plans to celebrate their new tradition either at home or at school.

Looking Ahead

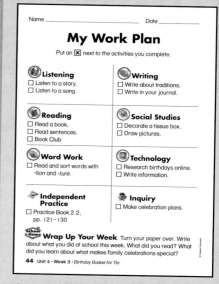

Name _____ Date _____

My Work Plan
Put an ☒ next to the activities you complete.

🎧 Listening
☐ Listen to a story.
☐ Listen to a song.

✏️ Writing
☐ Write about traditions.
☐ Write in your journal.

📖 Reading
☐ Read a book.
☐ Read sentences.
☐ Book Club

🌐 Social Studies
☐ Decorate a tissue box.
☐ Draw pictures.

📝 Word Work
☐ Read and sort words with *-tion* and *-ture*.

💻 Technology
☐ Research birthdays online.
☐ Write information.

✎ Independent Practice
☐ Practice Book 2.2, pp. 121–130

🎉 Inquiry
☐ Make celebration plans.

Wrap Up Your Week Turn your paper over. Write about what you did at school this week. What did you read? What did you learn about what makes family celebrations special?

44 Unit 6 · Week 3 · *Birthday Basket for Tía*

▲ **Group-Time Survival Guide**
p. 44, Weekly Contract

Birthday Basket for Tía (**350g**)

☑ Customize Your Plan *by Stran...*

ORAL LANGUAGE

Concept Development

Why are family celebrations special?

 to build oral vocabulary

angle   brilliant   celebration
create   custom   inspect
snapshot   tradition

BUILD

☐ **Question of the Week** Use the Morning Warm-Up! to introduce and discuss the question of the week. This week children will talk, sing, read, and write about family celebrations. **DAY 1** *350l*

☐ **Sing with Me Big Book** Sing a song about family traditions. Ask children to listen for the concept-related Amazing Words *celebration, custom, tradition.* **DAY 1** *350m*

Sing with Me Big Book

☐ **Build Background** Remind children of the question of the week. Then create a concept chart for children to add to throughout the week. **DAY 1** *350m*

DEVELOP

☐ **Question of the Day** Use the questions in the Morning Warm-Ups! to discuss lesson concepts and how they relate to the unit theme, Traditions. **DAY 2** *352a*, **DAY 3** *368a*, **DAY 4** *370a*, **DAY 5** *374a*

☐ **Share Literature** Read big books and read aloud selections that develop concepts, language, and vocabulary related to the lesson concept and the unit theme. Continue to develop this week's Amazing Words. **DAY 2** *352b*, **DAY 3** *368b*, **DAY 4** *370b*, **DAY 5** *374b*

CONNECT

☐ **Wrap Up Your Week!** Revisit the Question of the Week. Then connect concepts and vocabulary to next week's lesson. **DAY 5** *375b*

CHECK

☐ **Check Oral Vocabulary** To informally assess children's oral vocabulary, ask individuals to use some of this week's Amazing Words to tell you about the concept of the week—Traditions. **DAY 5** *374b*

PHONICS

🎯 **SYLLABLES** *-TION, -TURE* Some words consist of a base word and the ending syllable *-tion* or *-ture*. The letters *-tion* and *-ture* stand for the /shən/ and /chər/ sounds. Use structural cues to decode words with syllables *-tion, -ture.*

TEACH

☐ **Syllables** *-tion, -ture* Introduce the blending strategy for words with syllables *-tion, -ture.* Have children blend and sort words, then choose a word and use it in a sentence to demonstrate understanding. **DAY 1** *350n-350o*

☐ **Fluent Word Reading** Use the Fluent Word Reading Routine to develop children's word reading fluency. Use the Phonics Songs and Rhymes Chart for additional word reading practice. **DAY 2** *352c-352d*

Phonics Songs and Rhymes Chart 28

PRACTICE/APPLY

☐ **Decodable Reader 28** Practice reading words with syllables *-tion, -ture* in context. **DAY 1** *350q*

☐ ***A Birthday Basket for Tía*** Practice decoding words in context. **DAY 2** *354-367*

Decodable Reader 28

☐ **Homework** Practice Book 2.2 p. 123. **DAY 1** *350o*

☐ **Word Work Center** Practice syllables *-tion, -ture.* **ANY DAY** *350j*

Main Selection—Fiction

RETEACH/REVIEW

☐ **Review** Review words with this week's phonics skills. **DAY 5** *374c*

☐ **Reteach Lessons** If necessary, reteach syllables *-tion, -ture.* **DAY 5** *DI-66*

☐ **Spiral REVIEW** Review previously taught phonics skills. **DAY 1** *350o*, **DAY 3** *368c*, **DAY 4** *370c*

ASSESS

☐ **Sentence Reading** Assess children's ability to read words with syllables *-tion, -ture.* **DAY 5** *374e-374f*

① Use assessment data to determine your instructional focus.

② Preview this week's instruction by strand.

③ Choose instructional activities that meet the needs of your classroom.

SPELLING

SYLLABLES *-TION, -TURE* Some words consist of a base word and the ending syllable *-tion* or *-ture*. The letters *-tion* and *-ture* stand for the /shən/ and /chər/ sounds. Use structural cues to decode words with syllables *-tion, -ture*.

TEACH

❑ **Pretest** Before administering the pretest, model how to segment words with syllables *-tion, -ture* to spell them. Dictate the spelling words, segmenting them if necessary. Then have children check their pretests and correct misspelled words. **DAY 1** *350p*

PRACTICE/APPLY

❑ **Dictation** Have children write dictation sentences to practice spelling words. **DAY 2** *352d*

❑ **Write Words** Have children practice writing the spelling words by providing the missing end syllable and then writing a sentence using the word. **DAY 3** *368d*

❑ **Homework** Phonics and Spelling Practice Book pp. 109–112.
DAY 1 *350p*, **DAY 2** *352d*, **DAY 3** *368d*, **DAY 4** *370d*

RETEACH/REVIEW

❑ **Partner Review** Have pairs work together to read and write the spelling words. **DAY 4** *370d*

ASSESS

❑ **Posttest** Use dictation sentences to give the posttest for words with syllables *-tion, -ture*. **DAY 5** *374d*

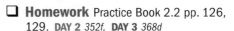

Spelling Words

Syllables *-tion, -ture*

1. mixture	7. caution
2. nation	8. station
3. section	9. fixture
4. future	10. motion
5. picture*	11. nature
6. action	12. feature

Challenge Words

13. furniture	15. tuition
14. adventure	

* Words from the Selection

VOCABULARY

 **STRATEGY CONTEXT CLUES** Homonyms are words that are pronounced and spelled the same, but have different meanings. Use context clues to figure out the meaning of homonyms.

LESSON VOCABULARY
aunt   bank   basket   collects   favorite   present

TEACH

❑ **Words to Know** Introduce and discuss this week's lesson vocabulary. **DAY 2** *352f*

❑ **Vocabulary Strategy Lesson** Use the lesson in the Student Edition to introduce/model *context clues*. **DAY 2** *352-353a*

Vocabulary Strategy Lesson

PRACTICE/APPLY

❑ **Words in Context** Read the lesson vocabulary in context. **DAY 2** *354-367*, **DAY 3** *354-369*

❑ **Lesson Vocabulary** Have children write a sentence using the lesson vocabulary words. **DAY 3** *368d*

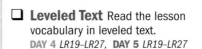
Main Selection—Fiction

❑ **Leveled Text** Read the lesson vocabulary in leveled text.
DAY 4 *LR19-LR27*, **DAY 5** *LR19-LR27*

❑ **Homework** Practice Book 2.2 pp. 126, 129. **DAY 2** *352f*, **DAY 3** *368d*

Leveled Readers

RETEACH/REVIEW

❑ **Words from Other Languages** Have children name non-English words they know and then write a sentence for each word. **DAY 3** *368e*

❑ **Review** Review this week's lesson vocabulary words. **DAY 5** *374c*

ASSESS

❑ **Selection Test** Use the Selection Test to determine children's understanding of the lesson vocabulary words. **DAY 3**

❑ **Sentence Reading** Assess children's ability to read this week's lesson vocabulary words. **DAY 5** *374e-374f*

HIGH-FREQUENCY WORDS

RETEACH/REVIEW

❑ **Spiral REVIEW** Review previously taught high-frequency words.
DAY 2 *352f*, **DAY 4** *370c*

☑ Customize Your Plan *by Strand*

COMPREHENSION

SKILL DRAW CONCLUSIONS To draw conclusions means to use clues from the words and pictures and what you know about the real world to make decisions.

STRATEGY SUMMARIZE When you summarize, you tell the most important parts of the story in the order that they happened.

TEACH

❑ **Skill/Strategy Lesson** Use the Skill/Strategy Lesson in the Student Edition to introduce *draw conclusions* and *summarize.* **DAY 1** *350r–351*

Skill/Strategy Lesson

PRACTICE/APPLY

❑ **Skills and Strategies in Context** Read *A Birthday Basket for Tía*, using the Guiding Comprehension questions to apply *draw conclusions* and *summarize.* **DAY 2** *354-367a*

Main Selection—Fiction

❑ **Reader Response** Use the questions on Student Edition p. 368 to discuss the selection. **DAY 3** *368g-369*

❑ **Skills and Strategies in Context** Read "Family Traditions: Birthdays," guiding children as they apply skills and strategies. **DAY 4** *370-373*

Paired Selection— Nonfiction

❑ **Leveled Text** Apply *draw conclusions* and *summarize* to read leveled text. **DAY 4** *LR19-LR27,* **DAY 5** *LR19-LR27*

❑ **Homework** Practice Book 2.2 pp. 124, 125. **DAY 1** *350-351,* **DAY 2** *352e*

Leveled Readers

ASSESS

❑ **Selection Test** Determine children's understanding of the main selection and assess their ability to *draw conclusions.* **DAY 3**

❑ **Story Reading** Have children read the passage "Tyler's Pictures." Ask questions that require them to *draw conclusions.* Then have them retell. **DAY 5** *374e-374g*

RETEACH/REVIEW

❑ **Reteach Lesson** If necessary, reteach *draw conclusions.* **DAY 5** *DI·66*

FLUENCY

SKILL READ WITH APPROPRIATE PHRASING Appropriate phrasing means pausing at the right places when you read. Punctuation marks, such as commas and periods, signal the right places to pause.

REREAD FOR FLUENCY

❑ **Oral Rereading** Have children read orally from Decodable Reader 28 or another text at their independent reading level. Listen as children read and provide corrective feedback regarding their oral reading and their use of the blending strategy. **DAY 1** *350q*

❑ **Paired Reading** Have pairs of children read orally from the main selection or another text at their independent reading level. Listen as children read and provide corrective feedback regarding oral reading and their use of the blending strategy. **DAY 2** *367a*

TEACH

❑ **Model** Use passages from *A Birthday Basket for Tía* to model reading with appropriate phrasing. **DAY 3** *368f,* **DAY 4** *373a*

PRACTICE/APPLY

❑ **Choral Reading** Have two groups choral read passages from *A Birthday Basket for Tía*, alternating paragraphs. Monitor progress and provide feedback regarding children's phrasing. **DAY 3** *368f,* **DAY 4** *373a*

❑ **Listening Center** Have children follow along with the AudioText for this week's selections. **ANY DAY** *350j*

❑ **Reading/Library Center** Have children build fluency by rereading Leveled Readers, Decodable Readers, or other text at their independent level. **ANY DAY** *350j*

❑ **Fluency Coach** Have children use Fluency Coach to listen to fluent reading or to practice reading on their own. **ANY DAY**

ASSESS

❑ **Story Reading** Take a one-minute timed sample of children's oral reading. Use the passage "Tyler's Pictures." **DAY 5** *374e-374g*

WRITING

Trait of the Week

ORGANIZATION/PARAGRAPHS Telling events in the right order holds your writing together.

TEACH

☐ **Write Together** Engage children in writing activities that develop language, grammar, and writing skills. Include independent writing as an extension of group writing activities.

> **Shared Writing** DAY 1 *351a*
> **Interactive Writing** DAY 2 *367b*
> **Writing Across the Curriculum** DAY 4 *373b*

☐ **Trait of the Week** Introduce and model the Trait of the Week, *organization/paragraphs*. DAY 3 *369a*

PRACTICE/APPLY

☐ **Write Now** Examine the model on Student Edition pp. 374–375. Then have children write reports. DAY 5 *374-375*

> **Prompt** *A Birthday Basket for Tía* tells about a special family event. Think about a special event your family has had. Now write a report telling about that event.

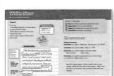
Write Now

☐ **Daily Journal Writing** Have children write about concepts and literature in their journals. **EVERY DAY** *350d-350e*

☐ **Writing Center** Have children write reports about their classmates' birthday traditions. **ANY DAY** *350k*

ASSESS

☐ **Scoring Rubric** Use a rubric to evaluate reports. DAY 5 *374-375*

RETEACH/REVIEW

☐ **The Grammar and Writing Book** Use pp. 212–217 of The Grammar and Writing Book to extend instruction. **ANY DAY**

The Grammar and Writing Book

SPEAKING AND LISTENING

TEACH

☐ **Understand Other Cultures** Have children use appropriate listening and speaking behaviors to discuss traditions and customs from their cultural backgrounds. DAY 4 *373d*

GRAMMAR

SKILL USE COMMAS Commas are used in addresses, dates, to begin and end a letter, and to separate three or more things in a sentence.

TEACH

☐ **Grammar Transparency 28** Use Grammar Transparency 28 to teach *using commas*. DAY 1 *351b*

Grammar Transparency 28

PRACTICE/APPLY

☐ **Develop the Concept** Review the concept of *using commas* and provide guided practice. DAY 2 *367c*

☐ **Apply to Writing** Have children use commas in writing. DAY 3 *369b*

☐ **Define/Practice** Review *commas*. Then have children use commas to separate items and names in sentences. DAY 4 *373c*

☐ **Write Now** Discuss the grammar lesson on Student Edition p. 375. Have children use commas in their reports about a special event. DAY 5 *374-375*

Write Now

☐ **Daily Fix-It** Have children find and correct errors in grammar, spelling, and punctuation.
DAY 1 *351b*, DAY 2 *367c*, DAY 3 *369b*, DAY 4 *373c*, DAY 5 *374-375*

☐ **Homework** The Grammar and Writing Practice Book pp. 109–112. DAY 2 *367c*, DAY 3 *369b*, DAY 4 *373c*, DAY 5 *374-375*

RETEACH/REVIEW

☐ **The Grammar and Writing Book** Use pp. 212–215 of The Grammar and Writing Book to extend instruction. **ANY DAY**

The Grammar and Writing Book

RESEARCH/INQUIRY

TEACH

☐ **Online Directories** Model how to use an online directory. Then have children locate links for special recipes. DAY 5 *375a*

☐ **Unit Inquiry Project** Allow time for children to make plans to celebrate their new tradition either at home or at school. **ANY DAY** *295*

Resources for
Differentiated Instruction

LEVELED READERS

▶ **Comprehension**
  ◎ **Skill** Draw Conclusions
  ◎ **Strategy** Summarize

▶ **Lesson Vocabulary**
  ◎ **Context Clues**

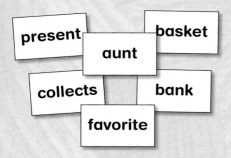

▶ **Social Studies Standards**
  • **Cultural Traditions**
  • **Celebrations**

ONLINE
PearsonSuccessNet.com

Use the Online Database of over 600 books to
• Download and print additional copies of this week's leveled readers
• Listen to readers being read online
• Search for more titles focused on this week's skills, topic, and content

---

On-Level Reader

Draw Conclusions

Read *Birthdays Around the World*. Write the answers to the questions below. Possible responses given.

1. What are important parts of all the birthday celebrations in this book?

special foods, games, friends and family to celebrate

2. Children in different countries eat different birthday food. What else is different about birthdays around the world?

play different games; have different activities

3. Do you think the children in this book enjoyed their birthday parties? Why or why not?

Yes. They look happy in the pictures and they all say good things about their parties.

◎ **On-Level Practice** TE p. LR23

Vocabulary

Unscramble the words and write them in the spaces below.

Words to Know
aunt bank basket collects favorite present

1. asbket
basket

2. eftaivor
favorite

3. nkab
bank

4. costclle
collects

5. tuan
aunt

6. prteens
present

7. Write a sentence using two or more vocabulary words.
Sentences will vary.

On-Level Practice TE p. LR24

Below-Level Reader

Draw Conclusions

Think about what you know about Chinese birthday celebrations after reading. Then answer the questions.

Write a few sentences that tell about what happened in the story. Possible responses given.

1. Why do you think new babies get gifts with tigers on them?

To protect the babies.

2. How do you know that birthdays are an important part of Chinese culture?

There are very special ways of celebrating each birthday.

3. How do you know that eating special foods is an important part of Chinese birthday celebrations?

Different foods are served at all the different celebrations.

4–5. Which of the birthday celebrations do you think you would like the most? Why?

Responses will vary.

◎ **Below-Level Practice** TE p. LR20

Vocabulary

Choose the word from the box that best fits each sentence. Each vocabulary word is used one time.

Words to Know
aunt bank basket collects favorite present

1. The basket was filled with toys.

2. A bank is a safe place to keep money.

3. My aunt gave me a birthday present.

4. Red is my favorite color.

5. My brother collects the gifts and puts them in a basket.

Write a word that means the same as the word *gift*.

6. present

Below-Level Practice TE p. LR21

Advanced

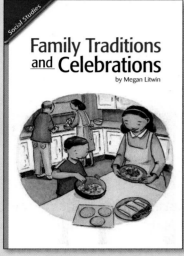

Social Studies

Family Traditions and Celebrations
by Megan Litwin

Advanced Reader

Draw Conclusions

What holiday are they celebrating? Use the information you learned about holidays in *Family Traditions and Celebrations* to complete the sentences below.

1. Alison is eating latkes, and her family is lighting a

menorah. Her family is celebrating **Hanukkah**

2. Jenny is blowing out candles, and her family is having a

party. Jenny is celebrating her **birthday**

3. Daryl's family is feasting for seven days, and Daryl's goal is Kuumba. Daryl's family is celebrating

Kwanzaa

4. Write a sentence that tells more of what you know about family traditions and celebrations.

Possible response given.

Family celebrations teach us
about who we are.

Advanced Practice TE p. LR26

Vocabulary

Write the word from the box next to its meaning.

Words to Know		
ancestors	celebrations	customs
festival	traditions	unique

1. **festival** — *n.* another word for celebration

2. **unique** — *adj.* one of a kind

3. **ancestors** — *n.* people from whom one is descended

4. **customs** — *n.* activities shared by people in a family or place

5. **celebrations** — *n.* gatherings to remember special events

6. **traditions** — *n.* information, beliefs, and values handed down from one generation to another

Advanced Practice TE p. LR27

Twelve Grapes for the New Year

ELL Reader

CONGRATULATIONS

ELL Poster 23

Teacher's Edition Notes

ELL notes throughout this lesson support instruction and reference additional resources at point of use.

ELL Teaching Guide pp. 190–196, 266–267
- Multilingual summaries of the main selection
- Comprehension lesson
- Vocabulary strategies and word cards
- ELL Reader 28 lesson

ELL and Transition Handbook

Ten Important Sentences
- Key ideas from every selection in the Student Edition
- Activities to build sentence power

More Reading

Readers' Theater Anthology
- Fluency practice
- Five scripts to build fluency
- Poetry for oral interpretation

Leveled Trade Books

- Extend reading tied to the unit concept
- Lessons in Trade Book Library Teaching Guide

School + Home

Homework
- Family Times Newsletter
- ELL Multilingual Selection Summaries

Take-Home Books
- Decodable Readers
- Leveled Readers

Literacy Centers

Let's Read Along

MATERIALS `SINGLES`
CD player, headphones, print copies of recorded pieces

LISTEN TO LITERATURE As children listen to the following recordings, have them follow along or read along in the print version.

AudioText
A Birthday Basket for Tía
"Family Traditions: Birthdays"

Sing with Me/Background Building Audio
"Family Tradition"

Phonics Songs and Rhymes Audio
"A Family Celebration"

A Family Celebration

A family celebration
Is almost like a vacation.
We plan our own recreation
That all of us enjoy.

Our family jamborees
Build future memories.
Our culture and history
Is something we all enjoy.

Audio CD **Phonics Songs and Rhymes Chart 28**

Read it Again!

MATERIALS `SINGLES` `PAIRS` `GROUPS`
collection of books for self-selected reading, reading logs

REREAD BOOKS Have children select previously read books from the appropriate book box and record titles of books they read in their logs. Use these previously read books:

- Decodable Readers
- Leveled Readers
- ELL Readers
- Stories written by classmates
- Books from the library

TEN IMPORTANT SENTENCES Have children read the Ten Important Sentences for *A Birthday Basket for Tía* and locate the sentences in the Student Edition.

BOOK CLUB Use p. 369 of the Student Edition to set up an "Author Study" of Pat Mora. Encourage the group to share their favorites.

Syllable Sort

MATERIALS `PAIRS`
word cards, copies of T-chart or Graphic Organizer 25, pencils

SYLLABLES *tion, ture* Children will use syllable patterns to read and sort words.

1. Place a stack of index cards with *tion* and *ture* words facedown. Some words to include are *motion, action, nation, future, picture, fixture,* and *mixture*.
2. Provide copies of a T-chart with column headings *tion* and *ture*.
3. Partners take turns choosing a word card and reading the word.
4. Then they write the word in the correct column on their T-chart.

 This interactive CD provides additional practice.

caution   structure

station   nature

tion	ture
caution	structure
station	nature

Scott Foresman Reading Street Centers Survival Kit

Use the *A Birthday Basket for Tía* materials
from the Reading Street Centers Survival Kit
to organize this week's centers.

Writing

Birthday Traditions

MATERIALS
paper, pencils

SINGLES
PAIRS

WRITE A REPORT Children write about their classmates' birthday traditions.

1. Pairs interview each other about special things their families do for birthdays.
2. Have individuals write a report about what they found out about their partner's birthday traditions.
3. Encourage volunteers to share their reports with the class.

LEVELED WRITING Encourage children to write at their own ability level. Some children will have trouble focusing on the topic. Others will be generally focused on the topic. Your best writers will be well focused on the topic.

Beverly's Birthday

Beverly's family decorates her house with paper lanterns for birthdays. She gets to eat an egg and noodles for good luck. Her parents bake her favorite kind of chocolate cake for her. Her grandparents always come over to her house for her birthday.

Social Studies

A Birthday Basket

MATERIALS
construction paper, art supplies, empty tissue boxes, paper strips, glue

SINGLES

MAKE A BIRTHDAY BASKET Children plan a birthday basket for a special friend or family member.

1. Children decide for whom they would like to make a birthday basket.
2. They decorate the tissue box and add a paper strip handle to make it look like a basket.
3. Then children draw pictures of the things the person would like and put the pictures in the basket.
4. The baskets can be displayed in the classroom.

Technology

Let's Celebrate

MATERIALS
computer with Internet access, paper, pencils, markers

SINGLES
PAIRS

EXPLORE A WEB SITE Have individuals or pairs of children use an online directory to research birthday celebrations around the world.

1. Have children use an online directory to find out about birthday celebrations in different cultures.
2. Children should record and illustrate what they learn.

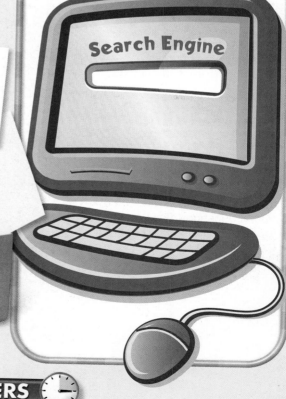

Search Engine

ALL CENTERS

Day 1
AT A GLANCE

Oral Vocabulary
"Family Tradition" 28

Phonics and Spelling
Syllables *-tion, -ture*
Spelling Pretest:
   Words with Syllables *-tion, -ture*

Read Apply Phonics [Word Wall]

Group Time < Differentiated Instruction

Listening Comprehension
Skill Draw Conclusions
Strategy Summarize

Shared Writing
Report

Grammar
Using Commas

Materials

- *Sing with Me Big Book*
- Letter Tiles
- Decodable Reader 28
- Student Edition 350–351
- Graphic Organizer 15
- Skill Transparency 28
- Writing Transparency 28
- Grammar Transparency 28

Take It to the NET
ONLINE
Professional Development
To learn more about spelling, go to PearsonSuccessNet.com and read "Questions Teachers Ask..." by S. Templeton and D. Morris.

Morning Warm-Up!

Today you will read about a birthday.

One friend had the freedom to come early to help set up a game.

The mother and father helped too.

Why are family celebrations special?

QUESTION OF THE WEEK Tell children they will talk, sing, read, and write about family celebrations. Write and read the message and discuss the question.

CONNECT CONCEPTS Ask questions to connect to other Unit 6 selections.

- In *Just Like Josh Gibson*, the grandmother is telling the story to her granddaughter. How can going to a baseball game be a family celebration?

- We learned about Flag Day and the Fourth of July in *Red, White, and Blue*. How does your family celebrate these holidays? What special things do you do?

REVIEW HIGH-FREQUENCY WORDS

- Circle the high-frequency words *birthday* and *freedom* in the message.

- Have children say and spell each word as they write it in the air.

Build Background Use the Day 1 instruction on ELL Poster 28 to assess knowledge and develop concepts.

ELL Poster 28

Oral Vocabulary

SHARE LITERATURE Display p. 28 of the *Sing with Me Big Book*. Tell children that the class is going to sing a song about family traditions. Read the title. Ask children to listen for the Amazing Words **tradition, custom,** and **celebration** as you sing. Then sing the song again and encourage children to sing and do the motions along with you, demonstrating their understanding of *tradition, custom,* and *celebration.*

**Sing with Me/
Background Building Audio**

Family Tradition

Tradition is important
To all kinds of cultures.
Tradition is important
To family groups too.
Each group celebration
And each conversation
And every family custom
Unites us like glue.

Sing with Me Big Book

BUILD BACKGROUND Remind children of the question of the week.

• Why are family celebrations special?

Draw a web or use Graphic Organizer 15. Label the middle circle of the web *Family Celebrations.* Draw four circles connected to the middle circle. Help children identify reasons why family celebrations are special. Display the web for use throughout the week.

• Do you have special food at family celebrations?

• How do people feel when the family is all together?

• Do you have special traditions at family celebrations?

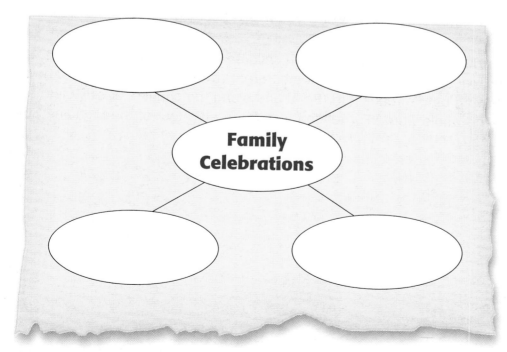

▲ **Graphic Organizer 15**

OBJECTIVE

● Build oral vocabulary.

to build oral vocabulary

Amazing Words	**MONITOR PROGRESS**
celebration custom tradition create inspect angle brilliant snapshot	**If...** children lack oral vocabulary experiences about the concept Traditions, **then...** use the Oral Vocabulary Routine below to teach *celebration.*

Oral Vocabulary ROUTINE

1 Introduce the Word Relate the word *celebration* to the song. Supply a child-friendly definition. Have children say the word. Example: A *celebration* is a party for a special day.

2 Demonstrate Provide an example to show meaning. Jill's birthday party was a real *celebration.*

3 Apply Have children demonstrate their understanding. Describe your favorite *celebration.*

4 Display the Word/Word Parts Write the word on a card. Display it. Point out the syllable *-tion* as you read the word. See p. DI·5 to teach *custom* and *tradition.*

ELL

Access Content Help children recognize the meanings of the English words *conversation* and *unites* in "Family Tradition" by asking them to make "talking motions" with their hands for the word *conversation.* Ask them to clasp their hands tightly in front of themselves to represent *unites.*

OBJECTIVES

- Use structural cues to decode words with syllables *-tion, -ture.*
- Blend, read, and sort words with syllables *-tion, -ture.*

Skills Trace

Syllables *-tion, -ture*	
Introduce/Teach	**TE: 2.6 350n–o, 352c–d**
Practice	TE: 2.6 350q; PB: 2.2 123; DR28
Reteach/Review	TE: 2.6 374c, 402c, DI·66; PB 2.2 138
Assess/Test	TE: 2.6 374e–g; Benchmark Test, Unit 6

Strategic Intervention

Use **Monitor Progress,** p. 350o, during Group Time after children have had more practice with syllables *-tion, -ture.*

Advanced

Use **Monitor Progress,** p. 350o, as a preassessment to determine whether this group of children would benefit from this instruction on syllables *-tion* and *-ture.*

Support Phonics The syllable *-tion* has similar forms in other languages, including French *(-tion),* Spanish *(-ción, -sión),* Haitian Creole *(-syon),* and Portuguese *(-çäo).* Children can look for cognates for *-tion* words in other languages. For example, the English word *direction* is *direction* in French, *dirección* in Spanish, *direksyon* in Haitian Creole, and *direçäo* in Portuguese.

See the Phonics Transition Lessons in the ELL and Transition Handbook.

Syllables *-tion, -ture*

TEACH/MODEL

Blending Strategy

ROUTINE

1 **Connect** Write *candle.* You studied words like this already. What do you know about reading this word? (This word ends in the syllable consonant plus *le.*) Today we'll learn about syllables *-tion* and *-ture.* The letters *-tion* and *-ture* stand for the /shən/ and /chər/ sounds.

2 **Model** Write *nation.* Read each chunk, or syllable, from left to right and then blend them to read the whole word. Divide *na/tion* to demonstrate. Remember that *-tion* stands for /shən/. What is the word? *(nation)* Let's blend this word together: /nā shən/.

3 **Group Practice** First, read each chunk, or syllable, from left to right. Then blend both syllables to read the whole word. Continue with *action, fixture, station, nature, motion, picture.*

4 **Review** What do you know about reading syllables *-tion* and *-ture?* The letters *-tion* and *-ture* stand for the /shən/ and /chər/ sounds.

BLEND WORDS

INDIVIDUALS BLEND WORDS Call on children to chunk and blend *future, section, lotion, caution, feature, fraction, creature.* Have them tell what they know about each word before reading it. (Read and blend the chunks, or syllables, and then read the whole word.) For feedback, refer to step four of the Blending Strategy Routine.

SORT WORDS

READ LONGER WORDS Write the words below. Have individuals sort and blend the words. Then have each child choose a word and use it in a sentence to demonstrate understanding. Provide help with meaning as needed.

fiction	**mention**	**nature**	**motion**	**furniture**
lotion	**portion**	**mixture**	**caption**	**adventure**

Vocabulary TIP

You may wish to explain the meanings of these words.

lecturing	speaking or talking
moisture	water spread in very small drops in the air
potion	a drink, especially one used in medicine
sculpture	a statue or carving

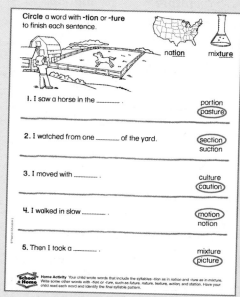

▲ **Practice Book 2.2** p. 123, Syllables *-tion, -ture*

Monitor Progress Check Word Reading Syllables *-tion, -ture*

Write the following words and have individuals read them.

potion	**moisture**	**caution**	**action**	**nature**
cautioned	**pictures**	**lecturing**	**sections**	**tuitions**
sculpture	**fraction**	**creature**	**station**	**fracture**

If... children cannot blend words with syllables *-tion, -ture* at this point,

then... continue to monitor their progress using other instructional opportunities during the week so that they can be successful with the Day 5 Assessment. See the Skills Trace on p. 350n.

SUCCESS PREDICTOR

Spiral REVIEW

- Row 2 reviews endings.
- Row 3 contrasts consonant blends.

▶ **Day 1 Check** Word Reading
Day 2 Check Lesson Vocabulary/ High-Frequency Words
Day 3 Check Retelling
Day 4 Check Fluency
Day 5 Assess Progress

Word Reading
SUCCESS PREDICTOR

OBJECTIVES

- Segment sounds and word parts to spell words.
- Spell words with *-tion, -ture.*

Spelling Words

Syllables *-tion, -ture*

1. mixture	7. caution
2. nation	8. station
3. section	9. fixture
4. future	10. motion
5. picture*	11. nature
6. action	12. feature

Challenge Words

13. furniture	15. tuition
14. adventure	

* **Words from the Selection**

Words with *-tion* and *-ture*

Generalization The final syllables in *mixture* and *nation* have the common syllable patterns **-ture** and **-tion**.

Sort the list words by **-ture** or **-tion**.

-ture	**-tion**
1. **mixture**	7. **nation**
2. **future**	8. **section**
3. **picture**	9. **action**
4. **fixture**	10. **station**
5. **nature**	11. **caution**
6. **feature**	12. **motion**

Challenge Words

-ture	**-tion**
13. **furniture**	15. **tuition**
14. **adventure**	

Spelling Words

1. mixture
2. nation
3. section
4. future
5. picture
6. action
7. caution
8. station
9. fixture
10. motion
11. nature
12. feature

Challenge Words

13. furniture
14. adventure
15. tuition

Home Activity Your child is learning to spell words with *-tion* and *-ture.* To practice at home, have your child look at the word, say it, spell it, and then write it on a piece of paper. Ask your child to point to the common syllable pattern.

▲ **Spelling Practice Book** p.109,

DAY 1

Support Spelling Before giving the spelling pretest, clarify the meaning of each spelling word with examples, such as saying *picture* while pointing to a picture, and illustrating *furniture* by pointing to a desk, chair, or table.

Spelling

PRETEST Syllables *-tion, -ture*

MODEL WRITING FOR WORD PARTS Each spelling word has the syllable *-tion* or *-ture.* Before administering the spelling pretest, model how to segment words with syllables *-tion, -ture* to spell them.

- You can spell words with syllables *-tion* and *-ture* by thinking about the syllables in each word. What syllables make up *puncture?* *(punc* and *ture)*
- Start with the sounds in the first syllable: *punc.* What letters spell /pungk/? Write *punc.*
- Next are the sounds in the second syllable: *ture.* What letters spell /chər/? Write *ture.*
- Now spell *puncture.*
- Repeat with *suction.*

PRETEST Dictate the spelling words. Segment the words for children if necessary. Have children check their pretests and correct misspelled words.

HOMEWORK Spelling Practice Book, p. 109

The History of Piñatas

Long ago, in the late 1200s, an explorer from Italy went to China. His name was Marco Polo. While in China, he learned about an early form of the piñata. He saw people in China making figures shaped like animals. They filled them with seeds. Then they covered them with colored paper and other decorations. They used colored sticks to break open the figures. The seeds spilled out. This was supposed to bring good luck.

When Marco Polo returned to Italy, he told people there what he had seen in China. Soon, Italian people were doing the same thing. This custom spread from Italy to Spain...

Birthday Basket for Tía

Decodable Reader 28

I Might Be

Written by Greg Morton
Illustrated by Brad Williams

Group Time

On-Level	**Strategic Intervention**	**Advanced**
Read Decodable Reader 28.	**Read** Decodable Reader 28.	**Read** Advanced Selection 28.
• Use p. 350q.	• Use the **Routine** on p. DI·34.	• Use the **Routine** on p. DI·35.

ⓘ Independent Activities

Fluency Reading Pair children to reread Leveled Readers or the ELL Reader from the previous week or other text at children's independent level.

Journal Writing List fun celebrations. Share writing.

Independent Reading See p. 350j for Reading/Library activities and suggestions.

Literacy Centers To practice Syllables *-tion, -ture,* you may use Word Work, p. 350j.

Practice Book 2.2 Syllables *-tion, -ture,* p. 123; Draw Conclusions, p. 124.

Break into small groups after Spelling and before the Comprehension lesson.

Decodable Reader 28

I Might Be
Written by Greg Morton
Illustrated by Brad Williams

Phonics Skill
Common Syllables -tion, -ture

future	picture(s)	mixture
action	stations	nation
locations	nature	motion

Apply Phonics

⦿PRACTICE Syllables *-tion, -ture*

HIGH-FREQUENCY WORDS Review *anything, builder,* and *people.*

READ DECODABLE READER 28

- Pages 98–99 Read aloud quietly with the group.
- Pages 100–101 Have the group read aloud without you.
- Pages 102–104 Select individuals to read aloud.

CHECK COMPREHENSION AND DECODING Have children retell the story to include characters, setting, and plot. Then have children locate words with syllables *-tion* and *-ture* in the story. Review *-tion* and *-ture* spelling patterns. Sort words according to their spelling patterns.

-tion	*-ture*
action	future
locations	mixture
motion	nature
nation	picture(s)
stations	

HOMEWORK Take-Home Decodable Reader 28

REREAD FOR FLUENCY

Oral Rereading

ROUTINE

1 **Read** Have children read the entire book orally.

2 **Reread** To achieve optimal fluency, children should reread the text three or four times.

3 **Provide Feedback** Listen as children read and provide feedback regarding their oral reading and their use of the blending strategy.

Monitor Progress

Decoding

If... children have difficulty decoding a word,	**then...** prompt them to blend the word.
	• What is the new word?
	• Is the new word a word you know?
	• Does it make sense in the story?

ELL

Access Content

Beginning Preview the story *I Might Be,* identifying and naming each job in the pictures and print. Have children repeat the words.

Intermediate Preview *I Might Be* and provide synonyms for unfamiliar words, such as *country, tall buildings,* and *movement* for *nation, skyscrapers,* and *motion.*

Advanced After reading *I Might Be,* point out that the word *skyscraper* is used to describe buildings that are so tall that they seem to be scraping the sky. Encourage children to name other figures of speech they have encountered in English and in their native languages.

- Draw conclusions.
- Summarize a story.

Skills Trace	
Draw Conclusions	
Introduce/Teach	TE: 2.2 283a–b, 284e; 2.3 345a–b, 346e; 2.6 350r, 350–351
Practice	TE: 2.2 288–289; 2.3 354–355; 2.6 362–363; PB: 2.1 94–95, 114–115, 127, 147; 2.2 37, 124–125
Reteach/Review	TE: 2.2 DI·68; 2.3 386–387, 444–445, DI·65; 2.4 104–105; 2.6 DI·66
Test	TE: 2.2 310e–g; 2.3 370e–g; 2.6 374e–g; Selection Tests: 2.2 37–40; 2.3 45–48, 2.6 109–112; Benchmark Test: Units 2–6

Empty Eggshells

Jorge asked Danny to come early to his party. "Help me make cascarones," he said. ●
"What are cascarones?" Danny wondered.
When Danny arrived he saw a carton of eggs. But they were just eggshells with a hole at the top—no eggs inside.
"What do we do with these?" Danny asked.
"First, we will paint the eggshells. Next, we will fill each egg with tiny bits of paper," Jorge told him. "Then my mother will glue paper over each hole." ●
Before the party, Jorge's father hid the eggs in the apartment. All the children went on an egg hunt, and all the eggs were found. Then—surprise! Jorge cracked one open over the top of Danny's head! The colored paper rained down! Danny laughed and laughed. Soon everyone at the party was cracking cascarones on one another's heads!

Skill Here you can draw the conclusion that Jorge and Danny are best friends. Jorge asked Danny to come early and help.

Strategy You might want to stop here and sum up what you have read so far. Who are the characters and what did they do? Don't forget to sum up again at the end.

Unit 6 A Birthday Basket for Tía · Skill Transparency 28

▲ **Skill Transparency 28**

Access Content

Beginning/Intermediate For a Picture It! lesson on drawing conclusions, see the ELL Teaching Guide, pp. 190–191.

Advanced Before children read "Empty Eggshells," make sure they know the meanings of *cascarones* and *cracked*.

◉ Draw Conclusions
◉ Summarize

TEACH/MODEL

INTRODUCE Recall *Red, White, and Blue.* Have students draw conclusions about how the astronauts might have felt when they landed on the moon. (Possible response: proud)

- What does our flag symbolize?

Read p. 350 with children. Explain the following:

- Drawing conclusions means figuring out something about a character or an event. Good readers use what they know about real life and what they have read to help them draw conclusions.
- Good readers summarize what they read. This helps them make sure they understand the text.

Use Skill Transparency 28 to teach drawing conclusions and summarizing.

SKILL Use the first four paragraphs to model drawing conclusions.

 MODEL I know that friends work together. So when I read that Jorge asked Danny to come to his house early, I can draw the conclusion that Jorge and Danny are good friends. I read that Jorge wants to make cascarones for his party and that he has empty eggshells. I know that parties have food and decorations. Since the eggshells are empty, I can conclude that Jorge will use them to make some kind of decoration.

STRATEGY Continue with paragraph 6 to model summarizing.

MODEL I know the clue words *first, next,* and *then* help me understand how the eggshells will be painted, filled, and glued. It's a good idea for me to stop and summarize, so I'm sure I understand this part.

Comprehension

Skill
Draw Conclusions

Strategy
Summarize

Draw Conclusions

- When you read, you can draw conclusions or figure out more about the characters and what happens in a story.
- Use what you have read and what you know about real life.
- Find words in the text to support your ideas.

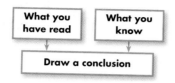

What you have read	What you know

↓ ↓

Draw a conclusion

Strategy: Summarize

Active readers summarize often to make sure they understand what they read. This will help you think about and draw conclusions.

Write

1. Read "Empty Eggshells." Make a graphic organizer. Use it to draw conclusions about Jorge and Danny.

2. Write a short summary of the story. Tell who the main characters are and what they did.

350

Empty Eggshells

Jorge asked Danny to come early to his party. "Help me make cascarones," he said.

"What are cascarones?" Danny wondered.

When Danny arrived he saw a carton of eggs. But they were just eggshells with a hole at the top—no eggs inside.

"What do we do with these?" Danny asked.

"First, we will paint the eggshells. Next, we will fill each egg with tiny bits of paper," Jorge told him. "Then my mother will glue paper over each hole."

Before the party, Jorge's father hid the eggs in the apartment. All the children went on an egg hunt, and all the eggs were found. Then—surprise! Jorge cracked one open over the top of Danny's head! The colored paper rained down! Danny laughed and laughed. Soon everyone at the party was cracking cascarones on one another's heads!

Skill Here you can draw the conclusion that Jorge and Danny are best friends. Jorge asked Danny to come early and help.

Strategy You might want to stop here and sum up what you have read so far. Who are the characters and what did they do? Don't forget to sum up again at the end.

351

PRACTICE

WRITE Work with children to complete the steps in the Write activity. Have children use the short summary to tell what the characters did in "Empty Eggshells."

Monitor Progress	**Compare and Contrast**
If... children are unable to complete **Write** on p. 350,	**then...** use Practice Book 2.2, p. 124, for additional practice.

CONNECT TO READING Encourage children to ask themselves these questions when they read.

- Do I know what to tell when I summarize?
- Do I know which events to leave out when I summarize?
- Do I use what I read and what I already know to draw conclusions?

Read the story. Look at the picture. Follow the directions.

The children were laughing and having fun. A paper piñata hung above them. One at a time, each child took a turn to swing. Finally, the piñata broke open. Candy and small toys fell to the ground. Everyone ran to grab a handful.

Circle the word that best finishes each sentence. Write the word on the line.

1. The children were _____ happy
   (happy) sad

2. They were playing a _____ game
   (game) sport

3. They were at a _____ party
   meeting (party)

4. Write a sentence to tell why the children swung at the piñata.

Possible response: They wanted it to break open so they could get the things inside.

School + Home Home Activity Your child read a passage and drew conclusions from the passage and its illustration. Read your child a favorite book. As you read, pause to discuss what is happening. Ask your child open-ended questions, such as "What's going on now?" and "What's this all about?"

▲ **Practice Book 2.2** p. 124, Draw Conclusions

OBJECTIVE
● Write a report.

DAILY FIX-IT

1. My favorit aunt collects
baskets?
My favorit<u>e</u> aunt collects baskets<u>.</u>

2. Where are we meeting?
she asked.
<u>"</u>Where are we meeting?<u>"</u>
she asked.

This week's practice sentences appear
on Daily Fix-It Transparency 28.

Strategic Intervention

Children who are not able to
write independently may draw
an illustration about the school
tradition and copy one or more of
the sentences.

Advanced

Have children write a report about
a family tradition and share this
report with the class.

Support Writing Before writing
about a different school tradition,
reread the Shared Writing report
and ask children to share ideas
about other traditions before
writing.

▲ **The Grammar and Writing Book**
For more instruction and practice,
use pp. 212–217.

Shared Writing

WRITE Report

GENERATE IDEAS Point out that just as families have traditions, schools have
traditions too. Ask children to think of an event that happens every year at your
school. Discuss what happens and why.

WRITE A REPORT Explain that the class will write a report about a school
tradition.

COMPREHENSION SKILL Have children
draw conclusions about why the school
has this tradition.

- Display Writing Transparency 28 and read
the title.
- Ask children to think of an event that
happens every year at school.
- Read the prompts.
- As children describe this school tradition,
record their responses in complete
sentences.

HANDWRITING While writing, model the
letter forms as shown on pp. TR14–17.

READ THE REPORT Have children read the
completed report aloud as you track the
print.

At Our School
Possible answers:
What We Do **Several times during the
year we have a food drive at our school.**
How We Do It **The students bring cans
and boxes of food to school. They
put the food into bags. A food
bank comes to pick up the food.**
Why We Do It **A food drive can help
people who do not have enough
food to eat. It also reminds us
how lucky we are.**

Unit 6 A Birthday Basket for Tia   Writing Model **28**

▲ **Writing Transparency 28**

INDEPENDENT WRITING

WRITE A REPORT Have children write their own report. Encourage them to use
words from the Word Wall and the Amazing Words board. Let children illustrate
their writing. You may gather children's work into a class book for self-selected
reading.

Grammar

TEACH/MODEL Use Commas

USE COMMAS Display Grammar Transparency 28. Read the definitions aloud.

• Commas are used in addresses. The address at the top of this letter needs a comma.

• Commas should be placed between the names of cities and states. Write a comma after the city *Syracuse*.

Continue modeling with the remainder of the letter.

PRACTICE

ADDRESS ENVELOPES Have children address envelopes. Be sure they include a comma between the city and state.

• Write your name on the middle of the envelope

• Write your street address below your name.

• Now write your city, state, and ZIP code. Be sure to include a comma between the city and state.

ADDITIONAL PRACTICE For additional practice, see pp. 212–217 of the Grammar and Writing Book.

Using Commas

Commas are used in addresses:
212 S. Oak Lane
Tucson, AZ 85742

Commas are used in dates:
January 31, 1929
Tuesday, June 14

Commas are used to begin and end a letter:
Dear Anna,
Love,
    Krysia

Commas are used to separate three or more things in a sentence.
Krysia wrote letters to Anna, Paul, and Aunt Beth.

Add commas where they are needed.

124 Maple Street
Syracuse, NY 13210
June 24, 2009

Dear Jaime,
    I am at my grandparents' ranch in Colorado. We come here every June. We swim, fish, and hike. I see all my cousins, aunts, and uncles. It is great. See you soon.
        Your friend,
        Tim

Unit 6 *A Birthday Basket for Tia*   Grammar **28**

▲ **Grammar Transparency 28**

Wrap Up Your Day!

✓ **COMMON SYLLABLES -tion, -ture** Write *mature* and *lotion* and ask children to decode the words.

✓ **SPELLING WORDS WITH -tion AND -ture** Have children name the letters for each sound in *adventure*. Write the letters as children write them in the air. Continue with *creation* and *capture*.

✓ **DRAW CONCLUSIONS** To help children draw conclusions, ask: In the story "Empty Eggshells," Danny came early to help Jorge. What kind of person do you think Danny is?

LET'S TALK ABOUT IT Recall that Jorge's family enjoyed the empty eggshell tradition. Review the Family Traditions web. Encourage children to discuss family birthday traditions.

 HOMEWORK Send home this week's Family Times newsletter.

PREVIEW Day 2

Tell children that tomorrow the class will read about a family celebration—a birthday party.

Day 2
AT A GLANCE

Share Literature
Magda's Tortillas

Phonics and Spelling
Syllables *-tion, -ture*
Spelling: Words with Syllables *-tion* and *-ture*

Build Background
Family Celebrations

Lesson Vocabulary
present · aunt · basket
collects · bank · favorite
More Words to Know
Piñata · ninetieth · Tía

Vocabulary
Skill Homonyms
Strategy Context Clues

Read
Group Time < Differentiated Instruction
A Birthday Basket for Tía

Interactive Writing
Write a Card

Grammar
Commas

Materials

- *Sing with Me Big Book*
- Big Book *Magda's Tortillas*
- Phonics Songs and Rhymes Chart 28
- Background Building Audio
- Graphic Organizer 16
- Tested Word Cards
- Student Edition 352–367

Morning Warm-Up!

Today we will read a story
about a girl named Cecilia. She
is having a party for her tía.
She must decide what gift to give her.
Have you ever been to a surprise party?

QUESTION OF THE DAY Encourage children to sing "Family Tradition" from the *Sing with Me Big Book* as you gather. Write and read the message and discuss the question.

REVIEW LONG *e: e, ea, ee, y*

- Read the first sentence of the message.
- Have children raise their hands when they hear a word with long *e*. *(we, read, story, she, party)*

Build Background Use the Day 2 instruction on ELL Poster 28 to preview lesson vocabulary.

ELL Poster 28

Share Literature

BUILD CONCEPTS

ITALICS Have children read the title. Identify the author. Ask children to locate words on the first page that are slanted, or italicized. Explain that these words are from another language. They are Spanish words. To show that these words are Spanish, they are written in a different way, in italics.

BUILD ORAL VOCABULARY Ask children what they know about cooking and making tortillas. Point out that cooks and chefs often **create** different kinds of foods. Suggest that as you read, children listen to find out what types of tortillas Magda creates.

- What types of tortillas do you think Magda will create? (different shapes, different flavors)

MONITOR LISTENING COMPREHENSION

- Do you think Magda could have made tortillas without her grandmother's help? Explain your answer. (Children will probably agree that any new tortilla maker would need help as he or she learns to roll and cut the dough.)

- What types of tortillas does Magda create? (heart, star, banana, hexagon, football, cloud, flower)

- Why do you think Abuela had a tear roll down her cheek? (Possible response: She was happy Magda liked her tortillas.)

Big Book

 **to build oral vocabulary**

Amazing Words	**MONITOR PROGRESS**
celebration custom tradition create inspect angle brilliant snapshot	**If...** children lack oral vocabulary experiences about the concept Traditions, **then...** use the Oral Vocabulary Routine. See p. DI·5 to teach *create*.

Build Concepts Cutting the tortillas is a main theme in *Magda's Tortillas*. Have children demonstrate their understanding of rolling and cutting circles with clay or play dough.

⚙ Syllables *-tion, -ture*

TEACH/MODEL

Fluent Word Reading   ROUTINE

1 **Connect** Write *motion* and *fracture.* You can read these words because you know how to read words with endings *-tion* and *-ture.* What syllables form *motion?* (*mo* and *tion*) Do the same with *fracture.*

2 **Model** When you come to a word with the ending *-tion* or *-ture*, look at the word and then read it. **Model reading *lecture, sculpture, edition, vacation.*** When you come to a new word, what are you going to do?

3 **Group Practice** Write *celebration, affection, adventure, furniture, collection.* Read these words. Look at the word, say the word to yourself, and then read the word aloud. **Allow 2–3 seconds previewing time.**

WORD READING

PHONICS SONGS AND RHYMES CHART 28 Frame each of the following words on Phonics Songs and Rhymes Chart 28. Call on individuals to read them. Guide children in previewing.

celebration	**vacation**	**recreation**
future	**culture**	

Sing "A Family Celebration" to the tune of "For He's a Jolly Good Fellow," or play the CD. Have children follow along on the chart as they sing. Then have individuals take turns pointing to and reading words with *-tion* and *-ture* endings on the chart.

Phonics Songs and Rhymes Audio

A Family Celebration

A family celebration
Is almost like a vacation.
We plan our own recreation
That all of us enjoy.

Our family jamborees
Build future memories.
Our culture and history
Is something we all enjoy.

Happy Birthday GRANDMA!

Phonics Songs and Rhymes Chart 28

SORT WORDS

INDIVIDUALS SORT WORDS WITH *-tion, -ture* Write *-tion* and *-ture* as headings in a two-column chart. Write the following words under the appropriate headings. Have all children complete the activity on paper. Ask individuals to read the completed lists. Provide feedback as necessary.

-tion	-ture
edition	lecture
creation	adventure
potion	puncture
addition	vulture
affection	mixture

Spelling

PRACTICE Syllables *-tion, -ture*

WRITE DICTATION SENTENCES Have children write these sentences. Repeat words slowly, allowing children to hear each sound. Children may use the Word Wall to help with spelling high-frequency words. **Word Wall**

We watched a motion picture about an adventure.

I like this furniture and light fixture.

There was lots of action at the fire station.

HOMEWORK Spelling Practice Book, p. 110

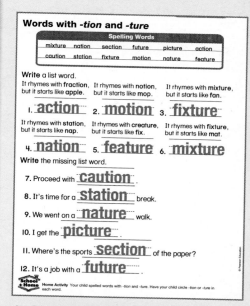
Birthday Basket for Tía   **352d**

OBJECTIVES

● Build background.
● Learn lesson vocabulary.

Read the story. Ask yourself **what is happening.** Answer each question.

Miss Booker stood by her door. She heard whispers inside. As she entered, the children yelled. For a minute Miss Booker didn't know what was going on. Then she looked around. Everyone was smiling and had on silly hats. They had even made a sign for this happy day.

1. Who is Miss Booker? _____ a teacher _____

2. Where is she? _____ her classroom; at school _____

3. Why didn't she know what was going on?

_____ The children planned a surprise. _____

4. **Draw** a picture of the sign the children made.
Children's artwork should show a sign with a message such as "Happy Birthday."

Home Activity Your child read a story and drew conclusions from the information in the story and illustration. Take turns reading another story with your child. Work together to figure out more about the characters and what happens in the story as you read.

▲ **Practice Book 2.2** p. 125, Draw Conclusions

Activate Prior Knowledge Draw simple pictures of a birthday cake, basket, and present. Ask children to name these objects in their home language and say the words in English.

Build Background

DISCUSS BIRTHDAY PARTIES Display a picture of someone blowing out candles at a birthday party, or draw a simple cake with candles on the board. Initiate a discussion by asking children if they have ever attended a birthday party.

● Have you ever gone to a surprise party?

● What is your favorite birthday memory?

● What do people do at birthday celebrations?

BACKGROUND BUILDING AUDIO Have children listen to the CD and share the new information they learned about birthday celebrations in different cultures.

Audio CD **Background Building Audio**

MAIN IDEA AND DETAILS Draw a main idea and details chart or display Graphic Organizer 16. Write *birthday party* at the top as the main idea. Ask children what they do and what they eat at a birthday party. Write their suggestions as supporting details on the graphic organizer.

```
Main Idea
              birthday party


                 Supporting Details

 play games and    sing Happy      eat cake and
 hit a piñata      Birthday        ice cream
```

▲ **Graphic Organizer 16**

CONNECT TO SELECTION Connect background information to *A Birthday Basket for Tía.*

When people go to a birthday party it is a custom to take a present. In the story we are going to read, a family is planning a celebration for a special relative. Someone creates a special basket for her. We'll find out what's in it.

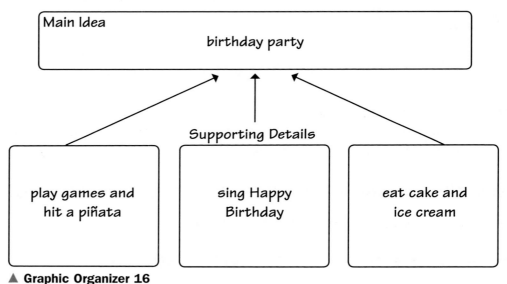

Vocabulary

LESSON VOCABULARY

STORY PREDICTION CHART Display Graphic Organizer 2 or create a chart. Write the story title and the vocabulary words in a box at the top. Write the sentence *I think this story might be about* and include a write-on line. In a box at the bottom, children draw a picture that shows what the story is actually about.

WORDS TO KNOW

T present A *present* is a gift. A present is something that someone gives you or that you give someone.

T aunt Your *aunt* is your father's sister, your mother's sister, or your uncle's wife.

T basket A *basket* is something to carry or store things in. Baskets can be made of straw, plastic, or strips of wood.

T collects If you *collect* things, you bring them together or gather them together.

T bank A *bank* is a place where people keep their money.

T favorite Your *favorite* thing is the one you like better than all the others.

MORE WORDS TO KNOW

piñata a decorated container filled with candy and toys that is hung at parties for blindfolded people to break open with a stick

ninetieth next after the 89th

tía Spanish word for aunt

T = Tested Word

- Children should be able to decode most words. To read *collects*, divide the word into syllables (col/lects) and have children blend the syllables with you.

- Have children share where they may have seen or heard some of these words.

Pick a word from the box to match each clue. Write the word on the line.

| aunt | bank | basket |
| collects | favorite | present |

1. present
2. basket
3. a place where people keep money — bank
4. the one you like best — favorite
5. Your mother's sister is your — aunt
6. saves — collects

Home Activity Your child used clues to identify and write vocabulary words learned this week. Ask your child to describe his or her dream birthday. Help your child write a description of the day. Encourage your child to use lesson vocabulary words in the writing.

▲ **Practice Book 2.2** p. 126, Lesson Vocabulary

Monitor Progress | Check Lesson Vocabulary

Write these words and have individuals read them.

| present | aunt | basket | collects | bank | favorite |
| birthday | today | door | family | laugh | |

If... children cannot read these words,

then... have them practice in pairs with word cards before reading the selection. Monitor their fluency with these words during reading, and provide additional practice opportunities before the Day 5 Assessment.

SUCCESS PREDICTOR

Day 1 Check Word Reading

▶ **Day 2** Check Lesson Vocabulary/High-Frequency Words

Day 3 Check Retelling

Day 4 Check Fluency

Day 5 Assess Progress

Spiral REVIEW

- Reviews previously taught high-frequency words and lesson vocabulary.

Word Reading

SUCCESS PREDICTOR

Vocabulary Strategy
for Homonyms

Words to Know

present

favorite

bank

basket

aunt

collects

Remember

Try the strategy. Then, if you need more help, use your glossary or a dictionary.

Context Clues When you read, you might come to a word you know, but the meaning doesn't make sense. The word may be a homonym. Homonyms are words that are pronounced and spelled the same but have different meanings. For example, *yard* means "space around a house." *Yard* also means "3 feet, or 36 inches." The words around the confusing word might help you.

1. If the meaning you know doesn't make sense, the word may be a homonym. Look at the nearby words.

2. Try to figure out another meaning for the homonym.

3. Try the meaning of the homonym in the sentence. Does it make sense?

Read "Picking a Present." Look for words that are homonyms. Use nearby words to figure out the meaning of each homonym.

Picking a Present

Is someone you know having a birthday soon? What will you give that person? It is not hard to think of a present. Ask yourself what the person likes. What is his or her favorite game? favorite hobby? favorite color? favorite food? See if the answers give you an idea.

You do not have to break your piggy bank to buy a present. Buy flowers at the grocery store. Find a basket or bowl at home. Arrange the flowers in it. This makes a nice present for your mother, grandmother, or aunt. Make a picture frame out of cardboard or wood. Decorate it. Put a picture of you or your family in it. This makes a good present for your father, grandfather, or uncle. Maybe this special person collects things such as baseball cards, photos, or rings. Decorate a box that has a lid. Find or draw pictures that match what the person collects.

So start thinking now. That birthday will be here soon!

Words to Write

Use your imagination. Write about a special gift you can give to a special friend or relative. Use words from the Words to Know list.

352

353

OBJECTIVE

Use context clues to determine the meaning of homonyms.

ELL

Access Content Use ELL Poster 28 to preteach the lesson vocabulary. Reinforce the words with the vocabulary activities and word cards in the ELL Teaching Guide, pp. 192–193. Choose from the following to meet children's language proficiency levels.

Beginning Use the list of Multilingual Lesson Vocabulary in the ELL Teaching Guide, pp. 276–283, and other home-language resources to provide translations.

Intermediate Have children add information they have learned about the vocabulary words to the birthday party web.

Advanced Teach the lesson on pp. 352–353. Have children determine whether any of the lesson vocabulary words have cognates in their home languages.

Vocabulary Strategy

TEACH/MODEL Context Clues

CONNECT Remind children of strategies to use when they come across words they don't understand.

- We can look in a dictionary or glossary.

- Sometimes we can get the meaning from word parts. We may understand the base word and prefix *(unmade, not made)* or the two shorter words in a compound *(snowman, a man made of snow).*

- We can look for context clues in the words and sentences around the unknown word. Today we will learn more about using context clues.

_____ syllables *-tion, -ture*   lesson/tested vocabulary

INTRODUCE THE STRATEGY

- Read and discuss the steps for using context clues on p. 352.

- Have children read "Picking a Present," paying attention to context clues to determine the meaning of highlighted words.

- Model using context clues to determine the meaning of *rings*.

 MODEL I know the word *rings* describes a noise. When I read the sentence *Maybe this special person collects things, such as baseball cards, photos, or rings*, *rings* does not describe a noise. I use context clues to figure out that in this sentence *rings* means "something you wear on your finger."

PRACTICE

- Have children determine the meanings of highlighted words in "Picking a Present" and explain the context clues they used.

- Point out that using context doesn't work with every word, and they may have to use the glossary or a dictionary to find the meaning of some words.

WRITE Children's writing should include lesson vocabulary to describe the special gift you can give a special friend or relative.

CONNECT TO READING Encourage children to use these strategies to determine the meaning of an unknown word.

- Look for context clues in nearby words or sentences.

- Use word parts.

- Use the glossary or a dictionary.

Group Time

On-Level	Strategic Intervention	Advanced
Read *Birthday Basket for Tía*	**Read** SI Decodable Reader 28.	**Read** *Birthday Basket for Tía*
• Use pp. 354–369.	• Read or listen to *A Birthday Basket for Tía*	• Use the **Routine** on p. DI·37.
	• Use the **Routine** on p. DI·36.	

ELL Place English language learners in the groups that correspond to their reading abilities in English.

ⓘ Independent Activities

Independent Reading See p. 350j for Reading/Library activities and suggestions.

Journal Writing Write about a special birthday. Share your writing.

Literacy Centers To provide experiences with *A Birthday Basket for Tía*, you may use the Writing Center on p. 350k.

Practice Book 2.2 Draw Conclusions, p. 125 Lesson Vocabulary, p. 126 Fact and Opinion, p. 127

DAY 2

Break into small groups after Vocabulary and before Writing.

2

A Birthday Basket for Tía

by Pat Mora

illustrated by Cecily Lang

Genre **Realistic fiction** is a story with characters and events that are like people and events in real life.

354

What will be in the birthday basket for Tía?

355

AudioText

Read
Prereading Strategies

PREVIEW AND PREDICT Have children read the title. Explain that *Tía* is a Spanish word, and ask if any children know the English translation. If necessary, explain that *Tía* means "aunt." Have children locate Tía in the cover illustration. Have children read the names of the author and illustrator. Invite children to take a picture walk to find objects that are in Tía's birthday basket. Ask them to tell whether they think Tía will appreciate the presents.

DISCUSS REALISTIC FICTION Remind children that realistic fiction tells a made-up story about events that could really happen. Read the definition of realistic fiction on p. 354 of the Student Edition. Have children use the story illustrations to name some realistic events in which the characters participate.

SET PURPOSE Call on volunteers to tell how they choose presents for their own family and friends. Then read aloud the question on p. 355. Ask what children would like to find out as they read the story.

ELL

Access Content Before reading, review the story summary in English and/or the home language. See the ELL Teaching Guide, pp. 194–196.

_____ syllables *-tion, -ture*   lesson/tested vocabulary

Today is secret day. I curl my cat into my arms and say, "Ssshh, Chica. Can you keep our secret, silly cat?"

Today is special day. Today is my great-aunt's ninetieth birthday. Ten, twenty, thirty, forty, fifty, sixty, seventy, eighty, ninety. Ninety years old. *¡Noventa años!*

356

At breakfast Mamá asks, "What is today, Cecilia?" I say, "Special day. Birthday day."

Mamá is cooking for the surprise party. I smell beans bubbling on the stove. Mamá is cutting fruit—pineapple, watermelon, mangoes. I sit in the backyard and watch Chica chase butterflies. I hear bees bzzzzz.

I draw <u>pictures</u> in the sand with a stick. I draw a <u>picture</u> of my <u>aunt</u>, my *Tía*. I say, "Chica, what will we give Tía?"

357

Guiding Comprehension

Character • Inferential

- **What do you know about Cecilia?**
She has a cat. She cares about her great-aunt.

Context Clues • Inferential

- **What does *noventa años* mean? How do you know?**
Noventa años means "ninety years." The translation appears in the same paragraph.

Draw Conclusions • Critical

- ***Text to World*** **To which culture do the characters in this story belong? How do you know?**
Readers can tell that the characters are Hispanic from the Spanish words, punctuation, accent marks, and illustrations.

▲ **Pages 356–357**
Have children read to find out information about the story characters.

Healthy Foods

Our bodies get energy from eating a variety of healthy foods. Ask children to identify healthy food they see on these pages. Discuss qualities of healthy foods (less sugar, less fat) and examples of smart snacks (vegetables, fruits). Ask children why our bodies need healthy food. (To build strong bones and muscles, to feel good, and so on)

Birthday Basket for Tía   **356–357**

Chica and I walk around the front yard and the backyard looking for a good present. We walk around the house. We look in Mamá's room. We look in my closet and drawers.

I say, "Chica, shall we give her my little pots, my piggy bank, my tin fish, my dancing puppet?"

I say, "Mamá, can Chica and I use this basket?"

Mamá asks, "Why, Cecilia?"

"It's a surprise for the surprise party," I answer. Chica jumps into the basket. "No," I say. "Not for you, silly cat. This is a birthday basket for Tía."

358

I put a book in the basket. When Tía comes to our house, she reads it to me. It's our favorite book. I sit close to her on the sofa. I smell her perfume. Sometimes Chica tries to read with us. She sits on the book. I say, "Silly cat. Books are not for sitting."

I put Tía's favorite mixing bowl on the book in the basket. Tía and I like to make *bizcochos*, sugary cookies for the family.

Tía says, "Cecilia, help me stir the cookie dough." She says, "Cecilia, help me roll the cookie dough." When we take the warm cookies from the oven, Tía says, "Cecilia, you are a very good cook."

359

▲ **Pages 358–359**
Have children read to learn how Cecilia decides what to put in Tía's basket.

Read each sentence.
Answer the questions.

1. Viv was late, so she missed the party.
Why did Viv miss the party?

She was late.

2. Because Jim forgot, he did not send a birthday card.
Why didn't Jim send a birthday card?

He forgot.

3. Mom burned the cake, so no one could eat it.
Why couldn't anyone eat the cake?

Mom burned it.

4. Because Al dropped the box, the gift broke.
Why did the gift break?

Al dropped the box.

5. Tim was sad because so many things went wrong.
Why was Tim sad?

So many things went wrong.

 Home Activity Your child read sentences to see what happened and answered questions about the cause of each event. Talk to your child about events of the day. Ask your child what happened and why. Have him or her draw a picture to show one thing that happened and write a sentence to tell why it happened.

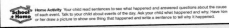

▲ **Practice Book 2.2** p. 127,
Cause and Effect

Skills in Context

(REVIEW) CAUSE AND EFFECT

- **Why does Cecilia include a book in Tía's basket?**
  She chooses the book because she and Tía like to read it together.

Monitor Progress	Cause and Effect
If... children have difficulty answering the question,	**then...** model how to identify cause and effect.

Think Aloud **MODEL** As I read, I look for what happened and why it happened. I know Cecilia put a book in Tía's basket, and I wonder why. I find out it is their favorite book to read together, so it will please Tía.

ASSESS Ask children why Cecilia gives Tía the mixing bowl. (Cecilia and Tía like to make *bizcochos* together.)

_____ Syllables *-tion, -ture*   ▢ lesson vocabulary

I put a flowerpot in the mixing bowl on the book in the basket. Tía and I like to grow flowers for the kitchen window. Chica likes to put her face in the flowers. "Silly cat," I say.

I put a teacup in the flowerpot that is in the mixing bowl on the book in the basket. When I'm sick, my aunt makes me hot mint tea, *hierbabuena*. She brings it to me in bed. She brings me a cookie too.

360

I put a red ball in the teacup that is in the flowerpot in the mixing bowl on the book in the basket. On warm days Tía sits outside and throws me the ball.

She says, "Cecilia, when I was a little girl in Mexico, my sisters and I played ball. We all wore long dresses and had long braids."

Chica and I go outside. I pick flowers to decorate Tía's basket. On summer days when I am swinging high up to the sky, Tía collects flowers for my room.

361

Guiding Comprehension

▲ **Pages 360–361**
Have children read to find out what else Tía and Cecilia like to do together.

Cause and Effect • Inferential
• **Why do you think Tía enjoys playing ball so much?**
It reminds her of her childhood in Mexico, when she played ball with her sisters.

Summarize • Inferential
• **What has happened in the story so far?**
Cecilia's family is planning a surprise birthday celebration for Cecilia's great-aunt. Cecilia is creating a birthday basket for Tía. Cecilia has chosen to include a book, a mixing bowl, a flowerpot, a teacup, a ball, and flowers in the basket.

Strategy Self-Check

Have children ask themselves these questions to check their reading.

Vocabulary Strategy
• Do I look for context clues?
• Do I use word parts?
• Do I use the glossary or a dictionary?

Summarize
• Do I know the most important events?
• Do I know which events to leave out?
• Do I use a few brief sentences to tell what has happened?

Mamá calls, "Cecilia, where are you?"

Chica and I run and hide our surprise.

I say, "Mamá, can you find the birthday basket for Tía?"

Mamá looks under the table. She looks in the refrigerator. She looks under my bed. She asks, "Chica, where is the birthday basket?"

Chica rubs against my closet door. Mamá and I laugh. I show her my surprise.

After my nap, Mamá and I fill a piñata with candy. We fill the living room with balloons. I hum, mmmmm, a little work song like the one Tía hums when she sets the table or makes my bed. I help Mamá set the table with flowers and tiny cakes.

362

"Here come the musicians," says Mamá. I open the front door. Our family and friends begin to arrive too.

I curl Chica into my arms. Then Mamá says, "Sshh, here comes Tía."

I rush to open the front door. "Tía! Tía!" I shout. She hugs me and says,

"Cecilia, *¿qué pasa?* What is this?"

363

▲ **Pages 362–363**
Have children read to find out what Cecilia and Mamá do to get ready for the party.

Piñatas

Time for **SOCIAL STUDIES**

Reread the last paragraph on p. 362. Ask what a piñata is and how it is used. Explain that the custom of piñatas at birthday parties began in Mexico. Ask children to name some other ways people celebrate birthdays. Ask if they know from which cultures the traditions come.

Skills in Context

🎯 DRAW CONCLUSIONS

• **Why is the family working hard to prepare for Tía's party?**
Possible responses: The party is important to the whole family. The family wants to show Tía how much they love her.

Monitor Progress	**Draw Conclusions**
If... children have difficulty answering the question,	**then...** model how to use what you already know to draw conclusions.

Think Aloud

MODEL I know from my own life that I would work hard on a party for someone I love, so I think that Cecilia's family works hard on Tía's party to show her how much they love her.

ASSESS Ask children whether Tía is really surprised or not. (Possible response: I think she's really surprised. She asks Cecilia what's going on.)

____ Syllables *-tion, -ture*   ☐ lesson vocabulary

"SURPRISE!" we all shout. "¡Feliz cumpleaños! Happy birthday!" The musicians begin to play their guitars and violins.

"Tía! Tía!" I say, "It's special day, birthday day! It's your ninetieth birthday surprise party!" Tía and I laugh.

364

365

Strategies in Context

🎯 SUMMARIZE

- **How would you summarize A Birthday Basket for Tía?**
Cecilia makes Tía a special birthday basket, and her family creates a surprise party to celebrate Tía's ninetieth birthday.

Monitor Progress	**Summarize**
If... children are unable to summarize the story,	**then...** model how to include the most important information in a few sentences.

Think Aloud

MODEL To use as few words as possible in my summary, I make a big statement that covers many events. For example, instead of naming everything Cecilia puts in the basket, I just say, "Cecilia makes Tía a special birthday basket."

ASSESS Have children summarize what happens on pp. 364–365.

▲ **Pages 364–365**
Have children read to find out what Tía does after everyone yells "Surprise!"

EXTEND SKILLS

Connect Experiences

For instruction on connecting experiences, discuss the following;

- When reading about another culture, connect it to what you already know about your culture.
- The musicians at the party are playing guitars and violins. These instruments are traditionally used to make music in Cecilia's culture.
- What instruments are used to make music in your culture?

Assess Have children find other details about Cecilia's culture and compare them to their own.

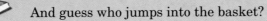

I give her the birthday basket. Everyone gets close to see what's inside. Slowly Tía smells the flowers. She looks at me and smiles. Then she takes the red ball out of the teacup and the teacup out of the flowerpot.

She pretends to take a sip of tea and we all laugh.

Carefully, Tía takes the flowerpot out of the bowl and the bowl off of the book. She doesn't say a word. She just stops and looks at me. Then she takes our favorite book out of the basket.

And guess who jumps into the basket?

366

Chica. Everyone laughs.

Then the music starts and my aunt surprises me. She takes my hands in hers. Without her cane, she starts to dance with me.

367

▲ **Pages 366–367**
Have children read to find out how Cecilia knows Tía liked her present.

Monitor Progress

Lesson Vocabulary

| **If...** children have a problem reading a new lesson vocabulary word, | **then...** use the Lesson Vocabulary Routine on p. 352f to reteach the problematic word. |

Guiding Comprehension

Cause and Effect • Inferential

• **How does Cecilia know that Tía likes her present?**
She knows Tía likes the present because Tía smiles and laughs and then gets up to dance with Cecilia without her cane.

Compare and Contrast • Critical

• *Text to Self* **What are some special traditions you and your family have to celebrate birthdays? How are they similar to and different from how Cecilia's family celebrates Tía's birthday?**
Children may give examples of customs their families follow, activities in which they participate, or special foods they eat.

Fluency

REREAD FOR FLUENCY

Paired Reading

ROUTINE

Reader 1 Begins Children read the entire book, switching readers at the end of each page.

Reader 2 Begins Have partners reread; now the other partner begins.

Reread For optimal fluency, children should reread three or four times.

Provide Feedback Listen to children read and provide corrective feedback regarding their oral reading and their use of the blending strategy.

OBJECTIVES

- Write a card.
- Identify commas.

Interactive Writing

WRITE Card

BRAINSTORM Use *A Birthday Basket for Tía* to encourage a discussion about preparing for a birthday party. Picture walk through the story and ask children to identify the things that Cecilia and her mother do to prepare for the party.

SHARE THE PEN Have children participate in writing and designing a birthday card. To begin, have one child suggest a saying for the front of the card. Write the saying on the front of a piece of folded construction paper. Invite individuals to write familiar letter-sounds, word parts, and high-frequency words. Ask questions such as:

- What is the first sound you hear in the word *happy?* (/h/)
- What letter stands for that sound? *(h)* Have a volunteer write *H.*
- What is the second sound you hear in the word *happy?* (/a/)
- What letter stands for that sound? *(a)* Have a volunteer write *a.*

Continue to have individuals make contributions for the inside of the card. Frequently reread what has been written while tracking the print.

READ THE CARD Read the completed card aloud, having children echo you.

Strategic Intervention

Have children copy one of the sentences from the card and design and illustrate their own card.

Advanced

Have children who are able to write complete sentences independently write a different type of card, e.g., an anniversary or thank you card.

Writing Support Before writing, display several birthday cards and point out key words that children may want to use in their own writing.

Beginning Have children copy *Happy Birthday* from the board to the front of their card. A more proficient English speaker can help a partner write the card.

Intermediate Help children create a web of words to use in writing the card.

Advanced Review children's cards and show where more details can be added to make the card more interesting.

Happy Birthday

Have a wonderful year!

May all your wishes come true!

Hope your day is perfect–just like you!

You deserve the best!

INDEPENDENT WRITING

WRITE A CARD Have children write their own birthday card. Let children design and illustrate their writing.

Support Grammar Demonstrate the function of commas by reading sentences aloud, pausing briefly after commas. Invite children to read aloud other sentences with commas. See the Grammar Transition lessons in the ELL and Transition Handbook.

Grammar

DEVELOP THE CONCEPT Using Commas

IDENTIFY COMMAS Write *Monday, June 2* on the board. Point to each word as you read it. Ask children to identify the comma in the sentence. Continue with *Dallas, TX.*

Commas are used in addresses and in dates. Where are commas used? (in dates and in addresses)

PRACTICE

WRITE COMMAS Display a calendar. Model writing the date, emphasizing where the comma is written.

MODEL This is today's date. Write *Tuesday, May 6.* A comma is written between the day of the week and the date. Here's another way to write today's date. Write *May 6, 2007.* A comma is written between the date and the year.

Have children name dates. Write them on the board. Ask individuals to write the commas in the correct places.

DAILY FIX-IT

3. Jordan colects baseball cards
   Jordan collects baseball cards.

4. My favrite aunt salls flowers.
   My favorite aunt sells flowers.

Using Commas
- **Commas** are used in addresses:
  St. Louis, MO 63119
- **Commas** are used in dates:
  May 10, 1946   Thursday, December 16
- **Commas** are used to begin and end a letter:
  Dear Grandpa,
  Love,
    Tony
- **Commas** are used to separate three or more things in a sentence.
  Tony bought stamps, paper, and a pen.

Add commas to the letter where they are needed.

307 Beach Drive
Southport, NC 28465

June 28, 2007

Dear Polly,
  I will be coming for a visit in July. I hope we can go to the beach again. I love looking for seashells. Could we also fish, swim, and skate? See you soon.
              Your cousin,
              Angela

Home Activity Your child learned about using commas. Collect pieces of mail. Look at the ads and the addresses on the envelopes. Have your child point out places where commas are used.

▲ **Grammar and Writing Practice Book** p. 109

Wrap Up Your Day!

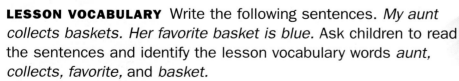

 LESSON VOCABULARY Write the following sentences. *My aunt collects baskets. Her favorite basket is blue.* Ask children to read the sentences and identify the lesson vocabulary words *aunt, collects, favorite,* and *basket.*

SUMMARIZE Have children work with a partner to summarize *A Birthday Basket for Tía.* Remind children to include the important parts of the story in the beginning, the middle, and the end.

LET'S TALK ABOUT IT Recall *A Birthday Basket for Tía.* Ask: What special things did Cecilia put in Tía's birthday basket? (flowers, red ball, teacup, flowerpot, bowl, and book) Encourage children to add to the family celebrations web.

PREVIEW Day 3

Tell children that tomorrow they will read about another special birthday celebration.

Share Literature
Magda's Tortillas

Phonics and Spelling
REVIEW Base Words and Endings

Spelling: Words with Syllables *-tion, -ture*

Vocabulary
Skill Words from Other Languages

Language Connections

Fluency
Read with Appropriate Phrasing

Writing Trait
Organization/Paragraphs

Grammar
Use Commas

Materials

- *Sing with Me Big Book*
- Big Book *Magda's Tortillas*
- Vocabulary Transparency 28
- Student Edition 368–369

Morning Warm~Up!

We will read about Magda again today.
Magda is helpful in the kitchen.
Magda works slowly,
while Abuela works quickly.
Magda may not make her tortillas
perfectly round, but people like them.
What would you like to learn
how to make?

QUESTION OF THE DAY Encourage children to sing "Family Tradition" from the *Sing with Me Big Book* as you gather. Write and read the message and discuss the question.

REVIEW SUFFIXES

- Point to *helpful* in the message. Ask children to identify the suffix in this word.

- Point to *slowly* in the message and ask children to identify the suffix in this word. Have children find two other words that have the *-ly* suffix. (*quickly, perfectly*)

Build Background Use the Day 3 instruction on ELL Poster 28 to support children's use of English to communicate about lesson concepts.

ELL Poster 28

Share Literature

LISTEN AND RESPOND

REALISTIC FICTION Recall what *Magda's Tortillas* is about. Review that realistic fiction is a story with characters and events that are like people and events in real life.

BUILD ORAL VOCABULARY Review that the class read the Big Book to find out about what types of tortillas Magda created. Ask that children listen today to find out what gets inspected. To **inspect** something means to check it. What is checked, or inspected, in *Magda's Tortillas?* (Magda's hands)

• Imagine your kitchen is inspected. What kinds of things might be checked? (Possible responses: cleanliness, items in the proper place, utensils, food)

Big Book

MONITOR LISTENING COMPREHENSION

• What does Magda present to be inspected? Who does the inspecting? (She presents her hands to her Abuela to be inspected.)

• What does Magda use to roll out the dough? (rolling pin)

• Why was Magda afraid to serve her tortillas? (She thought people would laugh at the funny shapes.)

• Do you think the other children want to learn how to make tortillas? How do you know? (Yes, the other children crowd around and say "Teach me, teach me.")

OBJECTIVES

● Discuss characteristics of realistic fiction.
● Set purpose for listening.
● Build oral vocabulary.

Amazing Words
to build oral vocabulary

	MONITOR PROGRESS
celebration	**If...** children lack oral vocabulary experiences about the concept Traditions,
custom	
tradition	
create	
inspect	
angle	**then...** use the Oral Vocabulary Routine. See p. DI·5 to teach *inspect*.
brilliant	
snapshot	

Listen and Respond Help children describe and demonstrate the actions conveyed by the word *inspect* by having a desk inspection. Give children time to clean and organize their desks and then take turns inspecting each other's desks.

3

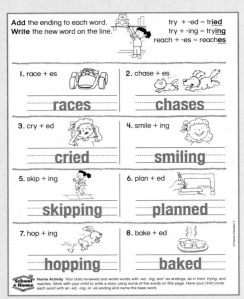

▲ **Practice Book 2.2** p. 128, Inflected Endings

Review Phonics

REVIEW INFLECTED ENDINGS

READ *-ed, -ing* WORDS Write *tried.* You can read this word because you know how to read base words and endings. You can cover the ending, read the base word, and then blend the base word and ending to read the whole word. What is the word? *(tried)* Remember that *-ed* is added to a base word to show that something has happened in the past.

Write *grabbing.* Remind children of the spelling changes that may be needed when endings are added to base words:

- Double the final consonant
- Drop *e* before adding the ending
- Change *y* to *i*

What is the base word in *tried? (try)* What was the spelling change? (*y* changed to *i*) Sometimes the final consonant is doubled before adding an ending. For example, the *b* in *grab* is doubled before the ending *-ing* is added. What is the word? *(grabbing)*

BUILD WORDS Write the words below. Have children read them and tell how the spelling changed when the endings were added.

base word	-ed	-ing
chop	chopped	chopping
cry	cried	crying
nod	nodded	nodding
dance	danced	dancing
dry	dried	drying
snap	snapped	snapping

Lesson Vocabulary

PRACTICE

CHOOSE AN EXAMPLE Write lesson vocabulary words on the board. Provide children with two examples. Have children write a complete sentence using the lesson vocabulary word and identifying which example is an example of the lesson vocabulary word.

- Which is a present—a toy you give your friend for her birthday or a book you check out of the library? (A present is a toy you give your friend for her birthday.)

- Which is your aunt—your mother's sister or your mother's mother? (Your aunt is your mother's sister.)

- Which is a basket—something you eat at a birthday party or something you can carry things in? (A basket is something you can carry things in.)

- Which is someone who collects something—a girl who picks up everyone's papers or a boy who loses his book? (Someone who collects something is a girl who picks up everyone's papers.)

- Which is a bank—a kind of cookie or a place to store your money? (A bank is a place to store your money.)

- Which is your favorite shirt—the shirt you didn't want to get or the shirt you wear all the time? (Your favorite shirt is the shirt you wear all the time.)

Spelling

PRACTICE Syllables *-tion, -ture*

FILL IN THE ENDING Have children practice spelling words by providing the missing syllables and writing a sentence for each word.

- Write the first syllable for each spelling word on a card (*mix, na, sec, fu, pic, ac, cau, sta, fix, mo, fea*).

- Display each card and have children copy the syllable. Ask children to provide the missing end syllable and then write a sentence using the word.

- Make sure children include both *nation* and *nature*.

HOMEWORK Spelling Practice Book, p. 111

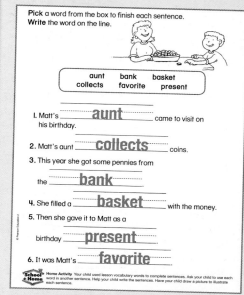

Pick a word from the box to finish each sentence. Write the word on the line.

| aunt | bank | basket |
| collects | favorite | present |

1. Matt's **aunt** came to visit on his birthday.
2. Matt's aunt **collects** coins.
3. This year she got some pennies from the **bank**
4. She filled a **basket** with the money.
5. Then she gave it to Matt as a birthday **present**
6. It was Matt's **favorite**

Home Activity Your child used lesson vocabulary words to complete sentences. Ask your child to use each word in another sentence. Help your child write the sentences. Have your child draw a picture to illustrate each sentence.

▲ **Practice Book 2.2** p. 129, Lesson Vocabulary

Spelling Words

Syllables *-tion, -ture*

1. mixture   7. caution
2. nation   8. station
3. section   9. fixture
4. future   10. motion
5. picture*   11. nature
6. action   12. feature

Challenge Words

13. furniture
14. adventure
15. tuition

* Words from the Selection

Words with *-tion* and *-ture*

Spelling Words					
mixture	nation	section	future	picture	action
caution	station	fixture	motion	nature	feature

Read the poster. Circle three spelling words and one word with a capitalization error. Write the words correctly.

> **Special double feature!**
> Packed with ACTION
> A superhero of the future saves the nation.
> Bring the family
> saturday at 1:00.

1. **feature**
2. **nation**
3. **family**
4. **Saturday**

Circle the word that is spelled correctly. Write it.

5. caution causion   **caution**
6. nater nature   **nature**
7. picture pichure   **picture**
8. section sectshion   **section**

Frequently Misspelled Words
special
family
really

Home Activity Your child identified misspelled words with *-tion* and *-ture*. Have your child underline these letter combinations in the list words.

▲ **Spelling Practice Book** p. 111

Birthday Basket for Tía   **368d**

3

Vocabulary

WORDS FROM OTHER LANGUAGES

DISCUSS WORDS FROM OTHER LANGUAGES Have children recall that in *A Birthday Basket for Tía* there were many words written in Spanish. We knew they were in Spanish because the print was different; the words were italicized. The first Spanish words were ¡*Noventa años!,* which means *Ninety years old!*

Write the following Spanish word and phrases on the board. Have children find the meaning of each word or phrase by looking through the story. Then have children use the word(s) in a sentence.

bizcochos   ¿Que pasa?   feliz cumpleaños

EXPAND SELECTION VOCABULARY Have children name other non-English words they know, and discuss the English words for these words. If children are having trouble identifying a non-English word, then encourage them to look through the story. Have children work with partners to write sentences for each non-English word. Invite volunteers to share their sentences.

OBJECTIVES

- Discuss meanings of words from other languages.
- Use words from other languages in sentences.

Strategic Intervention

Have children illustrate the meaning of *bizcochos.* Then help them write a caption using the word *bizcochos.*

Advanced

Have children use a Spanish translation dictionary to look up the meanings of *Tía* and *hierbabuena.* Encourage children to look up other words.

Extend Language Have children name words they know that translate easily into English. Create a list from *A Birthday Basket for Tía* and have children add words to the list. The list can be made into a class translation dictionary.

Group Time

DAY 3

On-Level	Strategic Intervention	Advanced
Read *A Birthday Basket for Tía.* • Use pp. 354–369.	**Read** or listen to *A Birthday Basket for Tía.* • Use the **Routine** on p. DI·38.	**Read** Self-Selected Reading. • Use the **Routine** on p. DI·39.

 Place English language learners in the groups that correspond to their reading abilities in English.

ⓘ Independent Activities

Independent Reading See p. 350j for Reading/Library activities and suggestions.

Journal Writing Write about a special gift you would like to give or get on a birthday. Share your writing.

Literacy Centers To provide experiences with *A Birthday Basket for Tía,* you may use the Writing Center on p. 350k.

Practice Book 2.2 Inflected Endings, p. 128

Break into small groups after Vocabulary and before Writing.

Fluency

READ WITH APPROPRIATE PHRASING

MODEL READING WITH APPROPRIATE PHRASING Use *A Birthday Basket for Tía.*

- Point to the quotation marks on p. 356. Quotation marks show that someone is talking. Read the part in the quotation marks the way someone would say it. I pause when I see commas.

- Ask children to follow along as you read the page, pausing at the commas and grouping the words.

- Have children read the page after you. Encourage them to read groups of words, not word-by-word. Continue in the same way with pp. 357–358.

REREAD FOR FLUENCY

Choral Reading

ROUTINE

1 **Select a Passage** For *A Birthday Basket for Tía,* use pp. 359–360.

2 **Divide into Groups** Assign each group a part to read. For this story, alternate paragraphs. The first group reads the first paragraph. The second group reads the next paragraph and so on.

3 **Model** Have children track the print as you read.

4 **Read Together** Have children read along with you.

5 **Independent Readings** Have the groups read aloud without you. Monitor progress and provide feedback. For optimal fluency, children should reread three to four times.

Monitor Progress	Fluency
If... children have difficulty reading with appropriate phrasing,	**then...** prompt: • Are there commas to tell me that a group of words belongs together? • Are there groups of words that should be read together? • Try to read groups of words, not word-by-word.
If... the class cannot read fluently without you,	**then...** continue to have them read along with you.

OBJECTIVE

- Read aloud fluently with appropriate phrasing.

Options for Oral Reading
Use *A Birthday Basket for Tía* or one of the following Leveled Readers.

On-Level

Very Special Birthdays

Strategic Intervention

Birthdays Around the World

Advanced

Family Traditions and Celebrations

Fluency Model the reading of phrases in the story, such as "pineapple, watermelon, mangoes" and "my aunt, my Tía," so that beginning English language learners can practice reading meaningfully.

Retelling Plan

- ☑ Week 1 assess Strategic Intervention students.
- ☑ Week 2 assess Advanced students.
- ☑ **This week assess Strategic Intervention students.**
- ☐ Week 4 assess On-Level students.
- ☐ Week 5 assess any students you have not yet checked during this unit.

Look Back and Write
Point out information from the text that answers the question. Then have children write a response to the question. For test practice, assign a 10–15 minute time limit. For assessment, see the Scoring Rubric at the bottom of this page.

Assessment Before retelling, help children name items shown. For more ideas on assessing comprehension, see the ELL and Transition Handbook.

Reader Response

TALK ABOUT IT Model a response. If I were making a birthday basket for my sister, I would put in her favorite foods (apples and cheese), her favorite flower (daisies), her favorite toy (blocks), and two things we could play with together (clay and paints).

1. RETELL Have children use the retelling strip in the Student Edition to retell the selection.

Monitor Progress **Check Retelling** Rubric 4 3 2 1

Have children retell *A Birthday Basket for Tía.*

If... children have difficulty retelling the story,

then... use the Retelling Cards and the Scoring Rubric for Retelling on pp. 368–369 to help them move toward fluent retelling.

SUCCESS PREDICTOR

| **Day 1** Check Word Reading | **Day 2** Check Lesson Vocabulary/High-Frequency Words | **▶ Day 3** Check Retelling | **Day 4** Check Fluency | **Day 5** Assess Progress |

---

2. **DRAW CONCLUSIONS** Model a response. Cecilia loves to spend time with Tía. She puts things in the basket that remind her of things they do together.

3. **SUMMARIZE** Model a response. Cecilia has decided to make a birthday basket for Tía. She has put a book, a mixing bowl, a flowerpot, a teacup, a red ball, and flowers in the basket.

LOOK BACK AND WRITE Read the writing prompt on p. 368 and model your thinking. I'll skim and scan the story. I'll look for what Cecilia first thought she might give Tía. Then I'll look for the things Cecilia finally decided to give Tía. Then I'll write my response. Have children write their responses.

Scoring Rubric **Look Back and Write**

Top-Score Response A top-score response will use details from the selection to list what Cecilia thought she would give to Tía and what she finally did give to Tía.

Example of a Top-Score Response Here are lists of things Cecilia thought of giving and what she really did give to Tía:

Might Give Tía	**Did Give Tía**
pots	book
piggy bank	mixing bowl
tin fish	flowers
dancing puppet	red ball
	teacup
	flowerpot

For additional rubrics, see p. WA10.

Reader Response

Open for Discussion Pretend you made a birthday basket for someone. What six things would you put into it? Why?

1. Use the pictures below to help retell the story. Retell

2. Think about the things Cecilia put into the basket for Tía. What conclusions can you draw about how Cecilia feels about her Tía? Draw Conclusions

3. Look back at page 362. Summarize what has happened so far in the story. Summarize

Look Back and Write What did Cecilia *first* think she might give to Tía? What things did Cecilia finally give to Tía? Make two lists. Use details from the story in your answer.

Meet the Author

Pat Mora

Read two more books by Pat Mora.

This Big Sky

Tomás and the Library Lady

Though Pat Mora grew up in Texas, she came from a home where both English and Spanish were spoken. When she started writing books, Ms. Mora realized she wanted to write about her experience as a Mexican American. "It was like opening a treasure chest," Ms. Mora says. "My whole Mexican heritage was something I could write about."

Ms. Mora tells students to write about what they love. She says, "The trick is how we bring everything that we are to the page—everything."

Retelling Strip

368

369

Scoring Rubric   Narrative Retelling

Rubric 4 3 2 1	**4**	**3**	**2**	**1**
Connections	Makes connections and generalizes beyond the text	Makes connections to other events, stories, or experiences	Makes a limited connection to another event, story, or experience	Makes no connection to another event, story, or experience
Author's Purpose	Elaborates on author's purpose	Tells author's purpose with some clarity	Makes some connection to author's purpose	Makes no connection to author's purpose
Characters	Describes the main character(s) and any character development	Identifies the main character(s) and gives some information about them	Inaccurately identifies some characters or gives little information about them	Inaccurately identifies the characters or gives no information about them
Setting	Describes the time and location	Identifies the time and location	Omits details of time or location	Is unable to identify time or location
Plot	Describes the events in sequence, using rich detail	Tells the plot with some errors in sequence that do not affect meaning	Tells parts of plot with gaps that affect meaning	Retelling has no sense of story

Use the Retelling Chart on p. TR20 to record retelling.

Selection Test To assess with *A Birthday Basket for Tía,* use Selection Tests, pp. 109–112.

Fresh Reads for Differentiated Test Practice For weekly leveled practice, use pp. 163–168.

Retelling

SUCCESS PREDICTOR

Writing Trait of the Week

INTRODUCE Organization/Paragraphs

DAILY FIX-IT

5. Aunt sue cullects dolls.
   Aunt <u>S</u>ue c<u>o</u>llects dolls.

6. Is that your faverite basket.
   Is that your fav<u>o</u>rite basket<u>?</u>

Connect to Unit Writing

Writing Trait

Have children use strategies for developing **organization/paragraphs** when they write a research report in the Unit Writing Workshop, pp. WA2–WA9.

ELL

Organization/Paragraphs Work with language learners to write strong paragraphs. Record their ideas and help them construct a topic sentence that "sets up" their paragraph. Then help them organize details in other sentences.

TALK ABOUT ORGANIZATION/PARAGRAPHS Explain to children that good organization holds a piece of writing together. A topic sentence that tells what a paragraph is about is one way to organize a paragraph. Point out that the author of *A Birthday Basket for Tía* uses some strong topic sentences to organize paragraphs. Then model your thinking.

Think Aloud

MODEL When I write, I can begin with a topic sentence to help me organize a paragraph. First, I write my main idea in the first sentence. Then I give details about the topic sentence in the rest of the paragraph. Here is a paragraph from *A Birthday Basket for Tía.*

> **Today is special day. Today is my great-aunt's ninetieth birthday. Ten, twenty, thirty, forty, fifty, sixty, seventy, eighty, ninety. Ninety years old.**

Help children recognize that the first sentence is a topic sentence. It states the idea that the paragraph is about. The rest of the paragraph gives details about that idea. Then read the following sentences from the story.

> **Then the music starts and my aunt surprises me. She takes my hands in hers. Without her cane, she starts to dance with me.**

What is the main idea of the paragraph? *(My aunt surprises me.)* Which is the topic sentence? *(first)* What details about the topic sentence does the author give in the rest of the paragraph? *(takes my hand in hers and dances without her cane)*

STRATEGY FOR DEVELOPING ORGANIZATION/PARAGRAPHS Have children choose the best topic sentence for a paragraph about a party.

> **Let me tell you about my favorite food.**
> **Colorful decorations help make a party fun.** *(best)*
> **I would like a pet for my birthday.**

PRACTICE

APPLY THE STRATEGY Have children choose one of the sentences from the activity above. Then have them use that as the topic sentence for an original paragraph. Remind them to include only details that support the topic sentence.

Grammar

OBJECTIVE

● Use commas in writing.

APPLY TO WRITING Commas

IMPROVE WRITING WITH COMMAS Have children recall that commas are used in addresses, in dates, in a letter, and to separate three or more things in a sentence. Remind children to use commas in their own writing.

Write *April 18 2007, Greenwood CA, June 2 2008.* Have children supply the commas. Remind children to use commas in their own writing.

April 18, 2007   **Greenwood, CA**   **June 2, 2008**

PRACTICE

WRITE WITH COMMAS Call on individuals to place commas where they are needed in addresses and dates. Have children write the current date and their address. Ask children to show proper placement of commas.

Using Commas

Write a letter to a friend or relative. **Tell** about something you did together. **Use** commas where they are needed. Possible answer:

June 6, 2008 ___ (date)

Dear Aunt Joyce, ___ (greeting)

(message) I liked the party very much. The cake, punch, and cookies were delicious. Thank you for inviting me.
___
___
___

(closing) Your niece,
(your name) Cindy

Home Activity Your child learned how to use commas in writing. Together name occasions when a person might send a note or letter and to whom. Have your child write greetings, such as *Dear Grandma*, and use commas correctly.

▲ **Grammar and Writing Practice Book** p. 110

Wrap Up Your Day!

 DRAW CONCLUSIONS Have children draw conclusions about what Tía's reaction was to the party and gifts. (She was happy.) What things did Tía do to show how happy she was?

 READ WITH APPROPRIATE PHRASING; GROUP WORDS APPROPRIATELY Remind children that good readers group words as they read. They group words that belong together and read in phrases. They don't read word-by-word.

LET'S TALK ABOUT IT Display the Family Celebrations Web from Day 1. Help children identify the ways that Cecilia's family celebrates. Who shows up? (family, friends, musicians) What decorations are used? (flowers, balloons) What foods do they make and eat? (beans, fruit, cake) What activities do they do? (dancing, piñata)

PREVIEW Day 4

Tell children that tomorrow they will listen to poems about special occasions.

Day 4
AT A GLANCE

Share Literature
Various poetry selections

Phonics and Spelling
Syllables –tion, –ture
Spelling: Words with Syllables –tion, –ture

Read Apply Phonics
Group Time < Differentiated Instruction

Fluency
Read with Appropriate Phrasing

Writing Across the Curriculum
Math Story

Grammar
Use Commas

Speaking and Listening
Understand Other Cultures

Materials
- *Sing with Me Big Book*
- Read Aloud Anthology
- Student Edition 370–373

Morning Warm~Up!

Today we will read about family birthday traditions.

When is your birthday?

Does your family have special birthday traditions?

QUESTION OF THE DAY Encourage children to sing "Family Tradition" from the *Sing with Me Big Book* as you gather. Write and read the message and discuss the question.

REVIEW QUESTION MARKS

- Ask children how many questions they see in the message.
- Have them offer their own questions about birthdays.

E L L

Extend Language Use the Day 4 instruction on ELL Poster 28 to extend and enrich language.

ELL Poster 28

Share Literature

CONNECT CONCEPTS

ACTIVATE PRIOR KNOWLEDGE Sing "Family Tradition" from the *Sing with Me Big Book.* Explain that today you will read several poems about families and traditions.

BUILD ORAL VOCABULARY Read the italicized stanza in "Ode to Family Photographs." Explain that **snapshot** is another name for *photograph.* Photographs are snapshots, or quick shots, of our lives. **Angle** in this poem means the point of view—the angles from which the pictures were taken. Then explain that if something is **brilliant,** it is shining brightly.

Read Aloud Anthology
Poetry Selections

REVIEW ORAL VOCABULARY After reading, review all the Amazing Words for the week. Have children take turns using them in sentences that tell about the concept for the week. Then talk about Amazing Words they learned in other weeks and connect them to the concept, as well. For example, ask:

- What is your favorite **annual holiday** or family celebration and why?
- Whom do you most like to **communicate** with at family parties?
- What sort of family **occasion** brings you the most **contentment** or **satisfaction**?

MONITOR LISTENING COMPREHENSION

- What do you think the poet means by *blackened* toast in "Happy Birthday, Mother Dearest"? (Possible response: The toast was burned.)
- Do you think the mother in "Happy Birthday, Mother Dearest" enjoyed her breakfast? (Possible response: Yes, even though it was weird and burned, her breakfast was made by a loving family.)
- Do you think Mama in "Ode to Family Photographs" is a good photographer? Explain. (Possible response: No, she takes pictures of people's feet, shows people with their eyes half-closed, and cuts off people's heads.)

OBJECTIVES

- Set purpose for listening.
- Build oral vocabulary.

Amazing Words to build oral vocabulary

	MONITOR PROGRESS
celebration custom tradition create inspect angle brilliant snapshot	**If...** children lack oral vocabulary experiences about the concept Traditions, **then...** use the Oral Vocabulary Routine. See p. DI·5 to teach *angle, brilliant,* and *snapshot.*

Connect Concepts To show their understanding of *snapshots* and *angles,* children can use a digital camera to take several *snapshots* of an object from different *angles.* Display the pictures on the computer and have children select the *angle* of the *snapshot* they like the best.

Spiral REVIEW

- Reviews contractions *'re, 've, 'd,* and irregular contractions.
- Reviews contractions *n't, 's, 'll, 'm.*
- Reviews high-frequency words *been, believe, caught, finally, today, tomorrow, whatever.*

Sentence Reading

REVIEW WORDS IN CONTEXT

READ DECODABLE AND HIGH-FREQUENCY WORDS IN CONTEXT Write these sentences. Call on individuals to read a sentence. Then randomly point to words and have children read them. To help you monitor word reading, high-frequency words are underlined and decodable words are circled.

Today we're going to the nature section of the shop.

I don't know whatever happened to my creature picture.

I'll finally get to hear the lecture about sculpture.

Tomorrow we'll see the action motion picture I've been waiting to see.

They'll make a mixture with the fish we've caught.

I can't believe the commotion at the station.

Monitor Progress	Word Reading
If... children are unable to read an underlined word,	**then...** read the word for them and spell it, having them echo you.
If... children are unable to read a circled word,	**then...** have them use the blending strategy they have learned for that word type.

ELL

Support Phonics For additional review, see the phonics activities in the ELL and Transition Handbook.

Spelling

PARTNER REVIEW Syllables *-tion, -ture*

READ AND WRITE Supply pairs of children with index cards on which the spelling words have been written. Have one child read a word while the other writes it. Then have children switch roles. Have them use the cards to check their spelling.

HOMEWORK Spelling Practice Book, p. 112

Group Time

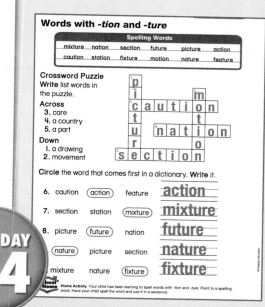

OBJECTIVE

● Spell words with syllables -tion, -ture.

Spelling Words

Syllables *-tion, -ture*

1.	mixture	7.	caution
2.	nation	8.	station
3.	section	9.	fixture
4.	future	10.	motion
5.	picture*	11.	nature
6.	action	12.	feature

Challenge Words

13.	furniture	15.	tuition
14.	adventure		

* Words from the Selection

Words with *-tion* and *-ture*

Spelling Words					
mixture	nation	section	future	picture	action
caution	station	fixture	motion	nature	feature

Crossword Puzzle
Write list words in the puzzle.
Across
3. care
4. a country
5. a part
Down
1. a drawing
2. movement

Circle the word that comes first in a dictionary. Write it.

6. caution (action) feature → **action**
7. section station (mixture) → **mixture**
8. picture (future) nation → **future**
(nature) picture section → **nature**
mixture nature (fixture) → **fixture**

Home Activity Your child has been learning to spell words with -tion and -ture. Point to a spelling word. Have your child spell the word and use it in a sentence.

▲ **Spelling Practice Book** p. 112

Group Time

On-Level	Strategic Intervention	Advanced
Read "Family Traditions." • Use pp. 370–373.	**Read** or listen to "Family Traditions." • Use the **Routine** on p. DI·40.	**Read** "Family Traditions." • Use the **Routine** on p. DI·41.

 Place English language learners in the groups that correspond to their reading abilities in English.

ⓘ Independent Activities

Fluency Reading Pair children to reread *A Birthday Basket for Tía.*

Journal Writing Write about your favorite birthday. Share writing.

Spelling Partner Review

Independent Reading See p. 350j for Reading/Library activities and suggestions.

Literacy Centers To provide listening opportunities, you may use the Listening Center on p. 350j. To extend social studies concepts, you may use the Social Studies Center on p. 350k.

Break into small groups after Spelling and before Fluency.

4

Reading Online

New Literacies: PearsonSuccessNet.com

Online Directories

Genre

- Online directories give links to Web sites about a topic you choose.
- You can use an online directory or a search engine to learn about a topic.

Text Features

- Directories list links to many topics. You may click on any link.
- Or you may type in a keyword and then click on the search button.
- Then you will get a list of links to Web sites about your topic.

Link to Social Studies

Interview members of your family about family traditions they remember celebrating.

For more practice

Take It to the Net

PearsonSuccessNet.com

370

Family Traditions: Birthdays

How can you find out more about birthdays? You can go to an Internet online directory. Here are some of the topics you might find listed there.

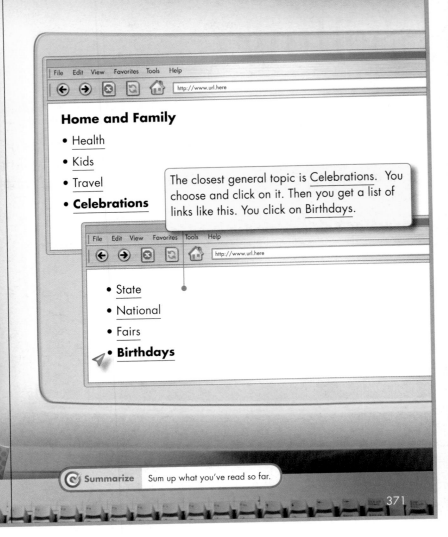

Home and Family
- Health
- Kids
- Travel
- **Celebrations**

The closest general topic is Celebrations. You choose and click on it. Then you get a list of links like this. You click on Birthdays.

- State
- National
- Fairs
- **Birthdays**

ⓒ **Summarize** Sum up what you've read so far.

371

Audio CD AudioText

OBJECTIVE

● Recognize text structure: nonfiction.

Read Social Studies in Reading

PREVIEW AND PREDICT Read the title. Have children preview the article. Encourage them to look at the art and Web sites listed. Ask children whether "Family Traditions: Birthdays" tells a story or provides information. The information in this article is about locating and using information on the Internet using electronic references. Have children read to learn how to search the Internet.

INFORMATIONAL TEXT Review that informational text is called nonfiction. Informational text often contains graphics and text features such as diagrams, maps, a table of contents, and an index. Point out that this article gives information about online directories that provide links to many topics.

VOCABULARY/HOMONYMS Review that some words are spelled and pronounced the same but have different meanings. Have children locate *links* on p. 370. What does *links* mean here—text or pictures that connect you to a new Web site or a golf course? Now have children locate *list* on p. 372. What does *list* mean—a "series of names, numbers, or items" or "tipping to one side"?

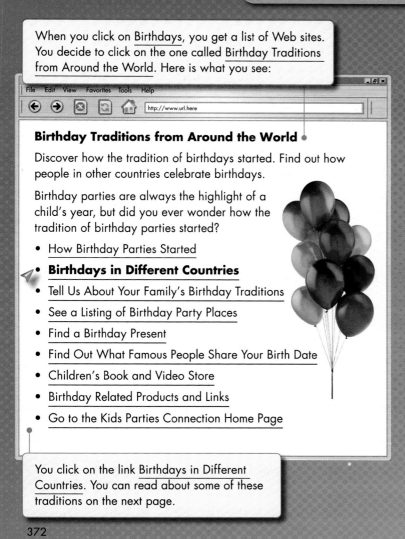

When you click on Birthdays, you get a list of Web sites. You decide to click on the one called Birthday Traditions from Around the World. Here is what you see:

Birthday Traditions from Around the World

Discover how the tradition of birthdays started. Find out how people in other countries celebrate birthdays.

Birthday parties are always the highlight of a child's year, but did you ever wonder how the tradition of birthday parties started?

- How Birthday Parties Started
- **Birthdays in Different Countries**
- Tell Us About Your Family's Birthday Traditions
- See a Listing of Birthday Party Places
- Find a Birthday Present
- Find Out What Famous People Share Your Birth Date
- Children's Book and Video Store
- Birthday Related Products and Links
- Go to the Kids Parties Connection Home Page

You click on the link Birthdays in Different Countries. You can read about some of these traditions on the next page.

372

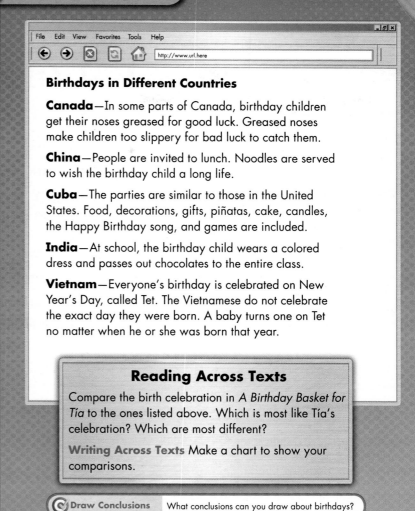

Birthdays in Different Countries

Canada—In some parts of Canada, birthday children get their noses greased for good luck. Greased noses make children too slippery for bad luck to catch them.

China—People are invited to lunch. Noodles are served to wish the birthday child a long life.

Cuba—The parties are similar to those in the United States. Food, decorations, gifts, piñatas, cake, candles, the Happy Birthday song, and games are included.

India—At school, the birthday child wears a colored dress and passes out chocolates to the entire class.

Vietnam—Everyone's birthday is celebrated on New Year's Day, called Tet. The Vietnamese do not celebrate the exact day they were born. A baby turns one on Tet no matter when he or she was born that year.

Reading Across Texts

Compare the birth celebration in *A Birthday Basket for Tía* to the ones listed above. Which is most like Tía's celebration? Which are most different?

Writing Across Texts Make a chart to show your comparisons.

Draw Conclusions What conclusions can you draw about birthdays?

373

BUILD CONCEPTS

Predict • Inferential

- **What might you find if you clicked on the link *Find Out What Famous People Share Your Birth Date?***
You might need to type in your birthday and then click to find out famous people that were born on the same day as you.

Supporting Details • Literal

- **Why do birthday children in Canada get their noses greased?**
for good luck

CONNECT TEXT TO TEXT

Discuss how birthdays are alike and different in the various countries. Help children identify the country that is most like Tía's celebration and the one that is most different.

Have children make a six-column chart. List Tía's Birthday, Canada, China, Cuba, India, and Vietnam as headings for the columns. Then help children list features of the celebrations under the appropriate headings, such as "greased nose" under Canada.

Activate Prior Knowledge Ask: How do you celebrate birthdays in your home country? Encourage children to share their birthday traditions with the class.

Birthday Basket for Tía **372–373**

OBJECTIVE

● Read aloud fluently with appropriate phrasing.

Options for Oral Reading

Use *A Birthday Basket for Tía* or one of the following Leveled Readers.

On-Level

Birthdays Around the World

Strategic Intervention

Very Special Birthdays

Advanced

Family Traditions and Celebrations

Assess Fluency English learners benefit from assisted reading, with modeling by the teacher or by a skilled classmate. When the English learner reads the passage aloud, the more proficient reader assists by providing feedback and encouragement.

Fluency

READ WITH APPROPRIATE PHRASING

MODEL READING WITH APPROPRIATE PHRASING Use *A Birthday Basket for Tía.*

- Point to the first sentence on p. 361. Remind children to read groups of words. When I come to a long sentence, I look for groups of words that belong together and should be read together, such as *in the teacup.* I try to read groups of words, not word-by-word.

- Ask children to follow along as you read the page with appropriate phrasing.

- Have children read the page after you. Encourage them to read groups of words, not word-by-word. Continue in the same way with pp. 362–363.

REREAD FOR FLUENCY

Choral Reading

ROUTINE

1 **Select a Passage** For *A Birthday Basket for Tía,* use pp. 364–367.

2 **Divide into Groups** Assign each group a part to read. For this story, alternate paragraphs. The first group reads the first paragraph. The second group reads the next paragraph and so on.

3 **Model** Have children track the print as you read.

4 **Read Together** Have children read along with you.

5 **Independent Readings** Have the groups read aloud without you. Monitor progress and provide feedback. For optimal fluency, children should reread three to four times.

Monitor Progress | **Check Fluency** WCPM

As children reread, monitor their progress toward their individual fluency goals. Current Goal: 90–100 words correct per minute. End-of-Year Goal: 90 words correct per minute.

If… children cannot read fluently at a rate of 90 words correct per minute,

then… make sure children practice with text at their independent level. Provide additional fluency practice, pairing nonfluent readers with fluent readers.

If… children already read at 90 words correct per minute,

then… they do not need to reread three to four times.

SUCCESS PREDICTOR

| **Day 1** Check Word Reading | **Day 2** Check Lesson Vocabulary/High-Frequency Words | **Day 3** Check Retelling | ▶ **Day 4 Check Fluency** | **Day 5** Assess Progress |

Writing Across the Curriculum

WRITE Math Story

DISCUSS Have children look at pp. 364–365 and discuss inviting children to a birthday party. Encourage them to use oral vocabulary, such as *celebration* and *tradition.*

SHARE THE PEN Have children participate in creating a math story. Draw 6 boys on one side of a table and 7 girls on the other side. Explain that the class will work together to write an illustrated math story. Review that a math story is a way to show information using a drawing and words. Tell children 6 boys and 7 girls have been invited to a party. Have children suggest sentences for a math story using these numbers. Invite individuals to help write sentences by discussing punctuation. Ask questions, such as the following:

- How does a sentence begin? (with a capital letter)
- What type of punctuation is written at the end of a statement? (period)
- What type of punctuation is at the end of a question? (question mark)

Continue having individuals contribute to writing the math story. Frequently reread the math story.

Words Correct Per Minute

SUCCESS PREDICTOR

DAILY FIX-IT

7. my aunt gave me a presint.

My aunt gave me a pres**e**nt.

8. i gave hir my piggy bank.

I gave h**e**r my piggy bank.

Using Commas

Mark the letter of the group of words or the date that uses commas correctly.

1. ⊗ A Littleton, CO 80120
   ○ B Littleton CO, 80120
   ○ C Littleton C,O 80120

2. ○ A November, 12 2007
   ○ B November 12 2007,
   ⊗ C November 12, 2007

3. ○ A Dear Aunt, Betty
   ○ B Dear, Aunt Betty
   ⊗ C Dear Aunt Betty,

4. ○ A ski sled, and skate
   ⊗ B ski, sled, and skate
   ○ C ski, sled and skate,

5. ⊗ A boots, hat, and mittens
   ○ B boots, hat and mittens,
   ○ C boots hat, and mittens

6. ○ A Your niece Monica,
   ⊗ B Your niece, Monica
   ○ C Your, niece Monica

Home Activity Your child prepared for taking tests on using commas. Ask your child to name three objects in the room. Have your child write a sentence using the objects. For example, *I see a chair, a picture, and a rug.*

▲ **Grammar and Writing Practice Book** p. 111

Grammar

REVIEW Using Commas

DEFINE COMMAS

- What punctuation do I use after the greeting and closing in a letter? **(comma)**
- Why do I write commas in a sentence that lists several items? **(to separate the items)**

PRACTICE

USE COMMAS Write *I opened a DVD a book a game and a toy on my birthday. Kara Ally Desi Sierra Madison and Nikki came to my party. We ate chicken strips apples cupcakes and ice cream.* Have individuals supply commas to separate the items and names in each sentence.

I opened a DVD, a book, a game, and a toy on my birthday.

Kara, Ally, Desi, Sierra, Madison, and Nikki came to my party.

We ate chicken strips, apples, cupcakes, and ice cream.

Speaking and Listening

UNDERSTAND OTHER CULTURES

DEMONSTRATE SPEAKING AND LISTENING Remind children of appropriate listening and speaking behaviors for a discussion. Then ask them to think about these behaviors as you discuss traditions and customs of various cultures.

Speakers	Listeners
• Face the group.	• Sit quietly.
• Speak loudly enough to be heard.	• Face the speaker.
• Speak clearly.	• Listen to what the speaker says.

CULTURE AND CUSTOMS Ask children if they have customs or traditions that reflect their cultural background. Allow each child to tell a story about a family tradition. Encourage children to demonstrate appropriate speaking and listening behaviors.

Wrap Up Your Day!

✓ **MAKE CONNECTIONS: TEXT TO SELF** The online directory explains birthday traditions in many countries. Does your family have a birthday tradition? Is it similar to one of the traditions listed in the online directory? Call on individuals to share traditions.

LET'S TALK ABOUT IT Discuss the birthday traditions described in the online directory and why family celebrations are special. Encourage children to add additional information to the birthday party web created earlier in the week.

PREVIEW Day 5

Remind children that they read about birthday celebrations around the world. Tell them that tomorrow they will hear about another special birthday celebration.

Day 5
AT A GLANCE

Share Literature
Poetry Selections

Phonics and Spelling

Review Syllables *-tion, -ture*

Lesson Vocabulary
present	aunt	basket
collects	bank	favorite

Monitor Progress
Spelling Test: Words with
Syllables *-tion, -ture*

Group Time < Differentiated Assessment

Writing and Grammar
Trait: Organization/Paragraphs
Commas

Research and Study Skills
Technology: Online Directories

Materials

- *Sing with Me Big Book*
- *Read Aloud Anthology*
- Reproducible Pages TE 374f–374g
- Student Edition 374–375

Morning Warm~Up!

This week we read about
birthday traditions and customs.
Celebrations create lasting memories.
Why are family celebrations special?

QUESTION OF THE DAY Encourage children to sing "Family Tradition" from the *Sing with Me Big Book* as you gather. Write and read the message and discuss the question.

REVIEW ORAL VOCABULARY Have children find a word in the message that

- is a synonym for *tradition*
- tells what celebrations create

Assess Vocabulary Use the Day 5 instruction on ELL Poster 28 to monitor children's progress with oral vocabulary.

ELL Poster 28

Share Literature

LISTEN AND RESPOND

USE PRIOR KNOWLEDGE Review that yesterday the class listened to the poem "Happy Birthday, Mother Dearest" to find out what the mother was served for breakfast. Suggest that today the class listen to "Seeing All My Family" to find out how the poet describes each of her family members.

MONITOR LISTENING COMPREHENSION

- How does the poet describe her Grandma? (Grandma is a sparkler.)

- The poet describes her dad as a banger firework. Why?
(He always talks too loud.)

- Do you think the poet described her family well? Why or why not?
(Possible response: Yes, she used fireworks names to describe each of their personalities.)

- What is the author's viewpoint? Why do you think the poet of "Seeing All My Family" compares her family members to different kinds of fireworks? (Possible response: Each member is special in a different way, and together they are as exciting to the poet as a brilliant fireworks show.)

Read Aloud Anthology
Poetry Selections

BUILD ORAL VOCABULARY

GENERATE DISCUSSION Recall how the poet in "Seeing All My Family" describes her family members as different kinds of fireworks. Have children discuss what sorts of things they could compare their family members to, such as foods, flowers, or animals. Have children use some of this week's Amazing Words as they share their ideas.

Monitor Progress | **Check Oral Vocabulary**

Remind children of the unit concept—Traditions. Ask them to tell you about the concept using some of this week's Amazing Words: *celebration, custom, tradition, create, inspect, angle, brilliant,* and *snapshot.*

If... children have difficulty using the Amazing Words,

then... ask more questions about the Read Aloud selection or the concept using the Amazing Words. Note which questions children can respond to. Reteach unknown words using the Oral Vocabulary routine on p. DI·1.

SUCCESS PREDICTOR

Amazing Words to build oral vocabulary

celebration	inspect
custom	angle
tradition	brilliant
create	snapshot

ELL

Extend Language Tell children that homonyms look and sound the same but have different meanings. Demonstrate this by writing the word *can.* Show the children a *can* and then tell them they *can* write their name. The word *can* has multiple meanings. *Can* means "metal container," and "ability to do something."

Oral Vocabulary

SUCCESS PREDICTOR

- Review syllables *-tion, -ture*.
- Review lesson vocabulary.

Syllables *-tion, -ture*

REVIEW

IDENTIFY WORDS WITH SYLLABLES *-tion, -ture* Write these sentences. Have children read each one aloud. Call on individuals to name and underline the words with syllables *-tion* and *-ture*.

Use <u>caution</u> when you set the <u>sculpture</u> beside the <u>furniture</u>.

A <u>vulture</u> is a <u>creature</u> that is sometimes in <u>motion</u>.

There was a lot of <u>action</u> at the <u>celebration</u>!

We show lots of <u>affection</u> in our <u>culture</u>.

Lesson Vocabulary

REVIEW

MEANING CLUES Write the following clues for children. Have children write a review word from p. 352 for each clue. Then read clues and answers together.

Tía is the Spanish word for _____. (aunt)

You can keep money in a _____. (bank)

The one you like best is your _____. (favorite)

Put your trash in the _____. (basket)

Another word for a gift is a _____. (present)

The opposite of gives away is _____. (collects)

Access Content For additional practice with lesson vocabulary, use the vocabulary strategies and word cards in the ELL Teaching Guide, pp. 192–193.

SPELLING TEST Syllables *-tion, -ture*

DICTATION SENTENCES Use these sentences to assess this week's spelling words.

1. The <u>nation</u> watched the first moon landing.
2. You may have a <u>section</u> of my book.
3. Nobody knows what will happen in the <u>future</u>.
4. We can make a meat and bean <u>mixture</u> for lunch.
5. Use <u>caution</u> when you are riding your bike.
6. I don't like the fast <u>motion</u> of that spinning ride.
7. The <u>feature</u> movie comes on in five minutes.
8. Uncle Bob works at the fire <u>station</u>.
9. Look at the <u>picture</u> I took of you.
10. It is fun to sit and look at <u>nature</u>.
11. I like to play sports with lots of <u>action</u>.
12. Dad replaced the old light <u>fixture</u>.

CHALLENGE WORDS

13. Mom painted the old <u>furniture</u>.
14. This summer we had an <u>adventure</u>.
15. Sam saves his money for <u>tuition</u>.

ASSESS

● Spell words with syllables *-tion, -ture*.

Spelling Words

Syllables *-tion, -ture*

1. mixture   7. caution
2. nation   8. station
3. section   9. fixture
4. future   10. motion
5. picture*   11. nature
6. action   12. feature

Challenge Words

13. furniture 15. tuition
14. adventure

* Words from the Selection

Group Time

On-Level

Read Set B Sentences and the Story.

• Use pp. 374e–374g.

Strategic Intervention

Read Set A Sentences.

• Use pp. 374e–374g.

• Use the **Routine** on p. DI·42.

Advanced

Read Set C Sentences.

• Use pp. 374e–374g.

• Use the **Routine** on p. DI·43.

ELL Place English language learners in the groups that correspond to their reading abilities in English.

DAY 5

(i) Independent Activities

Fluency Reading Children reread selections at their independent level.

Journal Writing Write about a tradition in your family.

Independent Reading See p. 350j for Reading/Library activities and suggestions.

Literacy Centers You may use the Technology Center on p. 350k to support this week's concepts and reading.

Practice Book 2.2 Online Directories, p. 130

Break into small groups after Spelling and before Grammar and Writing.

ASSESS

- Decode syllables -*tion*, -*ture.*
- Read lesson vocabulary words.
- Read aloud with appropriate speed and accuracy.
- Draw conclusions.
- Retell a story.

Differentiated Assessment

On-Level
Set B

Strategic Intervention
Set A

Advanced
Set C

Fluency Assessment Plan

☑ Week 1 assess Advanced students.

☑ Week 2 assess Strategic Intervention students.

☑ **This week assess On-Level students.**

☐ Week 4 assess Strategic Intervention students.

☐ Week 5 assess any students you have not yet checked during this unit.

Set individual fluency goals for children to enable them to reach the end-of-year goal.

- Current Goal: 90–100 wcpm
- End-of-Year Goal: 90 wcpm
- **ELL** Oral fluency depends not only on reading without halting but also on word recognition. After children read passages aloud for assessment, help them recognize unfamiliar English words and their meanings. Focus on each child's progress.

SENTENCE READING

ASSESS SYLLABLES -*tion*, -*ture* AND LESSON VOCABULARY WORDS Use one of the reproducible lists on p. 374f to assess children's ability to read words with syllables -*tion*, -*ture* and lesson vocabulary words. Call on individuals to read two sentences aloud. Have each child in the group read different sentences. Start over with sentence one if necessary.

RECORD SCORES Use the Sentence Reading Chart for this unit on p. WA19.

Monitor Progress	Syllables -*tion*, -*ture*
If... children have trouble reading syllables -*tion*, -*ture*,	**then...** use the Reteach Lessons on p. DI·66.
Lesson Vocabulary Words	
If... children cannot read a lesson vocabulary word,	**then...** mark the missed words on a lesson vocabulary word list and send the list home for additional word reading practice, or have the child practice with a fluent reader.

FLUENCY AND COMPREHENSION

ASSESS FLUENCY Take a one-minute sample of children's oral reading. See Monitoring Fluency, p. WA17. Have children read "Tyler's Pictures," the on-level fluency passage on p. 374g.

RECORD SCORES Record the number of words read correctly in one minute on the child's Fluency Progress Chart.

ASSESS COMPREHENSION Have the child read to the end of the passage. (If the child had difficulty with the passage, you may read it aloud.) Ask the child to draw conclusions about story events and have the child retell the passage. Use the Retelling Rubric on p. 368–369 to evaluate the child's retelling.

Monitor Progress	Fluency
If... a child does not achieve the fluency goal on the timed reading,	**then...** copy the passage and send it home with the child for additional fluency practice, or have the child practice with a fluent reader.
Draw Conclusions	
If... a child cannot draw conclusions,	**then...** use the Reteach Lesson on p. DI·66.

READ THE SENTENCES

Set A

1. I took a picture of my aunt at the station.
2. A culture in the nation does basket weaving.
3. One section of the bank features paintings.
4. Use caution when moving your favorite fixture.
5. Jordan collects plastic action creatures.
6. Ella gave me a mixture of lotions for a present.

Set B

1. The portions were a mixture of her favorite foods.
2. My aunt has a section of land that is a pasture.
3. Jill collects stamps from nations where she vacations.
4. The present was a picture of a calm nature scene.
5. In the future, Ned will move the sculpture in a basket.
6. The bank was full of motion on election day.

Set C

1. We had a celebration near the train station before my aunt left on her trip.
2. The picture did not capture the beauty of my favorite waterfall.
3. There is only a fraction of my tuition in the bank.
4. I had a notion that the adventure trip might be my birthday present.
5. Luke's arm has a fracture, and he collects signatures on the cast.
6. The basket held a collection of dollhouse furniture.

Monitor Progress   Syllables *-tion, -ture*
Lesson Vocabulary Words

374f

SUCCESS PREDICTOR

Tyler's Pictures

Tyler likes to take pictures. His mother lets him   9
use her new camera if he is very careful. The   19
camera lets him look at the pictures right after he   29
takes them. If Tyler does not like a photo, he can   40
remove it.   42

Tyler enjoys taking nature pictures of all   49
creatures, large or small. Sometimes he can   56
capture the moment of an animal in motion. These   65
action pictures are great. Once he got a picture of   75
a bird with its wings out.   81

Of course, he must use caution. He never gets   90
too close to an animal that may sting or bite him.   101
Once he thought he was taking a picture of some   111
ladybugs. When he saw the photo, there was a   120
snake curled up under a plant. That's one reason   129
he must be careful.   133

Taking photos is what Tyler likes to do. He   142
keeps a collection of his pictures in a book. Now   152
and then he looks at them and thinks about his   162
future.   163

See also Assessment Handbook, p. 361 •

Monitor Progress | Fluency Passage

SUCCESS PREDICTOR

Write Now
Writing and Grammar

Report

Prompt

A Birthday Basket for Tía tells about a special family event.
Think about a special event your family has had.
Now write a report telling about that event.

Student Model

Report is <u>organized</u> by beginning with the main idea.

Writer follows with details that tell more.

Writer saves the best fact for last.

My family had a reunion on Sunday, June 29. We met in Kent, Ohio. I met cousins I had never met before! We played softball, volleyball, and soccer. Then we had a picnic dinner. The best part was planning a reunion for next year.

374

Writer's Checklist

- **Focus** Do all sentences tell about a special family event?
- **Organization** Is the main idea stated first?
- **Support** Do the details tell more about the main idea?
- **Conventions** Are commas used correctly?

Grammar

Using Commas

Commas are used in addresses: San Antonio, TX 78250

Commas are used in dates: May 2, 1939

Commas are used to begin and end a letter.
  Dear Cecilia,   Yours truly,

Commas are used to separate three or more things in a sentence: Walk, skip, or run.

Read the report again. Write a quick note to your teacher telling her the date of the reunion. Begin and end the note properly. Use commas where they are needed.

375

Writing and Grammar

LOOK AT THE PROMPT Read p. 374 aloud. Have children select and discuss key words or phrases in the prompt. *(a special event your family has had, report, telling about that event)*

STRATEGIES TO DEVELOP ORGANIZATION/PARAGRAPHS Have children

- visualize the family event, write a list of details about it, and choose the details that best describe the event.
- first, write a main idea sentence that identifies their family event and then arrange detail sentences in an order that makes sense.
- underline the main idea in their first sentence, circle each detail that tells more about the main idea, and see if there are details that should be deleted.

See Scoring Rubric on p. WA11. Rubric 4 3 2 1

HINTS FOR BETTER WRITING Read p. 375 aloud. Use the checklist to help children revise their reports. Discuss the grammar lesson. (Answers: Responses will vary. The notes should have a salutation and a closing, with a comma after each. Make sure commas are used correctly elsewhere in their notes.)

DAILY FIX-IT

9. that was my favurite present.
   <u>T</u>hat was my fav<u>o</u>rite present.

10. i use a basket to collekt.
    <u>I</u> use a basket to colle<u>c</u>t.

Using Commas

Add commas where they are needed.

1. My seventh birthday party was on August 12, 2007.

2. I got games, puzzles, and some books.

3. We had cake, lemonade, and ice cream.

4. My sister will have a birthday on Thursday, November 29.

Add commas where they are needed.

5. 210 Juniper Street
    Pasadena, CA 91105

6. Mrs. Rose Yung
    712 Redwood Lane
    Portland, OR 97224

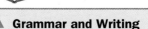

▲ **Grammar and Writing Practice Book** p. 112

- Use technology: online directories.

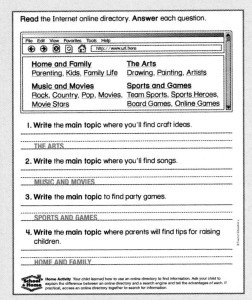

Practice Book 2.2 p. 130, Online Directories

Research/Study Skills

TEACH/MODEL Online Directories

MODEL USING AN ONLINE DIRECTORY Tell children that the Internet offers lots of information. Explain that typing your problem or question into an online directory often leads to lists of possible links to find that information. Wording your search correctly will help you locate the information more quickly.

Model how to use an online directory.

Think Aloud **MODEL** I can use an online directory to find the information I need to make my own piñata. First I type in *piñata*. I don't want to buy a piñata, but I want to make my own. I find a link that offers directions to make my own piñata, using a balloon, newspapers, and glue. I click on the link and find the directions.

FIND INFORMATION Have partners locate links for making cascarones and recipes for bizcochos.

PRACTICE

DEMONSTRATE USING AN ONLINE DIRECTORY Have partners locate an online directory that will help them make a chocolate birthday cake. Have them keyboard *birthday cake recipes* to find a list of links.

Access Content Guide children through the steps of finding information on the computer. Encourage children to find links in their home language as well as English.

Wrap Up Your Week!

LET'S TALK ABOUT Traditions

QUESTION OF THE WEEK Recall this week's question.

- Why are family celebrations special?

Display the Family Celebrations web started on Day 1. Review the web. Identify other ways families celebrate.

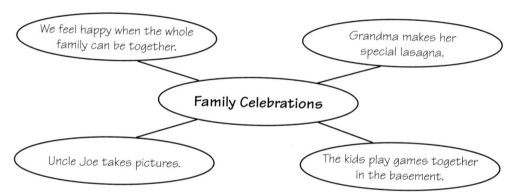

We feel happy when the whole family can be together.

Grandma makes her special lasagna.

Family Celebrations

Uncle Joe takes pictures.

The kids play games together in the basement.

CONNECT Use questions such as these to prompt a discussion.

- At family gatherings, there are often people of all ages. What do the children do at your celebrations? What do the grown-ups do?

- Cecilia, in *A Birthday Basket for Tía*, filled a piñata with candy. A piñata is a custom at some birthday parties. Would you like to go to a party that has a piñata? Why?

- Tía, the character in *A Birthday Basket for Tía,* is turning 90. Do you know anyone who is 90 years old? How would you celebrate that?

Build Background Use ELL Poster 29 to support the Preview activity.

You've learned	You've learned
008 Amazing Words **this week!**	**225** Amazing Words **so far this year!**

PREVIEW Tell children that next week they will read about more traditions.

PREVIEW Next Week

Assessment Checkpoints *for the Week*

Selection Assessment

Use pp. 109–112 of Selection Tests to check:

 Selection Understanding

  Comprehension Skill *Draw Conclusions*

Selection Vocabulary
aunt
bank
basket
collects
favorite
present

Leveled Assessment

- On-Level
- Strategic Intervention
- Advanced

Use pp. 163–168 of Fresh Reads for Differentiated Test Practice to check:

 Comprehension Skill *Draw Conclusions*

 REVIEW **Comprehension Skill** *Cause and Effect*

 Fluency *Words Correct Per Minute*

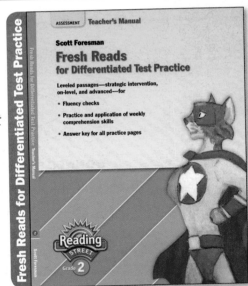

Managing Assessment

Use Assessment Handbook for:

 Weekly Assessment Blackline Masters for Monitoring Progress

 Observation Checklists

 Record-Keeping Forms

 Portfolio Assessment

Illinois

Planning Guide for Performance Descriptors

Cowboys

Reading Street Teacher's Edition pages	Grade 2 English Language Arts Performance Descriptors
Oral Language Build Concepts: 376l, 378a, 402a, 404a, 406a Share Literature: 376m, 378b, 402b, 404b, 406b	**1A.Stage B.7.** Use a variety of resources (e.g., context, previous experiences, dictionaries, glossaries, computer resources, ask others) to determine and clarify meanings of unfamiliar words. **1B.Stage B.1.** Read fiction and non-fiction materials for specific purposes.
Word Work **Phonics** Suffixes *-ness, -less*: 376n–376q, 378c–378d, 402c–402d, 404c–404d, 406c–406f **Spelling:** 376q, 378d, 402d, 404d, 406d	**1A.Stage B.4.** Use a variety of decoding strategies (e.g., phonics, word patterns, structural analysis, context clues) to recognize new words when reading age-appropriate material. **3A.Stage B.5.** Use correct spelling of high frequency words.
Reading **Comprehension** Cause and Effect: 376r–377, 380–401a, 402g, 404e–405, 406e Graphic Organizer: 376r–377, 380–401a, 402g **Vocabulary** Word Structure: 378–379 Time Words: 402e, 404e Compound Words: 378–379, 406b **Fluency** Paired Reading: 376q, 401a, 405a Choral Reading: 402f **Self-Selected Reading:** LR28–36, TR16–17 **Literature** Genre—Narrative Nonfiction: 380–381 Reader Response: 402g–402h	**1C.Stage B.4.** Use information in text or illustrations to generate questions about the cause of a specific effect. **1C.Stage B.14.** Select books appropriate to reading levels. **2B.Stage B.1.** Investigate self-selected/teacher-selected literature (e.g., picture books, nursery rhymes, fairy tales, poems, legends) from a variety of cultures. **3B.Stage B.1.** Use appropriate prewriting strategies (e.g., drawing, brainstorming, idea mapping, graphic organizers) to generate and organize ideas with teacher assistance. **5A.Stage B.4.** Use aids (e.g., KWL, webs, graphic organizers, technology) to locate and present information. **5C.Stage B.8.** Develop ideas by using details from pictures, diagrams, maps, and other graphic organizers.
Language Arts **Writing** Ad, Math Story, Respond to Literature, Labeled Picture: 377a, 401b, 402g, 405b, 406–407 **Six-Trait Writing** Sentences: 403a, 406–407 **Grammar, Usage, and Mechanics** Commas in Compound Sentences: 377b, 401c, 403b, 405c, 406–407 **Speaking/Listening** Listen to a Description: 405d **Research/Study** Thesaurus: 407a	**1A.Stage B.7.** Use a variety of resources (e.g., context, previous experiences, dictionaries, glossaries, computer resources, ask others) to determine and clarify meanings of unfamiliar words. **1C.Stage B.1.** Respond to analytical and interpretive questions based on information in text. **3B.Stage B.2.** Compose a focused story using picture(s) and/or basic text. **5A.Stage B.5.** Recognize that information is available through an organizational system (e.g., library, media center, classroom resources, available technology).
Unit Skills **Writing** Research Report: WA2–9 **Project/Wrap-Up:** 434–435	**3C.Stage B.4.** Experiment with different forms of writing (e.g., song, poetry, short fiction, recipes, diary, journal, directions). **5C.Stage B.5.** Create a report of ideas (e.g., drawing, using available technology, writing a story, letter, report).

This Week's Leveled Readers

Below-Level

1C.Stage B.4. Use information in text or illustrations to generate questions about the cause of a specific effect.

2A.Stage B.4. Identify the topic or main idea (theme).

Fiction

On-Level

1C.Stage B.4. Use information in text or illustrations to generate questions about the cause of a specific effect.

2A.Stage B.5. Distinguish between "make believe" and realistic narrative.

Fiction

Advanced

1C.Stage B.4. Use information in text or illustrations to generate questions about the cause of a specific effect.

1C.Stage B.8. Compare a broad range of books that have the same theme and topic.

Fiction

Content-Area Illinois Performance Descriptors in This Lesson

Social Studies

16C.Stage B.2. Describe how people made a living in the past.

16D.Stage B.5. List examples of past traditions found within the local community.

16D.Stage B.6. Interpret stories and folktales from the past to show various customs from groups of people in the past and the influence these customs had on their society.

17C.Stage B.2. Locate pictures showing ways that humans use the natural environment.

Math

6A.Stage B.2. Extend initial understanding of place value and the base-ten number system using multiple models.

6A.Stage B.4. Use cardinal and ordinal numbers appropriately.

7A.Stage B.2. Measure objects using standard units.

9A.Stage B.2. Describe and interpret direction and distance in navigating space, and apply concepts of direction and distance (e.g., nearer/farther).

Illinois!

A FAMOUS ILLINOISAN
Louis Sullivan

Louis Sullivan (1856–1924) was an architect and leader in the Chicago school of architecture. He believed that a structure's function involved more than simply meeting a practical need. Sullivan made the phrase "form follows function" popular. His first original design was the Chicago Auditorium Building. Architect Frank Lloyd Wright worked for Sullivan for six years.

Children can . . .
Research the Auditorium Building and draw a picture of how it might have looked in 1889 when it was first designed by Louis Sullivan.

A SPECIAL ILLINOIS PLACE
Chicago River

The Chicago River once flowed into Lake Michigan in the northeastern part of the state. A large storm in 1885 caused the river to pollute the lake, so workers built a canal to reverse the river's flow. The Chicago River now flows into the Illinois Waterway, which consists of the Chicago Sanitary and Ship Canal, the Des Plaines River, the Illinois River, and the Mississippi River.

Children can . . .
Write a few sentences about how it feels to be in a dirty or clean environment. Have them draw people's reactions to the Chicago River before and after engineers reversed its flow.

ILLINOIS FUN FACTS
Did You Know?

• Most of the land in Illinois is flat prairie. There are some plains in the western, northern, and southern parts of the state.

• The Illinois and Michigan Canal connected the Chicago and Illinois Rivers in 1848.

• Illinois is home to several types of flowers and trees, including walnut, cypress, white pine, and tamarack trees.

Children can . . .
Learn about the types of flowers and trees in their home state and make trading cards about them. Have children draw a picture of a plant on one side and write information about it on the other.

Unit 6
Traditions

CONCEPT QUESTION

How are traditions and celebrations important to our lives?

Week 1
Why are sports important in our country?

Week 2
What does our flag mean?

Week 3
Why are family celebrations special?

Week 4
Why should we learn about cowboys?

Week 5
What are some different ways that people celebrate?

CONNECT THE CONCEPT

▶ **Build Background**

buckaroo	lariat	occupation
climate	legend	rawhide
drover	livestock	

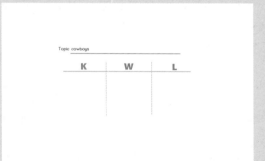

Topic cowboys

K	W	L

▶ **Social Studies Content**
American West, Cowboys, U.S. Growth, Transportation, Geography

▶ **Writing**
An Advertisement

Preview Your Week

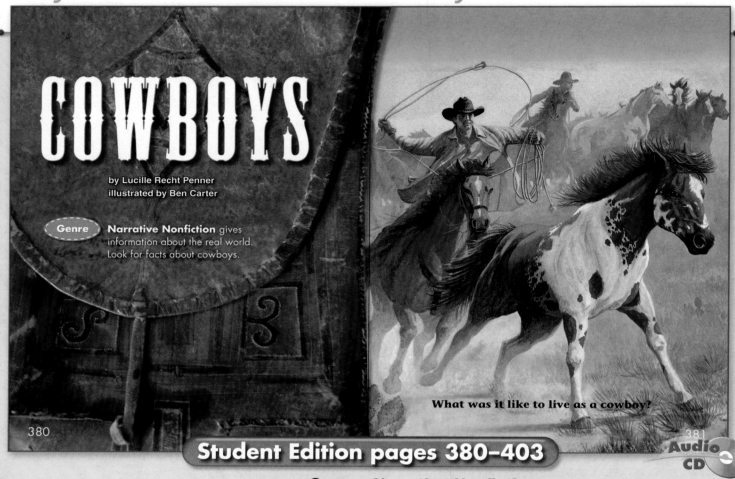

Student Edition pages 380–403

Genre	Narrative Nonfiction
Phonics	Suffixes *-ness, -less*
Vocabulary Strategy	Word Structure
Comprehension Skill	Cause and Effect
Comprehension Strategy	Graphic Organizer

Paired Selection

Reading Across Texts
Compare Information

Genre
Picture Encyclopedia

Text Features
Photographs
Captions

Social Studies in Reading

Picture Encyclopedia

- Picture encyclopedias provide information on many topics.
- There are many photos or pictures with captions.
- A reader can read the captions in any order.

Text Features
- In this article, the picture shows what a cowboy wears.
- The captions explain more about each part of a cowboy's outfit.

Link to Social Studies
Use the library or the Internet to find out more about cowboy equipment. Share your findings with the class.

COWBOY GEAR
from *The Cowboy's Handbook*
★ by Tod Cody ★

A cowboy's clothes and equipment had to be hard-wearing. There was no room for luggage on the trail drive, and most cowboys wore the same thing for months. Mud-caked and smelly, these clothes were often burned at the end of the journey.

READY TO HIT THE TRAIL!
What to Wear When You're Riding the Range

HAT
You can use it to signal to other cowboys, beat trail dust off your clothes, and hold food for your horse. A true cowboy wears his hat when he's sleeping.

PANTS
Cowboys originally refused to wear jeans because they were worn by miners and farm laborers. Pants (trousers) made of thick woolen material are more comfortable to wear on horseback.

BOOTS
The pointed toes and high heels are designed for riding, not for walking. That's why cowboys in the movies walk the way they do!

BANDANNA
Soak it in water, roll it up into a wad, and place it under your hat to keep cool during a hot spell. You can also use it to filter muddy water and blindfold a "spooked" horse.

CHAPS
These thick leather leg coverings will protect your legs from cow horns, rope burns, scrapes, and scratches. They also give a better grip to the saddle.

Reading Across Texts
What different information did each selection give about hats, bandannas, chaps, and boots?

Writing Across Texts
Write a paragraph explaining which piece of gear you think cowboys needed most.

Cause and Effect What effect do boots have on a cowboy's walk?

Student Edition pages 404–405

Read It
ONLINE
PearsonSuccessNet.com
• Student Edition
• Leveled Readers
• Decodable Reader

Integrate Social Studies Standards

• American West
• Cowboys
• U.S. Growth
• Transportation
• Geography

Leveled Readers

○ **Skill** Cause and Effect
○ **Strategy** Graphic Organizer
Lesson Vocabulary

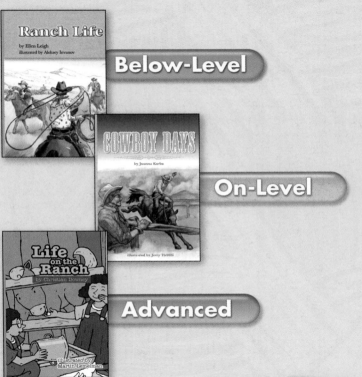

Below-Level

On-Level

Advanced

√ Read

Cowboys pp. 380–403

"Cowboy Gear" pp. 404–405

√ Read
Leveled Readers

Below-Level **On-Level** **Advanced**

• Support Concepts • Develop Concepts • Extend Concepts
• Social Studies Extension Activity

√ Read
ELL Reader

ELL Reader

What Does a Cowboy Do?

· Concept Vocabulary
· Text Support
· Language Enrichment

by Jesse Blackwell

√ Build Concept Vocabulary
Traditions, p. 376m

√ Teach Social Studies Concepts
Ranching, p. 398–399

√ Explore Social Studies Center
Compare Lists, p. 376k

Decodable Reader

Apply Phonics

· *Sandy and Randy*

Decodable Reader 29
Sandy and Randy
Written by Liz Hornby
Illustrated by Vince DeFrito

Weekly Plan

My Lesson Planner
ONLINE
PearsonSuccessNet.com

READING

90–120 minutes

TARGET SKILLS OF THE WEEK

- **Phonics**
  Suffixes *-ness, -less*

- **Comprehension Skill**
  Cause and Effect

- **Comprehension Strategy**
  Graphic Organizers

DAY 1   PAGES 376l–377b

Oral Language

QUESTION OF THE WEEK, 376l
Why should we learn about cowboys?

Oral Vocabulary/Share Literature, 376m
Sing with Me Big Book, Song 29
Amazing Words *climate, livestock, occupation*

Word Work

Phonics, 376n–376o
  Introduce Suffixes *-ness, -less* **T**

Spelling, 376p
Pretest

Comprehension/Vocabulary/Fluency

Read Decodable Reader 29

Grouping Options 376f–376g

Review High-Frequency Words
Check Comprehension
Reread for Fluency

Comprehension Skill/Strategy Lesson, 376r–377
  Cause and Effect **T**
  Graphic Organizers

DAY 2   PAGES 378a–401c

Oral Language

QUESTION OF THE DAY, 378a
How would you like to be a cowboy and ride a horse?

Oral Vocabulary/Share Literature, 378b
Read Aloud Anthology "B Is for Buckaroo"
Amazing Words *buckaroo, drover*

Word Work

Phonics, 378c–378d
  Review Suffixes *-ness, -less* **T**

Spelling, 378d
Dictation

Comprehension/Vocabulary/Fluency

Build Background, 378e
Cowboys

Lesson Vocabulary, 378f
Introduce *campfire, cattle, cowboy, galloped, herd, railroad, trails* **T**

Vocabulary Strategy Lesson, 378–379a
  Word Structure **T**

Read *Cowboys,* 380–401a

Grouping Options
376f–376g

  Cause and Effect **T**
  Graphic Organizers
  REVIEW Fact and Opinion **T**
Reread for Fluency

LANGUAGE ARTS

20–30 minutes

Trait of the Week

Sentences

Shared Writing, 377a
Ad

Grammar, 377b
Introduce Commas in Compound Sentences **T**

Interactive Writing, 401b
Math Story

Grammar, 401c
Practice Commas in Compound Sentences **T**

DAILY JOURNAL WRITING

Day 1 *Write about occupations.*

Day 2 *Write how you feel about horses.*

DAILY SOCIAL STUDIES CONNECTIONS

Day 1 Cowboys Concept Chart, 376m

Day 2 Time for Social Studies: Ranching, 398–399

DAILY SUCCESS PREDICTORS

for Adequate Yearly Progress

Monitor Progress and Corrective Feedback

Phonics
Check Word Reading, *376o*
Spiral **REVIEW** Phonics

Fluency
Check Lesson Vocabulary, *378f*
Spiral **REVIEW** High-Frequency Words

Grouping Options for Differentiated Instruction
Turn the page for the small group lesson plan.

DAY 3   PAGES 402a–403b

Oral Language

QUESTION OF THE DAY, 402a
Which letter is your favorite in this story?

Oral Vocabulary/Share Literature, 402b
Read Aloud Anthology "B Is for Buckaroo"
Amazing Word *lariat*

Word Work

Phonics, 402c
REVIEW Syllables *-tion, -ture* **T**

Lesson Vocabulary, 402d
Practice *campfire, cattle, cowboy, galloped, herd, railroad, trails* **T**

Spelling, 402d
Practice

Comprehension/Vocabulary/Fluency

Vocabulary, 402e
Time Words

Read *Cowboys,* 380–403

Grouping Options
376f–376g

Fluency, 402f
Read with Accuracy and Appropriate Pace

Reader Response, 402g

Trait of the Week, 403a
Introduce Sentences

Grammar, 403b
Write with Commas in Compound Sentences **T**

Day 3   *Write about a day on the trail.*

Day 3   Cowboys Concept Chart, 403b

DAY 4   PAGES 404a–405d

Oral Language

QUESTION OF THE DAY, 404a
Do cowboys have special items or clothes to make their job easier?

Oral Vocabulary/Share Literature, 404b
Read Aloud Anthology "Cowboy: An Album"
Amazing Words *legend, rawhide*

Word Work

Phonics, 404c
REVIEW Sentence Reading **T**

Spelling, 404d
Partner Review

Comprehension/Vocabulary/Fluency

Read "Cowboy Gear," 404–405
Leveled Readers

Grouping Options
376f–376g

Time Words
Reading Across Texts

Fluency, 405a
Read with Accuracy and Appropriate Pace

Writing Across the Curriculum, 405b
Labeled Picture

Grammar, 405c
Review Commas in Compound Sentences **T**

Speaking and Listening, 405d
Listen to a Description

Day 4   *List animals that live in your climate.*

Day 4   Social Studies Center: Compare Lists, 376k

DAY 5   PAGES 406a–407b

Oral Language

QUESTION OF THE DAY, 406a
Why should we learn about cowboys?

Oral Vocabulary/Share Literature, 406b
Read Aloud Anthology "Cowboy: An Album"
Amazing Words Review

Word Work

Phonics, 406c
Review Suffixes *-ness, -less* **T**

Lesson Vocabulary, 406c
Review *campfire, cattle, cowboy, galloped, herd, railroad, trails* **T**

Spelling, 406d
Test

Comprehension/Vocabulary/Fluency

Read Leveled Readers

Grouping Options 376f–376g

Monitor Progress, 406e–406g
Read the Sentences
Read the Story

Writing and Grammar, 406–407
Develop Sentences
Use Commas in Compound Sentences **T**

Research/Study Skills, 407a
Thesaurus

Day 5   *Write about cowboy life.*

Day 5   Revisit the Cowboys Concept Chart, 407b

KEY   = Target Skill   **T** = Tested Skill

Comprehension — Check Retelling, *402g*

Fluency — Check Fluency WCPM, *405a*
Spiral **REVIEW** Phonics, High-Frequency Words

Oral Vocabulary — Check Oral Vocabulary, *406b*
Assess Phonics, Lesson Vocabulary, Fluency, Comprehension, *406e*

SUCCESS PREDICTOR

Small Group Plan *for Differentiated Instruction*

Daily Plan
AT A GLANCE

Reading
Whole Group
- Oral Language
- Word Work
- Comprehension/Vocabulary

Group Time

Meet with small groups to provide:
- Skill Support
- Reading Support
- Fluency Practice

Read

This week's lessons for daily group time can be found behind the Differentiated Instruction (DI) tab on pp. DI·44–DI·53.

Whole Group
- Comprehension/Vocabulary
- Fluency

Language Arts
- Writing
- Grammar
- Speaking/Listening/Viewing
- Research/Study Skills

Use *My Sidewalks on Reading Street* for Tier III intensive reading intervention.

DAY 1

On-Level	Strategic Intervention	Advanced
Teacher-Led *Page 376q*	**Teacher-Led** *Page DI·44*	**Teacher-Led** *Page DI·45*
• **Read** Decodable Reader 29 • **Reread** for Fluency	• Blend Words with Suffixes *-ness, -less* • **Read** Decodable Reader 29 • **Reread** for Fluency	• Extend Word Reading • **Read** Advanced Selection 29 • Introduce Concept Inquiry

ⓘ Independent Activities
While you meet with small groups, have the rest of the class...

- Reread for fluency
- Write in their journals
- Read self-selected reading
- Visit the Word Work Center
- Complete Practice Book 2.2, pp. 133–134

DAY 2

On-Level	Strategic Intervention	Advanced
Teacher-Led *Pages 380–401*	**Teacher-Led** *Page DI·46*	**Teacher-Led** *Page DI·47*
• **Read** *Cowboys* • **Reread** for Fluency	• Blend Words with Suffixes *-ness, -less* • **Read** SI Decodable Reader 29 • **Read** or Listen to *Cowboys*	• **Read** *Cowboys* • Continue Concept Inquiry

ⓘ Independent Activities
While you meet with small groups, have the rest of the class...

- Read self-selected reading
- Write in their journals
- Visit the Listening Center
- Complete Practice Book 2.2, pp. 135–137

DAY 3

On-Level	Strategic Intervention	Advanced
Teacher-Led *Pages 380–403*	**Teacher-Led** *Page DI·48*	**Teacher-Led** *Page DI·49*
• **Reread** *Cowboys*	• **Reread** *Cowboys* • Read Words and Sentences • Review Cause and Effect and Graphic Organizer • **Reread** for Fluency	• Self-Selected Reading • Continue Concept Inquiry

ⓘ Independent Activities
While you meet with small groups, have the rest of the class...

- Read self-selected reading
- Write in their journals
- Visit the Writing Center
- Complete Practice Book 2.2, pp. 138–139

① Begin with whole class skill and strategy instruction.

② Meet with small groups to provide differentiated instruction.

③ Gather the whole class back together for fluency and language arts.

DAY 4

On-Level
Teacher-Led
Pages 404–405, LR31–LR33

- **Read** "Cowboy Gear"
- Practice with On-Level Reader *Cowboy Days*

Strategic Intervention
Teacher-Led
Pages DI · 50, LR28–LR30

- **Read** or Listen to "Cowboy Gear"
- **Reread** for Fluency
- Build Concepts
- Practice with Below-Level Reader *Ranch Life*

Advanced
Teacher-Led
Pages DI · 51, LR34–LR36

- **Read** "Cowboy Gear"
- Extend Vocabulary
- Continue Concept Inquiry
- Practice with Advanced Reader *Life on the Ranch*

ⓘ Independent Activities

While you meet with small groups, have the rest of the class…

- Reread for fluency
- Write in their journals
- Read self-selected reading
- Review spelling words with a partner
- Visit the Listening and Social Studies Centers

DAY 5

On-Level
Teacher-Led
Pages 406e–406g, LR31–LR33

- Sentence Reading, Set B
- Monitor Comprehension
- Practice with On-Level Reader *Cowboy Days*

Strategic Intervention
Teacher-Led
Pages DI · 52, LR28–LR30

- Practice Word Reading
- Sentence Reading, Set A
- Monitor Fluency and Comprehension
- Practice with Below-Level Reader *Ranch Life*

Advanced
Teacher-Led
Pages DI · 53, LR34–LR36

- Sentence Reading, Set C
- Monitor Comprehension
- Share Concept Inquiry
- Practice with Advanced Reader *Life on the Ranch*

ⓘ Independent Activities

While you meet with small groups, have the rest of the class…

- Reread for fluency
- Write in their journals
- Read self-selected reading
- Visit the Technology Center
- Complete Practice Book 2.2, p. 140

Grouping Place English language learners in the groups that correspond to their reading abilities in English.

Use the appropriate Leveled Reader or other text at children's instructional level.

TIP Send home the appropriate Multilingual Summary of the main selection on Day 1.

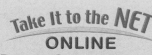

Take It to the NET ONLINE
PearsonSuccessNet.com

Connie Juel
For research on decodable text, see the article "The Influence of Basal Readers on First Grade Reading" by Scott Foresman author Connie Juel along with D. Roper-Schnieder.

TEACHER TALK

Paired reading is a method of repeated reading in which two children take turns reading aloud to each other.

Be sure to schedule time for children to work on the unit inquiry project "Research Traditions." This week children should prepare materials they need for the tradition.

Looking Ahead

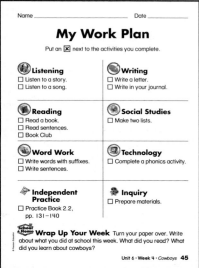

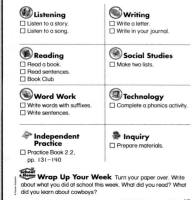

▲ **Group-Time Survival Guide**
p. 45, Weekly Contract

☑ Customize Your Plan *by Strand*

ORAL LANGUAGE

Concept Development

Why should we learn about cowboys?

 *to build oral vocabulary*

buckaroo	climate	drover
lariat	legend	livestock
occupation	rawhide	

BUILD

❑ **Question of the Week** Use the Morning Warm-Up! to introduce and discuss the question of the week. This week children will talk, sing, read, and write about cowboys. **DAY 1** *376l*

❑ **Sing with Me Big Book** Sing a song about cowboys. Ask children to listen for the concept-related Amazing Words *climate, livestock, occupation.* **DAY 1** *376m*

❑ **Build Background** Remind children of the question of the week. Then create a concept chart for children to add to throughout the week. **DAY 1** *376m*

Sing with Me Big Book

DEVELOP

❑ **Question of the Day** Use the questions in the Morning Warm-Ups! to discuss lesson concepts and how they relate to the unit theme, Traditions. **DAY 2** *378a,* **DAY 3** *402a,* **DAY 4** *404a,* **DAY 5** *406a*

❑ **Share Literature** Read big books and read aloud selections that develop concepts, language, and vocabulary related to the lesson concept and the unit theme. Continue to develop this week's Amazing Words. **DAY 2** *378b,* **DAY 3** *402b,* **DAY 4** *404b,* **DAY 5** *406b*

CONNECT

❑ **Wrap Up Your Week!** Revisit the Question of the Week. Then connect concepts and vocabulary to next week's lesson. **DAY 5** *407b*

CHECK

❑ **Check Oral Vocabulary** To informally assess children's oral vocabulary, ask individuals to use some of this week's Amazing Words to tell you about the concept of the week—Traditions. **DAY 5** *406b*

PHONICS

 SUFFIXES -*NESS*, -*LESS* Some words consist of a base word and the ending syllable -*less* or -*ness*. The suffix -*less* means *"without."* The suffix -*ness* means *"the quality of being _____."*

TEACH

❑ **Suffixes -*ness*, -*less*** Introduce the blending strategy for words with suffixes -*ness*, -*less*. Then have children blend and build words, adding the suffixes to each base word, reading the new words, and supplying their meanings. **DAY 1** *376n–376o*

❑ **Fluent Word Reading** Use the Fluent Word Reading Routine to develop children's word reading fluency. Use the Phonics Songs and Rhymes Chart for additional word reading practice. **DAY 2** *378c-378d*

Phonics Songs and Rhymes Chart 29

PRACTICE/APPLY

❑ **Decodable Reader 29** Practice reading words with suffixes -*ness*, -*less* in context. **DAY 1** *376q*

❑ ***Cowboys*** Practice decoding words in context. **DAY 2** *380–401*

Decodable Reader 29

❑ **Homework** Practice Book 2.2 p. 133. **DAY 1** *376o*

❑ **Word Work Center** Practice suffixes -*ness*, -*less*. **ANY DAY** *376j*

Main Selection—Nonfiction

RETEACH/REVIEW

❑ **Review** Review words with this week's phonics skills. **DAY 5** *406c*

❑ **Reteach Lessons** If necessary, reteach suffixes -*ness*, -*less*. **DAY 5** *DI·67*

❑ **Spiral REVIEW** Review previously taught phonics skills. **DAY 1** *376o,* **DAY 3** *402c,* **DAY 4** *404c*

ASSESS

❑ **Sentence Reading** Assess children's ability to read words with suffixes -*ness*, -*less*. **DAY 5** *406e-406f*

① Use assessment data to determine your instructional focus.

② Preview this week's instruction by strand.

③ Choose instructional activities that meet the needs of your classroom.

SPELLING

SUFFIXES -NESS, -LESS Some words consist of a base word and the ending syllable *-less* or *-ness*. The suffix *-less* means *"without."* The suffix *-ness* means *"the quality of being ____."*

TEACH

❑ **Pretest** Before administering the pretest, model how to segment words with suffixes to spell them. Dictate the spelling words, segmenting them if necessary. Then have children check their pretests and correct misspelled words. **DAY 1** *376p*

PRACTICE/APPLY

❑ **Dictation** Have children write dictation sentences to practice spelling words. **DAY 2** *378d*

❑ **Write Words** Have children practice writing the spelling words by using an outline of a cow or another animal to write sentences inside the cow that use the spelling words. **DAY 3** *402d*

❑ **Homework** Phonics and Spelling Practice Book pp. 113–116. **DAY 1** *376p*, **DAY 2** *378d*, **DAY 3** *402d*, **DAY 4** *404d*

RETEACH/REVIEW

❑ **Partner Review** Have pairs work together to read and write the spelling words. **DAY 4** *404d*

ASSESS

❑ **Posttest** Use dictation sentences to give the posttest for words with suffixes *-ness, -less*. **DAY 5** *406d*

Spelling Words

Suffixes

1. kindness
2. careless
3. goodness
4. useless
5. fearless*
6. darkness
7. sadness
8. sickness
9. helpless
10. thankless
11. fitness
12. weakness

Challenge Words

13. awareness
14. eagerness
15. wireless

* Words from the Selection

VOCABULARY

🔍 **STRATEGY WORD STRUCTURE** A compound word is made of two small words. Use the small words to figure out the compound word.

LESSON VOCABULARY

campfire   cattle   cowboy   galloped
herd   railroad   trails

TEACH

❑ **Words to Know** Introduce and discuss this week's lesson vocabulary. **DAY 2** *378f*

❑ **Vocabulary Strategy Lesson** Use the lesson in the Student Edition to introduce/ model *word structure*. **DAY 2** *378-379a*

Vocabulary Strategy Lesson

PRACTICE/APPLY

❑ **Words in Context** Read the lesson vocabulary in context. **DAY 2** *380-401*, **DAY 3** *380-403*

❑ **Lesson Vocabulary** Have children write using vocabulary words. **DAY 3** *402d*

Main Selection—Nonfiction

❑ **Leveled Text** Read the lesson vocabulary in leveled text. **DAY 4** *LR28-LR36*, **DAY 5** *LR28-LR36*

❑ **Homework** Practice Book 2.2 pp. 136, 139. **DAY 2** *378f*, **DAY 3** *402d*

Leveled Readers

RETEACH/REVIEW

❑ **Time Words** Discuss and use time words. **DAY 3** *402e*

❑ **Review** Review this week's lesson vocabulary words. **DAY 5** *406c*

ASSESS

❑ **Selection Test** Use the Selection Test to determine children's understanding of the lesson vocabulary words. **DAY 3**

❑ **Sentence Reading** Assess children's ability to read this week's lesson vocabulary words. **DAY 5** *406e-406f*

HIGH-FREQUENCY WORDS

RETEACH/REVIEW

❑ **Spiral REVIEW** Review previously taught high-frequency words. **DAY 2** *378f*, **DAY 4** *404c*

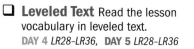

☑ Customize Your Plan *by Strand*

COMPREHENSION

SKILL CAUSE AND EFFECT The *effect* is what happens in the story. The *cause* is the reason why something happens. When you read, ask yourself what happens and why it happens.

STRATEGY GRAPHIC ORGANIZER A graphic organizer is a chart, diagram, outline, or time line that helps you put information in order, to organize as you read.

TEACH

❑ **Skill/Strategy Lesson** Use the Skill/ Strategy Lesson in the Student Edition to introduce *cause and effect* and *graphic organizer.* **DAY 1** *376r-377*

Skill/Strategy Lesson

PRACTICE/APPLY

❑ **Skills and Strategies in Context** Read *Cowboys,* using the Guiding Comprehension questions to apply *cause and effect* and *graphic organizer.* **DAY 2** *380-401a*

❑ **Reader Response** Use the questions on Student Edition p. 402 to discuss the selection. **DAY 3** *402g-403*

Main Selection—Nonfiction

❑ **Skills and Strategies in Context** Read "Cowboy Gear," guiding children as they apply skills and strategies. **DAY 4** *404e-405*

❑ **Leveled Text** Apply *cause and effect* and *graphic organizer* to read leveled text. **DAY 4** *LR28-LR36,* **DAY 5** *LR28-LR36*

Paired Selection— Nonfiction

❑ **Homework** Practice Book 2.2 pp. 134, 135. **DAY 1** *376-377,* **DAY 2** *378e*

Leveled Readers

ASSESS

❑ **Selection Test** Determine children's understanding of the main selection and assess their ability to identify *cause and effect.* **DAY 3**

❑ **Story Reading** Have children read the passage "Maggie's Wish." Ask questions that require them to identify *cause and effect.* Then have them retell. **DAY 5** *406e-406g*

RETEACH/REVIEW

❑ **Reteach Lesson** If necessary, reteach *cause and effect.* **DAY 5** *DI·67*

FLUENCY

SKILL READ WITH ACCURACY AND APPROPRIATE PACE When you read, try to read each word correctly. Try not to change any words or leave any words out. Read at a pace you would use if you were speaking.

REREAD FOR FLUENCY

❑ **Paired Reading** Have pairs of children read orally from Decodable Reader 29, the main selection or another text at their independent reading level. Listen to children read and provide corrective feedback regarding their oral reading and their use of the blending strategy. **DAY 1** *376q,* **DAY 2** *401a*

TEACH

❑ **Model** Use passages from *Cowboys* to model reading with accuracy and appropriate pace. **DAY 3** *402f,* **DAY 4** *405a*

PRACTICE/APPLY

❑ **Choral Reading** Have two groups choral read passages, alternating paragraphs, from *Cowboys.* Monitor progress and provide feedback regarding children's accuracy and pace. **DAY 3** *402f*

❑ **Paired Reading** Have pairs of children read passages from *Cowboys,* switching readers at the end of each page. Monitor progress and provide feedback regarding children's accuracy and pace. **DAY 4** *405a*

❑ **Listening Center** Have children follow along with the AudioText for this week's selections. **ANY DAY** *376j*

❑ **Reading/Library Center** Have children build fluency by rereading Leveled Readers, Decodable Readers, or other text at their independent level. **ANY DAY** *376j*

❑ **Fluency Coach** Have children use Fluency Coach to listen to fluent reading or to practice reading on their own. **ANY DAY**

ASSESS

❑ **Story Reading** Take a one-minute timed sample of children's oral reading. Use the passage "Maggie's Wish." **DAY 5** *406e-406g*

1 Use assessment data to determine your instructional focus.

2 Preview this week's instruction by strand.

3 Choose instructional activities that meet the needs of your classroom.

WRITING

Trait of the Week

SENTENCES Good writers use different kinds of sentences. A mix of short and longer sentences gives writing rhythm and style.

TEACH

☐ **Write Together** Engage children in writing activities that develop language, grammar, and writing skills. Include independent writing as an extension of group writing activities.

      Shared Writing DAY 1 *377a*
      Interactive Writing DAY 2 *401b*
      Writing Across the Curriculum DAY 4 *405b*

☐ **Trait of the Week** Introduce and model the Trait of the Week, *sentences.* DAY 3 *403a*

PRACTICE/APPLY

☐ **Write Now** Examine the model on Student Edition pp. 406–407. Then have children write ads. DAY 5 *406–407*

    Prompt *Cowboys* describes a cowboy's job. Think about a job you know. Now write an ad that tells the requirements of the job.

Write Now

☐ **Daily Journal Writing** Have children write about concepts and literature in their journals. **EVERY DAY** *376d–376e*

☐ **Writing Center** Have children write letters describing what it might be like to be cowboys on a long cattle drive. **ANY DAY** *376k*

ASSESS

☐ **Scoring Rubric** Use a rubric to evaluate children's ads. DAY 5 *406–407*

RETEACH/REVIEW

☐ **The Grammar and Writing Book** Use pp. 218–223 of The Grammar and Writing

The Grammar and Writing Book

SPEAKING AND LISTENING

TEACH

☐ **Listen to a Description** Remind children of appropriate listening and speaking behaviors as they describe an item. DAY 4 *405d*

GRAMMAR

SKILL COMMAS IN COMPOUND SENTENCES Sometimes two sentences have ideas that go together. These sentences can be combined using a comma and a connecting word, such as *and* or *but.*

TEACH

☐ **Grammar Transparency 29** Use Grammar Transparency 29 to teach *commas in compound sentences.* DAY 1 *377b*

Grammar Transparency 29

PRACTICE/APPLY

☐ **Develop the Concept** Review the concept of commas in compound sentences and provide guided practice. DAY 2 *401c*

☐ **Apply to Writing** Have children use commas in compound sentences in writing. DAY 3 *403b*

☐ **Define/Practice** Review the definition of *commas.* Then have children add commas and connecting words to make compound sentences. DAY 4 *405c*

☐ **Write Now** Discuss the grammar lesson on Student Edition p. 407. Have children appropriately place commas in compound sentences in advertisements that they write telling the requirements needed for a job. DAY 5 *406–407*

Write Now

☐ **Daily Fix-It** Have children find and correct errors in grammar, spelling, and punctuation. DAY 1 *377b*, DAY 2 *401c*, DAY 3 *403b*, DAY 4 *405c*, DAY 5 *406–407*

☐ **Homework** The Grammar and Writing Practice Book pp. 113–116. DAY 2 *401c*, DAY 3 *403b*, DAY 4 *405c*, DAY 5 *406–407*

RETEACH/REVIEW

☐ **The Grammar and Writing Book** Use pp. 218–221 of The Grammar and Writing Book to extend instruction. **ANY DAY**

The Grammar and Writing Book

RESEARCH/INQUIRY

TEACH

☐ **Thesaurus** Model how to use a thesaurus. Then have children use a thesaurus to look up synonyms for several words. DAY 5 *407a*

☐ **Unit Inquiry Project** Allow time for children to prepare materials they need for their research projects on a tradition. **ANY DAY** *295*

Resources for Differentiated Instruction

LEVELED READERS

▶ **Comprehension**
- 🎯 **Skill** Cause and Effect
- 🎯 **Strategy** Graphic Organizer

▶ **Lesson Vocabulary**
- 🎯 Word Structure

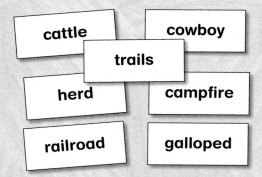

cattle	cowboy
trails	
herd	campfire
railroad	galloped

▶ **Social Studies Standards**
- **American West**
- **Cowboys**
- **U.S. Growth**
- **Transportation**
- **Geography**

Leveled Reader Database ONLINE

PearsonSuccessNet.com

Use the Online Database of over 600 books to
- Download and print additional copies of this week's leveled readers
- Listen to the readers being read online
- Search for more titles focused on this week's skills, topic, and content

On-Level

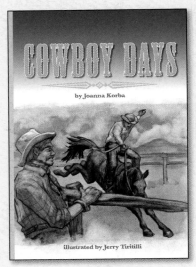

On-Level Reader

Cause and Effect

Each sentence below tells a **cause**.
Write a sentence that tells the **effect**.
Use *Cowboy Days* to help you.

1. CAUSE: Jeannie Grigsby hears a lot about Great Uncle Carl, the cowboy.
EFFECT:
She tells others about him.

2. CAUSE: The land along the trail drive is very dusty.
EFFECT:
The cattle kick up dust.

3. CAUSE: Someone tells Carl about a show called a rodeo.
EFFECT:
He spends his life performing.

4. CAUSE: Ranchers used barbed wire fences to keep the cattle together.
EFFECT:
Ranchers didn't need cowboys to keep cattle together.

On-Level Practice TE p. LR32

Vocabulary

Circle the word that best completes the sentence and write it in the space.

Words to Know
| campfire | cattle | cowboy | galloped |
| herd | railroad | trails | |

1. Many cows make up one large **herd**.
campfire (herd)

2. The cattle **galloped** across the dry land.
(galloped) railroad

3. Great Uncle Carl was once a **cowboy**.
railroad (cowboy)

4. The cowboys led the cattle on dusty **trails**.
(trails) railroad

5. At night, the cowboys cooked over a **campfire**.
(campfire) herd

6. The **railroad** changed the life of the cowboy.
trails (railroad)

On-Level Practice TE p. LR33

Strategic Intervention

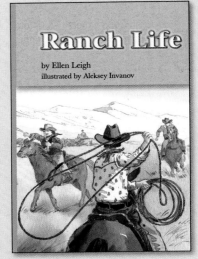

Ranch Life
by Ellen Leigh
illustrated by Aleksey Invanov

Below-Level Reader

Cause and Effect

The sentences on the left tell a **cause**.
The sentences on the right tell an **effect**.
Draw a line to match each cause with its effect.

Cause
1. Emma plants seeds.
2. Emma's friends and family live far away.
3. The cattle must get to town.
4. A railroad might be built near the ranch.

Effect
a. Papa hired cowboys to bring his cattle together.
b. Vegetables will soon grow.
c. The ranch might not need cowboys anymore.
d. Emma stays in touch with family and friends by writing letters.

5. Read the sentence below.
CAUSE: It is hot and sunny today.
Write a sentence to tell an effect.
EFFECT: Possible response given.
I will go to the beach.

Below-Level Practice TE p. LR29

Vocabulary

Look at each picture. Which word tells about it?
Circle the correct word for each picture.

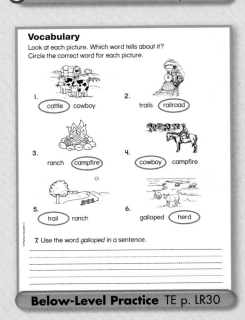

1. (cattle) cowboy
2. trails (railroad)
3. ranch (campfire)
4. (cowboy) campfire
5. (trail) ranch
6. galloped (herd)

7. Use the word *galloped* in a sentence.

Below-Level Practice TE p. LR30

Advanced

Advanced Reader

Cause and Effect

Write the missing **cause** or **effect**.
Use *Life on the Ranch* to help you.

1. CAUSE: The cows ate all the grass in one pasture.
   EFFECT:

   Uncle Leo had to move the cows.

2. CAUSE:

   The crops don't get enough rain.
   EFFECT: The crops die.

3. CAUSE: The wheat ripens in late summer.
   EFFECT:

   The Ramirezes harvest it.

4. CAUSE:

   Angela brushed Linda the brown cow.
   EFFECT: Linda the brown cow's coat became shiny.

5. CAUSE: Mimi's new puppy was hiding.
   EFFECT:

   The girls look for the puppy.

Advanced Practice TE p. LR35

Vocabulary

Complete each sentence with a word from the box.

Words to Know			
chores	climate	livestock	occupation
pasture	ranch	stalls	tractor

1.-2. Angela and Maria know they are too young to drive a

tractor on the **ranch**.

3. The **climate** is mostly warm where they live.

4. Before they go to school, the girls have to do their

chores.

5.-6. Mr. Ramirez's **occupation** is to sell items

grown on the **farm**.

7. The girls chose their own cows for the **livestock**

show.

Advanced Practice TE p. LR36

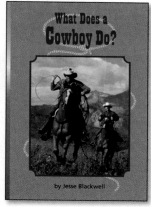

ELL Reader

ELL Poster 29

Teacher's Edition Notes

ELL notes throughout this lesson support instruction and reference additional resources at point of use.

ELL Teaching Guide pp. 197–203, 268–269

- Multilingual summaries of the main selection
- Comprehension lesson
- Vocabulary strategies and word cards
- ELL Reader 29 lesson

ELL and Transition Handbook

Ten Important Sentences

- Key ideas from every selection in the Student Edition
- Activities to build sentence power

More Reading

Readers' Theater Anthology

- Fluency practice
- Five scripts to build fluency
- Poetry for oral interpretation

Leveled Trade Books

- Extend reading tied to the unit concept
- Lessons in Trade Book Library Teaching Guide

School + Home

Homework

- Family Times Newsletter
- ELL Multilingual Selection Summaries

Take-Home Books

- Decodable Readers
- Leveled Readers

Literacy Centers

Listening

Let's Read
Along

MATERIALS
CD player, headphones, print copies of recorded pieces

`SINGLES` `PAIRS`

LISTEN TO LITERATURE As children listen to the following recordings, have them follow along or read along in the print version.

AudioText
Cowboys
"Cowboy Gear"

Sing with Me/Background Building
"Occupation Cowboy"

Phonics Songs and Rhymes Audio
"A Cowboy's Life"

A Cowboy's Life

In the old days, fearless cowboys
Roamed all over the West.
They all had countless talents,
And always did their best.

They faced loneliness and weariness
But they could all agree
That cheerfulness was easy
'Cause they loved the wide prairie.

Audio CD **Phonics Songs and Rhymes Chart 29**

Reading/Library

Read It
Again!

MATERIALS
collection of books for self-selected reading, books about cowboys, reading logs

`SINGLES` `PAIRS` `GROUPS`

REREAD BOOKS Have children select previously read books from the appropriate book box and record titles of books they read in their logs. Use these previously read books:

- Decodable Readers
- Leveled Readers
- ELL Readers
- Stories written by classmates
- Books from the library

TEN IMPORTANT SENTENCES Have children read the Ten Important Sentences for *Cowboys* and locate the sentences in the Student Edition.

BOOK CLUB Encourage groups to read books about cowboys. Ask each group to make a web that gives details about life on the trail.

Word Work

Word
Building

MATERIALS
sentence cards, paper, pencils

`PAIRS`

SUFFIXES *ness, less* Have children make words with the suffixes *ness, less*.

1. Write sentences such as this on index cards: Thank you for your kind_____. *(less, ness).*
2. Have children work in pairs to read the sentence and choose the correct suffix. Then have one child write and read aloud the completed sentence. Have the other child tell how many syllables are in the new word.

 This interactive CD provides additional practice.

Thank you for your kind____(less, ness).

Don't be thought____ (less, ness) with your friends.

1. Thank you for your kindness.
2. It was hard to see in the darkness.
3. Carla tore her pants because she was careless.
4. Don't be thoughtless with your friends.

Scott Foresman Reading Street Centers Survival Kit
Use the *Cowboys* materials
from the Reading Street Centers Survival Kit
to organize this week's centers.

Writing

Social Studies

Technology

Life on the Trail

MATERIALS
paper, pencils

`SINGLES`
`GROUPS`

WRITE A LETTER Children imagine that they are cowboys on a long cattle drive.

1. Have children discuss what they might include in letters they write home, such as how they sleep and eat and troubles they have along the way.
2. Have each child write a letter.
3. Display the letters in the classroom.

LEVELED WRITING Encourage children to write at their own ability level. Some may only write a sentence or two. Others will be able to write a letter with an opening and closing. Your best students will be able to write an engaging and well-organized letter.

May 18

Dear Mom and Dad,
    Working on a cattle drive is hard. I wear all my clothes and lie down on the ground to sleep. We eat good food like beans and meat. I can't wait to come home and see you all again.
Your son, Alex

Pack for the JOURNEY

MATERIALS
copies of T-chart or Graphic Organizer 25, pencils

`PAIRS`

COMPARE LISTS Children compare what cowboys would take on an 1800s trail drive with what children would bring on a trip now.

1. Have children use *Cowboys* to list things that cowboys brought along on their trail drives.
2. Then have pairs of children list things they would pack for a journey.
3. Ask pairs to compare the two lists.

Things Cowboys Brought	Things We Would Bring
• hats	• clothes
• bandannas	• toothbrush
• chaps	• games
• boots	• jacket
• food	• sunglasses
• water	• pajamas
• cards	• books
• bedroll	

Focus Phonics

MATERIALS
computer, Phonics Practice Activities CD-ROM

`PAIRS`

USE A CD-ROM Have pairs of children use a CD-ROM.

1. Have children turn on the computer and open the Phonics Practice Activities CD-ROM.
2. Working with a partner, have children read and complete one of the CD-ROM activities.

Phonics Activities CD

`ALL CENTERS`

Day 1
AT A GLANCE

Oral Vocabulary
"Occupation: Cowboy" 29

Phonics and Spelling
Suffixes -ness and -less

Spelling Pretest: Words with suffixes -ness and -less

Read Apply Phonics [Word Wall]

[Group Time] < Differentiated Instruction

Comprehension
Skill Cause and Effect
Strategy Graphic Organizer

Shared Writing
Ad

Grammar
Commas in Compound Sentences

Materials
- *Sing with Me Big Book*
- Letter Tiles
- Decodable Reader 29
- Skill Transparency 29
- Student Edition 376–377
- Graphic Organizer 3
- Writing Transparency 29
- Grammar Transparency 29

Take It to the NET™
ONLINE
Professional Development
To learn more about informational text, go to PearsonSuccessNet.com and read "A Classroom Study..." by Kamil and Lane.

Morning Warm-Up!

Many cowboys work long hours.

They don't mind getting dirty.

What kinds of clothes do they wear?

Why should we learn about cowboys?

QUESTION OF THE WEEK Tell children they will talk, sing, read, and write about cowboys. Write and read the message and discuss the question.

CONNECT CONCEPT Ask questions to connect to other Unit 6 selections.

- How are the soldiers in *Red, White, and Blue* like cowboys?

- Cowboys wear special clothing to do their job. What kind of special clothes did the players wear to do their job in "Pepper Davis, Play Ball?"

REVIEW HIGH-FREQUENCY WORDS

- Circle the high-frequency words *many, hours,* and *clothes* in the message.

- Have children find the contraction in the message and identify the two words that make up the contraction.

Build Background Use the Day 1 instruction on ELL Poster 29 to assess knowledge and develop concepts.

ELL Poster 29

Oral Vocabulary

SHARE LITERATURE Display p. 29 of the *Sing with Me Big Book.* Tell children that the class is going to sing a song about cowboys. Read the title. Ask children to listen for the Amazing Words **occupation, livestock,** and **climate** as you sing.

Occupation: Cowboy
Oh, a cowboy's occupation
Was so tough.
He drove cattle down the trail.
It was rough.
Oh, the livestock could be frisky,
And the climate made things risky,
What a hard-working cowboy,
Sure enough.

Sing to the tune of
If You're Happy and You Know It!

Unit 6
Traditions

Week 4
Cowboys

Oral Vocabulary
occupation
livestock
climate

29

Sing with Me Big Book

- Being a cowboy is one kind of occupation. What are some other occupations you can think of? (Possible response: firefighter, police officer, astronaut, scientist, artist)

- Remember what a cowboy does and look at the picture that goes with the song. What kind of livestock does a cowboy take care of? (cattle)

- The climate is the kind of weather a place has. What is the climate in the song? (rainy with thunder and lightning)

**Sing with Me/
Background Building Audio**

BUILD BACKGROUND Remind children of the question of the week.

- Why should we learn about cowboys?

Draw a K-W-L chart or use Graphic Organizer 3. Help children identify what they know about cowboys and what they want to know about cowboys. Display the chart for use throughout the week.

- What do cowboys wear?
- What do cowboys do all day?

Topic *Cowboys*

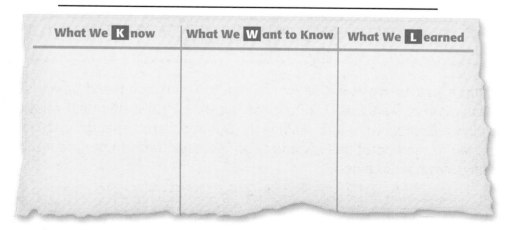

What We **K**now	What We **W**ant to Know	What We **L**earned

▲ **Graphic Organizer 3**

Amazing Words **to build oral vocabulary**

	MONITOR PROGRESS
climate **livestock** **occupation** buckaroo drover lariat legend rawhide	**If...** children lack oral vocabulary experiences about the concept Traditions, **then...** use the Oral Vocabulary Routine below to teach *climate*.

Oral Vocabulary ROUTINE

1. **Introduce the Word** Relate the word *climate* to the song. Supply a child-friendly definition. Have children say the word. Example: *Climate* is the type of weather that happens in a particular place.

2. **Demonstrate** Provide an example to show meaning. The desert has a hot, dry *climate.*

3. **Apply** Have children demonstrate their understanding. What is your favorite type of *climate?*

4. **Display the Word/Letter-Sounds** Write the word on a card. Display it. Point out the long *i* sound in the first syllable. See p. DI·6 to teach *livestock* and *occupation.*

Access Content Help children recognize the meanings of the English words *cattle* and *climate* in "Occupation: Cowboy" by asking them to point to the cattle and the rain in the *Sing with Me Big Book* as the words are sung.

OBJECTIVES

- Use structural cues to decode words with suffixes *-less* and *-ness*.
- Blend, read, and build words with suffixes *-less* and *-ness*.

Skills Trace	
Suffixes	
Introduce/Teach	TE: 2.6 376n–o, 378c–d
Practice	TE 2.6 376q; PB; 2.2 133, 148; DR29
Reteach/Review	TE: 2.6 406c, 426c, DI·67
Assess/Test	TE: 2.6 406e–g Benchmark Test, Unit 6

Strategic Intervention

Use **Monitor Progress,** p. 376o, during Group Time after children have had more practice with suffixes.

Advanced

Use **Monitor Progress,** p. 376o, as a preassessment to determine whether this group of children would benefit from this instruction on suffixes.

ELL

Support Phonics Speakers of monosyllabic languages such as Cantonese, Hmong, Khmer, Korean, and Vietnamese may have difficulty understanding that multisyllabic words are single words. Help children practice saying and writing words with suffixes as single words, such as *goodness* and *careless*.

See the Phonics Transition Lessons in the ELL and Transition Handbook.

⊙ Suffixes

TEACH/MODEL

Blending Strategy

ROUTINE

1 **Connect** Write *useful* and *sadly*. You studied words like this already. What do you know about reading these words? (They have a base word and a suffix.) Today we'll learn about adding suffixes *-less* and *-ness* to the end of words. Each suffix has a special meaning.

- *-less*   without
- *-ness*   the quality of being _____

2 **Model** Write *kindness.* This is a two-syllable word made from the base word *kind* and the suffix *-ness.* You can chunk the word into its parts—the base word and the suffix. Then cover the suffix, read the base word, and then blend the base word and the suffix to read the whole word. This is how I blend this word. Cover the suffix to read the base word; uncover and read the ending. Blend the two parts. Let's blend this word together: /kīnd/ /nes/, *kindness.* What does it mean? *(the quality of being kind)* Repeat with *careless.* Some words have two suffixes added. Add *-ly* to *careless,* and model blending:

care, less, ly—carelessly. Have children blend the word with you.

3 **Group Practice** First, chunk the word into its parts—the base word and the suffix. Then read the base word, read the suffix, and blend the two parts. Continue with *sadness, friendless, laziness, hopelessly, usefulness.*

4 **Review** What do you know about reading words with suffixes? Chunk the word, read the base word, read the suffix or suffixes, and then blend the parts.

BLEND WORDS

INDIVIDUALS BLEND WORDS Call on children to chunk and blend *darkness, painless, fitness, weakness, bottomless, sickness.* Have them tell what they know about each word before reading it. (Suffixes form separate syllables that are added to the end of base words.) For feedback, refer to step four of the Blending Strategy Routine.

BUILD WORDS

READ LONGER WORDS Write the suffixes *-less* and *-ness* as headings for a two-column chart. Write the base words in each column. Have children add the suffix to each base word, read the new word, and supply its meaning. Have the completed lists reread.

-less	*-ness*
thought	quick
cord	sick
friend	still
spot	dark
fear	sad

Vocabulary TiP

You may wish to explain the meanings of these words.

awareness being aware; noticing
pointless without a point; without meaning

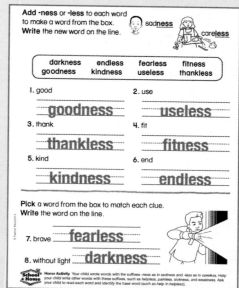

Add *-ness* or *-less* to each word to make a word from the box. Write the new word on the line. sad**ness** care**less**

darkness	endless	fearless	fitness
goodness	kindness	useless	thankless

1. good **goodness** 2. use **useless**
3. thank **thankless** 4. fit **fitness**
5. kind **kindness** 6. end **endless**

Pick a word from the box to match each clue. Write the word on the line.

7. brave **fearless**
8. without light **darkness**

Home Activity Your child wrote words with the suffixes *-ness* as in *sadness* and *-less* as in *careless*. Help your child write other words with these suffixes, such as *helpless*, *painless*, *sickness*, and *weakness*. Ask your child to read each word and identify the base word (such as *help* in *helpless*).

▲ **Practice Book 2.2** p. 133, Suffixes

Monitor Progress — Check Word Reading Suffixes

Write the following words and have individuals read them.

thoughtless	**useless**	**pointless**	**brightness**	**illness**
fearless	**lonely**	**actor**	**graceful**	**teacher**
painlessly	**watchfulness**	**carefully**	**gentleness**	**awareness**

If... children cannot blend words with syllables *-less, -ness* at this point,

then... continue to monitor their progress using other instructional opportunities during the week so that they can be successful with the Day 5 Assessment. See the Skills Trace on p. 376n.

SUCCESS PREDICTOR

Spiral REVIEW

● Row 2 reviews suffixes *-ly, -ful, -er, -or.*
● Row 3 reviews multisyllabic words.

▶**Day 1** Check Word Reading
Day 2 Check Lesson Vocabulary/High-Frequency Words
Day 3 Check Retelling
Day 4 Check Fluency
Day 5 Assess Progress

Word Reading

SUCCESS PREDICTOR

- Segment sounds and word parts to spell words.
- Spell words with suffixes *-less, -ness*.

Spelling Words

Suffixes

1. kindness
2. careless
3. goodness
4. useless
5. fearless*
6. darkness
7. sadness
8. sickness
9. helpless
10. thankless
11. fitness
12. weakness

Challenge Words

13. awareness
14. eagerness
15. wireless

* Word from the Selection

Suffixes *-ness* and *-less*

Generalization When *-ness* or *-less* is added to most base words, the base word stays the same: **kindness**, **careless**.

Sort the list words by *-ness* and *-less*.

-ness	-less
1. kindness	8. careless
2. goodness	9. useless
3. darkness	10. fearless
4. sadness	11. helpless
5. sickness	12. thankless
6. fitness	
7. weakness	

Spelling Words
1. kindness
2. careless
3. goodness
4. useless
5. fearless
6. darkness
7. sadness
8. sickness
9. helpless
10. thankless
11. fitness
12. weakness

Challenge Words
13. awareness
14. eagerness
15. wireless

Challenge Words

-ness	-less
13. awareness	15. wireless
14. eagerness	

School + Home **Home Activity** Your child is learning to spell words with *-ness* and *-less*. To practice at home, have your child write the list word and circle the base word. Ask if the base word stayed the same.

▲ **Spelling Practice Book** p. 113

Support Spelling Before giving the spelling pretest, clarify the meaning of each spelling word with examples, such as pretending to cry to illustrate *sadness,* and pointing to a picture of an athlete or a gym for *fitness*.

Spelling

PRETEST Suffixes

MODEL WRITING FOR WORD PARTS Each spelling word ends with a suffix. Before administering the spelling pretest, model how to segment suffixes to spell them.

- You can spell words with suffixes by thinking about the base word and the suffix. What base word and suffix make up *countless? (count* and *-less)*
- Start with the sounds in the base word: *count.* What letters spell /kount/? Write *count.*
- Now add the suffix *-less.* Add *less.*
- Now spell *countless.*
- Repeat with *smallness.*

PRETEST Dictate the spelling words. Segment the words for children if necessary. Have children check their pretests and correct misspelled words.

HOMEWORK Spelling Practice Book, p. 113

Wild West Show

Cowboys

William Frederick "Buffalo Bill" Cody was born in Iowa in 1846, but he grew up in Kansas. At the age of eleven, Cody got a job herding cattle as a wagon driver. This wouldn't be his only occupation. By the time William Cody was fourteen he had worked as a fur trapper, a miner, and a Pony Express rider during the Civil War. After the war ended, Cody made his living as a buffalo hunter. This is how he earned the nickname Buffalo Bill.

When he was 26, Buffalo Bill started the Wild West

Decodable Reader 29

Sandy and Randy
Written by Liz Mardry
Illustrated by Vince DeFlate

Group Time

On-Level	Strategic Intervention	Advanced
Read Decodable Reader 29. • Use p. 376q.	**Read** Decodable Reader 29. • Use the **Routine** on p. DI•44.	**Read** Advanced Selection 29. • Use the **Routine** on p. DI•45.

DAY 1

ELL Place English language learners in the groups that correspond to their reading abilities in English.

(i) Independent Activities

Fluency Reading Pair children to reread Leveled Readers or the ELL Reader from the previous week or other text at children's independent level.

Journal Writing Write about occupations. Share writing.

Independent Reading See p. 376j for Reading/Library activities and suggestions.

Literacy Centers To practice Suffixes, you may use Word Work, p. 376j.

Practice Book 2.2 Suffixes, p. 133; Cause and Effect, p. 134

Break into small groups after Spelling and before the Comprehension lesson.

Apply Phonics

⟳ PRACTICE Suffixes

HIGH-FREQUENCY WORDS Review *colorless, laughed,* and *though.*

READ DECODABLE READER 29

- Pages 106–107 Read aloud quietly with the group.
- Pages 108–109 Have the group read aloud with you.
- Pages 110–112 Select individuals to read aloud.

CHECK COMPREHENSION AND DECODING Have children retell the story to include characters, setting, and plot. Then have children locate words with syllables *-less* and *-ness* in the story. Review *-less* and *-ness* spelling patterns. Sort words according to their spelling patterns.

-ness	-less
brightness	colorless
darkness	helpless
goodness	useless
kindness	
sadness	
sweetness	
weakness	

HOMEWORK Take-Home Decodable Reader 29

REREAD FOR FLUENCY

Paired Reading

ROUTINE

1 **Reader 1 Begins** Children read the entire selection, switching readers at the end of each page.

2 **Reader 2 Begins** Have partners reread; now the other partner begins.

3 **Reread** For optimal fluency, children should reread three or four times.

4 **Provide Feedback** Listen to children read and provide corrective feedback regarding their oral reading and their use of the blending strategy.

OBJECTIVES

- Apply knowledge of letter-sounds and word parts to decode unknown words when reading.
- Use context with letter-sounds and word parts to confirm the identification of unknown words.
- Practice fluency in paired reading.

Monitor Progress

Decoding

If... children have difficulty decoding a word,	**then...** prompt them to blend the word.
	• What is the new word?
	• Is the new word a word you know?
	• Does it make sense in the story?

E L L

Access Content
Beginning Preview the book *Sandy and Randy,* identifying *grab* and *pack* in the pictures and print. Have children repeat the words and use gestures to act out the meanings.

Intermediate Preview *Sandy and Randy* and point out *-less* and *-ness* words, such as *colorless, useless,* and *brightness.* Facilitate a discussion, using these words to build conversational fluency.

Advanced After reading *Sandy and Randy,* have partners take turns retelling the story.

THE
STAGECOACH DRIVER

Being a stagecoach driver was a hard job. A driver had to take care of a stagecoach full of people. A stagecoach would sometimes get stuck or tip over because it traveled on muddy trails and rocky roads. And sometimes stagecoaches were robbed.

Charley Parkhurst was a stagecoach driver. He was a small person with a patch over one eye. He did not talk much. Charley drove stagecoaches for 20 years. When he died, people found out that Charley was a woman!

Charlotte Parkhurst wanted to drive a stagecoach. But women were not allowed, so Charlotte changed her name to Charley. She put on men's clothes. For 20 years she acted like a man. No one knew her secret.

Skill Here is a clue word —*because*. It signals a cause and effect. It tells why stagecoaches sometimes got stuck or tipped over.

Strategy Here is another clue word—*so*. If you made a graphic organizer, what would you write in it?

Unit 6 Cowboys   Skill Transparency 29

▲ **Skill Transparency 29**

Access Content
Beginning/Intermediate For a Picture It! lesson on cause and effect, see the ELL Teaching Guide, pp. 197–198.

Advanced Before children read "The Stagecoach Driver," make sure they know the meanings of *stagecoach*, *patch*, and *trails*.

Cause and Effect
Graphic Organizer

TEACH/MODEL

INTRODUCE Recall *A Birthday Basket for Tía*. Have students discuss what caused the musicians to begin to play their guitars and violins. (Possible response: Tía entered the room.)

- What would have happened if Tía had not entered the room?

Read p. 376 with children. Explain the following:

- Good readers understand what happened in a story and why it happened. Sometimes there are clue words to help figure this out. Look for the clue words *because, so*, and *since*.

- It is important to understand what you read. A graphic organizer can help you understand what happened in a story and why it happened.

Use Skill Transparency 29 to teach cause and effect and graphic organizers.

SKILL Use paragraph one to model using clue words to identify cause and effect.

 Think Aloud

MODEL I know I should keep track of what happens in a story. It is also helpful to know why it happened. I read that stagecoaches would sometimes get stuck. The clue word *because* helps me identify why: stagecoaches could get stuck *because* they traveled on muddy trails.

STRATEGY Continue with paragraph three to model using a graphic organizer.

Think Aloud

MODEL I can use a graphic organizer to understand what happened in a story and why it happened. I will use the graphic organizer shown on p. 376. When I read the word *so* in the second sentence, I know it is a clue that tells what happened. I will write *Charlotte changed her name* in the first box for *What happened*. Now I will reread to find out why she changed her name. The text says women were not allowed to be stagecoach drivers. I will write that in the box for *Why It Happened*.

Comprehension

Skill
Cause and Effect

Strategy
Graphic Organizers

Cause and Effect

- As you read, look for what happened and why it happened.
- Clue words help you figure out what happened and why. *Because, so,* and *since* are clue words.

Strategy: Graphic Organizers

Good readers use graphic organizers. A graphic organizer can help you understand what you read. A chart like this one can help you keep track of what happened and why it happened.

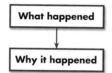

What happened

↓

Why it happened

Write to Read ✏

1. Read "The Stagecoach Driver." Look for clue words that tell what happened and why it happened.

2. Make a chart like the one above. Fill in your chart to show what happened and why it happened.

376

THE STAGECOACH DRIVER

Being a stagecoach driver was a hard job. A driver had to take care of a stagecoach full of people. A stagecoach would sometimes get stuck or tip over because it traveled on muddy trails and rocky roads. And sometimes stagecoaches were robbed.

Charley Parkhurst was a stagecoach driver. He was a small person with a patch over one eye. He did not talk much. Charley drove stagecoaches for 20 years. When he died, people found out that Charley was a woman!

Charlotte Parkhurst wanted to drive a stagecoach. But women were not allowed, so Charlotte changed her name to Charley. She put on men's clothes. For 20 years she acted like a man. No one knew her secret.

Skill Here is a clue word —*because.* It signals a cause and effect. It tells why stagecoaches sometimes got stuck or tipped over.

Strategy Here is another clue word—*so.* If you made a graphic organizer, what would you write in it?

377

PRACTICE

WRITE Work with children to complete the steps in the Write activity. Have children use the completed graphic organizer to tell what happened and why it happened in "The Stagecoach Driver."

Monitor Progress	Cause and Effect
If... children are unable to complete **Write** on p. 376,	**then...** use Practice Book 2.2, p. 134, for additional practice.

CONNECT TO READING Encourage children to ask themselves these questions when they read.

- Do I look for what happened and why it happened as I read?
- Do I look for clue words such as *because, so,* and *since*?
- Do I use a graphic organizer to help me understand what I read?

Look at each picture.
Answer the questions.

1. Why did the horse go up on two legs?

It saw a snake.

2. Why did the fire go out?

The rain put it out.

3. Why did the wagon stop moving?

The wheel broke.

4. Why did the cowboy's hat come off?

The wind blew it off.

Home Activity Your child looked at pictures to see what happened and the cause of each event. With your child, look at pictures in a book or magazine. Discuss what is going on in the pictures. Ask your child to tell why these things happened.

▲ **Practice Book 2.2** p. 134, Cause and Effect

1

● **LANGUAGE ARTS** ●

OBJECTIVE

● Write an ad.

DAILY FIX-IT

1. A hurd wandered the trails?
   A h**e**rd wandered the trails**.**

2. "We will visit dr. Hino today,
   Mom said.

   "We will visit **D**r. Hino today**,**"
   Mom said.

This week's practice sentences appear on Daily Fix-It Transparency 29.

Strategic Intervention

Children who are not able to write independently may draw an illustration of a cowboy and label the horse and clothing.

Advanced

Have children write an ad for a cowboy. Encourage one partner in a group to pretend to be the cowboy answering the ad. The other partner should interview the cowboy.

Support Writing Have children look at the illustrations in nonfiction books about cowboys for visual support as they write.

▲ **The Grammar and Writing Book**
For more instruction and practice, use pp. 218–223.

Shared Writing

WRITE Ad

GENERATE IDEAS Ask children to imagine that they need to hire some cowboys. Have children share what they know about cowboys and the work they do, including what they wear and ride.

WRITE AN AD Explain that the class will write an ad about cowboys that explains what cowboys do, wear, and ride and why.

COMPREHENSION SKILL Have children think about what a cowboy wears. What causes a cowboy to wear a hat and a bandanna?

● Display Writing Transparency 29 and read the title.

● Ask children to think about cowboys. What do cowboys do and why? What do they wear and why? What do cowboys ride and why?

● Read the prompts.

● As children describe what cowboys do, wear, and ride, record their responses.

HANDWRITING While writing, model the letter forms as shown on pp. TR14–TR17.

READ THE AD Have children read the completed ad aloud as you track the print.

Wanted: Cowboys

Possible answers:
What Cowboys Do and Why

Cowboys herd cattle together.

They used to take cattle on trail drives.

What Cowboys Wear and Why

Cowboys wear hats. Hats protect their

heads from sun and rain. Cowboys wear boots. Boots protect their feet.

What Cowboys Ride and Why

Cowboys ride horses. Horses help cowboys herd the cattle.

Unit 6 Cowboys   Writing Model **29**

▲ **Writing Transparency 29**

INDEPENDENT WRITING

WRITE AN AD Have children write their own ad for a cowboy. Encourage them to use words from the Word Wall and the Amazing Words board. Let children illustrate their writing. You may wish to gather children's work and display the ads in the classified section of a class newspaper.

ADDITIONAL PRACTICE For additional practice, use pp. 218–223 in the Grammar and Writing Book.

Grammar

TEACH/MODEL Commas in Compound Sentences

COMBINE SIMPLE SENTENCES Display Grammar Transparency 29. Read the definition aloud.

- We can combine these two simple sentences to make a more interesting compound sentence.
- Write the first sentence, add a comma and the word *and*, and then add the second sentence.

Continue modeling with items 2–3.

PRACTICE

ADD A COMMA Have children combine simple sentences. Write two simple sentences on the board. Have children complete the steps to create a compound sentence.

- Read the two sentences. Decide how these two sentences can be made into a compound sentence.
- Decide which connecting word you will use.
- Add a comma as you combine and rewrite the sentences.

Commas in Compound Sentences

Sometimes two sentences have ideas that go together. These sentences can be combined using a comma and a connecting word, such as **and** or **but**. The combined sentence is called a **compound sentence**.

Every summer we get together. Grandpa tells us stories.
Every summer we get together, and Grandpa tells us stories.

He tells the same stories. We like hearing them again.
He tells the same stories, but we like hearing them again.

Use the word in ( ) and a comma to combine each pair of sentences. **Write** the new sentence on the lines.

1. We sit close together. We don't say a word. (and)
We sit close together, and we don't say a word.

2. Cindy likes the scary stories. I like the funny ones. (but)
Cindy likes the scary stories, but I like the funny ones.

3. Grandpa uses different voices. He acts out all the parts. (and)
Grandpa uses different voices, and he acts out all the parts.

Unit 6 Cowboys   Grammar **29**

▲ **Grammar Transparency 29**

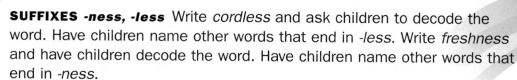

Wrap Up Your Day!

PREVIEW Day 2

✓ **SUFFIXES -ness, -less** Write *cordless* and ask children to decode the word. Have children name other words that end in *-less*. Write *freshness* and have children decode the word. Have children name other words that end in *-ness*.

✓ **SPELLING WORDS WITH SUFFIXES -ness -less** Have children add the suffix *-ness* to base words *ill* and *bright*. Have children add the suffix *-less* to base words *hope* and *use*.

✓ **CAUSE AND EFFECT** To help children identify cause and effect, ask: Why did Charlotte Parkhurst change her name to Charley? (because she wanted to drive a stagecoach) What clue word helped you find the cause? (so)

LET'S TALK ABOUT IT Recall what people knew about cowboys. Review and add to the KWL chart.

 HOMEWORK Send home this week's Family Times newsletter.

Tell children that tomorrow the class will read about cowboys.

Day 2

AT A GLANCE

Materials

- *Sing with Me Big Book*
- *Read Aloud Anthology*
- *Phonics Songs and Rhymes Chart 29*
- *Background Building Audio*
- *Graphic Organizer 25*
- *Tested Word Cards*
- *Student Edition 378–401*

Morning Warm~Up!

Today we will read about cowboys.
They ride horses and round up cows.
Cowboys like to be outside.
How would you like to be a
cowboy and ride a horse?

QUESTION OF THE DAY Encourage children to sing "Occupation: Cowboy" from the *Sing with Me Big Book* as you gather. Write and read the message and discuss the question.

REVIEW DIPHTHONGS *ou, ow*/ou/

- Reread the second and third sentences of the message.
- Have children raise their hands when they hear a word with the /ou/ sound. *(about, round, cows, cowboys, outside, how)*

Build Background Use the Day 2 instruction on ELL Poster 29 to preview lesson vocabulary words.

ELL Poster 29

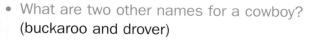
Share Literature

BUILD CONCEPTS

EXPOSITORY NONFICTION/ABC BOOKS Read the title and subtitle. Identify the author. Tell children this is an alphabet book. Each page will have a letter of the alphabet on it and a word related to a cowboy that starts with that letter.

BUILD ORAL VOCABULARY Ask children what they know about cowboys. Point out that **buckaroo** is another name for cowboy. **Drover** is also another name for cowboy because cowboys *drove* cattle along a trail. Suggest that as you read, children listen to find out what the letter *R* is for.

Read Aloud Anthology
B Is for Buckaroo

- What are two other names for a cowboy? (buckaroo and drover)

MONITOR LISTENING COMPREHENSION

- What does the letter *R* stand for in this ABC book? (rodeo)

- The letter *H* stands for *hat*. What were the names of some of the hats mentioned in this story? (Stetson, Ten Gallon, Boss of the Plains)

- Did you hear other words for *cowboy?* (vaquero, Will Rogers, Pecos Bill, Annie Oakley)

- What does the letter *C* stand for in this ABC book? What does it mean? (chuck wagon; wagon where the food was cooked and served)

 **Amazing Words** to build oral vocabulary

	MONITOR PROGRESS
climate **livestock** **occupation** **buckaroo** **drover** **lariat** **legend** **rawhide**	**If…** children lack oral vocabulary experiences about the concept Traditions, **then…** use the Oral Vocabulary Routine. See p. DI•6 to teach *buckaroo* and *drover*.

Build Concepts Have children demonstrate their understanding of ABC books by creating the first three pages of their own cowboy ABC book. Have children illustrate the *A* is for Andalusia, *B* is for buckaroo, and *C* is for chuck wagon pages.

Suffixes

- Review words with suffixes *-ness*, *-less*.
- Read and sort words with suffixes *-ness, -less*.

TEACH/MODEL

Fluent Word Reading

ROUTINE

1 **Connect** Write *sweetness.* You can read this word because you know how to read words with suffixes. What base word and suffix form *sweetness?* (*sweet* and *ness*) Do the same with *jobless.*

2 **Model** When you come to a word with a suffix, look at the base word and suffix and blend the two word parts together to read it. Model reading *emptiness, rudeness, weariness, harmless.* When you come to a new word with a suffix, what are you going to do?

3 **Group Practice** Write *pointless, thoughtfulness, tireless, ageless, redness, shameless.* Read these words. Look at the word, say the word to yourself, and then read the word aloud. Allow 2–3 seconds previewing time.

Strategic Intervention

Use **Strategic Intervention Decodable Reader 29** for more practice with suffixes.

ELL

Support Phonics Invite children to name the items pictured in the art for "A Cowboy's Life" as you replay the Phonics Songs and Rhymes Audio CD.

WORD READING

PHONICS SONGS AND RHYMES CHART 29 Frame each of the following words on Phonics Songs and Rhymes Chart 29. Call on individuals to read them. Guide children in previewing.

fearless	**countless**	**loneliness**
weariness	**cheerfulness**	

Sing "A Cowboy's Life" to the tune of "The Yellow Rose of Texas," or play the CD. Have children follow along on the chart as they sing. Then have individuals take turns circling and reading words with suffixes on the chart.

Phonics Songs and Rhymes Audio

A Cowboy's Life

In the old days, fearless cowboys
Roamed all over the West.
They all had countless talents,
And always did their best.

They faced loneliness and weariness
But they could all agree
That cheerfulness was easy
'Cause they loved the wide prairie.

Phonics Songs and Rhymes Chart 29

SORT WORDS

INDIVIDUALS SORT WORDS WITH SUFFIXES Write suffixes -*ness* and -*less* as headings for a two-column chart. Write the base words in each column. Have all children complete the activity on paper by writing each base word and adding the suffix. Ask individuals to read the completed lists and tell what each word means. Provide feedback as necessary.

-ness	-less
mad	tooth
late	flight
still	shape
sore	meat
sharp	speech

Spelling

PRACTICE Suffixes

WRITE DICTATION SENTENCES Have children write these sentences. Repeat words slowly, allowing children to hear each sound. Children may use the Word Wall to help with spelling high-frequency words. [Word Wall]

Dad wants us to show kindness and goodness to people.
Fitness will help prevent sickness and weakness.
"I am fearless in the darkness!" I told my sister.

HOMEWORK Spelling Practice Book, p. 114

Spelling Words

Suffixes

1. kindness	7. sadness
2. careless	8. sickness
3. goodness	9. helpless
4. useless	10. thankless
5. fearless*	11. fitness
6. darkness	12. weakness

Challenge Words

13. awareness 15. wireless
14. eagerness

* Words from the Selection

Suffixes -ness and -less

Spelling Words					
kindness	careless	goodness	useless	fearless	darkness
sadness	sickness	helpless	thankless	fitness	weakness

Write a list word that means the same as each word or phrase.

sorrow	being fit	being good
1. sadness	2. fitness	3. goodness

without help	being kind	not rewarded
4. helpless	5. kindness	6. thankless

Write a list word to finish each sentence.

7. Grandma has a **weakness** for sweets.
8. His **sickness** caused a high fever.
9. I stumbled in the **darkness** .
10. It's **useless** to look for his ring in the lake.
11. The **fearless** firefighters rescued the little boy.
12. I was **careless** and dropped my model airplane.

School + Home **Home Activity** Your child used spelling words in sentences. Have your child make up new sentences, using the list words.

▲ **Spelling Practice Book** p. 114

OBJECTIVES

- Build background.
- Learn lesson vocabulary.

Read each sentence. **Answer** the questions.

1. The family wanted new land, so they moved West.
   Why did the family move West?

   They wanted new land.

2. Because the hills were steep, the ox got tired.
   Why did the ox get tired?

   The hills were steep.

3. They came to a pond, so they stopped for water.
   Why did they stop for water?

   They came to a pond.

4. The trail turned to mud because of the rain.
   Why did the trail turn to mud?

   The rain turned it to mud.

5. The wagon got stuck in the mud.
   Why did the wagon get stuck?

   It was muddy.

Home Activity Your child answered questions about why things happened. Work with your child to write a story about a trip or drive you have taken together. As you plan your story, discuss what happened and why these things happened. Encourage your child to add an illustrated cover to the story.

▲ **Practice Book 2.2** p. 135, Cause and Effect

Build Background Draw a simple picture of a horse and campfire. Ask children to name these objects in their home language and say the words in English.

Build Background

DISCUSS COWBOYS Display a picture of a cowboy from long ago. Initiate discussion by asking children what they know about cowboys.

- What do cowboys do?
- What do cowboys wear? Why?
- Have you ever seen a cowboy movie?

BACKGROUND BUILDING AUDIO Have children listen to the CD and share the new information they learned about life on a ranch in the Old West and ranching today.

Background Building Audio

COMPLETE A GRAPHIC ORGANIZER Draw a T-chart or display Graphic Organizer 25. Write *clothes cowboys wore* and *what cowboys did* as the headings in the T-chart. Ask children to suggest cowboy clothing and activities. Write their suggestions in the appropriate columns of the chart.

clothes cowboys wore	what cowboys did
cowboy hats	herded cattle
boots	slept outside
bandannas or scarves	slept in bunkhouses
	rode horses

▲ **Graphic Organizer 25**

CONNECT TO SELECTION Connect background information to *Cowboys*.

Today we still have cattle ranches. Long ago, cowboys lived and worked on cattle ranches and took care of the livestock. We are about to read a story about cowboys. We'll find out about their occupation and what life was like for them.

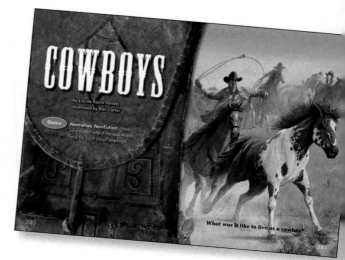

Vocabulary

LESSON VOCABULARY

WORD RATING CHART Create word rating charts using the categories *Know, Have Seen,* and *Don't Know,* or use Graphic Organizer 4.

WORDS TO KNOW

T **cattle** *Cattle* are animals raised for their meat, milk, or skins. Cows and bulls are *cattle.*

T **trails** A *trail* is a path across a field or through the woods.

T **cowboy** A *cowboy* is a person who works on a cattle ranch. *Cowboys* also take part in rodeos.

T **herd** A *herd* is a group of the same kind of animal that is kept or fed together.

T **campfire** a fire in a camp used for cooking or warmth

T **railroad** A *railroad* is a road or track of two steel rails. Trains run on *railroads.*

T **galloped** To *gallop* is to run very fast.

MORE WORDS TO KNOW

roundup the act of driving or bringing cattle together from long distances

chuckwagon a wagon that carries food and cooking equipment for cowboys

bellowed made a loud, deep noise like a roar

T = Tested Word

- Children should be able to decode most words. To read *cattle,* divide the word into syllables (*cat/tle*) and have children blend the syllables with you.

- Read each word and have children check one of the three columns: *Know* (know and can use), *Have Seen* (have seen or heard the word; don't know the meaning), *Don't Know.*

- Have children review their charts at the end of the week and make changes to their ratings.

▲ **Practice Book 2.2** p. 136, Lesson Vocabulary

Word	Know	Have Seen	Don't Know
cattle	✓		
trails	✓		
cowboy	✓		
herd			✓
campfire	✓		
railroad		✓	
galloped			✓

▲ **Graphic Organizer 4**

Monitor Progress | **Check Lesson Vocabulary**

Write these words and have individuals read them.

cattle	**trails**	**cowboy**	**herd**	**campfire**	**railroad**
galloped	**stars**	**money**	**clothes**	**caught**	**many**

If... children cannot read these words,

then... have them practice in pairs with word cards before reading the selection. Monitor their fluency with these words during reading, and provide additional practice opportunities before the Day 5 Assessment.

SUCCESS PREDICTOR

Spiral REVIEW

● Reviews previously taught high-frequency words and lesson vocabulary.

Day 1 Check Word Reading	▶**Day 2** Check Lesson Vocabulary/High-Frequency Words	**Day 3** Check Retelling	**Day 4** Check Fluency	**Day 5** Assess Progress

Word Reading

SUCCESS PREDICTOR

Vocabulary Strategy
for Compound Words

Words to Know

cowboy
cattle
campfire
herd
trails
railroad
galloped

Remember

Try the strategy. Then, if you need more help, use your glossary or a dictionary.

Word Structure When you are reading, you may come across a long word that you don't know. If the long word is made up of two small words, then it is probably a compound word. The two small words can help you figure out the meaning of the compound word.

1. Look for the two small words in a long word.

2. Think about what each small word means. Put those meanings together. Does this help you understand the compound word?

3. Try the new meaning in the sentence. Does it make sense?

Read "Like a Cowboy." Look for compound words. Use the meanings of the small words in each compound word to help you figure out the new meaning.

378

LIKE A COWBOY

What was it like to be a cowboy long ago? To find out, some people stay on a ranch. They ride horses, and they chase and rope cattle, or cows. At night around a campfire, they tell stories and sing songs. They even take a herd of cattle on a cattle drive.

Long ago, cowboys took herds of cattle on cattle drives. They traveled on trails that ran from Texas to Kansas. From there, railroad trails took the cattle to cities in the East. The trail was a thousand miles long. The cattle drive lasted for months.

The cattle drive at the ranch today lasts only a day or two. Still, the cattle drive gives people an idea of what it was like to be a cowboy. They can imagine how hard the cowboys worked on the trail. They can imagine how happy the cowboys were as they galloped into town after a long cattle drive.

Words to Write

Would you like to be a cowboy or a cowgirl? Why or why not? Write your ideas. Use words from the Words to Know list.

379

OBJECTIVE

⊙ Use compound words to determine the meaning of unfamiliar words.

ELL

Access Content Use ELL Poster 29 to preteach the lesson vocabulary. Reinforce the words with the vocabulary activities and word cards in the ELL Teaching Guide, pp. 199–200. Choose from the following to meet children's language proficiency levels.

Beginning Use the list of Multilingual Lesson Vocabulary in the ELL Teaching Guide, pp. 276–283, and other home-language resources to provide translations.

Intermediate Have children add to the cowboy graphic organizer.

Advanced Teach the lesson on pp. 378–379. Have children find home-language terms for *cowboy, cattle,* and *campfire.*

Resource for home-language words may include parents, bilingual staff members, and bilingual dictionaries.

Vocabulary Strategy

TEACH/MODEL Word Structure

CONNECT Remind children of strategies to use when they come across words they don't understand.

- We can look in a dictionary or glossary.
- We can look for context clues in the words and sentences around the unknown word.
- Sometimes we can get the meaning from word parts. We may understand the base word and suffix *(graceful, full of grace),* or the two smaller words in a compound word *(campfire, a fire at camp).* Today we will learn more about using word parts.

INTRODUCE THE STRATEGY

- Read and discuss the steps for using word structure on p. 378.

- Have children read "Like a Cowboy," paying attention to word structure to determine the meaning of highlighted words.

- Model using word structure to determine the meaning of *campfire*.

MODEL When I come to the word *campfire*, I know that this word is made of two smaller words, *camp* and *fire*. Knowing what those two words mean helps me know that a campfire is a fire that you have while camping.

PRACTICE

- Have children determine the meanings of highlighted words in "Like a Cowboy" and explain the word structure clues they used.

- Point out that using word structure doesn't work with every word, and they may still have to use the glossary or a dictionary to find the meaning of some words.

WRITE Children's writing about whether they would like to be a cowboy or cowgirl should include lesson vocabulary.

CONNECT TO READING Encourage children to use these strategies to determine the meaning of an unknown word.

- Look for context clues in nearby words or sentences.

- Use word parts.

- Use the glossary or a dictionary.

Group Time

On-Level	Strategic Intervention	Advanced
Read *Cowboys.*	**Read** SI Decodable Reader 29.	**Read** *Cowboys.*
• Use pp. 380–403.	• Read or listen to *Cowboys.*	• Use the **Routine** on p. DI•47.
	• Use the **Routine** on p. DI•46.	

 ELL Place English language learners in the groups that correspond to their reading abilities in English.

DAY 2

ⓘ Independent Activities

Independent Reading See p. 376j for Reading/Library activities and suggestions.

Journal Writing Write how you feel about horses. Share your writing.

Literacy Centers To provide experiences with *Cowboys,* you may use the Writing Center on p. 376k.

Practice Book 2.2 Cause and Effect, p. 135; Lesson Vocabulary, p. 136; Fact and Opinion, p. 137

Break into small groups after Vocabulary and before Writing.

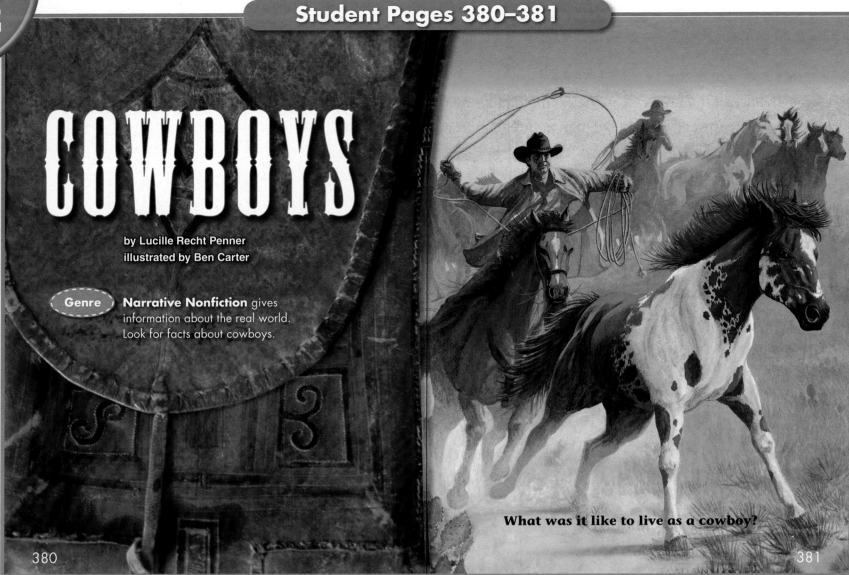

COWBOYS

by Lucille Recht Penner
illustrated by Ben Carter

Genre **Narrative Nonfiction** gives information about the real world. Look for facts about cowboys.

380

What was it like to live as a cowboy?

381

 **AudioText**

Read
Prereading Strategies

PREVIEW AND PREDICT Have children read the selection title. Invite them to tell what they know about a cowboy's job. Call on volunteers to read the names of the author and illustrator. Challenge children to look at the illustrations and predict what they will learn about cowboys from this selection.

DISCUSS NARRATIVE NONFICTION Read the definition of narrative nonfiction on p. 380 of the Student Edition. Make sure children understand that this selection will teach them about real people. Explain that it gives information about an important part of United States history.

SET PURPOSE Read aloud the question on p. 381. Ask what other questions children would like answered in the selection.

 **ELL**

Access Content Before reading, review the story summary in English and/or the home language. See the ELL Teaching Guide, pp. 201–203.

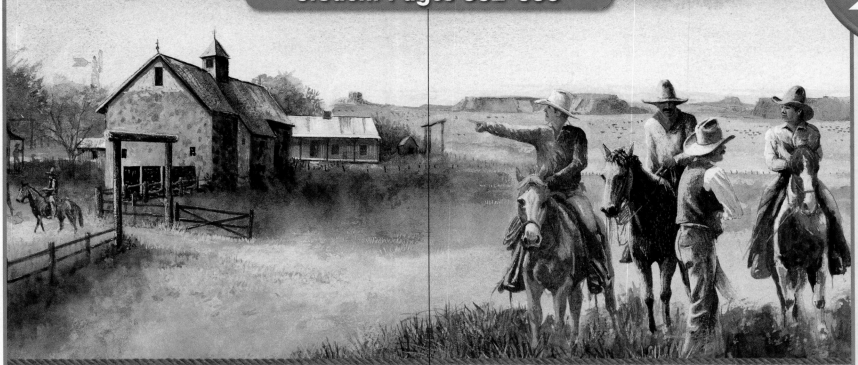

If you were out west about a hundred years ago, you might have heard a cowboy yelling—*ti yi yippy yay!*—as he rode across the plains.

What was it like to be a cowboy way back then? Cowboys lived on cattle ranches. A ranch had a house for the rancher and his family, barns for animals, and a bunkhouse where the cowboys slept.

382

The rancher owned thousands of cattle. They wandered for miles looking for grass and water.

Twice a year, the cowboys drove all the cattle together. This was called a roundup. The cowboys counted the baby calves that had been born since the last roundup. The biggest cattle were chosen to sell at market.

383

Guiding Comprehension

Setting • Literal
- **What time and place is the author writing about?**
The author is writing about the Old West about 100 years ago.

Cause and Effect • Inferential
- **Why did ranchers need cowboys?**
Since ranchers owned thousands of cattle that wandered for miles looking for grass and water, they probably needed cowboys to keep an eye on the cattle. They also needed them at roundup time.

▲ **Pages 382–383**
Have children read to find out why ranchers needed cowboys.

Monitor Progress

Decoding

If... children come to a word they don't know,	**then...** remind them to:
	1. Blend the word.
	2. Decide if the word makes sense.
	3. Look in a dictionary for more help.

A roundup was hard work. The cattle were wild and fast. They had long, sharp, dangerous horns. Cowboys called them Longhorns. If you made a Longhorn mad, it would charge at you. A cowboy didn't want to get close to an angry Longhorn.

So he made a loop in the end of his rope. Then he twirled it over his head and let it fly. When he caught the Longhorn, he could tell that it belonged to his ranch.

How could he tell? It was easy. Each rancher put a special mark called a brand on his cows. Baby calves didn't have brands, yet. They didn't need them. A baby calf always followed its mother.

Every ranch had its own name and its own brand. The Rocking Chair Ranch brand looked like a rocking chair. The Flying V Ranch brand looked like this: ∿

384

385

▲ **Pages 384–385**
Have children read to learn why ranchers branded cattle.

Monitor Progress

Lesson Vocabulary

| **If...** children have a problem reading a new lesson vocabulary word, | **then...** use the Lesson Vocabulary on p. 378f to reteach the problematic word. |

Guiding Comprehension

Cause and Effect • Inferential
- **Why was it important for cowboys to learn to rope Longhorns?**
  They needed to be able to catch the Longhorns without being hurt by them.

Details and Facts • Literal
- **What was the purpose of branding cattle?**
  The brand showed who owned the cattle.

Make Judgments • Critical
- **Did the Flying V Ranch have a good brand? Why or why not?**
  Children may say yes, because the symbol looks something like a V with wings so other ranchers could easily connect the brand with the name of the ranch. Children may say no, because some people might think that the symbol does not look like a V.

___ Suffixes –ness, –less

lesson/tested vocabulary

After the roundup was over, it was time to sell the Longhorns. That meant taking them to big market towns. Back then, there were no roads across the wide plains—only dusty trails that cattle had made with their hooves as they tramped along. Some trails were a thousand miles long! Since cattle could walk only fifteen miles a day, the long, hard trip often lasted months. It was called a trail drive. There was a lot to do to get ready.

At the beginning of a trail day, one cowboy rode out in front of the herd. "Come on, boys," he called

to the cattle. A few big Longhorns started after him. They bellowed and swung their heads from side to side. Other cattle followed, and soon they were all on their way.

Cattle didn't like so much walking. After a while, they wanted to turn around and go home. Cowboys rode up and down the sides of the herd to keep them in line. A few cowboys rode at the end of the herd to make sure no cattle were left behind.

386

387

Guiding Comprehension

Cause and Effect • Inferential
- **Why did cowboys go on trail drives?**
  They had to take cattle from a ranch in the country to a large town that had a marketplace where the cattle could be sold.

Graphic Sources • Inferential
- **What is the occupation of each cowboy in the picture?**
  The cowboy in front is leading the herd. The cowboys riding beside the Longhorns are keeping them in line. The cowboys at the rear are watching to make sure no cattle are left behind.

Summarize • Inferential
- **What have you learned from the selection so far?**
  About 100 years ago, ranchers in the Old West hired cowboys to take care of their cattle. Each ranch had its own brand. Twice a year, cowboys took cattle on a trail drive to a market town where the cattle could be sold.

▲ **Pages 386–387**
Have children read to find out how cattle got from a ranch to the market.

Strategy Self-Check

Have children ask themselves these questions to check their reading.

Vocabulary Strategy
- Do I look for context clues?
- Do I use word parts?
- Do I use the glossary or a dictionary?

Graphic Organizer
- Do I look for what happens and why it happened?
- Do I look for clue words like *because* and *so*?
- Do I use a graphic organizer to help me understand what I read?

2

It was hot on the trail. Cowboys wore hats with wide brims to keep the sun out of their eyes. When it rained, the brims made good umbrellas. Around their necks, cowboys wore red bandannas. When it got dusty, they pulled the bandannas over their noses.

388

Leather leggings—called chaps—were tied over their pants to keep out thorns and cactus spines. High leather boots kept out dirt and pebbles. Cowboy boots had handles called "mule ears." The cowboy grabbed the mule ears to pull his boots off and on.

389

▲ **Pages 388–389**
Have children read to find out why cowboys dressed the way they did.

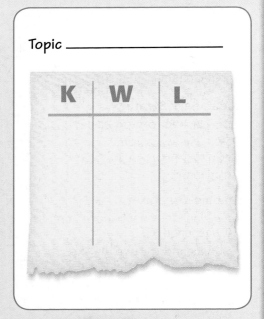

Topic _____

K	W	L

▲ **Graphic Organizer 3**

Strategies in Context

GRAPHIC ORGANIZER

- **Why did cowboys dress the way they did?**
  Their hats protected them from sun and rain. Their bandannas protected them from dust. Their chaps protected them from thorns and cactus spines. Their high leather boots kept out dirt and pebbles.

Monitor Progress	**Graphic Organizer**
If... children are unable to answer the question,	**then...** model how to use a K-W-L Chart.

Think Aloud **MODEL** In the K-column, I wrote that cowboys wear hats and boots. In the W-column, I wrote that I wanted to know more about how cowboys dress. In the L-column, I'll write about what I learned: Cowboys wear hats with brims, bandannas, chaps, and high leather boots to protect them from thorns, dirt, and pebbles and the sunny, rainy, dusty climate.

ASSESS Have children continue to use K-W-L Charts to record information.

____ Suffixes –ness, –less   lesson/tested vocabulary

What else did a cowboy need on his trail? A good horse. Cowboys spent the whole day on horseback. They rode little horses called cow ponies. A good cow pony was <u>fearless</u>. It could cross rough ground in the blackest night. It could swim a deep, wide river.

It could crash right through the bushes after a runaway cow. The cowboy had to hold on tight!

Every day the herd tramped the hot, dry plains. Two or three big steers were the leaders. They always walked in front. The cowboys got to know them well. They gave them pet names, like "Old Grumpy" and "Starface."

Cows could get in trouble. Sometimes one got stuck in the mud. The cowboy roped it and pulled it out. A cow might get hurt on the trail. A cowboy took care of that, too.

390

391

Guiding Comprehension

▲ **Pages 390–391**
Have children read to find out what makes a good cow pony.

Summarize • Inferential

- **What makes a good cow pony?**
A good cow pony is brave. It is sure-footed and able to swim. It can see well, even at night, and is tough enough to carry a cowboy for a whole day.

Make Judgments • Critical

- **Do you think a cowboy could be good at his occupation if he did not have a good cow pony? Why or why not?**
No. A cowboy and his pony are a team. A cowboy needs a pony that can take him wherever he has to go.

Visualize • Inferential

- **What can you tell about the climate and landforms along the trail?**
It is hot, dry, and dusty. Most of the land is flat and grassy, but there are also hills and muddy holes.

TIME FOR Science

Climate
Have children study the illustrations to draw conclusions about the climate of the dry, dusty plains. Plains receive more rainfall than desert areas but less than forested regions. They are characterized by mostly flat land, few trees, and different kinds of grass. Plains are often good places to grow crops. Animals common to American plains are bison, prairie dogs, rodents, and many species of birds.

At night the cowboys stopped to let the cattle eat, drink, and sleep. It was time for the cowboys to eat, too. "Cookie" had a hot meal ready for them. That's what cowboys called the cook.

Cookie drove a special wagon called the chuckwagon. It had drawers for flour, salt, beans, and pots and pans. A water barrel was tied underneath.

Cookie gave every cowboy a big helping of biscuits, steak, gravy, and beans. He cooked the same meal almost every night, but the cowboys didn't mind. It tasted good!

There were no tables or chairs, so the cowboys sat right on the ground. After dinner they played cards or read by the flickering light of the campfire. The nights were chilly and bright with stars.

392

393

▲ **Pages 392–393**
Have children read to find out how cowboys got food during a trail drive.

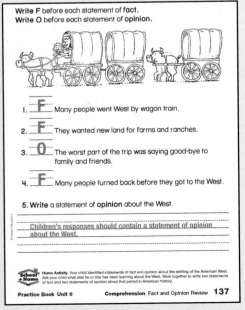

Write **F** before each statement of **fact**.
Write **O** before each statement of **opinion**.

1. **F** Many people went West by wagon train.

2. **F** They wanted new land for farms and ranches.

3. **O** The worst part of the trip was saying good-bye to family and friends.

4. **F** Many people turned back before they got to the West.

5. Write a statement of **opinion** about the West.

Children's responses should contain a statement of opinion about the West.

Practice Book Unit 6   Comprehension Fact and Opinion Review **137**

▲ **Practice Book 2.2** p. 137, Fact and Opinion

Skills in Context

REVIEW **FACT AND OPINION**

- **Is it a fact or an opinion that the cook drove a chuckwagon? Why?**
  It is a fact because you can prove that it is true or false.

Monitor Progress	Fact and Opinion
If... children are unable to answer the question,	**then...** model how to identify facts and opinions.

Think Aloud — **MODEL** I know that a fact is something I can check by looking it up in a book or other resource. I can find out whether cooks drove a chuckwagon, so it is a fact.

ASSESS Have children identify other facts on these pages.

____ Suffixes -ness, -less

lesson/tested vocabulary

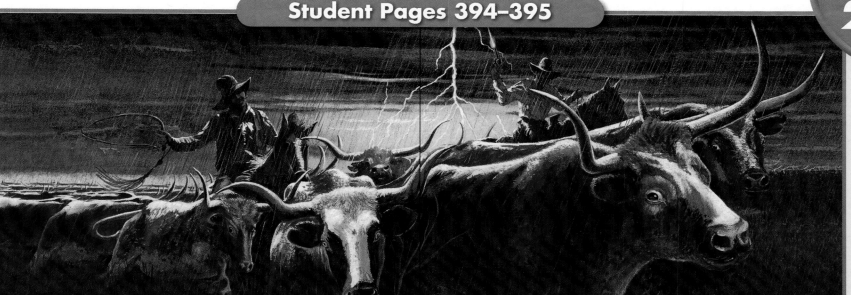

But the cowboys didn't stay up late. They were tired. At bedtime, they just pulled off their boots and crawled into their bedrolls. A cowboy never wore pajamas. What about a pillow? He used his saddle.

Trail drives were dangerous. Many things could go wrong. The herd might stampede if there was a loud noise—like a sudden crash of thunder. A stampede was scary. Cattle ran wildly in all directions, rolling their eyes and bellowing with fear. The ground shook under them. The bravest cowboys galloped to the front of the herd. They had to make

the leaders turn. They shouted at them and fired their six shooters in the air. They tried to make the cattle run in a circle until they calmed down.

Sometimes they'd run into rustlers. A rustler was a cow thief. Rustlers hid behind rocks and jumped out at the cattle to make them stampede. While the cowboys were trying to catch the terrified cattle and calm them down, the rustlers drove off as many as they could.

394

395

Skills in Context

CAUSE AND EFFECT

- **What can cause a stampede?**
  A loud noise like a sudden crash of thunder can cause a stampede.

Monitor Progress	Cause and Effect
If... children are unable to answer the questions,	then... model how to determine the cause.

Think Aloud

MODEL To find the cause, I can ask, "Why does a stampede happen?" The text says that a stampede happens when cattle are frightened by a loud noise. The cause is a loud noise, and the effect is a stampede.

ASSESS Ask children why rustlers made cattle stampede. Have them use a cause and effect graphic organizer if necessary. (The rustlers scared the cattle by jumping suddenly, which caused the cattle to stampede. While the cowboys were busy trying to stop the stampede, the rustlers were able to drive off many cattle.)

▲ **Pages 394–395**
Have children read to find out what causes a stampede.

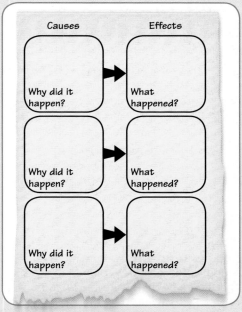

▲ **Graphic Organizer 19**

When the herd came to a big river, the cowboys in front galloped right into the water. The cattle plunged in after them. The cattle swam mostly under water. Sometimes the cowboys could see only the tips of their black noses and their long white horns.

Most cowboys didn't know how to swim. If a cowboy fell into the water, he grabbed the horse's tail and held on tight until they reached shore.

Trail drives often went through Indian Territory. The Indians charged ten cents a head to let the cattle cross their land. If the cowboys didn't pay, there might be a fight. But usually the money was handed over and the herd plodded on.

396   397

▲ **Pages 396–397**
Have children read to find out how cowboys got the herd across wide rivers.

Guiding Comprehension

Details and Facts • Literal
- **How did cowboys get the herd across wide rivers?**
  The cowboys in front galloped into the water, and the cattle followed.

Visualize • Inferential
- **Imagine that you are standing on the other side of a river watching the cattle cross. What would you see and hear?**
  Children may say they would see the noses and horns of the cattle, the swimming horses, and cowboys holding onto their horses. They would hear splashing, animal sounds, and the shouts of the cowboys.

Graphic Sources • Inferential
- **Which cowboy in the picture has fallen off his horse? How do you know?**
  The cowboy holding his horse's tail fell off his horse. The text says most cowboys couldn't swim so they grabbed their horses' tails if they fell off.

Access Content Pantomime the action words *galloped, plunged, swam,* and *plodded.* Then write the words on cards. Invite children to choose a card, read the word, and act out the appropriate motion.

_____ Suffixes –*ness,* –*less*   lesson/tested vocabulary

398

At last, the noisy, dusty cattle stamped into a market town. The cowboys drove them into pens near the railroad tracks. Then they got their pay. It was time for fun!

What do you think most cowboys wanted first? A bath! The barber had a big tub in the back of the shop. For a dollar, you could soak and soak. A boy kept throwing in pails of hot water. Ahh-h-h! Next it was time for a shave, a haircut, and some new clothes.

Tonight, the cowboys would sleep in real beds and eat dinner at a real table. They would sing, dance, and have fun with their friends.

But soon they would be heading back to Longhorn country. There would be many more hot days in the saddle. There would be many more cold nights under the stars.

399

▲ **Pages 398–399**
Have children read to find out what cowboys did at the end of a trail drive.

Guiding Comprehension

Details and Facts • Inferential

- **How did cowboys celebrate the end of a trail drive?**
They got a bath, a shave, a haircut, and new clothes. Then they went out to eat dinner and have fun with their friends.

Visualize • Critical

- **Imagine that you lived in a market town in the Old West. What would it be like on the day the cowboys brought their herd into town?**
Children may say the town would be dusty from all the cattle going down the dirt streets. It would be filled with the sounds of the cattle's hooves and the sounds of the cowboys' shouts. Later, the town would be crowded and noisy because the cowboys were celebrating.

Analyze • Critical

- *Text to Self* **What would you like best about being a cowboy?**
Children may share that they would enjoy traveling or taking care of cattle.

Ranching
Time for SOCIAL STUDIES

Modern ranchers use machines to harvest hay for animals to eat. They transport animals using trains and trucks. Most ranches have telephones and Internet access, so workers can communicate with others. Ask children what they have learned about the work cowhands did in the old days. Have them explain how they think the job is different for modern cowhands. Ask them which parts of the job have probably stayed the same.

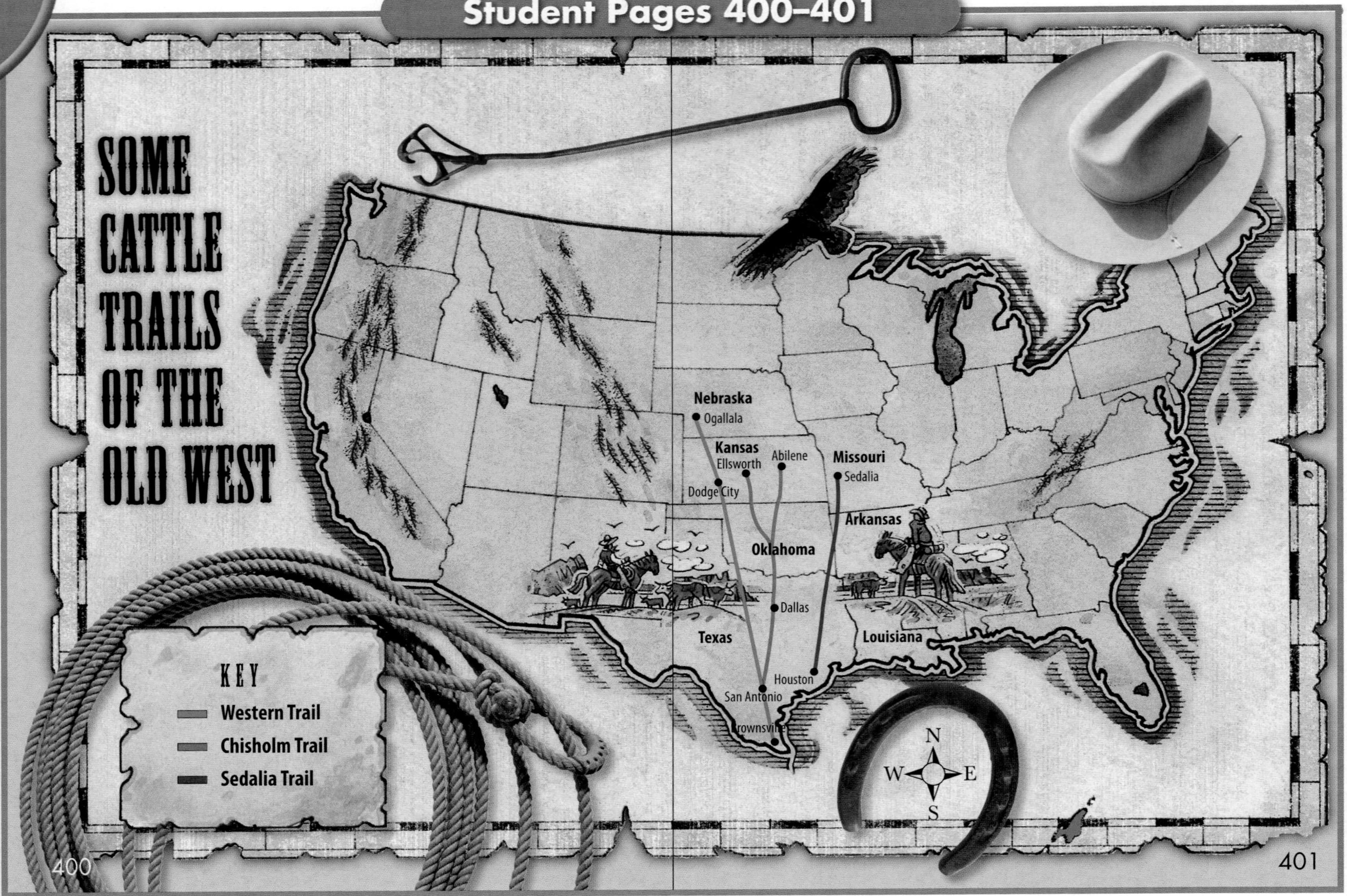

SOME CATTLE TRAILS OF THE OLD WEST

Nebraska
• Ogallala

Kansas
Ellsworth • Abilene

Missouri
• Sedalia

Dodge City

Arkansas

Oklahoma

Dallas •

Texas

Louisiana

Houston •
San Antonio •

Brownsville

KEY

— Western Trail
— Chisholm Trail
— Sedalia Trail

N
W — E
S

400

401

▲ **Pages 400–401**
Have children examine the map to
see cattle trails of the Old West.

EXTEND SKILLS

Graphic Sources

For instruction in using graphic sources,
such as reading a map, discuss the
following:

• Point out the map key. Explain that
the symbols in the key tell what the
features on the map mean. Have
children use the key to identify where
the Western Trail is.

• Point out the compass rose. Explain
that it shows direction on a map. Ask
if the Sedalia Trail ran east or west
of the Chisholm Trail.

Assess Have children use the key
and compass rose to describe the
three trails.

____ Suffixes –ness, –less

⬛ lesson/tested vocabulary

Guiding Comprehension

Graphic Sources • Inferential

• **If you were in Houston, which trail would you use to take cattle to Missouri?**
You would take the Sedalia Trail.

Graphic Sources • Inferential

• **If you were going from Ellsworth, Kansas, to San Antonio, Texas, in which direction would you be traveling?**
You would be traveling south.

Author's Purpose • Inferential

• **Why do you think the author included this map?**
This map shows the trails the cowboys might have taken during their cattle drives.

Fluency

REREAD FOR FLUENCY

Paired Reading

ROUTINE

Reader 1 Begins Children read the entire book, switching readers at the end of each page.

Reader 2 Begins Have partners reread; now the other partner begins.

Reread For optimal fluency, children should reread three or four times.

Provide Feedback Listen to children read and provide corrective feedback regarding their oral reading and their use of the blending strategy.

OBJECTIVES

● Write a math story.
● Identify commas.

Strategic Intervention

Have children copy the math story, solve it, and illustrate their writing.

Advanced

Have children who are able to write complete sentences independently write a more advanced math story. Partners can exchange and solve math stories.

Writing Support Before writing, reread the class math story and point out key words that children may want to incorporate in their own writing.

Beginning Provide a writing framework that children can copy, and fill in missing numbers to create a math story.

Intermediate Help children work in small groups to discuss what they will write, as one group member takes notes. Children can refer to these notes when they write.

Advanced Encourage children to do a "think-aloud" with a partner to discuss what they are planning to write.

Support Grammar Children may have difficulty recognizing the clauses in a compound sentence. Give them additional practice finding the subject and verb within each independent clause. See the Grammar Transition lessons in the ELL and Transition Handbook.

Interactive Writing

WRITE Math Story

BRAINSTORM Use *Cowboys* to encourage a discussion about cowboys and cattle. Picture walk through the selection and ask children to identify the things that cowboys did with cattle.

SHARE THE PEN Have children participate in writing a math story about cattle. To begin, have a child state something about cattle. Create a number story about it. Write the math story, inviting individuals to write familiar letter-sounds, word parts, and high-frequency words. Ask questions such as:

• What is the first syllable in *cattle?* (/kat/)

• What letters stand for /kat/? *(cat)*

• Have a volunteer write *cat.*

• The last syllable in *cattle* is consonant plus *le.*

• What letters stand for that syllable? *(tle)*

• Have a volunteer write *tle.* Have children blend *cat, tle, cattle.*

Continue to have individuals make contributions. Frequently reread what has been written while tracking the print.

READ THE MATH STORY Read the completed math story, having children echo you.

Math Story

There are 38 cattle on a ranch. A rustler took away 24 cattle. How many cattle are left?

INDEPENDENT WRITING

WRITE A MATH STORY Have children write their own math stories about cattle. Let children illustrate their writing.

Grammar

DEVELOP THE CONCEPT
Commas in Compound Sentences

IDENTIFY COMMAS IN COMPOUND SENTENCES Write these two sentences on the board. *Cowboys tell stories. They read by the campfire.* Point to each word as you read it. Ask children to add a word and a comma to combine these sentences. Add a comma and the word *and*. Change the capital *T* to a lowercase *t*.

Sometimes two sentences can be combined into one sentence. Sentences can be combined with a comma and a connecting word, such as *and* or *but*. The combined sentence is called a compound sentence. What do you call two sentences put together with a comma and a connecting word? (a compound sentence)

PRACTICE

COMBINE SENTENCES Write these two sentences on the board. *Cowboys eat outside. They cook supper over an open fire.*

MODEL I can use a comma with the word *and* to combine these two sentences. Write a comma and the word *and* between the two sentences. Change the capital *T* to a lowercase *t*. Now instead of two short sentences, I have a compound sentence.

Have children practice combining other simple sentences by using a comma and a connecting word.

DAILY FIX-IT

3. Were sitting by the camfire.
   We're sitting by the campfire.

4. The Cowboy rode the tails.
   The cowboy rode the trails.

Commas in Compound Sentences

Sometimes sentences have ideas that go together. These sentences can be combined using a comma and a connecting word, such as **and** or **but**. The combined sentence is called a **compound sentence.**

I want to be a cowboy. I want to ride the range.
I want to be a cowboy, **and** I want to ride the range.

I try to rope cattle. I always miss.
I try to rope cattle, **but** I always miss.

Use the word in ( ) and a comma to combine each pair of sentences. **Write** the new sentence on the lines.

1. I have a cow pony. I need a hat. (but)

   I have a cow pony, but I need a hat.

2. I eat beans. I cook them on a fire. (and)

   I eat beans, and I cook them on a fire.

3. The work is hard. There is time for fun around the campfire. (but)

   The work is hard, but there is time

   for fun around the campfire.

Home Activity Your child learned about commas in compound sentences. Ask your child to combine these sentences, using a comma and the word and: Cowboys wear boots. They wear hats.

▲ **Grammar and Writing Practice Book** p. 113

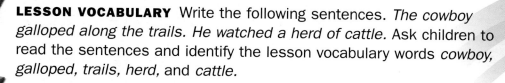

Wrap Up Your Day!

✓ **LESSON VOCABULARY** Write the following sentences. *The cowboy galloped along the trails. He watched a herd of cattle.* Ask children to read the sentences and identify the lesson vocabulary words *cowboy, galloped, trails, herd,* and *cattle.*

✓ **GRAPHIC ORGANIZER** Point to the KWL chart. Have children identify what the *K, W,* and *L* stand for. (What We <u>K</u>now, What We <u>W</u>ant to Know, What We <u>L</u>earned)

LET'S TALK ABOUT IT Recall *Cowboys.* Ask: Why should we learn about cowboys? How does knowing about them help us today? (Responses will vary.) Encourage children to add to their KWL chart.

PREVIEW Day 3

Tell children that tomorrow they will hear another story about cowboys.

Share Literature

B Is for Buckaroo

Phonics and Spelling

REVIEW Syllables *-tion, -ture*

Spelling: Words with Suffixes *-ness, -less*

Vocabulary

Skill Time Words

Fluency

Read with Accuracy and Appropriate Rate

Writing Trait

Sentences

Grammar

Commas in Compound Sentences

Materials

- *Sing with Me Big Book*
- *Read Aloud Anthology*
- Student Edition 402–403

Morning Warm~Up!

Today we're going to listen to the cowboy alphabet again. I'll read and you listen. Let's listen for the letters of the alphabet. Which letter is your favorite in this story?

QUESTION OF THE DAY Encourage children to sing "Occupation: Cowboy" from the *Sing with Me Big Book* as you gather. Write and read the message and discuss the question.

REVIEW CONTRACTIONS

- Point to *we're* in the message. Review that *we're* is a shorter way of saying *we are.*

- Ask children to point to other contractions in the morning message. Identify the two words that make up each contraction.

Build Background Use the Day 3 instruction on ELL Poster 29 to support children's use of English to communicate about lesson concepts.

ELL Poster 29

Share Literature

LISTEN AND RESPOND

BUILD ORAL VOCABULARY Review that yesterday the class listened to find out what the letter *R* stood for. Ask children if they remember what the letter *R* stood for. (rodeo) Remind them that *L* stood for **lariat,** a loop of coiled rope. Ask that children listen today to find out another name for lariat.

Read Aloud Anthology
B is for Buckaroo

MONITOR LISTENING COMPREHENSION

- What are two names for a loop of coiled rope that is used to catch cattle? (lariat or lasso)

- What cowboy gear is mentioned on the *G* page? (boots, hats, jeans, and chaps)

- Two trails are mentioned on the *T* page. Which trails are they? (Goodnight and Santa Fe)

- What people were talked about in this story? What were they famous for? (Will Rogers: He did fancy tricks with his lasso to thrill kids at the Wild West Show; Annie Oakley: She was a sharp shooter in the Wild West Show; Pecos Bill: He is a cowboy legend who rode a cyclone without a saddle and sang songs to quiet the cattle.)

OBJECTIVES

- Set purpose for listening.
- Build oral vocabulary.

Amazing Words
to build oral vocabulary

	MONITOR PROGRESS
climate livestock occupation buckaroo drover lariat legend rawhide	**If...** children lack oral vocabulary experiences about the concept Traditions, **then...** use the Oral Vocabulary Routine. See p. DI·6 to teach *lariat*.

Listen and Respond Help children describe and demonstrate the actions of using a *lariat*. Give children a piece of rope; have them coil it and practice tossing it at a target.

3

OBJECTIVES

- Review syllables *-tion*, and *-ture*.
- Blend, read, and use *-tion, -ture* words.
- Recognize lesson vocabulary.
- Spell words with suffixes *-ness, -less.*

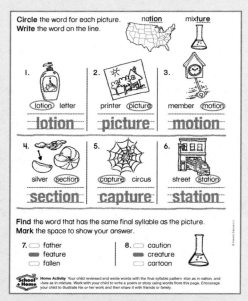

▲ **Practice Book 2.2** p. 138, Syllables *-tion, -ture*

Review Phonics

REVIEW SYLLABLES *-tion, -ture*

READ *-tion, -ture* WORDS Write *action.* You can read this word because you know how to read words with more than one syllable. Read each syllable from left to right and then blend them to read the whole word. Divide *ac/tion* to demonstrate. Remember that *-tion* stands for /shən/. What is the word? (*action*)

Repeat with *picture*, making sure that children recognize that the letters *-ture* can stand for /chər/.

BLEND AND USE WORDS Write the words below. Have children blend the words. Then have each child choose a word and use it in a sentence to demonstrate understanding. Provide help with meaning as needed.

| nation | nature | fraction | station | fixture |
| motion | caution | mixture | feature | fracture |

Lesson Vocabulary

PRACTICE

COMPLETE SENTENCES Provide sentences such as the following. Write lesson vocabulary words on the board. Have children write the lesson vocabulary word that completes each sentence.

- The _____ took care of a cow that had an injured leg. (cowboy)
- We rode down many _____. (trails)
- When the horse _____, it ran very fast. (galloped)
- We made sure the _____ didn't run away. (cattle)
- She sat close to the _____ to stay warm. (campfire)
- There were many cows in the _____. (herd)
- You can ride a _____ train across the country. (railroad)

Spelling

PRACTICE Suffixes *-ness, -less*

MAKE A HERD Have children provide a sentence for each spelling word.

- Give each child a sheet of paper with the outline of a cow on it.
- Have children write sentences inside each cow that use the spelling words. Ask them to underline the spelling words.
- Display the class "herd" on a bulletin board or the wall.

HOMEWORK Spelling Practice Book, p. 115

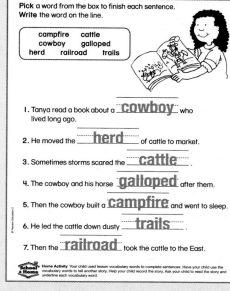

Pick a word from the box to finish each sentence. Write the word on the line.

campfire	cattle
cowboy	galloped
herd	railroad	trails

1. Tanya read a book about a **cowboy** who lived long ago.
2. He moved the **herd** of cattle to market.
3. Sometimes storms scared the **cattle**.
4. The cowboy and his horse **galloped** after them.
5. Then the cowboy built a **campfire** and went to sleep.
6. He led the cattle down dusty **trails**.
7. Then the **railroad** took the cattle to the East.

School + Home Home Activity Your child used lesson vocabulary words to complete sentences. Have your child use the vocabulary words to tell another story. Help your child record the story. Ask your child to read the story and underline each vocabulary word.

▲ **Practice Book 2.2** p. 139, Lesson Vocabulary

Spelling Words

Suffixes *-ness, -less*

1. kindness
2. careless
3. goodness
4. useless
5. fearless*
6. darkness
7. sadness
8. sickness
9. helpless
10. thankless
11. fitness
12. weakness

Challenge Words

13. awareness
14. eagerness
15. wireless

* Word from the Selection

Suffixes *-ness* and *-less*

Spelling Words					
kindness	careless	goodness	useless	fearless	darkness
sadness	sickness	helpless	thankless	fitness	weakness

Read the story. **Circle** three spelling mistakes. **Write** the words correctly. Write the run-on sentence as two separate sentences.

Frequently Misspelled Words
again
very
then

Last night I heard a scratchy noise in the (darknes) My fearless sister got up she turned on the light. My hamster was scratching under my bed. I hadn't put him back in his cage. I won't be so (carless) (agin).

1. **darkness** 2. **careless** 3. **again**
4. **My fearless sister got up.**
   She turned on the light.

Circle the word that is spelled correctly. **Write** it.

5. (sickness) / sicknes **sickness**   6. usless / (useless) **useless**
7. (weakness) / weekness **weakness**   8. (sadness) / sadnes **sadness**

School + Home Home Activity Your child identified misspelled words with *-ness* and *-less*. Have your child pronounce a list word and then spell the base word and the suffix separately.

▲ **Spelling Practice Book** p. 115

OBJECTIVES

- Discuss meanings of time words.
- Use time words in sentences.

Strategic Intervention

Have children illustrate the meaning of *twice a year.* Then help them write a caption using the words *twice a year.*

Advanced

Have children work with a partner to identify other time words. They can use a dictionary to confirm their meanings.

Extend Language Help children practice using time words. Write the phrase they use on paper and have children illustrate it.

Vocabulary

TIME WORDS

DISCUSS TIME WORDS Have children recall that *Cowboys* refers to a time long ago. Explain that some words represent time, such as the words *long ago.* Write the following sentence and discuss the time words *once each week.* Then have children think of more time words.

I have piano lessons once each week.

EXPAND SELECTION VOCABULARY Discuss with children the meaning of each phrase listed below. Use each phrase in a sample sentence. Have children work with partners to write their own sentences for each phrase. Invite volunteers to share their sentences.

a hundred years ago   at the beginning

Group Time

DAY
3

On-Level	**Strategic Intervention**	**Advanced**
Read *Cowboys.*	*Read* or listen to *Cowboys.*	*Read* Self-Selected Reading.
• Use pp. 380–403.	• Use the **Routine** on p. DI•48.	• Use the **Routine** on p. DI•49.

 Place English language learners in the groups that correspond to their reading abilities in English.

ⓘ Independent Activities

Independent Reading See p. 376j for Reading/Library activities and suggestions.

Journal Writing Pretend you are on a trail drive. Write about a day on the trail. Share your writing.

Literacy Centers To provide experiences with *Cowboys,* you may use the Writing Center on p. 376k.

Practice Book 2.2 Syllables *-tion, -ture,* p. 138; Lesson Vocabulary, p. 139

Break into small groups after Vocabulary and before Writing.

Fluency

READ WITH ACCURACY AND APPROPRIATE PACE

MODEL READING WITH ACCURACY AND APPROPRIATE PACE Use *Cowboys.*

- Point to the first sentence on p. 384. Good readers read without making mistakes. They don't leave out words. They read with accuracy.

- Ask children to follow along as you read the page with accuracy and at an appropriate pace.

- Have children read the page after you. Encourage them to read at a similar pace. Continue in the same way with pp. 385–386.

REREAD FOR FLUENCY

Choral Reading

ROUTINE

1 **Select a Passage** For *Cowboys,* use pp. 394–396.

2 **Divide into Groups** Assign each group a part to read. For this selection, alternate paragraphs. The first group reads the first paragraph. The second group reads the next paragraph and so on.

3 **Model** Have children track the print as you read.

4 **Read Together** Have children read along with you.

5 **Independent Readings** Have the groups read aloud without you. Monitor progress and provide feedback. For optimal fluency, children should reread three to four times.

Monitor Progress	Fluency
If... children have difficulty reading,	**then...** prompt: • Are you reading too fast? • Are you skipping any words? • Try to read at a good pace, not too fast and not too slow.
If... the class cannot read fluently without you,	**then...** continue to have them read along with you.

OBJECTIVE

- Read aloud fluently with accuracy and appropriate pace.

Options for Oral Reading
Use *Cowboys* or one of the following Leveled Readers.

On-Level

Cowboy Days

Strategic Intervention

Ranch Life

Advanced

Life on the Ranch

ELL

Fluency Model the reading of phrases in the story, such as "let it fly" and "wild and fast," so that beginning English language learners can practice reading at an appropriate pace.

Fluency Coach CD To develop fluent readers, use Fluency Coach.

Retelling Plan
- ☑ Week 1 assess Strategic Intervention students.
- ☑ Week 2 assess Advanced students.
- ☑ Week 3 assess Strategic Intervention students.
- ☑ **This week assess On-Level students**.
- ☐ Week 5 assess any students you have not yet checked during this unit.

Look Back and Write
Point out information from the text that answers the question. Then have children write a response to the question. For test practice, assign a 10–15 minute time limit. For assessment, see the Scoring Rubric at the bottom of this page.

Assessment Focus on comprehension and whether each child can provide good information about the selection, rather than mistakes in English. For more ideas on assessing comprehension, see the ELL and Transition Handbook.

Reader Response

TALK ABOUT IT Model a response. It would have been fun to sit around the campfire and play cards. It would have been hard to use a saddle for a pillow.

1. RETELL Have children use the retelling strip in the Student Edition to retell the selection.

Monitor Progress **Check Retelling** Rubric 4 3 2 1

Have children retell *Cowboys*.

If... children have difficulty retelling the selection,

then... use the Retelling Cards and the Scoring Rubric for Retelling on p. 402–403 to help them move toward fluent retelling.

SUCCESS PREDICTOR

Day 1 Check Word Reading · **Day 2** Check Lesson Vocabulary/High-Frequency Words · ▶**Day 3 Check Retelling** · **Day 4** Check Fluency · **Day 5** Assess Progress

2. 🔄 **CAUSE AND EFFECT** Model a response. It could make the cattle run in a stampede.

3. 🔄 **GRAPHIC ORGANIZERS** Model a response. I'll write *What I Know About Cowboys* in the center circle. In the outer circles I'll write some of the things we learned in *Cowboys,* such as *work hard, ride horses, wear protective clothing, take care of livestock,* and *go on trail drives.*

LOOK BACK AND WRITE Read the writing prompt on p. 402 and model your thinking. I'll look back at pages 394–397 and reread them. I'll look for trail drive dangers. Then I'll write my response in a list. Have children write their responses.

Scoring Rubric | **Look Back and Write**

Top-Score Response A top-score response will list details from pp. 394–397 of the selection about dangers that cowboys might face on a trail drive.
Example of a Top-Score Response Here is a list of trail drive dangers that might have helped cowboys:

Trail Drive Dangers
stampedes
rustlers
rivers

For additional rubrics, see p. WA10.

Reader Response

Open for Discussion Would you have liked a cowboy's job? What part would have been fun? What part might have made you pack up your gear and go away?

1. Use the pictures below to help summarize what you learned about cowboys. **Summarize**

2. What effect might a noisy thunderstorm have during a trail drive? Look back on pages 394 and 395 to help you answer. **Cause/Effect**

3. If you were to make a web to organize what you know about cowboys, what headings would you put in the smaller circles? in the main circle? **Graphic Organizers**

Look Back and Write A list of "Trail Drive Dangers" might have helped cowboys. Make a list for them. Use information on pages 391 to 397 to help you.

Meet the Author and the Illustrator
Lucille Recht Penner and Ben Carter

Read other books written by Lucille Recht Penner or illustrated by Ben Carter.

Lucille Recht Penner often writes about life long ago. She tries to show how "people just like you" lived in the past. Ms. Penner likes to write about cowboys. People were adventurous and brave in the Old West. They were willing to do hard things even when they didn't know what would happen to them.

Ms. Penner reads many books about a subject before she begins writing. Then she chooses the most interesting and unusual parts to include in the book.

Ben Carter has been an artist since he graduated from college. He is of Native American descent, and his books often draw upon his heritage.

X Marks the Spot!

Wilma Mankiller: Principal Chief of the Cherokee Nation

Retelling Strip

402

403

Scoring Rubric | Expository Retelling

Rubric 4 3 2 1	4	3	2	1
Connections	Makes connections and generalizes beyond the text	Makes connections to other events, texts, or experiences	Makes a limited connection to another event, text, or experience	Makes no connection to another event, text, or experience
Author's Purpose	Elaborates on author's purpose	Tells author's purpose with some clarity	Makes some connection to author's purpose	Makes no connection to author's purpose
Topic	Describes the main topic	Identifies the main topic with some details early in retelling	Identifies the main topic	Retelling has no sense of topic
Important Ideas	Gives accurate information about ideas using key vocabulary	Gives accurate information about ideas with some key vocabulary	Gives limited or inaccurate information about ideas	Gives no information about ideas
Conclusions	Draws conclusions and makes inferences to generalize beyond the text	Draws conclusions about the text	Is able to tell some learnings about the text	Is unable to draw conclusions or make inferences about the text

Use the Retelling Chart on p. TR21 to record retelling.

Selection Test To assess with *Cowboys* use Selection Tests, pp. 113–116.

Fresh Reads for Differentiated Test Practice For weekly leveled practice, use pp. 169–174.

Retelling

SUCCESS PREDICTOR

3

DAILY FIX-IT

5. How many cattel are in
   the herd.
   How many catt<u>le</u> are in
   the herd<u>?</u>

6. The Cowboy gallupped.
   The <u>c</u>owboy gall<u>op</u>ed.

Connect to Unit Writing

Writing Trait

Have children use strategies for developing **sentences** when they write a research report in the Unit Writing Workshop, pp. WA2–WA9.

Sentences Have language learners read their sentences aloud to check rhythm, completeness, and sense. Point out opportunities to change a declarative sentence to another type or to vary sentence beginnings.

Writing Trait of the Week

INTRODUCE Sentences

TALK ABOUT SENTENCES Explain to children that good writers use different kinds of sentences, such as questions, commands, and exclamations. This gives the writing rhythm and style. Write these sentences about *Cowboys* on the board. Then model your thinking.

> **How exciting the lives of cowboys were! Every day brought new adventures. What did a cowboy need on the trail? A cowboy needed a good horse, protective clothing, and food. Tell me if you want to be a cowboy.**

Think Aloud

MODEL The first sentence is an exclamation that shows excitement. The next sentence states a fact. The third sentence asks a question and involves readers. The fourth sentence states other facts. The last sentence gives readers a command. Notice how these types of sentences are punctuated. Questions are followed by a question mark. Commands and statements end with a period. Exclamations end with an exclamation mark.

STRATEGY FOR DEVELOPING SENTENCES On the board, write the following sentences. Work with children to change each into the type indicated in parentheses. Point out the end marks.

> **Sometimes cowboys got bored.** *Question (Did cowboys sometimes get bored?)*
>
> **Cow ponies worked hard.** *Exclamation (How hard cow ponies worked!)*
>
> **You can learn more about cowboys in museums.**
> *Command (Learn more about cowboys in museums.)*
>
> **Has my dad seen many old movies about cowboys?**
> *Statement (My dad has seen many old movies about cowboys.)*

PRACTICE

APPLY THE STRATEGY Ask children to list facts they learned about cowboys. Then have them use the list to write one statement, one question, one command, and one exclamation. Remind them to use the correct end punctuation for each type of sentence.

Grammar

APPLY TO WRITING
Commas in Compound Sentences

IMPROVE WRITING WITH COMMAS Have children recall that sometimes two sentences have ideas that go together, and they can be combined into one. These sentences can be combined with a comma and a connecting word, such as *and* or *but*. Write these two simple sentences and review how to connect them by writing a comma and the word *and*. Remind children to use commas to connect sentences in their own writing.

Uncle Henry always shows us pictures.

We like to see them.

Uncle Henry always shows us pictures, and we like to see them.

PRACTICE

WRITE WITH COMMAS Write several related simple sentences. Ask children to select two sentences to combine. Have children write the two sentences and use a comma and a connecting word to create a compound sentence.

Commas in Compound Sentences

Add a comma where it is needed. **Circle** the word that joins the two sentences.

1. Jill wants to be a pilot, but she is afraid to fly.

2. Alan wants to be a vet, and he loves animals

Tell what you would like to be and why.
Combine sentences.
Use a comma and the word *and* or *but*.

Possible answer: I would like to be a teacher, and I would like to help children learn. I want to teach math and reading, but I don't want to teach science.

Home Activity Your child learned how to use commas in compound sentences in writing. Have your child point out places in a book where compound sentences are used. Ask your child to point to the commas and the word *and* or *but*.

▲ **Grammar and Writing Practice Book** p. 114

Wrap Up Your Day!

✓ **CAUSE AND EFFECT** Recall the *J* in "B Is for Buckaroo." What causes the jinglebob, the little bell on a spur, to jingle? (When cowboys walk, dance, and play it moves and jingles.)

✓ **READ WITH ACCURACY AND APPROPRIATE PACE** Remind children that fluent readers read at a good pace—not too fast and not too slow.

LET'S TALK ABOUT IT Display the K-W-L chart from Day 1. Help children add to the *L* column and add any further information they may want to know about cowboys. Why should we learn about cowboys?

PREVIEW Day 4

Tell children that tomorrow they will listen to a story about the things cowboys use and wear.

Day 4
AT A GLANCE

Share Literature
Cowboy: An Album

Phonics and Spelling
Suffixes *-ness*, *-less*
Spelling: Words with Suffixes

Read
 Group Time < Differentiated Instruction
"Cowboy Gear"

Fluency
Read with Accuracy and Appropriate Pace

Writing Across the Curriculum
Labeled Picture

Grammar
Commas

Speaking and Listening
Listen to a Description

Materials

- *Sing with Me Big Book*
- *Read Aloud Anthology*
- Student Edition 404–405

Morning Warm-Up!

Today we will read more about cowboys.

We know cowboys work hard.

They often sleep outside by a campfire.

Do cowboys have special items or clothes to make their job easier?

QUESTION OF THE DAY Encourage children to sing "Occupation: Cowboy" from the *Sing with Me Big Book* as you gather. Write and read the message and discuss the question.

REVIEW COMPOUND WORDS

- Ask children how many compound words they see in the message. (three)
- Have them identify the two smaller words that make up each compound word. (cow-boys, out-side, camp-fire)

Extend Language Use the Day 4 instruction on ELL Poster 29 to extend and enrich language.

ELL Poster 29

Share Literature

CONNECT CONCEPTS

ACTIVATE PRIOR KNOWLEDGE Recall the story *Cowboys*. Recall what the cowboys wore and what they did in the story. Explain that today children will listen to more information about cowboys—*Cowboy: An Album* by Linda Granfield.

Read Aloud Anthology
Cowboy: An Album

BUILD ORAL VOCABULARY Reread the first paragraph. Explain that cowboys of the Old West are **legends.** They are legendary, or famous, because of the many stories told about them. Times have changed and so has a cowboy's equipment. Cowboys used to use rope made of **rawhide.** Rawhide is untanned cattle skin. Today rope is generally made of nylon, not rawhide. Ask children to listen to the story to find out other changes that have been made in cattle ranching.

REVIEW ORAL VOCABULARY After reading, review all the Amazing Words for the week. Have children take turns using them in sentences that tell about the concept for the week. Then talk about Amazing Words they learned in other weeks and connect them to the concept, as well. For example, ask:

- What sorts of **contraptions** would cowboys today have on a cattle drive that they didn't have 100 years ago?

- Would you like to be a **professional** cowboy? Why or why not?

- What do you think would be the most **terrifying incident** that could happen on a trail drive?

MONITOR LISTENING COMPREHENSION

- Besides horseback, what other forms of transportation do modern cowboys use to do daily chores? (You may find cowboys on snowmobiles, in trucks, and in helicopters.)

- Why do ranch owners sometimes need to subdivide and rent out their land to make a living? (Cattle prices rise and fall and ranch owners need to make a living.)

- Why do cattlemen continue to ranch? (Possible response: They have pride in keeping the cowboy tradition. A cowboy's life represents honesty, independence, a work ethic, and a respect for the land that they wish to pass down to their children.)

Amazing Words to build oral vocabulary

	MONITOR PROGRESS
climate livestock occupation buckaroo drover lariat **legend** **rawhide**	**If...** children lack oral vocabulary experiences about the concept Traditions, **then...** use the Oral Vocabulary Routine. See p. DI•6 to teach *legend* and *rawhide*.

Connect Concepts Bring in *rawhide* dog treats to show children what rawhide is. Show children where they can find books about legends in the library. Legends can be found in the 300s section using the Dewey Decimal classification system.

Sentence Reading

REVIEW WORDS IN CONTEXT

READ DECODABLE AND HIGH-FREQUENCY WORDS IN CONTEXT Write these sentences. Call on individuals to read a sentence. Then randomly point to words and have children read them. To help you monitor word reading, high-frequency words are underlined and decodable words are circled.

(Peach) is their (fastest) selling (breakfast) (tea).

The youngest of his three (tireless) daughters (teaches) (reading).

I went (running) for half an hour and (breathed) in and out in the (stillness).

I've seen many (feathers), but this is the (prettiest) (eagle) (feather)!

Did you buy the (gingerbread) (spread) and (peanuts) for the (feast)?

I like (sitting) alone in the (meadow) when the (weather) is (cloudless) and a bit (warmer).

Monitor Progress	Word Reading
If... children are unable to read an underlined word,	**then...** read the word for them and spell it, having them echo you.
If... children are unable to read a circled word,	**then...** have them use the blending strategy they have learned for that word type.

Support Phonics For additional review, see the phonics activities in the ELL and Transition Handbook.

Spelling

PARTNER REVIEW Suffixes

READ AND WRITE Supply pairs of children with index cards on which the spelling words have been written. Have one child read a word while the other writes it. Then have children switch roles. Have them use the cards to check their spelling.

HOMEWORK Spelling Practice Book, p. 116

OBJECTIVE

● Spell words with suffixes
-ness, -less.

Spelling Words

Suffixes

1. **kindness**   7. **sadness**
2. **careless**   8. **sickness**
3. **goodness**   9. **helpless**
4. **useless**   10. **thankless**
5. **fearless***   11. **fitness**
6. **darkness**   12. **weakness**

Challenge Words

13. **awareness** 15. **wireless**
14. **eagerness**

* Word from the Selection

Group Time

On-Level	Strategic Intervention	Advanced
Read "Cowboy Gear." • Use pp. 404–405.	**Read** or listen to "Cowboy Gear." • Use the **Routine** on p. DI•50.	**Read** "Cowboy Gear." • Use the **Routine** on p. DI•51.

ELL Place English language learners in the groups that correspond to their reading abilities in English.

DAY 4

(i) Independent Activities

Fluency Reading Pair children to reread *Cowboys.*

Journal Writing List animals that live in your climate. Share writing.

Spelling Partner Review

Independent Reading See p. 376j for Reading/Library activities and suggestions.

Literacy Centers To provide listening opportunities, you may use the Listening Center on p. 376j. To extend social studies concepts, you may use the Social Studies Center on p. 376k.

Break into small groups after Spelling and before Fluency.

Suffixes -ness and -less

Spelling Words					
kindness	careless	goodness	useless	fearless	darkness
sadness	sickness	helpless	thankless	fitness	weakness

Finish the list words. **Read** the word in the shaded boxes to find something that grows on reefs.

| weakness |
| careless |
| sickness |
| helpless |
| goodness |

1. s i c k n e s s
2. g o o d n e s s
3. c a r e l e s s
4. w e a k n e s s
5. h e l p l e s s

Fill the chart with list words.

Base Word	-ness	-less
6. sad	sadness	
7. use		useless
8. dark	darkness	
9. thank		thankless
fit	fitness	
fear		fearless
kind	kindness	

Home Activity Your child has been learning to spell words with -ness and -less. Help your child look in schoolbooks or library books for examples of words with these suffixes.

▲ **Spelling Practice Book** p. 116

Audio
CD   **Audio Text**

Read
Social Studies
in Reading

PREVIEW AND PREDICT Read the title and author's name. Have children preview the selection and name the articles of clothing shown in the photograph. (hat, bandanna, chaps, boots, pants) Then ask children to predict whether "Cowboy Gear" tells a story or provides information. Have children read to learn what a cowboy wears.

INFORMATIONAL TEXT Review that selections about real people doing real things are called nonfiction. Point out that the photograph in this picture encyclopedia article gives information about real things and that the sentences next to the photograph provide information about what is pictured.

VOCABULARY/TIME WORDS Review that some words, such as *beginning* and *end*, tell when something happens. Have children locate the time phrase "at the end" on p. 404. What do cowboys often do at the end of the journey? Why?

Social Studies in Reading

Picture Encyclopedia

Genre

- Picture encyclopedias provide information on many topics.
- There are many photos or pictures with captions.
- A reader can read the captions in any order.

Text Features

- In this article, the picture shows what a cowboy wears.
- The captions explain more about each part of a cowboy's outfit.

Link to Social Studies

Use the library or the Internet to find out more about cowboy equipment. Share your findings with the class.

COWBOY GEAR

from *The Cowboy's Handbook*

★ by Tod Cody ★

A cowboy's clothes and equipment had to be hard-wearing. There was no room for luggage on the trail drive, and most cowboys wore the same thing for months. Mud-caked and smelly, these clothes were often burned at the end of the journey.

404

READY TO HIT THE TRAIL!
What to Wear When You're Riding the Range

HAT
You can use it to signal to other cowboys, beat trail dust off your clothes, and hold food for your horse. A true cowboy wears his hat when he's sleeping.

PANTS
Cowboys originally refused to wear jeans because they were worn by miners and farm laborers. Pants (trousers) made of thick woolen material are more comfortable to wear on horseback.

BOOTS
The pointed toes and high heels are designed for riding, not for walking. That's why cowboys in the movies walk the way they do!

BANDANNA
Soak it in water, roll it up into a wad, and place it under your hat to keep cool during a hot spell. You can also use it to filter muddy water and blindfold a "spooked" horse.

CHAPS
These thick leather leg-coverings will protect your legs from cow horns, rope burns, scrapes, and scratches. They also give a better grip to the saddle.

Reading Across Texts
What different information did each selection give about hats, bandannas, chaps, and boots?

Writing Across Texts
Write a paragraph explaining which piece of gear you think cowboys needed most.

Cause and Effect What effect do boots have on a cowboy's walk?

405

BUILD CONCEPTS

Details • Literal

- **Why did cowboys wear chaps?**
to grip the saddle and to protect their legs from rope burns, scratches, and cow horns

Cause and Effect • Inferential

- **Why did a cowboy's clothes have to be hard-wearing?**
There was no room to carry additional clothes, and cowboys wore the same clothes for months.

CONNECT TEXT TO TEXT

Have children reread the description of cowboy clothes on pp. 388–389 to compare information.

Discuss with children which piece of clothing they think is the most important and why. Explain that children can have different opinions and that they should write about why they chose the one they did.

E L L

Activate Prior Knowledge Ask: Have you ever worn a cowboy hat or boots? Have children share their experiences. If children have not seen a cowboy hat or boots, bring in the items or photographs of them to show the class.

Options for Oral Reading

Use *Cowboys* or one of the following Leveled Readers.

On-Level

Cowboy Days

Strategic Intervention

Ranch Life

Advanced

Life on the Ranch

E L L

Assess Fluency Read interesting sentences aloud to English language learners frequently, adding think-aloud comments to explain how cues such as letter patterns in words, phrases or other "chunks" of words, and punctuation can help you understand and read fluently.

 To develop fluent readers, use Fluency Coach.

Fluency

READ WITH ACCURACY AND APPROPRIATE PACE

MODEL READING WITH ACCURACY AND APPROPRIATE PACE Use *Cowboys.*

- Point to the first sentence on p. 392. Review that good readers read at an appropriate pace. I'll read this page aloud at a good pace, not too fast and not too slow.

- Ask children to follow along as you read the page with accuracy and appropriate pace.

- Have children read the page after you. Encourage them to read at a similar pace. Continue in the same way with pp. 393–394.

REREAD FOR FLUENCY

Paired Reading

ROUTINE

1 **Select a Passage** For *Cowboys,* use pp. 388–391.

2 **Reader 1 Begins** Have children read, switching readers at the end of each page.

3 **Reader 2 Begins** Have partners reread; now the other partner begins.

4 **Reread** For optimal fluency, children should reread three or four times with attention to accuracy and pace.

5 **Provide Feedback** Listen as children read and provide corrective feedback regarding their oral reading and their use of the blending strategy.

Monitor Progress | Check Fluency WCPM

As children reread, monitor their progress toward their individual fluency goals. Current Goal: 90–100 words correct per minute. End-of-Year Goal: 90 words correct per minute.

If... children cannot read fluently at a rate of 90–100 words correct per minute,

then... make sure children practice with text at their independent level. Provide additional fluency practice, pairing nonfluent readers with fluent readers.

If... children already read at 90 words correct per minute,

then... they do not need to reread three to four times.

SUCCESS PREDICTOR

Day 1 Check Word Reading

Day 2 Check Lesson Vocabulary/High-Frequency Words

Day 3 Check Retelling

▶ **Day 4 Check Fluency**

Day 5 Assess Progress

Writing Across the Curriculum

WRITE Labeled Picture

DISCUSS Have children look at pp. 404–405 and name the clothing cowboys wore. Encourage them to use lesson vocabulary, such as *cowboy, trails, galloped.*

SHARE THE PEN Have children participate in creating a labeled picture. To begin, draw a simple picture of a cowboy. Explain that the class will work together to write labels for the cowboy's clothing. Explain that a labeled picture is a way to show information. Call on an individual to name something a cowboy wears. Write the label, inviting individuals to help spell the word by writing familiar letter-sounds. Ask questions, such as the following:

- What is the first sound you hear in the word *bandanna*? (/b/)
- What letter stands for that sound? *(b)* Have a volunteer write *b.*
- What is the beginning sound you hear in the word *chaps*? (/ch/)
- What letters stand for that sound? *(ch)* Have a volunteer write *ch.*

Continue having individuals contribute to writing labels. Frequently reread the labels.

OBJECTIVE

● Create a labeled picture.

Advanced

Encourage children to choose a profession that wears a uniform, such as police officers or chefs, and make a labeled picture of the clothes they wear.

ELL

Home Language Connection
Invite children to find out the names for the clothes in their home languages. List the names on a multilingual diagram.

Resources for home-language words may include parents, bilingual staff members, or bilingual dictionaries.

Words Correct Per Minute

SUCCESS PREDICTOR

Grammar

REVIEW Commas

DAILY FIX-IT

7. We built a camp fire?
   We built a <u>campfire.</u>

8. did you see the herd of cattle.
   <u>D</u>id you see the herd of cattle<u>?</u>

Commas in Compound Sentences

Mark the letter of the compound sentence that shows how to correctly combine the two sentences.

1. Longhorn cattle have long horns. These horns are sharp and dangerous.
   ○ **A** Longhorn cattle have long horns, these horns are sharp and dangerous.
   ⊗ **B** Longhorn cattle have long horns, and these horns are sharp and dangerous.
   ○ **C** Longhorn cattle have long horns and, these horns are sharp and dangerous.

2. A few big steers are leaders. They walk in front of the herd.
   ○ **A** A few big steers are leaders and, they walk in front of the herd.
   ○ **B** A few big steers are leaders but, they walk in front of the herd.
   ⊗ **C** A few big steers are leaders, and they walk in front of the herd.

3. Some cows get stuck in mud. They are not left behind.
   ○ **A** Some cows get stuck in mud, they are not left behind.
   ○ **B** Some cows get stuck in mud and, they are not left behind.
   ⊗ **C** Some cows get stuck in mud, but they are not left behind.

4. Cattle walk slowly. They run fast.
   ⊗ **A** Cattle walk slowly, but they run fast.
   ○ **B** Cattle walk slowly, and, they run fast.
   ○ **C** Cattle walk slowly and, they run fast.

 Home Activity Your child prepared for taking tests on commas in compound sentences. Ask your child to choose one of the numbered pairs of sentences on this page and to combine the two sentences to make a compound sentence.

▲ **Grammar and Writing Practice Book** p. 115

REVIEW COMMAS

● What do you use to combine two simple sentences? (a comma and a connecting word)

● Name two connecting words. (*and, but*)

PRACTICE

ADD COMMAS Write *The night air was chilly. I had a warm blanket.* Have individuals add a comma and a connecting word and then rewrite these two simple sentences into a compound sentence.

The night air was chilly. I had a warm blanket.

The night air was chilly, but I had a warm blanket.

Speaking and Listening

LISTEN TO A DESCRIPTION

OBJECTIVES

● Speak to communicate information.
● Listen for details.

DEMONSTRATE SPEAKING AND LISTENING Remind children of appropriate listening and speaking behaviors for a discussion. Then ask them to think about these behaviors as you discuss descriptive words.

Speakers	Listeners
• Use interesting words.	• Face the speaker.
• Remember your audience's interests.	• Listen for the most important things.

DESCRIBE NATURE Gather several interesting items (e.g., feather, pine cone, shell, rock, leaf). Allow each child to select and describe one of the items to the class. Encourage speakers to use descriptive words. Invite listeners to close their eyes and picture the item in their mind as it is being described.

Wrap Up Your Day!

✓ **MAKING CONNECTIONS** Compare the items of clothing mentioned in *Cowboy Gear* to what people wear today. How are cowboy clothes similar to and different from clothes you and people around you wear? (Possible response: We wear boots in winter and bandannas when we go to camp. Our boots are designed for walking though.)

LET'S TALK ABOUT IT Discuss cowboys and the clothes they wore. Why should we learn about cowboys? Have children add additional information to the cowboy web created earlier in the week.

PREVIEW Day 5

Remind children that today they read about cowboy gear and discussed the importance of cowboys. Tell them that tomorrow they will hear more about cowboys.

Share Literature
Cowboy: An Album

Phonics and Spelling

Review Suffixes *-ness, -less*

Lesson Vocabulary
cattle   trails   cowboy
herd   campfire   railroad
galloped

Monitor Progress
Spelling Test: Words with Suffixes
    -ness, -less

Group Time < Differentiated Assessment

Writing and Grammar
Trait: Sentences
Commas

Research and Study Skills
Thesaurus

Materials

- *Sing with Me Big Book*
- *Read Aloud Anthology*
- Reproducible Pages TE pp. 406f–406g
- Student Edition 406–407

Morning Warm~Up!

This week we read about cowboys.
A cowboy's occupation is taking care
of livestock. Livestock can be cattle,
horses, sheep, hogs, or goats.
Why should we learn about cowboys?

QUESTION OF THE DAY Encourage children to sing "Occupation: Cowboy" from the *Sing with Me Big Book* as you gather. Write and read the message and discuss the question.

REVIEW ORAL VOCABULARY Have children name a word(s) in the message that

- describes a cowboy's occupation
- describes what taking care of livestock is
- describes livestock
- names an animal that cowboys ride

Assess Vocabulary Use the Day 5 instruction on ELL Poster 29 to monitor children's progress with oral vocabulary.

ELL Poster 29

Share Literature

LISTEN AND RESPOND

USE PRIOR KNOWLEDGE Review that yesterday the class listened to find out what changes have been made in cattle ranching. Suggest that today the class listen to find out what is slowly creeping into the cowboy's workplace.

MONITOR LISTENING COMPREHENSION

- What is creeping into the cowboy's workplace? (condominiums and modern subdivisions)

- During which seasons do cowboys work especially hard? (Possible response: They work hard during spring calving season, during roundup and branding times, and during the cold winter months.)

- Is the cowboy of the Old West in danger of being forgotten? Explain. (Most children will say no; there are plenty of stories being told about these cowboys of long ago.)

Read Aloud Anthology
Cowboy: An Album

BUILD ORAL VOCABULARY

GENERATE DISCUSSION Recall how the cowboy tradition has changed from 100 years ago. Today, cowboys might use snowmobiles and walkie-talkies to herd cattle. Invite children to predict how cowboys will do their jobs 100 years from now. Have children use some of this week's Amazing Words as they talk about the cowboy of the future.

Monitor Progress | Check Oral Vocabulary

Remind children of the unit concept—Traditions. Ask them to tell you about the concept using some of this week's Amazing Words: *climate, livestock, occupation, buckaroo, drover, lariat, legend,* and *rawhide.*

If... children have difficulty using the Amazing Words,

then... ask more questions about the Read Aloud selection or the concept using the Amazing Words. Note which questions children can respond to. Reteach unknown words using the Oral Vocabulary routine on p. DI·1.

SUCCESS PREDICTOR

Day 1 Check Word Reading	Day 2 Check Lesson Vocabulary/High-Frequency Words	Day 3 Check Retelling	Day 4 Check Fluency	▶ Day 5 Check Oral Vocabulary Assess Progress

OBJECTIVES

- Set purpose for listening.
- Build oral vocabulary.

Amazing Words to build oral vocabulary

climate	drover
livestock	lariat
occupation	legend
buckaroo	rawhide

Extend Language Remind children that a compound word is made up of two smaller words. Write *ball, bed, water, room, fall* on index cards or sentence strips. Have children put them together to make compound words.

Oral Vocabulary

SUCCESS PREDICTOR

OBJECTIVES
- Review words with suffixes *-ness, -less.*
- Review lesson vocabulary.

Suffixes

REVIEW

IDENTIFY WORDS WITH SUFFIXES Write these sentences. Have children read each one aloud. Call on individuals to name and underline the words with suffixes and identify the base word and suffix in each.

It is <u>useless</u> to call on that <u>cordless</u> phone.

Treat people with <u>kindness</u> or you may be <u>friendless</u>.

Good <u>fitness</u> can make you feel <u>ageless</u> and <u>tireless</u>!

She acted <u>fearless</u> during her <u>illness</u>.

Lesson Vocabulary

REVIEW

COMPLETE THE RHYME Read the rhyme, leaving blanks for missing words. Ask children to complete each line with one of the Words to Know from p. 378. Then reread the rhyme.

A _____ has a tough job, I'd say. (cowboy)

He can move a big _____ along its way. (herd)

Across the _____ he rides—"yipee yi yay!" (trails)

He keeps the _____ moving all day (cattle)

To the _____ station, but he does not stay. (railroad)

At night around the _____ he sings. (campfire)

He has _____ for miles and seen many things! (galloped)

Access Content For additional practice with lesson vocabulary, use the vocabulary strategies and word cards in the ELL Teaching Guide, pp. 199–200.

SPELLING TEST Suffixes

DICTATION SENTENCES Use these sentences to assess this week's spelling words.

1. I felt <u>helpless</u> when Bill scraped his knee.
2. Feeding my dog is never a <u>thankless</u> job!
3. <u>Darkness</u> falls after sunset.
4. The broken vase is <u>useless</u>.
5. Thank you for your <u>kindness</u>.
6. The new <u>fitness</u> center is open.
7. The superhero was <u>fearless</u>!
8. Don't be <u>careless</u> with your homework.
9. Eating too little food may cause <u>weakness</u>.
10. "Oh my <u>goodness</u>, you've grown!" said Grandma.
11. Her <u>sadness</u> went away when she found her puppy.
12. <u>Sickness</u> means your body needs to rest.

CHALLENGE WORDS

13. "Passing the ball takes skill and <u>awareness</u>," said the coach.
14. Sue's <u>eagerness</u> to help made me feel good.
15. Dad made a <u>wireless</u> call from his cell phone.

ASSESS

● Spell words with suffixes -ness, -less.

Spelling Words

Suffixes

1.	**kindness**	7.	**sadness**
2.	**careless**	8.	**sickness**
3.	**goodness**	9.	**helpless**
4.	**useless**	10.	**thankless**
5.	**fearless** *	11.	**fitness**
6.	**darkness**	12.	**weakness**

Challenge Words

13. **awareness** 15. **wireless**
14. **eagerness**

* **Word from the Selection**

Group Time

On-Level	Strategic Intervention	Advanced
Read Set B Sentences.	**Read** Set A Sentences and the Story.	**Read** Set C Sentences.
• Use pp. 406e–406g.	• Use pp. 406e–406g.	• Use pp. 406e–406g.
	• Use the **Routine** on p. DI•52.	• Use the **Routine** on p. DI•53.

DAY 5

 Place English language learners in the groups that correspond to their reading abilities in English.

(i) Independent Activities

Fluency Reading Children reread selections at their independent level.

Journal Writing Write about cowboy life. Share writing.

Independent Reading See p. 376j for Reading/Library activities and suggestions.

Literacy Centers You may use the Technology Center on p. 376k to support this week's concepts and reading.

Practice Book 2.2 Thesaurus, p. 140

Break into small groups after Spelling and before Grammar and Writing.

5

- Decode suffixes *-ness, -less.*
- Read lesson vocabulary words.
- Read aloud with appropriate speed and accuracy.
- Recognize cause and effect.
- Retell a story.

Differentiated Assessment

On-Level
Set B

Strategic Intervention
Set A

Advanced
Set C

Fluency Assessment Plan

☑ Week 1 assess Advanced students.

☑ Week 2 assess Strategic Intervention students.

☑ Week 3 assess On-Level students.

☑ **This week assess Strategic Intervention students.**

☐ Week 5 assess any students you have not yet checked during this unit.

Set individual fluency goals for children to enable them to reach the end-of-year goal.

- Current Goal: 90–100 wcpm
- End-of-Year Goal: 90 wcpm
- **ELL** Fluency, particularly for English learners reading texts in English, develops gradually and through much practice. Focus on each child's improvement rather than solely monitoring the number of words correct per minute.

SENTENCE READING

ASSESS SUFFIXES *-ness, -less* AND LESSON VOCABULARY WORDS Use one of the reproducible lists on p. 406f to assess children's ability to read suffixes *-ness, -less* and lesson vocabulary words. Call on individuals to read two sentences aloud. Have each child in the group read different sentences. Start over with sentence one if necessary.

RECORD SCORES Use the Sentence Reading Chart for this unit on p. WA19.

Monitor Progress	Suffixes *-ness, -less*
If... children have trouble reading suffixes *-ness, -less,*	**then...** use the Reteach Lessons on p. DI•67.
Lesson Vocabulary Words	
If... children cannot read a lesson vocabulary word,	**then...** mark the missed words on a lesson vocabulary word list and send the list home for additional word reading practice, or have the child practice with a fluent reader.

FLUENCY AND COMPREHENSION

ASSESS FLUENCY Take a one-minute sample of children's oral reading. See Monitoring Fluency, p. WA17. Have children read "Maggie's Wish," the on-level fluency passage on p. 406g.

RECORD SCORES Record the number of words read correctly in a minute on the child's Fluency Progress Chart.

ASSESS COMPREHENSION Have the child read to the end of the passage. (If the child had difficulty with the passage, you may read it aloud.) Ask about causes and effects in the story and have the child retell the passage. Use the Retelling Rubric on p. 368–369 to evaluate the child's retelling.

Monitor Progress	Fluency
If... a child does not achieve the fluency goal on the timed reading,	**then...** copy the passage and send it home with the child for additional fluency practice, or have the child practice with a fluent reader.
Cause and Effect	
If... a child cannot recognize cause and effect,	**then...** use the Reteach Lesson on p. DI•67.

READ THE SENTENCES

Set A

1. The endless smaller trails were useless.
2. The lifeless railroad station was spotless.
3. The cow's illness filled the cowboy with sadness.
4. The tasteless campfire food was harmless.
5. Sickness made the homeless herd of cattle slow.
6. The fearless horse galloped into the darkness.

Set B

1. The cloudless night at the campfire was noiseless.
2. The cowboy galloped on rainless days and slept under the brightness of the moon.
3. The motionless railroad train was hopeless.
4. The helpless herd was clueless about the flood.
5. The dirtless jogging trails have a springy softness.
6. Colorless rocks matched the paleness of the cattle.

Set C

1. It was hopeless trying to escape the loudness of the railroad train.
2. Some were careless due to the herd's quickness.
3. I felt a soreness in my muscles after running on the trails for a fitness workout.
4. The cowboy felt coldness after the campfire went out and the warmness disappeared.
5. Caring for cattle is a thankless job, but the kindness of people makes it happen.
6. The priceless horse galloped into greatness.

Monitor Progress | Suffixes *-ness, -less*
Lesson Vocabulary Words

406f

SUCCESS PREDICTOR

Maggie's Wish

Maggie wished she had a dog. Her mom said   9
she couldn't have one because they're too much   17
trouble. Maggie knew it was useless to keep   25
asking.   26

One rainy night, Maggie heard scratching at the   34
door. There in the darkness sat a little dog with 44
sadness in its eyes. Maggie took the helpless dog 53
into the warmness of the house. She dried off the 63
dog because it was soaking wet.   69

"May we keep the dog? I think it's homeless."   78
Maggie asked.   80

"You have to try to find its owner first," said her   91
mom.   92

The little dog was quiet as it slept in a cozy   103
corner on a blanket. The next day, Maggie put an   113
ad in the paper. No one claimed the dog.   122

Maggie's mom let her keep the dog because   130
Maggie showed it such kindness. Because the   137
dog's fur had such softness, Maggie named her   145
Fluffy. Maggie loved her priceless little dog.   152

See also Assessment Handbook, p. 363 • REPRODUCIBLE PAGE

Monitor Progress   Fluency Passage

Write Now
Writing and Grammar

Ad

Prompt

Cowboys describes a cowboy's job. Think about a job you know. Now write an ad that tells the requirements of the job.

Writing Trait

Use different types of **sentences** to make your ad interesting.

Ad names job in title.

Student Model

> Wanted: Mechanics
>
> Do you like cars and trucks?
>
> Are you a trained mechanic?
>
> If so, we need you! Our garage
>
> rebuilds engines. The hours are
>
> from 8 to 4 Monday through
>
> Friday. You can apply online, or
>
> you can visit us in person.

Writer speaks directly to reader, using you.

Ad has different types of sentences.

406

Writer's Checklist

- **Focus** Do all sentences tell about a job?
- **Organization** Is the job named at the beginning?
- **Support** Do sentences tell details about the job?
- **Conventions** Are commas used correctly?

Grammar

Commas in Compound Sentences

Two sentences with ideas that go together can be combined using a comma and a connecting word, such as **and** or **but**. The combined sentence is called a **compound sentence.**

A cowpony crossed rough ground. It swam deep rivers.

A cowpony crossed rough ground, **and** it swam deep rivers.

Write the compound sentence in the ad.

407

Writing and Grammar

LOOK AT THE PROMPT Read p. 406 aloud. Have children select and discuss key words or phrases in the prompt. *(a job you know, ad, tells the requirements of the job)*

STRATEGIES TO DEVELOP SENTENCES Have children

- consider beginning their ads with a question, exclamation, or command for impact and sentence variety.
- underline short sentences in their ads and combine any related pairs to make compound sentences.
- count how many short and long sentences they have in their ads to make sure they have a mix of both.

See Scoring Rubric on p. WA12. **Rubric** 4 3 2 1

HINTS FOR BETTER WRITING Read p. 407 aloud. Use the checklist to help children revise their ads. Discuss the grammar lesson. (Answer: *You can apply online, or you can visit us in person.*) Have children write compound sentences correctly in their ads.

DAILY FIX-IT

9. Fore couboys sat around.
   Four cowboys sat around.

10. The horses gallopped away
    The horses galloped away.

Commas in Compound Sentences

Add a comma where it is needed. Circle the word that joins the two sentences.

1. Uncle Kyle has a ranch and he raises horses.

2. Some horses are cow ponies but some are wild mustangs.

3. I chose a cow pony and I rode around the ranch.

4. Later I brushed the cow pony but Uncle Kyle fed her.

Use the word in ( ) and a comma to combine each pair of sentences. **Write** the new sentence on the lines.

5. Aunt Liz served beans. I asked for more. (and)

   Aunt Liz served beans, and I
   asked for more.

6. The ranch is a great place. I must leave soon. (but)

   The ranch is a great place,
   but I must leave soon.

▲ **Grammar and Writing Practice Book** p. 116

OBJECTIVE

● Use a thesaurus.

Research/Study Skills

TEACH/MODEL Thesaurus

MODEL USING A THESAURUS Write the word *occupation* on the board. Explain that a thesaurus is a book of synonyms. People use a thesaurus when they want to find synonyms—words with the same meaning or almost the same meaning as another word.

Model how to find synonyms for *occupation. Occupation* means "job" or "career."

MODEL I can use this thesaurus to find words that mean the same as *occupation*. First, I go to the *o* pages. Next, I find where the *occ* words begin. Now I find *occupation*.

IDENTIFY SYNONYMS Call on individuals to identify and read synonyms for *ranch* (*farm*) and *market* (*bazaar*).

PRACTICE

DEMONSTRATE USING A THESAURUS Invite children to use a thesaurus to look up synonyms for two words. Encourage children to use the synonyms in sentences.

Name _____   Cowboys

Read the synonyms for **good** and **wet**. **Write** the answer to each question.

| good | 1 able, expert, skilled; 2 caring, honest; 3 healthful |
| wet | damp, soaked, soggy, sopping, flooded |

1. Which words could you use instead of *good* in this sentence?
   The cook fixed the cowboys a good dinner.

   healthful or tasty

2. Which words could you use instead of *good* in this sentence?
   The cowboy was a good person.

   caring or honest

3. Which words could you use instead of *good* in this sentence?
   The cowboy was a good rider and never fell off his horse.

   able, expert, or skilled

4. Which words could you use instead of *wet* in this sentence?
   After three days of rain, the cattle trail was wet.

   soaked, sopping, or flooded

5. Why would a thesaurus be helpful when writing?

   You could find words to make your writing more colorful and exact.

▲ **Practice Book 2.2** p. 140, Thesaurus

Access Content Help children locate a word of their choice in the thesaurus. Read synonyms with the child. Have the child use the synonym in a sentence.

Wrap Up Your Week!

LET'S TALK ABOUT Traditions

QUESTION OF THE WEEK Recall this week's question.

• Why should we learn about cowboys?

Display the K-W-L chart started on Day 1. Review information and add any additional information.

Topic *Cowboys*

What We **K** now	What We **W** ant to Know	What We **L** earned
Cowboys ride horses.	Why do cowboys wear those leather pants?	Leather chaps protect their legs from rope burns.
Cowboys wear boots.	Why do cowboys wear that scarf?	Bandannas keep dust out of their noses.
Cowboys wear hats.	What do cowboys do all day?	Cowboys take care of livestock.
Cowboys work hard.		

CONNECT Use questions such as these to prompt a discussion.

• What kind of livestock do the cowboys in this story work with? What other animals can be livestock?

• The climate is very hot and dry in the selection *Cowboys.* How did the cowboys' clothes help them deal with this type of climate?

Build Background Use ELL Poster 30 to support the Preview activity.

| You've learned **008** *Amazing Words* **this week!** | You've learned **233** *Amazing Words* **so far this year!** |

PREVIEW Tell children that next week they will read about more traditions and how people celebrate in different ways.

PREVIEW Next Week

Assessment Checkpoints *for the Week*

Selection Assessment

Use pp. 113–116 of Selection Tests **to check:**

 Selection Understanding

  Comprehension Skill *Cause and Effect*

 Selection Vocabulary
campfire
cattle
cowboy
galloped
herd
railroad
trails

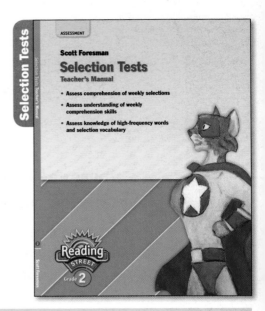

ASSESSMENT

Scott Foresman
Selection Tests
Teacher's Manual

• Assess comprehension of weekly selections
• Assess understanding of weekly comprehension skills
• Assess knowledge of high-frequency words and selection vocabulary

Selection Tests

Reading STREET Grade 2

Leveled Assessment

 On-Level

Strategic Intervention

Advanced

Use pp.169–174 of Fresh Reads for Differentiated Test Practice **to check:**

 Comprehension Skill *Cause and Effect*

 REVIEW **Comprehension Skill** *Fact and Opinion*

 Fluency *Words Correct Per Minute*

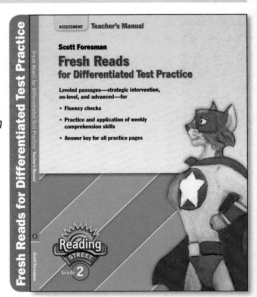

ASSESSMENT | Teacher's Manual

Scott Foresman
Fresh Reads
for Differentiated Test Practice

Leveled passages—strategic intervention, on-level, and advanced—for
• Fluency checks
• Practice and application of weekly comprehension skills
• Answer key for all practice pages

Fresh Reads for Differentiated Test Practice

Reading STREET Grade 2

Managing Assessment

Use Assessment Handbook **for:**

 Weekly Assessment Blackline Masters for Monitoring Progress

 Observation Checklists

 Record-Keeping Forms

 Portfolio Assessment

ASSESSMENT

Scott Foresman
Assessment Handbook

• Suggestions for preparing students for high-stake tests
• Ideas for classroom-based assessment
• Forms in English and Spanish for students to record interests and progress
• Forms in English and Spanish for teachers to record observations of students' reading and writing abilities and progress
• Monitoring Progress forms reproduced from *Reading Street Teacher's Editions*

Assessment Handbook

Reading STREET Grades K–2

Illinois

Planning Guide for Performance Descriptors

Jingle Dancer

Reading Street Teacher's Edition pages	Grade 2 English Language Arts Performance Descriptors
Oral Language Build Concepts: 408l, 410a, 426a, 428a, 432a Share Literature: 408m, 410b, 426b, 428b, 432b	**1A.Stage B.4.** Use a variety of decoding strategies (e.g., phonics, word patterns, structural analysis, context clues) to recognize new words when reading age-appropriate material. **1B.Stage B.1.** Read fiction and non-fiction materials for specific purposes.
Word Work **Phonics** Prefixes *mis-, mid-:* 408n–408q, 410c–410d, 426c–426d, 428c–428d, 432c–432f **Spelling:** 408p, 410d, 426d, 428d, 432d	**1A.Stage B.4.** Use a variety of decoding strategies (e.g., phonics, word patterns, structural analysis, context clues) to recognize new words when reading age-appropriate material. **3A.Stage B.6.** Use phonemic clues, phonetic and/or developmental spelling to spell unfamiliar words.
Reading **Comprehension** Character, Setting, and Plot: 408r–409, 412–425a, 426g, 432e Prior Knowledge: 408r–409, 412–425, 426g **Vocabulary** Context Clues: 410–411 Homonyms: 426e, 428–429 Unfamiliar Words: 410–411, 432b **Fluency** Oral Rereading: 408q, 425a Choral Reading: 426f, 431a **Self-Selected Reading:** LR37–45, TR16–17 **Literature** Genre—Realistic Fiction: 412–413 Reader Response: 426g–426h	**1B.Stage B.1.** Read fiction and non-fiction materials for specific purposes. **1B.Stage B.2.** Use clues (e.g., titles, pictures, themes, prior knowledge, graphs) to make and justify predictions before, during and after reading. **1C.Stage B.14.** Select books appropriate to reading levels. **2A.Stage B.1.** Describe and compare characters, settings, and/or events in stories or pictures. **2A.Stage B.3.** Define unfamiliar vocabulary. **2B.Stage B.5.** Apply text variations (e.g., change setting, alter a character, rewrite the ending). **4B.Stage B.1.** Demonstrate awareness of situation and setting for the oral message. **5A.Stage B.2.** Discuss prior knowledge of topic.
Language Arts **Writing** Story, Essay, Respond to Literature, Map: 409a, 425b, 426g, 431b, 432–433 **Six-Trait Writing** Organization/Paragraphs: 427a, 432–433 **Grammar, Usage, and Mechanics** The Paragraph: 409b, 425c, 427b, 431c **Speaking/Viewing** Listen for Speaker's Purpose: 431d **Research/Study** Time Line: 433a	**2A.Stage B.8.** Recognize that prose is written in sentences and organized in paragraphs. **3B.Stage B.2.** Compose a focused story using picture(s) and/or basic text. **4A.Stage B.7.** Demonstrate the ability to listen for different purposes (e.g., entertainment, information, social interaction). **5C.Stage B.3.** Use life experiences as sources of information for written reports, letters, and stories.
Unit Skills **Writing** Research Report: WA2–9 **Project/Wrap-Up:** 434–435	**3C.Stage B.4.** Experiment with different forms of writing (e.g., song, poetry, short fiction, recipes, diary, journal, directions). **5C.Stage B.5.** Create a report of ideas (e.g., drawing, using available technology, writing a story, letter, report).

This Week's Leveled Readers

Below-Level	On-Level	Advanced
 Fiction	**Fiction**	**Fiction**
2A.Stage B.1. Describe and compare characters, settings, and/or events in stories or pictures. **2A.Stage B.4.** Identify the topic or main idea (theme).	**2A.Stage B.1.** Describe and compare characters, settings, and/or events in stories or pictures. **2B.Stage B.4.** Make a reasonable judgment with support from the text.	**1B.Stage B.2.** Use clues (e.g., titles, pictures, themes, prior knowledge, graphs) to make and justify predictions before, during and after reading. **2A.Stage B.1.** Describe and compare characters, settings, and/or events in stories or pictures.

Content-Area Illinois Performance Descriptors in This Lesson

Social Studies

14E.Stage B.2. Tell about food from other countries.

14F.Stage B.1. Identify an example of behavior that shows someone showing good citizenship (e.g., recycling, being honest when being questioned).

18A.Stage B.1. Describe how communities within a culture are similar.

18A.Stage B.2. Identify cultural traits.

18A.Stage B.3. Identify symbols of local culture.

18B.Stage B.4. Tell about the role of families in the community.

Science

12F.Stage B.1. Apply scientific inquiries or technological designs to describe the main bodies in the solar system: relating Earth's dependence on the Sun for heat and light; modeling the phases of the Moon.

12F.Stage B.2. Apply scientific inquiries or technological designs to explain the seasonal and annual motions of the Earth and other planets in relation to the Sun: modeling the Earth's motion in relation to the Sun during the day, night, year.

Math

6A.Stage B.4. Use cardinal and ordinal numbers appropriately.

Illinois!

A FAMOUS ILLINOISAN
Harold Washington

Harold Washington (1922–1987) was the first African American mayor of Chicago and served from 1983 to 1987. Washington attended Roosevelt University and then earned a law degree from the Northwestern University School of Law. In 1953 he became a lawyer. Before being elected mayor, Washington served in the Illinois House of Representatives from 1965 to 1976, the Illinois State Senate from 1976 to 1980, and the U.S. House of Representatives from 1981 to 1983.

Children can . . .
Create a time line of events in Harold Washington's political career, starting with his law degree in 1952 and ending with his election as mayor of Chicago.

A SPECIAL ILLINOIS PLACE
Naperville

Naperville is located on the west branch of the DuPage River in northeastern Illinois. The community was named for its founder, Captain Joseph Naper. Naperville grew in population and industry after the arrival of the Chicago, Burlington, and Quincy Railroad in 1864. It became a city in 1890.

Children can . . .
Learn more about trade and rail transportation. Have them make a picture list of goods that are transported by rail and label each picture with a one word description.

ILLINOIS FUN FACTS
Did You Know?

- Illinois has more than seven hundred airports.

- The General Assembly of Illinois is made up of 59 members of the Senate and 118 members of the House of Representatives.

- As a boy, Abraham Lincoln lived in a log cabin in Kentucky.

Children can . . .
Learn more about Abraham Lincoln's childhood and the time period during which he grew up. Have them draw or make a toy that a child of the nineteenth century might have played with.

Unit 6
Traditions

CONCEPT QUESTION

How are traditions and celebrations important to our lives?

Week 1

Why are sports important in our country?

Week 2

What does our flag mean?

Week 3

Why are family celebrations special?

Week 4

Why should we learn about cowboys?

Week 5

What are some different ways that people celebrate?

Week 5

EXPAND THE CONCEPT

What are some different ways that people celebrate?

Time for SOCIAL STUDIES

Jingle Dancer

by Cynthia Leitich Smith
illustrated by Cornelius Van Wright and Ying-Hwa Hu

Genre

Realistic fiction is a story that...

Social Studies in Reading

Photo Essay

Genre
- A photo essay includes text and many photos on one topic.

Text Features
- In this selection, the photos show what happens during Buffalo Days.
- The captions tell about the photos.

Link to Social Studies
Use the library or the Internet to find out about other powwow activities. Organize a classroom powwow to talk about the rules and affairs of your classroom.

CELEBRATING THE BUFFALO DAYS
from *Buffalo Days* by Diane Hoyt-Goldsmith

Every summer the Crow nation holds a special gathering to celebrate the Buffalo Days. The Crow Fair and Rodeo is something that everyone looks forward to all year long. The fair began in 1904 as a way to encourage ranching and farming. Over the years, it has become a celebration of Native American traditions. People who come to the fair are able to experience a way of life that existed during the Buffalo Days.

The Crow Fair and Rodeo is called the Tipi Capital of the World. People put up more than a thousand tipis on the fairgrounds.

During the third week in August, Crow people from all over the reservation gather to put up their tipis. They hold a powwow that lasts for many days, with dance contests, drumming, and giveaways. There are rodeo competitions and horse races every day. People from other tribes all over North America come to share in the fun.

Graphic Organizers If it will help, make a graphic organizer.

428   429

CONNECT THE CONCEPT

▶ **Build Background**

ceremony	*evergreen*	*multicolored*
compliment	*festival*	*sash*
culture	*fidget*	

How [child A] Celebrates Birthdays	How [child B] Celebrates Birthdays
1.	1.
2.	2.

▶ **Social Studies Content**
Native American Culture: Powwow Ceremony, Family History

▶ **Writing**
A Story

Preview Your Week

What are some different ways that people celebrate?

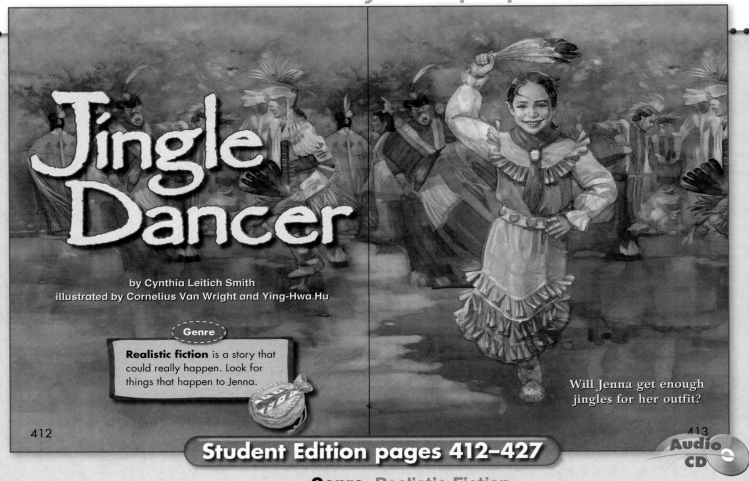

Jingle Dancer

by Cynthia Leitich Smith
illustrated by Cornelius Van Wright and Ying-Hwa Hu

Genre

Realistic fiction is a story that could really happen. Look for things that happen to Jenna.

412

Will Jenna get enough jingles for her outfit?

413

Student Edition pages 412–427

Genre	Realistic Fiction
Phonics	Prefixes *mis-, mid-*
Vocabulary Strategy	Context Clues
Comprehension Skill	Character, Setting, and Plot
Comprehension Strategy	Prior Knowledge

Paired Selection

Reading Across Texts
Compare Traditions

Genre
Photo Essay

Text Features
Photographs
Captions

Social Studies in Reading

Photo Essay

Genre
A photo essay includes text and many photos on one topic.

Text Features
- In this selection, the photos show what happens during Buffalo Days.
- The captions tell about the photos.

Link to Social Studies
Use the library or the Internet to find out about other powwow activities. Organize a classroom powwow to talk about the rules and affairs of your classroom.

Celebrating the BUFFALO DAYS

from *Buffalo Days*
by Diane Hoyt-Goldsmith

Every summer the Crow nation holds a special gathering to celebrate the Buffalo Days. The Crow Fair and Rodeo is something that everyone looks forward to all year long. The fair began in 1904 as a way to encourage ranching and farming. Over the years, it has become a celebration of Native American traditions. People who come to the fair are able to experience a way of life that existed during the Buffalo Days.

The Crow Fair and Rodeo is called the Tipi Capital of the World. People put up more than a thousand tipis on the fairgrounds.

During the third week in August, Crow people from all over the reservation gather to put up their tipis. They hold a powwow that lasts for many days, with dance contests, drumming, and giveaways. There are rodeo competitions and horse races every day. People from other tribes all over North America come to share in the fun.

Graphic Organizers If it will help, make a graphic organizer.

428

Student Edition pages 428–431

Read It
ONLINE
PearsonSuccessNet.com

- Student Edition
- Leveled Readers
- Decodable Reader

Leveled Readers

◎ **Skill** Character, Setting, and Plot

◎ **Strategy** Prior Knowledge

Lesson Vocabulary

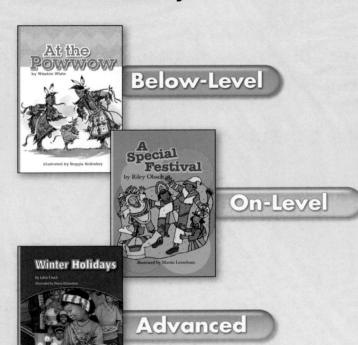

Below-Level

On-Level

Advanced

ELL Reader

- Concept Vocabulary
- Text Support
- Language Enrichment

A Wild Onion Dinner
by Celeste Keys

Illustrated by Fabricio Vanden Broeck

Decodable Readers

Apply Phonics

- *Hiking the Hard Way*

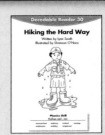

Decodable Reader 30
Hiking the Hard Way
Written by Lynn South
Illustrated by Shannon O'Hara

Time for
SOCIAL STUDIES

Integrate Social Studies Standards

- Native American Culture
- Family History

✓ Read

Jingle Dancer pp. 412–427

"Celebrating the Buffalo Days" pp. 428–431

✓ Read

Leveled Readers

Below-Level | On-Level | Advanced

- Support Concepts
- Develop Concepts
- Extend Concepts
- Social Studies Extension Activity

✓ Read

ELL Reader

A Wild Onion Dinner

✓ Build **Concept Vocabulary**
Traditions, p. 408m

✓ Teach **Social Studies Concepts**
Powwows, p. 414–415

✓ Explore **Social Studies Center**
Celebration Sounds, p. 408k

Weekly Plan

READING

90–120 minutes

TARGET SKILLS OF THE WEEK

Phonics
Prefixes *mis-, mid-*

Comprehension Skill
Character, Setting, and Plot

Comprehension Strategy
Prior Knowledge

LANGUAGE ARTS

20–30 minutes

Trait of the Week

Organization/Paragraphs

DAILY JOURNAL WRITING

DAILY SOCIAL STUDIES CONNECTIONS

DAILY SUCCESS PREDICTORS
for Adequate Yearly Progress

408d

DAY 1 PAGES 408l–409b

Oral Language

QUESTION OF THE WEEK, 408l
What are some different ways that people celebrate?

Oral Vocabulary/Share Literature, 408m
Sing with Me Big Book, Song 30
Amazing Words *ceremony, culture, festival*

Word Work

Phonics, 408n–408o
Introduce Prefixes *mis-, mid-* **T**

Spelling, 408p
Pretest

Comprehension/Vocabulary/Fluency

Read Decodable Reader 30

Grouping Options 408f–408g

Review High-Frequency Words
Check Comprehension
Reread for Fluency

**Comprehension Skill/Strategy
Lesson,** 408r–409
Character, Setting, and Plot **T**
Prior Knowledge

Shared Writing, 409a
Story

Grammar, 409b
Introduce the Paragraph **T**

Day 1 *Write about a festival.*

Day 1 Birthday Celebration Concept Chart, 408m

DAY 2 PAGES 410a–425c

Oral Language

QUESTION OF THE DAY, 410a
What sounds make you happy?

Oral Vocabulary/Share Literature, 410b
Big Book *Magda's Tortillas*
Amazing Word *compliment*

Word Work

Phonics, 410c–410d
Review Prefixes *mis-, mid-* **T**

Spelling, 410d
Dictation

Comprehension/Vocabulary/Fluency

Build Background, 410e
Powwows

Lesson Vocabulary, 410f
Introduce *borrow, clattering, drum, jingles, silver, voice* **T**

Vocabulary Strategy Lesson, 410–411a
Context Clues **T**

Read *Jingle Dancer,* 412–425a

Grouping Options
408f–408g

Character, Setting,
and Plot **T**
Prior Knowledge
REVIEW Cause and Effect **T**
Reread for Fluency

Interactive Writing, 425b
Essay

Grammar, 425c
Practice the Paragraph **T**

Day 2 *Write about the best compliment you ever received.*

Day 2 Time for Social Studies: Powwows, 414–415

Monitor Progress and Corrective Feedback

Phonics
Check Word Reading, *408o*
Spiral REVIEW Phonics

Fluency
Check Lesson Vocabulary, *410f*
Spiral REVIEW High-Frequency Words

Grouping Options for Differentiated Instruction
Turn the page for the small group lesson plan.

DAY 3 PAGES 426a–427b

Oral Language

QUESTION OF THE DAY, 426a
Is there someone special that you imitate?

Oral Vocabulary/Share Literature, 426b
Big Book *Magda's Tortillas*
Amazing Word *fidget*

Word Work

Phonics, 426c
REVIEW Suffixes *-less, -ness* **T**

Lesson Vocabulary, 426d
Practice *borrow, clattering, drum, jingles, silver, voice* **T**

Spelling, 426d
Practice

Comprehension/Vocabulary/Fluency

Vocabulary, 426e
Homonyms

Read *Jingle Dancer,* 412–427

Grouping Options
408f–408g

Fluency, 426f
Read with Appropriate Phrasing

Reader Response, 426g

Trait of the Week, 427a
Introduce Organization/Paragraphs

Grammar, 427b
Write the Paragraph **T**

Day 3 *Write about a time when you borrowed something.*

Day 3 Birthday Celebration Concept Chart, 427b

DAY 4 PAGES 428a–431d

Oral Language

QUESTION OF THE DAY, 428a
Do you invite family and friends to your home for celebrations?

Oral Vocabulary/Share Literature, 428b
Read Aloud Anthology "Bringing the Light"
Amazing Words *evergreen, multicolored, sash*

Word Work

Phonics, 428c
REVIEW Sentence Reading **T**

Spelling, 428d
Partner Review

Comprehension/Vocabulary/Fluency

Read "Celebrating the Buffalo Days," 428–431
Leveled Readers

Grouping Options
408f–408g

Homonyms
Reading Across Texts

Fluency, 431a
Read with Appropriate Phrasing

Writing Across the Curriculum, 431b
Map

Grammar, 431c
Review the Paragraph **T**

Speaking and Listening, 431d
Listen for Speaker's Purpose

Day 4 *Describe a special ceremony.*

Day 4 Social Studies Center: Celebration Sounds, 408k

DAY 5 PAGES 432a–433b

Oral Language

QUESTION OF THE DAY, 432a
What are some different ways that people celebrate?

Oral Vocabulary/Share Literature, 432a
Read Aloud Anthology "Bringing the Light"
Amazing Words Review

Word Work

Phonics, 432c
Review Prefixes *mis-, mid-* **T**

Lesson Vocabulary, 432c
Review *borrow, clattering, drum, jingles, silver, voice* **T**

Spelling, 432d
Test

Comprehension/Vocabulary/Fluency

Read Leveled Readers

Grouping Options 408f–408g

Monitor Progress, 432e–432g
Read the Sentences
Read the Story

Writing and Grammar, 432–433
Develop Organization/Paragraphs
Use the Paragraph **T**

Research/Study Skills, 433a
Time Line

Day 5 *Write about dancing.*

Day 5 Revisit the Birthday Celebration Concept Chart, 433b

KEY ◉ = Target Skill **T** = Tested Skill

Check Retelling, *426g*

Check Fluency WCPM, *431a*
Spiral REVIEW Phonics,
High-Frequency Words

Check Oral Vocabulary, *432b*
Assess Phonics,
Lesson Vocabulary, Fluency,
Comprehension, *432e*

SUCCESS PREDICTOR

Small Group Plan *for Differentiated Instruction*

Daily Plan AT A GLANCE

Reading
Whole Group
- Oral Language
- Word Work
- Comprehension/Vocabulary

Group Time

Meet with small groups to provide:
- Skill Support
- Reading Support
- Fluency Practice

Read

This week's lessons for daily group time can be found behind the Differentiated Instruction (DI) tab on pp. DI·54–DI·63.

Whole Group
- Comprehension/Vocabulary
- Fluency

Language Arts
- Writing
- Grammar
- Speaking/Listening/Viewing
- Research/Study Skills

Use *My Sidewalks on Reading Street* for Tier III intensive reading intervention.

DAY 1

On-Level	Strategic Intervention	Advanced
Teacher-Led *Page 408q*	**Teacher-Led** *Page DI · 54*	**Teacher-Led** *Page DI · 55*
• **Read** Decodable Reader 30 • **Reread** for Fluency	• Blend Words with Prefixes *mis-, mid-* • **Read** Decodable Reader 30 • **Reread** for Fluency	• Extend Word Reading • **Read** Advanced Selection 30 • Introduce Concept Inquiry

(i) Independent Activities

While you meet with small groups, have the rest of the class...

- Reread for fluency
- Write in their journals
- Read self-selected reading
- Visit the Word Work Center
- Complete Practice Book 2.2, pp. 143–144

DAY 2

On-Level	Strategic Intervention	Advanced
Teacher-Led *Pages 412–425*	**Teacher-Led** *Page DI · 56*	**Teacher-Led** *Page DI · 57*
• **Read** *Jingle Dancer* • **Reread** for Fluency	• Blend Words with Prefixes *mis-, mid-* • **Read** SI Decodable Reader 30 • **Read** or Listen to *Jingle Dancer*	• **Read** *Jingle Dancer* • Continue Concept Inquiry

(i) Independent Activities

While you meet with small groups, have the rest of the class...

- Read self-selected reading
- Write in their journals
- Visit the Listening Center
- Complete Practice Book 2.2, pp. 145–147

DAY 3

On-Level	Strategic Intervention	Advanced
Teacher-Led *Pages 412–427*	**Teacher-Led** *Page DI · 58*	**Teacher-Led** *Page DI · 59*
• **Reread** *Jingle Dancer*	• **Reread** *Jingle Dancer* • Read Words and Sentences • Review Character, Setting, and Plot/Prior Knowledge • **Reread** for Fluency	• Self-Selected Reading • Continue Concept Inquiry

(i) Independent Activities

While you meet with small groups, have the rest of the class...

- Read self-selected reading
- Write in their journals
- Visit the Writing Center
- Complete Practice Book 2.2, pp. 148–149

① Begin with whole class skill and strategy instruction.

② Meet with small groups to provide differentiated instruction.

③ Gather the whole class back together for fluency and language arts.

DAY 4

On-Level
Teacher-Led
Pages 428–431, LR40–LR42
- **Read** "Celebrating the Buffalo Days"
- Practice with On-Level Reader *A Special Festival*

Strategic Intervention
Teacher-Led
Pages DI·60, LR37–LR39
- **Read** or Listen to "Celebrating the Buffalo Days"
- **Reread** for Fluency
- Build Concepts
- Practice with Below-Level Reader *At the Powwow*

Advanced
Teacher-Led
Pages DI·61, LR43–LR45
- **Read** "Celebrating the Buffalo Days"
- Extend Vocabulary
- Continue Concept Inquiry
- Practice with Advanced Reader *Winter Holidays*

i Independent Activities
While you meet with small groups, have the rest of the class...

- Reread for fluency
- Write in their journals
- Read self-selected reading
- Review spelling words with a partner
- Visit the Listening and Social Studies Centers

DAY 5

On-Level
Teacher-Led
Pages 432e–432g, LR40–LR42
- Sentence Reading, Set B
- Monitor Fluency and Comprehension
- Practice with On-Level Reader *A Special Festival*

Strategic Intervention
Teacher-Led
Pages DI·62, LR37–LR39
- Practice Word Reading
- Sentence Reading, Set A
- Monitor Fluency and Comprehension
- Practice with Below-Level Reader *At the Powwow*

Advanced
Teacher-Led
Pages DI·63, LR43–LR45
- Sentence Reading, Set C
- Monitor Fluency and Comprehension
- Share Concept Inquiry
- Practice with Advanced Reader *Winter Holidays*

i Independent Activities
While you meet with small groups, have the rest of the class...

- Reread for fluency
- Write in their journals
- Read self-selected reading
- Visit the Technology Center
- Complete Practice Book 2.2, p. 150

ELL

Grouping Place English language learners in the groups that correspond to their reading abilities in English.

Use the appropriate Leveled Reader or other text at children's instructional level.

TIP Send home the appropriate Multilingual Summary of the main selection on Day 1.

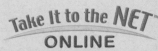
Take It to the NET
ONLINE
PearsonSuccessNet.com

Sharon Vaughn
For research on intervention, see the article "Group Size and Time Allotted to Intervention" by Scott Foresman author S. Vaughn and by S. Linan-Thompson.

TEACHER TALK
In **Readers' Theater,** children read text aloud dramatically to an audience, with minimal or no props.

Be sure to schedule time for children to work on the unit inquiry project "Research Traditions." This week children should present their plans and traditions to the class.

Looking Ahead

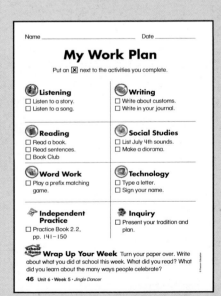

▲ **Group-Time Survival Guide**
p. 46, Weekly Contract

Jingle Dancer **408g**

Customize Your Plan *by Strand*

Concept Development

SOCIAL STUDIES

What are some different ways that people celebrate?

 *to build oral vocabulary*

ceremony	compliment	culture
evergreen	festival	fidget
multicolored	sash	

BUILD

❑ **Question of the Week** Use the Morning Warm-Up! to introduce and discuss the question of the week. This week children will talk, sing, read, and write about how people celebrate in different ways. **DAY 1** *408l*

❑ **Sing with Me Big Book** Sing a song about a festival. Ask children to listen for the concept-related Amazing Words *ceremony, festival, culture.* **DAY 1** *408m*

❑ **Build Background** Remind children of the question of the week. Then create a concept chart for children to add to throughout the week. **DAY 1** *408m*

Sing with Me Big Book

DEVELOP

❑ **Question of the Day** Use the questions in the Morning Warm-Ups! to discuss lesson concepts and how they relate to the unit theme, Traditions. **DAY 2** *410a*, **DAY 3** *426a*, **DAY 4** *428a*, **DAY 5** *432a*

❑ **Share Literature** Read big books and read aloud selections that develop concepts, language, and vocabulary related to the lesson concept and the unit theme. Continue to develop this week's Amazing Words. **DAY 2** *410b*, **DAY 3** *426b*, **DAY 4** *428b*, **DAY 5** *432b*

CONNECT

❑ **Wrap Up Your Week!** Revisit the Question of the Week. **DAY 5** *433b*

CHECK

❑ **Check Oral Vocabulary** To informally assess children's oral vocabulary, ask individuals to use some of this week's Amazing Words to tell you about the concept of the week—Traditions. **DAY 5** *432b*

PREFIXES *MIS-*, *MID-* Some words consist of a base word and the prefix *mis-* or *mid-*. The prefix *mis-* means "*not* or *wrong*." The prefix *mid-* means "*half* or *middle*."

TEACH

❑ **Prefixes *mis-*, *mid-*** Introduce the blending strategy for words that begin with prefixes *mis-*, *mid-*. Then have children blend and build words, by adding the prefix to each base word, read the new word, and supply its meaning. **DAY 1** *408n-408o*

❑ **Fluent Word Reading** Use the Fluent Word Reading Routine to develop children's word reading fluency. Use the Phonics Songs and Rhymes Chart for additional word reading practice. **DAY 2** *410c-410d*

Phonics Songs and Rhymes Chart 30

PRACTICE/APPLY

❑ **Decodable Reader 30** Practice reading words with prefixes *mis-*, *mid-* in context. **DAY 1** *408q*

❑ *Jingle Dancer* Practice decoding words in context. **DAY 2** *412-425*

Decodable Reader 30

❑ **Homework** Practice Book 2.2 p. 143. **DAY 1** *408o*

❑ **Word Work Center** Practice prefixes *mis-*, *mid-*. **ANY DAY** *408j*

Main Selection—Fiction

RETEACH/REVIEW

❑ **Review** Review words with this week's phonics skills. **DAY 5** *432c*

❑ **Reteach Lessons** If necessary, reteach prefixes *mis- mid-*. **DAY 5** *DI·68*

❑ **Spiral REVIEW** Review previously taught phonics skills. **DAY 1** *408o*, **DAY 3** *426c*, **DAY 4** *428c*

ASSESS

❑ **Sentence Reading** Assess children's ability to read words with prefixes *mis-*, *mid-*. **DAY 5** *432e-432f*

① Use assessment data to determine your instructional focus.

② Preview this week's instruction by strand.

③ Choose instructional activities that meet the needs of your classroom.

SPELLING

PREFIXES MIS-, MID- Some words consist of a base word and the prefix *mis-* or *mid-*. The prefix *mis-* means "not or wrong." The prefix *mid-* means "half or middle."

TEACH

❑ **Pretest** Before administering the pretest, model how to segment prefixes *mis-*, *mid-* to spell them. Dictate the spelling words, segmenting them if necessary. Then have children check their pretests and correct misspelled words. **DAY 1** *408p*

PRACTICE/APPLY

❑ **Dictation** Have children write dictation sentences to practice spelling words. **DAY 2** *410d*

❑ **Write Words** Have children practice by writing the spelling words with prefixes that mean something has been done wrong and that mean "middle." **DAY 3** *426d*

❑ **Homework** Phonics and Spelling Practice Book pp. 117–120. **DAY 1** *408p*, **DAY 2** *410d*, **DAY 3** *426d*, **DAY 4** *428d*

RETEACH/REVIEW

❑ **Partner Review** Have pairs work together to read and write the spelling words. **DAY 4** *428d*

ASSESS

❑ **Posttest** Use dictation sentences to give the posttest for words with prefixes *mis-*, *mid-*. **DAY 5** *432d*

Spelling Words

Prefixes

1. midair	7. midweek*
2. misplace	8. misbehave
3. mislead	9. midyear
4. midway*	10. mismatch
5. misprint	11. misdeed
6. midday*	12. mistake

Challenge Words

13. midstream	15. misbehavior
14. midnight	

* Words from the Selection

VOCABULARY

🔄 **STRATEGY CONTEXT CLUES** Context clues are the words and sentences around an unfamiliar word. Use context clues to help you figure out a word's meaning.

LESSON VOCABULARY
borrow   clattering   drum   jingles   silver   voice

TEACH

❑ **Words to Know** Introduce and discuss this week's lesson vocabulary. **DAY 2** *410f*

❑ **Vocabulary Strategy** Use the vocabulary strategy in the Student Edition to introduce/model *context clues*. **DAY 2** *410-411a*

Vocabulary Strategy Lesson

PRACTICE/APPLY

❑ **Words in Context** Read the lesson vocabulary in context. **DAY 2** *412-425*, **DAY 3** *412-427*

❑ **Lesson Vocabulary** Write and answer questions that use lesson vocabulary. **DAY 3** *426d*

Main Selection—Fiction

❑ **Leveled Text** Read the lesson vocabulary in leveled text. **DAY 4** *LR37-LR45*, **DAY 5** *LR37-LR45*

❑ **Homework** Practice Book 2.2 pp. 146, 149. **DAY 2** *410f*, **DAY 3** *426d*

Leveled Readers

RETEACH/REVIEW

❑ **Homonyms** Have partners write sentences with the homonyms *fair*, *bank*, and *duck*. **DAY 3** *426e*

❑ **Review** Review this week's lesson vocabulary words. **DAY 5** *432c*

ASSESS

❑ **Selection Test** Use the Selection Test to determine children's understanding of the lesson vocabulary words. **DAY 3**

❑ **Sentence Reading** Assess children's ability to read this week's lesson vocabulary words. **DAY 5** *432e-432f*

HIGH-FREQUENCY WORDS

RETEACH/REVIEW

❑ **Spiral REVIEW** Review previously taught high-frequency words. **DAY 2** *410f*, **DAY 4** *428c*

☑ **Customize Your Plan** *by Strand*

COMPREHENSION	FLUENCY

COMPREHENSION

SKILL CHARACTER, SETTING, AND PLOT Characters are the people or animals in a story. The setting is where and when a story takes place. What happens in the beginning, middle, and end of a story makes up the plot.

STRATEGY PRIOR KNOWLEDGE Prior knowledge is what you already know. Use prior knowledge to figure out the meaning of what you are reading.

TEACH

☐ **Skill/Strategy Lesson** Use the Skill/Strategy Lesson in the Student Edition to introduce *character, setting, and plot,* and *prior knowledge.* DAY 1 *408r–409*

Skill/Strategy Lesson

PRACTICE/APPLY

☐ **Skills and Strategies in Context** Read *Jingle Dancer,* using the Guiding Comprehension questions to apply *character, setting, and plot* and *prior knowledge.* DAY 2 *412–425a*

Main Selection—Fiction

☐ **Reader Response** Use the questions on Student Edition p. 426 to discuss the selection. DAY 3 *426g–427*

☐ **Skills and Strategies in Context** Read "Celebrating the Buffalo Days," guiding children as they apply skills and strategies. DAY 4 *428-431*

Paired Selection—Nonfiction

☐ **Leveled Text** Apply *character, setting, and plot* and *prior knowledge* to read leveled text. DAY 4 *LR37–LR45,* DAY 5 *LR37–LR45*

Leveled Readers

☐ **Homework** Practice Book 2.2 pp. 144, 145. DAY 1 *408-409,* DAY 2 *410e*

ASSESS

☐ **Selection Test** Determine children's understanding of the main selection and assess their ability to identify *character, setting, and plot.* DAY 3

☐ **Story Reading** Have children read the passage "The Spelling Bee." Ask questions about the character, setting and plot. Then have them retell. DAY 5 *432e-432g*

RETEACH/REVIEW

☐ **Reteach Lesson** If necessary, reteach *character, setting and plot.* DAY 5 *DI-68*

FLUENCY

SKILL READ WITH APPROPRIATE PHRASING Appropriate phrasing means pausing at the right places when you read. Punctuation marks, such as commas and periods, signal the right places to pause.

REREAD FOR FLUENCY

☐ **Oral Rereading** Have children read orally from Decodable Reader 30 or another text at their independent reading level. Listen as children read and provide corrective feedback regarding their oral reading and their use of the blending strategy. DAY 1 *408q*

☐ **Paired Reading** Have pairs of children read orally from the main selection or another text at their independent reading level. Listen as children read and provide corrective feedback regarding their oral reading and their use of the blending strategy. DAY 2 *425a*

TEACH

☐ **Model** Use passages from *Jingle Dancer* to model reading with appropriate phrasing. DAY 3 *426f,* DAY 4 *431a*

PRACTICE/APPLY

☐ **Choral Reading** Have groups choral read parts from *Jingle Dancer.* Monitor progress and provide feedback regarding children's phrasing. DAY 3 *426f,* DAY 4 *431a*

☐ **Listening Center** Have children follow along with the AudioText for this week's selections. **ANY DAY** *408j*

☐ **Reading/Library Center** Have children build fluency by rereading Leveled Readers, Decodable Readers, or other text at their independent level. **ANY DAY** *408j*

☐ **Fluency Coach** Have children use Fluency Coach to listen to fluent reading or to practice reading on their own. **ANY DAY**

ASSESS

☐ **Story Reading** Take a one-minute timed sample of children's oral reading. Use the passage "The Spelling Bee." DAY 5 *432e-432g*

WRITING

Trait of the Week

ORGANIZATION/PARAGRAPHS Organization holds your writing together. Your story should have a beginning, middle, and an end.

TEACH

☐ **Write Together** Engage children in writing activities that develop language, grammar, and writing skills. Include independent writing as an extension of group writing activities.

　　Shared Writing DAY 1 *409a*
　　Interactive Writing DAY 2 *425b*
　　Writing Across the Curriculum DAY 4 *431b*

☐ **Trait of the Week** Introduce and model the Trait of the Week, *organization/paragraphs*. DAY 3 *427a*

PRACTICE/APPLY

☐ **Write Now** Examine the model on Student Edition pp. 432–433. Then have children write stories. DAY 5 *432-433*

Write Now

　　Prompt *Jingle Dancer* tells the story of Jenna's search for jingles. Think about something else Jenna might want to find or do. Now write a story that tells what Jenna wants and how she gets it.

☐ **Daily Journal Writing** Have children write about concepts and literature in their journals. EVERY DAY *408d-408e*

☐ **Writing Center** Have children write a report about Native American customs. ANY DAY *408k*

ASSESS

☐ **Scoring Rubric** Use a rubric to evaluate stories. DAY 5 *432-433*

RETEACH/REVIEW

☐ **The Grammar and Writing Book** Use pp. 224–229 of The Grammar and Writing Book to extend instruction. ANY DAY

The Grammar and Writing Book

SPEAKING AND LISTENING

TEACH

☐ **Listen for Speaker's Purpose** Remind children of appropriate listening and speaking behaviors as they role play a discussion with their families about getting a pet. DAY 4 *431d*

GRAMMAR

SKILL　INDENT PARAGRAPHS A paragraph is a group of sentences about the same idea. The first sentence of a paragraph is indented.

TEACH

☐ **Grammar Transparency 30** Use Grammar Transparency 30 to teach *paragraph indentation*. DAY 1 *409b*

Grammar Transparency 30

PRACTICE/APPLY

☐ **Develop the Concept** Review the concept of *paragraph indentation* and provide guided practice. DAY 2 *425c*

☐ **Apply to Writing** Have children use indented paragraphs in writing. DAY 3 *427b*

☐ **Define/Practice** Review the definition of *indented paragraphs*. Then have children write sentences in indented paragraph form. DAY 4 *431c*

☐ **Write Now** Discuss the grammar lesson on Student Edition p. 433. Have children write paragraphs in a story. DAY 5 *432-433*

Write Now

☐ **Daily Fix-It** Have children find and correct errors in grammar, spelling, and punctuation. DAY 1 *409b*, DAY 2 *425c*, DAY 3 *427b*, DAY 4 *431c*, DAY 5 *432-433*

☐ **Homework** The Grammar and Writing Practice Book pp. 117–120. DAY 2 *425c*, DAY 3 *427b*, DAY 4 *431c*, DAY 5 *432-433*

RETEACH/REVIEW

☐ **The Grammar and Writing Book** Use pp. 224–227 of The Grammar and Writing Book to extend instruction. ANY DAY

The Grammar and Writing Book

RESEARCH/INQUIRY

TEACH

☐ **Time Line** Model how to read and create a time line. Then have partners create a time line of a favorite book. DAY 5 *433a*

☐ **Unit Inquiry Project** Allow time for children to present their plans and traditions to the class. ANY DAY *295*

Resources for Differentiated Instruction

LEVELED READERS

▶ **Comprehension**
- 🎯 **Skill** Character, Setting, and Plot
- 🎯 **Strategy** Prior Knowledge

▶ **Lesson Vocabulary**
- 🎯 Context Clues

clattering	jingles
drum	voice
borrow	silver

▶ **Social Studies Standards**
- Native American Culture: Powwow Ceremony
- Family History

Leveled Reader Database
ONLINE
PearsonSuccessNet.com

Use the Online Database of over 600 books to
- Download and print additional copies of this week's leveled readers
- Listen to the readers being read online
- Search for more titles focused on this week's skills, topic, and content

---

On-Level

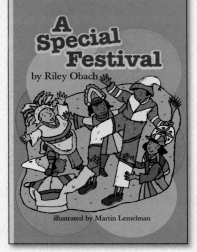

A Special Festival
by Riley Obach

illustrated by Martin Lemelman

On-Level Reader

Character, Setting, Plot
Think about the story *A Special Festival*. Circle the answer to the questions below.

1. What does Zeke like to do?
   sew   cook   (play music)

2. Where does Zeke hope to go for summer vacation?
   music   camp   (the Bahamas)   Florida

3. Which character or characters in the story live in the Bahamas?
   Zeke   Goombay family   (Gramps)

Possible responses given.
4-6. Write a few sentences that tell what happened in the beginning, middle, and end of the story.

<u>Zeke thinks about what he did last summer; Zeke's parents sew and cook special things, they all go to the Goombay Festival.</u>

On-Level Practice TE p. LR41

Vocabulary
Write a word from the box that fits on each group of lines. Write one letter on each line. Then, find a secret message. Write each letter that has a number under its line on the same number line on question 7.

Words to Know
borrow   clattering   drum   jingle   silver   voice

1. d r u m
       6
2. s i l v e r
   3   9
3. c l a t t e r i n g
   1   7   8
4. b o r r o w
         5
5. v o i c e
           4
6. j i n g l e
         2
7. c e l e b r a t e !
   1 2 3 4 5 6 7 8 9

On-Level Practice TE p. LR42

Strategic Intervention

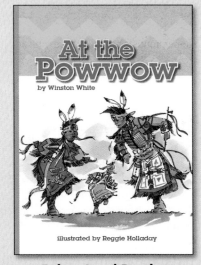

At the POWWOW
by Winston White

illustrated by Reggie Holladay

Below-Level Reader

Character, Setting, Plot
Draw a picture of Ben at a powwow. Show how Ben feels.

1–2.

Write a few sentences that tell about what happened in the story. Possible responses given.

3. Beginning: <u>Ben's family put on special clothes.</u>
4. Middle: <u>Everyone danced together.</u>
5. End: <u>Ben's family eats together.</u>

Below-Level Practice TE p. LR38

Vocabulary
Circle the word that best fits into each sentence. Then, write it on the line.

1. Sally plays the <u>drum</u>
   drain   (drum)   dress

2. My new ring is made out of <u>silver</u>
   slip   sling   (silver)

3. Please don't talk in such a loud <u>voice</u>
   vest   choice   (voice)

4. Can I <u>borrow</u> your pencil to write a letter?
   (borrow)   bored   broom

Circle the words that describe a sound.

5. (Jingle)   Very   (Clattering)   Class   Clown   Jump

Below-Level Practice TE p. LR39

Advanced

Advanced Reader

Character, Setting, Plot
Think about the story *Winter Holidays*. Then circle the answer to each question.

1. What do Selene and Anneka have in common?
(like holidays)   live in America   have blond hair

2. How are Selene and Anneka different?
one is a boy   one is much older   (from different countries)

3. What are the two cities where the story takes place?
(Chicago)   (Stockholm)   New York

4. When does the story take place?
in the future   in the past   (a little while ago)

5. Write a sentence that tells what happened at the end of the story. Possible response given.

The girls wrote and thanked each other for sharing their winter holidays.

Advanced Practice TE p. LR44

Vocabulary
Write the word next to its definition.

Words to Know

carols	famine	festival	geraniums
Middle Ages	ornaments	siblings	value

1. **geraniums** — *n.* red summertime flowers
2. **siblings** — *n.* brothers and sisters
3. **carols** — *n.* songs of joy
4. **famine** — *n.* great shortage of food
5. **ornaments** — *n.* pretty holiday objects
6. **value** — *n.* desirable quality
7. **Middle Ages** — *n.* period of European history from A.D. 500 to 1500
8. **festival** — *n.* celebration

Advanced Practice TE p. LR45

ELL Reader

ELL Poster 30

Teacher's Edition Notes
ELL notes throughout this lesson support instruction and reference additional resources at point of use.

ELL Teaching Guide pp. 204–210, 270–271
- Multilingual summaries of the main selection
- Comprehension lesson
- Vocabulary strategies and word cards
- ELL Reader 30 lesson

ELL and Transition Handbook

Ten Important Sentences
- Key ideas from every selection in the Student Edition
- Activities to build sentence power

More Reading

Readers' Theater Anthology
- Fluency practice
- Five scripts to build fluency
- Poetry for oral interpretation

Leveled Trade Books

Below-Level

On-Level

Advanced

- Extend reading tied to the unit concept
- Lessons in Trade Book Library Teaching Guide

School + Home

Homework
- Family Times Newsletter
- ELL Multilingual Selection Summaries

Take-Home Books
- Decodable Readers
- Leveled Readers

Literacy Centers

 Listening

Let's Read
Along

MATERIALS SINGLES
CD player, headphones, print copies of recorded pieces

LISTEN TO LITERATURE As children listen to the following recordings, have them follow along or read along in the print version.

AudioText
Jingle Dancer
"Celebrating the Buffalo Days"

Sing with Me/Background Building Audio
"Festival Time"

Phonics Songs and Rhymes Audio
"Powwow"

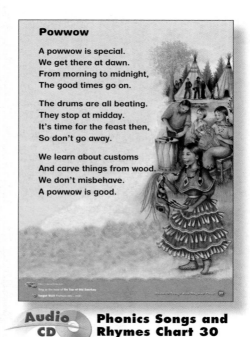

Powwow

A powwow is special.
We get there at dawn.
From morning to midnight,
The good times go on.

The drums are all beating.
They stop at midday.
It's time for the feast then,
So don't go away.

We learn about customs
And carve things from wood.
We don't misbehave.
A powwow is good.

Audio CD **Phonics Songs and Rhymes Chart 30**

 Reading/Library

Read It
Again!

MATERIALS SINGLES PAIRS GROUPS
collection of books for self-selected reading, reading logs

REREAD BOOKS Have children select previously read books from the appropriate book box and record titles of books they read in their logs. Use these previously read books:

- Decodable Readers
- Leveled Readers
- ELL Readers
- Stories written by classmates
- Books from the library

TEN IMPORTANT SENTENCES Have children read the Ten Important Sentences for *Jingle Dancer* and locate the sentences in the Student Edition.

BOOK CLUB Have children read books about different cultures that use dances for special celebrations. Have children write about one of the dances.

 Word Work

Mix and
Match

MATERIALS PAIRS GROUPS
prefix and base word cards

PREFIXES mis-, mid- Have two or more children play a match game.

1. Make cards for the prefixes *mis-* and *mid-*. Also make cards with base words that can be combined with these prefixes. Place word cards facedown and prefix cards faceup.
2. Have children turn over a card and match it with a prefix. If they can make and read a word, the word card stays faceup. If not, the word card is placed facedown at the bottom of the pile.
3. Children take turns picking a card and trying to make a word. The game ends when all word cards have been matched with a prefix.

Phonics Activities CD This interactive CD provides additional practice.

mis   mid

lead   match   behave

night   way   summer

Scott Foresman Reading Street Centers Survival Kit

Use the *Jingle Dancer* materials
from the Reading Street Centers Survival Kit
to organize this week's centers.

 Writing

 Social Studies

Technology

Culture Report

MATERIALS `SINGLES`
paper, pencils, books or videos about Native American culture

WRITE A REPORT Have children find information about Native American customs.

1. Children read books or watch videos to find facts about a Native American group's dances, music, celebrations, clothing, or food.
2. Then they write a report, using the facts they found.

LEVELED WRITING Encourage children to write at their own ability level. Some may only list the facts they found. Others will be able to paraphrase the facts with some organization. Your best writers will write a report with greater detail and attention to mechanics and spelling.

Sights and Sounds

MATERIALS `SINGLES`
paper, pencils, shoeboxes, art supplies, glue

CELEBRATION SOUNDS Review the sounds of the powwow ceremony: the tink of jingles, the brum of the drum, the hey-ah-ho-o of the song.

1. Children make a list of July Fourth sounds.
2. Then they choose one sound and make a diorama that shows the activity associated with the sound.
3. Display children's dioramas in the classroom.

Write a Letter

MATERIALS `SINGLES`
computer, printer

WRITE TO A CHARACTER Have individuals write a letter to a character in *Jingle Dancer*.

1. Have children turn on the computer and open a word processing program.
2. Children then type a short letter to a character from the selection.
3. Have children print out their letters.
4. Remind children to sign their names after the closing.

June 7, 2007
Dear Jenna,

How was the powwow? Did everyone like your dance? Who taught you how to dance?

Your friend,
Mary Jenkins

<u>Sioux Powwows</u>

Some Sioux still do dances like the Sun Dance. A powwow is a celebration with some of these dances. Dancers wear outfits with beads and feathers. People dance to drums. Families sometimes travel far to get to powwows.

boom boom boom

ALL CENTERS

Oral Vocabulary
"Festival Time" 30

Phonics and Spelling
Prefixes *mis-, mid-*

Spelling Pretest: Words with prefixes *mis-* and *mid-*

 Read Apply Phonics **Word Wall**

Group Time < Differentiated Instruction

Listening Comprehension
Skill Character, Setting, and Plot
Strategy Prior Knowledge

Shared Writing
Story

Grammar
Indent Paragraphs

Materials

- *Sing with Me Big Book*
- Letter Tiles
- Decodable Reader 30
- Student Edition 408–409
- Graphic Organizer 25
- Skill Transparency 30
- Writing Transparency 30
- Grammar Transparency 30

Take It to the NET
ONLINE

Professional Development
To learn more about text for beginning readers, go to PearsonSuccessNet.com and read the article "Analyzing Beginning Reading Programs" by M. Stein and others.

Morning Warm-Up!

How often does your family get together?
Many people get together to celebrate special occasions.
People all around the world celebrate.
What are some different ways that people celebrate?

QUESTION OF THE WEEK Tell children they will talk, sing, read, and write about how people celebrate in different ways. Write and read the message and discuss the question.

CONNECT CONCEPTS Ask questions to connect to other Unit 6 selections.

- How did the family in *A Birthday Basket for Tía* celebrate Tía's birthday?

- In *Red, White, and Blue,* we talked about celebrating the flag. Do you think people from other countries celebrate their flag? How do you think they celebrate?

REVIEW HIGH-FREQUENCY WORDS

- Circle the high-frequency words *family, often, together,* and *world* in the message.

- Underline the statements in the message. Circle the questions in the message.

Build Background Use the Day 1 instruction on ELL Poster 30 to assess knowledge and develop concepts.

ELL Poster 30

Oral Vocabulary

SHARE LITERATURE Display p. 30 of the *Sing with Me Big Book.* Tell children that the class is going to sing a song about a festival. Read the title. Ask children to listen for the Amazing Words **ceremony, festival,** and **culture** as you sing.

- A ceremony is a special act or set of acts done for a special occasion. What are some ceremonies you have gone to? (Possible response: wedding, school graduation, cultural holiday)

- A festival is a day when people eat and celebrate together, often to remember something important that happened before. What are some things people might do during a festival? (Possible response: eat special foods, wear costumes, perform dances)

- The culture of a people is its beliefs, customs, arts, and tools. What are some things that are important to your culture? (Children might name favorite foods, activities, books, or television shows.)

Festival Time
There's a festival.
Please come along with me.
We'll attend a ceremony.
There's a lot to do and see.
We can learn about a culture.
What a fun time it will be
At the festival.

Sing with Me Big Book

 **Sing with Me/ Background Building Audio**

BUILD BACKGROUND Remind children of the question of the week.

- What are some different ways that people celebrate?

Draw a T-chart or use Graphic Organizer 25.

Label the columns with the help of two children from your class. Ask these two children to tell you how they celebrate birthdays in their family. Display the chart for use throughout the week.

- What kinds of activities do you do for your birthday?
- Who helps you celebrate your birthday?

How [child A] Celebrates Birthdays	How [child B] Celebrates Birthdays
1.	1.
2.	2.

▲ **Graphic Organizer 25**

OBJECTIVE
- Build oral vocabulary.

Amazing Words to build oral vocabulary

	MONITOR PROGRESS
ceremony culture festival compliment fidget evergreen multicolored sash	**If...** children lack oral vocabulary experiences about the concept Traditions, **then...** use the Oral Vocabulary Routine below to teach *ceremony.*

Oral Vocabulary ROUTINE

1 Introduce the Word Relate the word *ceremony* to the song. Supply a child-friendly definition. Have children say the word. Example: A *ceremony* is something that people do to celebrate a special occasion.

2 Demonstrate Provide an example to show meaning. My aunt's wedding *ceremony* was held outdoors.

3 Apply Have children demonstrate their understanding. What type of *ceremonies* have you been to?

4 Display the Word/Word Parts Write the word on a card. Display it. Clap the four word parts in *cer-e-mo-ny* as you say the word. See p. DI·7 to teach *culture* and *festival.*

ELL

Access Content Help children recognize the meanings of the English words *come along* and *see* in "Festival Time" by motioning with your hand for them to join you at *come along* and pointing to your eyes at *see.*

OBJECTIVES

- Use structural cues to decode words with prefixes *mis-, mid-*.
- Blend, read, and build words with prefixes *mis-, mid-*.

Skills Trace

Prefixes *mis-, mid-*

Introduce/Teach	TE: 2.6 408n–o, 410c–d
Practice	TE: 2.6 408q; PB: 2.2 143; DR30
Reteach/Review	TE: 2.6 432c DI-68
Assess/Test	TE: 2.6 432e–g; Benchmark Test: Unit 6

Strategic Intervention

Use **Monitor Progress,** p. 408o, during Group Time after children have had more practice with prefixes.

Advanced

Use **Monitor Progress,** p. 408o, as a preassessment to determine whether this group of children would benefit from this instruction on prefixes.

 ELL

Support Phonics Point out to Spanish speakers that the prefix *mid-* is related to the Spanish word *medio,* which means "half" or "middle." As examples, use cognates such as *midnight/medianoche* and *midday/mediodía.*

See the Phonics Transition Lessons in the ELL and Transition Handbook.

Prefixes *mis-, mid-*

TEACH/MODEL

Blending Strategy

ROUTINE

① Connect Write *repaint* and *disagree.* What do you know about reading these words? (They have a base word and a prefix.) Today we'll learn about adding prefixes *mis-* and *mid-* to the beginning of words. Each prefix has a special meaning.

- *mis-*   not or wrong
- *mid-*   half or middle

② Model Write *misplace.* This is a two-syllable word made from the base word *place* and the prefix *mis-.* You can chunk the word into its parts—the prefix and the base word. Then cover the prefix, then read the base word, read the prefix, and blend the two together to read the word. This is how I blend this word. Cover the prefix to read the base word *place,* uncover and read the prefix and

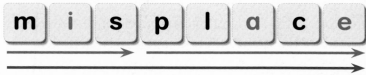

base word. Blend the two parts. Let's blend this word together: /mis/ / plās/, *misplace.* Repeat with *midnight.*

③ Group Practice First, chunk the word. Then read the prefix, read the base word, and blend the two parts. Continue with *midway, mistake, midlife, mislead, midair, misprint.*

④ Review What do you know about reading words with prefixes? Chunk the word, read the prefix, read the base word, and then blend the two parts.

BLEND WORDS

INDIVIDUALS BLEND WORDS Call on individuals to chunk and blend the words *midday, misdeed, midyear, misfit, mismatch, midweek.* Have them tell what they know about each word before reading it. (Prefixes form separate syllables that are added to the beginning of base words.) For feedback, refer to step four of the Blending Strategy Routine.

BUILD WORDS

READ LONGER WORDS Write the prefixes *mis-* and *mid-* as headings for a two-column chart. Write several base words in each column. Have children add the prefix to each base word, read the new word, and supply its meaning. Have the completed lists reread.

mid-	*mis-*
stream	judge
point	give
size	mark
air	file

Read the clues. Write mid or mis to finish the word.

midair   misplace

1. middle of the week — **mid** week
2. an error — **mis** take
3. act badly — **mis** behave
4. noon — **mid** day
5. about July 1 — **mid** year
6. an error in printing — **mis** print
7. a wrong act — **mis** deed
8. middle of winter — **mid** winter
9. make a spelling error — **mis** spell
10. middle of the ship — **mid** ship

School + Home Home Activity Your child wrote words with the prefixes mid- (as in midair) and mis- (as in misplace). Together, name other words with the prefixes mid- and mis-, such as midway, midsize, mislead, misfile, and misdirect. Write the words. Ask your child to pronounce them and identify the prefixes.

▲ **Practice Book 2.2** p. 143, Prefixes

Monitor Progress | Check Word Reading Prefixes

Write the following words and have individuals read them.

midlife	**mistype**	**miscopy**	**midsummer**	**misshape**
reread	**prepaid**	**unfold**	**dislike**	**misjudge**
midafternoon	**helpfulness**	**hopefully**	**aimlessly**	**misleading**

If… children cannot blend words with prefixes at this point,

then… continue to monitor their progress using other instructional opportunities during the week so that they can be successful with the Day 5 Assessment. See the Skills Trace on p. 408n.

SUCCESS PREDICTOR

Spiral REVIEW

- Row 2 reviews prefixes *un-, re-, pre-, dis-*.
- Row 3 reviews multisyllabic words.

▶ **Day 1 Check** Word Reading	**Day 2** Check Lesson Vocabulary/ High-Frequency Words	**Day 3** Check Retelling	**Day 4** Check Fluency	**Day 5** Assess Progress

Word Reading

SUCCESS PREDICTOR

OBJECTIVES

- Segment sounds and word parts to spell words.
- Spell words with prefixes *mis-, mid-*.

Spelling Words

Prefixes

1. midair
2. misplace
3. mislead
4. midway*
5. misprint
6. midday*
7. midweek*
8. misbehave
9. midyear
10. mismatch
11. misdeed
12. mistake

Challenge Words

13. midstream
14. midnight
15. misbehavior

* Words from the Selection

Prefixes *mis-* and *mid-*

Generalization When **mis-** and **mid-** are added to words, make no change in the spelling of the base word: mid + air = **midair**.

Sort the list words by **mis-** and **mid-**.

mis-	mid-
1. misplace	8. midair
2. mislead	9. midway
3. misprint	10. midday
4. misbehave	11. midweek
5. mismatch	12. midyear
6. misdeed	
7. mistake	

Spelling Words
1. midair
2. misplace
3. mislead
4. midway
5. misprint
6. midday
7. midweek
8. misbehave
9. midyear
10. mismatch
11. misdeed
12. mistake

Challenge Words
13. midstream
14. midnight
15. misbehavior

Challenge Words

mis-	mid-
13. misbehavior	14. midstream
	15. midnight

Home Activity Your child is learning to spell words with the prefixes mis- and mid-. To practice at home, ask your child to identify the prefixes for each word. Then ask your child to spell each list word.

▲ **Spelling Practice Book** p. 117

Support Spelling Before giving the spelling pretest, clarify the meaning of each spelling word with examples, such as writing 2 + 2 = 5 to illustrate *mistake* and pointing to Wednesdays on a calendar as examples of *midweek*.

Spelling

PRETEST Prefixes

MODEL WRITING FOR WORD PARTS Each spelling word begins with a prefix. Before administering the spelling pretest, model how to segment prefixes to spell them.

- You can spell words with prefixes by thinking about the base word and the prefix. What prefix and base word make up *midpoint*? (*mid-* and *point*)
- Start with the prefix *mid-*. Write *mid*.
- Then think of the sounds in the base word: *point*. What letters spell /point/? Write *point*.
- Now spell *midpoint*.
- Repeat with *misspell*.

PRETEST Dictate the spelling words. Segment the words for children if necessary. Have children check their pretests and correct misspelled words.

HOMEWORK Spelling Practice Book, p. 117

Group Time

On-Level	Strategic Intervention	Advanced
Read Decodable Reader 30.	**Read** Decodable Reader 30.	**Read** Advanced Selection 30.
• Use p. 408q.	• Use the **Routine** on p. DI•54.	• Use the **Routine** on p. DI•55.

ELL Place English language learners in the groups that correspond to their reading abilities in English.

ⓘ Independent Activities

Fluency Reading Pair children to reread Leveled Readers or the ELL Reader from the previous week or other text at children's independent level.

Journal Writing Write about a festival. Share writing.

Independent Reading See p. 408j for Reading/Library activities and suggestions.

Literacy Centers To practice prefixes, you may use Word Work, p. 408j.

Practice Book 2.2 Prefixes, p. 143; Character, Setting, Plot, p. 144

Break into small groups after Spelling and before the Comprehension lesson.

DAY 1

Apply Phonics

◉ PRACTICE Prefixes

HIGH-FREQUENCY WORDS Review *doesn't*, *through*, and *water*.

READ DECODABLE READER 30

- Pages 114–115 Read aloud quietly with the group.
- Pages 116–117 Have the group read aloud without you.
- Pages 118–120 Select individuals to read aloud.

CHECK COMPREHENSION AND DECODING Ask children the following questions about *Hiking the Hard Way*:

- Where does the story take place? (on a bus, on a hike)
- What went wrong for Danny? (His boots were mismatched, he did not have his water bottle, he slipped midstream and got wet, and he forgot his lunch.)

Then have children locate words with prefixes *mis-* and *mid-* in the story. Review *mis-* and *mid-* spelling patterns. Sort words according to their spelling patterns.

mid-	*mis-*
midday	mislaid
midstream	mismatched
midway	misplaced
	misstep

HOMEWORK Take-Home Decodable Reader 30

REREAD FOR FLUENCY

Oral Rereading

ROUTINE

1 **Read** Have children read the entire selection orally.

2 **Reread** To achieve optimal fluency, children should reread the text three or four times.

3 **Provide Feedback** Listen as children read and provide corrective feedback regarding their oral reading and their use of the blending strategy.

Monitor Progress

Decoding

If... children have difficulty decoding a word,	**then...** prompt them to blend the word.
	• What is the new word?
	• Is the new word a word you know?
	• Does it make sense in the story?

Access Content

Beginning Lead children on a noun walk through *Hiking the Hard Way*, identifying people, places, and things, such as *Danny*, *backpack*, *boots*, *troop*, *bus*, and *stream*.

Intermediate Aid comprehension by providing synonyms for unfamiliar words, such as *packed* and *group* for *loaded* and *troop*.

Advanced After reading *Hiking the Hard Way*, have partners take turns retelling what made Danny's hike difficult.

OBJECTIVES

- Identify character, setting, plot.
- Use prior knowledge.

Skills Trace

Character, Setting, Plot

Introduce/Teach	TE: 2.1 13a–b, 14e, 69a–b, 70e; 2.3 403a–b, 404e; 2.4 96r, 96–97; 2.5 208r, 208–209; 2.6 408r, 408–409
Practice	TE: 2.1 18–19, 82–83; 2.3 414–415; 2.4 114–115; 2.5 222–223; 2.6 420–421; PB: 2.1 4–5, 24–25, 134–135; 2.2 34–35, 74–75, 144–145
Reteach/Review	TE: 2.1 140–141, DI·64, DI·66; 2.2 178–179; 2.3 DI·67; 2.4 18–19, DI·67; 2.5 196–197, DI·66; 2.6 DI·68; PB: 2.1 47, 57; 2.2 7, 67, 87
Test	TE: 2.1 40e–g, 95e–g; 2.3 424e–g; 2.4 122e–g; 2.5 232e–g; 2.6 432e–g; Selection Test: 2.1 1–4, 9–12; 2.3 53–56; 2.4 73–76; 2.5 89–92; 2.6 117–120; Benchmark Test: Units 1–5

POWWOW!

Mike's family could not often spend much time together. Mike had drum lessons. His sister played soccer. His mother and father had jobs. They were all very busy. ●

"Come on," his father called one day. "We are all going to the powwow." Once a year, Mike's family and other Native Americans came together for this big fair.

At the powwow they watched the Fancy Shawl dancing. Then they walked all around. They saw the beautiful art and jewelry. They stopped at Aunt Numa's stand to get fry bread with beans and cheese. "Are you up for a big night of dancing and singing?" she asked. ●

"Yes!" was their answer.

It was dark when the family left. Tomorrow Mike would have his drum lesson. His sister had a soccer game. His mother and father would go to work. But today, at the powwow, they had fun being together.

Strategy Does this remind you of anything you are familiar with? Use what you know to help you understand this family.

Skill This is a good spot to ask yourself: Who are the characters in the story? Where does the story take place?

Unit 6 Jingle Dancer   Skill Transparency 30

▲ Skill Transparency 30

Access Content

Beginning/Intermediate For a Picture It! Lesson on character, setting, and plot, see the ELL Teaching Guide, pp. 204–205.

Advanced Before children read *Jingle Dancer*, make sure they know the meanings of *glimpse*, *pale*, and *case*.

Character, Setting, Plot
Prior Knowledge

TEACH/MODEL

INTRODUCE Recall *A Birthday Basket for Tía*. Remind children that this story told about a girl named Cecilia as she prepared for her aunt's birthday.

- What character traits describe Cecilia?

Read p. 408 with children. Explain the following:

- Good readers can identify the characters in a story. They also know where and when the story takes place. Good readers can place events of a story in order from beginning to end.
- We can use prior knowledge to help us understand what we read. We can make connections from our lives to the story.

Use Skill Transparency 30 to teach character, setting, and plot and prior knowledge.

SKILL Use paragraphs 1–3 to model character, setting, and plot.

MODEL First, I'll identify the characters in this story—Mike and his family members—and describe them. Next, I'll find where this story takes place—at a powwow. Then I'll notice the events and put them in order.

STRATEGY Continue to the end of the story to model using prior knowledge.

MODEL I will decide if I know any characters like those in the story. I'll think about the setting and decide if I have ever been to a place like a powwow. Have I ever had an experience like the one in the story? What did I do? How did I react? Did I behave like the characters in the story?

Jingle Dancer

Comprehension

Skill
Character,
Setting, Plot

Strategy
Prior Knowledge

 # Character, Setting, Plot

A story has characters, a plot, and a setting.

- Characters can be animals or people. An author tells about the characters.
- The setting tells where and when a story takes place.
- The plot is what happens throughout the story.

Story Title		
Characters	**Setting**	**Plot**
		beginning:
		middle:
		end:

Strategy: Prior Knowledge

Good readers use what they already know to help them understand what they read. As you read, use what you know to help you understand the characters and the plot.

Write to Read

1. Read "Powwow!" Make a chart like the one above to describe each part of the story.

2. Choose one thing about "Powwow!" that reminds you of something or someone you know. Write about it.

408

POWWOW!

Mike's family could not often spend much time together. Mike had drum lessons. His sister played soccer. His mother and father had jobs. They were all very busy.

"Come on," his father called one day. "We are all going to the powwow." Once a year, Mike's family and other Native Americans came together for this big fair.

At the powwow they watched the Fancy Shawl dancing. Then they walked all around. They saw the beautiful art and jewelry. They stopped at Aunt Numa's stand to get fry bread with beans and cheese. "Are you up for a big night of dancing and singing?" she asked.

"Yes!" was their answer.

It was dark when the family left. Tomorrow Mike would have his drum lesson. His sister had a soccer game. His mother and father would go to work. But today, at the powwow, they had fun being together.

Strategy Does this remind you of anything you are familiar with? Use what you know to help you understand this family.

Skill This is a good spot to ask yourself: Who are the characters in the story? Where does the story take place?

409

PRACTICE

WRITE Work with children to complete the steps in the Write activity. Have children describe the characters in "Powwow."

Monitor Progress	**Character, Setting, and Plot**
If... children are unable to complete **Write** on p. 408,	**then...** use Practice Book 2.2, p. 144, for additional practice.

CONNECT TO READING Encourage children to ask themselves these questions when they read.

- Who are the characters in the story? What are they like?
- Do I remember the order in which things happened?
- Does this story relate to anything that has happened in my life?

Read the story. Follow the directions.

Anna was excited to be visiting the small village where her grandparents lived. It was Saturday night and the villagers were having a dance. Anna's grandmother had showed her the steps. As the band began to play, Anna hummed. Then her grandfather took her hand, and they began to spin!

1. **Underline** the part of the story that tells where the story takes place.

2. **Circle** the words that tell when the story takes place.

3. **Underline** the word that tells how Anna feels.

4. **Write** a sentence to tell what Anna does when she hears the music.

She hummed.

5. **Draw** a picture of what happens at the end of the story.

Children's artwork should show a girl dancing with her grandfather.

Home Activity Your child read a story and answered questions about its characters, setting, and plot. Work with your child to write a story about a celebration or holiday. Before you begin, talk about who will be in the story, where and when it will take place, and what will happen.

▲ **Practice Book 2.2** p. 144, Character, Setting, Plot

DAILY FIX-IT

1. May i borrow your bell.

   May I borrow your bell?

2. It is february," Matt said.

   "It is February," Matt said.

This week's practice sentences appear on Daily Fix-It Transparency 30.

Strategic Intervention

Children who are not able to write independently may create an illustrated storyboard and orally share their story with a friend.

Advanced

Have children write a description of their Thanksgiving tradition in an unusual setting—for example, space, underwater, or in a hot-air balloon.

E L L

Support Writing Let Beginning English speakers dictate words, phrases, or sentences about their Thanksgiving tradition to a teacher or a more proficient English speaker.

▲ **The Grammar and Writing Book**
For more instruction and practice, use pp. 224–229.

Shared Writing

WRITE Story

GENERATE IDEAS Ask children to tell about things that they usually do at Thanksgiving, both at school and at home. Prompt them by reading aloud the words in the box. Write children's ideas on the board.

WRITE A STORY Explain that the class will write a story about the Thanksgiving traditions they observe at school and at home. When they are finished, ask them who the characters are and what the setting is in their story.

 COMPREHENSION SKILL Have children think of the setting of their Thanksgiving tradition.

- Display Writing Transparency 30 and read the title.

- Read the words in the box as children follow along.

- Discuss who should be in their story, where the story takes place, and what happens in their story.

- As children tell the story of this Thanksgiving tradition, write the story in logical sequence.

HANDWRITING While writing, model the letter forms as shown on pp. TR14–17.

READ THE STORY Have children read the completed story aloud as you track the print.

A Story

Thanksgiving Traditions

holiday	relatives	dinner	school
parade	home	turkey	watch
friends	football	eat	pumpkin pie

Possible answer:
At school we learn about the first Thanksgiving.

Thanksgiving is always a holiday from school.

We eat turkey, sweet potatoes, cranberry sauce,

green beans, and pumpkin pie. Many relatives

and friends come to our home. Sometimes we watch football games on television.

Unit 6 Jingle Dancer   Writing Model **30**

▲ **Writing Transparency 30**

INDEPENDENT WRITING

WRITE A STORY Have children write their own story of a Thanksgiving tradition. Encourage them to use words from the Word Wall and the Amazing Words board. Remind children to develop a beginning, middle, and end as they compose their first drafts. Let children illustrate their writing. You may gather children's work into a class traditions book for self-selected reading.

Grammar

TEACH/MODEL Indent Paragraphs

PARAGRAPHS Display Grammar Transparency 30. Read the definition aloud.

- Sentences within a paragraph are all about the same idea. Find the sentence that does not belong with the other four sentences.
- Number the sentences in an order that makes sense.
- Write these sentences in paragraph form. Be sure to indent the first sentence.

PRACTICE

IDENTIFY NEW PARAGRAPHS Give children a newspaper and a highlighter. Ask children to find an article. Encourage children to highlight the indented area of every paragraph within the article.

ADDITIONAL PRACTICE For additional practice, use pp. 224–229 in the Grammar and Writing Book.

Wrap Up Your Day!

✓ **PREFIXES *mis-* AND *mid-*** Write *mishap* and ask children to decode the word. Have children name other words that begin with *mis-*. Write *midwinter* and have children decode the word. Have children name other words that begin with *mid-*.

✓ **SPELLING WORDS WITH PREFIXES *mis-* AND *mid-*** Have children add the prefix *mis-* to base words *fortune* and *judge*. Have children add the prefix *mid-* to base words *summer* and *point*.

✓ **CHARACTER, SETTING, PLOT** To help children recognize the importance of story elements, ask: What are the characters like in "Powwow"? Have children retell the events of "Powwow" in order.

LET'S TALK ABOUT IT Recall how different people celebrate. What were some of the things Mike's family did at the Powwow? (walked around, ate, danced, sang, looked at art and jewelry)

HOMEWORK Send home this week's Family Times newsletter.

PREVIEW Day 2

Tell children that tomorrow the class will read about traditions of Native American dancers.

Day 2
AT A GLANCE

Share Literature
Magda's Tortillas

Phonics and Spelling
 Prefixes *mis-* and *mid-*
Spelling: Words with Prefixes *mis-* and *mid-*

Build Background
Powwows

Lesson Vocabulary
clattering   jingles   drum
voice   borrow   silver
More Words to Know
moccasins   shuffled   regalia

Vocabulary
Skill Unfamiliar Words
Strategy Context Clues

Read

Group Time < Differentiated Instruction

Jingle Dancer

Interactive Writing
Essay

Grammar
Paragraph

Materials

- *Sing with Me Big Book*
- Big Book *Magda's Tortillas*
- Phonics Songs and Rhymes Chart 30
- Background Building Audio
- Graphic Organizers 5, 8
- Tested Word Cards
- Student Edition 410–425

Morning Warm~Up!

Today we will read about a girl who wants to dance at a powwow. She is grateful that people give her jingles. The jingles make a lovely sound. What sounds make you happy?

QUESTION OF THE DAY Encourage children to sing "Festival Time" from the *Sing with Me Big Book* as you gather. Write and read the message and discuss the question.

REVIEW SUFFIXES *-ful* AND *-ly*

- Read the second and third sentences of the message.
- Have children raise their hands when they hear a word with the suffixes *-ly* or *-ful*. (*grateful, lovely*)

ELL

Build Background Use the Day 2 instruction on ELL Poster 30 to preview lesson vocabulary words.

ELL Poster 30

Share Literature

BUILD CONCEPTS

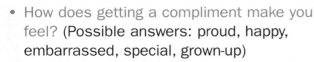

REALISTIC FICTION Have children read the title. Identify the author. Review that books about people doing things that could really happen are realistic fiction.

BUILD ORAL VOCABULARY Ask children to recall when someone told them they did a great job at something. When someone pays you a **compliment,** they are saying nice things. Magda's *abuela* says something nice to Magda about her tortilla making. Suggest that as you read, children listen to find out the compliment Abuela gives Magda.

Big Book

- How does getting a compliment make you feel? (Possible answers: proud, happy, embarrassed, special, grown-up)

MONITOR LISTENING COMPREHENSION

- What is the compliment Magda hears from her abuela? (Magda is an artist.)

- How does Magda feel when she hears this compliment? (Magda feels very special and very grown-up.)

- How will Magda remember this day and her special tortillas now that they have been eaten? (She can look at the photo of the tortillas that Tío Manuel took for the family photo album.)

- Why do you think Magda hugs her abuela after she compliments Magda's tortilla making? (Possible responses: Magda is grateful. She loves her abuela. She is happy about the time they spent together.)

Amazing Words to build oral vocabulary

	MONITOR PROGRESS
ceremony culture festival **compliment** fidget evergreen multicolored sash	**If...** children lack oral vocabulary experiences about the concept Traditions, **then...** use the Oral Vocabulary Routine. See p. DI·7 to teach *compliment.*

Build Concepts Write these compliments on individual index cards. *That is a beautiful sweater! You are very creative! You have neat handwriting! You are so athletic—I wish I could run that fast!* Have children demonstrate giving and receiving these compliments.

2

⊚ Prefixes *mis-, mid-*

TEACH/MODEL

Fluent Word Reading

ROUTINE

1 **Connect** Write *midday.* You can read this word because you know how to read words with prefixes. What prefix and base word form *midday? (mid-* and *day)* Do the same with *mismatch.*

2 **Model** When you come to a word with a prefix, figure out the base word. Then read the prefix and base word and blend the two word parts together to read it. Model reading *misapply, misdirect, midship, midtown, mislabel, midweek.* When you come to a new word with a prefix, what are you going to do?

3 **Group Practice** Write *midafternoon, misinform, midstream, mistrust.* Read these words. Look at the word, say the word to yourself, and then read the word aloud. Allow 2–3 seconds previewing time.

WORD READING

PHONICS SONGS AND RHYMES CHART 30 Frame each of the following words on Phonics Songs and Rhymes Chart 30. Call on individuals to read them. Guide children in previewing.

midnight   midday   misbehave

Sing "Powwow" to the tune of "On Top of Old Smokey," or play the CD. Have children follow along on the chart as they sing. Then have individuals take turns pointing to and reading words with prefixes on the chart.

 **Phonics Songs and Rhymes Audio**

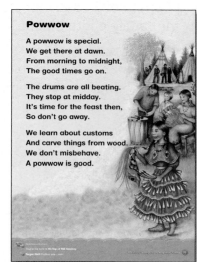

Powwow

A powwow is special.
We get there at dawn.
From morning to midnight,
The good times go on.

The drums are all beating.
They stop at midday.
It's time for the feast then,
So don't go away.

We learn about customs
And carve things from wood.
We don't misbehave.
A powwow is good.

Phonics Songs and Rhymes Chart 30

BUILD WORDS

INDIVIDUALS BUILD WORDS WITH PREFIXES Write prefixes *mid-* and *mis-* as headings for a two-column chart. Write the base word in each column. Have children add the prefix to each base word, read the new word, and supply its meaning. Have completed lists reread.

mid-	*mis-*
way	match
sentence	label
week	compute
	report

Spelling

PRACTICE Prefixes

WRITE DICTATION SENTENCES Have children write these sentences. Repeat words slowly, allowing children to hear each sound. Children may use the Word Wall to help with spelling high-frequency words. **Word Wall**

He kicked the football in midair at the midweek game.
The mistake in the newspaper was just a misprint.
A misdeed can be the result of misbehavior.
If you misplace a sock you might get a mismatch!

HOMEWORK Spelling Practice Book, p. 118

Spelling Words

Prefixes

1. midair
2. misplace
3. mislead
4. midway*
5. misprint
6. midday*
7. midweek*
8. misbehave
9. midyear
10. mismatch
11. misdeed
12. mistake

Challenge Words

13. midstream
14. midnight
15. misbehavior

* Words from the Selection

Prefixes *mis-* and *mid-*

Spelling Words

| midair | misplace | mislead | midway | misprint | midday |
| midweek | misbehave | midyear | mismatch | misdeed | mistake |

Write a list word by adding mid- or mis to each base word.

match
1. mismatch

print
2. misprint

week
3. midweek

air
4. midair

behave
5. misbehave

deed
6. misdeed

year
7. midyear

way
8. midway

Write the missing list word to complete each phrase.

9. misplace your keys
10. make a mistake
11. mislead people
12. midday nap

Home Activity Your child wrote spelling words in sentences. Take turns with your child using the words in new sentences.

▲ **Spelling Practice Book** p. 118

Read the story. **Answer** the questions.

Ved peeked into the living room. It was filled with friends and family. Everyone had come for the feast. Ved felt left out. No one even knew he was there. Then his mother called to him. Ved flew into her arms. A smile filled his face.

1. Where did the story take place?

__in Ved's living room__

2. At first, how did Ved feel about the party?

__He felt left out.__

3. Underline the sentence that tells what Ved's mother did.
4. Circle the sentence that tells what Ved did then.
5. Draw a picture that shows how Ved felt at the end of the story.

Children's artwork should show that Ved is very happy.

Home Activity Your child read a story and answered questions about its characters, setting, and plot. Read a favorite story with your child. Ask your child to tell where and when it takes place. Then discuss how the characters affect what happens in the story.

▲ **Practice Book 2.2** p. 145, Character, Setting, Plot

Build Background Draw simple pictures of a drum and feet on the board. Ask children to name these objects in their home language and say the words in English.

Build Background

DISCUSS POWWOWS Display a picture of someone dancing at a powwow. Initiate a discussion by asking children what they know about Native American powwows.

● Have you ever gone to a powwow?
● What do people do at a powwow ceremony?
● What do people wear at a powwow?

BACKGROUND BUILDING AUDIO Have children listen to the CD and share the new information they learned about the sights, sounds, and smells of a powwow ceremony.

 **Background Building Audio**

COMPLETE A VOCABULARY FRAME Draw a vocabulary frame or display Graphic Organizer 5. Write *powwow* in the Word box. Ask children to suggest possible definitions of *powwow*. Have them use *powwow* in a sentence. After children verify the definition with a dictionary, they can use *powwow* in another sentence.

> (powwow)   ( )
> Word   Symbol
>
> Predicted definition: A powwow is a Native American celebration.
> One good sentence: I am going to a powwow.
> Verified definition: a North American Indian ceremony that includes dancing and eating
> Another good sentence: The costumes I saw at the powwow were beautiful.

▲ **Graphic Organizer 5**

CONNECT TO SELECTION Connect background information to *Jingle Dancer*.

When people go to powwows they often dance. Jenna is a character in the story we are about to read. She wants to dance at a powwow. We'll find out whether or not Jenna gets to dance during the ceremony.

Vocabulary

LESSON VOCABULARY

VOCABULARY FRAME Display Graphic Organizer 5 or create vocabulary frame pages with two boxes at the top. One box is for the vocabulary word and the other is to draw a picture. Children predict the definition of the word and write a sentence using it. Then children verify the definition and write another good sentence.

WORDS TO KNOW

T drum A *drum* is a musical instrument that makes a sound when it is beaten. A *drum* is hollow with a cover stretched tight over either or both ends.

T clattering making a noise like plates or silverware striking together

T voice Your *voice* is the sound you make with your mouth. You use your *voice* when you speak, sing, or shout.

T jingles to make or cause to make sounds like bells

T silver *Silver* is a shiny white metal. *Silver* is used to make coins, jewelry, and other things.

T borrow If you *borrow* something, you get it from a person just for a while.

MORE WORDS TO KNOW

moccasins a soft leather shoe without an attached heel
regalia fine clothes
shuffled dragged your feet while walking

T = Tested Word

- Children should break *clattering, silver, jingles,* and *borrow* into syllables.
- Invite children to identify words that represent sounds.
- Have children share where they may have seen or heard some of these words.

---

ck a word from the box to match each clue.
ite the word on the line.

| borrow | clattering | drum |
| jingles | silver | voice |

1. drum

2. silver

3. opposite of lend — borrow

4. rattling noise — clattering

5. musical sounds like little bells — jingles

6. what you hear when someone talks — voice

Home Activity Your child used clues to identify lesson vocabulary words. Ask your child to read the list of words. Work with your child to write sentences to describe the sounds he or she might hear at a celebration or party. Try to use as many vocabulary words as possible.

▲ **Practice Book 2.2** p. 146, Lesson Vocabulary

| drum | |
| Word | Symbol |

Predicted definition:
    A drum is something you hit.

One good sentence: I like to play the drum.

Verified definition:
    A drum is a musical instrument
    that makes a sound when it is hit.

Another good sentence:
    I hear the drum when the band marches.

▲ **Graphic Organizer 5**

Monitor Progress — Check Lesson Vocabulary

Write these words and have individuals read them.

| clattering | jingles | drum | voice | borrow | silver |
| enough | animals | aunt | above | family | |

If… children cannot read these words,

then… have them practice in pairs with word cards before reading the selection. Monitor their fluency with these words during reading, and provide additional practice opportunities before the Day 5 Assessment.

SUCCESS PREDICTOR

Day 1 Check Word Reading

▶ Day 2 Check Lesson Vocabulary/High-Frequency Words

Day 3 Check Retelling

Day 4 Check Fluency

Day 5 Assess Progress

Spiral REVIEW

- Reviews previously taught high-frequency and lesson vocabulary words.

Word Reading

SUCCESS PREDICTOR

drum

clattering

voice

jingles

silver

borrow

Remember

Try the strategy. Then, if you need more help, use your glossary or a dictionary.

Vocabulary Strategy
for Unfamiliar Words

Context Clues When you come to a word you don't know during reading, what can you do? You can look for clues in the words and sentences around the word. This strategy can help you figure out the meaning of the word.

1. Read the words and sentences around the word you don't know. Sometimes the author gives you an explanation.

2. If not, predict a meaning for the word.

3. Try that meaning in the sentence. Does it make sense?

Read "Fiona's Feet." Look for clues in nearby words and sentences to help you understand the meanings of the vocabulary words.

410

Fiona's Feet

Fiona loves to dance. As soon as she hears the sounds of the fiddle, the pipes, and the drum, her feet start to move. When Fiona wears her hard shoes, her feet make a clattering noise. Tap, tap, tappity, tappity, tap. It is as though her feet are talking in a loud, happy voice. But when Fiona wears her soft shoes, her feet make no noise at all. That is the way it is supposed to be. But Fiona wishes her feet had a voice then too.

One morning as Fiona was eating her porridge, her sister walked into the kitchen. Fiona heard a faint sound, like the jingles of a bell. The sound made her think of snowflakes.

"Moira," asked Fiona, "what is making that sound?"

Moira showed Fiona her earrings. They were tiny silver bells that jingled when Moira walked. Fiona had an idea.

"May I borrow the bells?" she asked.

That night when Fiona danced in her soft shoes, her feet made a tinkling sound. Jingle, jingle, jingle, jingle. It was as though her feet were talking in a small, sweet voice.

Words to Write

Describe something else that jingles. Use words from the Words to Know list.

411

OBJECTIVE

Use context clues to determine the meaning of unfamiliar words.

ELL

Access Content Use ELL Poster 30 to preteach the lesson vocabulary. Reinforce the words with the vocabulary activities and word cards in the ELL Teaching Guide, pp. 206–207. Choose from the following to meet children's language proficiency levels.

Beginning If children are unfamiliar with the word *clattering*, point out the clues in the first paragraph on p. 411 that describe a *clattering* noise.

Intermediate Have children create a list of noises. Begin the list with *clattering* and *jingles*. Encourage children to name other words that describe noises.

Advanced Teach the lesson on pp. 410–411. Have children add information they learned about the vocabulary words to the Powwow web.

Vocabulary Strategy

TEACH/MODEL Context Clues

CONNECT Remind children of strategies to use when they come across words they don't understand.

• We can look in a dictionary or glossary.

• Sometimes we can get the meaning from word parts. We may understand the base word and prefix (*replay,* play again) or the two smaller words in a compound word (*lunchbox,* a box for lunch).

• We can look for context clues in the words and sentences around the unknown word. Today we will learn more about using context clues.

INTRODUCE THE STRATEGY

- Read and discuss the steps for using context clues on p. 410.

- Have children read "Fiona's Feet," paying attention to context clues to determine the meaning of highlighted words.

- Model using context clues to determine the meaning of *clattering*.

MODEL The word *clattering* describes a noise. The next sentence shows that it's a tap, tap, tappity sound. It goes on to say that the noise is loud and happy. *Clattering* must mean "making a loud tapping."

PRACTICE

- Have children determine the meanings of highlighted words in "Fiona's Feet" and explain the context clues they used.

- Point out that using context clues doesn't work with every word, and they may still have to use the glossary or a dictionary to find the meaning of some words.

WRITE Children's writing should include lesson vocabulary in a description of something that jingles, such as bells, wind chimes, keys, or coins.

CONNECT TO READING Encourage children to use these strategies to determine the meaning of an unknown word.

- Look for context clues in nearby words or sentences.

- Use word parts.

- Use the glossary or a dictionary.

Group Time

DAY 2

On-Level	Strategic Intervention	Advanced
Read *Jingle Dancer.*	**Read** SI Decodable Reader 30.	**Read** *Jingle Dancer.*
• Use pp. 412–427.	• Read or listen to *Jingle Dancer.*	• Use the **Routine** on p. DI•57.
	• Use the **Routine** on p. DI•56.	

ELL Place English language learners in the groups that correspond to their reading abilities in English.

(i) Independent Activities

Independent Reading See p. 408j for Reading/Library activities and suggestions.

Journal Writing Write about the best compliment you ever received. How did it make you feel? Share your writing.

Literacy Centers To provide experiences with *Jingle Dancer,* you may use the Writing Center on p. 408k.

Practice Book 2.2 Character, Setting, Plot, p. 145; Lesson Vocabulary, p. 146; Cause and Effect, p. 147

Break into small groups after Vocabulary and before Writing.

Jingle Dancer

by Cynthia Leitich Smith
illustrated by Cornelius Van Wright and Ying-Hwa Hu

Genre

Realistic fiction is a story that could really happen. Look for things that happen to Jenna.

412

Will Jenna get enough jingles for her outfit?

413

 **AudioText**

Read
Prereading Strategies

PREVIEW AND PREDICT Have children read the selection title and the names of the author and illustrators. Call attention to the illustration and ask who children think jingle dancers are and what they do. Have children point to the parts of the dancer's costume that jingle. Then invite them to take a picture walk through the book and make predictions about what will happen in the story.

DISCUSS REALISTIC FICTION Read the definition of realistic fiction on p. 412 of the Student Edition. Have children review the illustrations and tell what makes the story seem realistic.

SET PURPOSE Call on volunteers to tell what they know about Native American dances. Then read the question on p. 413. Ask what children would like to learn about jingle dancers.

ELL

Access Content Before reading, review the story summary in English and/or the home language. See the ELL Teaching Guide, pp. 208–210.

____ Prefixes *mis-, mid-*   lesson/tested vocabulary

Tink, tink, tink, tink, sang cone-shaped jingles sewn to Grandma Wolfe's dress. Every Grandma bounce-step brought clattering *tinks* as light blurred silver against jingles of tin.

414

Jenna daydreamed at the kitchen table, tasting honey on fry bread, her heart beating to the *brum, brum, brum, brum* of the powwow drum.

As Moon kissed Sun good night, Jenna shifted her head on Grandma Wolfe's shoulder. "I want to jingle dance, too."

"Next powwow, you could dance Girls," Grandma Wolfe answered. "But we don't have enough time to mail-order tins for rolling jingles."

Again and again, Jenna watched a videotape of Grandma Wolfe jingle dancing. When Grandma bounce-stepped on TV, Jenna bounce-stepped on family room carpet.

But Jenna's dress would not be able to sing. It needed four rows of jingles.

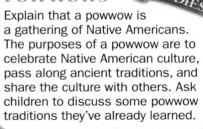

415

Strategies in Context

🎯 PRIOR KNOWLEDGE

- **What does the picture on p. 414 make you think of? Why?**
  Children may say it reminds them of Native Americans because sometimes Native Americans wear feathers and colorful clothes when they dance.

Monitor Progress	🎯 **Prior Knowledge**
If… children have difficulty connecting ideas from the story to things they know,	**then…** model making connections to prior knowledge.

 Think Aloud **MODEL** The dancer makes me think of cultural celebrations in which people do traditional dances. I think this dancer must be a Native American because I know Native Americans use feathers in their costumes for special ceremonies.

ASSESS Have children start and maintain a class K-W-L Chart.

▲ **Pages 414–415**
Have children read to find out what the woman in the illustration is doing.

Powwows
Explain that a powwow is a gathering of Native Americans. The purposes of a powwow are to celebrate Native American culture, pass along ancient traditions, and share the culture with others. Ask children to discuss some powwow traditions they've already learned.

Time for **SOCIAL STUDIES**

Jingle Dancer **414–415**

As Sun fetched morning, Jenna danced east to Great-aunt Sis's porch. Jenna's bounce-steps crunched autumn leaves, but her steps didn't jingle.

Once again, Great-aunt Sis told Jenna a Muscogee Creek story about Bat. Although other animals had said he was too small to make a difference, Bat won a ball game by flying high and catching a ball in his teeth.

Rising sunlight reached through a windowpane and flashed against . . . what was it, hanging in Aunt Sis's bedroom?

Jingles on a dress too long quiet.

"May I borrow enough jingles to make a row?" Jenna asked, not wanting to take so many that Aunt Sis's dress would lose its voice.

"You may," Aunt Sis answered, rubbing her calves. "My legs don't work so good anymore. Will you dance for me?"

"I will," said Jenna with a kiss on Aunt Sis's cheek.

Now Jenna's dress needed three more rows.

416

417

▲ **Pages 416–417**
Have children read to find out what happens when Jenna goes to visit Great-aunt Sis.

Read each sentence.
Answer the questions.

1. Kiko planned a party because she wanted to do something with friends on New Year's Day. **Why** did Kiko plan a party?

She wanted to do something
with friends on New Year's Day.

2. Kiko called her friends so they would know what time to come to the party. **Why** did Kiko call her friends?

She called so they would know
what time to come to the party.

3. Because Kiko wanted the party to be fun, she got some games to play. **Why** did Kiko get games for the party?

She wanted the party to be fun.

 Home Activity Your child read sentences about things that happened and wrote about why those things happened (cause and effect). Work with your child to write sentences about what people do to prepare for celebrations and why they do those things. Ask your child to illustrate the writing.

Practice Book Unit 6   **Comprehension** Cause and Effect Review   **147**

▲ **Practice Book 2.2** p. 147,
Cause and Effect

Skills in Context

REVIEW CAUSE AND EFFECT

- **Why does Great-aunt Sis give Jenna some of her jingles?**
  Great-aunt Sis is older. She does not dance much anymore because she has problems with her legs. If Jenna is wearing jingles Aunt Sis once used, Aunt Sis will feel a little like she is dancing herself.

Monitor Progress	Cause and Effect
If... children have difficulty answering the question,	**then...** model how to identify a cause and effect.

 Think Aloud

MODEL To find the reason, or cause, I ask, "Why did it happen?" I can figure that out from what Aunt Sis says. She says her legs "don't work so good." Then she asks Jenna to dance for her.

ASSESS Ask children why Jenna took only one row of Aunt Sis's jingles. (Possible response: She didn't want Aunt Sis's dress to lose all its jingles.)

_____ Prefixes *mis-*, *mid-*   ☐ lesson/tested vocabulary

As Sun arrived at <u>midcircle</u>, Jenna skipped south to Mrs. Scott's brand-new duplex. At Jenna's side, jingles clinked.

Mrs. Scott led Jenna into the kitchen. Once again, Jenna rolled dough, and Mrs. Scott fried it.

"May I borrow enough jingles to make a row?" Jenna asked, not wanting to take so many that Mrs. Scott's dress would lose its voice.

"You may," Mrs. Scott answered, tossing flour with her apron. "At powwow, I'll be busy selling fry bread and Indian tacos. Will you dance for me?"

"I will," said Jenna with a high five.

Now Jenna's dress needed two more rows.

418

419

Guiding Comprehension

Summarize • Inferential

- **How does Jenna get her second row of jingles?**
  Jenna visits her neighbor, Mrs. Scott. While she helps Mrs. Scott cook, she asks to borrow a row of jingles. Mrs. Scott lends Jenna a row of jingles and asks Jenna to dance for her.

Cause and Effect • Inferential

- **Why won't Mrs. Scott be dancing at the powwow?**
  Since she will be selling traditional food at the powwow, she will not have time for dancing.

Details and Facts • Inferential

- **How many rows does Jenna have now? How many more rows does she need?**
  Jenna has two rows of jingles, and she needs two more rows.

▲ **Pages 418–419**
Have children read to find out how Jenna gets her second set of jingles.

EXTEND SKILLS

Imagery

For instruction in imagery, discuss the following;

- Imagery is a word picture.
- Authors often use imagery to present an idea or a fact in a more interesting way.
- Jenna visited Mrs. Scott "as Sun arrived at midcircle." Describe the image the words make you see. What time was it?

Assess Have children find another example of imagery in the selection so far, describe the image, and tell what it means.

As Sun caught a glimpse of Moon, Jenna strolled west to Cousin Elizabeth's apartment. At Jenna's side, jingles clanked.

Elizabeth had arrived home late from the law firm. Once again, Jenna helped Elizabeth carry in her files.

"May I borrow enough jingles to make a row?" Jenna asked, not wanting to take so many that Elizabeth's dress would lose its voice.

"You may," Elizabeth answered, burrowing through her messy closet for her jingle dress. "This weekend, I'm working on a big case and can't go to powwow. Will you dance for me?"

"I will," said Jenna, clasping her cousin's hands.

Now Jenna's dress needed one more row of jingles, but she didn't know which way to turn.

As Moon glowed pale, Jenna shuffled north to Grandma Wolfe's. At Jenna's side, jingles sat silent. High above, clouds wavered like worried ghosts.

When Jenna tugged open the door, jingles sang, *tink, tink, tink, tink.* Grandma Wolfe was jingle dancing on TV. Jenna breathed in every *hey-ah-ho-o* of a powwow song. Her heart beat *brum, brum, brum, brum* to the pounding of the drum.

420

421

▲ **Pages 420–421**
Have children read to find out how Jenna gets her third row of jingles.

Strategy Self-Check

Have children ask themselves these questions to check their reading.

Vocabulary Strategy
• Do I look for context clues?
• Do I use word parts?
• Do I use the glossary or a dictionary?

Prior Knowledge
• Do I know who the characters are and what they are like?
• Do I remember the order in which things happened?
• Do I think about how this story relates to things that have happened in my life?

Guiding Comprehension

Draw Conclusions • Critical
• **About what time is it now? How do you know?**
It is early evening. Both the Sun and Moon are in the sky, and Elizabeth has just come home from work.

Sequence • Literal
• **What does Jenna do before asking Elizabeth for some jingles?**
Jenna helps Elizabeth carry the files she has brought home from work.

Summarize • Inferential
• **What has happened in the story so far?**
Grandma said Jenna may dance at the powwow, but there is no time to buy the four rows of jingles Jenna needs to complete her costume. Jenna really wants to wear jingles so she borrows jingles from Great-aunt Sis, her neighbor Mrs. Scott, and her cousin Elizabeth. So far she has three of the four rows she needs.

_____ Prefixes *mis-, mid-*   ☐ lesson/tested vocabulary

On family room carpet, beaded moccasins waited for Jenna's feet. She shucked off a sneaker and slipped on a moccasin that long before had danced with Grandma Wolfe.

Jenna knew where to find her fourth row.

"May I borrow enough jingles to make a row?" Jenna asked, not wanting to take so many that Grandma Wolfe's dress would lose its voice.

"You may," Grandma said with a hug.

Now Jenna's dress could sing.

Every night that week, Jenna helped Grandma Wolfe sew on jingles and bring together the dance regalia.

Every night, Jenna practiced her bounce-steps.

422

423

Skills in Context

🎯 CHARACTER, SETTING, AND PLOT

- **Who are the characters in this story? Where are they? What does the main character do?**

The characters are Jenna, Grandma Wolfe, Aunt Sis, Mrs. Scott, and Cousin Elizabeth. They all live in different homes in the same community. The main character, Jenna, asks each of the other characters to lend her some jingles.

Monitor Progress	Character, Setting, and Plot
If... children have difficulty identifying the character, setting, and plot,	**then...** model how to answer the question.

 Think Aloud

MODEL I flip through the story to find the names of the different characters. I see that Jenna visits each of the other characters in her home. They must all live in different homes in the same community. I see that Jenna asks each of them the same question to see if she can borrow their jingles.

ASSESS Have children use Graphic Organizer 8 to record characters, setting, and plot.

▲ **Pages 422–423**
Have children read to find out more about Jenna's dance costume.

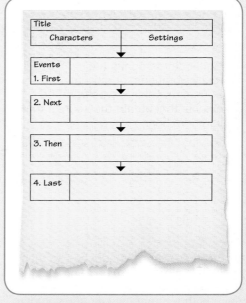

▲ **Graphic Organizer 8**

Jingle Dancer 422–423

Brum, brum, brum, brum, sounded the drum at the powwow the next weekend. As light blurred silver, Jenna jingle danced

. . . for Great-aunt Sis, whose legs ached,

. . . for Mrs. Scott, who sold fry bread,

. . . for Elizabeth, who worked on her big case,

. . . and for Grandma Wolfe, who warmed like Sun.
Tink, tink, tink, tink.

424

425

▲ **Pages 424–425**
Have children read to decide what makes Jenna's costume special.

Sounds TIME FOR **Science**

Explain that sounds are really vibrations, or movements. Sounds travel in waves from the objects that create the sounds that listeners hear.

Access Content Model how to read the sound words *brum* and *tink* with expression, so the words reflect the sounds they stand for. List and compare other sound words in English and in children's first languages.

_____ Prefixes *mis-, mid-*   lesson/tested vocabulary

Guiding Comprehension

Draw Conclusions • Critical

- **What makes Jenna's costume really special?**
People Jenna cares about have given her the jingles for her costume. The borrowed jingles are symbols that connect Jenna to the special people she will be dancing for.

Compare and Contrast • Inferential

- *Text to Text* **How are Jenna in *Jingle Dancer* and Cecilia in *A Birthday Basket for Tía* alike?**
Children may say that both girls learn about family customs and traditions from older female relatives. Jenna learns about bounce-dancing by watching Grandma Wolfe, and Grandma Wolfe gives her moccasins and helps her sew jingles on her dress. Cecilia learns to make sugar cookies called *bizcoches*, grow flowers, and enjoy reading from Tía.

Fluency

REREAD FOR FLUENCY

Paired Reading

ROUTINE

1 **Reader 1 Begins** Children read the entire book, switching readers at the end of each page.

2 **Reader 2 Begins** Have partners reread; now the other partner begins.

3 **Reread** For optimal fluency, children should reread three or four times.

4 **Provide Feedback** Listen to children read and provide corrective feedback regarding their oral reading and their use of the blending strategy.

Interactive Writing

WRITE Essay

BRAINSTORM Use *Jingle Dancer* to encourage a discussion about festivals. Picture walk through the book and ask children to identify the things people are doing to prepare for the powwow.

SHARE THE PEN Have children participate in writing an essay about a festival. To begin, have a child name a festival or ceremony. Have the class repeat it. Invite individuals to write familiar letter-sounds, word parts, and high-frequency words. Ask questions such as:

- What is the first sound you hear in the word *festival*? (/f/)
- What letter stands for that sound? *(f)* Have a volunteer write *f*.
- What is the second sound you hear in the word *festival*? (/e/)
- What letter stands for that sound? *(e)* Have a volunteer write *e*.

Continue to have individuals make contributions. Frequently reread what has been written while tracking the print.

READ THE ESSAY Read the completed essay aloud, having children echo you.

The Town Festival

There are many kinds of food to eat at the town festival. The music makes everyone happy, and many people dance. Everyone has fun.

INDEPENDENT WRITING

WRITE AN ESSAY Have children write their own essay about a festival they have attended, heard about, or read about. Let children illustrate their writing.

Strategic Intervention

Have children copy the essay and illustrate their writing.

Advanced

Have children who are able to write complete sentences independently write their own essay about a festival. Children may also design a poster for the festival, inviting other people to attend.

Writing Support Before writing, children might share ideas in their home languages.

Beginning Have children draw a picture of a festival. Have children label the picture or dictate a sentence that accompanies the picture.

Intermediate Help children create a word list to use when writing their essay.

Advanced Have children work in small groups to discuss what they will write as one group member takes notes. Children can refer to these notes when they write.

Support Grammar The writing systems of children's home languages may have different conventions for indicating paragraphs. Have children practice finding paragraph indents in classroom texts. See the Grammar Transition lessons in the ELL and Transition Handbook.

Grammar

DEVELOP THE CONCEPT The Paragraph

IDENTIFY PARAGRAPHS Write this short paragraph on the board, being sure to indent the first sentence. *The band at the festival is great! The music has a great sound. People are singing and dancing.* Point to each word as you read it. Ask children to identify the beginning of the paragraph.

A paragraph is a group of sentences about the same idea. The beginning of every paragraph should be indented. What should you do at the beginning of every paragraph? (indent)

PRACTICE

IDENTIFY PARAGRAPHS Have children look at a newspaper. Tell children they are going to identify the beginning of paragraphs.

Think Aloud

MODEL This is a newspaper article. I can find the beginning of each paragraph because it is indented. I look for the indented part and know that this is where a new paragraph, and a new idea, starts.

Have children use a highlighter and locate the indented places within a newspaper article. Invite children to count the number of paragraphs in the article.

The Paragraph

A **paragraph** is a group of sentences about the same idea. The sentences are in an order that makes sense. One sentence gives the main idea. The other sentences give details about the main idea. The first sentence of a paragraph is indented.

Every August my relatives get together for a picnic. My aunts, uncles, and cousins come. Grandma and Grandpa come. People come from far and near. We meet at a big park.

Cross out the sentence that does not tell about the same idea. **Write** the other sentences in the correct order to make a paragraph. **Indent** the first sentence.

1. First we all open our picnic baskets.
2. Then children play, and grown-ups talk.
3. I don't like grapes.
4. Soon we must leave.
5. Next we eat chicken and fruit.

First we all open our picnic baskets.

Next we eat chicken and fruit. Then children

play, and grown-ups talk. Soon we must leave.

Home Activity Your child learned about the paragraph. As you look through a book together, ask your child to point out paragraphs. Have your child explain how he or she knew they were paragraphs.

▲ **Grammar and Writing Practice Book** p. 117

Wrap Up Your Day!

 LESSON VOCABULARY Write the following question on the board. *A voice yelled downstairs, "May I borrow your silver bracelet?"* Ask children to read the question and identify the lesson vocabulary words *voice*, *borrow*, and *silver*.

 PRIOR KNOWLEDGE Why did Jenna have to borrow jingles? (It was too late to order them.) Have children tell about a time when a relative or neighbor helped them do something.

LET'S TALK ABOUT IT Recall *Jingle Dancer*. Ask: How did Jenna celebrate at the powwow? (She jingle danced.) Encourage children to tell about a time when they celebrated something.

PREVIEW Day 3

Tell children that tomorrow they will hear more about Magda.

Day 3

AT A GLANCE

Share Literature
Magda's Tortillas

Phonics and Spelling
REVIEW Suffixes *-ness*, *-less*

Spelling: Words with Prefixes *mis-* and *mid-*

Vocabulary
Skill Homonyms

Fluency
Read with Appropriate Phrasing

Writing Trait
Organization/Paragraphs

Grammar
Paragraph

Materials

- *Sing with Me Big Book*
- Big Book *Magda's Tortillas*
- Graphic Organizer 25
- Student Edition 426–427

Morning Warm~Up!

Today we will read *Magda's Tortillas* again. Magda tried to imitate her abuela.

She pinned her hair in a bun like her abuela.

She flapped her apron and tried to tie it without looking.

Is there someone special that you imitate?

QUESTION OF THE DAY Encourage children to sing "Festival Time" from the *Sing with Me Big Book* as you gather. Write and read the message and discuss the question.

REVIEW ENDINGS

- Point to the word *tried* in the message. Ask children to identify the base word and the ending of this word.

- Review the ending *-ed*. Have children locate and identify other words in the morning message that have this ending. *(pinned, flapped, tried)*

Build Background Use the Day 3 instruction on ELL Poster 30 to support children's use of English to communicate about lesson concepts.

ELL Poster 30

Share Literature

LISTEN AND RESPOND

BUILD ORAL VOCABULARY Review that yesterday the class listened to find out the compliment Abuela gave Magda. Tell children that sometimes people are uncomfortable when people compliment them. They may get embarrassed and **fidget.** When someone fidgets, they appear nervous and restless. Magda does not fidget when her abuela compliments her—she is proud. Magda fidgets early in the day. Ask that children listen today to find out when and why Magda fidgets.

Big Book

MONITOR LISTENING COMPREHENSION

- Why is Magda fidgeting at the beginning of this story? (She is so excited—it is her birthday, and she is having her first tortilla-making lesson.)

- What are the Spanish words for a *little heart*? *(un corazoncito)*

- Who tells Magda she made a hexagon? How does he know that? (her older brother Eduardo; he knows everything about geometry)

- Why does Magda hide behind Abuela when the tortillas are served? Why does she peek out from behind Abuela? (Magda is afraid everyone will laugh at her tortillas. She hears everyone screaming, and she wants to see what the fuss is about.)

Amazing Words
to build oral vocabulary

	MONITOR PROGRESS
ceremony culture festival compliment **fidget** evergreen multicolored sash	**If...** children lack oral vocabulary experiences about the concept Traditions, **then...** use the Oral Vocabulary Routine. See p. DI·7 to teach *fidget*.

E L L

Listen and Respond Help children describe and demonstrate the action conveyed by the word *fidgeted* in *Magda's Tortillas.*

OBJECTIVES

- Review suffixes *-less* and *-ness*.
- Blend, read, and sort *-less, -ness* words.
- Recognize lesson vocabulary.
- Spell words with prefixes *mis-, mid-*.

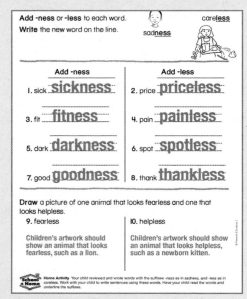

▲ **Practice Book 2.2** p. 148, Suffixes *-less, -ness*

Review Phonics

REVIEW SUFFIXES *-less, -ness*

READ WORDS WITH SUFFIXES Write *helpless* and *happiness.* Look at these words. You can read these words because you know how to read words with suffixes. You can cover the suffix, read the base word, and then blend the base word and the suffix to read the whole word. What are the words? *(helpless, happiness)* Remind children of the meaning of each suffix and have them provide meanings for *joyless, sleepless, shyness,* and *illness.*

- *-less*   without
- *-ness*   the state of being _____

BUILD WORDS Write the suffixes *-less* and *-ness* as headings for a two-column chart or use Graphic Organizer 25. Write several base words in each column. Have children add the suffix to each base word, read the new word, and supply its meaning.

-less	*-ness*
thankless	kindness
useless	goodness
fearless	awareness
careless	darkness
thoughtless	fitness

Lesson Vocabulary

PRACTICE

ANSWER QUESTIONS Write on the board questions that use each of the lesson vocabulary words. Have children read the questions and answer them in groups.

- What kinds of things can make *clattering* noises?
- What are some things that a *drum* can be used for?
- What do different kinds of *voices* sound like?
- Do you let people *borrow* your things? Why or why not?
- What are some *silver* things you've seen?
- When do you like to hear something that *jingles?*

Spelling

PRACTICE Prefixes *mis-, mid-*

GIVE CLUES Have children practice by writing the spelling words that

- mean something has been done wrong *(mismatch, misbehave, mislead, misprint, misplace, misbehavior, misdeed, mistake).*
- mean "middle" *(midyear, midday, midweek, midnight, midair, midstream, midway).*

HOMEWORK Spelling Practice Book, p. 119

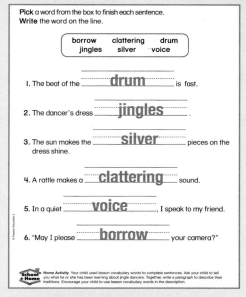

▲ **Practice Book 2.2** p. 149, Lesson Vocabulary

Spelling Words

Prefixes *mid-, mis-*

1.	**midair**	7.	**midweek***
2.	**misplace**	8.	**misbehave**
3.	**mislead**	9.	**midyear**
4.	**midway***	10.	**mismatch**
5.	**misprint**	11.	**misdeed**
6.	**midday***	12.	**mistake**

Challenge Words

13. **midstream**
14. **midnight**
15. **misbehavior**

* Words from the Selection

Prefixes *mis-* and *mid-*
Read the notice. **Circle** three spelling mistakes and a word with a capitalization error. **Write** the words correctly.

Notice: There was a *misprint* in last week's newsletter. The class book fair will **not** be *misweek.* It will be after school on *friday.* We are sorry about the mistake. We didn't mean to mislead you. We hope *evry* student can come!

Spelling Words

midair	misplace
mislead	midway
misprint	midday
midweek	misbehave
midyear	mismatch
misdeed	mistake

1. misprint   2. midweek
3. every   4. Friday

Frequently Misspelled Words

every
whole
could

Circle the word that is spelled correctly. **Write** the word.

5. (midway)   middway   5. midway
6. misbehav   (misbehave)   6. misbehave
7. (mislead)   misleed   7. mislead
8. (misplace)   misplase   8. misplace

Home Activity Your child identified misspelled words with *mis-* and *mid-.* Pronounce a list word. Have your child spell the base word and the prefix separately.

▲ **Spelling Practice Book** p. 119

Jingle Dancer   **426d**

Strategic Intervention

Have children illustrate the two meanings of *fair.* Then help them write a caption using the word *fair* for each picture.

Advanced

Have children use a dictionary to list other meanings of *bank,* such as "a place to store money" and "the ground next to a river."

Extend Language Help children practice telling which meaning of *duck* makes sense in each sentence by paying attention to the words around it.

Vocabulary

HOMONYMS

DISCUSS HOMONYMS Explain that some words have more than one meaning. Write the following sentence pair and discuss the two meanings of *calves*— "baby cows" and "the lower back part of the leg." Then have children think of their own sentences, using each meaning.

The barn is full of calves.

My calves ache from running the race.

EXPAND LESSON VOCABULARY Discuss with children the two meanings of each word listed below. Give an example of each meaning. Have partners write sentences, using each meaning of each word. Invite volunteers to share their sentences.

fair   bank   duck

Group Time

On-Level	Strategic Intervention	Advanced
Read *Jingle Dancer.*	**Read** or listen to *Jingle Dancer.*	**Read** Self-Selected Reading.
• Use pp. 412–427.	• Use the **Routine** on p. DI·58.	• Use the **Routine** on p. DI·59.

DAY 3

ELL Place English language learners in the groups that correspond to their reading abilities in English.

ⓘ Independent Activities

Independent Reading See p. 408j for Reading/Library activities and suggestions.

Journal Writing Write about a time when you borrowed something. Share your writing.

Literacy Centers To provide experiences with *Jingle Dancer,* you may use the Writing Center on p. 408k.

Practice Book 2.2 Suffixes -*ness,* -*less,* p. 148; Lesson Vocabulary, p. 149

Break into small groups after Vocabulary and before Writing.

Fluency

READ WITH APPROPRIATE PHRASING

MODEL READING WITH APPROPRIATE PHRASING Use *Jingle Dancer.*

- Point to the italicized words in the first sentence on p. 414. These italicized words represent a sound. I'll read these words together. The words in the rest of the sentence can be grouped together too.

- Ask children to follow along as you read the rest of the page with appropriate phrasing.

- Have children read the page after you. Encourage them to read groups of words and use appropriate phrasing. Continue in the same way with p. 415.

REREAD FOR FLUENCY

Choral Reading

ROUTINE

1 **Select a Passage** For *Jingle Dancer,* use pp. 416–419.

2 **Divide into Groups** Assign each group a part to read. For this story, alternate paragraphs. The first group reads the first paragraph. The second group reads the next paragraph and so on.

3 **Model** Have children track the print as you read.

4 **Read Together** Have children read along with you.

5 **Independent Readings** Have the groups read aloud without you. Monitor progress and provide feedback. For optimal fluency, children should reread three to four times.

Monitor Progress	Fluency
If... children have difficulty reading with appropriate phrasing,	**then...** prompt: • Are there commas to tell me that a group of words belongs together? • Are there groups of words that should be read together? • Try to read groups of words, not word-by-word.
If... the class cannot read fluently without you,	**then...** continue to have them read along with you.

OBJECTIVE

- Read aloud fluently with appropriate phrasing.

Options for Oral Reading

Use *Jingle Dancer* or one of the following Leveled Readers.

On-Level

A Special Friend

Strategic Intervention

At the Powwow

Advanced

Winter Holidays

Fluency Model the reading of phrases in the story, such as "bounce-stepped" and "jingle dance" so that beginning English language learners can practice reading with appropriate phrasing.

Reader Response

TALK ABOUT IT Model a response. This is the first time Jenna gets to dance at the powwow. I imagine I would hear the sounds of drums and the jingles. I would see people dressed in colorful clothes with feathers and beads. I would see Jenna's friends and relatives at the powwow.

1. **RETELL** Have children use the retelling strip in the Student Edition to retell the selection.

Retelling Plan

☑ Week 1 assess Strategic Intervention students.

☑ Week 2 assess Advanced students.

☑ Week 3 assess Strategic Intervention students.

☑ Week 4 assess On-Level students.

☑ **This week assess any students you have not yet checked during this unit.**

Look Back and Write Point out information from the text that answers the question. Then have children write a response to the question. For test practice, assign a 10–15 minute time limit. For assessment, see the Scoring Rubric at the bottom of this page.

Monitor Progress | **Check Retelling** Rubric 4 3 2 1

Have children retell *Jingle Dancer.*

If... children have difficulty retelling the story,

then... use the Retelling Cards and the Scoring Rubric for Retelling on pp. 426–427 to help them move toward fluent retelling.

 SUCCESS PREDICTOR

Day 1 Check Word Reading | Day 2 Check Lesson Vocabulary/High-Frequency Words | ▶ **Day 3 Check Retelling** | Day 4 Check Fluency | Day 5 Assess Progress

---

2. **CHARACTER, PLOT, SETTING** Model a response. Jenna is a Native American girl who lives in a community with other Native Americans. She needs jingles for her dress so she can dance at the powwow. She borrows jingles from other people who won't be able to dance.

3. **PRIOR KNOWLEDGE** Model a response. I knew that they held powwows together. That helped me understand why dancing at the powwow was important to Jenna.

LOOK BACK AND WRITE Read the writing prompt on p. 426 and model your thinking. I'll look back through the story. I'll look for reasons why Jenna didn't get all four rows of jingles from one person. Then I'll write my response. Have children write their responses.

Assessment Let beginning English language learners listen to other retellings before attempting their own. For more ideas on assessing comprehension, see the ELL and Transition Handbook.

Scoring Rubric | **Look Back and Write**

Top-Score Response A top-score response will use details from the selection to tell why Jenna did not get all four rows of jingles from one person's dress.

Example of a Top-Score Response Jenna didn't get all four rows of jingles from one person's dress because she did not want the other dresses to lose their voice, their sound, or their jingle. If she borrowed only one row of jingles from each person, there would still be plenty of jingles left on each dress to make noise.

For additional rubrics, see p. WA10.

Reader Response

Open for Discussion Why is the powwow so important to Jenna? Describe the sights and sounds you would experience if you accompanied Jenna.

1. Use the pictures below to retell Jenna's story.
Retell

2. Who is Jenna, where is she, and what problem does she have? How did she solve her problem?
Character/Plot/Setting

3. What did you already know about Native Americans that helped you understand the story?
Prior Knowledge

 Look Back and Write Why didn't Jenna get all four rows of jingles from one person's dress? Look back at the story. Use details from the story in your answer.

Meet the Author and the Illustrators

Cynthia Leitich Smith
Cornelius Van Wright and **Ying-Hwa Hu**

Read more books by Cynthia Leitich Smith or illustrated by Mr. Van Wright and Ms. Hu.

Indian Shoes

Cynthia Leitich Smith is a member of the Creek Nation, just like Jenna in *Jingle Dancer*. "*Jingle Dancer* was one of my first stories for young readers. I had gone to law school. But at my first job, I found myself scribbling stories during my lunch hour. My real dream was to become a fiction writer. So I did."

Cornelius Van Wright and **Ying-Hwa Hu** are a husband-and-wife artist team. Mr. Van Wright says about children's art, "There are so many different kinds of kids—all kinds of shapes and sizes. What beauty! What freedom!"

Mei-Mei Loves the Morning

Retelling Strip

426

427

Scoring Rubric | Narrative Retelling

Rubric 4 3 2 1	4	3	2	1
Connections	Makes connections and generalizes beyond the text	Makes connections to other events, stories, or experiences	Makes a limited connection to another event, story, or experience	Makes no connection to another event, story, or experience
Author's Purpose	Elaborates on author's purpose	Tells author's purpose with some clarity	Makes some connection to author's purpose	Makes no connection to author's purpose
Characters	Describes the main character(s) and any character development	Identifies the main character(s) and gives some information about them	Inaccurately identifies some characters or gives little information about them	Inaccurately identifies the characters or gives no information about them
Setting	Describes the time and location	Identifies the time and location	Omits details of time or location	Is unable to identify time or location
Plot	Describes the events in sequence, using rich detail	Tells the plot with some errors in sequence that do not affect meaning	Tells parts of plot with gaps that affect meaning	Retelling has no sense of story

Use the Retelling Chart on p. TR20 to record retelling.

Selection Test To assess with *Jingle Dancer,* use Selection Tests, pp. 117–120.

Fresh Reads for Differentiated Test Practice For weekly leveled practice, use pp. 175–180.

Retelling

SUCCESS PREDICTOR

DAILY FIX-IT

5. The drumms were clatterin.
   The dru<u>m</u>s were clatterin<u>g</u>.

6. are the jingle bells sliver?
   <u>A</u>re the jingle bells si<u>l</u>ver?

Connect to Unit Writing

Writing Trait

Have children use strategies for developing **organization/paragraphs** when they write a research report in the Unit Writing Workshop, pp. WA2–WA9.

ELL

Organization/Paragraphs Make sure English learners can decode words in the prompt. Work with children to complete a cloze sentence that addresses the prompt and could be used to launch a piece of writing (e.g., *The minute I was in front of the audience, I _____.*).

Writing Trait of the Week

INTRODUCE Organization/Paragraphs

TALK ABOUT ORGANIZATION/PARAGRAPHS Explain to children that a good writer tells what happens in the right order. This organization holds writing together. A good beginning sentence helps organize a paragraph. A good ending tells what happens last or sums up the paragraph. Ask children to think about how the author describes the events in *Jingle Dancer*. Then model your thinking.

 MODEL In Jingle Dancer, Jenna goes through several steps to get jingles for her dress. The story ends as Jenna dances for the women who gave her jingles. Write the following and read it aloud:

> **Jenna's dress needed four rows of jingles. She got a row from Aunt Sis. Then she got her second row from Mrs. Scott. Elizabeth gave Jenna the third row. Grandma Wolfe gave Jenna the last row of jingles.**

Read the following sentences and work with children to identify which sentence would be the best conclusion to the paragraph above. After discussion, write the first sentence on the board to conclude the paragraph.

Now Jenna's dress could sing. (This is the best conclusion.)

Grandma was a good dancer.

Elizabeth couldn't go to Powwow.

STRATEGY FOR DEVELOPING ORGANIZATION/PARAGRAPHS Ask children to complete the concluding sentence for the paragraph below.

> **Jenna collected jingles from four women—Aunt Sis, Mrs. Scott, Elizabeth, and Grandma Wolfe. Each woman asked Jenna to jingle dance for her. That weekend Jenna_____ .** (Possible response: *That weekend Jenna went to the powwow and danced for all four women.*)

PRACTICE

APPLY THE STRATEGY Ask children to write a paragraph about a time they performed for an audience. Remind them that their concluding sentence should describe the last event or sum up the experience.

Grammar

OBJECTIVE

- Use paragraphs in writing.

APPLY TO WRITING The Paragraph

IMPROVE WRITING WITH PARAGRAPHS Have children recall that a paragraph is a group of sentences about the same idea. One sentence sometimes tells the main idea and the other sentences are in an order that makes sense. Remind children that the first sentence of a paragraph is indented, or moved in a little.

Write the following sentences on the board. Have children number the sentences in an order that makes sense. Encourage children to copy the sentences in that order to write a paragraph. Remind them to indent the first sentence.

Have you tried the baklava?

The crust is flaky.

The food at this festival is delicious.

It is right out of the oven and still warm.

PRACTICE

WRITE A PARAGRAPH Brainstorm several ideas for a paragraph. Invite children to write a three- or four-sentence paragraph about a topic of their choice. Remind children to indent the first sentence of their paragraph.

The Paragraph

Write 1, 2, or 3 after each sentence to show the correct order.

1. Last we eat tasty treats. — 3

2. Our family has birthday celebrations. — 1

3. We shout, "¡Feliz cumpleaños!" — 2

Write a paragraph. **Tell** about something special you do with your family, friends, or neighbors. Indent the first sentence.
Possible answer:
We have a big block party in our neighborhood. Everyone brings food. There is music and dancing. We all have fun.

Home Activity Your child learned how to use the paragraph in writing. Have your child read the paragraph he or she wrote on this page. Then ask your child to point to the place where the paragraph is indented.

▲ **Grammar and Writing Practice Book** p. 118

Wrap Up Your Day!

 CHARACTER, SETTING, PLOT Have children recall the main characters in *Magda's Tortillas* and tell where this story takes place. (Magda, Magda's abuela; in Abuela's kitchen)

 READ WITH APPROPRIATE PHRASING Remind children that good readers group words as they read. They don't read word-by-word.

LET'S TALK ABOUT IT Display the Birthday T-Chart from Day 1. Where would Magda and her birthday celebration fit on this chart? Is her celebration more like Birthday Child A or Birthday Child B? Why?

PREVIEW Day 4

Tell children that tomorrow they will read a story about a Native American festival.

Share Literature

"Bringing the Light"

Phonics and Spelling

Prefixes *mis-, mid-*

Spelling: Words with Prefixes *mis-, mid-*

Read

 **Group Time** < Differentiated Instruction

"Celebrating the Buffalo Days"

Fluency

Read with Appropriate Phrasing

Writing Across the Curriculum

Map

Grammar

Paragraphs

Speaking and Listening

Listen for Speaker's Purpose

Materials

- *Sing with Me Big Book*
- *Read Aloud Anthology*
- Student Edition 428–431

Morning Warm-Up!

Today we will read about another Native American celebration. Family celebrations are a joyful time and bring us happiness. Do you invite family and friends to your home for celebrations?

QUESTION OF THE DAY Encourage children to sing "Festival Time" from the *Sing with Me Big Book* as you gather. Write and read the message and discuss the question.

REVIEW SUFFIXES

- Ask children to identify words with suffixes *-ful* and *-ness* in the morning message.

- Have children name the word and suffix. (joy-ful, happy-ness) Note the spelling change in *happiness*.

Extend Language Use the Day 4 instruction on ELL Poster 30 to extend and enrich language.

ELL Poster 30

Share Literature

CONNECT CONCEPTS

ACTIVATE PRIOR KNOWLEDGE Recall Jenna and how she gathered enough jingles to make her own jingle dance dress. Explain that you will read another story about someone who needs to put together a costume to carry on a family tradition—"Bringing the Light" by Elizabeth Gawlick.

Read Aloud Anthology
Bringing the Light

BUILD ORAL VOCABULARY Read the second paragraph. Explain that Karin needs to put together a special outfit. She needs a **sash.** A *sash* is a broad band of cloth, a large fabric belt that is usually worn around the waist. Karin is looking for a red sash. **Multicolored** means "many-colored." Karin also needs **evergreen** branches. Evergreen branches are from trees that stay green year round—often pine or spruce. Ask children to listen to find out if Karin finds evergreen branches for her costume.

REVIEW ORAL VOCABULARY After reading, review all the Amazing Words for the week. Have children take turns using them in sentences that tell about the concept for the week. Then talk about Amazing Words they learned in other weeks and connect them to the concept, as well. For example, ask:

- Does your family have any **unusual,** or out of the ordinary, **traditions**? Explain.

- What sorts of **customs** and **symbols** do people use at family **celebrations**?

- Have you ever been to a **foreign** place during a holiday? How did you **celebrate**?

MONITOR LISTENING COMPREHENSION

- Does Karin find evergreen branches to use for her costume? Explain. (**Karin** finds some scraggly-looking plants with strange branches and thick green leaves. They aren't at all like evergreens, but they are the best she can find.)

- What is multicolored in this story? (a boy's poncho)

- Karin's family moves to a tiny village in the mountains of Peru in South America. Where did they live before? (Sweden)

- Do you think Karin's parents are happy? Explain. (Possible response: Yes, because Karin carries on this family tradition even though they are far from home and living in another country.)

OBJECTIVES

- Set purpose for listening.
- Build oral vocabulary.

Amazing Words to build oral vocabulary

	MONITOR PROGRESS
ceremony culture festival compliment fidget **evergreen** **multicolored** **sash**	**If…** children lack oral vocabulary experiences about the concept Traditions, **then…** use the Oral Vocabulary Routine. See p. DI·7 to teach *evergreen, multicolored,* and *sash.*

ELL

Connect Concepts To show their understanding of *multicolored* and *sash,* children can create a multicolored sash. Give children several pieces of colored fabrics. Children can combine them to create a multicolored sash.

Spiral REVIEW

- Reviews syllables *-tion, -ture.*
- Reviews vowels *aw, au, augh, al.*
- Reviews high-frequency words *clothes, hours, money, neighbor, only, question, taught.*

Sentence Reading

REVIEW WORDS IN CONTEXT

READ DECODABLE AND HIGH-FREQUENCY WORDS IN CONTEXT Write these sentences. Call on individuals to read a sentence. Then randomly point to review words and have children read them. To help you monitor word reading, high-frequency words are underlined and decodable words are circled.

My neighbor and I had quite an adventure selling clothes at the midyear auction.

Mrs. Rauls taught us to draw with chalk.

I finally caught the baseball after hours of awkward mistakes.

We paid our money and saw an action picture.

The only thing Mom said was, "It's always naughty to misbehave."

I have a question about the culture show in August.

Monitor Progress	Word Reading
If... children are unable to read an underlined word,	**then...** read the word for them and spell it, having them echo you.
If... children are unable to read a circled word,	**then...** have them use the blending strategy they have learned for that word type.

Support Phonics For additional review, see the phonics activities in the ELL and Transition Handbook.

Spelling

PARTNER REVIEW Prefixes

READ AND WRITE Supply pairs of children with index cards on which the spelling words have been written. Have one child read a word while the other writes it. Then have children switch roles. Have them use the cards to check their spelling.

HOMEWORK Spelling Practice Book, p. 120

Group Time

On-Level	Strategic Intervention	Advanced
Read "Celebrating the Buffalo Days."	**Read** or listen to "Celebrating the Buffalo Days."	**Read** "Celebrating the Buffalo Days."
• Use pp. 428–431.	• Use the **Routine** on p. DI·60.	• Use the **Routine** on p. DI·61.

 Place English language learners in the groups that correspond to their reading abilities in English.

(i) Independent Activities

Fluency Reading Pair children to reread *Jingle Dancer.*

Journal Writing Describe a special ceremony. Share writing.

Spelling Partner Review

Independent Reading See p. 408j for Reading/Library activities and suggestions.

Literacy Centers To provide listening opportunities, you may use the Listening Center on p. 408j. To extend social studies concepts, you may use the Social Studies Center on p. 408k.

Break into small groups after Spelling and before Fluency.

OBJECTIVE

● Spell words with prefixes *mis-, mid-.*

Spelling Words

Prefixes

1. **midair**	7. **midweek**＊
2. **misplace**	8. **misbehave**
3. **mislead**	9. **midyear**
4. **midway**＊	10. **mismatch**
5. **misprint**	11. **misdeed**
6. **midday**＊	12. **mistake**

Challenge Words

13. **midstream**
14. **midnight**
15. **misbehavior**

＊ Words from the Selection

Prefixes *mis-* and *mid-*

Spelling Words					
midair	misplace	mislead	midway	misprint	midday
midweek	misbehave	midyear	mismatch	misdeed	mistake

Unscramble each word.

kimdeew	dealmis
1. midweek	2. mislead
habvesime	ramiid
3. misbehave	4. midair
eesiddm	stamike
5. misdeed	6. mistake

Write the list word.

7. This word rhymes with **trace**, but starts with **pl**. Add the prefix **mis-**.   7. misplace

8. This word rhymes with **clear**, but starts with **y**. Add the prefix **mid-**.   8. midyear

9. This word rhymes with **scratch**, but starts with **m**. Add the prefix **mis-**.   9. mismatch

10. This word rhymes with **stay**, but starts with **w**. Add the prefix **mid-**.   10. midway

Home Activity Your child is learning to spell words with mis- and mid-. Take turns with your child thinking of a base word and adding mis- or mid- to make a list word.

▲ **Spelling Practice Book** p. 120

Social Studies in Reading

Photo Essay

Genre
• A photo essay includes text and many photos on one topic.

Text Features
• In this selection, the photos show what happens during Buffalo Days.
• The captions tell about the photos.

Link to Social Studies
Use the library or the Internet to find out about other powwow activities. Organize a classroom powwow to talk about the rules and affairs of your classroom.

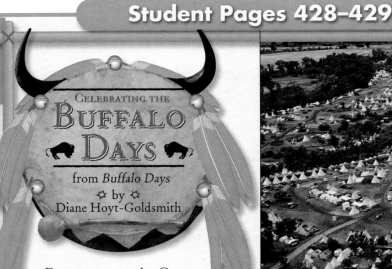

CELEBRATING THE
BUFFALO DAYS

from *Buffalo Days*
☆ by ☆
Diane Hoyt-Goldsmith

The Crow Fair and Rodeo is called the Tipi Capital of the World. People put up more than a thousand tipis on the fairgrounds.

Every summer the Crow nation holds a special gathering to celebrate the Buffalo Days. The Crow Fair and Rodeo is something that everyone looks forward to all year long. The fair began in 1904 as a way to encourage ranching and farming. Over the years, it has become a celebration of Native American traditions. People who come to the fair are able to experience a way of life that existed during the Buffalo Days.

During the third week in August, Crow people from all over the reservation gather to put up their tipis. They hold a powwow that lasts for many days, with dance contests, drumming, and giveaways. There are rodeo competitions and horse races every day. People from other tribes all over North America come to share in the fun.

 **Graphic Organizers** If it will help, make a graphic organizer.

428

429

Audio CD AudioText

Read
Social Studies in Reading

PREVIEW AND PREDICT Read the title and author's name. Have children preview the photo essay and name the objects in the photographs. (tipis, outfits) Then ask them to predict whether "Celebrating the Buffalo Days" tells a story or provides information. Have children read to learn how the Crow Nation celebrate Buffalo Days.

INFORMATIONAL TEXT Review that selections about real people doing real things are called *nonfiction.* Point out that the photographs in this article give information about real things and that the sentences under each photograph provide information about what is pictured.

VOCABULARY/HOMONYMS Review that some words are spelled the same and sound the same but have different meanings. Have children locate *fair* on p. 428. What does *fair* mean—"light color," "honest," or "a gathering"?

Kalsey BirdinGround wears a Jingle Dance dress. The jingles on her dress are made from the tops of tin cans that have been shaped into cones.

Marilyn Blacksmith wears an outfit for the Fancy Shawl Dance. There are mink tails braided into her hair, and she wears a white eagle feather.

Each day during the Crow Fair, hundreds of Native American dancers from all over the West compete in different categories. People of all ages come to perform and to watch. For everyone, it is a time to celebrate the best of their traditions and to keep those traditions alive.

Gary Plenty Buffalo wears a Grass Dance outfit. His headdress is made of porcupine hair and he wears eagle feathers.

Marcia Blacksmith wears a traditional Crow dress decorated with elk teeth. She holds a fan of hawk feathers and a handbag decorated with beadwork.

Reading Across Texts
Modern Native American powwows celebrate old traditions. What are some that you read about in *Jingle Dancer* and in this selection?

Writing Across Texts
Make a list of traditions celebrated at powwows. If you wish, draw pictures to illustrate your list.

 Graphic Organizers What can you add to your graphic organizer?

430

431

BUILD CONCEPTS

Draw Conclusions • Critical
- **Why do you think the Crow People want to keep traditions alive?**
They are proud of their traditions and the skills it takes to compete in them.

Personal Response • Critical
- **If you had a chance, in which event would you compete? Why?**
Answers will vary.

CONNECT TEXT TO TEXT

Ask which tradition is mentioned in both Jingle Dancer and "Celebrating the Buffalo Days." Then ask which other traditions are mentioned in "Celebrating the Buffalo Days."

Have children make a list of the traditions they just discussed. Suggest that they draw pictures to illustrate their lists or to choose one event to illustrate.

Sound
Sound is produced when materials vibrate. The type of sound produced depends on the materials through which the vibration occurs. Encourage children to create their own sounds by making a rubber band guitar, playing a ruler, and hitting bottles of water filled with varying amounts of water with a metal spoon.

ELL

Activate Prior Knowledge Ask: Have you ever attended a festival? Have children share their experience with words or by drawing pictures.

OBJECTIVE

- Read aloud fluently with appropriate phrasing.

Options for Oral Reading

Use *Jingle Dancer* or one of the following Leveled Readers.

On-Level

A Special Friend

Strategic Intervention

At the Powwow

Advanced

Winter Holidays

Assess Fluency Build children's fluency by encouraging them to repeatedly read aloud passages from familiar and favorite selections, including books that reflect their cultures.

Fluency

READ WITH APPROPRIATE PHRASING

MODEL READING WITH APPROPRIATE PHRASING Use *Jingle Dancer.*

- Direct children to the first sentence on p. 420. Review that good readers group words appropriately. When I read, I group words together. I do not read word-by-word. I read at a good pace and pause at the commas.
- Ask children to follow along as you read the paragraph.
- Have children read the paragraph after you. Encourage them to group words appropriately. Continue in the same way with the rest of p. 420.

REREAD FOR FLUENCY

Choral Reading

ROUTINE

1 **Select a Passage** For *Jingle Dancer,* use pp. 423–425.

2 **Divide into Groups** Assign each group a part to read. For this story, alternate paragraphs on the first page. The first group reads the first paragraph. The second group reads the next paragraph and so on. On pp. 424–425, alternate reading the parts under the pictures.

3 **Model** Have children track the print as you read.

4 **Read Together** Have children read along with you.

5 **Independent Readings** Have the groups read aloud without you. Monitor progress and provide feedback. For optimal fluency, children should reread three to four times.

Monitor Progress | Check Fluency WCPM

As children reread, monitor their progress toward their individual fluency goals. Current Goal: 90–100 words correct per minute. End-of-Year Goal: 90 words correct per minute.

If... children cannot read fluently at a rate of 90–100 words correct per minute,

then... make sure children practice with text at their independent level. Provide additional fluency practice, pairing nonfluent readers with fluent readers.

If... children already read at 90 words correct per minute,

then... they do not need to reread three to four times.

SUCCESS PREDICTOR

Day 1 Check Word Reading

Day 2 Check Lesson Vocabulary/High-Frequency Words

Day 3 Check Retelling

▶ **Day 4 Check Fluency**

Day 5 Assess Progress

Writing Across the Curriculum

WRITE Map

BRAINSTORM Have children look at pp. 428–431 and name the different areas they might find at a powwow. Encourage them to use lesson vocabulary, such as *festival* and *ceremony*.

SHARE THE PEN Have children participate in creating a map. To begin, draw an outline map of powwow grounds and explain that the class will work together to write labels for the map. Explain that a map is a way to show location and direction. Call on an individual to name an area of a powwow. Write the label, inviting individuals to help spell the word by writing familiar letter-sounds. Ask questions, such as the following:

- What is the first sound you hear in the word *booth*? (/b/)
- What letter stands for that sound? *(b)* Have a volunteer write *b.*
- What vowel sound do you hear in *booth*? (/ü/)
- What letters stand for that vowel sound? *(oo)* Have a volunteer write *oo.*

Continue having individuals contribute to labeling the map. Frequently reread the labels.

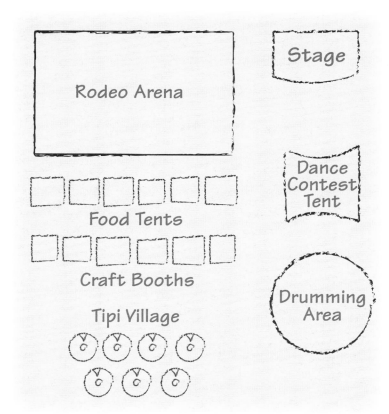

OBJECTIVE

● Identify a paragraph.

DAILY FIX-IT

7. My voise craked last night.
My voi_c_e crac_k_ed last night.

8. He playing the drom loudly.
He _played_ the dr_u_m loudly.

The Paragraph

Read the paragraph. **Mark** the letter of the sentence that answers the question.

Grandma is a terrific baker. She has won many prizes. At the fair last year, her cherry pie won first place. I like to make cakes. Grandma won the grand prize with her cookies. Once a food company had a contest.

1. What was done to the first sentence of the paragraph?
   ○ A It was kept long.
   ⊗ B It was indented.
   ○ C It had quotation marks added.

2. Which sentence gives the main idea of the paragraph?
   ⊗ A Grandma is a terrific baker.
   ○ B She has won many prizes.
   ○ C I like to make cakes.

3. What sentence does not belong?
   ○ A Grandma is a terrific baker.
   ⊗ B I like to make cakes.
   ○ C Once a food company had a contest.

4. Which sentence is out of order?
   ○ A She has won many prizes.
   ○ B At the fair last year, her cherry pie won first place.
   ⊗ C Once a food company had a contest.

5. What sentence would be a good way to end the paragraph?
   ○ A I wonder if Grandma will win again.
   ○ B Grandma is tired of baking pies.
   ⊗ C I'm lucky to have a grandma who bakes so well.

 Home Activity Your child prepared for taking tests on the paragraph. Ask your child to write a paragraph about something he or she does well. Have your child read the paragraph to you.

▲ **Grammar and Writing Practice Book** p. 119

Grammar

REVIEW Paragraph

DEFINE PARAGRAPH

- What is a group of sentences about the same idea called? (paragraph)
- How is the first sentence of a paragraph written? (indented)

PRACTICE

WRITE PARAGRAPH Copy the following sentences on the board. _Marc performed a dance on Saturday. The family had a great time at the Crow Fair and Rodeo. Marc's family arrived on Friday afternoon and set up their tipi. He wore a grass dance outfit and an eagle feather._ Have children organize and then write these sentences in paragraph form. Remind them to indent the first sentence. Share completed paragraphs.

> **Marc's family arrived on Friday afternoon and set up their tipi. Marc performed a dance on Saturday. He wore a grass dance outfit and an eagle feather. The family had a great time at the Crow Fair and Rodeo.**

Speaking and Listening

LISTEN FOR SPEAKER'S PURPOSE

DEMONSTRATE SPEAKING AND LISTENING Remind children of appropriate listening and speaking behaviors for a discussion. Then ask them to think about these behaviors as you discuss family pets.

Speakers	Listeners
• Stand up straight.	• Identify the speaker's purpose.
• Choose appropriate language.	• Interpret the speaker's purpose.
• Speak clearly.	• Evaluate the quality of a project or report.
• Focus on the listeners.	

ASK FOR A PET Invite children to role play a discussion with their families about getting a pet. Speakers should choose appropriate language, offer clear reasoning, and focus on the listeners. Listeners should listen to identify the speaker's purpose and to evaluate their performance.

Wrap Up Your Day!

✓ **MAKE CONNECTIONS: TEXT TO TEXT** Review "Celebrating the Buffalo Days" and *Jingle Dancer.* How are The Crow Fair and Rodeo in "Celebrating the Buffalo Days" and the powwow Jenna attended in *Jingle Dancer* the same? (both had dancing)

LET'S TALK ABOUT IT Discuss Buffalo Days and the Crow Nation celebration. Invite children to add information to the powwow web created earlier in the week.

PREVIEW Day 5

Remind children that today they read about the Crow Nation and how they celebrate Buffalo Days. Tell them that tomorrow they will hear about a little girl and a special celebration.

Day 5
AT A GLANCE

Share Literature
"Bringing the Light"

Phonics and Spelling
Review Prefixes *mis-*, *mid-*

Lesson Vocabulary
clattering   jingles   drum
voice   borrow   silver

Monitor Progress
Spelling Test: Words with Prefixes
   mis-, *mid-*

Group Time < Differentiated
           Assessment

Writing and Grammar
Trait: Organization/Paragraphs
Paragraphs

Research and Study Skills
Time Line

Materials

- *Sing with Me Big Book*
- *Read Aloud Anthology*
- Reproducible Pages TE 432f–432g
- Student Edition 432–433

Morning Warm-Up!

This week we read about festivals. We read about a ceremony called a powwow. We learned how the Crow Nation celebrates Buffalo Days. What are some different ways that people celebrate?

QUESTION OF THE DAY Encourage children to sing "Festival Time" from the *Sing with Me Big Book* as you gather. Write and read the message and discuss the question.

REVIEW ORAL VOCABULARY Have children identify words in the message that name

- what a powwow is
- a synonym for festival
- the Crow Nation festival
- the tribe that celebrates Buffalo Days

Assess Vocabulary Use the Day 5 instruction on ELL Poster 30 to monitor children's progress with oral vocabulary.

ELL Poster 30

Share Literature

LISTEN AND RESPOND

USE PRIOR KNOWLEDGE Review that yesterday the class listened to find out if Karin finds the materials she needs to put together her Lucia costume. Suggest that today the class listen for words from other languages.

MONITOR LISTENING COMPREHENSION

- What color is *blanco?* (white)

- Karin doesn't know many Spanish words. How does she find the market? (Possible response: When she tries to ask a boy where the market is, she doesn't understand his answer. She looks confused so the boy takes her there.)

Read Aloud Anthology
Bringing the Light

BUILD ORAL VOCABULARY

GENERATE DISCUSSION Recall how important it was for Karin to keep up the family tradition of "Bringing the Light." Although she had to use different materials in her new home, she was able to perform the ceremony. Invite children to discuss family traditions or ceremonies that are important to them. Have children use some of this week's Amazing Words as they talk about their own family traditions.

Monitor Progress | Check Oral Vocabulary

Remind children of the unit concept—Traditions. Ask them to tell you about the concept using some of this week's Amazing Words: *ceremony, culture, festival, compliment, fidget, evergreen, multicolored,* and *sash.*

If... children have difficulty using the Amazing Words,

then... ask more questions about the Read Aloud selection or the concept using the Amazing Words. Note which questions children can respond to. Reteach unknown words using the Oral Vocabulary routine on p. DI·1.

SUCCESS PREDICTOR

| Day 1 Check Word Reading | Day 2 Check Lesson Vocabulary/High-Frequency Words | Day 3 Check Retelling | Day 4 Check Fluency | ▶ Day 5 Check Oral Vocabulary Assess Progress |

OBJECTIVES

- Set purpose for listening.
- Build oral vocabulary.

Amazing Words to build oral vocabulary

ceremony	fidget
culture	evergreen
festival	multicolored
compliment	sash

ELL

Extend Language Ask children to name three to five words in their home language and then say what the words mean in English.

5

⟳ Prefixes mis-, mid-

REVIEW

IDENTIFY WORDS WITH PREFIXES Write these sentences. Have children read each one aloud. Call on individuals to name and underline the words with prefixes and identify the base word and prefix in each.

The <u>midyear</u> test was full of <u>mistakes</u> and <u>misprints</u>.

<u>Midwinter</u> afternoons can be as dark as <u>midnight</u>.

He said he <u>misunderstood</u> the rules about <u>misconduct</u> and <u>misbehavior</u>.

Did you <u>misplace</u> the toy boat we wanted to sail <u>midstream</u>?

Lesson Vocabulary

REVIEW

MEANING CLUES Read the following clues for children. Have children write a review word from p. 410 for each clue. Check by reading clues and answers together.

The opposite of *lend* is _____. (borrow)

These go together: gold and _____. (silver)

This is something you beat. (drum)

This is the sound a bell makes. (jingle)

You use your _____ to talk. (voice)

Another word for *banging* is _____. (clattering)

Access Content For additional practice with lesson vocabulary, use the vocabulary strategies and word cards in the ELL Teaching Guide, pp. 206–207.

SPELLING TEST Prefixes

DICTATION SENTENCES Use these sentences to assess this week's spelling words.

1. Our <u>midyear</u> break starts next week.
2. I hope I didn't <u>misplace</u> my homework.
3. The zip code on the letter had a <u>misprint</u>.
4. We are <u>midway</u> through the year.
5. We eat a <u>midday</u> snack in our class.
6. The striped shirt and checked pants are a <u>mismatch</u>.
7. A <u>misdeed</u> can happen when you don't think clearly.
8. Slow down so you don't make a <u>mistake</u>.
9. Today is our <u>midweek</u> quiz.
10. The kite flew in <u>midair</u> and then came back down again.
11. Read the problem carefully so it does not <u>mislead</u> you.
12. If you <u>misbehave</u>, then you cannot come over.

CHALLENGE WORDS

13. His toy boat floated <u>midstream</u>.
14. Dad's plane will land at <u>midnight</u>.
15. Mom said, "No <u>misbehavior</u> at the store!"

ASSESS

● Spell words with prefixes *mis-, mid-*.

Spelling Words

Prefixes mid-, mis-

1. **midair**	7. **midweek** *
2. **misplace**	8. **misbehave**
3. **mislead**	9. **midyear**
4. **midway** *	10. **mismatch**
5. **misprint**	11. **misdeed**
6. **midday** *	12. **mistake**

Challenge Words

13. **midstream**
14. **midnight**
15. **misbehavior**

* Words from the Selection

Group Time

On-Level	**Strategic Intervention**	**Advanced**
Read Set B Sentences and the Story for rechecking.	**Read** Set A Sentences and the Story for rechecking.	**Read** Set C Sentences and the Story for rechecking.
• Use pp. 432e–432g.	• Use pp. 432e–432g.	• Use pp. 432e–432g.
	• Use the **Routine** on p. DI·62.	• Use the **Routine** on p. DI·63.

ELL Place English language learners in the groups that correspond to their reading abilities in English.

DAY 5

(i) Independent Activities

Fluency Reading Children reread selections at their independent level.

Journal Writing Write about dancing. Share writing.

Independent Reading See p. 408j for Reading/Library activities and suggestions.

Literacy Centers You may use the Technology Center on p. 408k to support this week's concepts and reading.

Practice Book 2.2 Time Line, p. 150

Break into small groups after Spelling and before Grammar and Writing.

ASSESS

- Decode prefixes *mis-, mid-*.
- Read lesson vocabulary words.
- Read aloud with appropriate speed and accuracy.
- Recognize character, setting, and plot.
- Retell a story.

Differentiated Assessment

Fluency Assessment Plan

☑ Week 1 assess Advanced students.

☑ Week 2 assess Strategic Intervention students.

☑ Week 3 assess On-Level students.

☑ Week 4 assess Strategic Intervention students.

☑ **This week assess any students you have not yet checked during this unit.**

Set individual fluency goals for children to enable them to reach the end-of-year goal.

- Current Goal: 90–100 wcpm
- End-of-Year Goal: 90 wcpm
- **ELL** Measuring a child's oral reading speed—words per minute—provides a low-stress informal assessment of fluency. Such an assessment should not take the place of more formal measures of words correct per minute.

SENTENCE READING

ASSESS PREFIXES *mis-, mid-* AND LESSON VOCABULARY WORDS Use one of the reproducible lists on p. 432f to assess children's ability to read prefixes *mis-, mid-* and lesson vocabulary words. Call on individuals to read two sentences aloud. Have each child in the group read different sentences. Start over with sentence one if necessary.

RECORD SCORES Use the Sentence Reading Chart for this unit on p. 435k.

Monitor Progress	Prefixes *mis-, mid-*
If... children have trouble reading prefixes *mis-, mid-*,	**then...** use the Reteach Lessons on p. DI·68.
Lesson Vocabulary Words	
If... children cannot read a lesson vocabulary word,	**then...** mark the missed words on a lesson vocabulary word list and send the list home for additional word reading practice, or have the child practice with a fluent reader.

FLUENCY AND COMPREHENSION

ASSESS FLUENCY Take a one-minute sample of children's oral reading. See Monitoring Fluency, p. 435i. Have children read "The Spelling Bee," the on-level fluency passage on p. 432g.

RECORD SCORES Record the number of words read correctly in one minute on the child's Fluency Progress Chart.

ASSESS COMPREHENSION Have the child read to the end of the passage. (If the child had difficulty with the passage, you may read it aloud.) Ask about the characters, setting, and plot and have the child retell the passage. Use the Retelling Rubric on p. 426g to evaluate the child's retelling.

Monitor Progress	Fluency
If... a child does not achieve the fluency goal on the timed reading,	**then...** copy the passage and send it home with the child for additional fluency practice, or have the child practice with a fluent reader.
Character, Setting, Plot	
If... a child cannot recognize character, setting, and plot,	**then...** use the Reteach Lesson on p. DI·68.

READ THE SENTENCES

Set A

1. Do not misuse silver found in the Midwest.
2. At midpoint in the day, a voice misnamed her.
3. It was a mistake to borrow the midsize car.
4. The drum was mispriced at midweek.
5. I lost the mismatched jingle bells in midsummer.
6. She misspoke due to the midday clattering.

Set B

1. I misplaced my silver necklace in midwinter.
2. The midstate band misplaced their drums.
3. We heard her voice misspell the word during the midweek spelling bee.
4. Do not misbehave and jingle the bells at midnight.
5. I misfiled my Midwest map but will borrow one.
6. The clattering at midweek caused Sue to misdate the letter.

Set C

1. Bess miscounted her money and had to borrow some midway through her trip.
2. Deb misunderstood and took the jingle bells to midship.
3. The voice on the radio misled people in the Midwest.
4. There was a misprint about the price of the drum in the Mideast paper.
5. The clattering caused the police to misdirect traffic at midmorning.
6. It was a mistake to drop the silver ring in midair.

Monitor Progress Prefixes *mis-, mid-*
Lesson Vocabulary Words

SUCCESS
PREDICTOR

The Spelling Bee

Juan lived in a large Midwest city. It was	9
midsummer, and he noticed a sign in the library	18
about a spelling bee in one week. The prize was a	29
new bike. He copied the time and day on a piece	40
of paper. Juan was great at spelling. He hardly	49
ever misspelled a word.	53

Juan studied spelling words every day. One day	61
he stayed up until midnight. By midweek, he had	70
learned to spell many new words.	76

On the day of the spelling bee, he was ready by	87
midmorning. He went to the library, but only the	96
workers were there. He checked the sign. Oh, no!	105
He had misprinted the date. The spelling bee	113
wasn't until the next day.	118

Juan tried to look at the bright side. Because he	128
miswrote the day, he'd have one more day to	137
study. So he learned to spell more words and	146
that helped him win the spelling bee! Sometimes a	155
mistake can be a good thing, he thought.	163

See also Assessment Handbook, p. 365 • REPRODUCIBLE PAGE

Monitor Progress | Fluency Passage

SUCCESS PREDICTOR

Write Now
Writing and Grammar

Story

Prompt

Jingle Dancer tells the story of Jenna's search for jingles. Think about something else Jenna might want to find or do. Now write a story that tells what Jenna wants and how she gets it.

Writing Trait

Organize your story with a beginning, middle, and end.

Student Model

First sentence of paragraph is indented. →

Strong verbs clearly show story actions.

Story has beginning, middle, and end.

> Jenna wanted to sing in the choir, but first she had to try out. She asked Aunt Sis for help. Every day she practiced her song while Aunt Sis listened. At the tryout, Jenna pretended she was singing for Aunt Sis. The director smiled and welcomed Jenna to the choir.

432

Writer's Checklist

- **Focus** Is every sentence needed to tell the story?
- **Organization** Does the story have a beginning, middle, and end?
- **Support** Do details explain clearly what is happening?
- **Conventions** Are spelling, capitalization, and punctuation correct?

Grammar

The Paragraph

A **paragraph** is a group of sentences about the same idea. The sentences are in an order that makes sense. One sentence gives the main idea. The other sentences give details about the main idea. The first sentence of a paragraph is indented.

. . . .

Copy the story from page 432. Circle the sentence that gives the main idea. Underline the sentences that give details.

433

Writing and Grammar

LOOK AT THE PROMPT Read p. 432 aloud. Have children select and discuss key words or phrases in the prompt. (*something else Jenna might want to find or do, story, tells what Jenna wants and how she gets it*)

STRATEGIES TO DEVELOP ORGANIZATION/PARAGRAPHS Have children

- make a story map with boxes labeled *Beginning, Middle,* and *End* to help them organize their story details before they begin writing.

- write sentences using details from each box.

- exchange stories with a partner and read each other's story aloud to see if the organization makes sense.

  See Scoring Rubric on p. WA12. [Rubric 4 3 2 1]

HINTS FOR BETTER WRITING Read p. 433 aloud. Use the checklist to help children revise their stories. Discuss the grammar lesson. (Answers: Children should circle the first sentence in the paragraph and underline the second through fifth sentences.) Have children write correct paragraphs in their stories.

DAILY FIX-IT

9. I cant hear your voise.
   I can't hear your voice.

10. May i borro your silver ring?
    May I borrow your silver ring?

The Paragraph

Draw a line through the sentence that does not belong in each group.

1. I want to be a jingle dancer.
   ~~Jenna wants to be a ballet dancer.~~
   I will dance at the powwow.
   I will dance to the beat of the drums.

2. Grandma will help me make jingles.
   ~~Grandma will make a video.~~
   I need four rows of jingles.
   We will sew them on my dress.

Write the sentences in the correct order to make a paragraph. **Indent** the first sentence.

3. Soon I heard the drums beat.
4. Time for the powwow had come.
5. I jingle danced.

~~Time for the powwow had come. Soon I heard the drums beat. I jingle danced.~~

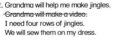 Home Activity Your child reviewed the paragraph. Read a story together. Have your child choose a paragraph and read the sentence that is the main idea.

▲ **Grammar and Writing Practice Book** p. 120

Mary made this time line about her life. **Use** the time line to answer the questions.

Start dance
lessons
Born   Ray is   Move   Move
              born   to Kansas   to Texas

1996 1997 1998 1999 2000   2002 2003 2004 2005   2006
                              2001

1. What are the first and last years marked on the time line?

1996   2006

2. When was Mary born? **1997**

3. When was Ray born? **1999**

4. What happened in 2006?

Mary moved to Texas.

5. How long did Mary live in Kansas? **five years**

▲ **Practice Book 2.2** p. 150,
Time Line

Access Content As you draw and label the time line, discuss each event using sequence words. For example: *First, Jenna daydreamed. Second, she borrowed jingles. Next, she...*

Research/Study Skills

TEACH/MODEL Time Line

MODEL USING A TIME LINE Draw and label a simple time line of the events in *Jingle Dancer.* Explain that a time line is a line divided into periods of time. It is labeled to show the order in which events happened. Time lines are read from left to right.

Model how to label a time line.

Think Aloud **MODEL** I'll make a time line to show the events in *Jingle Dancer.* I want to show only the important events in the story. In the beginning, Jenna daydreams about jingle dancing at the powwow. I'll write that as the first event on the time line on the far left side. Then, I'll write the other events of the story in order.

LABEL EVENTS Call on individuals to identify the people Jenna visited and the order they were visited. Add these events to the time line.

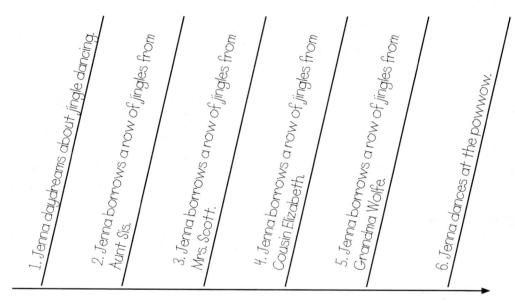

Time Line

PRACTICE

CREATE YOUR OWN TIME LINE Have partners work together to create a time line of a favorite book. Have children identify the beginning, middle, and ending of the story and label these events on a time line.

Wrap Up Your Week!

LET'S TALK ABOUT Traditions

QUESTION OF THE WEEK Recall this week's question.

• What are some different ways people celebrate?

Display the Birthday graphic organizer started on Day 1. Review how the two children celebrate their birthdays. Compare celebrations.

Name of child	Name of child
Chocolate cake with candles	Ice cream cake
Vanilla ice cream	Out to dinner with family
Piñata	Games
Family/friends for dinner	Pin the Tail on the Donkey
Breakfast in bed	Friends for pizza

CONNECT Use questions such as these to prompt a discussion.

• Birthday parties are small festivals. Have you ever been to a large festival?

• Have you ever had a piñata at a party? What culture usually has piñatas?

• Jenna, the character in *Jingle Dancer,* was going to a festival. She was going to dance in a special ceremony. What kinds of ceremonies have you attended? Have you been to a wedding ceremony?

You've learned	You've learned
008 Amazing Words	**241** Amazing Words
this week!	so far this year!

Assessment Checkpoints *for the Week*

Selection Assessment

Use pp. 117–120 of Selection Tests to check:

 Selection Understanding

  Comprehension Skill *Character, Setting, and Plot*

Selection Vocabulary
borrow
clattering
drum
jingles
silver
voice

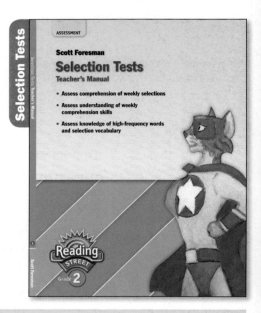

Leveled Assessment

On-Level

Strategic Intervention

Advanced

Use pp. 175–180 of Fresh Reads for Differentiated Test Practice to check:

 Comprehension Skill *Character, Setting, and Plot*

 REVIEW Comprehension Skill *Cause and Effect*

Fluency *Words Correct Per Minute*

Managing Assessment

Use Assessment Handbook for:

 Weekly Assessment Blackline Masters for Monitoring Progress

 Observation Checklists

 Record-Keeping Forms

Portfolio Assessment

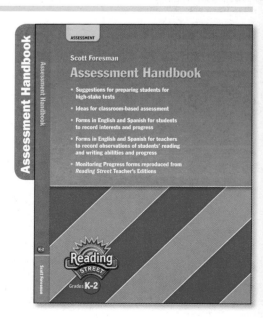

Unit 6
Concept Wrap-Up

Children are ready to express their understanding of the unit concept question through discussion and wrap-up activities and to take the Unit 6 Benchmark Test.

Unit Wrap-Up

Use the Unit Wrap-Up on pp. 434–435 to discuss the unit theme, Traditions, and to have children show their understanding of the theme through cross-curricular activities.

Unit Inquiry Project

On p. 295 you assigned children a unit-long inquiry project, to research old traditions in order to create a new tradition. Children have investigated, analyzed, and synthesized information during the unit as they prepared their plans. Schedule time for children to present their projects. The project rubric can be found below.

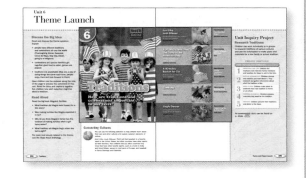

Unit Inquiry Project Rubric

4	3	2	1
• Research is organized and list of resources is useful. Plans for celebration are complete. Materials are gathered and used. • Presentation is logical and informative.	• Research is accurate but not thorough. Most sources are relevant to inquiry question. Materials are incomplete. • Presentation contains information but lacks organization.	• Research is not accurate and contains little information. Plans are incomplete, and many materials are missing. • Presentation is not understandable and does not relate to subject.	• Research is not organized and does not relate to inquiry question. Plans are incomplete and materials are not gathered. • Does not make presentation.

Unit 6
Wrap-Up

TRADITIONS

Discuss the Big Idea

Are traditions and celebrations important in our lives?

Help children relate the theme question for this unit to the selections and their own experiences. Write the questions and prompt discussion with questions such as the following. Then assign the Wrap-Up activities.

- **How are traditions and celebrations important to people in the selections we read?** (Possible answers: *Just Like Josh Gibson* The tradition of playing baseball was important to the little girl in this story. *Red, White, and Blue* For over two hundred years, our flag of red, white, and blue has stood for the United States. *A Birthday Basket for Tía* Tía's birthday basket was filled with things that reminded Cecilia of good times with her aunt. *Cowboys* Cowboys are part of the American tradition of workers. *Jingle Dancer* Jenna participated in a Native American tradition, dancing.)

- **Why do you think people like to have special celebrations and traditions?** (Possible response: People enjoy doing the same things and celebrating in the same ways. People enjoy celebrating special events and anniversaries of events.)

A Grand New Flag

connect to ART

Design a flag for your family. Think about what colors might help show something important. What symbols or pictures would help others learn about your family? Paint your design. Then show your flag to a friend. Explain what you want it to show.

434

How are traditions and celebrations important to our lives?

A Curious Culture

connect to WRITING

You read about many cultures and traditions in this unit. Which one did you find most interesting or surprising? Write a paragraph or two about it. Tell what you learned that was important.

Another Birthday Basket

connect to SOCIAL STUDIES

Suppose a character you read about in *Just Like Josh Gibson* or in *Jingle Dancer* wanted to make a present as the girl did in *A Birthday Basket for Tía*. Who would the character make it for? What would the present be? Why would the person like it? Draw a picture of the present. Tell a partner about it.

435

ACTIVITIES

A Grand New Flag

Draw and Explain Before children begin, brainstorm symbols that children can use on their flags. You might also display other examples of flags from around the world to inspire children's use of color and symbol.

A Curious Culture

Write As children write, remind them that their writing is personal and reflects how they feel about the tradition. Have them list at least one thing they learned and tell why they thought it was important to them.

Another Birthday Basket

Draw and Discuss Have children choose a character to make the present and one to receive it. Then have children decide what kinds of things that character might need or find special. Suggest they label their pictures "A Present for _____"

Glossary

Glossary

Aa

adventure (uhd VEN cher) An **adventure** is an exciting or unusual thing to do: Riding a raft down the river was a great **adventure**. *NOUN*

afternoon (af ter NOON) The **afternoon** is the part of the day between morning and evening: On Saturday we played all **afternoon**. *NOUN*

America (uh MAIR uh kuh) **America** is another name for North **America**. Some people use the name **America** to mean the United States. *NOUN*

America

American Revolution (uh MAIR uh kuhn rev uh LOO shuhn) The **American Revolution** was a series of protests and acts of American colonists from 1763 to 1783 against England. It is also known as the Revolutionary War.

angry (ANG gree) If you are **angry**, you feel upset or mad: Dad was **angry** when he saw the broken car window. *ADJECTIVE*

assistant (uh SIS tuhnt) An **assistant** is a helper: I was her **assistant** in the library. *NOUN*

aunt (ANT or AHNT) Your **aunt** is your father's sister, your mother's sister, or your uncle's wife. *NOUN*

Bb

bank[1] (BANK) A **bank** is a place where people keep their money: My brother has a **bank** for nickels and pennies. *NOUN*

436

bank[2] (BANK) The **bank** of a river or lake is the ground beside it: He sat on the river **bank**. *NOUN*

bases (BAY sez)
1. A **base** is the bottom of something: The metal **bases** of the floor lamps might scratch the floor. *NOUN*
2. A **base** is also an object in some games: After hitting a home run, the player ran the **bases**. *NOUN*

basket (BAS kuht)
1. A **basket** is something to carry or store things in. **Baskets** are made of straw, plastic, or strips of wood. *NOUN*
2. In basketball a **basket** is used as a goal. The **basket** is made of a metal ring with a net hanging from it. *NOUN*

basket

bellowed (BELL ohd) To **bellow** is to make a loud, deep noise: The moose **bellowed** angrily at the man. *VERB*

birthday (BERTH day) A **birthday** is the day that a person was born or something was started: Our country's **birthday** is July 4th. *NOUN*

blame (BLAYM) To **blame** is to hold someone responsible for something bad or wrong. *VERB*

blankets (BLANG kuhts) **Blankets** are soft, warm coverings for beds: We bought new, wool **blankets**. *NOUN*

437

bleachers (BLEE cherz) **Bleachers** are benches for people attending games or other outdoor events. *NOUN*

block (BLOK)
1. A **block** is a thick piece of wood or plastic: My little brother held one green **block** and two blue ones. *NOUN*
2. If you **block** something, you fill it so that nothing can pass by: I saw a large truck **block** traffic. *VERB*
3. A **block** is also an area of a city that has a street on each side: I walked down the **block** to my friend's house. *NOUN*

borrow (BAR oh or BOR oh) If you **borrow** something, you get it from a person or place just for a while: I like to **borrow** books from the library. *VERB*

branches (BRANCH ez)
1. **Branches** are the part of the tree that grow out from the trunk: Swings hung from the tree's **branches**. *NOUN*
2. **Branches** are small parts of something: The **branches** of the river had quiet water. *NOUN*

brooding (BROOD ing) **Brooding** is to hang over as if to cover: The **brooding** storm clouds settled over the town. *ADJECTIVE*

building (BIL ding) A **building** is something that has been built. A **building** has walls and a roof. Schools, houses, and barns are **buildings**. *NOUN*

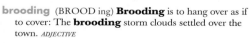
building

438

bulges (BUHL jez) **Bulges** are an outward swelling: The air in the man's jaws made **bulges** in his cheeks. *NOUN*

bumpy (BUHM pee) If something is **bumpy**, it is rough or has a lot of bumps: This street is too **bumpy** to skate on. *ADJECTIVE*

burning (BERN ing) **Burning** means to be on fire: Dad carefully watched the **burning** leaves. *ADJECTIVE*

Cc

campfire (KAMP fyr) A **campfire** is an outdoor fire used for cooking or staying warm. *NOUN*

cattle (KAT uhl) **Cattle** are animals raised for their meat, milk, or skins. Cows and bulls are **cattle**. *NOUN PLURAL*

chased (CHAYST) When you **chase** someone or something, you run after them: The children **chased** the ball down the hill. *VERB*

chewing

cheers (CHEERZ) When you **cheer**, you call out or yell loudly to show you like something: She **cheers** for her team. *VERB*

chewing (CHOO ing) When you **chew** something, you crush it with your teeth: He was **chewing** the nuts. *VERB*

chuckle (CHUK uhl) When you **chuckle**, you laugh softly: She will **chuckle** when she sees her gift. *VERB*

439

chuckwagon (CHUK WAG uhn) A **chuckwagon** is a wagon or truck that carries food and cooking equipment for cowhands. *NOUN*

clattering (KLAT tuhr ing) **Clattering** is having a loud, rattling noise: The **clattering** dishes woke me up. *ADJECTIVE*

climbed (KLYMD) When you **climb**, you go up something, usually by using your hands and feet: The children **climbed** into the bus. *VERB*

clubhouse (KLUB HOWSS) A **clubhouse** is a building used by a group of people joined together for some special reason. *NOUN*

clung (KLUNG)
1. If you **clung**, you held tightly to someone or something: He **clung** to his father's hand. *VERB*
2. **Clung** means to have stuck to something: The vine **clung** to the wall. *VERB*

collects (kuh LEKTS) If you **collect** things, you bring them together or gather them together: The student **collects** the crayons. *VERB*

colonies (KOL uh neez) A **colony** is a group of people who leave their own country to settle in another land but who still remain citizens of their own country: The thirteen British **colonies** became the United States of America. *NOUN*

Congress (KONG gris) **Congress** is the national legislative body of the United States. **Congress** has two parts, the Senate and the House of Representatives. *NOUN*

cowboy

cowboy (KOW boi) A **cowboy** is a person who works on a cattle ranch. **Cowboys** also take part in rodeos. *NOUN*

crawls (KRAWLZ) When you **crawl** you move on your hands and knees or with your body close to the ground: The lizard **crawls** across the floor. *VERB*

cycle (SY kuhl) A **cycle** is a series of events that repeats itself in the same order over and over again: A frog's life **cycle** begins as an egg. *NOUN*

Dd

dripping

downhearted (DOWN HART id) To be **downhearted** is to be depressed or discouraged: The team was **downhearted** because we lost the last game. *ADJECTIVE*

dripping (DRIP ing) When something **drips**, it falls in drops: The rain was **dripping** on the roof. *VERB*

drum (DRUHM) A **drum** is a musical instrument that makes a sound when it is beaten. A **drum** is hollow with a cover stretched tight over each end. *NOUN*

drum

dugout (DUHG OWT) A **dugout** is a small shelter at the side of a baseball field, used by players not on the field: The team sat in the **dugout** while the batters took turns. *NOUN*

Ee

exploring (ek SPLOR ing) When you are **exploring**, you are traveling to discover new areas: Astronauts are **exploring** outer space. *VERB*

Ff

fair

fair[1] (FAIR) If you are **fair**, you go by the rules. People who are **fair** treat everyone the same: Try to be **fair** in everything you do. *ADJECTIVE*

fair[2] (FAIR) A **fair** is an outdoor show of farm animals and other things: We enjoyed ourselves at the county **fair**. *NOUN*

favorite (FAY ver it)
1. Your **favorite** thing is the one you like better than all the others: What is your **favorite** color? *ADJECTIVE*
2. A **favorite** is a person or thing that you like very much: Pizza is a **favorite** with me. *NOUN*

feverishly (FEE vuhr ish lee) When something is done **feverishly**, it is done in an excited or restless way: We packed **feverishly** for the trip. *ADVERB*

field (FEE uhld) A **field** is a piece of land used for a special purpose: The football **field** needs to be mowed. *NOUN*

fierce (FEERS) When something is **fierce**, it is very great or strong: A **fierce** wind blew the tree house down. *ADJECTIVE*

fingers (FING gerz) Your **fingers** are the five end parts of your hand. *NOUN*

fingers

fireproof (FYR proof) A thing that is **fireproof** is almost impossible to burn: Steel and concrete are **fireproof**. *ADJECTIVE*

flag

flag (FLAG) A **flag** is a piece of colored cloth with stars or other symbols on it. Every country and state has its own **flag**. *NOUN*

flashes (FLASH ez) To **flash** is to give a light or flame: The light **flashes** on and off. *VERB*

forties (FOR teez) The **forties** are the 1940s: My granddad was born in the **forties**. *NOUN*

freedom (FREE duhm) **Freedom** is not being under someone else's control or rule. *NOUN*

fruit

fruit (FROOT) **Fruit** is the part of a tree, bush, or vine that has seeds in it and is good to eat. Apples, oranges, strawberries, and bananas are **fruit**. *NOUN*

Gg

galloped (GAL uhpt) To **gallop** is to run very fast: The horse **galloped** down the road. *VERB*

Glossary

giant

giant (JY uhnt)
1. In stories, a **giant** is a person who is very large. *NOUN*
2. If something is **giant**, it is much bigger than usual: We made a **giant** sandwich for lunch. *ADJECTIVE*

glee (GLEE) **Glee** is a feeling of great delight or lively joy: The children at the party laughed with **glee** at the clown. *NOUN*

grabbed (GRABD) When you **grab** something, you take it suddenly: The dog **grabbed** the bone. *VERB*

greatest (GRAYT est) If something is the **greatest**, it is the best and most important: He thought it was the **greatest** book he had ever read. *ADJECTIVE*

Hh

harvest (HAR vist)
1. A **harvest** is the ripe crops that are picked after the growing season is over: The corn **harvest** was poor after the hot, dry summer. *NOUN*
2. When you **harvest**, you gather in the crops and store them: We **harvest** the apples in late fall. *VERB*

hatchet (HACH it) A **hatchet** is a small ax with a handle about a foot long, for use with one hand: Dad chopped the log with a **hatchet**. *NOUN*

herd

herd (HERD) A **herd** is a group of the same kind of animals: We saw a **herd** of cows when we drove through the country. *NOUN*

444

hydrant (HY druhnt) A **hydrant** is a large water pipe that sticks up out of the ground. It has places where firefighters can connect hoses. *NOUN*

Ii

ideas (eye DEE uhz) **Ideas** are thoughts or plans: The class had different **ideas** on how to spend the money. *NOUN*

important (im PORT uhnt) Something that is **important** has a lot of meaning or worth: Learning to read is **important**. *ADJECTIVE*

insect

insects (IN sekts) **Insects** are small animals with six legs and bodies that have three parts. Most **insects** have four wings. Flies, bees, butterflies, and mosquitoes are **insects**. *NOUN*

Jj

jingle (JING uhl)
1. To **jingle** is to make or cause a sound like little bells. *VERB*
2. A **jingle** is a cone-shaped piece of tin sewn in rows onto a Native American dress. *NOUN*

Ll

lightning (LYT ning) **Lightning** is a flash of electricity in the sky. The sound that usually comes after a flash of **lightning** is thunder. *NOUN*

445

Louisville slugger (LOO ee vil SLUG ger) A **Louisville slugger** is one kind of a baseball bat. *NOUN*

Mm

masks (MASKS) **Masks** are coverings that hide or protect your face: The firefighters wear gas **masks**. *NOUN*

moccasins

moccasins (MOK uh suhnz) A **moccasin** is a soft leather shoe or sandal, often without an attached heel. Many Native Americans wore **moccasins**, often made of deer hide. *NOUN*

Nn

nicknames (NIK naymz) **Nicknames** are names used instead of real names: Ed is a **nickname** for Edward. *NOUN*

ninetieth (NYN tee ith) **Ninetieth** is next after the 89th: Great-grandmother celebrated her **ninetieth** birthday. *ADJECTIVE*

nudging (NUJ ing) **Nudging** means to give a slight push: The mother cat was **nudging** her kittens along. *VERB*

Oo

outrigger (OWT RIG er) An **outrigger** is a framework that sticks out from the side of a light boat, canoe, or other vehicle to keep it from turning over: The **outrigger** helped to steady the fire truck. *NOUN*

446

Pp

patchwork (PACH werk) **Patchwork** is pieces of cloth of various colors or shapes sewed together: Mother made the quilt from **patchwork**. *NOUN*

piñata

picnic (PIK nik) A **picnic** is a party with a meal outdoors: Our class had a **picnic** at the park. *NOUN*

piñata (pee NYAH tuh) A **piñata** is a decorated shape filled with candy, fruit, and small toys and hung at holiday time in Mexico and other Latin American countries. Blindfolded children swing sticks in order to break the **piñata** to get what is inside. *NOUN*

plate (PLAYT)
1. A **plate** is a dish that is almost flat and is usually round. We eat food from **plates**. *NOUN*
2. A **plate** is a hard rubber slab that a baseball player stands beside to hit the ball. *NOUN*

pond

pond (POND) A **pond** is water with land all around it. A **pond** is smaller than a lake and does not have waves. *NOUN*

pounds (POWNDZ) To **pound** is to hit something hard again and again: She **pounds** the door with her fist. *VERB*

pours (PORZ) When it **pours**, it rains a lot: The rain **pours** down on the city. *VERB*

447

Glossary

powerful (POW er fuhl) **Powerful** is being strong and having great force: The runner had **powerful** legs. *ADJECTIVE*

practice (PRAK tiss) A **practice** is a training session: Coach says that to play the game, you must go to **practice**. *NOUN*

present[1] (PREZ uhnt) Another word for **present** is *here*. If you are **present**, you are not absent: Every member of the class is **present** today. *ADJECTIVE*

present[2] (PREZ uhnt) A **present** is a gift. A **present** is something that someone gives you or that you give someone: His uncle sent him a birthday **present**. *NOUN*

present

pressing (PRESS ing)
1. **Pressing** is pushing something in a steady way: The child is **pressing** the elevator button. *VERB*
2. When you **press** clothes, you make them smooth with a hot iron: I was **pressing** my shirt to get out the wrinkles. *VERB*

pretended (pri TEND ed) To **pretend** is to make believe that something is real when it is not: We **pretended** that we were camping. *VERB*

Qq

quickly (KWIK lee) **Quickly** means in a short time: When I asked him a question, he answered **quickly**. *ADVERB*

448

quilt (KWILT) A **quilt** is a soft covering for a bed. A **quilt** is usually made from two pieces of cloth sewn together with soft material between them. *NOUN*

quilt

Rr

railroad (RAYL rohd) A **railroad** is a road or track of two steel rails. Trains run on **railroads**. *NOUN*

regalia (ri GAY lee uh) **Regalia** are the decorations of any society: He wore the **regalia** of the Lakota Indians. *NOUN*

roar (ROR) A **roar** is a loud, deep sound: The **roar** of the lion frightened some people at the zoo. *NOUN*

rolling (ROHL ling) **Rolling** is making deep loud sounds: The **rolling** thunder woke the baby. *ADJECTIVE*

root (ROOT)
1. The **root** is the part of a plant that grows underground. A plant gets food and water through its **roots**. *NOUN*
2. A **root** is usually called a base word. It is a word from which other words are made. In the words *rounder* and *roundest*, the **root** is *round*. *NOUN*

roundup (ROWND up) A **roundup** is the act of driving or bringing cattle together from long distances. *NOUN*

Ss

sailed (SAYLD) When something **sails**, it travels on the water or through the air: The ball **sailed** out of the ballpark. *VERB*

449

---

scent (SENT) A **scent** is a nice smell: Helen loved the **scent** of freshly baked cookies. *NOUN*

sewer (SOO er) A **sewer** is an underground drain that carries away waste water and trash. *NOUN*

shed (SHED) To **shed** is to let hair, skin, or fur fall off: The dog **shed** on the rug. *VERB*

shuffled (SHUF uhld) To **shuffle** is to scrape or drag your feet while walking: We **shuffled** along the slippery sidewalk. *VERB*

signmaker (SYN mayk er) A **signmaker** makes marks or words on a sign that tell you what to do or not to do. *NOUN*

silver (SIL ver) **Silver** is a shiny white metal. **Silver** is used to make coins, jewelry, and other things. *NOUN*

skin (SKIN) **Skin** is the outside covering of human and animal bodies, plants, fruits, and seeds: Her **skin** was red from too much sun. *NOUN*

smooth (SMOOTH) When something is **smooth**, it has an even surface. Something that is **smooth** is not bumpy or rough: The road was very **smooth**. *ADJECTIVE*

soar

soar (SOR) To **soar** is to fly at a great height: Did you see the kite **soar** in the air? *VERB*

450

soil

soil[1] (SOIL) **Soil** is the top layer of the earth. **Soil** is dirt: Our garden has such rich **soil** that almost anything will grow in it. *NOUN*

soil[2] (SOIL) If you **soil** something, you make it dirty: The dust will **soil** her white gloves. *VERB*

spawn (SPAWN) **Spawn** is the eggs of fish, frogs, shellfish, and other animals growing or living in water. *NOUN*

special (SPESH uhl)
1. If something is **special**, it is unusual or different in some way: Your birthday is a **special** day. *ADJECTIVE*
2. A **special** is a TV show produced for one showing: I saw a TV **special** on wolves. *NOUN*

spectators (SPEK tay ters) A **spectator** is someone who looks on without taking part. There were many **spectators** at the ball game. *NOUN*

stars (STARZ)
1. **Stars** are the very bright points of light that shine in the sky at night: On a clear night, the **stars** are very bright. *NOUN*
2. **Stars** are also shapes that have five or six points: I drew **stars** on the paper. *NOUN*

451

Glossary

station (STAY shuhn) A **station** is a building or place used for a special reason: The man went to the police **station**. *NOUN*

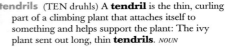
storm

stitched (STICHT) To **stitch** is to sew or fasten something with **stitches**: Mom **stitched** the hole in my sweater. *VERB*

storm (STORM) A **storm** is a strong wind with rain, snow, or hail. Some **storms** have lightning and thunder. *NOUN*

stray (STRAY) A **stray** is a lost animal: That cat is a **stray** that we took in. *NOUN*

stripes (STRYPS) **Stripes** are long, narrow bands of color: Our flag has seven red **stripes** and six white **stripes**. *NOUN*

strong (STRAWNG) Something that is **strong** has power. A **strong** person can lift and carry things that are heavy. **Strong** means not weak: A **strong** wind blew down the tree. *ADJECTIVE*

stuffing (STUF ing) **Stuffing** is material used to fill or pack something: The **stuffing** is coming out of the pillow. *NOUN*

Tt

tantrum (TAN truhm) A **tantrum** is a sudden, childish outburst of bad temper or ill humor: The girl had a **tantrum** when she couldn't get her way. *NOUN*

452

tears (TEERZ) **Tears** are drops of salty water that come from your eye. **Tears** fall when you cry. *NOUN*

tendrils (TEN druhls) A **tendril** is the thin, curling part of a climbing plant that attaches itself to something and helps support the plant: The ivy plant sent out long, thin **tendrils**. *NOUN*

tendrils

threw (THROO) When you **threw** something, you sent it through the air: She **threw** the ball back to him. *VERB*

thunder (THUHN der) **Thunder** is the loud noise from the sky that comes after a flash of lightning. *NOUN*

tía (TEE uh) **Tía** is the Spanish word for aunt: My **tía** is my mother's sister. *NOUN*

tightly (TYT lee) When something is tied **tightly**, it is firmly tied: The rope was tied **tightly**. *ADVERB*

townspeople (TOWNZ pee puhl) **Townspeople** are the men, women, and children who live in a village or town: The **townspeople** enjoyed the fair. *NOUN*

trails (TRAYLZ) **Trails** are paths across fields or through the woods: Two **trails** led to the river. *NOUN*

treat (TREET) A **treat** is a gift of food, drink, a free ticket, or the like: She gave us **treats** on the last day of school. *NOUN*

453

trouble (TRUHB uhl)
1. **Trouble** is something that makes you upset, bothers you, or gives you pain: I had a lot of **trouble** working those math problems. *NOUN*
2. If you are in **trouble**, people are angry or upset with you: You will be in **trouble** if you knock that can of paint over. *NOUN*

truest (TROO ist) To be **true** is to be faithful and loyal: She is the **truest** friend I have. *ADJECTIVE*

trunks (TRUHNGKS) **Trunks** are large boxes for carrying clothes. *NOUN*

trunks

Uu

unpacked (uhn PAKT) To **unpack** is to take things out that were packed in a box, trunk, or other container: He **unpacked** his clothes. *VERB*

usually (YOO zhoo uhl lee) **Usually** tells how something is seen, found, or happening most of the time: We **usually** eat at six o'clock. *ADVERB*

Vv

vegetarians (vej uh TAIR ee uhns) A **vegetarian** is someone who eats vegetables but no meat: **Vegetarians** like to eat fruit. *NOUN*

vine (VYN) A **vine** is a plant that grows along the ground. Some **vines** climb up walls and fences. Pumpkins, melons, and grapes grow on **vines**. *NOUN*

454

voice (VOISS) Your **voice** is the sound you make with your mouth. You use your **voice** when you speak, sing, or shout. *NOUN*

Ww

wagged (WAGD) To **wag** is to move from side to side or up and down: The dog **wagged** her tail. *VERB*

wisdom (WIZ duhm) **Wisdom** is knowledge and good judgment based on experience: The leader's **wisdom** guided the group through the woods. *NOUN*

wither (WITH er) To **wither** is to make or become dry and lifeless; dry up: The hot sun will **wither** the plants. *VERB*

wondered (WUHN derd) When you **wondered** about something, you wanted to know about it: He **wondered** what time it was. *VERB*

wrapped

wonderful (WUHN der fuhl) If something is **wonderful**, you like it very much: The ocean was a **wonderful** sight. *ADJECTIVE*

wrapped (RAPT) When you **wrap** something, you cover it up, usually with paper: We **wrapped** presents all morning. *VERB*

455

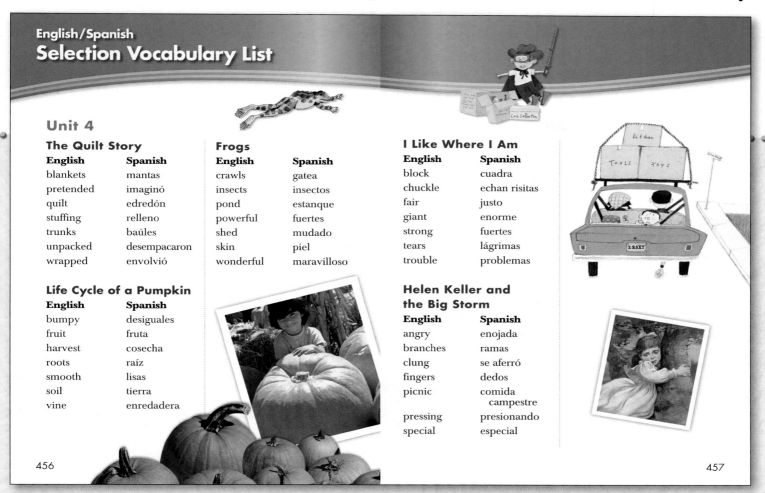

English/Spanish
Selection Vocabulary List

Unit 4

The Quilt Story

English	Spanish
blankets	mantas
pretended	imaginó
quilt	edredón
stuffing	relleno
trunks	baúles
unpacked	desempacaron
wrapped	envolvió

Life Cycle of a Pumpkin

English	Spanish
bumpy	desiguales
fruit	fruta
harvest	cosecha
roots	raíz
smooth	lisas
soil	tierra
vine	enredadera

Frogs

English	Spanish
crawls	gatea
insects	insectos
pond	estanque
powerful	fuertes
shed	mudado
skin	piel
wonderful	maravilloso

I Like Where I Am

English	Spanish
block	cuadra
chuckle	echan risitas
fair	justo
giant	enorme
strong	fuertes
tears	lágrimas
trouble	problemas

Helen Keller and the Big Storm

English	Spanish
angry	enojada
branches	ramas
clung	se aferró
fingers	dedos
picnic	comida campestre
pressing	presionando
special	especial

456

457

Unit 5

Firefighter!

English	Spanish
building	edificio
burning	ardiente
masks	máscaras
quickly	rápidamente
roar	rugido
station	estación
tightly	bien

One Dark Night

English	Spanish
lightning	relámpago
flashes	destella
pounds	golpea
pours	llueve a cántaros
rolling	retumbando
storm	tormenta
thunder	truenos

Bad Dog, Dodger!

English	Spanish
chased	persiguieron
chewing	mordiendo
dripping	goteando
grabbed	agarró
practice	entrenamiento
treat	galletas (de perro)
wagged	meneó

Horace and Morris but mostly Dolores

English	Spanish
adventure	aventura
climbed	subieron
clubhouse	casa del club
exploring	explorando
greatest	mejores
truest	más verdaderos
wondered	se preguntaba

The Signmaker's Assistant

English	Spanish
afternoon	tarde
blame	culpen
ideas	idea
important	importante
signmaker	rotulista
townspeople	ciudadanos

458

459

English/Spanish Selection Vocabulary List

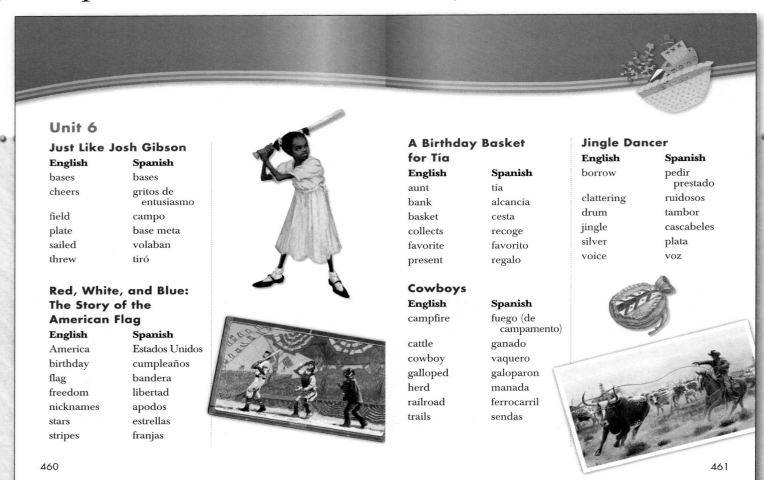

Unit 6

Just Like Josh Gibson

English	Spanish
bases	bases
cheers	gritos de entusiasmo
field	campo
plate	base meta
sailed	volaban
threw	tiró

Red, White, and Blue: The Story of the American Flag

English	Spanish
America	Estados Unidos
birthday	cumpleaños
flag	bandera
freedom	libertad
nicknames	apodos
stars	estrellas
stripes	franjas

460

A Birthday Basket for Tía

English	Spanish
aunt	tía
bank	alcancía
basket	cesta
collects	recoge
favorite	favorito
present	regalo

Cowboys

English	Spanish
campfire	fuego (de campamento)
cattle	ganado
cowboy	vaquero
galloped	galoparon
herd	manada
railroad	ferrocarril
trails	sendas

Jingle Dancer

English	Spanish
borrow	pedir prestado
clattering	ruidosos
drum	tambor
jingle	cascabeles
silver	plata
voice	voz

461

Acknowledgments

Text

Page 16: *The Quilt Story* by Tony Johnston and illustrated by Tomie dePaola. Text Copyright © Tony Johnston, 1985. Illustrations Copyright © Tomie dePaola, 1985. Published by arrangement with G.P. Putnam's Sons, a division of Penguin Young Readers Group, a member of Penguin Group (USA) Inc. All rights reserved.

Page 46: *The Life Cycle of a Pumpkin* by Ron Fridell and Patricia Walsh. Harcourt Global Library, art of Harcourt Education Ltd. Reprinted by permission.

Page 62: From *Where Fish Go in Winter And Other Great Mysteries* by Amy Goldman Koss, copyright © 1987 by Amy Goldman Koss, text. Used by permission of Dial Books for Young Readers, A Division of Penguin Young Readers Group, A Member of Penguin Group (USA) Inc., 345 Hudson Street, New York, NY 10014. All rights reserved.

Page 70: From *Frogs* by Gail Gibbons. Copyright © 1993 by Gail Gibbons. All rights reserved. Reprinted from *Frogs* by permission of Holiday House, Inc.

Page 90: From *Life Cycles* by Michael Elsohn Ross; illustrated by Gustav Moore. Text copyright © 2001 by Michael Elsohn Ross; illustrations copyright © 2001 by Gustav Moore. Used by permission of Millbrook Press, a division of Lerner Publishing Group. All rights reserved.

Page 100: *I Like Where I Am* by Jessica Harper and illustrated by Brian Karas. Text Copyright © Jessica Harper 2004. Illustrations Copyright © Brian Karas, 2004 Published by arrangement with G.P. Putnam's Sons, a division of Penguin Young Readers Group, a member of Penguin Group (USA) Inc. All rights reserved.

Page 128: Reprinted with the permission of Aladdin Paperbacks, an imprint of Simon & Schuster Children's Publishing Division from *Helen Keller and the Big Storm* by Patricia Lakin. Copyright © 2002 Patricia Lakin.

Page 144: Reprinted with the permission of Aladdin Paperbacks, an imprint of Simon & Schuster Children's Publishing Division from *Wind* by Marion Dane Bauer. Copyright © 2003 Marion Dane Bauer.

Page 158: *Fire Fighter!* by Angela Royston. Copyright © 1998 Dorling Kindersley Limited, London. Reprinted by permission.

Page 184: *One Dark Night* written by Hazel Hutchins and illustrations by Susan Hartung. Text copyright © 2001 by Hazel Hutchins. Illustrations copyright © 2001 by Susan Hartung. Published by arrangement with Viking Children's Books, a division of Penguin Young Readers Group, a member of Penguin Group (USA) Inc.

Page 204: Isabel Joshlin Glaser for "Adoption". Reprinted from *Y ou and Me* by Salley Mavor, 1997. Reprinted by permission of Isabel Joshlin Glaser.

Page 205: *"The Stray Cat"* by Eve Merriam. Used by permission of Marian Reiner.

Page 212: Reprinted with the permission of Margaret K. McElderry Books, an imprint of Simon & Schuster Children's Publishing Division from *Bad Dog, Dodger!* by Barbara Abercrombie. Text copyright © 2002 Barbara Abercrombie.

Page 238: From *Horace and Morris but Mostly Dolores.* Text copyright © 1999 by James Howe. Illustrations copyright © 1999 by Amy Walrod. Reprinted with permission of Atheneum Books for Young Readers, Simon & Schuster Children's Publishing Division. All rights reserved.

Page 268: *The Signmaker's Assistant* by Tedd Arnold. Copyright © 1992 by Tedd Arnold. Published by arrangement with Dial Books for Young Readers, a division of Penguin Young Readers Group, a member of Penguin Group (USA) Inc..

Page 286: Action Without Borders Web site, www.idealist.org/kt/youthorgs.html. Reprinted by permission.

Page 300: From *Just Like Josh Gibson.* Text copyright © 2004 by Angela Johnson. Illustrations copyright © 2004 by Beth Peck. Reprinted with permission of Simon & Schuster Books for Young Readers, Simon & Schuster Children's Publishing Division. All rights reserved.

Page 326: *Red, White, And Blue* by John Herman, and illustrated by Robin Roraback. Text Copyright © John Herman, 1998. Illustration Copyright © Robin Roraback, 1998. Published by arrangement with Grosset & Dunlap, a division of Penguin Young Readers Group, a member of Penguin Group (USA) Inc. All rights reserved.

Page 354: From *A Birthday Basket for Tía.* Text copyright © 1992 by Pat Mora. Illustrations copyright © 1992 by Cecily Lang. Reprinted with permission of Simon & Schuster Books for Young Readers, Simon & Schuster Children's Publishing Division. All rights reserved.

Page 370: From www.kidparties.com/traditions.htm. Reprinted by permission.

Page 380: *Cowboys* by Lucille Recht Penner, illustrated by Ben Carter, Grosset & Dunlap, 1996.

Page 404: From *The Cowboy's Handbook* by Tod Cody, copyright © 1996 by Breslich & Foss, entire text and compilation of illustrations. Used by permission of Cobblehill Books, an affiliate of Dutton Children's Books, A Division of Penguin Young Readers Group, A Member of Penguin Group (USA) Inc., 345 Hudson Street, New York, NY 10014. All rights reserved.

Page 412: *Jingle Dancer* by Cynthia Leitich Smith, illustrated by Cornelius Van Wright and Ying-Hwa Hu. Text copyright © 2000 by Cynthia Leitich Smith. Illustrations copyright © 2000 by Cornelius Van Wright and Ying-Hwa Hu.

Page 428: From "Celebrating the Buffalo Days" from *Buffalo Days* by Diane Hoyt-Goldsmith, Photographs by Lawrence Migdale, Illustrations by Ted Furlo. Text copyright © 1997 by Diane Hoyt-Goldsmith. Photographs copyright © 1997 by Lawrence Migdale. All rights reserved. Reprinted from *Buffalo Days* by permission of Holiday House, Inc.

Illustrations

89, 117, 129, 150-151, 174-177, 212-225, 250, 292-293, 345, 403, 434-435 Laura Ovresat; **128-140** Troy Howell; **206** Jui Ishida; **214-226** Diane Greenseid; **316-319** Clint Hansen; **326-336, 340-342** Shannan Stirnweiss; **338, 400-401** Derek Grinnell

Photographs

Every effort has been made to secure permission and provide appropriate credit for photographic material. The publisher deeply regrets any omission and pledges to correct errors called to its attention in subsequent editions.

Unless otherwise acknowledged, all photographs are the property of Scott Foresman, a division of Pearson Education.

Photo locators denoted as follows: Top (T), Center (C), Bottom (B), Left (L), Right (R), Background (Bkgd).

10 Man on the Moon (A Day in the Life of Bob). ©2002 Simon Bartram. First published in Great Britain by Templar Publishing. Reproduced by permission of the publisher/Candlewick Press, Inc., Cambridge, MA; **13** Corbis; **15** ©Michael Boys/Corbis; **34** Getty Images; **35** (CR, BR) Getty Images, (TR) ©Cape Cod Travel; **36** (TR, BR) ©Cape Cod Travel; **37** ©Lee Snider/Corbis; **38** ©Amy Dykens/Cape Cod Travel; **39** ©Cape Cod Travel; **43** ©Renee Lynn/Corbis; **45** (TR, BR) Getty Images; **46** (Bkgd) Getty Images, (TR) ©Royalty-Free/Corbis; **48** (CR) ©Royalty-Free/Corbis, (TC) ©Ben Klaffe; **49** (TL) Getty Images, (TR) ©Dwight R. Kuhn; **50** (TL, TR) ©Dwight R. Kuhn; **51** (TC) ©Shmuel Thaler/Index Stock Imagery, (CR) ©Dwight R. Kuhn; **52** (T) ©Steve Solum/Index Stock Imagery, (CR) ©Ben Klaffe; **53** (T, TR) ©Dwight R. Kuhn; **54** (T, BR) ©Ben Klaffe; **55** (T) ©Reuters/Corbis, (CR) ©Dwight R. Kuhn; **56** (T) ©Dwight R. Kuhn, (CR) Getty Images; **57** (T) ©Barry Lewis/Corbis, (CR) ©Matthew Klein/Corbis; **58** (TL) ©Tony Freeman/PhotoEdit, (TR) ©Royalty-Free/Corbis; **59** ©Richard Hamilton Smith/Corbis; **60** ©Dwight R. Kuhn; **61** (BL) ©Dwight R. Kuhn, (BR) ©Ben Klaffe, (TL) ©Matthew Klein/Corbis, (TC) ©Royalty-Free/Corbis, (BC) Getty Images, (CL) ©Alex Cohn; **63** ©David Aubrey/Corbis; **65** ©Royalty-Free/Corbis; **67** (BL) ©Royalty-Free/Corbis, (BC) ©Richard Cummins/Corbis; **68-69** Getty Images; **97** ©Royalty-Free/Corbis; **99** (TR) Corbis, (CR, BR) Getty Images; **118** ©Craig Aurness/Corbis; **125** ©DK Images; **126-127** ©G.K. & Vikki Hart/ PhotoDisc; **130** (BL) Getty Images, (TR) ©Royalty-Free/Corbis; **131** ©Bettmann/Corbis; **132** (TL) Getty Images, (C) ©Bettmann/ Corbis; **133** (TL) ©Bettman/Corbis, (TR) ©Siede Preis/Getty Images, (T) Getty Images; **135** ©Royalty-Free/Corbis; **141** (TC) ©Royalty-Free/Corbis, (R) Getty Images, (C) Corbis; **142** (BR) ©Bettmann/Corbis, (TL) Getty Images; **143** (TR) ©Siede Preis/Getty Images, (BR) ©Royalty-Free/Corbis, (BC) ©Bettman/Corbis, (T) Getty Images, (B) ©First Light/Corbis; **144** ©Kevin Anthony Horgan/Getty Images; **145** (BL) ©Martin Barraud/Getty Images, (CR) ©Geostock/Getty Images; **146** (TC) ©Guy Grenier/ Masterfile Corporation, (TL) ©Michael Melford/Getty Images, (TR) Getty Images, (CL) ©Alan R. Moller/Getty Images, (BL) ©Guy Motil/Corbis, (BR) ©Randy Faris/Corbis; **147** (TR) ©Stan Osolinski/Getty Images, (CL) ©World Perspectives/Getty Images, (CR) Getty Images, (Bkgd) ©Stephen Frink/Getty Images; **148** ©Bettman/Corbis; **151** ©Geostock/Getty Images; **152** ©Jim Sugar/Corbis; **155** ©DK Images; **157-158** ©Tim Ross/Index Stock Imagery; **159** (Bkgd) ©Mark Barrett/Index Stock Imagery, (B) ©Walter Bibikow/Index Stock Imagery; **160** (BL) ©Royalty-Free/Corbis, (TL) ©Roberts Company, Inc., (TR) Lynton Gardiner/©DK Images, (BL) Michal Heron/©DK Images, (R) Richard Leeney/©DK Images; **161** (BC) Getty Images, (TL) Michal Heron/©DK Images, (R) ©DK Images; **162** (TR, BR) ©DK Images; **163** (TR) Lynton Gardiner/©DK Images; **164** ©Jim Pickerell/Stock Connection; **165** Lynton Gardiner/©DK Images; **166** ©James McLoughlin; **167** (BR) ©Rubberball Productions/Getty Images, (BC) Corbis; **168** Getty Images; **169-170** ©Lynton Gardiner/©DK Images; **171** Getty Images; **172** ©Roberts Company, Inc.; **173** (B) ©Richard Leeney/©DK Images, (TR) Corbis; **174** (TC) ©Roberts Company, Inc., (Bkgd) ©Comstock Images/Getty Images; **175** ©Royalty-Free/Corbis; **176** ©Comstock Images/Getty Images; **179** ©DK Images; **181** Getty Images; **183** ©Rob Matheson/Corbis; **203** ©Pat Doyle/Corbis; **209, 211** Getty Images; **227** (TL) ©Comstock Inc., (BC) ©Robert Dowling/Corbis; **229** (BL) ©Jim Craigmyle/Corbis, (BR) ©Tracy Morgan/©DK Images, (TR) ©Cydney Conger/Corbis; **230** (BC) ©Burke/Triolo Productions/FoodPix, (TR) ©Jim Craigmyle/Corbis; **231** (B) ©Tracy Morgan/©DK Images, (T) ©Jim Craigmyle/Corbis; **235** (BL, BR) Getty Images; **237** Getty Images; **257** (TL) ©Hans Neleman/Getty Images, (T) Photo of James Howe used with permission of Simon & Schuster, Inc. ©John Maggiotto, (BL) Getty Images; **258** (BR) Getty Images, (C) ©Bob Thomas/Getty Images; **259** (TR) ©Lori Adamski Peek/Getty Images, (BR) ©Bob Gomel/Corbis; **260** (TR) ©Tim Pannell/Corbis, (BR) ©Charles Gupton/Corbis; **261** ©Lori Adamski Peek/Getty Images; **265** (TR, BC) Getty Images; **267** ©Royalty-Free/Corbis; **286** ©Tom Stewart/Corbis; **287** (TR) Getty Images, (CR) Jacob Taposchaner/Taxi/Getty Images; **292** ©Tom Brakefield/Corbis; **293** (T) ©Joseph Van Os/Getty Images, (BR) Getty Images; **294** ©Ariel Skelley/Corbis; **297** ©Royalty-Free/Corbis; **299** (T) ©Royalty-Free/Corbis, (BR) ©Ariel Skelley/Corbis; **315** Illustration Works, Inc.; **317** Library of Congress; **323** (TR) ©Royalty-Free/Corbis, (BR) ©Jim Cummins/Corbis; **325** (CR) Corbis, (BR) ©Jerry Tobias/Corbis; **330** (BL) Stock Montage Inc., (TR) ©Bettmann/ Corbis, (CR) ©PoodlesRock/Corbis; **334** (T) Composite photograph of the 190 year-old Star-Spangled Banner, the flag that inspired the national anthem. Smithsonian's National Museum of American History, ©2002/Smithsonian Institution; **335** Corbis; **336** (T) The Granger Collection, NY; **338** ©Bjorn G. Bolstad/Photo Researchers, Inc.; **340** (BL) Corbis; **343** Digital Vision; **347** ©Terence Beddis/Getty Images; **348** (BR) ©Bettmann/Corbis, (BL) Stock Montage Inc.; **349** Digital Vision; **353** (BR) Brand X Pictures, (TR) Getty Images; **369** Corbis; **370** ©Jose L. Pelaez/Corbis; **372** Getty Images; **377** Corbis; **379** (TR) ©Jules Frazier/Getty Images, (BR) ©Macduff Everton/Corbis; **380** ©Guillaud Jean Michel/Sygma/Corbis; **382** Getty Images; **400** (TR) ©Jules Frazier/Getty Images, (B) Getty Images; **401-402** ©Jules Frazier/Getty Images; **403** Getty Images; **404** (B, TR) Getty Images, (TR) ©C Squared Studios/Getty Images, (BR) Brand X Pictures; **405** Getty Images; **409** ©Lindsay Hebberd/Corbis; **411** (T) ©Werner Forman/Corbis, (B) Getty Images; **428** (L, T) ©Lawrence Migdale, (C) Getty Images, (BC) ©C Squared Studios/Getty Images; **429** ©Lawrence Migdale; **431** ©Lawrence Migdale; **434** ©Ariel Skelley/Corbis; **435** Getty Images; **436** ©Ira Rubin/Getty Images; **437** ©Thinkstock/Getty Images; **438** ©Craig Aurness/Corbis; **439** image100; **441** (BR) Getty Images, (BL) ©Richard H. Johnston/Getty Images; **442** ©Patrick Ward/Corbis; **443** (CL) Corbis, (BL, TR) Getty Images; **444** (BL) Getty Images, (TL) ©Brian Hagiwara/Getty Images; **445** ©G.K. & Vikki Hart/PhotoDisc; **446** ©Werner Forman/Corbis; **447** (CL) ©Betsie Van der Meer/Getty Images, (CL) ©R. Derek Smith/Getty Images; **448-449** Getty Images; **450** ©Guy Grenier/Masterfile Corporation; **451** ©David Aubrey/Corbis; **452** ©Alan R. Moller/Getty Images; **453** ©Kevin Schafer/Corbis; **454** Corbis; **455** ©Jose Luis Pelaez, Inc./Corbis

Glossary

The contents of this glossary have been adapted from *My First Dictionary.* Copyright © 2000, Pearson Education, Inc.

462

463

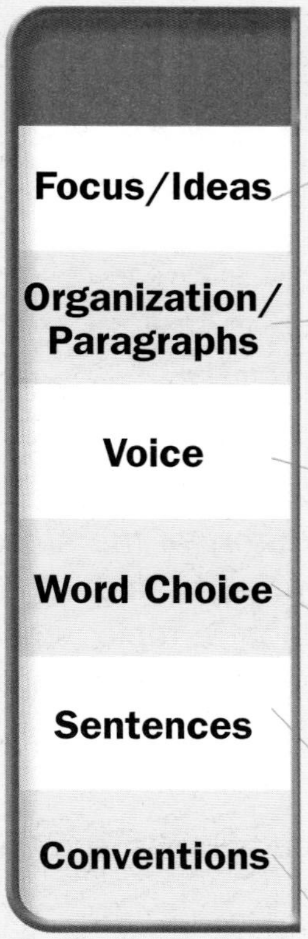

Writing Traits

- **Focus/Ideas** refers to the main purpose for writing and the details that make the subject clear and interesting. It includes development of ideas through support and elaboration.

- **Organization/Paragraphs** refers to the overall structure of a piece of writing that guides readers. Within that structure, transitions show how ideas, sentences, and paragraphs are connected.

- **Voice** shows the writer's unique personality and establishes a connection between writer and reader. Voice, which contributes to style, should be suited to the audience and the purpose for writing.

- **Word Choice** is the use of precise, vivid words to communicate effectively and naturally. It helps create style through the use of specific nouns, lively verbs and adjectives, and accurate, well-placed modifiers.

- **Sentences** covers strong, well-built sentences that vary in length and type. Skillfully written sentences have pleasing rhythms and flow fluently.

- **Conventions** refers to mechanical correctness and includes grammar, usage, spelling, punctuation, capitalization, and paragraphing.

Focus/Ideas

Organization/
Paragraphs

Voice

Word Choice

Sentences

Conventions

Writing Workshop

Research Report

Writing Prompt: Traditions

Think of a tradition that is important to your family, school, community, or country. It might be a game, holiday, symbol, or celebration. Write about the tradition and what makes it important. Find facts about its history in books or magazines or on the Internet.

Purpose: Inform

Audience: People who don't know about the tradition

READ LIKE A WRITER

Ask children to look back at *Red, White, and Blue: The Story of the American Flag.* Point out that before writing this article, the writer had to find information about our flag. Explain that searching for information about a topic is called research. Tell children that they will write a research report about a tradition.

SHOW THE MODEL AND RUBRIC

GUIDED WRITING Read the model aloud. Point out the paragraphs and the indent at the beginning of each paragraph.

- Note that each paragraph begins with a sentence that tells the main idea and is followed by sentences that give details about the main idea.
- Discuss the facts that the writer presents in the report. Remind children that a research report gives accurate facts.
- Discuss how the model reflects traits of good writing.

Martin Luther King, Jr., Day

Martin Luther King, Jr., was an important African American leader. He believed that all Americans should have the same rights. He made speeches, wrote books, and led peaceful marches. After King was killed in 1968, many people wanted a holiday to honor him.

In 1983, Congress said that Martin Luther King, Jr., Day would be celebrated on the third Monday in January. The first Martin Luther King, Jr., Day was on January 20, 1986.

A national holiday is a great honor. The birthdays of only two Americans have been made national holidays. King was the second person, but do you know who the first person was? It was George Washington. He was our first President.

Unit 6 Research Report • PREWRITE   Writing Process **31**

▲ **Writing Transparency** WP31

Traits of a Good Research Report

Focus/Ideas	Report sticks to the topic and gives facts.
Organization/ Paragraphs	Writer organizes related facts into paragraphs and begins each paragraph with a main idea sentence.
Voice	Report is interesting. Writer knows about the topic.
Word Choice	Writer uses powerful words. (*rights, peaceful, honor*)
Sentences	Writer uses short and long sentences, including a compound sentence.
Conventions	Writer uses good grammar, capitalization, and spelling.

Unit 6 Research Report • PREWRITE   Writing Process **32**

▲ **Writing Transparency** WP32

Writing

Writing Trait of the Week

Writing Workshop

Rubrics

Assessment

Assessment

Student Tips for Making Top Scores in Writing Tests

1 **Use words such as these to connect ideas, sentences, or paragraphs.**

first	last	before	now
next	finally	after	then

2 **Write a good beginning. Make readers want to read more.**
- I peeked in the room and screamed.
- Never try to mess with an angry bee.
- When I was four, I saw a purple dog.
- Have you ever heard of a talking tree?

3 **Focus on the topic.**
If a word or sentence is not about the topic, get rid of it.

4 **Organize your ideas.**
Have a plan in mind before you start writing. Your plan can be a list or a web. Your writing will go faster if you spend time planning first.

5 **Support your ideas.**
- Use examples and details to make your ideas clear.
- Use vivid words that create pictures.
- Try not to use dull *(get, go, say),* unclear *(thing, stuff, lots of),* or overused *(really, very)* words.
- Use a voice that your readers will understand.

6 **Make writing conventions as error-free as possible.**
Proofread your work carefully. Read it three times. Look for correct punctuation, then capitalization, and finally spelling.

7 **Write an ending that wraps things up. "The end" is not a good ending.**
- That's why I don't eat grapes anymore.
- I still think Chip is the best cat ever.
- My bedroom was never the same again.
- Next time I'll wear my raincoat.

FINDING A TOPIC

GO TO THE LIBRARY Suggest that children look in books and magazines and on the Internet to find out about traditions they might use as their topics.

NARROW THE CHOICE Have children ask questions about the ideas they have chosen. They might ask: Will I find enough information about this topic? Too much information? Is the topic too big? Too difficult? Would it be interesting to readers?

Think Aloud **MODEL** Birthday parties might be hard to write about. It is a big topic, and it might be too general. My family always goes to the movies on Saturday afternoon, so that is our tradition. Still, I don't think I could gather enough information to write about a report about that. Basketball would be a good topic if I focused on its early history. I think that would be interesting to readers.

PREWRITING STRATEGY

USE A K-W-L CHART Use Writing Transparency WP33 to show how to find facts for a report.

Think Aloud **MODEL** Writers can use a K-W-L chart to find out what they already know and what they want to find out about a topic. This writer wrote what he knows about basketball's history in the K column. Then he wrote questions that he wants to answer in the W column. When he found the answers to the questions, he wrote the answers in the L column. Now the writer has facts that he can use in his research report.

PREWRITING ACTIVITY Have children use the K-W-L Chart graphic organizer on Grammar and Writing Practice Book p. 180 to help them organize their ideas.

Topic Ideas

**birthday parties
Saturday afternoon movies
basketball**

K-W-L Chart

Fill out this K-W-L chart to help you organize your ideas.

What I Know	What I Want to Know	What I Learned
Basketball is an American tradition.	Who invented basketball?	James Naismith, a PE teacher
Many people like to watch basketball.	When and where was it invented?	in 1891, in Springfield, Massachusetts
Many people like to play basketball.	How has it changed?	wooden baskets became metal hoops with nets
		soccer ball became bigger ball
		new rules added

Unit 6 Research Report • PREWRITE   Writing Process **33**

▲ **Writing Transparency** WP33

Guided Writing

Some children will need additional guidance as they plan and write their reports. You might give these children the option of writing a group report under your supervision or pair them with a more able writer.

K-W-L Chart

Fill out this K-W-L chart to help you organize your ideas.

What I Know	What I Want to Know	What I Learned
Answers will vary.		

▲ **Grammar and Writing Practice Book** p. 180

Traditions   **WA3**

Think Like a Writer

Find Many Facts Explain that when writers research a topic, they generally find much more information than they will be able to use in their writing. They do this because they can't be sure of exactly what they will need until they begin writing. With many facts available to them, they can choose the best ones to include in their draft.

Support Writing If children include home-language words in their drafts, help them find replacement words in English. Resources can include

• conversations with you
• other home-language speakers
• bilingual dictionaries
• online translation sources

Eliminate Wordiness

Don't use more words than are needed.
• Take out phrases such as *kind of, I think that,* and *it seems like.*
• Don't use *a lot of.* Use *many* or another word.
• Don't use two words that mean the same thing: great big, little tiny.
• Don't use several words when you can use one word: moved with great slowness, move slowly.

Look at each pair of sentences. **Write** the words that are left out in the second sentence.
  1. Aaron is wearing a great big cowboy hat.
     Aaron is wearing a big cowboy hat.

  ~~great~~

  2. I think that Beth is kind of excited.
     Beth is excited.

  ~~I think that; kind of~~

Look at each pair of sentences. **Circle** the word that is different in the second sentence. **Write** the words that the word replaced.
  3. The children played a lot of baseball games.
     The children played (ten) baseball games.

  ~~a lot of~~

  4. She carried the flag with a great deal of care.
     She carried the flag (carefully.)

  ~~with a great deal of care~~

▲ **Grammar and Writing Practice Book** p. 181

WRITING THE FIRST DRAFT

GUIDED WRITING Have children review their K-W-L Charts to help them organize their ideas as they write their first drafts. Remind them to do the following.

• Choose the facts that they want to include in their report.

• Think of a good way to organize the facts.

• Put the facts in paragraphs.

• Consider how they will introduce and conclude their report.

Wordy Sentences

Tía wore a tiny little hat.

She has a lot of hats.

Her hats are blue in color.

ELIMINATE WORDINESS Explain that *wordiness* means using more words than are necessary. Write the sentences on the board. Ask children how the sentences could be rewritten to be less wordy, that is, to say the same thing using fewer words. (*Tía wore a tiny hat.* or *Tía wore a little hat. She has many hats. Her hats are blue.*) Remind children to avoid wordiness in their reports.

DRAFTING STRATEGIES

PUT FACTS IN GROUPS Suggest that children divide a sheet of paper into thirds and write the facts that go together in each section. In the first draft, they should get their ideas on paper quickly. They can worry about spelling and punctuation later.

PRACTICE ELIMINATING WORDINESS Have children use Grammar and Writing Practice Book p. 181 to practice eliminating wordiness in their writing.

REVISING STRATEGIES

GUIDED WRITING Use Writing Transparency WP34 to model how to revise a research report.

MODEL This is part of the research report on basketball. In the first paragraph, the writer took out the third sentence because it does not tell about the same idea as the other sentences. He saw three short, choppy sentences that all began with *He,* so he combined them to make one longer, smoother sentence. In the second paragraph, the writer took out the words *a lot of* in the second sentence because they weren't necessary.

Revising Marks	
Take Out	⌐
Add	^
Small Letter	/

Basketball

James Naismith was a PE teacher in Springfield, Massachusetts. In the winter, it was too cold and snowy for his students to play sports outside. ~~Baseball is played outside.~~ Naismith needed a team sport that they could play inside. He took a soccer ball. ^He hung two wooden baskets from a railing. ^and ^He ^made up a new game. His PE students played the first basketball game in December 1891.

Soon metal hoops with nets replaced the wooden baskets and the soccer balls were replaced with bigger balls. In the 1930s, ~~a lot of~~ new rules were added to the game. Basketball became more faster and more exciting.

[Unit 6 Research Report • REVISE] Writing Process **34**

▲ **Writing Transparency** WP34

WRITER'S CRAFT Paragraph

ELABORATION Explain to children that they should organize sentences about the same idea into a paragraph. Remind them that all the sentences in a paragraph must tell about this idea. Write the following paragraph on the board. Ask children to identify the sentence that does not belong.

> **Dad and I go to the park every Sunday afternoon. We play soccer with friends and relatives.** ~~Last Sunday it rained.~~ **Everyone gets tired and dirty, but we have fun.**

TIP Indent the first sentence in a paragraph. Think of that space as a signal to reader. It says, "A new idea begins here."

ADDITIONAL SUPPORT Point out how deleting the off-topic sentence improved the writing model on Writing Transparency WP34. Use Grammar and Writing Practice Book p. 182 to improve paragraphs.

APPLY WRITER'S CRAFT Have children examine paragraphs in their writing.

- Encourage them to look for and remove sentences that do not tell about the same idea as the other sentences in the paragraph.
- Write the Revising Checklist on the board or make copies to distribute. Children can use this checklist to revise their research reports.

Revising Checklist

- ✔ Does the report stick to the topic?
- ✔ Are the facts complete and accurate?
- ✔ Did I organize the facts into paragraphs?
- ✔ Do the sentences in each paragraph tell about the same idea?

Extend Language To help children find specific words to use in their reports, work with them to develop topical word webs that include vivid adjectives and strong verbs. Suggest that they look in bilingual or beginning dictionaries for possible words.

Writing Trait: Paragraph
- All the sentences in a paragraph must tell about the same idea.
- The sentences in a paragraph must be in an order that makes sense.
- One sentence in a paragraph gives the main idea, and the other sentences give details about the main idea.
- The first sentence of a paragraph is indented.

Read the sentences below. **Cross out** the sentence that does not tell about the same idea. **Write** the other sentences in the correct order to make a paragraph. **Indent** the first sentence.

> Chris swung her bat at the ball.
> She waited for the first pitch.
> Chris raced to first base.
> ~~Her team won five games.~~
> Whack! The bat hit the ball.
> It was Chris's turn to bat.

It was Chris's turn to bat. She waited for the first pitch. Chris swung her bat at the ball. Whack! The bat hit the ball. Chris raced to first base.

▲ **Grammar and Writing Practice Book** p. 182

EDITING STRATEGY

ONE THING AT A TIME Show children how to look first for spelling errors, next for missing capital letters, then for incorrect or missing punctuation, and finally for grammar errors as they proofread their work. Model this strategy using Writing Transparency WP35.

Think Aloud

MODEL This is another part of the research report on basketball. First, I'll look for spelling errors. The last sentence has a misspelled word. The writer has changed *Thayd* to the contraction *They'd*. Next, I'll look for missing capital letters. There are no missing capital letters. Next, I'll look for incorrect or missing punctuation. There should be a comma in the first sentence because it is a compound sentence. There should be quotation marks after *Naismith* in the last sentence. The writer has made both corrections. Finally, I'll look for grammar errors and other mistakes. The *more* in front of *faster* is incorrect and should be taken out. A new paragraph should begin with the fourth sentence.

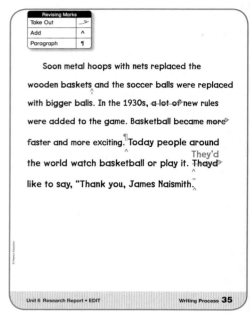

▲ **Writing Transparency** WP35

Write the Editing Checklist on the board or make copies to distribute. Children can use this checklist to edit their research reports.

Tech Talk ONLINE If children are using a computer to type their research reports, they may find these tips useful.

- Use a search engine to find information about your topic on the Internet. Make sure you get your facts from accurate, reliable sources, such as an encyclopedia or other reference book.

- If your work is more than a single page, you may wish to use the header or footer feature in the menu to include a page number.

Monitor Progress

Differentiated Instruction

If... children have trouble using commas in compound sentences,	then... review the grammar lesson on p. 377b.

Editing Checklist

- ✔ Did I spell words correctly, including contractions?

- ✔ Did I indent the first sentence in each paragraph?

- ✔ Does each sentence begin with a capital letter and end with a punctuation mark?

Support Writing When reviewing a child's draft, focus on ideas more than errors. If you find consistent spelling errors, choose one or two skills for attention during editing. Reinforce the skills with the appropriate Phonics Transition lessons in the ELL and Transition Handbook.

SELF-EVALUATION

Prepare children to fill out a Self-Evaluation Guide. Display Writing Transparency WP36 to model the self-evaluation process.

Think Aloud

MODEL I used facts in my paragraphs. Sentences in my paragraphs are arranged in order and are focused on the topic. I would mark *Yes* for numbers 1, 2, and 3. I like the sentence *Basketball became faster and more exciting.* If I could write the report again, I would tell which things made the game faster and more exciting.

Assign Grammar and Writing Practice Book p. 183. Children can save their Self-Evaluation Guides and their work in a portfolio to monitor their development as writers. Encourage them to build on their skills and note areas to improve.

Basketball

James Naismith was a PE teacher in Springfield, Massachusetts. In the winter, it was too cold and snowy for his students to play sports outside. Naismith needed a team sport that they could play inside. He took a soccer ball, hung two wooden baskets from a railing, and made up a new game. His PE students played the first basketball game in December 1891.

Soon metal hoops with nets replaced the wooden baskets, and the soccer balls were replaced with bigger balls. In the 1930s, new rules were added to the game. Basketball became faster and more exciting.

Today people around the world watch basketball or play it. They'd like to say, "Thank you, James Naismith."

Unit 6 Research Report • PUBLISH   Writing Process **36**

▲ **Writing Transparency** W36

Ideas for Publishing

Class Book Children can add illustrations to their reports and make a class book to put in the reading center.

Author's Chair Children can read their reports aloud in small groups. Encourage them to first explain why they chose their topic.

Self-Evaluation Guide

Check *Yes* or *No* about paragraphs in your research report.

	Yes	No
1. I organized my facts in paragraphs.		
2. The sentences in my paragraphs are in an order that makes sense.		
3. The sentences in each paragraph tell about the same idea.		

Answer the questions.

4. What is the best part of your research report?

Answers will vary.

5. What is one thing you would change about this research report if you could write it again?

Answers will vary.

▲ **Grammar and Writing Practice Book** p. 183

Scoring Rubric | Research Report

Rubric 4 3 2 1	4	3	2	1
Focus/Ideas	Research report well focused on topic with many accurate facts	Research report focused on topic with accurate facts	Research report mostly focused on topic with some accurate facts	Research report with no focus and few facts
Organization/ Paragraphs	Presents facts in clearly organized way	Presents facts in organized way	Presents facts in somewhat organized way	Little organization of facts
Voice	Shows strong grasp of topic; clear tone	Shows good grasp of topic; clear tone	Shows reasonable grasp of topic; tone uneven	No grasp of topic; no tone
Word Choice	Uses vivid, specific words	Uses some vivid, specific words	Uses few vivid, specific words	Dull word choice
Sentences	Complete, accurate sentences; variety of sentences	Complete, accurate sentences; some variety	Choppy sentences; little variety	Incomplete sentences; no variety
Conventions	Shows good understanding of writing conventions	Shows understanding of most writing conventions	Shows understanding of some writing conventions	Contains serious errors that may prevent understanding

For 6-, 5-, and 3-point Scoring Rubrics, see pp. WA13–WA16.

Writing Workshop

Research Report
Differentiated Instruction

WRITING PROMPT: Traditions

Think of a tradition that is important to your family, school, community, or country. It might be a game, holiday, symbol, or celebration. Write about the tradition and what makes it important. Find facts about its history in books or magazines or on the Internet.

Purpose: Inform

Audience: People who don't know about the tradition

Pick One

MODIFY INSTRUCTION

ALTERNATIVE PROMPTS

ALTERNATIVE PROMPT: Expository Writing

Strategic Intervention Think of something your family always does on a holiday or another special occasion. Draw a picture showing what your family does. Then write a paragraph that describes what is happening in the picture and why.

On-Level Imagine that you are nominating the tradition you chose for an award as Top Tradition. Focus on the question of why the tradition is important and support your answer with facts, examples, and reasons. Remember, you are competing against many other traditions, so build a strong argument for yours.

Advanced Write a research report about a tradition (food, celebration, game, clothing, music) in another country or culture that is new to you. Use three sources to find out about the tradition. Describe the tradition, tell about its history, and explain why people continue to follow it.

Strategic Intervention

MODIFY THE PROMPT

Help emerging writers choose a topic. Remind them that a tradition may be a food, celebration, game, type of clothing, or style of music. Have them use an encyclopedia, either print or electronic, to research the tradition they choose.

1 PREWRITE **2** DRAFT **3** REVISE **4** EDIT **5** PUBLISH

PREWRITING SUPPORT

- Allow more time for prewriting. Films, picture books, guest speakers, and Internet searches are some ways to create interest in research topics.

- Work with children to narrow their topics.

American Traditions

National Holidays

Thanksgiving

- Let children dictate to you what they want to say in their research reports. Take notes that they can use for their reports. Circle words that could supply a focus for each paragraph.

OPTIONS

- Give children the option of writing a group report under your supervision.

CHECK PROGRESS Segment the assignment into manageable pieces. Check work at intervals, such as graphic organizers and first drafts, to make sure writing is on track.

MODIFY THE PROMPT

Expect advanced writers to produce a complete research report with a clear focus on the topic and accurate facts that support the topic. They should organize the facts into paragraphs. Sentences in each paragraph should relate to the same idea and be in an order that makes sense. The research report should be 150–200 words and contain facts from two or three sources.

APPLY SKILLS

- As children revise their work, have them consider some ways to improve it.

    Check to see that the sentences in each paragraph tell about the same idea.

    Combine some short, choppy sentences to make compound sentences.

    Avoid wordiness by using as few words as possible to say what they want to say.

OPTIONS

- Work with children to create their own class rubrics. Follow these steps.

    1. Read examples of class research reports and rank them 1–4, with 4 the highest.

    2. Discuss how they arrived at each rank.

    3. Isolate the six traits and make a rubric based on them.

CHECK PROGRESS Discuss children's Self-Evaluation Guide. Work with children to monitor their growth and identify their strengths and weaknesses as writers.

MODIFY THE PROMPT

Have beginning speakers dictate their reports to you or to another proficient speaker to record. In the revising step, have children focus on one or two sentences in their reports that they can improve.

BUILD BACKGROUND

- Write the word *research* on the board. Remind children that research is searching for information about a topic. Point out that while a story can be made up, a research report should contain facts. Facts are statements that can be proven to be true. Discuss the list of Key Features of a research report that appears in the left column of p. WA2.

OPTIONS

- As children write their research reports, guide them toward books, magazines, or Web sites that provide comprehension support through features such as the following.

    detailed photographs or illustrations

    strong picture/text correspondence

- For more suggestions on scaffolding the Writing Workshop, see the ELL and Transition Handbook.

CHECK PROGRESS You may need to explain certain traits and help children fill out their Self-Evaluation Guides. Downplay conventions and focus more on ideas. Recognize examples of vocabulary growth and efforts to use language in more complex ways.

Scoring Rubric | Look Back and Write

2 points The response indicates that the student has a complete understanding of the reading concept embodied in the task. The response is accurate, complete, and fulfills all the requirements of the task. Necessary support and/or examples are included, and the information given is clearly text-based.

1 point The response indicates that the student has a partial understanding of the reading concept embodied in the task. The response includes information that is essentially correct and text-based, but the information is too general or too simplistic. Some of the support and/or examples may be incomplete or omitted.

0 points The response indicates that the student does not demonstrate an understanding of the reading concept embodied in the task. The student has either failed to respond or has provided a response that is inaccurate or has insufficient information.

Scoring Rubric | Look Back and Write

4 points The response indicates that the student has a thorough understanding of the reading concept embodied in the task. The response is accurate, complete, and fulfills all the requirements of the task. Necessary support and/or examples are included, and the information is clearly text-based.

3 points The response indicates that the student has an understanding of the reading concept embodied in the task. The response is accurate and fulfills all the requirements of the task, but the required support and/or details are not complete or clearly text-based.

2 points The response indicates that the student has a partial understanding of the reading concept embodied in the task. The response that includes information is essentially correct and text-based, but the information is too general or too simplistic. Some of the support and/or examples and requirements of the task may be incomplete or omitted.

1 point The response indicates that the student has a very limited understanding of the reading concept embodied in the task. The response is incomplete, may exhibit many flaws, and may not address all requirements of the task.

0 points The response indicates that the student does not demonstrate an understanding of the reading concept embodied in the task. The student has either failed to respond or has provided a response that is inaccurate or has insufficient information.

Writing Trait Rubric — Josh Gibson, pp. 320–321

	4	3	2	1
Sentence	Clear, interesting, unique sentences	Clear sentences	Some sentences clear	Most sentences unclear
	Exceptional sentence variety in facts	Some sentence variety in facts	Needs more sentence variety in facts	Little or no sentence variety in facts

Writing Trait Rubric — Red, White, and Blue, pp. 348–349

	4	3	2	1
Conventions	Excellent control of grammar, capitalization, and punctuation	Good control of grammar, capitalization, and punctuation	Limited control of grammar, capitalization, and punctuation	Poor control of grammar, capitalization, and punctuation
	No errors or only minor errors in answers	No serious errors in answers that affect understanding	Few distracting errors in answers	Many errors in answers that affect understanding

Writing Trait Rubric — Birthday Basket for Tía, pp. 374–375

	4	3	2	1
Organization/ Paragraphs	Ideas well developed from beginning to end; strong closure	Ideas that progress from beginning to end; good closure	Some sense of movement from beginning to end; weak closure	No sense of movement from beginning to end or closure
	Report organized with exceptional logic	Report organized adequately	Report not clearly organized	Report not organized

Writing Trait Rubric — *Cowboys,* pp. 406–407

	4	3	2	1
Sentences	Clear, interesting, unique sentences	Clear sentences	Some sentences clear	Most sentences unclear
	Exceptional sentence variety in news report	Some sentence variety in news report	Needs more sentence variety in news report	Little or no sentence variety in news report

Writing Trait Rubric — *Jingle Dancer,* pp. 432–433

	4	3	2	1
Organization/ Paragraphs	Excellent main idea sentence; many vivid supporting details	Good main idea sentence; good supporting details	Adequate main idea sentence; some supporting details	No main idea sentence; few supporting details
	Story organized with exceptional logic	Story organized adequately	Story not clearly organized	Story not organized

Scoring Rubric — Narrative Writing

	6	5	4	3	2	1
Focus/Ideas	Excellent, focused narrative; well elaborated with quality details	Good, focused narrative; elaborated with telling details	Narrative focused; adequate elaboration	Generally focused narrative; some supporting details	Sometimes unfocused narrative; needs more supporting details	Rambling narrative; lacks development and detail
Organization/ Paragraphs	Strong beginning, middle, and end; appropriate order words	Coherent beginning, middle, and end; some order words	Beginning, middle, and end easily identifiable	Recognizable beginning, middle, and end; some order words	Little direction from beginning to end; few order words	Lacks beginning, middle, end; incorrect or no order words
Voice	Writer closely involved; engaging personality	Reveals personality	Pleasant but not compelling voice	Sincere voice but not fully engaged	Little writer involvement, personality	Careless writing with no feeling
Word Choice	Vivid, precise words that bring story to life	Clear words to bring story to life	Some specific word pictures	Language adequate but lacks color	Generally limited or redundant language	Vague, dull, or misused words
Sentences	Excellent variety of sentences; natural rhythm	Varied lengths, styles; generally smooth	Correct sentences with some variations in style	Correctly constructed sentences; some variety	May have simple, awkward, or wordy sentences; little variety	Choppy; many incomplete or run-on sentences
Conventions	Excellent control; few or no errors	No serious errors to affect understanding	General mastery of conventions but some errors	Reasonable control; few distracting errors	Weak control; enough errors to affect understanding	Many errors that prevent understanding

Scoring Rubric — Narrative Writing

	5	4	3	2	1
Focus/Ideas	Excellent, focused narrative; well elaborated with quality details	Good, focused narrative; elaborated with telling details	Generally focused narrative; some supporting details	Sometimes unfocused narrative; needs more supporting details	Rambling narrative; lacks development and detail
Organization/ Paragraphs	Strong beginning, middle, and end; appropriate order words	Coherent beginning, middle, and end; some order words	Recognizable beginning, middle, and end; some order words	Little direction from beginning to end; few order words	Lacks beginning, middle, end; incorrect or no order words
Voice	Writer closely involved; engaging personality	Reveals personality	Sincere voice but not fully engaged	Little writer involvement, personality	Careless writing with no feeling
Word Choice	Vivid, precise words that bring story to life	Clear words to bring story to life	Language adequate but lacks color	Generally limited or redundant language	Vague, dull, or misused words
Sentences	Excellent variety of sentences; natural rhythm	Varied lengths, styles; generally smooth	Correctly constructed sentences; some variety	May have simple, awkward, or wordy sentences; little variety	Choppy; many incomplete or run-on sentences
Conventions	Excellent control; few or no errors	No serious errors to affect understanding	Reasonable control; few distracting errors	Weak control; enough errors to affect understanding	Many errors that prevent understanding

Scoring Rubric — Narrative Writing

	3	2	1
Focus/Ideas	Excellent, focused narrative; well elaborated with quality details	Generally focused narrative; some supporting details	Rambling narrative; lacks development and detail
Organization/ Paragraphs	Strong beginning, middle, and end; appropriate order words	Recognizable beginning, middle, and end; some order words	Lacks beginning, middle, end; incorrect or no order words
Voice	Writer closely involved; engaging personality	Sincere voice but not fully engaged	Careless writing with no feeling
Word Choice	Vivid, precise words that bring story to life	Language adequate but lacks color	Vague, dull, or misused words
Sentences	Excellent variety of sentences; natural rhythm	Correctly constructed sentences; some variety	Choppy; many incomplete or run-on sentences
Conventions	Excellent control; few or no errors	Reasonable control; few distracting errors	Many errors that prevent understanding

Scoring Rubric — Descriptive Writing

	6	5	4	3	2	1
Focus/Ideas	Excellent, focused description; well elaborated with quality details	Good, focused description; elaborated with telling details	Description focused; good elaboration	Generally focused description; some supporting details	Sometimes unfocused description; needs more supporting details	Rambling description; lacks development and detail
Organization/ Paragraphs	Compelling ideas enhanced by order, structure, and transitions	Appealing order, structure, and transitions	Structure identifiable and suitable; transitions used	Adequate order, structure, and some transitions to guide reader	Little direction from beginning to end; few transitions	Lacks direction and identifiable structure; no transitions
Voice	Writer closely involved; engaging personality	Reveals personality	Pleasant but not compelling voice	Sincere voice but not fully engaged	Little writer involvement, personality	Careless writing with no feeling
Word Choice	Vivid, precise words that create memorable pictures	Clear, interesting words to bring description to life	Some specific word pictures	Language adequate; appeals to senses	Generally limited or redundant language	Vague, dull, or misused words
Sentences	Excellent variety of sentences; natural rhythm	Varied lengths, styles; generally smooth	Correct sentences with variations in style	Correctly constructed sentences; some variety	May have simple, awkward, or wordy sentences; little variety	Choppy; many incomplete run-on sentences
Conventions	Excellent control; few or no errors	No serious errors to affect understanding	General mastery of conventions but some errors	Reasonable control; few distracting errors	Weak control; enough errors to affect understanding	Many errors that prevent understanding

Scoring Rubric — Descriptive Writing

	5	4	3	2	1
Focus/Ideas	Excellent, focused description; well elaborated with quality details	Good, focused description; elaborated with telling details	Generally focused description; some supporting details	Sometimes unfocused description; needs more supporting details	Rambling description; lacks development and detail
Organization/ Paragraphs	Compelling ideas enhanced by order, structure, and transitions	Appealing order, structure, and transitions	Adequate order, structure, and some transitions to guide reader	Little direction from beginning to end; few transitions	Lacks direction and identifiable structure; no transitions
Voice	Writer closely involved; engaging personality	Reveals personality	Sincere voice but not fully engaged	Little writer involvement, personality	Careless writing with no feeling
Word Choice	Vivid, precise words that create memorable pictures	Clear, interesting words to bring description to life	Language adequate; appeals to senses	Generally limited or redundant language	Vague, dull, or misused words
Sentences	Excellent variety of sentences; natural rhythm	Varied lengths, styles; generally smooth	Correctly constructed sentences; some variety	May have simple, awkward, or wordy sentences; little variety	Choppy; many incomplete or run-on sentences
Conventions	Excellent control; few or no errors	No serious errors to affect understanding	Reasonable control; few distracting errors	Weak control; enough errors to affect understanding	Many errors that prevent understanding

Scoring Rubric — Descriptive Writing

	3	2	1
Focus/Ideas	Excellent, focused description; well elaborated with quality details	Generally focused description; some supporting details	Rambling description; lacks development and detail
Organization/ Paragraphs	Compelling ideas enhanced by order, structure, and transitions	Adequate order, structure, and some transitions to guide reader	Lacks direction and identifiable structure; no transitions
Voice	Writer closely involved; engaging personality	Sincere voice but not fully engaged	Careless writing with no feeling
Word Choice	Vivid, precise words that create memorable pictures	Language adequate; appeals to senses	Vague, dull, or misused words
Sentences	Excellent variety of sentences; natural rhythm	Correctly constructed sentences; some variety	Choppy; many incomplete or run-on sentences
Conventions	Excellent control; few or no errors	Reasonable control; few distracting errors	Many errors that prevent understanding

Scoring Rubric — Persuasive Writing

	6	5	4	3	2	1
Focus/Ideas	Persuasive argument carefully built with quality details	Persuasive argument well supported with details	Persuasive argument focused; good elaboration	Persuasive argument with one or two convincing details	Persuasive piece sometimes unfocused; needs more support	Rambling persuasive argument; lacks development and detail
Organization/ Paragraphs	Information chosen and arranged for maximum effect	Evident progression of persuasive ideas	Progression and structure evident	Information arranged in a logical way with some lapses	Little structure or direction	No identifiable structure
Voice	Writer closely involved; persuasive but not overbearing	Maintains persuasive tone	Persuasive but not compelling voice	Sometimes uses persuasive voice	Little writer involvement, personality	Shows little conviction
Word Choice	Persuasive words carefully chosen for impact	Argument supported by persuasive language	Uses some persuasive words	Occasional persuasive language	Generally limited or redundant language	Vague, dull, or misused words; no persuasive words
Sentences	Excellent variety of sentences; natural rhythm	Varied lengths, styles; generally smooth	Correct sentences with variations in style	Carefully constructed sentences; some variety	Simple, awkward, or wordy sentences; little variety	Choppy; many incomplete or run-on sentences
Conventions	Excellent control; few or no errors	No serious errors to affect understanding	General mastery of conventions but some errors	Reasonable control; few distracting errors	Weak control; enough errors to affect understanding	Many errors that prevent understanding

Scoring Rubric — Persuasive Writing

	5	4	3	2	1
Focus/Ideas	Persuasive argument carefully built with quality details	Persuasive argument well supported with details	Persuasive argument with one or two convincing details	Persuasive piece sometimes unfocused; needs more support	Rambling persuasive argument; lacks development and detail
Organization/ Paragraphs	Information chosen and arranged for maximum effect	Evident progression of persuasive ideas	Information arranged in a logical way with some lapses	Little structure or direction	No identifiable structure
Voice	Writer closely involved; persuasive but not overbearing	Maintains persuasive tone	Sometimes uses persuasive voice	Little writer involvement, personality	Shows little conviction
Word Choice	Persuasive words carefully chosen for impact	Argument supported by persuasive language	Occasional persuasive language	Generally limited or redundant language	Vague, dull, or misused words; no persuasive words
Sentences	Excellent variety of sentences; natural rhythm	Varied lengths, styles; generally smooth	Carefully constructed sentences; some variety	Simple, awkward, or wordy sentences; little variety	Choppy; many incomplete or run-on sentences
Conventions	Excellent control; few or no errors	No serious errors to affect understanding	Reasonable control; few distracting errors	Weak control; enough errors to affect understanding	Many errors that prevent understanding

Scoring Rubric — Persuasive Writing

	3	2	1
Focus/Ideas	Persuasive argument carefully built with quality details	Persuasive argument with one or two convincing details	Rambling persuasive argument; lacks development and detail
Organization/ Paragraphs	Information chosen and arranged for maximum effect	Information arranged in a logical way with some lapses	No identifiable structure
Voice	Writer closely involved; persuasive but not overbearing	Sometimes uses persuasive voice	Shows little conviction
Word Choice	Persuasive words carefully chosen for impact	Occasional persuasive language	Vague, dull, or misused words; no persuasive words
Sentences	Excellent variety of sentences; natural rhythm	Carefully constructed sentences; some variety	Choppy; many incomplete or run-on sentences
Conventions	Excellent control; few or no errors	Reasonable control; few distracting errors	Many errors that prevent understanding

Scoring Rubric — Expository Writing

	6	5	4	3	2	1
Focus/Ideas	Insightful, focused exposition; well elaborated with quality details	Informed, focused exposition; elaborated with telling details	Exposition focused, good elaboration	Generally focused exposition; some supporting details	Sometimes unfocused exposition needs more supporting details	Rambling exposition; lacks development and detail
Organization/ Paragraphs	Logical, consistent flow of ideas; good transitions	Logical sequencing of ideas; uses transitions	Ideas sequenced with some transitions	Sequenced ideas with some transitions	Little direction from beginning to end; few order words	Lacks structure and transitions
Voice	Writer closely involved; informative voice well suited to topic	Reveals personality; voice suited to topic	Pleasant but not compelling voice	Sincere voice suited to topic	Little writer involvement, personality	Careless writing with no feeling
Word Choice	Vivid, precise words to express ideas	Clear words to express ideas	Words correct and adequate	Language adequate but may lack precision	Generally limited or redundant language	Vague, dull, or misused words
Sentences	Strong topic sentence; fluent, varied structures	Good topic sentence; smooth sentence structure	Correct sentences that are sometimes fluent	Topic sentence correctly constructed; some sentence variety	Topic sentence unclear or missing; wordy, awkward sentences	No topic sentence; many incomplete or run-on sentences
Conventions	Excellent control; few or no errors	No serious errors to affect understanding	General mastery of conventions but some errors	Reasonable control; few distracting errors	Weak control; enough errors to affect understanding	Many errors that prevent understanding

Scoring Rubric — Expository Writing

	5	4	3	2	1
Focus/Ideas	Insightful, focused exposition; well elaborated with quality details	Informed, focused exposition; elaborated with telling details	Generally focused exposition; some supporting details	Sometimes unfocused exposition needs more supporting details	Rambling exposition; lacks development and detail
Organization/ Paragraphs	Logical, consistent flow of ideas; good transitions	Logical sequencing of ideas; uses transitions	Sequenced ideas with some transitions	Little direction from beginning to end; few order words	Lacks structure and transitions
Voice	Writer closely involved; informative voice well suited to topic	Reveals personality; voice suited to topic	Language adequate but may lack precision	Little writer involvement, personality	Careless writing with no feeling
Word Choice	Vivid, precise words to express ideas	Clear words to express ideas	Topic sentence correctly constructed; some sentence variety	Generally limited or redundant language	Vague, dull, or misused words
Sentences	Strong topic sentence; fluent, varied structures	Good topic sentence; smooth sentence structure	Sincere voice suited to topic	Topic sentence unclear or missing; wordy, awkward sentences	No topic sentence; many incomplete or run-on sentences
Conventions	Excellent control; few or no errors	No serious errors to affect understanding	Reasonable control; few distracting errors	Weak control; enough errors to affect understanding	Many errors that prevent understanding

Scoring Rubric — Expository Writing

	3	2	1
Focus/Ideas	Insightful, focused exposition; well elaborated with quality details	Generally focused exposition; some supporting details	Rambling exposition; lacks development and detail
Organization/ Paragraphs	Logical, consistent flow of ideas; good transitions	Sequenced ideas with some transitions	Lacks structure and transitions
Voice	Writer closely involved; informative voice well suited to topic	Sincere voice suited to topic	Careless writing with no feeling
Word Choice	Vivid, precise words to express ideas	Language adequate but may lack precision	Vague, dull, or misused words
Sentences	Strong topic sentence; fluent, varied structures	Topic sentence correctly constructed; some sentence variety	No topic sentence; many incomplete or run-on sentences
Conventions	Excellent control; few or no errors	Reasonable control; few distracting errors	Many errors that prevent understanding

Unit 6
Monitoring Fluency

Ongoing assessment of a child's reading fluency is one of the most valuable measures we have of children's reading skills. One of the most effective ways to assess fluency is taking timed samples of children's oral reading and measuring the number of words correct per minute (wcpm).

How to Measure Words Correct Per Minute—wcpm

Choose a Text
Start by choosing a text for the child to read. The text should be:
- narrative
- unfamiliar
- on grade level

Make a copy of the text for yourself and have one for the child.

Timed Reading of the Text
Tell the child: As you read this aloud, I want you to do your best reading and to read as quickly as you can. That doesn't mean it's a race. Just do your best, fast reading. When I say begin, start reading.

As the child reads, follow along in your copy. Mark words that are read incorrectly.

Incorrect	Correct
• omissions	• self-corrections within 3 seconds
• substitutions	• repeated words
• mispronunciations	
• reversals	

After One Minute
At the end of one minute, draw a line after the last word that was read. Have the child finish reading but don't count any words beyond one minute. Arrive at the words correct per minute—wcpm—by counting the total number of words that the child read correctly in one minute.

Fluency Goals
Grade 2 End-of-Year Goal = 90 wcpm

Target goals by unit

Unit 1 50 to 60 wcpm	**Unit 4** 74 to 84 wcpm
Unit 2 58 to 68 wcpm	**Unit 5** 82 to 92 wcpm
Unit 3 66 to 76 wcpm	**Unit 6** 90 to 100 wcpm

More Frequent Monitoring
You may want to monitor some children more frequently because they are falling far below grade-level benchmarks or they have a result that doesn't seem to align with their previous performance. Follow the same steps above, but choose 2 or 3 additional texts.

Fluency Progress Chart Copy the chart on the next page. Use it to record each child's progress across the year.

Fluency Progress Chart, Grade 2

Name _____

WCPM

	1	2	3	4	5	6	7	8	9	10	11	12	13	14	15	16	17	18	19	20	21	22	23	24	25	26	27	28	29	30
125																														
120																														
115																														
110																														
105																														
100																														
95																														
90																														
85																														
80																														
75																														
70																														
65																														
60																														
55																														
50																														
45																														
40																														
35																														
30																														

Timed Reading

Sentence Reading Chart

Unit 6

	Phonics		Lesson Vocabulary		Reteach ✓	Reassess: Words Correct
	Total Words	Words Correct	Total Words	Words Correct		
Week 1 *Just Like Josh Gibson* A B C						
Contractions *'re, 've, 'd*	4					
Lesson Vocabulary			2			
Week 2 *Red, White and Blue: The Story of the American Flag* A B C						
Base Words and Endings	4					
Lesson Vocabulary			2			
Week 3 *A Birthday Basket for Tía* A B C						
Syllables *-tion, -ture*	4					
Lesson Vocabulary			2			
Week 4 *Cowboys* A B C						
Suffixes *-ness, -less*	4					
Lesson Vocabulary			2			
Week 5 *Jingle Dancer* A B C						
Prefixes *mis-, mid-*	4					
Lesson Vocabulary			2			
Unit Scores	20		10			

- **RECORD SCORES** Use this chart to record scores for the Day 5 Sentence Reading Assessment. Circle A, B, or C to record which set of sentences was used.
- **RETEACH PHONICS SKILLS** If the child is unable to read all the tested phonics words, then reteach the phonics skills using the Reteach lessons on pp. DI·64–DI·68.

- **PRACTICE LESSON VOCABULARY** If the child is unable to read all the tested high-frequency words, then provide additional practice for the week's words. See pp. 320e, 348e, 374e, 406e, and 432e.
- **REASSESS** Use the same set of sentences or an easier set for reassessment.

Unit 6
Assess and Regroup

FYI In Grade 2 there are opportunities for regrouping every five weeks—at the end of Units 2, 3, 4, and 5. These options offer sensitivity to each child's progress although some teachers may prefer to regroup less frequently.

End-of-Year Performance

There is no need to regroup at the end of Unit 6. To assess children's end-of-year performance, consider their scores for

- Unit 6 Sentence Reading (Day 5 Assessments)
- Fluency (WCPM)
- Unit 6 Benchmark Test

Group Time

On-Level	Strategic Intervention	Advanced
Children's performance is On-Level if they	**Children's performance is below level if they**	**Children's performance is advanced if they**
• score 80% or better on their cumulative Unit Scores for Sentence Reading for phonics and lesson vocabulary	• score 60% or lower on their cumulative Unit Scores for Sentence Reading for phonics and lesson vocabulary, regardless of their fluency scores	• score 100% on their cumulative Unit Scores for Sentence Reading for phonics and lesson vocabulary
• meet the current benchmark for fluency (90–100 WCPM), reading On-Level text such as Student Edition selections	• do not meet the current benchmark for fluency (90–100 WCPM)	• score 95% on the Unit 6 Benchmark Test
• score 80% or better on the Unit 6 Benchmark Test	• score below 80% on their cumulative Unit Scores for Sentence Reading for phonics and lesson vocabulary AND have fluency scores below the current benchmark of 90–100 WCPM	• read above grade-level material (90–100 WCPM) with speed, accuracy, and expression. You may try them out on one of the Advanced Selections.
• are capable of working in the On-Level group based on teacher judgment	• score below 60% on the Unit 6 Benchmark Test	• use expansive vocabulary and ease of language in retelling
	• are struggling to keep up with the On-Level group based on teacher judgment	• are capable of handling the problem solving and the investigative work of the Advanced group based on teacher judgment

QUESTIONS TO CONSIDER

- What types of test questions did the child miss? Are they specific to a particular skill or strategy?
- Does the child have adequate background knowledge to understand the test passages or selections for retelling?
- Has the child's performance met expectations for daily lessons and assessments with little or no reteaching?
- Is the child performing more like children in another group?
- Does the child read for enjoyment, different purposes, and with varied interests?

Benchmark Fluency Scores

Current Goal: 90–100 WCPM

End-of-Year Goal: 90 WCPM

Unit Scores for Sentence Reading

Phonics	Lesson Vocabulary
100% = **20**	100% = **10**
80% = **16**	80% = **8**
60% = **12**	60% = **6**

Leveled Readers

Table of Contents

Three of the Greats

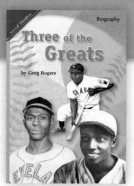

COMPARE AND CONTRAST

VISUALIZE

LESSON VOCABULARY bases, cheers, field, plate, sailed, threw

SUMMARY This nonfiction book explores the lives and careers of three great African American baseball players.

INTRODUCE THE BOOK

BUILD BACKGROUND Engage children in a discussion of baseball. Have them share what they know about the sport as well as their experiences playing or watching the game. Ask: What happens during a baseball game? Who are some of your favorite baseball players?

PREVIEW/TAKE A PICTURE WALK Have children preview the book, looking at the photographs. Call special attention to the photographs on pages 6, 7 and 11. Point out the labels on the photographs and help children say the names of these players. Ask: What do you think these three men have to do with this book?

TEACH/REVIEW VOCABULARY Say each of the vocabulary words aloud with the children and discuss the definitions. Ask children what they think these words have in common. Remind children of your discussion about baseball and use these words in context as you describe the sights and sounds of a baseball game.

ELL Use photographs or pantomime to help children understand the meanings of the vocabulary words.

TARGET SKILL AND STRATEGY

COMPARE AND CONTRAST Explain to children what it means to *compare* and *contrast*. As you read about Satchel Paige and James Bell, encourage children to describe ways in which these men were the same and different. Use a Venn Diagram to help children organize their ideas.

VISUALIZE Prior to reading, prompt children to form pictures in their minds using what they already know about baseball. Have them picture their favorite teams or players and encourage children to describe what they see.

READ THE BOOK

Use the following questions to support comprehension.

PAGE 3 How was baseball in the past different from today? *(African American players were not allowed to play in the major leagues. They played in separate baseball leagues called the Negro leagues.)*

PAGE 4 Why were African American baseball players not allowed to join the major leagues? *(because of their skin color)*

PAGE 12 How have Satchel Paige, James Bell, and Josh Gibson been honored for their skill? *(They have been included in the Baseball Hall of Fame)*

TALK ABOUT THE BOOK

READER RESPONSE

1. Responses should include that today, African American players play in the major leagues but in the past they played in the Negro leagues. Use the chart to organize ideas.
2. Reponses should reflect James Bell's speed.
3. Answers may vary but should reflect comprehension of word meaning in the context of baseball.
4. Responses may vary, but should include that these were skilled players who made the game of baseball exciting.

RESPONSE OPTIONS

WRITING Provide children with more information about other important and famous baseball players, of any races, both past and present. Have each child choose one baseball player to study and gather information from books as well as the Internet.

CONTENT CONNECTIONS

SOCIAL STUDIES Tell children that baseball is called the "Great American Pastime" and ask them to share why they think the sport is referred to in this way.

Time for SOCIAL STUDIES

Name _____

Compare and Contrast

In the book *Three of the Greats*, you learned about Satchel Paige and Josh Gibson. Compare and contrast these baseball players. Use the chart below to organize the facts. Write two facts for each player. Then, write one fact that they share.

Satchel Paige	Both	Josh Gibson

114

Name _____

Vocabulary

Choose a word from the box to complete the following story about baseball. Write the word on the line. The first one has been done for you.

Words to Know
bases   cheers   field   plate   sailed   threw

Playing baseball is a lot of fun, but I was nervous when

I got up to the _____ **plate** _____. The pitcher

_____ the ball. I hit it as hard as I could.

The ball _____ high through the air. It

landed far out in the _____. I ran around

the _____ as fast as I could. I heard loud

_____ from the crowd. I scored a home run!

© Pearson Education 2

115

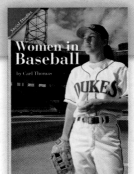

Women in Baseball

👁 **COMPARE AND CONTRAST**

👁 **VISUALIZE**

LESSON VOCABULARY athlete, bases, cheers, field, plate, sailed, threw

---

SUMMARY This nonfiction book explores the history of women in baseball, from the late 1800s to present day.

INTRODUCE THE BOOK

BUILD BACKGROUND Engage children in a discussion of baseball. Ask: Who are some of your favorite baseball players? Do you know of any women baseball players?

PREVIEW/TAKE A PICTURE WALK Have the children preview the book, looking at the pictures. Point out the photographs on pages 4–5 and 8–9. Ask: Who or what do you think these groups of women are? Why are they wearing uniforms?

TEACH/REVIEW VOCABULARY Have children practice looking up the definitions of the vocabulary words in the glossary and then write the words and definitions on their own papers. For extra practice, help children think of and write short sentences using the words.

TARGET SKILL AND STRATEGY

👁 **COMPARE AND CONTRAST** Remind the children what it means to *compare* and *contrast.* Then turn to page 9 and look at the uniforms the women are wearing. Have children describe how these uniforms are similar to and different from baseball uniforms today.

👁 **VISUALIZE** Prior to reading, prompt children to form pictures in their minds using what they already know about baseball. Encourage children to describe what they see. Read the first sentence of the book and ask: What pictures do you see in your mind when you think of baseball?

ELL Allow children to describe their mental pictures in their native languages.

READ THE BOOK

Use the following questions to support comprehension.

PAGE 3 How long have women been playing baseball? *(more than 100 years)*

PAGE 5 Why was the All-American Girls Professional Baseball League started in 1943? *(because many men went off to war, and most women did not go)*

PAGE 15 The author says that baseball is not just for boys and men. How do we know this? *(Responses will vary, but should include information from the text. Women have been playing baseball for a long time, and there are many examples of women involved in this sport.)*

TALK ABOUT THE BOOK

READER RESPONSE

1. Prior to 1948 women's baseball was getting increasingly popular and the AAGPBL was formed; after 1948 attendance dropped and the league soon ended. Girls and women continue to play baseball and softball.

2. Possible response: images of large numbers of fans and cheering

3. Possible response: moved quickly

4. Many men went off to war, and women began to play professional baseball.

RESPONSE OPTIONS

WRITING Have children make a time line of the events surrounding women in baseball using the information provided in the text. Help children gather this information from the text and show them how to organize the dates along their time lines. Guide them in using the book to write a short sentence or two for each date. Children can then illustrate their time lines.

CONTENT CONNECTIONS

Time for **SOCIAL STUDIES**

SOCIAL STUDIES Provide children with additional information on women in sports. Encourage them to use the library or the Internet to research women's involvement in other sports that interest them. Then have children share the information with the rest of the class.

Name _____

Compare and Contrast

Use the chart below to compare and contrast baseball with another sport, like basketball, soccer, or football. Write the name of the sport you choose on the line provided.

Baseball	Both	_____

114

Name _____

Vocabulary

Pretend that you are playing baseball. Write a short story using each of the words in the word box once. The story has been started for you.

> ### Words to Know
>
> athlete bases cheers field plate sailed threw

When I first got to the game, I heard all of the loud

_____

_____ from the crowd.

_____

_____

_____

_____

_____

_____

_____

_____

_____

_____

_____

_____

_____

_____

_____

115

Baseball Heroes

↻ **COMPARE AND CONTRAST**

↻ **VISUALIZE**

LESSON VOCABULARY athletes, banned, challenges, effort, prejudice, record, rookie, talented

---

SUMMARY This biography highlights the baseball careers of Jackie Robinson, Willie Mays, and Hank Aaron.

INTRODUCE THE BOOK

BUILD BACKGROUND Invite children to discuss their own heroes. Remind them that a hero might be a sports or other public figure, but could also be a friend or family member from their own lives. Ask: What things do heroes do that make us admire them? Why is your hero special to you?

PREVIEW/USE TEXT FEATURES Have children preview the book, looking at the photographs and other features in the book. Call specific attention to the table of contents and have children read the names of the chapters. Ask: Who or what do you think each chapter will be about?

TEACH/REVIEW VOCABULARY Ask children to practice looking up the vocabulary words in the glossary at the back of the book. Have children write the words on their own papers and help them think of sentences using each word.

ELL Have children share information about heroes in their home countries. Why are these people heroes?

TARGET SKILL AND STRATEGY

↻ **COMPARE AND CONTRAST** As you read, help children take notes on each of the baseball players. Once you have gathered this information, remind children what it means to *compare* and *contrast*. Create a Venn Diagram with three intersecting circles to organize the similarities and differences between the three players discussed in the book.

↻ **VISUALIZE** Remind the children that they can form pictures in their heads to better understand the information in the book as they read. Pause after reading page 12 and have children create pictures in their minds as you reread the first two paragraphs on the page.

READ THE BOOK

Use the following questions to support comprehension.

PAGES 4–5 Why were African American players banned from professional major league baseball? What is this called? *(They were black. prejudice)*

PAGE 12 Why do you think Willie Mays won so many awards during his career? *(Responses will vary: He was a talented player, made excellent plays, played so many years.)*

TALK ABOUT THE BOOK

READER RESPONSE

1. Major leagues used to be all white; players were paid better than in the Negro leagues; the Negro leagues were for African American players; players were not paid as well; many Negro league players were just as talented as major league players; the Negro leagues ended but the major leagues continue.

2. Responses will vary, but should include descriptions of Willie Mays catching the ball with his bare hand.

3. skillful, able to do something very well; Responses will vary.

4. Answers will vary.

RESPONSE OPTIONS

WRITING Have children write a news article about one of the famous plays or games of Jackie Robinson, Willie May, or Hank Aaron as described in the book. Encourage them to use descriptive language and to create interesting headlines for their articles.

CONTENT CONNECTIONS

SOCIAL STUDIES Work with children to research other important African American figures in sports, music, or literature. Discuss these people's challenges as well as their accomplishments, and create a bulletin board to share this information.

Time for SOCIAL STUDIES

Name _____

Compare and Contrast

In the book *Baseball Heroes*, you learned about Jackie Robinson and Hank Aaron. Compare and contrast these two baseball players. Use the chart below to organize the facts. Write two facts for each player. Then list one fact that they share.

Jackie Robinson	Both	Hank Aaron

114

Name _____

Vocabulary

Write the word from the box next to its meaning.

Words to Know
athletes   banned   challenges   effort
prejudice   record   rookie   talented

1. _____   *n.* player in his or her first year of professional athletics; beginner

2. _____   *n.* difficulties

3. _____   *adj.* skillful; able to do something very well

4. _____   *n.* a hard try

5. _____   *v.* forbidden by law

6. _____   *n.* the best number, rate, or speed yet reached

7. _____   *n.* people trained in sports

8. _____   *n.* an unreasonable dislike of a group of people

115

Happy Birthday, America!

Happy Birthday, ★★
★★★America!
by Vita Richman

◎ **FACT AND OPINION**

◎ **MONITOR AND FIX UP**

LESSON VOCABULARY America, birthday, flag, freedom, nicknames, stars, stripes

SUMMARY This informational text describes how people in the United States celebrate the Fourth of July. By showing the connection of the nation's flag to the holiday, the book supports and extends the lesson concept of the meaning of the American flag.

INTRODUCE THE BOOK

BUILD BACKGROUND Show children a large calendar page for July, and circle July 4. Say it for the class, and ask children what comes to mind when they think of it.

PREVIEW/TAKE A PICTURE WALK Invite children to take a picture walk through the book. Encourage them to call out any ideas that the pictures evoke.

TEACH/REVIEW VOCABULARY Write the word *birthday* on the board, and ask a volunteer to explain its meaning in his or her own words. Repeat the activity for the remaining vocabulary words.

ⒺⓁⓁ Make a set of vocabulary word cards. Ask children to sort the cards by the number of syllables in each word.

TARGET SKILL AND STRATEGY

◎ **FACT AND OPINION** Remind children that a statement of *fact* can be proved true or false, while a statement of *opinion* cannot. Have children read the first sentence on page 11. Explain that this is a statement of fact because it can be proved true or false. Point out that the next two sentences are examples that help prove that the statement is true.

◎ **MONITOR AND FIX UP** Suggest that the children ask themselves questions as they read. *What does this section mean? Does this make sense?* Remind them that they can reread parts of the book that they do not, at first, understand. Have children read the last sentence on page 12, and suggest that they reread page 4 to help them remember.

READ THE BOOK

Use the following questions to support comprehension.

PAGE 6 Is the first sentence on the page a statement of fact or opinion? Why? *(It is a statement of fact because it can be proved true or false.)*

PAGE 7 Is Uncle Sam a real person? *(No, he is a symbol. People dress up as this symbol.)*

PAGE 9 Why do people wave flags when they watch a parade on the Fourth of July? *(Waving a flag shows you are proud and happy to be an American.)*

TALK ABOUT THE BOOK

READER RESPONSE

1. Possible response: He is a "good" symbol is an opinion.
2. Possible responses: symbol of America; Philadelphia; Independence Hall; made in 1752; cracked; last rang in 1846; still has a crack
3. Possible response: Our flag's design is made up of stars and stripes.
4. Possible response: It explains that Uncle Sam is sometimes shown as a cartoon.

RESPONSE OPTIONS

WRITING Invite children to think about ways to celebrate the Fourth of July. Encourage children to write a few sentences to tell about their ideas. You might suggest a sentence starter, such as: "On the Fourth of July, we _____."

CONTENT CONNECTIONS

Time for
SOCIAL
STUDIES

SOCIAL STUDIES Help children research how their community celebrates the Fourth of July. Encourage children to make posters that inform others about the community's festivities.

Name _____

Fact and Opinion

Each sentence below is a statement of opinion. **Rewrite** them so it is a statement of fact. The first one has been done for you.

1. Opinion: The American flag is a terrific symbol.
Fact:

_____

The American flag is a symbol.

2. Opinion: The Fourth of July is the most important holiday.
Fact:

_____

_____

3. Opinion: Uncle Sam is a funny American symbol.
Fact:

_____

_____

4. Opinion: The Liberty Bell rang loudly on July 4, 1776.
Fact:

_____

_____

5. Opinion: After a parade, some people should have a barbecue.
Fact:

_____

_____

© Pearson Education 2

118

Name _____

Vocabulary

Read each word.

Draw a line to the picture that best shows the meaning of the word.

1. flag

a.

2. stripes

b.

3. America

c.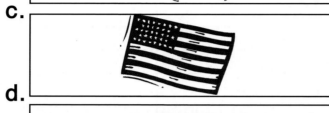

4. stars

d.

Read each sentence. Write a word from the box that best fits each sentence.

birthday   freedom   nicknames

_____

5. The Stars and Stripes is one of the _____ for the American flag.

_____

6. July 4 is America's _____ .

_____

7. America gained its _____ from England many years ago.

119

Red, White and Blue
On-Level Reader

Heroes of the
American Biography
Revolution

Unit 6 Week 2

Heroes of the American . . .

SUMMARY Many people helped the United States gain its independence from Britain. Four such people were Benjamin Franklin, George Washington, Margaret Corbin, and Dicey Langston.

INTRODUCE THE BOOK

BUILD BACKGROUND Explain that the American Revolution led to the United States becoming an independent country—free from English rule. Encourage children to share what they know about the American Revolution.

PREVIEW/TAKE A PICTURE WALK Ask children to explain what they notice about the pictures. Confirm that the pictures are illustrations that show people or events from long ago. Let children predict what they might learn, based on these illustrations.

TEACH/REVIEW VOCABULARY Write the word *America* in the center of a word web. In the surrounding circles, write *flag, stars, stripes, freedom,* and *birthday.* Encourage children to explain how each word relates to *America.*

ELL Help children recognize smaller words in *birthday (birth* and *day), freedom (free),* and *nickname (name).* Use these smaller words to build on the meanings of the larger vocabulary words.

TARGET SKILL AND STRATEGY

📀 **FACT AND OPINION** Remind children that an *opinion* tells how someone feels. Opinions are not right or wrong. A fact, however, can be right or wrong. Encourage children to consider the information in the book as fact or opinion.

📀 **MONITOR AND FIX UP** As children read, encourage them to pause after each page and to think about what they've learned. If they feel they do not understand the main idea, encourage them to reread the text.

READ THE BOOK

Use the following questions to support comprehension.

PAGE 6 What information on this page is fact, and what information is opinion? *(Most of the information is fact except for: He invented useful things.)*

PAGE 8 What job did George Washington have during the American Revolution? *(He was not President, but he was in charge of the army during the American Revolution.)*

PAGE 13 How did Dicey Langston get the nickname Daring Dicey? *(At 15, she warned Americans of a British attack.)*

TALK ABOUT THE BOOK

READER RESPONSE

1. Possible responses: This is an opinion. She was a hero is a fact; she was the *bravest* is an opinion.
2. Possible responses for web: wrote books; invented swim fins; invented glasses; studied lightning and electricity; asked France to help the Colonies; helped America
3. Possible response: The Fourth of July is the day that America declared its independence from Britain.
4. Possible response: On this map from 1775, only thirteen states are identified. Today, we have 50 states.

RESPONSE OPTIONS

WRITING Ask children whom in this book they would like to learn more about. Ask children to write about why they chose this person.

CONTENT CONNECTIONS

SOCIAL STUDIES Talk about why the people in this book are considered heroes. Then ask children to think about other people they consider heroes. Encourage children to draw a picture of a hero and write about why that person is a hero.

Time for SOCIAL STUDIES

Name _____

Fact and Opinion

Read each sentence. Decide if it is a statement of fact or a statement of opinion.
Write the letter **F** on the line if the sentence is a statement of fact.
Write the letter **O** on the line if the sentence is a statement of opinion.

_____ 1. Benjamin Franklin was born in Boston in 1706.

_____ 2. Benjamin Franklin was an interesting man with many talents.

_____ 3. George Washington was a terrific leader of the American Revolution.

_____ 4. George Washington would become the first President of the United States.

_____ 5. Deborah Sampson dressed as a soldier during the American Revolution.

_____ 6. She was an amazing woman and admired by all.

_____ 7. Dicey Langston was the bravest person of the American Revolution.

_____ 8. Sybil Ludington was a hero at the age of 16.

118

© Pearson Education 2

Name _____

Vocabulary

Read each sentence. Choose a word from the box that best fits the sentence. Write one letter on each line.

Words to Know			
America	birthday	flag	freedom
nickname	stars	stripes	

1. The ___ ___ ___ ___ ___ on the flag stand for the states.

2. The flag also has thirteen ___ ___ ___ ___ ___ ___ ___.

3. The American Revolution was fought for America's

___ ___ ___ ___ ___ ___ ___ from English rule.

4. The new country became known as the United States of

___ ___ ___ ___ ___ ___ ___.

5. Daring Dicey was the ___ ___ ___ ___ ___ ___ ___ ___ for Dicey Langston.

Home of the Brave

Home of the Brave by Barbara Wood

🔘 **FACT AND OPINION**

🔘 **MONITOR AND FIX UP**

LESSON VOCABULARY colony, continents, democracy, government, history, independence, symbol

SUMMARY Long ago, America was a group of thirteen colonies, ruled by Britain. The colonies wanted to form their own government and be free from British rule, so the colonists started the American Revolution. Once their freedom had been gained, the Founding Fathers looked for a new form of government. They chose a form of democracy, which the United States still has today.

INTRODUCE THE BOOK

BUILD BACKGROUND Discuss the image on the book cover. Ask: Why is this building important? Lead children to recognize that some people who work for the United States government work in this building, the U.S. Capitol.

PREVIEW/TAKE A PICTURE WALK Have children open the book to page 8. Explain that this picture shows a government in Greece. Encourage children to look through the book for other examples of government.

TEACH/REVIEW VOCABULARY Write each word on the board, and invite children to read it with you. Have children share their ideas about what each word means.

ELL Label pictures in the book with vocabulary words that best represent them. For example, the illustration on page 4 shows a historical event. Label this picture *history*.

TARGET SKILL AND STRATEGY

🔘 **FACT AND OPINION** Remind children that an *opinion* tells how someone feels. Opinions are not right or wrong. A *fact,* however, can be right or wrong. For example, on page 7, *Creating a new government was not easy* is an opinion. *Americans living in different parts of the country had different needs* is a fact.

🔘 **MONITOR AND FIX UP** As children read, encourage them to pause after each page and to think about what they've learned. If they feel they do not understand the main idea, encourage them to reread the text.

READ THE BOOK

Use the following questions to support comprehension.

PAGE 5 How did the colonists feel about British rule? Were their feelings fact or opinion? *(They felt British rules were unfair. Their feelings were opinions.)*

PAGE 9 Why were some Americans given the name Founding Fathers? *(The Founding Fathers established— or founded—the government of the United States.)*

PAGE 15 Why is the Statue of Liberty a good symbol for America? *(The Statue represents freedom, and people in America enjoy many freedoms and rights.)*

TALK ABOUT THE BOOK

READER RESPONSE

1. Possible response: Facts: In a democracy, all citizens eighteen years of age and over have the right to vote. Voting is free. No one knows how each person voted. Opinions: Will vary.

2. Accept all reasonable responses, making sure that children identify freedom of speech and freedom of religion.

3. Possible response: the U.S. Capitol, the Statue of Liberty, the United States flag

4. the original thirteen colonies

RESPONSE OPTIONS

WRITING Invite each child to write another title for this book and then a few sentences about what it tells about the book.

CONTENT CONNECTIONS

Time for **SOCIAL STUDIES**

SOCIAL STUDIES Introduce children to memorials in Washington, D.C., that symbolize America's past and democratic government, such as the White House, the Lincoln Memorial, the Washington Monument, the Jefferson Memorial, and the U.S. Capitol.

Name _____

Fact and Opinion

Each sentence below is a statement of fact about the United States. On the line below each sentence, write a statement of opinion about this information.

Hint: start your sentence with **"I think . . ."**

I. Fact: The United States was once thirteen colonies ruled by Britain.

My Opinion:

_____

- -

_____

2. Fact: Colonists fought against Britain in the American Revolution.

My Opinion:

_____

- -

_____

3. Fact: The United States formed a type of democratic government.

My Opinion:

_____

- -

_____

4. Fact: People's rights in the United States are protected by law.

My Opinion:

_____

- -

_____

© Pearson Education 2

118

Name _____

Vocabulary

Read each definition on the right.
Draw a line to match the words with their meanings.

1. democracy   **a.** a group of settlers ruled by
                                    another country

2. continent   **b.** one of the seven large areas
                                    of land on earth

3. symbol   **c.** a type of government

4. colony   **d.** an image that reminds us of
                                    an idea

5. history   **e.** how a country is ruled

6. independence   **f.** a record of events from the
                                    past

7. government   **g.** freedom from control of
                                    another person or country

© Pearson Education 2

119

Very Special Birthdays

Very Special Birthdays
by Jessica Quilty
illustrated by Nicole Wong

DRAW CONCLUSIONS

SUMMARIZE

LESSON VOCABULARY aunt, bank, basket, collects, favorite, present

SUMMARY This informational book describes how Chinese families celebrate birthdays. It supports the lesson concept of family celebrations as traditions.

INTRODUCE THE BOOK

BUILD BACKGROUND Invite children to discuss how their own families or cultures celebrate birthdays. Ask if anybody knows of any special ways that birthdays might be celebrated in the Chinese culture. Let them know that in Chinese culture, different birthdays are celebrated in different ways, and tell them that they will be learning more about that in the book.

PREVIEW/READ THE HEADINGS Have children look through the book. Point out the first heading *Birthdays Are Special.* Ask children to look for other headings. Afterward, ask them what they think they will learn by reading the book based on the headings.

TEACH/REVIEW VOCABULARY Review the lesson vocabulary. Have children use the words in sentences that relate to the idea of birthdays or birthday parties.

ELL To help make sure children understand the vocabulary, invite them to point to the pictures in the book that illustrate or relate to the words.

TARGET SKILL AND STRATEGY

DRAW CONCLUSIONS Review with children that to *draw a conclusion* is to use what you read and what you already know to figure out more about the book. Based on what they already know, ask children to draw a conclusion about the importance of birthdays in China. Have the children fill in a web diagram with facts that support their conclusion.

SUMMARIZE Discuss that to *summarize* something is to put the most important idea in your own words. After each section of the book, ask children to write a sentence that tells what the most important idea is in that section. After reading the complete book, have children use their own sentences to help them write a sentence that summarizes the whole book.

READ THE BOOK

Use the following questions to support comprehension.

PAGE 5 Why are babies given red eggs? *(Red means happiness; eggs mean new life. People want the new babies to be happy.)*

PAGE 10 What kind of noodles are served at birthday celebrations? Why? *(long noodles for a long life)*

PAGE 12 Why do you think food is so important in Chinese birthday celebrations? *(Possible response: You need food to live, and the birthday celebrations honor life.)*

TALK ABOUT THE BOOK

READER RESPONSE
1. Red is for happiness. So the red paper around money means good or happy fortune.
2. One Month: Red Egg party, lots of family, telling baby's name, presents. Sixtieth: lots of family, sharing eggs, noodles, and peaches for long life.
3. Possible responses: A picnic basket holds food. A basketball is thrown into a hoop or basket.
4. It tells you that birthdays and children will be discussed.

RESPONSE OPTIONS

WRITING Invite children to suppose they have been to a Chinese birthday party. Have children use index cards to create postcards describing what happened at the party.

CONTENT CONNECTIONS

Time for
SOCIAL STUDIES

SOCIAL STUDIES Encourage children to find out more about Chinese celebrations. Display books and articles on the topic. Have small groups share information about what they learned.

Name_____

Draw Conclusions

Think about what you know about Chinese birthday celebrations after reading. Then answer the questions.

Write a few sentences that tell about what happened in the story.

1. Why do you think new babies get gifts with tigers on them?

_____

- -

_____

2. How do you know that birthdays are an important part of Chinese culture?

_____

- -

_____
_____

- -

_____

3. How do you know that eating special foods is an important part of Chinese birthday celebrations?

_____

- -

_____
_____

- -

_____

4-5. Which of the birthday celebrations do you think you would like the most? Why?

_____

- -

_____
_____

- -

_____

© Pearson Education 2

122

Name_____

Vocabulary

Choose the word from the box that best fits each sentence. Each vocabulary word is used one time.

Words to Know
aunt   bank   basket   collects   favorite   present

_____
1. The _____ was filled with toys.

_____
2. A _____ is a safe place to keep money.

_____
3. My _____ gave me a birthday present.

_____
4. Red is my _____ color.

_____
5. My brother _____ the gifts and puts them in a basket.

Write a word that means the same as the word *gift*.

_____
6. _____

© Pearson Education 2

123

Birthdays Around the World

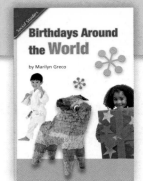

Birthdays Around the World

by Marilyn Greco

⊚ **DRAW CONCLUSIONS**

⊚ **SUMMARIZE**

LESSON VOCABULARY aunt, bank, basket, collects, favorite, present

SUMMARY This informational book shows how children around the world celebrate their birthdays. It extends the lesson concept of family celebrations as traditions.

INTRODUCE THE BOOK

BUILD BACKGROUND Invite children to share the ways that they celebrate their birthdays. Present the idea that people in different countries might celebrate their birthdays in different ways. Ask them to share any information they have about how children from other cultures celebrate their birthdays.

PREVIEW/TAKE A PICTURE WALK Have children preview the book. Are there mostly photos or drawings? Do they think the book is about real life, or a made-up story? Why? Ask them what information they get from the headings on each page spread (the name of a country). Have children discuss what they think they will learn from the book. Note that the book includes a glossary.

ELL In their home language, have children make a list of the items they see in the pictures. As they read, have them write the word or words that have the same meaning as each word on their list.

TEACH/REVIEW VOCABULARY Review the vocabulary by asking a question for each vocabulary word. For example: What would you call your mother's sister?

TARGET SKILL AND STRATEGY

⊚ **DRAW CONCLUSIONS** Remind children that they can use what they already know to draw a conclusion. Ask children to *draw a conclusion* about the importance of families in celebrating birthdays in the five countries they will read about. Have them write the conclusion in a web diagram. As they read, children should fill in the diagram with facts that support their conclusion.

⊚ **SUMMARIZE** After they read each section on a country, children can write a sentence that tells the most important idea in that section. After reading the complete book, have children use their sentences to help them write a new sentence that summarizes the whole book.

READ THE BOOK

Use the following questions to support comprehension.

PAGE 5 How would you describe Aisha after reading about her? *(Possible responses: She likes to have fun. She is thoughtful toward others.)*

PAGE 11 What will Victor do with the money he gets for his birthday? *(put it in the bank)*

PAGE 15 What is a reason that birthdays are celebrated in so many different places? *(People want to show how happy they are that the birthday person was born.)*

TALK ABOUT THE BOOK

READER RESPONSE
1. Some of the children get sung to, and there is a Tagalog birthday song on page 11.
2. Foods: cakes, BBQ, pies, candy, nuts, roast pig, beans and rice
3. Responses will vary.
4. Responses will vary.

RESPONSE OPTIONS

WRITING Have children write a paragraph about what a perfect birthday celebration would be to them.

CONTENT CONNECTIONS

SOCIAL STUDIES Suggest that children learn more about the countries they read about in this book. They can use classroom books, the library, or the Internet when appropriate. Afterward, they should share what they learned.

Time for SOCIAL STUDIES

Name_____

Draw Conclusions

Read *Birthdays Around the World*. Write the answers to the questions below.

1. What are important parts of all the birthday celebrations in this book?

_____

_____

_____

_____

_____

_____

2. Children in different countries eat different birthday food. What else is different about birthdays around the world?

_____

_____

_____

_____

_____

_____

3. Do you think the children in this book enjoyed their birthday parties? Why or why not?

_____

_____

_____

_____

_____

_____

122

Name_____

Vocabulary

Unscramble the words and write them in the spaces below.

Words to Know
aunt bank basket collects favorite present

1. asbket

_____

_____

2. eftaivor

_____

_____

3. nkab

_____

_____

4. costclle

_____

_____

5. tuan

_____

_____

6. prteens

_____

_____

7. Write a sentence using two or more vocabulary words.

_____

_____

_____

_____

123

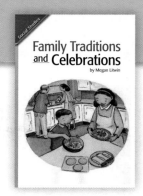

Family Traditions and Celebrations

➤ **DRAW CONCLUSIONS**

➤ **SUMMARIZE**

LESSON VOCABULARY ancestors, celebrations, customs, festival, traditions, unique

SUMMARY This book explains the importance of family celebrations as a way of sharing time together and maintaining family traditions. It supports the lesson concept of family celebrations as traditions.

INTRODUCE THE BOOK

BUILD BACKGROUND Have children share their experiences with family celebrations. Ask: Did your grandparents celebrate this way too?

PREVIEW/TAKE A PICTURE WALK Have children preview the pictures and headings. Ask: What do the headings tell you about what you will read?

TEACH/REVIEW VOCABULARY Reinforce word meaning by having children give an example sentence for each vocabulary word, such as *My great-grandfather is one of my ancestors.*

TARGET SKILL AND STRATEGY

➤ **DRAW CONCLUSIONS** Tell children that they should use what they have read and what they know about real life to help them draw conclusions about what happens in the book. Model: "On page 4, I read that birthdays are important in Jenny's family. I know that, in my family, we celebrate birthdays to show people we love them and that we think they are special. I think Jenny's family must be a loving family."

➤ **SUMMARIZE** Remind children that readers can use their own words to tell the important things that happen in a book. Model the following on page 5: I read that Jenny's cake has eight candles, that the candles are used up to age sixteen, and that they use number candles for older people, because it would be hard to use a lot of candles. I ask, "What is this paragraph mostly about?" I will use my own words to tell what happens: Jenny's family uses birthday candles on their birthday cakes. As children read, have them tell the main idea of a paragraph by asking: What is this paragraph mostly about?

ELL Have children start a KWL chart. In the preview, have them list what they know about each of the six celebrations and what they want to learn. During reading, have them list what they learned. After reading, have them write a sentence summarizing the book based on their notes.

READ THE BOOK

Use the following questions to support comprehension.

PAGE 4 Why are celebrations important to our lives? *(They are a way for us to spend time with family and a way to remember important events.)*

PAGE 10 Why does Daryl have to be careful when he lights the candles? *(He could burn himself or start a fire.)*

PAGE 16 How will Peter be like his older relatives? *(He will pass on family stories too.)*

TALK ABOUT THE BOOK

READER RESPONSE
1. so that they can see the bright colors against the dark sky
2. food, music, dancing, giving small gifts, lighting candles, stating goals
3. Customs are shared by family members, while traditions are passed from generation to generation.
4. Responses will vary.

RESPONSE OPTIONS

WRITING Have children write a sentence to summarize why family traditions and celebrations are important.

CONTENT CONNECTIONS

SOCIAL STUDIES Have children do guided research on the Internet to find out information about how birthdays are celebrated in another culture.

Name_____

Draw Conclusions

What holiday are they celebrating? Use the information you learned about holidays in *Family Traditions and Celebrations* to complete the sentences below.

1. Alison is eating latkes, and her family is lighting a

_____

menorah. Her family is celebrating _____.

2. Jenny is blowing out candles, and her family is having a

_____

party. Jenny is celebrating her _____.

3. Daryl's family is feasting for seven days, and Daryl's goal is Kuumba. Daryl's family is celebrating

_____

_____.

4. Write a sentence that tells more of what you know about family traditions and celebrations.

_____

_____

_____

_____

© Pearson Education 2

122

Name_____

Vocabulary

Write the word from the box next to its meaning.

Words to Know		
ancestors	celebrations	customs
festival	traditions	unique

1. _____ *n.* another word for celebration

2. _____ *adj.* one of a kind

3. _____ *n.* people from whom one is descended

4. _____ *n.* activities shared by people in a family or place

5. _____ *n.* gatherings to remember special events

6. _____ *n.* information, beliefs, and values handed down from one generation to another

© Pearson Education 2

123

Ranch Life

Ranch Life
by Ellen Leigh
illustrated by Aleksey Ivanov

◎ **CAUSE AND EFFECT**

◎ **GRAPHIC ORGANIZERS**

LESSON VOCABULARY campfire, cattle, cowboy, galloped, herd, railroad, trail

SUMMARY Eight-year-old Emma lives on a ranch in the American West, more than a hundred years ago. This historical fiction gives readers a glimpse of ranch life.

INTRODUCE THE BOOK

BUILD BACKGROUND Write the word *cowboy* on the board, and invite children to describe images and ideas that this word evokes. Then ask children what job cowboys served and list their ideas.

PREVIEW/TAKE A PICTURE WALK Ask children to share their ideas about what a ranch looks like. Ask: What scenery do you expect to see? What buildings? What animals? What might people wear? Have children then view the pictures to confirm and amend ideas.

TEACH/REVIEW VOCABULARY Have children close their eyes, and tell them to listen as you say the vocabulary words. Encourage children to picture the words in their minds as you say them.

ELL Ahead of time, create simple picture cards for each vocabulary word and label each card. Present each card, one at a time. Point to the picture, then point to the word and say it aloud. Point to the picture again, and have children say the word with you.

TARGET SKILL AND STRATEGY

◎ **CAUSE AND EFFECT** Remind children that one event often causes another event to happen. The first event is called the *cause.* The result of that cause, or the second event, is the *effect.* For example, on page 6, the story says Emma was proud. That's an effect. What caused Emma to be proud? *(She finished sewing her apron.)*

◎ **GRAPHIC ORGANIZERS** Remind children that *graphic organizers* are useful tools that will help them better understand what they read. Graphic organizers help readers organize information in more structured ways. Suggest that children add information to a graphic organizer as they read to aid comprehension.

READ THE BOOK

Use the following questions to support comprehension.

PAGE 4 What is the result, or the effect, of Papa turning over the soil in the garden? *(The soil is now ready for planting.)*

PAGE 6 How is the task described here the same yet different for Emma and Mama? Write your ideas in a Venn diagram. *(Mama: sews sheets and clothes; Both: they both sew; Emma: sews an apron for herself)*

PAGE 8 How does Emma feel about the cowboys? *(Emma likes to watch the cowboys keep the cattle from running away.)*

TALK ABOUT THE BOOK

READER RESPONSE
1. Possible responses: The cowboys would no longer be needed at the ranch because trains could take the cattle to town.
2. Possible responses: Outdoor Jobs: planting, bringing in water, fishing; Indoor Jobs: cooking, sewing, writing letters
3. Possible response: cows, roundup, fireplace
4. Responses will vary. Children should include details about ranch life that they read about in the book.

RESPONSE OPTIONS

WRITING Emma writes letters to people "back East." Invite children to imagine they live on a ranch, and have them describe what their life is like.

CONTENT CONNECTIONS

SOCIAL STUDIES Display a map of the United States. Recall that some of Emma's friends and family are "back East." Point to the East Coast of the United States. Then point to western states, such as Montana, Wyoming, and Texas, and explain that many states in the West have cattle ranches.

Time for **SOCIAL STUDIES**

Name _____

Cause and Effect

The sentences on the left tell a **cause**.
The sentences on the right tell an **effect**.
Draw a line to match each cause with its effect.

Cause	**Effect**
1. Emma plants seeds.	**a.** Papa hired cowboys to bring his cattle together.
2. Emma's friends and family live far away.	**b.** Vegetables will soon grow.
3. The cattle must get to town.	**c.** The ranch might not need cowboys anymore.
4. A railroad might be built near the ranch.	**d.** Emma stays in touch with family and friends by writing letters.

5. Read the sentence below.
CAUSE: It is hot and sunny today.
Write a sentence to tell an effect.
EFFECT:

_____

- -

_____

_____

- -

_____

126

Name _____

Vocabulary

Look at each picture. Which word tells about it?
Circle the correct word for each picture.

1.   cattle   cowboy

2.   trails   railroad

3.   ranch   campfire

4.   cowboy   campfire

5.   trail   ranch

6.   galloped   herd

7. Use the word *galloped* in a sentence.

_____

_____

_____

127

COWBOY DAYS
by Joanna Korba
illustrated by Jerry Tiritilli

⊙ **CAUSE AND EFFECT**

⊙ **GRAPHIC ORGANIZERS**

LESSON VOCABULARY campfire, cattle, cowboy, galloped, herd, railroad, trails

Cowboy Days

SUMMARY A girl tells about a great uncle from 150 years ago who was once a cowboy. She explains what cowboy life was like and how it has changed.

INTRODUCE THE BOOK

BUILD BACKGROUND Write the word *cowboy* on the board, and read it with the class. Invite children to share their ideas about cowboys. Explain that there were lots of cowboys 150 years ago.

PREVIEW/TAKE A PICTURE WALK Ask children who the girl and the man in the illustration on page 3 might be. Help children recognize the man as they preview the illustrations. Afterward, ask children if they have any new ideas about the girl on page 3.

TEACH/REVIEW VOCABULARY Ask children which vocabulary word appears in the book title. Have them explain how the other vocabulary words might relate to cowboys.

ELL Write each word on a self-stick note. Work with children to look through the book for pictures that illustrate each word. Place the self-stick notes on the pictures to reinforce meaning.

TARGET SKILL AND STRATEGY

⊙ **CAUSE AND EFFECT** Review *cause* and *effect,* using this example: On page 8, a clap of thunder or a sudden noise is a cause; the effect of the noise is a cattle stampede.

⊙ **GRAPHIC ORGANIZERS** Share with children that *graphic organizers* help readers organize and view information. Suggest to children that they add information to a graphic organizer as they read to aid comprehension.

READ THE BOOK

Use the following questions to support comprehension.

PAGE 3 Why does Jeannie Grigsby tell us about Carl Grigsby? *(She has heard many stories about him. He was a cowboy. She thinks others would like to hear about cowboy life.)*

PAGE 7 What was a trail drive like? Write ideas in a word web. *(Center circle: trail drive; Outer circles, possible responses: 3,000 longhorns; three months on the trail; dusty; stampede)*

PAGE 9 Why did Carl think sitting around the campfire was the best part of the trail drive? *(It was a time to rest. It was a time to relax. It was a time to talk and eat.)*

TALK ABOUT THE BOOK

READER RESPONSE

1. Possible responses: Barbed wire prevented cattle from straying onto other ranches. Cowboys were no longer needed to keep the cattle on their own ranch. Carl put up fences, which made him sad.

2. Possible responses: Past: cowboys mostly men; cowboys moved cattle; cowboys fixed fences. Present: cowboys called cowhands, many are women; trucks move cattle; machines fix fences.

3. Possible responses: railroad, campfire, longhorn, sunset, cowhands

4. Answers will vary. Riding a horse should be included, but accept all reasonable answers. Make sure children's answers include support from the text.

RESPONSE OPTIONS

WRITING Explain to children that Carl kept a journal when he was on a cattle drive. Ask children to each write a few sentences that tell what happens during one day on the trail. Let children illustrate their journal entries.

CONTENT CONNECTION

TIME FOR Science

SCIENCE Ask children to describe the land of the range and the cattle drive, drawing their ideas from information in the book. Work with children to compare the hot, dry plains of the range to other places in the United States, such as forests, mountains, wetlands, and coasts.

Name _____

Cause and Effect

Each sentence below tells a **cause**.
Write a sentence that tells the **effect**.
Use *Cowboy Days* to help you.

1. CAUSE: Jeannie Grigsby hears a lot about Great Uncle Carl, the cowboy.
   EFFECT:

   _____

   -

   _____

2. CAUSE: The land along the trail drive is very dusty.
   EFFECT:

   _____

   -

   _____

3. CAUSE: Someone tells Carl about a show called a rodeo.
   EFFECT:

   _____

   -

   _____

4. CAUSE: Ranchers used barbed wire fences to keep the cattle together.
   EFFECT:

   _____

   -

   _____

   -

   _____

© Pearson Education 2

126

Name _____

Vocabulary

Circle the word that best completes the sentence and write it in the space.

Words to Know			
campfire	cattle	cowboy	galloped
herd	railroad	trails	

_____

1. Many cows make up one large _____ .

      campfire   herd

_____

2. The cattle _____ across the dry land.

      galloped   railroad

_____

3. Great Uncle Carl was once a _____ .

      railroad   cowboy

_____

4. The cowboys led the cattle on dusty _____ .

      trails   railroad

_____

5. At night, the cowboys cooked over a _____ .

      campfire   herd

_____

6. The _____ changed the life of the cowboy.

      trails   railroad

127

Life on the Ranch by Christian Downey
illustrated by Martin Lemelman

🔘 **CAUSE AND EFFECT**

🔘 **GRAPHIC ORGANIZERS**

LESSON VOCABULARY chores, climate, livestock, occupation, pasture, ranch, stalls, tractor

Life on the Ranch

SUMMARY Sisters Maria and Angela Ramirez live on a modern-day ranch. Their family raises cattle and pigs and grows wheat and a few other crops. Maria and Angela have many chores to do on the ranch, but they don't mind. They enjoy life on a ranch.

INTRODUCE THE BOOK

BUILD BACKGROUND Say the word *ranch,* and invite children to share any images that come to mind. Share with children that a ranch is similar to a farm. People grow crops and raise animals. Most ranches, unlike farms, raise cattle (or cows) for meat.

PREVIEW/TAKE A PICTURE WALK Discuss with children who the main characters are. *(two girls)* Ask children if they think the girls like living on the ranch. How can they tell?

TEACH/REVIEW VOCABULARY Discuss the meanings of the words. Invite children to consider how the words relate to life on a ranch. Encourage children to use each word in a sentence that tells about a ranch.

ELL Help children recognize the two smaller words that make up the compound words *cowboy, campfire,* and *railroad.* Show children pictures of each smaller word, and then help them figure out what the compound words mean.

TARGET SKILL AND STRATEGY

🔘 **CAUSE AND EFFECT** Review with children that one event often causes another event to happen. The first event is called the *cause.* The result of that cause, or the second event, is the *effect.* For example, on page 5, rain is a cause; the effect of enough rain is that crops will grow.

🔘 **GRAPHIC ORGANIZERS** Share with children that *graphic organizers* help readers organize and view information in more structured ways. Suggest to children that they jot down information within graphic organizers as they read to aid comprehension.

READ THE BOOK

Use the following questions to support comprehension.

PAGE 8 Why do you think wheat is the biggest crop the Ramirez family grows on the ranch? *(The hot, dry climate is perfect for growing wheat.)*

PAGE 9 How is wheat made into bread? Draw a flow chart to show the steps. *(Step 1: Wheat is grown. Step 2: Wheat is harvested. Step 3: Wheat is taken to the mill. Step 4: Wheat is made into flour. Step 5: Flour is made into bread.)*

PAGES 10–11 What do you think the word *livestock* means? *(Livestock are animals, such as cows, pigs, and chickens, that are raised on a farm or ranch.)*

TALK ABOUT THE BOOK

READER RESPONSE

1. Possible responses: Ice and snow could kill the crops. If the crops die, the family has no food to sell or eat. Life would become difficult.
2. Possible responses: Crops: wheat, soybeans, corn; Animals: horses, cows, pigs, dogs, chickens
3. Responses will vary.
4. Possible response: Mrs. Ramirez wants her girls to feel proud, whether they win or lose.

RESPONSE OPTIONS

WRITING Suggest to children that Maria and Angela are interviewed by the local newspaper because their cows won blue ribbons. Have children write two questions to ask Maria and Angela. Then ask children to write answers for their questions.

CONTENT CONNECTIONS

SOCIAL STUDIES Ask children to call out foods they enjoy. Then diagram how the food came to be. For example, if children call out *ice cream,* diagram that ice cream is made from milk, which comes from dairy cows on a farm.

Time for SOCIAL STUDIES

Name _____

Cause and Effect

Write the missing **cause** or **effect**.
Use *Life on the Ranch* to help you.

I. CAUSE: The cows ate all the grass in one pasture.
   EFFECT:

_____

_____

2. CAUSE:

_____

_____

   EFFECT: The crops die.

3. CAUSE: The wheat ripens in late summer.
   EFFECT:

_____

_____

4. CAUSE:

_____

_____

   EFFECT: Linda the brown cow's coat became shiny.

5. CAUSE: Mimi's new puppy was hiding.
   EFFECT:

_____

_____

126

Name _____

Vocabulary

Complete each sentence with a word from the box.

Words to Know			
chores	climate	livestock	occupation
pasture	ranch	stalls	tractor

1.-2. Angela and Maria know they are too young to drive a

_____   _____

---------------------------------   ---------------------------------

_____ on the _____ .

_____

----

3. The _____ is mostly warm where they live.

4. Before they go to school, the girls have to do their

_____

_____ .

_____

5.-6. Mr. Ramirez's _____ is to sell items

_____

----

grown on the _____ .

_____

----

7. The girls chose their own cows for the _____

show.

127

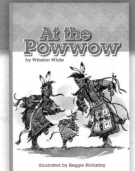

At the Powwow

SUMMARY A Native American boy attends a powwow ceremony with his family and learns about some of his tribe's traditions.

INTRODUCE THE BOOK

BUILD BACKGROUND Discuss any knowledge children might have of a powwow. If they have never heard of one, let them know that it is a Native American celebration, and they will be learning more about it in this book. Tell them that whole families participate in the powwows. Ask them if there are any celebrations that their families like to attend.

ELL Invite children to tell the class about any celebrations that are particularly important to their families.

PREVIEW/TAKE A PICTURE WALK Invite children to look at the pictures in the book. Ask them to tell you where most of the story takes place. What do they think they will learn in this story? Why?

TEACH/REVIEW VOCABULARY Challenge children to use as many vocabulary words as possible in one sentence. Example: "I would like to *borrow* your *silver drum.*"

TARGET SKILL AND STRATEGY

CHARACTER, SETTING, PLOT Review with children that *characters* are *who* is in the story, *setting* is *where* the story takes place, and *plot* is *what* happens in the story. Let children know they should be paying attention to how the characters are feeling. They should also notice how the setting of a powwow affects the characters and what happens in the story.

PRIOR KNOWLEDGE Tell children to think about what they already know about Native American culture and family celebrations. Discuss and display a KWL chart. Help them to fill in the first two columns. After reading the text, work together to fill in the last column. Then, ask children if they thought filling in the chart helped them to better understand what they were reading.

READ THE BOOK

Use these questions to support comprehension.

PAGE 3 Do you think Ben has been to many powwows? Why or why not? *(He has not been to many powwows. He asks his grandmother to tell him about them.)*

PAGE 5 What do Ben's parents do to get ready for the powwow? *(put on special costumes)*

PAGE 11 How does Ben feel at the end of the powwow? *(happy that he got to spend a special day with his family)*

TALK ABOUT THE BOOK

READER RESPONSE
1. Setting: powwow; Characters: Ben, Gram, Mom, Dad
2. Answers will vary.
3. Possible responses: rattling, banging, clanking
4. Possible response: Drums are important to Native Americans like our beating hearts are important to our bodies.

RESPONSE OPTIONS

VISUAL Have children draw pictures of a special celebration day they spent with their own families. Then, have them write a few sentences about what is happening in the picture.

CONTENT CONNECTIONS

SOCIAL STUDIES Provide books or Internet access for children to explore how different Native American groups celebrate powwows. Invite children to share the information they've learned with each other.

Time for SOCIAL STUDIES

Name_____

Character, Setting, Plot

Draw a picture of Ben at a powwow. Show how Ben feels.

1–2.

Write a few sentences that tell about what happened in the story.

3. Beginning: _____

4. Middle: _____

5. End: _____

130

Name_____

Vocabulary

Circle the word that best fits into each sentence. Then, write it on the line.

_____

1. Sally plays the _____.

    drain   drum   dress

_____

2. My new ring is made out of _____.

    slip   sling   silver

_____

3. Please don't talk in such a loud_____.

    vest   choice   voice

_____

4. Can I _____ your pencil to write a letter?

    borrow   bored   broom

Circle the words that describe a sound.

5. Jingle   Very   Clattering   Class   Clown   Jump

© Pearson Education 2

131

A Special Festival
by Riley Obach
illustrated by Martin Lemelman

◎ **CHARACTER, SETTING, PLOT**

◎ **PRIOR KNOWLEDGE**

LESSON VOCABULARY borrow, clattering, drum, jingle, silver, voice

A Special Festival

SUMMARY A Bahamian American boy is surprised when his grandfather comes to celebrate Bahamian culture at the Goombay Festival. The story supports the lesson concept of celebrations in different cultures.

INTRODUCE THE BOOK

BUILD BACKGROUND Ask children to describe cultural celebrations that they know of.

PREVIEW/TAKE A PICTURE WALK Have children preview the pictures. Ask: Whom is this story about? Have children read the heading and view the photo on page 16. Ask: Is this part of the story? What is this page about?

TEACH/REVIEW VOCABULARY Give children sets of vocabulary word cards. On the board, write: I heard the _____ of pots and pans. I shook the bells to make them _____. I play the _____ in my band. I use my _____ to sing. You may _____ my bike until Monday. I have a _____ ring. Read each sentence aloud. Have children show the correct word card.

TARGETED SKILL AND STRATEGY

◎ **CHARACTER, SETTING, PLOT** Review these literary elements with children. Remind them to keep them in mind as they read the book. How do the *characters* change? How do the *settings* influence characters' actions? What are the major elements in the *plot*?

◎ **PRIOR KNOWLEDGE** Remind children that successful readers use what they already know to help them understand what they read. Model text-to-self connections (page 3): This is like the summers I spent with my aunt when I was a child. Text-to-world connections (page 7): Conch chowder reminds me of soup called clam chowder. Text-to-text connections (page 5): Doesn't Zeke remind you of the character in the book we read yesterday?

ELL Assign each child a partner. Give these action words from the story to each pair: *swam, chatted, hugged, whispered, groaned.* Have one child act out each word and have the other say the correct word.

READ THE BOOK

Use the following questions to support comprehension.

PAGE 4 Why did Gramps let Zeke play the drum only at home? *(Possible response: Zeke was too young to play well enough in public.)*

PAGE 9 Why did Dad and Mom talk about everything except why they were going to the airport? *(They wanted to surprise Zeke.)*

PAGE 15 What did the writer of this story want you to learn? *(Possible response: Cultural celebrations are very important to people.)*

TALK ABOUT THE BOOK

READER RESPONSE
1. The settings include Zeke's home and the Goombay Festival. Zeke thinks about the Bahamas.
2. Responses will vary.
3. Possible responses: The pans made a lot of noise. The garbage collectors made a loud, rattling noise.
4. Celebration in the story: Special foods (conch chowder), costumes, music, dancing, and family; My family's celebration: Answers will vary but may include music, food, family, friends.

RESPONSE OPTIONS

WRITING Have children describe their favorite cultural celebration and how they help to celebrate.

CONTENT CONNECTIONS

ART Have children share the celebrations they described in the Reader Response. Have children work together to paint a mural that depicts one of the celebrations they discussed.

Character, Setting, Plot

Think about the story *A Special Festival*. Circle the answer to the questions below.

1. What does Zeke like to do?

    sew   cook   play music

2. Where does Zeke hope to go for summer vacation?

    music   camp   the Bahamas   Florida

3. Which character or characters in the story live in

the Bahamas?

    Zeke   Goombay family   Gramps

4-6. Write a few sentences that tell what happened in the beginning, middle, and end of the story.

_____

_____

_____

_____

_____

_____

130

Name_____

Vocabulary

Write a word from the box that fits on each group of lines. Write one letter on each line. Then, find a secret message. Write each letter that has a number under its line on the same number line on question 7.

Words to Know

| borrow | clattering | drum | jingle | silver | voice |

1. __d__ __r__ __u__ __m__
      6

2. __s__ __ __ __ __
    3   9

3. __ __ __ __ __ __ __ __ __g__
  1   7   8

4. __ __ __ __ __ __w__
  5

5. __ __i__ __ __
     4

6. __j__ __ __ __ __
        2

7. __ __ __ __ __ __r__ __ __ __!
  1 2 3 4 5 6 7 8 9

131

Winter Holidays

Winter Holidays
by Lana Cruce
Illustrated by Diana Kizlauskas

◉ **CHARACTER, SETTING, PLOT**

◉ **PRIOR KNOWLEDGE**

LESSON VOCABULARY carols, famine, festival, geraniums, Middle Ages, ornaments, siblings, value

SUMMARY An African American girl and her Swedish pen pal teach each other about celebrations that are important in their cultures.

INTRODUCE THE BOOK

BUILD BACKGROUND Discuss what kind of celebrations take place during the winter. Invite children to talk about anything special that their family does for these celebrations. Introduce the idea that people in different cultures and places might participate in different kinds of celebrations.

ELL Ask children to share home language words about celebrations. Or one child may interview another child about celebrations.

PREVIEW/TAKE A PICTURE WALK Invite children to look at the pictures in the book. Ask them who they think the main characters in the story will be and what they think might happen.

TEACH/REVIEW VOCABULARY Invite children to play a game of charades. Give each child a vocabulary word. That child will act out the word while the other children guess what it is. If there are not enough words for each child, divide the group into teams and have each team act out a word.

TARGET SKILL AND STRATEGY

◉ **CHARACTER, SETTING, PLOT** Have children describe *character*, *setting*, and *plot* in their own words. To help them, suggest they pay close attention to what the two main characters learn in this story and how they are affected by their settings. Have them focus on how the characters are alike and different.

◉ **PRIOR KNOWLEDGE** Ask children how the discussion they had during Build Background might help them better understand the holidays that will be celebrated in the book. Suggest they compare the celebrations they read about in the story with those they celebrate at home.

READ THE BOOK

Use the following questions to support comprehension.

PAGE 5 How are Anneka and Selene alike? *(same age, both have younger sisters, like to write letters, draw, and play make-believe)*

PAGE 10 Why do you think Anneka wanted to tell Selene about St. Lucia? *(Answers will vary, but should be supported by text.)*

PAGE 18 How are Kwanzaa and St. Lucia similar? *(They are both about celebrating your history and being with family.)*

TALK ABOUT THE BOOK

READER RESPONSE
1. Possible response: proud of culture and heritage; likes family togetherness; thinks about history; has a good imagination
2. Answers will vary.
3. celebration, party
4. Possible response: It's fun to make things; they are a nice surprise.

RESPONSE OPTIONS

WRITING Invite children to imagine they have a pen pal in another country. What would they want to tell that person about American celebrations? Have each child write a letter to their imaginary pen pal. Afterwards, they can share their writing with each other.

CONTENT CONNECTIONS

Time for
SOCIAL STUDIES

SOCIAL STUDIES Display books that give information on how holidays around the world are celebrated. Invite children to pick a holiday and find out more about it. They can use the classroom books, a library, or the Internet when appropriate.

Character, Setting, Plot

Think about the story *Winter Holidays*. Then circle the answer to each question.

1. What do Selene and Anneka have in common?

like holidays live in America have blond hair

2. How are Selene and Anneka different?

one is a boy one is much older from different countries

3. What are the two cities where the story takes place?

Chicago   Stockholm   New York

4. When does the story take place?

in the future in the past a little while ago

5. Write a sentence that tells what happened at the end of the story.

_____

_____

_____

_____

© Pearson Education 2

130

Name_____

Vocabulary

Write the word next to its definition.

Words to Know			
carols	famine	festival	geraniums
Middle Ages	ornaments	siblings	value

1. _____ *n.* red summertime flowers

2. _____ *n.* brothers and sisters

3. _____ *n.* songs of joy

4. _____ *n.* great shortage of food

5. _____ *n.* pretty holiday objects

6. _____ *n.* desirable quality

7. _____ *n.* period of European history from A.D. 500 to 1500

8. _____ *n.* celebration

© Pearson Education 2

131

Answer Key for Below-Level Reader Practice

Three of the Greats   LR1

Compare and Contrast, LR2

Possible response given. Satchel Paige: great pitcher, over 20 years; Both: African American; Josh Gibson: great hitter, 17 years

Vocabulary, LR3

threw, sailed, field, bases, cheers

Happy Birthday, America!   LR10

Fact and Opinion, LR11

2. The Fourth of July is a holiday. **3.** Uncle Sam is an American symbol. **4.** The Liberty Bell rang on July 4, 1776. **5.** After a parade, some people have a barbeque.

Vocabulary, LR12

1. c **2.** d **3.** b **4.** a **5.** nicknames **6.** birthday **7.** freedom

Very Special Birthdays   LR19

Draw Conclusions, LR20

Possible response given. **1.** to protect the babies. **2.** There are very special ways of celebrating each birthday. **3.** Different foods are served at all the different celebrations. **4–5.** Responses will vary.

Vocabulary, LR21

1. basket **2.** bank **3.** aunt **4.** favorite **5.** collects **6.** gift

Ranch Life   LR28

Cause and Effect, LR29

1. b **2.** d **3.** a **4.** c **5.** Possible response given. I will go to the beach.

Vocabulary, LR30

1. cattle **2.** railroad **3.** campfire **4.** cowboy **5.** trail **6.** herd **7.** Sentences will vary.

At the Powwow   LR37

Character, Setting, Plot, LR38

Possible responses given. **1–2.** Pictures will vary. **3.** Ben's family put on special clothes. **4.** Everyone danced together. **5.** Ben's family eats together.

Vocabulary, LR39

1. drum **2.** silver **3.** voice **4.** borrow **5.** Jingle, Clattering

Women in Baseball   LR4

◎ Compare and Contrast, LR5

Possible responses given. Baseball: hit ball with bat, run around the bases; Both: women play; Soccer: kick ball, run up and down the field

Vocabulary, LR6

cheers

Heroes of the American Revolution   LR13

◎ Realism/Fantasy, LR14

1. F **2.** O **3.** O **4.** F **5.** F **6.** O **7.** O **8.** F

Vocabulary, LR15

1. stars **2.** stripes **3.** freedom **4.** America **5.** nickname

Birthdays Around the World   LR22

◎ Draw Conclusions, LR23

Possible responses given. **1.** special foods, games, friends and family to celebrate **2.** play different games; have different activities **3.** Yes. They look happy in the pictures and they all say good things about their parties.

Vocabulary, LR24

1. basket **2.** favorite **3.** bank **4.** collects **5.** aunt **6.** present

Cowboy Days   LR31

◎ Cause and Effect, LR32

1. She tells others about him. **2.** The cattle kick up dust. **3.** He spends his life performing. **4.** Ranchers didn't need cowboys to keep cattle together.

Vocabulary, LR33

1. herd **2.** galloped **3.** cowboy **4.** trails **5.** campfire **6.** railroad **7.** Sentences will vary.

A Special Festival   LR40

◎ Character, Setting, Plot, LR41

1. play music **2.** the Bahamas **3.** Gramps. **4–6.** Possible responses given. Zeke thinks about what he did last summer; Zeke's parents sew and cook special things; they all go to the Goombay Festival

Vocabulary, LR42

2. silver **3.** clattering **4.** borrow **5.** voice **6.** jingle **7.** celebrate

Baseball Heroes   LR7

🎯 Main Idea, LR8
Possible responses given. Jackie Robinson: played for the Dodgers, great hitter; Both: faced many challenges; Hank Aaron: played for the Braves and the Brewers, set many records

Vocabulary, LR9
rookie, challenges, talented, effort, banned, record, athletes, prejudice

Home of the Brave   LR16

🎯 Fact and Opinion, LR17
Answers will vary.

Vocabulary, LR18
1. c **2.** b **3.** d **4.** a **5.** f **6.** g **7.** e

Family Traditions
and Celebrations   LR25

🎯 Draw Conclusions, LR26
1. Hanukkah **2.** birthday **3.** Kwanzaa **4–5.** Possible response given. Family celebrations teach us about who we are.

Vocabulary, LR27
1. festival **2.** unique **3.** ancestors **4.** customs **5.** celebrations **6.** traditions

Life on the Ranch   LR34

🎯 Cause and Effect, LR35
1. Uncle Leo had to move the cows. **2.** The crops don't get enough rain. **3.** The Ramirezes harvest it. **4.** Angela brushed Linda the brown cow. **5.** The girls look for the puppy.

Vocabulary, LR36
1. tractor **2.** ranch **3.** climate **4.** chores **5.** occupation **6.** farm **7.** livestock

Winter Holidays   LR43

🎯 Character, Setting, Plot, LR44
1. like holidays **2.** from different countries **3.** Chicago, Stockholm **4.** a little while ago **5.** Possible response given. The girls wrote and thanked each other for sharing their winter holidays.

Vocabulary, LR45
1. geraniums **2.** siblings **3.** carols **4.** famine **5.** ornaments **6.** value **7.** Middle Ages **8.** festival

Differentiated Instruction

Table of Contents

Continued on back of tab

Daily **Group Time** Lessons, continued

Let's Learn Amazing Words

TEACH/MODEL

Oral Vocabulary

ROUTINE

1 **Introduce the Word** Relate the word to the song or story in which it appears. Supply a child-friendly definition. Have children say the word. Example:

- In the song each game is a *challenge*. A *challenge* is a hard task or a test of someone's abilities. You can also *challenge* someone by inviting or daring him or her to do something, such as take part in a competition. Say the word *challenge* with me, *challenge*.

2 **Demonstrate** Provide familiar examples to demonstrate meaning. When possible, use gestures to help convey meaning. Examples:

- Running in the 5K race was a *challenge*. It was a *challenge* to write a two-page report. Our school will *challenge* another school to a basketball game.

3 **Apply** Have children demonstrate understanding with a simple activity. Suggestions for step 3 activities appear on the next page. Example:

- Tell me something that is a *challenge* for you. How else might one school *challenge* another?

4 **Display the Word/Letter-Sounds** Write the word on a card and display it on a classroom Amazing Words board. Have children identify some familiar letter-sounds or word parts. Example:

- This word is *challenge*. Run your hand under the two word parts *chal-lenge* as you read the word.

Use the Oral Vocabulary Routine along with the definitions, examples, letter-sounds, and word parts that are provided on the following pages to introduce each Amazing Word.

ABOUT ORAL VOCABULARY A child's oral vocabulary development is a predictor of future reading success. Oral vocabulary development now boosts children's comprehension as they become fluent readers. Oral vocabulary is informally assessed.

ACTIVITIES

To allow children to demonstrate understanding of the Amazing Words, use activities such as these in step 3 of the Routine.

ANSWER QUESTIONS Would you prefer to have a *festive* day or an *ordinary* day? Why?

CREATE EXAMPLES What is something a good *citizen* might do?

MAKE CHOICES If any of the things I name can *hatch*, say *hatch*; if not, say nothing: a train, a chicken, a jar of jam, a snake, a tadpole, a horse.

PANTOMIME Show me how an eagle *soars*, a rocket, an airplane.

PERSONAL CONTEXT Some people are *fond* of fishing. Tell about something you are *fond* of. Use the word *fond* when you tell about it.

SYNONYMS AND ANTONYMS Name a word that means the opposite of *genuine*; name a word that means about the same as *genuine*.

Monitor Progress | Check Oral Vocabulary

To monitor understanding of concepts and vocabulary that have been explicitly taught each week:

- Display the week's paired selection in the Student Edition. (In some cases you may prefer to use the opening pages of the first selection.)
- Remind the child of the concept that the class has been talking about that week.
- Ask the child to tell you about the paired selection illustrations using some of the week's Amazing Words.

If... a child has difficulty using the Amazing Words,

then... ask questions about the illustration using the Amazing Words. Note which questions the child can respond to. Reteach unknown words using the Oral Vocabulary Routine.

SUCCESS PREDICTOR

Amazing Words

to build oral vocabulary

Definitions, examples, and **letter-sounds** to use with the Oral Vocabulary Routine on p. DI·1

USE WITH

DAY 1

1 **ATHLETE** An *athlete* is somebody who uses skills and abilities to compete in sports.

2 **Examples:** The basketball players were skilled *athletes.* The fastest *athletes* competed in the race.

4 **Letter-Sounds:** Children can decode the word *athlete.*

1 **CHALLENGE** A *challenge* is a test of someone's abilities. You can also *challenge* someone by daring him or her to do something.

2 **Examples:** Pitching a perfect game was her biggest *challenge.* The other team will *challenge* us to a rematch if we win.

4 **Word Parts:** Run your hand under the two word parts in *chal-lenge* as you read the word.

1 **EFFORT** *Effort* is the physical and mental energy you use to do something or to achieve a goal.

2 **Examples:** The men used a lot of *effort* to move the refrigerator onto the truck. She put forth her best *effort.*

4 **Letter-Sounds:** Point out that the *e* stands for its short vowel sound.

DAY 2

1 **DAINTY** *Dainty* means delicate and pretty.

2 **Examples:** The dress had a *dainty* lace collar. You could eat the *dainty* cookies in one bite.

4 **Letter-Sounds:** Children can decode the word *dainty.*

DAY 3

1 **DISGUISE** A *disguise* can be clothes or make-up someone wears to change the way he or she looks so he or she won't be recognized. When you change your appearance so you won't be recognized, you *disguise* yourself.

2 **Examples:** The spy wore a *disguise* so she wouldn't be recognized. He wore a wig and a beard to *disguise* himself.

4 **Word Parts:** Run your hand under the two word parts in *dis-guise* as you read the word.

DAY 4

1 **CHAMPION** A *champion* is the winner of a game or competition.

2 **Examples:** The *champions* had ten wins and no losses. Our team practiced hard because we wanted to beat last year's *champions.*

4 **Word Parts:** Run your hand under the three word parts in *cham-pi-ons* as you read the word.

1 **PROFESSIONAL** *Professional* describes a type of job in which people are paid for their skill and training.

2 **Examples:** My uncle is a *professional* basketball player. I want to be a *professional* singer when I grow up.

4 **Letter-Sounds:** Point out the sound the *ss* stands for as you read *professional.*

1 **SHORTSTOP** *Shortstop* is the infield position on a baseball team between second and third base.

2 **Examples:** I would prefer playing *shortstop* rather than third base. Our baseball team has the best *shortstop* in the league.

4 **Word Parts:** Children can decode the compound word *shortstop.*

Definitions, examples, and **letter-sounds** to use with the Oral Vocabulary Routine on p. DI·1

Amazing Words **to build oral vocabulary**

USE WITH

DAY 1

1 **HISTORY** *History* is all that has happened in the life of a people, a country, or a field of study such as science or art.

2 **Examples:** In school we will study the *history* of the United States. I like to learn about the *history* of the Plains Indians. My brother takes a class in art *history*.

4 **Word Parts:** Run your hand under the three word parts in *his-tor-y* as you read the word.

1 **INDEPENDENCE** *Independence* means freedom from being controlled by other people or countries.

2 **Examples:** The United States declared *independence* from England over 200 years ago. The Fourth of July is *Independence* Day in the United States.

4 **Word Parts:** Clap the four word parts in *in-de-pend-ence* as you read the word.

1 **SYMBOL** A *symbol* is something, such as a sign, a mark, or an object that stands for something else.

2 **Examples:** A red traffic light is a *symbol* for stop. A flag can be a *symbol* for a country or a state. A star on a map is a *symbol* for a capital city.

4 **Letter-Sounds:** Point out how the *y* stands for short *i* sound in the first syllable of symbol.

DAY 2

1 **PATRIOTIC** If someone shows love and loyalty to his or her country, that person is *patriotic*.

2 **Examples:** People who fly the flag of their country are *patriotic*. It is *patriotic* to support and defend your country. *Patriotic* men and women sometimes run for governor or senator.

4 **Word Parts:** Run your hand under the four word parts in *pa-tri-ot-ic* as you read the word.

1 **UNFURL** To *unfurl* something means to unroll it or spread it out.

2 **Examples:** When you *unfurl* the flag, you can see the stars and stripes. Mom *unfurled* the blanket and put it on the bed.

4 **Letter-Sounds:** Children can decode *unfurl*.

DAY 3

1 **FRAYED** When something is *frayed*, it is worn away on the edges, and threads are hanging loose.

2 **Examples:** His jeans were *frayed* at the bottom. The old rug was *frayed* around the edges.

4 **Letter-Sounds:** Children can decode *frayed*.

DAY 4

1 **ALLEGIANCE** *Allegiance* is the loyalty or faithfulness a person feels to his or her country, a leader, a friend, or family.

2 **Examples:** He joined the army because of his *allegiance* to his country. The children said the Pledge of *Allegiance* to the flag of the United States.

4 **Word Parts:** Run your hand under the three word parts in *al-le-giance* as you read the word.

1 **INDIVISIBLE** If something is *indivisible*, it cannot be divided, or separated into parts.

2 **Examples:** The states of the United States are *indivisible*. The team is so united that they are *indivisible*.

4 **Word Parts:** Run your hand under the five word parts in *in-di-vis-i-ble* as you read the word.

Amazing Words to build oral vocabulary

Definitions, examples, and **letter-sounds** to use with the Oral Vocabulary Routine on p. DI·1

USE WITH

DAY 1

1 **CELEBRATION** A *celebration* can be a party or other activity in which people might eat, play music, and have a good time together to show happiness about a special day or when something good happens.

2 **Examples:** We always have a *celebration* for our birthdays. There was a *celebration* when my brother graduated from college.

4 **Word Parts:** Point out the syllable *-tion* as you read the word.

1 **CUSTOM** A *custom* is something that people always do or have done for a long time.

2 **Examples:** It is our *custom* to drink warm milk at night. We have a *custom* of walking around the block after dinner.

4 **Word Parts:** Run your hand under the two word parts in *cus-tom* as you read the word.

1 **TRADITION** *Tradition* is a custom or belief that is handed down from generation to generation. For example, children get their *tradition* from parents who got it from the grandparents.

2 **Examples:** Our family has a *tradition* of singing around the piano on holidays. It is *tradition* to eat turkey on Thanksgiving.

4 **Letter-Sounds:** Point out the syllable *-tion* as you read *tradition*.

DAY 2

1 **CREATE** If you *create* something, you make something that hasn't been made before.

2 **Examples:** She likes to *create* vases from clay. My dad *creates* delicious new recipes for dinner. The new grocery store will *create* many new jobs for people.

4 **Word Parts:** Point out that *cre-ate* has two syllables, not one.

DAY 3

1 **INSPECT** When you *inspect* something, you look at it very carefully.

2 **Examples:** Mom will *inspect* my room after I clean it to make sure I did a good job. You should *inspect* clothes before you buy them to make sure they are well-made.

4 **Letter-Sounds:** Children should be able to decode *inspect*.

DAY 4

1 **ANGLE** The way you look at something is the *angle* from which you see it.

2 **Example:** The seats were on the side at a bad *angle*, so we couldn't see the screen very well.

4 **Letter-Sounds:** Children can decode *angle*.

1 **BRILLIANT** If something is *brilliant*, it is very bright and sparkling.

2 **Examples:** The diamond ring was *brilliant*. The colored lights in the night parade were *brilliant*.

4 **Letter-Sounds:** Point out the sound that *iant* stands for in *brilliant*.

1 **SNAPSHOT** A *snapshot* is a simple picture taken with a camera.

2 **Examples:** I took a *snapshot* of my birthday cake. It was difficult to take good *snapshots* from the moving car.

4 **Word Parts:** Children can decode the compound word *snapshot*.

Definitions, examples, and letter-sounds to use with the Oral Vocabulary Routine on p. DI·1

Amazing Words **to build oral vocabulary**

USE WITH

DAY 1

1 **CLIMATE** *Climate* is the kind of weather that happens in a particular place.

2 **Examples:** The desert has a dry *climate*. There is a lot of rain in a rain forest *climate*. Florida has a much warmer *climate* than Michigan has.

4 **Letter-Sounds:** Point out the long *i* sound in the first syllable.

1 **LIVESTOCK** Animals such as cows or chickens that are raised on farms are called *livestock*.

2 **Examples:** The rancher's *livestock* grazed in the fields. It was Jeff's responsibility to feed the *livestock* each morning.

4 **Word Parts:** Point out the two words in the compound word *livestock*.

1 **OCCUPATION** A person's *occupation* is the work that person does to earn a living.

2 **Examples:** A firefighter has a dangerous *occupation*. My sister changed her *occupation* from a teacher to a lawyer.

4 **Word Parts:** Run your hand under the four word parts in *oc-cu-pa-tion* as you read the word.

DAY 2

1 **BUCKAROO** *Buckaroo* is another name for cowboy or cowhand.

2 **Examples:** The *buckaroo* rode the wild horse. The *buckaroo* rounded up the cattle and put them into the corral.

4 **Word Parts:** Run your hand under the three word parts in *buck-a-roo* as you read the word.

1 **DROVER** *Drover* is another name for a cowboy who herds droves of cattle along a trail.

2 **Examples:** The *drover* rode his horse and made sure the cattle stayed on the trail. The *drover* chased after the calf that ran away.

4 **Letter-Sounds:** Children can decode *drover*.

DAY 3

1 **LARIAT** A *lariat* is another name for a lasso, or stiff rope with a sliding loop at one end used for catching horses or cows.

2 **Examples:** The drover threw the *lariat* and caught the cow around the neck. It takes a lot of practice for a cowboy to learn how to use a *lariat* to catch a horse.

4 **Word Parts:** Run your hand under the three word parts in *lar-i-at* as you read the word.

DAY 4

1 **LEGEND** A *legend* is a story that has been passed down through the years that many people believe. A *legend* can also be a famous person who is greatly admired for his or her talents.

2 **Examples:** There is a *legend* about a cowboy in the Old West who could catch any wild horse. Davy Crockett is a *legend* in American history.

4 **Letter-Sounds:** Point out the soft *g* sound in *legend* as you read the word.

1 **RAWHIDE** *Rawhide* is an animal hide that has not been tanned, or made into leather.

2 **Examples:** The cowboys used a rope made of *rawhide*. After the *rawhide* is tanned into leather, it will be made into a jacket.

4 **Word Parts:** Children can decode the compound word *rawhide*.

Amazing Words

to build oral vocabulary

Definitions, examples, and letter-sounds to use with the Oral Vocabulary Routine on p. DI·1

USE WITH

DAY 1

1 **CEREMONY** A *ceremony* is something that people do to celebrate a special occasion. Examples are a wedding *ceremony* or a *ceremony* to officially open a new park.

2 **Examples:** My aunt's wedding *ceremony* was held outdoors. The mayor attended the groundbreaking *ceremony* for the new playground.

4 **Word Parts:** Clap the four word parts in *cer-e-mo-ny* as you read the word.

1 **CULTURE** We call the beliefs, customs, and behaviors of groups of people at a certain time their *culture*.

2 **Examples:** The Japanese tea ceremony is a part of their *culture*. There are many Native American *cultures* in the United States.

4 **Letter-Sounds:** Children can decode the word *culture*.

1 **FESTIVAL** A *festival* is a program of entertainment often held annually.

2 **Examples:** People have *festivals* to celebrate religious holidays. In August our town has a corn *festival*.

4 **Word Parts:** Run your hand under the three word parts in *fes-ti-val* as you read the word.

DAY 2

1 **COMPLIMENT** A *compliment* is something kind said about you, or praise given to someone else.

2 **Examples:** My mother paid me a *compliment* on my art project by saying she liked the pastel colors I used. I give my little brother a *compliment* when he does something good.

4 **Word Parts:** Run your hand under the three word parts in *com-pli-ment* as you read the word.

DAY 3

1 **FIDGET** When you move around in a restless way, you *fidget*.

2 **Examples:** I always *fidget* when I am supposed to sit still. Mom said I should not *fidget* when we are at the concert.

4 **Letter-Sounds:** Point out the soft *g* sound as you read the word *fidget*.

DAY 4

1 **EVERGREEN** *Evergreen* is a word used to describe a type of tree or shrub that stays green all year long, such as pine trees.

2 **Examples:** The *evergreen* branches looked pretty with snow on them. We used *evergreen* clippings to make a wreath for our door.

4 **Word Parts:** Children can decode the compound word *evergreen*.

1 **MULTICOLORED** If something has many different colors, we say it is *multicolored*.

2 **Examples:** In the winter, I wear a *multicolored* scarf. The *multicolored* picture contained reds, blues, greens, and yellows.

4 **Word Parts:** Run your hand under the four word parts in *mul-ti-col-ored* as you read the word.

1 **SASH** A *sash* is a long piece of cloth that can be tied around your waist or worn over one shoulder. A *sash* is like a scarf.

2 **Examples:** She wore a red *sash* around her waist as part of her costume.

4 **Letter-Sounds:** Children can decode *sash*.

SUCCESS PREDICTOR

Grade 2
Oral Vocabulary Words

UNIT 1 Exploration
UNIT 2 Working Together
UNIT 3 Creative Ideas
UNIT 4 Our Changing World
UNIT 5 Responsibility
UNIT 6 Traditions

DEVELOP LANGUAGE

Exploration	Working Together	Creative Ideas	Our Changing World	Responsibility	Traditions
brittle	avalanche	construct	concentration	caretaker	athlete
creature	blustery	contraption	frown	community	challenge
dart	courageous	daydream	homeland	instrument	champion
decision	fast-paced	foolproof	patient	lug	dainty
investigate	hazard	project	preserve	operation	disguise
rural	instinct	scrap	represent	responsible	effort
underground	rescue	sidekick	tough	supplies	professional
urban	skittish	unique	valuable	teamwork	shortstop
ascend	actuate	correspond	adapt	concern	allegiance
descend	aloft	cove	ancient	fragile	frayed
enormous	compete	deaf	annual	growth	history
journey	contribute	footprint	bury	litter	independence
launch	deserve	imitate	massive	pellets	indivisible
meteorite	mope	postage	nutrients	pollute	patriotic
orbit	recreation	sign language	sprout	protection	symbol
universe	tinker	transport	undisturbed	release	unfurl
detective	coax	boast	appearance	behavior	angle
fascinating	conflict	consume	canopy	companion	brilliant
galaxy	inhabit	contentment	forage	confident	celebration
identify	ramp	cure	forepaw	consider	create
slimy	resolve	gloat	pursue	cooperate	custom
tranquil	serape	incident	restless	obedient	inspect
underneath	startle	prey	stage	properly	snapshot
wildlife	vacation	shrewd	transform	reprimand	tradition
arid	depend	snicker	accent	advantage	buckaroo
discovery	familiar	abundant	adjust	appreciate	climate
dunes	insist	assist	foreign	communicate	drover
forbidding	miserable	beam	forlorn	defiant	lariat
haven	partnership	dismay	landmark	demand	legend
landform	solution	efficient	quiver	ferocious	livestock
ledge	struggle	forever	tease	firmly	occupation
precipitation	survival	generous	unexpected	respect	rawhide
delicate	banquet	situation	breeze	apologize	ceremony
exhibit	decorate	accomplish	condition	citizen	compliment
genius	dine	excel	funnel	hoard	culture
inquire	flare	opportunity	predict	interrupt	evergreen
resist	glimmer	original	sparkle	judgment	festival
satisfaction	holiday	process	swirl	protest	fidget
stun	participate	research	terrifying	scold	multicolored
sturdy	whispery	scientist	whip	troublemaker	sash
		unusual			

REMEMBER that oral vocabulary is informally assessed.

Babe Didrikson

There are many women in sports today, but it wasn't always this way. It was different back in the 1920s and 1930s. Then it was rare to find a woman athlete.

One of the first women in sports was Babe Didrikson. Her real first name was Mildred. She grew up in Texas. She loved to play sports as a child. She especially liked to play baseball with the boys who lived near her.

Young Mildred was a good baseball player. That might be the reason she got the name "Babe." Babe Ruth was a famous baseball player. He hit a lot of home runs, and Mildred hit a lot of home runs too.

Didrikson played many other sports and was good at all of them. She played basketball. She also played golf and became a women's golf champion. They say that someone once asked Didrikson if there was anything she didn't play. She answered, "Dolls."

When she was twenty-one, Didrikson went to the 1932 Olympic Games. She entered three track and field events and won three medals—two gold and one silver. Not everyone cheered for her because some people thought that sports should only be for men. But that didn't stop Didrikson. With her bravery and effort, she changed the way people thought about women in sports.

ADVANCED SELECTION 26   VOCABULARY: athlete, effort

A Gift from France

The Statue of Liberty was opened to the public on October 28, 1886. Thousands came to see it. It was an important day in American history.

Since then, the statue has welcomed millions of people to New York Harbor and the United States as a symbol of our country. However, it was made in France. The Statue of Liberty was a gift from the people of France to the people of the United States.

An artist named Bartholdi designed the statue. He came to the United States in 1871. At that time in history, people traveling from Europe to our country came by ship. When Bartholdi's ship steamed into New York Harbor, it was an exciting time for him. As he looked from the deck, he saw an old fort on an island in the harbor. He knew immediately that this was the place for his statue. Everyone who sailed into New York Harbor would see it. The government owned the island. The island already belonged to the people. It was perfect!

Picking the place to put the statue was the easy part. It cost a lot of money to make such a large monument. It took a long time for the French people to raise the money.

Finally, the statue was finished. More than one hundred years later, the Statue of Liberty continues to be an important symbol of freedom and independence.

ADVANCED SELECTION 27 **VOCABULARY:** symbol, independence, history

The History of Piñatas

Long ago, an explorer from Italy went to China on an adventure. His name was Marco Polo. While in China, he saw people making figures shaped like animals. They filled them with seeds and covered them with colored paper and other decorations. They used colored sticks to break open the figures, and the seeds spilled out to bring good luck. This was an early form of the piñata.

When Marco Polo returned to Italy, he told people what he had seen in China. Soon Italian people were doing the same thing. This custom spread from Italy to Spain, and Spanish people brought this custom with them to Mexico.

Today, the custom of breaking a piñata is still a common tradition in Mexico. In fact, a birthday celebration in Mexico is not complete without a piñata. Piñatas are pretty to look at, but they are made to be broken. There are candies and other surprises, such as small toys and coins, inside. Every child at the party gets a turn to try to break open the piñata with a stick. An adult hangs the piñata up outside so it can swing freely. Each child wears a blindfold to make it harder to break the piñata. When the piñata breaks open, the treats fall out, and the children rush to pick up as much as they can. Often there's a bowl of extra treats to make sure that everyone enjoys the celebration.

ADVANCED SELECTION 28   VOCABULARY: custom, tradition, celebration

Wild West Show

William Frederick "Buffalo Bill" Cody was born in Iowa in 1846, but he grew up in Kansas. At the age of eleven, Cody got a job herding livestock as a wagon driver. However, this wouldn't be his only occupation. By the time William Cody was fourteen, he had worked as a fur trapper, a miner, and a Pony Express rider. After the War, Cody made his living in the Army as a buffalo hunter. This is how he earned the nickname Buffalo Bill.

When he was twenty-six, Buffalo Bill started the Wild West Show. Buffalo Bill and other real cowboys and cowgirls, such as Annie Oakley and "Wild Bill" Hickok, performed ranching and roping tricks for audiences that didn't live on or near ranches. They also performed fearless bronco-riding tricks. The Wild West Show introduced people to what they thought was the cowboy way of life. As the show became very popular, Buffalo Bill took it all across the United States and Europe.

People loved the Wild West Show. They thought they were seeing the way things really happened in the Wild West. They thought they were watching history.

However, the Wild West Show was more than history. Buffalo Bill showed people what they wanted to see rather than what the West was really like. He was a showman who used his eagerness and skill to educate and entertain. Even today, some of our ideas about the Old West come from Buffalo Bill's Wild West Show.

ADVANCED SELECTION 29   VOCABULARY: livestock, occupation

Native American Music

Music is an important part of the Native American culture. Native Americans have their own kinds of instruments and songs and often use drums and rattles to make their music.

Some Native American drums are made from dried animal skins that are tied to four sticks or stretched tightly over hollow logs and sewn.

Another Native American drum is a water drum. Some water drums use hollow logs. Others use big iron pots. The log or pot is filled with water, and the animal skin is stretched over the top.

Wooden boxes make good square drums. Native Americans who live on the Pacific Coast make this kind of drum. Some are big enough for people to sit on. They play the drum with their feet.

Native Americans also make rattles using many different materials. Turtle shells or buffalo horns are filled with pebbles to make rattles. Shaking the rattle in midair makes the rattling sound.

Some Native American tribes still use these drums and rattles. When they have a festival or ceremony, they play them. This music helps to keep their culture alive.

ADVANCED SELECTION 30   VOCABULARY: culture, ceremony, festival

Group Time

DAY 1

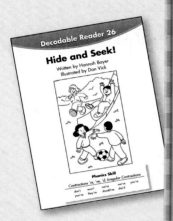

Decodable Reader 26
Hide and Seek!
Written by Hannah Bayer
Illustrated by Dan Vick

1 **Word Work**

CONTRACTIONS Reteach p. 296n. Additional words to blend:

| they're | I'd | they've | they'd | don't |

Then have children read and write the word pairs shown below and name the contraction they can form. Then have them write the contractions and identify which letter or letters were left out to form the contraction.

he had	he'd
where did	where'd
you have	you've
we are	we're

SPELLING Reteach p. 296p. Model spelling *don't* and *they're.* You may wish to give children fewer words to learn.

2 **Read** Decodable Reader 26

BEFORE READING Review the contractions on p. 296q and have children blend these story words: *don't, we've, won't, behind, counting, ducked, muttered.* Be sure children understand the meanings of words such as *ducked.*

DURING READING Use p. 296q.

Monitor Progress	Word and Story Reading
If... children have difficulty with any of these words,	**then...** reteach them by modeling. Have children practice the words, with feedback from you, until they can read them independently.
If... children have difficulty reading the story individually,	**then...** read a page aloud as children follow along. Then have the group reread the page. Continue reading in this way before children read individually.

3 **Reread** for Fluency

Use the Oral Rereading Routine, p. 296q, and text at each child's independent reading level.

MORE READING FOR
Group Time

Use this Leveled Reader or other text at children's instructional level.

Below-Level

Reviews
- Lesson vocabulary *bases, cheers, field, plate, sailed, threw*
- Compare and contrast

Check this database for additional titles.

Leveled Reader Database

ONLINE

PearsonSuccessNet.com

Advanced

ROUTINE

DAY 1

1 Word Work

Contractions Practice using words with the contractions *'re, 've,* and *'d.* If children know the words on first read, they may need no further practice. Practice items:

we're	**they're**	**we've**	**she'd**	**could've**
they've	**I've**	**you're**	**I'd**	**we'd**
you'd	**he'd**	**they'd**	**you've**	

Have children write the words on cards and sort by contractions. Then have individuals choose several words to use in a sentence

2 Read Advanced Selection 26

BEFORE READING Have children identify this oral vocabulary word: *athlete*.

DURING READING Children may read silently. Provide guidance as needed.

AFTER READING Have children recall the events in the selection. (Babe Didrikson played sports as a child. She became a famous athlete and changed the way people thought about women and sports.) Ask:

- Why were there very few women athletes in the 1920s and 1930s?
- Do you like to play or watch any sports? Why?

On the back of the selection page have children write a short poem about a sport they enjoy.

DI•9

3 Extend Concepts Through Inquiry

IDENTIFY QUESTIONS Have children choose two famous women athletes to compare and contrast. During the week, they should learn more about their choices from reading, studying pictures, and talking with adults or older children. On Day 5 they will share what they learned. Guide children in brainstorming possible choices.

- Think about your choices. Are they alike in some ways? Are they different in some ways?

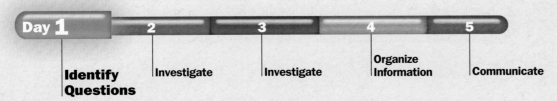

Day 1	2	3	4	5
Identify Questions	Investigate	Investigate	**Organize Information**	Communicate

MORE READING FOR
Group Time

Use this Leveled Reader or other text at children's instructional level.

Advanced

Reviews
- Concept vocabulary
- Compare and contrast

Group Time

DAY 2

Audio CD AudioText

Strategic Intervention

ROUTINE

1 Word Work

🎯 **CONTRACTIONS** Reteach pp. 298c–298d. Additional words to blend:

should've	they're	she'd	you're
you'd	you've	I'd	would've

LESSON VOCABULARY Reteach p. 298f. Have individuals practice reading the words from word cards.

2 Read Strategic Intervention Decodable Reader 26

BEFORE READING Before reading, review *bases, cheers, field, plate, sailed,* and *threw.* Point out quotation marks throughout the story, when the speaker changes, and who is speaking.

AFTER READING Check comprehension by having children retell the story, including the characters, setting, and plot.

Have children locate contractions in the story. List words children name. Review the contraction spelling patterns. Have children sort the words they found below *'re, 've, 'd,* and *irregular.*

're	've	'd	irregular
they're	I've	he'd	don't
we're			won't

3 Reread Josh Gibson

BEFORE READING Have children practice the words below—first as a group and then individually. Then use Guiding Comprehension, pp. 300–313, to monitor understanding.

slugger	baseballs	forties	supposed
practicing	imagine	especially	nothing

Monitor Progress	Word and Story Reading
If... children have difficulty with any of these words,	**then...** reteach them by modeling. Have children practice the words, with feedback from you, until they can read them independently.
If... children have difficulty reading the story individually,	**then...** have them follow along in their books as they listen to the AudioText. You may also have them read pages of the selection aloud together, first with you and then without you, before reading individually.

ROUTINE

1 Read *Josh Gibson*

DURING READING Have children read silently to p. 307. Provide guidance as needed. Ask:

- Why did Grandmama always pretend she was Josh Gibson?
- Why do you think the boys said, "Too bad she's a girl"?

Have children read silently to p. 313. Then ask:

- Why did Grandmama wear a dress to play baseball?

COMPARE AND CONTRAST Have children compare and contrast Grandmama and Josh Gibson. Discuss how the acceptance of women athletes has changed sports.

- Why do you think there are more women athletes today?
- Do you look up to any women athletes? Who are they?

Children can work with a partner to complete a Venn diagram (Graphic Organizer 17) to compare and contrast Grandmama and Josh Gibson.

VISUALIZE Children can visualize what the park looked like the day that Grandmama was allowed to play in the game with the boys. Have them describe the crowd cheering for Grandmama as she hit the ball out of the park.

RESPONSE Ask children to imagine they are famous athletes. Have them write a diary entry for one day in their life.

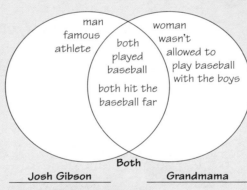

man famous athlete | both played baseball both hit the baseball far | woman wasn't allowed to play baseball with the boys

Both

Josh Gibson   Grandmama

▲ **Graphic Organizer 17**

Can a girl really hit a baseball just like Josh Gibson?

301

Audio CD   **AudioText**

3 Extend Concepts Through Inquiry

INVESTIGATE Guide children in choosing material at their independent reading level to explore their topic. Help children decide how they will present their information. Children may use a chart or other graphic organizer, a written format, photographs, drawings, or posters.

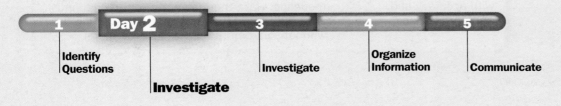

1 Identify Questions | **Day 2** | 3 Investigate | 4 Organize Information | 5 Communicate

Investigate

Group Time

Just Like
JOSH GIBSON
by Angela Johnson
illustrated by Beth Peck

Genre **Realistic fiction** stories are made up but could
really happen. Look for things that really could
have happened to a little girl.

300

Audio CD AudioText

MORE READING FOR
Group Time

Use this Leveled
Reader or other
text at children's
instructional level.

Below-Level

Reviews
• Lesson vocabulary *bases,
cheers, field, plate, sailed, threw*
• Compare and contrast

Strategic Intervention

ROUTINE

1 Word Work

REVIEW VOWELS *aw, au, augh, al* Review p. 314c, using these
additional words. Have children sort the words into *aw, au, augh,*
and *al* lists.

| taught | daughter | sauce | naughty | draw | wall |
| chalk | caught | ball | jaw | talk | August |

REVIEW SENTENCE READING Have individuals read these
sentences to review decoding skills.

> **She taught her daughter how to make the sauce.**
> **It is naughty to draw on the wall with chalk.**
> **I caught the ball so he did not stay on first base.**
> **Paul hurt his jaw and could not talk until August.**

2 Comprehension

COMPARE AND CONTRAST/VISUALIZE Reteach pp. 296r and
296–297. Have children respond to the Connect to Reading
questions after completing step 3 Reread for Fluency.
• Now read the story again quietly, picturing in your mind what
people look like or what is happening and compare and contrast
what you read with what you already know. When you have
finished, I'd like you to tell me what clue words helped you
compare and contrast.

3 Reread for Fluency

READ WITH ACCURACY AND APPROPRIATE PACE Teach p. 314f
using text at children's independent level. Reading options
include Student Edition selections, Decodable Readers, Strategic
Intervention Decodable Readers, and Leveled Readers.

Monitor Progress	Fluency
If... children have difficulty reading with accuracy and appropriate pace,	**then...** have them determine if they are reading too fast or too slow and provide additional modeling. Have them listen to your model and then read aloud together, first with you and then without you, before reading individually.

Advanced

1 Read Self-Selected Reading

BEFORE READING Have children select a trade book or Leveled Reader to read independently. Guide children in selecting books of appropriate difficulty.

AFTER READING When they have finished, have each child select an interesting fact about an athlete to read aloud to a partner.

DAY 3

2 Extend Concepts Through Inquiry

INVESTIGATE Give children time to investigate the athletes they are comparing and to begin preparing their information.

1	2	Day 3	4	5
Identify Questions	Investigate	Investigate	Organize Information	Communicate

Trade Books for Self-Selected Reading

LIVING THE GOLD-MEDAL LIFE: INSPIRATIONS FROM FEMALE ATHLETES by Mary Lee Tracy and Ginny McCabe, Standard Publishing Company, 2003

GREAT WOMEN ATHLETES by Darice Bailer, Random House Books for Young Readers, 2001

MORE READING FOR
Group Time

Use this Leveled Reader or other text at children's instructional level.

Advanced

Reviews
• Concept vocabulary
• Compare and contrast

Group Time

DAY 4

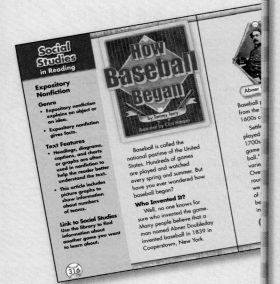

AudioText

Strategic Intervention

ROUTINE

1 Read "How Baseball Began"

BEFORE READING Have children practice the words below—first as a group and then individually. Then use Social Studies in Reading, pp. 316–319.

national	pastime	wondered	believed
probably	developed	official	professional

Monitor Progress	Word and Selection Reading
If... children have difficulty with any of these words,	**then...** have them practice in pairs reading word cards before reading the selection.
If... children have difficulty reading the selection individually,	**then...** have them follow along in their books as they listen to the AudioText. You may also have them read pages of the selection aloud together, first with you and then without you, before reading individually.

2 Reread for Fluency

Preteach p. 319a, using text at children's independent reading level. Reading options include Student Edition selections, Decodable Readers, Strategic Intervention Decodable Readers, and Leveled Readers.

3 Build Concepts

Use the Oral Vocabulary Routine, pp. DI·1–DI·3, and the Oral Vocabulary Words on p. DI·8.

MORE READING FOR
Group Time

Use this Leveled Reader or other text at children's instructional level.

Below-Level

Reviews
- Lesson vocabulary *bases, cheers, field, plate, sailed, threw*
- Compare and contrast

Advanced

ROUTINE

1 Read "How Baseball Began"

AFTER READING Ask:
- Have you ever played baseball? Did you follow all of the rules?
- Why don't players throw a ball at a runner anymore?
- Why do you think baseball has become such a popular sport?

2 Vocabulary

Extend vocabulary with questions such as these:
- Would you like to be a *professional athlete* someday? Why or why not?
- In baseball, where is the *shortstop* position?
- Have you ever faced a *challenge*? Explain.

Encourage children to use the words in their writing.

3 Extend Concepts Through Inquiry

ORGANIZE INFORMATION Give children time to continue reading about the athletes they are comparing. Remind them that tomorrow they will share their information. By now they should have begun putting the information in a presentation format.

1	2	3	Day 4	5
Identify Questions	Investigate	Investigate	Organize Information	Communicate

In rounders, players threw the ball at runners. If a runner got hit, he was out.

Abner Doubleday

Baseball probably developed from the English game of the 1600s called "rounders."

Settlers living in America played rounders in the 1700s. They also called the game "town ball" and "base ball." Rules of the game varied from place to place. Over the years, the game of rounders became the game we now call baseball. One of the biggest differences between the two games is in how the batter is put out.

In baseball, players tag runners to put them out.

Compare and Contrast   What two games are being compared?

317

Audio CD   **AudioText**

Josh Gibson
Group Time

ROUTINE

DAY 5

1 Word Work

CONTRACTIONS Have children read aloud as you track the print. Call on individuals to blend the underlined words.

I <u>don't</u> know if <u>you've</u> finished the race or if <u>you're</u> still running it. She'd said that <u>he'd</u> paint tonight, but it <u>won't</u> be dry until later. <u>I've</u> had a cold like <u>you've</u> had, and it <u>won't</u> go away. He'd better call soon so we'll know if <u>they've</u> decided to come.

LESSON VOCABULARY Use p. 298f to review *bases, cheers, field, plate, sailed, threw.*

Monitor Progress	Lesson Vocabulary
If... children have difficulty with any of these words,	**then...** reteach them by modeling. Have children practice the words, with feedback from you, until they can read them independently.

2 Monitor Progress

SENTENCE READING SET A Use Set A on reproducible p. 320f to assess children's ability to read decodable and lesson vocabulary words in sentences.

COMPREHENSION To assess comprehension, have each child read Strategic Intervention Decodable Reader 26 or other text at the child's independent level. Ask children to compare and contrast people, places, and things in the story and have them retell the story.

MORE READING FOR
Group Time

Use this Leveled Reader or other text at children's instructional level.

Below-Level

Reviews
• Lesson vocabulary *bases, cheers, field, plate, sailed, threw*
• Compare and contrast

Advanced

1 Monitor Progress

SENTENCE READING SET C Use Set C on reproducible page 320f to assess children's ability to read decodable and lesson vocabulary words in sentences. If you have any questions about whether children have mastered this week's skills, have them read the Set B sentences.

COMMUNICATE Have each child read "Luke and Carlos" on reproducible p. 320g. Ask them to compare and contrast the characters and then retell the passage. Use the Retelling Rubric on p. 314–315 to evaluate the child's retelling.

2 Extend Concepts Through INquiry

COMMUNICATE Have children share their comparison of two female athletes.

1	2	3	4	Day 5
Identify Questions	Investigate	Investigate	Organize Information	

Communicate

MORE READING FOR
Group Time

Use this Leveled Reader or other text at children's instructional level.

Advanced

Reviews
• Concept vocabulary
• Compare and contrast

Red, White, and Blue
Group Time

ROUTINE

1 Word Work

INFLECTED ENDINGS Reteach p. 322n. Additional words to blend:

hopping glued thornier richest tries

Then make a six-column chart and make word cards for each of the words shown below. Have children choose a card, read the word, and write it under the appropriate heading. Have children tell how the spelling changed when the ending was added.

base word	-s or -es	-ed	-ing	-er	-est
drop	drops	dropped	dropping		
crazy	X	X	X	crazier	craziest
float	floats	floated	floating	X	X

SPELLING Reteach p. 322p. Model spelling *planned* and *crying.* You may wish to give children fewer words to learn.

2 Read Decodable Reader 27

BEFORE READING Review the words with inflected endings on p. 322q and have children blend these story words: *biggest, excited, coming, helped, peeking, pointed, prettiest, returns.* Be sure children understand meanings of words such as *returns.*

DURING READING Use p. 322q.

Monitor Progress	Word and Story Reading
If... children have difficulty with any of these words,	**then...** reteach them by modeling. Have children practice the words, with feedback from you, until they can read them independently.
If... children have difficulty reading the story individually,	**then...** read a page aloud as children follow along. Then have the group reread the page. Continue reading in this way before children read individually.

3 Reread for Fluency

Use the Paired Reading Routine, p. 322q, and text at each child's independent reading level.

MORE READING FOR
Group Time

Use this Leveled Reader or other text at children's instructional level.

Below-Level

Reviews
• Lesson vocabulary *America, birthday, flag, freedom, nicknames, stars, stripes*
• Fact and opinion

Check this database for additional titles.

Leveled Reader Database

ONLINE
PearsonSuccessNet.com

Advanced

ROUTINE

DAY 1

1 Word Work

🎯 **INFLECTED ENDINGS** Practice with words that have inflected endings. If children know the words on first read, they may need no further practice. Practice items:

cruelest	slower	catches	longest	wringing
presented	shortest	doing	hears	prettier
being	farthest	taller	walked	tougher

Have children write five more words with inflected endings. Then have individuals choose several words to use in a sentence.

2 Read Advanced Selection 27

BEFORE READING Have children identify these oral vocabulary words: *history, independence, symbol.*

DURING READING Children may read silently. Provide guidance as needed.

AFTER READING Have children decide whether the information in this selection can be proven, or if it explains someone's feelings or beliefs. (The information in this selection can be proven so it is fact, not opinion.) Ask:

- Why do you think the artist wanted everyone who sailed into the harbor to see the Statue of Liberty?
- Have you ever visited the Statue of Liberty? Tell about it.

On the back of the selection page have children draw something else that symbolizes freedom and write about it.

3 Extend Concepts Through Inquiry

IDENTIFY QUESTIONS Have children choose another national monument to research. During the week, they should learn more about the monument from reading, studying pictures, and talking with adults or older children. On Day 5 they will share what they learned. Guide children in brainstorming possible choices.

- Think about other important monuments in our country. Where are they located? Why are they important?

A Gift from France

The Statue of Liberty was opened to the public on October 28, 1886. Thousands came to see it. It was an important day in American history.

Since then, the statue has welcomed millions of people to New York Harbor and the United States as a symbol of our country. However, it was made in France. The Statue of Liberty was a gift from the people of France to the people of the United States.

An artist named Bartholdi designed the statue. He came to the United States in 1871. At that time in history, people traveling from Europe to our country came by ship. When Bartholdi's ship streamed into New York Harbor, it was an exciting time for him. As he looked from the deck, he saw an old fort on an island in the harbor. He knew immediately that this was the place for his statue. Everyone who sailed into New York Harbor would see it.

The government owned the island. The island already belonged to the people. It was perfect!

Picking the place to put the statue was the easy part. It cost a lot of money to make such a large monument. It took a long time for the French people to raise the money.

Finally, the statue was finished. More than one hundred years later, the Statue of Liberty continues to be an important symbol of freedom and independence.

DI•10

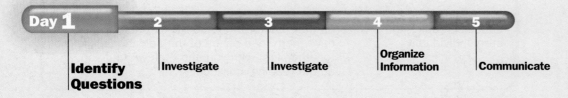

Day **1**   **2**   **3**   **4**   **5**

Identify Questions | Investigate | Investigate | **Organize Information** | Communicate

---

MORE READING FOR
Group Time

Use this Leveled Reader or other text at children's instructional level.

Advanced

Reviews
- Concept vocabulary
- Fact and opinion

Red, White, and Blue
Group Time

DAY 2

AudioText

ROUTINE

1 Word Work

INFLECTED ENDINGS Reteach p. 324c. Additional words to blend:

sleepiest	braver	pinches	rubbing
hammered	rides	looked	hardest

LESSON VOCABULARY Reteach p. 324f. Have individuals practice reading the words from word cards.

2 Read Strategic Intervention Decodable Reader 27

BEFORE READING Before reading, review *America, birthday, flag, freedom, nicknames, stars,* and *stripes.* Do a picture walk and have children predict what the story will be about.

AFTER READING Check comprehension by having children retell the story, including the characters, setting, and plot.

Have children locate words with inflected endings in the story. List words children name. Have children sort the words they found.

-est: *biggest, happiest, loneliest, nicest*

-ed: *cried, danced, liked, purred, replied, scampered, shouted, started, stopped, thrilled, tried, trusted*

-ing: *crying, dancing, hopping, singing, skipping, talking*

-er: *sadder*

3 Reread Red, White, and Blue

BEFORE READING Have children practice the words below—first as a group and then individually. Then use Guiding Comprehension, pp. 326–343, to monitor understanding.

parades	colonies	revolution	famous
general	soldiers	decision	president

Monitor Progress	Word and Story Reading
If... children have difficulty with any of these words,	**then...** reteach them by modeling. Have children practice the words, with feedback from you, until they can read them independently.
If... children have difficulty reading the story individually,	**then...** have them follow along in their books as they listen to the AudioText. You may also have them read pages of the selection aloud together, first with you and then without you, before reading individually.

Advanced

1 Read *Red, White, and Blue*

DURING READING Have children read silently to p. 335. Provide guidance as needed. Ask:

- Why do you think Betsy Ross made changes to the General's idea?
- Why is "The Star-Spangled Banner" the national anthem for our country?

Have children read silently to p. 343. Then ask:

- Do you think Abraham Lincoln made the right decision? Why or why not?
- Why do you think the astronauts put the flag on the moon?

FACT AND OPINION Have children decide whether this selection is fact or opinion. (fact) Discuss other places where the U.S. flag is flown, such as at sporting events and banks.

- Why is the U.S. flag flown in front of schools?
- Where else can you see a U.S. flag flown?
- Do you agree that the flag should be flown at these places? Explain.

MONITOR AND FIX UP Children can work with a partner to reread any difficult parts of the story.

RESPONSE Ask children to imagine they are going to design a flag for a new country. Have them draw a picture of the flag and explain what the colors represent.

2 Extend Concepts Through Inquiry

INVESTIGATE Guide children in choosing material at their independent reading level to explore the monument they chose. Some books that may be appropriate are *Our National Monuments* by Eleanor Ayer or *Monuments Help Us Remember: A Building Block Book* by Lee Sullivan Hill.

Help children decide how they will present their information. Children may use a story web or other graphic organizer, a written format, posters, models, or dramatic presentations.

How did the American flag change over the years?

327

AudioText

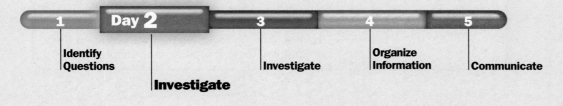

1	**Day 2**	3	4	5
Identify Questions		Investigate	Organize Information	Communicate
	Investigate			

Red, White, and Blue
Group Time

DAY **3**

AudioText

Strategic Intervention

ROUTINE

1 Word Work

REVIEW **CONTRACTIONS** Review p. 344c, using these additional words. Have children write each contraction and the two words they stand for.

you're	won't	we're	we've	they're	should've
they'd	I'd	you've	don't	she'd	you'd

REVIEW **SENTENCE READING** Have individuals read these sentences to review decoding skills.

You're saying that you won't go unless we're coming too?
We've got to know if they're at the airport yet—
they should've called.
They'd said I'd love to see what you've got in that box.
Don't you think she'd go swimming if you'd opened the pool?

2 Comprehension

FACT AND OPINION/MONITOR AND FIX UP Reteach pp. 322r and 322–323. Have children respond to the Connect to Reading questions after completing step 3 Reread for Fluency.
* Now read the story again quietly and keep track of statements of fact and statements of opinion by stopping during reading and rereading what you don't understand. When you have finished, I'd like you to tell me some facts and opinions in the story and the clue words that helped you.

3 Reread for Fluency

READ SILENTLY WITH FLUENCY AND ACCURACY Teach p. 344f, using text at children's independent level. Reading options include Student Edition selections, Decodable Readers, Strategic Intervention Decodable Readers, and Leveled Readers.

Monitor Progress	Fluency
If… children have difficulty reading with fluency and accuracy,	**then…** prompt them to read groups of words, not word-by-word, and provide additional modeling. Have them listen to your model and then read aloud together, first with you and then without you, before reading individually.

MORE READING FOR
Group Time

Use this Leveled Reader or other text at children's instructional level.

Below-Level

Reviews
• Lesson vocabulary *America, birthday, flag, freedom, nicknames, stars, stripes*
• Fact and opinion

Advanced

ROUTINE

DAY 3

1 Read Self-Selected Reading

BEFORE READING Have children select a trade book or Leveled Reader to read independently. Guide children in selecting books of appropriate difficulty.

AFTER READING When they have finished, have children write about a monument they would design to represent their community or school.

2 Extend Concepts Through INquiry

INVESTIGATE Give children time to investigate the national monument they have chosen and to begin preparing their information.

1	2	Day 3	4	5
Identify Questions	Investigate	Investigate	Organize Information	Communicate

Trade Books for Self-Selected Reading

OUR NATIONAL MONUMENTS by Eleanor Ayer, Rebound by Sagebrush, 1999

MONUMENTS HELP US REMEMBER: A BUILDING BLOCK BOOK by Lee Sullivan Hill, Carolrhoda Books, 2000

MORE READING FOR
Group Time

Use this Leveled Reader or other text at children's instructional level.

Advanced

Reviews
- Concept vocabulary
- Fact and opinion

DAY
4

Poetry | **You're a Grand Old Flag**

Song

Genre
- A song is a poem set to music.
- Songs often use rhyme. In each verse of this song, the first two lines rhyme, and the third and fifth lines rhyme.
- Songs often express the songwriter's feelings. As you read, think about how the songwriter feels about the flag.

Link to Writing
Write words to a song about something you feel is important. It could be a poem set to a familiar tune. Share your song with your classmates.

You're a Grand Old Flag
by George M. Cohan

You're a grand old flag,
You're a high flying flag
And forever in peace may you wave.
You're the emblem of the land I love.
The home of the free and the brave.

Ev'ry heart beats true
'Neath the red, white, and blue,
Where there's never a boast or brag,
Should auld acquaintance be forgot,
Keep your eye on the grand old flag.

346

Audio CD **AudioText**

MORE READING FOR
Group Time

Use this Leveled Reader or other text at children's instructional level.

Below-Level

Reviews
- Lesson vocabulary *America, birthday, flag, freedom, nicknames, stars, stripes*
- Fact and opinion

Strategic Intervention

ROUTINE

1 Read "You're a Grand Old Flag"

BEFORE READING Have children practice the words below—first as a group and then individually. Then use Poetry, pp. 346–347.

emblem   boast   there's   acquaintance

Monitor Progress	Word and Selection Reading
If... children have difficulty with any of these words,	**then...** have them practice in pairs reading word cards before reading the selection.
If... children have difficulty reading the selection individually,	**then...** have them follow along in their books as they listen to the AudioText. You may also have them read pages of the selection aloud together, first with you and then without you, before reading individually.

2 Reread for Fluency

Preteach p. 347a, using text at children's independent reading level. Reading options include Student Edition selections, Decodable Readers, Strategic Intervention Decodable Readers, and Leveled Readers.

3 Build Concepts

Use the Oral Vocabulary Routine, pp. DI·1–DI·2, DI·4, and the Oral Vocabulary Words on p. DI·8.

Advanced

ROUTINE

1 Read "You're a Grand Old Flag"

AFTER READING Ask:
- Why would the flag wave in peace?
- What is an emblem?
- What is meant by the "home of the free and the brave"?

2 Vocabulary

Extend vocabulary with questions such as these:
- Why is it important to learn about *history*?
- What is a *symbol* you see every day?
- What are some ways you can be *patriotic*?
- How can you show your *independence* at home or at school?

Encourage children to use the words in their writing.

3 Extend Concepts Through INQuiry

ORGANIZE INFORMATION Give children time to continue reading about the monument they have chosen. Remind them that tomorrow they will share their information. By now they should have begun putting the information in a presentation format.

1	2	3	Day 4	5
Identify Questions	Investigate	Investigate	Organize Information	Communicate

Reading Across Texts
"You're a Grand Old Flag" is one song about the flag of the United States. What other song about the flag did you read about in *Red, White, and Blue*?
Writing Across Texts Make a list of other patriotic songs that you know.

Monitor and Fix Up *If you are confused, remember to go back and reread.*

347

AudioText

MORE READING FOR
Group Time

Use this Leveled Reader or other text at children's instructional level.

Advanced

Reviews
- Concept vocabulary
- Fact and opinion

Red, White, and Blue
Group Time

Strategic Intervention

1 Word Work

INFLECTED ENDINGS Have children read aloud as you track the print. Call on individuals to blend the underlined words.

We <u>dragged</u> the box instead of <u>picking</u> it up and <u>carrying</u> it.
Our kite <u>lasted</u> <u>longer</u> in the air and flew <u>higher</u>
  than the other kites.
Tito was <u>telling</u> the <u>silliest</u> joke when I <u>walked</u> into the room.
She <u>sits</u> and <u>reads</u> books for the <u>longest</u> time.

LESSON VOCABULARY Use p. 324f to review *America, birthday, flag, freedom, nicknames, stars, stripes.*

Monitor Progress	Lesson Vocabulary
If... children have difficulty with any of these words,	**then...** reteach them by modeling. Have children practice the words, with feedback from you, until they can read them independently.

2 Monitor Progress

SENTENCE READING SET A Use Set A on reproducible page 348f to assess children's ability to read decodable and lesson vocabulary words in sentences.

COMPREHENSION To assess comprehension, have each child read Strategic Intervention Decodable Reader 27 or other text at the child's independent level. Have children identify facts and opinions in the story and have them retell the story.

MORE READING FOR
Group Time

Use this Leveled Reader or other text at children's instructional level.

Below-Level

Reviews
• Lesson vocabulary *America, birthday, flag, freedom, nicknames, stars, stripes*
• Fact and opinion

Advanced

ROUTINE

DAY **5**

1 Monitor Progress

SENTENCE READING SET C Use Set C on reproducible p. 348f to assess children's ability to read decodable and lesson vocabulary words in sentences. If you have any questions about whether children have mastered this week's skills, have them read the Set B sentences.

COMPREHENSION Have each child read "The Grand Canyon" on reproducible p. 348g. Ask whether the information can be proven or if it is a statement of someone's feelings and beliefs (fact or opinion). Have the child retell the passage. Use the Retelling Rubric on p. 314–315 to evaluate the child's retelling.

2 Extend Concepts Through **INquiry**

COMMUNICATE Have children share their presentation about a national monument.

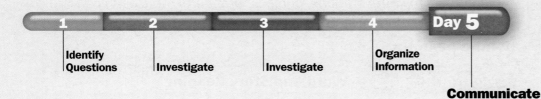

1	2	3	4	Day 5
Identify Questions	Investigate	Investigate	Organize Information	**Communicate**

MORE READING FOR
Group Time

Use this Leveled Reader or other text at children's instructional level.

Advanced

Reviews
• Concept vocabulary
• Fact and opinion

Group Time

ROUTINE

DAY 1

1 Word Work

SYLLABLES *-tion, -ture* Reteach p. 350n. Additional words to blend:

vacation   culture   future   affection

Then have children sort the following *-tion* and *-ture* words and circle the letters that stand for those syllables.

section   action   mixture   caution   edition

lotion   feature   furniture   sculpture

SPELLING Reteach p. 350p. Model spelling *action* and *feature*. You may wish to give children fewer words to learn.

2 Read Decodable Reader 28

BEFORE READING Review words with syllables *-tion* and *-ture* on p. 350q and have children blend these story words: *future, locations, mixture, stations, choices, firefighter, houses, nicely.* Be sure children understand meanings of words such as *locations*.

DURING READING Use p. 350q.

Monitor Progress	Word and Story Reading
If... children have difficulty with any of these words,	**then...** reteach them by modeling. Have children practice the words, with feedback from you, until they can read them independently.
If... children have difficulty reading the story individually,	**then...** read a page aloud as children follow along. Then have the group reread the page. Continue reading in this way before children read individually.

3 Reread for Fluency

Use the Oral Rereading Routine, p. 350q, and text at each child's independent reading level.

Decodable Reader 28

I Might Be

Written by Greg Morton
Illustrated by Brad Williams

Phonics Skill
Common Syllables -tion, -ture

future	picture(s)	mixture
action	stations	nation
locations	nature	motion

MORE READING FOR
Group Time

Very Special Birthdays

Use this Leveled Reader or other text at children's instructional level.

Below-Level

Reviews
- Lesson vocabulary *aunt, bank, basket, collects, favorite, present*
- Draw conclusions

Check this database for additional titles.

Leveled Reader Database

ONLINE

PearsonSuccessNet.com

Advanced

DAY 1

1 Word Work

⊙ **SYLLABLES** Practice using words that contain the syllables *-tion* and *-ture*. If children know the words on first read, they may need no further practice. Practice items:

question	mixture	traction	nature	furniture
ration	creature	motion	potion	adventure
station	feature	tuition	caution	fracture

Have children write the words in a list and sort by syllables. Then have individuals choose several words to use in a sentence.

2 Read Advanced Selection 28

BEFORE READING Have children identify these story words: *celebration, custom, tradition.*

DURING READING Children may read silently. Provide guidance as needed.

AFTER READING Have children recall the two most important ideas in the selection. (Piñatas have been around for many years. Several countries have their own versions.) Ask:
- Which version of the piñata would you prefer? Why?
- What would you like to find inside of your piñata?

On the back of the selection page have children draw a picture of their piñata.

The History of Piñatas

Long ago, an explorer from Italy went to China on an adventure. His name was Marco Polo. While in China, he saw people making figures shaped like animals. They filled them with seeds and covered them with colored paper and other decorations. They used colored sticks to break open the figures, and the seeds spilled out to bring good luck. This was an early form of the piñata.

When Marco Polo returned to Italy, he told people what he had seen in China. Soon Italian people were doing the same thing. This custom spread from Italy to Spain, and Spanish people brought this custom with them to Mexico.

Today, the custom of breaking a piñata is still a common tradition in Mexico. In fact, a birthday celebration in Mexico is not complete without a piñata. Piñatas are pretty to look at, but they are made to be broken. There are candies and other surprises, such as small toys and coins, inside. Every child at the party gets a turn to try to break open the piñata with a stick. An adult hangs the piñata up outside so it can swing freely. Each child wears a blindfold to make it harder to break the piñata. When the piñata breaks open, the treats fall out, and the children rush to pick up as much as they can. Often there's a bowl of extra treats to make sure that everyone enjoys the celebration.

DI•11

3 Extend Concepts Through Inquiry

IDENTIFY QUESTIONS Have children choose two traditions or customs to investigate. During the week, they should learn more about their choices from reading, studying pictures, and talking with adults or older children. On Day 5 they will share what they learned. Guide children in brainstorming possible choices.
- Think about your choices. In which countries are these traditions practiced? Do you practice them in your own family?

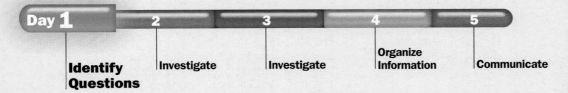

Day 1	2	3	4	5
Identify Questions	Investigate	Investigate	Organize Information	Communicate

MORE READING FOR
Group Time

Use this Leveled Reader or other text at children's instructional level.

Advanced

Reviews
- Concept vocabulary
- Draw conclusions

Group Time

DAY 2

AudioText

Strategic Intervention

ROUTINE

1 Word Work

SYLLABLES *-tion, -ture* Reteach p. 352c–352d. Additional words to blend:

location	action	nature	picture	fixture
mention	station	fracture	caution	capture

LESSON VOCABULARY Reteach p. 352f. Have individuals practice reading the words from word cards.

2 Read Strategic Intervention Decodable Reader 28

BEFORE READING Before reading, review *aunt, bank, basket, collects, favorite,* and *present.* Lead children on a picture walk through the story and discuss what is happening in each picture.

AFTER READING Check comprehension by having children retell the story, including the characters, setting, and plot.

Have children locate *-ture* and *-tion* words in the story. List words children name. Review the *-ture* and *-tion* spelling patterns. Have children sort the words they found below action and *captured.*

action	captured
caution	future
mentioned	picture
motion	
nation	
section	
station	

3 Reread *A Birthday Basket for Tía*

BEFORE READING Have children practice the words below—first as a group and then individually. Then use Guiding Comprehension, pp. 354–367, to monitor understanding.

ninetieth	special	surprise	bubbling
butterflies	drawers	sugary	musicians

Monitor Progress	Word and Story Reading
If... children have difficulty with any of these words,	**then...** reteach them by modeling. Have children practice the words, with feedback from you, until they can read them independently.
If... children have difficulty reading the story individually,	**then...** have them follow along in their books as they listen to the AudioText. You may also have them read pages of the selection aloud together, first with you and then without you, before reading individually.

Advanced

1 Read *A Birthday Basket for Tía*

DURING READING Have children read silently to p. 361. Provide guidance as needed. Ask:

- Why do you think Cecilia wants to give her aunt a present?

Have children read silently to p. 367. Then ask:

- Do these family members care about each other? How do you know?

DRAW CONCLUSIONS Have children discuss what kind of relationship Tía and Cecilia have. (a close, loving relationship) Discuss how family members show love for each other.

- Why do you think Cecilia put those things in the basket for Tía?
- What would you like to find in a birthday basket?

SUMMARIZE Children can complete a story sequence chart. Draw a chart or distribute copies of Graphic Organizer 7.

RESPONSE Ask children to plan a party for someone special. Have them list the guests, food, decorations, and gifts.

Beginning
Cecilia decides to make a birthday basket for Tía.

↓

Middle
Cecilia prepares the birthday basket. Cecilia and her family decorate and prepare for the surprise party.

↓

End
Tía enjoys her party and her birthday basket.

▲ **Graphic Organizer 7**

Audio CD **AudioText**

2 Extend Concepts Through Inquiry

INVESTIGATE Guide children in choosing material at their independent reading level to explore their traditions. Some books that may be appropriate are *Children Just Like Me: Celebrations!* by Anabel Kindersley and Barnabas Kindersley or *Wake Up, World!: A Day in the Life of Children Around the World* by Beatrice Hollyer.

Help children decide how they will present their information. Children may use photographs, posters, music, drawings, or models.

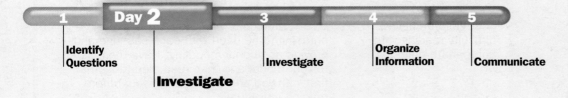

1	Day 2	3	4	5
Identify Questions	Investigate	Investigate	Organize Information	Communicate

Group Time

DAY 3

Audio CD AudioText

354

Realistic fiction is a story with characters and events that are like people and events in real life.

Genre

Strategic Intervention

ROUTINE

1 Word Work

REVIEW **BASE WORDS AND ENDINGS *-ed, -ing*** Review p. 368c, using these additional words. Have children write the words and circle the inflected endings.

ended	making	erupted	picked	drumming
fitted	hiking	climbed	rolling	landed
worked	cleaning			

REVIEW **SENTENCE READING** Have individuals read these sentences to review decoding skills.

I was tired of making so many mistakes on my homework. They picked the sweetest strawberries from the rolling hills. While hiking we climbed to see the volcano that erupted. My room was the neatest in the house because I worked hard cleaning it.

2 Comprehension

DRAW CONCLUSIONS/SUMMARIZE Reteach pp. 350r and 350–351. Have children respond to the Connect to Reading questions after completing step 3 Reread for Fluency.
• Now read the story again quietly. When you have finished, I'd like you to summarize the story and tell me why the characters acted the way they did.

3 Reread for Fluency

READ WITH APPROPRIATE PHRASING Teach p. 368f, using text at children's independent level. Reading options include Student Edition selections, Decodable Readers, Strategic Intervention Decodable Readers, and Leveled Readers.

Monitor Progress	Fluency
If... children have difficulty reading with appropriate phrasing,	**then...** discuss with them the appropriate phrasing to be used with each passage and provide additional modeling. Have them listen to your model and then read aloud together, first with you and then without you, before reading individually.

MORE READING FOR
Group Time

Use this Leveled Reader or other text at children's instructional level.

Below-Level

Reviews
• Lesson vocabulary *aunt, bank, basket, collects, favorite, present*
• Draw conclusions

DAY 3

Advanced

ROUTINE

1 Read Self-Selected Reading

BEFORE READING Have children select a trade book or Leveled Reader to read independently. Guide children in selecting books of appropriate difficulty.

AFTER READING When they have finished, have each child select an interesting tradition or custom to share with a partner.

2 Extend Concepts Through Inquiry

INVESTIGATE Give children time to investigate the traditions and customs they are learning about and to begin preparing their information.

1	2	Day 3	4	5
Identify Questions	Investigate	Investigate	Organize Information	Communicate

Trade Books for Self-Selected Reading

CHILDREN JUST LIKE ME: CELEBRATIONS! by Anabel Kindersley and Barnabas Kindersley, DK Publishing Inc., 1997

WAKE UP, WORLD!: A DAY IN THE LIFE OF CHILDREN AROUND THE WORLD by Beatrice Hollyer, Henry Holt & Company, 1999

MORE READING FOR
Group Time

Use this Leveled Reader or other text at children's instructional level.

Advanced

Reviews
- Concept vocabulary
- Draw conclusions

Group Time

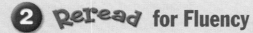

Strategic Intervention

ROUTINE

① Read "Family Traditions: Birthdays"

BEFORE READING Have children practice the words below—first as a group and then individually. Then use Reading Online, pp. 370–373.

tradition   slippery   celebration   similar

Monitor Progress	Word and Selection Reading
If… children have difficulty with any of these words,	**then…** have them practice in pairs reading word cards before reading the selection.
If… children have difficulty reading the selection individually,	**then…** have them follow along in their books as they listen to the AudioText. You may also have them read pages of the selection aloud together, first with you and then without you, before reading individually.

② Reread for Fluency

Preteach p. 373a, using text at children's independent reading level. Reading options include Student Edition selections, Decodable Readers, Strategic Intervention Decodable Readers, and Leveled Readers.

③ Build Concepts

Use the Oral Vocabulary Routine, pp. DI·1–DI·2, DI·5, and the Oral Vocabulary Words on p. DI·8.

AudioText

MORE READING FOR

Group Time

Use this Leveled Reader or other text at children's instructional level.

Below-Level

Reviews
• Lesson vocabulary *aunt, bank, basket, collects, favorite, present*
• Draw conclusions

Advanced

1 Read "Family Traditions: Birthdays"

AFTER READING Ask:
- Have you ever searched for birthday information on the Internet? Tell about it.
- Why do you think people all over the world celebrate birthdays?
- Recall how birthdays are celebrated in different countries. Which birthday tradition would you most enjoy? Explain.

2 Vocabulary

Extend vocabulary with questions such as these:
- Have you ever taken *snapshots* yourself? If so, from what *angle*?
- What kinds of things do you like to *create*?
- What *tradition* or *custom* does your family practice on your birthday?
- Do you have a favorite *celebration*? Tell about it.

Encourage children to use the words in their writing.

3 Extend Concepts Through Inquiry

ORGANIZE INFORMATION Give children time to continue reading about the customs or traditions they are comparing. Remind them that tomorrow they will share their information. By now they should have begun putting the information in a presentation format.

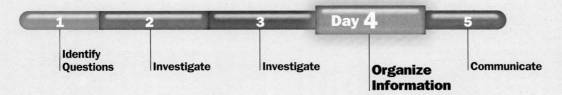

1	2	3	Day 4	5
Identify Questions	Investigate	Investigate	Organize Information	Communicate

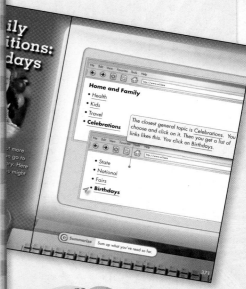

DAY 4

AudioText

MORE READING FOR

Group Time

Use this Leveled Reader or other text at children's instructional level.

Advanced

Reviews
- Concept vocabulary
- Draw conclusions

Group Time

Strategic Intervention

DAY 5

1 Word Work

SYLLABLES *-tion, -ture* Have children read aloud as you track the print. Call on individuals to blend the underlined words.

I forgot to <u>mention</u> the <u>location</u> of the <u>picture</u>.
Use <u>caution</u> and limit <u>motion</u> because of your <u>fracture</u>.
We went to the bus <u>station</u> to pick up the <u>furniture</u> and <u>fixtures</u> Grandma shipped.
He is making a <u>feature</u> film about <u>nature</u> in <u>action</u>.

LESSON VOCABULARY Use p. 352f to review *aunt, bank, basket, collects, favorite, present.*

Monitor Progress	Lesson Vocabulary
If... children have difficulty with any of these words,	**then...** reteach them by modeling. Have children practice the words, with feedback from you, until they can read them independently.

2 Monitor Progress

SENTENCE READING SET A Use Set A on reproducible page 374f to assess children's ability to read decodable and lesson vocabulary words in sentences.

COMPREHENSION To assess comprehension, have each child read Strategic Intervention Decodable Reader 28 or other text at the child's independent level. Ask children to draw conclusions about a choice a character made and have them retell the events in order.

MORE READING FOR
Group Time

Use this Leveled Reader or other text at children's instructional level.

Below-Level

Reviews
• Lesson vocabulary *aunt, bank, basket, collects, favorite, present*
• Draw conclusions

Advanced

ROUTINE

DAY 5

1 Monitor Progress

SENTENCE READING SET C Use Set C on reproducible page 374f to assess children's ability to read decodable and lesson vocabulary words in sentences. If you have any questions about whether children have mastered this week's skills, have them read the Set B sentences.

COMPREHENSION Have each child read "Tyler's Pictures" on reproducible page 374g. Ask what Tyler might be thinking about the future. Then have the child retell the passage. Use the Retelling Rubric on p. 368–369 to evaluate the child's retelling.

2 Extend Concepts Through **Inquiry**

COMMUNICATE Have children share their presentation on the customs or traditions they have studied.

1	2	3	4	Day 5
Identify Questions	Investigate	Investigate	Organize Information	

Communicate

MORE READING FOR
Group Time

Use this Leveled Reader or other text at children's instructional level.

Advanced

Reviews
• Concept vocabulary
• Draw conclusions

Group Time

DAY 1

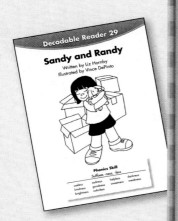

Strategic Intervention

ROUTINE

1 Word Work

SUFFIXES *-less, -ness* Reteach p. 376n. Additional words to blend:

pointless   hopeless   gentleness   worthless   fondness

Then have children sort the following *-less* and *-ness* words and circle the suffixes.

greatness	**weakness**	**tenderness**	**speechless**
loudness	**joyless**	**tireless**	
goodness	**fullness**	**mindless**	

SPELLING Reteach p. 376p. Model spelling *useless* and *goodness*. You may wish to give children fewer words to learn.

2 Read Decodable Reader 29

BEFORE READING Review the *-less* and *-ness* words on p. 376q and have children blend these story words: *brightness, colorless, sweetness, weakness, useless, moving, darkness, goodness.* Be sure children understand meanings of words such as *useless.*

DURING READING Use p. 376q.

Monitor Progress	Word and Story Reading
If... children have difficulty with any of these words,	**then...** reteach them by modeling. Have children practice the words, with feedback from you, until they can read them independently.
If... children have difficulty reading the story individually,	**then...** read a page aloud as children follow along. Then have the group reread the page. Continue reading in this way before children read individually.

3 Reread for Fluency

Use the Paired Reading Routine, p. 376q, and text at each child's independent reading level.

MORE READING FOR
Group Time

Use this Leveled Reader or other text at children's instructional level.

Below-Level

Reviews
• Lesson vocabulary *campfire, cattle, cowboy, galloped, herd, railroad, trails*
• Cause and effect

Check this database for additional titles.

ONLINE
PearsonSuccessNet.com

Advanced

ROUTINE

1 Word Work

🔊 **SUFFIXES** Practice using words ending in the suffixes *-ness* and *-less*. If children know the words on first read, they may need no further practice. Practice items:

alertness	craziness	regardless	cheapness
shameless	tasteless	harshness	effortless
foolishness	gracefulness	heartless	carefulness

Have children think of other words with these suffixes. Then have individuals choose several words to use in a sentence.

2 Read Advanced Selection 29

BEFORE READING Have children identify this oral vocabulary word: *occupation*.

DURING READING Children may read silently. Provide guidance as needed.

AFTER READING Have children recall the events of the selection. (Buffalo Bill worked many jobs when he was young. He started the Wild West Show when he was older. People enjoyed the show and thought they were learning about history.) Ask:

- Do you think Buffalo Bill enjoyed his job? Why or why not?
- Why do you think the Wild West Show was mostly for fun and not based on history?

On the back of the selection page have children write a short description of Buffalo Bill.

3 Extend Concepts Through Inquiry

IDENTIFY QUESTIONS Have children develop a play about the Old West. During the week, they should learn more about the Old West from reading, studying pictures, and talking with adults or older children. On Day 5 they will share their play. Guide children in brainstorming possible choices.

- Think about how the Old West used to be. How did people travel? What kinds of jobs did they do?

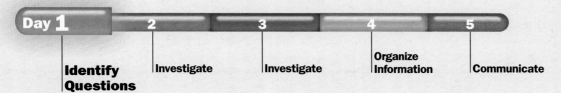

Day 1	2	3	4	5
Identify Questions	Investigate	Investigate	Organize Information	Communicate

---

Wild West Show

William Frederick "Buffalo Bill" Cody was born in Iowa in 1846, but he grew up in Kansas. At the age of eleven, Cody got a job herding livestock as a wagon driver. However, this wouldn't be his only occupation. By the time William Cody was fourteen, he had worked as a fur trapper, a miner, and a Pony Express rider. After the War, Buffalo Bill made his living in the Army as a buffalo hunter. This is how he earned the nickname Buffalo Bill.

When he was twenty-six, Buffalo Bill started the Wild West Show. Buffalo Bill and other real cowboys and cowgirls, such as Annie Oakley and "Wild Bill" Hickok, performed ranching and roping tricks for audiences that didn't live on or near ranches. They also performed fearless broncoriding tricks. The Wild West Show introduced people to what they thought was the cowboy way of life. As the show became very popular, Buffalo Bill took it all across the United States and Europe.

People loved the Wild West Show. They thought they were seeing the way things really happened in the Wild West. They thought they were watching history. However, the Wild West Show was more than history. Buffalo Bill showed people what they wanted to see rather than what the West was really like. He was a showman who used his eagerness and skill to educate and entertain. Even today, some of our ideas about the Old West come from Buffalo Bill's Wild West Show.

DI•12

Group Time

ROUTINE

DAY 2

1 Word Work

SUFFIXES *-less, -ness* Reteach pp. 378c–378d. Additional words to blend:

laziness	friendless	rudeness	emptiness
helpless	careless	madness	happiness

LESSON VOCABULARY Reteach p. 378f. Have individuals practice reading the words from word cards.

2 Read Strategic Intervention Decodable Reader 29

BEFORE READING Before reading, review *campfire, cattle, cowboy, galloped, herd, railroad,* and *trails.* Page through the story and have children make predictions about what will happen in the darkness.

AFTER READING Check comprehension by having children retell the story, including the characters, setting, and plot.

Have children locate *-less* and *-ness* words in the story. List words children name. Review the *-less* and *-ness* spelling patterns. Have children sort the words they found below *brightness* and *helpless.*

brightness	**helpless**
darkness	restless
goodness	sleepless
kindness	useless

In the Darkness

Written by Joel Grand
Illustrated by Vivian Mendez

Strategic Intervention
Decodable Reader 29

Phonics Skill
Suffixes -ness, -less

3 Read Cowboys

BEFORE READING Have children practice the words below—first as a group and then individually. Then use Guiding Comprehension, pp. 380–401, to monitor understanding.

bunkhouse	thousands	calves	belonged
umbrellas	bandannas	leather	throwing

AudioText

Monitor Progress	Word and Story Reading
If... children have difficulty with any of these words,	**then...** reteach them by modeling. Have children practice the words, with feedback from you, until they can read them independently.
If... children have difficulty reading the story individually,	**then...** have them follow along in their books as they listen to the AudioText. You may also have them read pages of the selection aloud together, first with you and then without you, before reading individually.

Advanced

1 Read *Cowboys*

DURING READING Have children read silently to p. 389. Provide guidance as needed. Ask:

- How was transportation different in the Old West?
- How did the cowboys' clothing help them?

Have children read silently to p. 401. Then ask:

- Do you think cowboys had tough jobs to do? Why or why not?

CAUSE AND EFFECT Have children tell what caused the cowboys to get excited on the last day of the trail. (They could take a bath, eat at a table, and sleep in a bed.) Discuss how our lives are different from a cowboy's life.

- What would you enjoy the most if you were a cowboy?
- What would you enjoy the least?

GRAPHIC ORGANIZER
Children can work with a partner to complete a KWL chart. Draw a chart or distribute copies of Graphic Organizer 3.

RESPONSE Ask children to imagine they are cowboys in the Old West. Write a journal entry about their last day on the trail.

Topic _____

K	W	L
Cowboys rode horses in the Old West.	How did cowboys take baths?	Cowboys didn't take baths until the end of a trail drive.

▲ **Graphic Organizer 3**

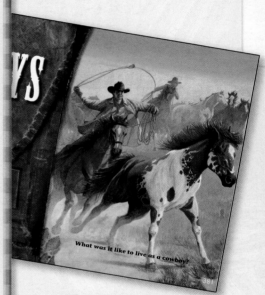

What was it like to live as a cowboy?

Audio CD **AudioText**

2 Extend Concepts Through **Inquiry**

INVESTIGATE Guide children in choosing material at their independent reading level. Books that may be appropriate are *Bandannas, Chaps, and Ten-Gallon Hats* by Bobbie Kalman or *Longhorn on the Move* by Neil Morris, Ting Morris, and Anna Clarke.

Help children decide how they will present their information. Children may use photographs, drawings, or models as props for their plays.

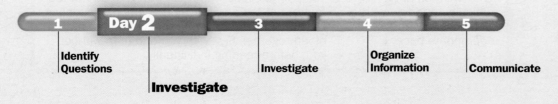

1	**Day 2**	3	4	5
Identify Questions	Investigate	Investigate	Organize Information	Communicate

Cowboys
Group Time

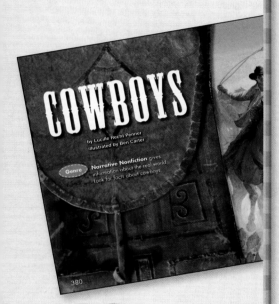

COWBOYS
by Lucille Recht Penner
illustrated by Ben Carter

Genre Narrative Nonfiction gives information about the real world. Look for facts about cowboys.

380

Audio CD AudioText

MORE READING FOR
Group Time

Use this Leveled Reader or other text at children's instructional level.

Below-Level

Reviews
• Lesson vocabulary *campfire, cattle, cowboy, galloped, herd, railroad, trails*
• Cause and effect

Strategic Intervention

ROUTINE

1 Word Work

REVIEW SYLLABLES **-tion, -ture** Review p. 402c, using these additional words. Have children sort the words into -*tion* and -*ture* lists.

mention	location	future	pictures	creatures
nature	caution	fraction	mixture	captured
fractured	station			

REVIEW SENTENCE READING Have individuals read these sentences to review decoding skills.

Did he mention the location of future meetings?
Sid wants to take pictures of creatures in nature.
Use caution when making even a fraction of that mixture.
The police captured the robber and took him to the station.
The girl fractured her toe.

2 Comprehension

CAUSE AND EFFECT/GRAPHIC ORGANIZER Reteach pp. 376r and 376–377. Have children respond to the Connect to Reading questions after completing step 3 Reread for Fluency.
• Now read the story again quietly. When you have finished, I'd like you to tell me why the mom stayed in her son's room and how you could show this cause and effect relationship in a graphic organizer.

3 Reread for Fluency

READ WITH ACCURACY AND APPROPRIATE PACE Teach p. 402f using text at children's independent level. Reading options include Student Edition selections, Decodable Readers, Strategic Intervention Decodable Readers, and Leveled Readers.

Monitor Progress	Fluency
If... children have difficulty reading with accuracy and appropriate pace,	**then...** discuss with them how to read not too fast or not too slow. Provide additional modeling. Have them listen to your model and then read aloud together, first with you and then without you, before reading individually.

Advanced

ROUTINE

1 Read Self-Selected Reading

BEFORE READING Have children select a trade book or Leveled Reader to read independently. Guide children in selecting books of appropriate difficulty.

AFTER READING When they have finished, have each child select an interesting passage to read aloud to a partner.

2 Extend Concepts Through Inquiry

INVESTIGATE Give children time to investigate the ways of the Old West and to begin preparing their information.

1	2	Day 3	4	5
Identify Questions	Investigate	Investigate	Organize Information	Communicate

DAY **3**

Trade Books for Self-Selected Reading

BANDANNAS, CHAPS, AND TEN-GALLON HATS by Bobbie Kalman, Crabtree Publishing Company, 1999

LONGHORN ON THE MOVE by Neil Morris, Ting Morris, and Anna Clarke, Marshall Cavendish Corp., 1994

MORE READING FOR
Group Time

Use this Leveled Reader or other text at children's instructional level.

Advanced

Reviews
• Concept vocabulary
• Cause and effect

Cowboys
Group Time

DAY
4

Strategic Intervention

ROUTINE

1 Read "Cowboy Gear"

BEFORE READING Have children practice the words below—first as a group and then individually. Then use Social Studies in Reading, pp. 404–405.

| equipment | luggage | journey | designed |
| originally | miners | laborers | material |

Monitor Progress	Word and Selection Reading
If... children have difficulty with any of these words,	**then...** have them practice in pairs reading word cards before reading the selection.
If... children have difficulty reading the selection individually,	**then...** have them follow along in their books as they listen to the AudioText. You may also have them read pages of the selection aloud together, first with you and then without you, before reading individually.

2 Reread for Fluency

Preteach p. 405a, using text at children's independent reading level. Reading options include Student Edition selections, Decodable Readers, Strategic Intervention Decodable Readers, and Leveled Readers.

3 Build Concepts

Use the Oral Vocabulary Routine, pp. DI·1–DI·2, DI·6, and the Oral Vocabulary Words on p. DI·8.

AudioText

MORE READING FOR
Group Time

Use this Leveled Reader or other text at children's instructional level.

Below-Level

Reviews
- Lesson vocabulary *campfire, cattle, cowboy, galloped, herd, railroad, trails*
- Cause and effect

ROUTINE

1 Read "Cowboy Gear"

AFTER READING Ask:
- Why do you think the cowboys didn't just wash their clothes at the end of a journey instead of burning them?
- Which pieces of clothing helped cowboys with their jobs?
- Which piece of clothing do you think you would most like to wear? Why?

2 Vocabulary

Extend vocabulary with questions such as these:
- Who are some *legends* from the Old West?
- What are some things that are made from *rawhide*?
- Would you rather live in a warm or cold *climate*? Why?
- What are some types of *livestock*?

Encourage children to use the words in their writing.

3 Extend Concepts Through Inquiry

ORGANIZE INFORMATION Give children time to continue reading about the ways of the Old West. Remind them that tomorrow they will share their information. By now they should have begun putting the information in a presentation format.

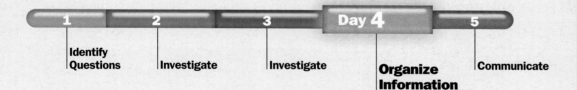

1	2	3	Day 4	5
Identify Questions	Investigate	Investigate	**Organize Information**	Communicate

DAY **4**

405

 Audio CD   AudioText

MORE READING FOR
Group Time

Use this Leveled Reader or other text at children's instructional level.

Advanced

Reviews
- Concept vocabulary
- Cause and effect

Cowboys
Group Time

Strategic Intervention

ROUTINE

1 Word Work

🎯 **SUFFIXES -less, -ness** Have children read aloud as you track the print. Call on individuals to blend the underlined words.

My friend Kiko is full of <u>kindness</u>, <u>gentleness</u>, and <u>sweetness</u>.
I would rather be <u>penniless</u> than <u>friendless</u> or <u>heartless</u>.
Grandpa says he feels <u>ageless</u> because of his good <u>fitness</u>
and no <u>sickness</u>.
The <u>fearless</u> leader led his men into the <u>darkness</u> with
great <u>awareness</u>.

LESSON VOCABULARY Use p. 378f to review *campfire, cattle, cowboy, galloped, herd, railroad, trails.*

Monitor Progress	Lesson Vocabulary
If... children have difficulty with any of these words,	**then...** reteach them by modeling. Have children practice the words, with feedback from you, until they can read them independently.

2 Monitor Progress

SENTENCE READING SET A Use Set A on reproducible page 406f to assess children's ability to read decodable and lesson vocabulary words in sentences.

COMPREHENSION To assess comprehension, have each child read Strategic Intervention Decodable Reader 29 or other text at the child's independent level. Have children identify the cause and effect relationships in the story and then have them retell the story.

MORE READING FOR
Group Time

Use this Leveled Reader or other text at children's instructional level.

Below-Level

Reviews
• Lesson vocabulary *campfire, cattle, cowboy, galloped, herd, railroad, trails*
• Cause and effect

Advanced

ROUTINE

DAY 5

1 Monitor Progress

SENTENCE READING SET C Use Set C on reproducible p. 406f to assess children's ability to read decodable and lesson vocabulary words in sentences. If you have any questions about whether childen have mastered this week's skills, have them read the Set B sentences.

COMPREHENSION Have each child read "Maggie's Wish" on reproducible p. 406g. Ask the child to name some effects of Maggie's kindness and then retell the passage. Use the Retelling Rubric on p. 368–369 to evaluate the child's retelling.

2 Extend Concepts Through **Inquiry**

COMMUNICATE Have children perform their plays about the Old West.

1	2	3	4	Day 5
Identify Questions	Investigate	Investigate	Organize Information	Communicate

---

MORE READING FOR
Group Time

Use this Leveled Reader or other text at children's instructional level.

Advanced

Reviews
- Concept vocabulary
- Cause and effect

Group Time

DAY 1

Strategic Intervention

ROUTINE

① Word Work

PREFIXES *mis-, mid-* Reteach p. 408n. Additional words to blend:

| midtown | midday | misstep | misplace | midyear |

Then have children sort the following *mis-* and *mid-* words and circle the prefixes.

| midnight | mislead | midway | mislaid | misspoke |
| midline | misfile | midsummer | mistreat | mismatch |

SPELLING Reteach p. 408p. Model spelling *misbehave* and *midday*. You may wish to give children fewer words to learn.

② Read Decodable Reader 30

BEFORE READING Review the *mis-* and *mid-* words on p. 408q and have children blend these story words: *midday, midstream, midway, mislaid, mismatched, misstep, bottles, darkness.* Be sure children understand meanings of words such as *misstep.*

DURING READING Use p. 408q.

Monitor Progress	Word and Story Reading
If... children have difficulty with any of these words,	**then...** reteach them by modeling. Have children practice the words, with feedback from you, until they can read them independently.
If... children have difficulty reading the story individually,	**then...** read a page aloud as children follow along. Then have the group reread the page. Continue reading in this way before children read individually.

③ Reread for Fluency

Use the Oral Rereading Routine, p. 408q, and text at each child's independent reading level.

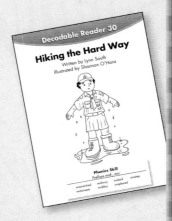

Decodable Reader 30

Hiking the Hard Way
Written by Lynn South
Illustrated by Shannon O'Hara

Phonics Skill
Prefixes *mid-, mis-*

MORE READING FOR
Group Time

Use this Leveled Reader or other text at children's instructional level.

Below-Level

Reviews
- Lesson vocabulary *borrow, clattering, drum, jingles, silver, voice*
- Character, setting, plot

Check this database for additional titles.

Leveled Reader
Database

ONLINE

PearsonSuccessNet.com

DAY 1

Advanced

ROUTINE

1 Word Work

PREFIXES Practice using words that contain the prefixes *mis-* and *mid-*. If children know the words on first read, they may need no further practice. Practice items:

mistook	midterm	misbehave	miscount	miscommunicate
midsummer	mischief	midpoint	Midwestern	midsection
misplace	midtown	misapply	misjudge	misinform

Have children write each word on two cards and play a matching game. Then have individuals choose several words to use in a sentence.

2 Read Advanced Selection 30

BEFORE READING Have children identify these vocabulary words: *ceremony, culture, festival.*

DURING READING Children may read silently. Provide guidance as needed.

AFTER READING Have children recall the two most important ideas in the selection. (Music is an important part of the Native American culture. This music helps to keep their culture alive.) Ask:

- Which of these drums seems like it would make the best sound? Why?
- Have you ever made an instrument? Tell about it.

On the back of the selection page have children write a riddle about one type of drum or rattle.

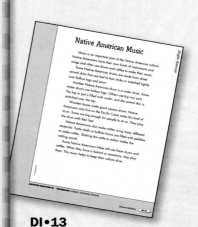

DI•13

3 Extend Concepts Through Inquiry

IDENTIFY QUESTIONS Have children find out more about other instruments used in Native American music, such as the flute. During the week, they should learn more about the instruments from reading, studying pictures, listening to music, and talking with adults or older children. On Day 5 they will share what they learned. Guide children in brainstorming possible choices.

- Think about Native American music. What does a flute sound like? How is it made?

Day 1	2	3	4	5
Identify Questions	Investigate	Investigate	Organize Information	Communicate

MORE READING FOR
Group Time

Use this Leveled Reader or other text at children's instructional level.

Advanced

Reviews
- Concept vocabulary
- Character, setting, plot

Jingle Dancer

Group Time

Audio CD — **AudioText**

Strategic Intervention

ROUTINE

1 Word Work

PREFIXES *mis-, mid-* Reteach p. 410c–410d. Additional words to blend:

midweek	midsummer	misquote	misguided
misread	midair	midlife	misinform

LESSON VOCABULARY Reteach p. 410f. Have individuals practice reading the words from word cards.

2 Read Strategic Intervention Decodable Reader 30

BEFORE READING Before reading, review *borrow, clattering, drum, jingles, silver,* and *voice.* Have children predict what they think will happen in "The Big Sale."

AFTER READING Check comprehension by having children retell the story, including the characters, setting, and plot.

Have children locate words with prefixes *mis-* and *mid-* in the story. List words children name. Review the *mis-* and *mid-* spelling patterns. Have children sort the words they found below *midday* and *misleading.*

midday	misleading
midnight	misprint
midtown	
midweek	
midyear	

3 Read *Jingle Dancer*

BEFORE READING Have children practice the words below—first as a group and then individually. Then use Guiding Comprehension, pp. 412–425, to monitor understanding.

sewn	blurred	videotape	duplex
dough	answered	burrowing	breathed

Monitor Progress	Word and Story Reading
If... children have difficulty with any of these words,	**then...** reteach them by modeling. Have children practice the words, with feedback from you, until they can read them independently.
If... children have difficulty reading the story individually,	**then...** have them follow along in their books as they listen to the AudioText. You may also have them read pages of the selection aloud together, first with you and then without you, before reading individually.

Advanced

1 Read *Jingle Dancer*

DURING READING Have children read silently to p. 419. Provide guidance as needed. Ask:

- Why does Jenna ask more than one woman for jingles?

Have children read silently to p. 425. Then ask:

- How would you describe Jenna's relationship with the women in her community?

CHARACTER, SETTING, PLOT Have children recall the characters, setting, and plot of the story. (Jenna is the main character. The story takes place in her town, and she wants to become a jingle dancer, but doesn't have enough jingles.) Discuss how to solve a problem. Ask:

- What is the first thing you should do when you have a problem?
- How would you have solved Jenna's problem differently?

Children can work together to complete a story elements chart. Distribute copies of Graphic Organizer 10.

> **This story is about:** Jenna, who wants to become a jingle dancer
> **This story takes place:** in Jenna's town
> **The action begins when:** Jenna wants to become a jingle dancer, but she doesn't have enough jingles.
> **Then:** Jenna borrows one row of jingles from her great aunt.

▲ **Graphic Organizer 10**

PRIOR KNOWLEDGE Children can work with a partner to discuss what they already know about problem-solving.

RESPONSE Ask children to find objects around the classroom that they could use as jingles.

2 Extend Concepts Through Inquiry

INVESTIGATE Guide children in choosing material at their independent reading level to explore Native American music.

Help children decide how they will present their information. Children may use a graphic organizer, a written or musical format, photographs, drawings, or models.

Will Jenna get enough jingles for her outfit?

413

Audio CD AudioText

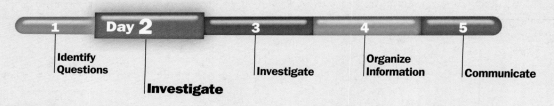

1	Day 2	3	4	5
Identify Questions	Investigate	Investigate	Organize Information	Communicate

Jingle Dancer

Group Time

DAY 3

MORE READING FOR

Group Time

Use this Leveled Reader or other text at children's instructional level.

Below-Level

Reviews
- Lesson vocabulary *borrow, clattering, drum, jingles, silver, voice*
- Character, setting, plot

Strategic Intervention

ROUTINE

1 Word Work

REVIEW **SUFFIXES *-less, -ness*** Review p. 426c, using these additional words. Have children sort the words into *-less* and *-ness* lists.

kindness	**fairness**	**goodness**	**fearless**	**darkness**
harmless	**helpless**	**hopeless**	**happiness**	**spotless**

REVIEW **SENTENCE READING** Have individuals read these sentences to review decoding skills.

Everyone must be treated with kindness and fairness.
The fearless owl flew in the darkness.
The harmless trapped animal felt helpless and hopeless.
The owner felt happiness from having a spotless diner.

2 Comprehension

CHARACTER, SETTING, PLOT/PRIOR KNOWLEDGE Reteach pp. 408r and 408–409. Have children respond to the Connect to Reading questions after completing step 3 Reread for Fluency.

- Now read the story again quietly. When you have finished, I'd like you to use what you already know to tell me who the story is about, where and when it takes place, and what happens.

3 Reread for Fluency

READ WITH APPROPRIATE PHRASING Teach p. 426f, using text at children's independent level. Reading options include Student Edition selections, Decodable Readers, Strategic Intervention Decodable Readers, and Leveled Readers.

Monitor Progress	Fluency
If... children have difficulty reading with appropriate phrasing,	**then...** discuss with them the appropriate phrasing to be used with each passage and provide additional modeling. Have them listen to your model and then read aloud together, first with you and then without you, before reading individually.

Advanced

ROUTINE

1 Read Self-Selected Reading

BEFORE READING Have children select a trade book or Leveled Reader to read independently. Guide children in selecting books of appropriate difficulty.

AFTER READING When they have finished, have each child share an interesting fact about Native American music with a partner.

2 Extend Concepts Through Inquiry

INVESTIGATE Give children time to investigate Native American music and to begin preparing their information.

1	2	Day 3	4	5
Identify Questions	Investigate	Investigate	Organize Information	Communicate

Trade Books for Self-Selected Reading

THE STORY OF THE FIRST FLUTE: BASED ON AN ANCIENT CHEROKEE LEGEND by Hawk Hurst, Lindley Sharp, Parkway Publishers, 2002

THE FLUTE PLAYER: AN APACHE FOLKTALE by Michael Lacapa, Rising Moon Books, 1995

MORE READING FOR
Group Time

Use this Leveled Reader or other text at children's instructional level.

Advanced

Reviews
• Concept vocabulary
• Character, setting, plot

Jingle Dancer
Group Time

DAY **4**

AudioText

MORE READING FOR
Group Time

Use this Leveled Reader or other text at children's instructional level.

Below-Level

Reviews
- Lesson vocabulary *borrow, clattering, drum, jingles, silver, voice*
- Character, setting, plot

Strategic Intervention

ROUTINE

1 Read "Celebrating the Buffalo Days"

BEFORE READING Have children practice the words below—first as a group and then individually. Then use Social Studies in Reading, pp. 428–431.

encourage   traditions   experience   reservation

Monitor Progress	Word and Selection Reading
If... children have difficulty with any of these words,	**then...** have them practice in pairs reading word cards before reading the selection.
If... children have difficulty reading the selection individually,	**then...** have them follow along in their books as they listen to the AudioText. You may also have them read pages of the selection aloud together, first with you and then without you, before reading individually.

2 Reread for Fluency

Preteach p. 431a, using text at children's independent reading level. Reading options include Student Edition selections, Decodable Readers, Strategic Intervention Decodable Readers, and Leveled Readers.

3 Build Concepts

Use the Oral Vocabulary Routine, pp. DI·1–DI·2, DI·7, and the Oral Vocabulary Words on p. DI·8.

Advanced

ROUTINE

DAY 4

1 Read "Celebrating the Buffalo Days"

AFTER READING Ask:
- What are some things that are used to make Native American clothing?
- Would you like to go to the Crow Fair? Why or why not?
- What are some of your family's traditions?

2 Vocabulary

Extend vocabulary with questions such as these:
- What *compliment* could you give a friend?
- Which kind of tree do you like better, an *evergreen* or a *spruce?* Why?
- Describe something you have admired that is *multicolored*.
- How is a *sash* usually worn? How else could you wear a sash?

Encourage children to use the words in their writing.

3 Extend Concepts Through Inquiry

ORGANIZE INFORMATION Give children time to continue reading about Native American music. Remind them that tomorrow they will share their information. By now they should have begun putting the information in a presentation format.

The Crow Fair and Rodeo is called the Tipi Capital of the World. People put up more than a thousand tipis on the fairgrounds.

During the third week in August, Crow people from all over the reservation gather to put up their tipis. They hold a powwow that lasts for many days, with dance contests, drumming, and giveaways. There are rodeo competitions and horse races every day. People from other tribes all over North America come to share in the fun.

Graphic Organizers If it will help, make a graphic organizer.

1	2	3	Day 4	5
Identify Questions	Investigate	Investigate	Organize Information	Communicate

AudioText

MORE READING FOR
Group Time

Use this Leveled Reader or other text at children's instructional level.

Advanced

Reviews
- Concept vocabulary
- Character, setting, plot

Jingle Dancer

Group Time

Strategic Intervention

ROUTINE

1 Word Work

↻ **PREFIXES *mis-, mid-*** Have children read aloud as you track the print. Call on individuals to blend the underlined words.

The <u>midterm</u> test is taken <u>midyear</u>.
The <u>misprint</u> was a big <u>mistake</u>!
<u>Midway</u> through our game, I tossed the ball in <u>midair</u>.
I <u>misplaced</u> what we need for our <u>midsummer</u> trip.

LESSON VOCABULARY Use p. 410f to review *borrow, clattering, drum, jingles, silver, voice.*

Monitor Progress	Lesson Vocabulary
If... children have difficulty with any of these words,	**then...** reteach them by modeling. Have children practice the words, with feedback from you, until they can read them independently.

2 Monitor Progress

SENTENCE READING SET A Use Set A on reproducible p. 432f to assess children's ability to read decodable and lesson vocabulary words in sentences.

COMPREHENSION To assess comprehension, have each child read Strategic Intervention Decodable Reader 30 or other text at the child's independent level. Ask who the characters are and when and where the story takes place (setting). Then have the child retell the story.

MORE READING FOR
Group Time

Use this Leveled Reader or other text at children's instructional level.

Below-Level

Reviews
• Lesson vocabulary *borrow, clattering, drum, jingles, silver, voice*
• Character, setting, plot

Advanced

DAY 5

1 Monitor Progress

SENTENCE READING SET C Use Set C on reproducible page 432f to assess children's ability to read decodable and lesson vocabulary words in sentences. If you have any questions about whether children have mastered this week's skills, have them read the Set B sentences.

COMPREHENSION Have each child read "The Spelling Bee" on reproducible page 432g. Ask who the characters are, when the story takes place, and what happens. Then have the child retell the passage. Use the Retelling Rubric on p. 426g to evaluate the child's retelling.

2 Extend Concepts Through Inquiry

COMMUNICATE Have children share their information about Native American music and instruments.

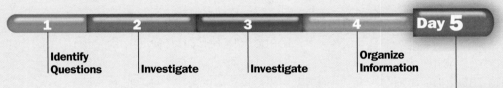

1	2	3	4	Day 5
Identify Questions	Investigate	Investigate	Organize Information	

Communicate

MORE READING FOR
Group Time

Use this Leveled Reader or other text at children's instructional level.

Advanced

Reviews
- Concept vocabulary
- Character, setting, plot

Just Like Josh Gibson

Contractions 're, 've, 'd

1 TEACH

Remind children that a contraction is a word that is made by putting two words together and leaving out a letter or letters. An apostrophe is used in place of the missing letters. Write the following word pairs and words in columns on the board:

you are   I've
they had   they'd
I have   you're

Ask volunteers to draw a line between each word pair and its corresponding contraction. Have children circle the letter or letters in the word pair that are replaced by the apostrophe.

Then write *don't* and *won't* on the board. Write *do not* and *will not* below them. Explain that *don't* and *won't* are irregular contractions. Say: *Don't* is the contraction for *do not*. *Won't* is the contraction for *will not*.

2 PRACTICE AND ASSESS

Write the sentences below on the board. Have children rewrite each sentence by using a contraction for the underlined words.

We are going home soon.
I would like to read that book.
We do not want to stay late.
I wish she would sit by me.
You are so nice.
I have never been late.
He will not ride with us.

Have children read their sentences aloud. Guide children to understand that using a contraction for the word pair does not change the meaning of a sentence.

Just Like Josh Gibson

Compare and Contrast

1 TEACH

Write the following words on the board:

like   both   alike   same
different   however   although   but

Remind children that authors sometimes use these clue words when they are writing about things being alike or different. Ask children which words an author might use to tell how things are alike. *(like, both, alike, same)* Ask which words an author might use to tell how things are different. *(different, however, although, but)*

Ask volunteers to use the words above in sentences to tell how two things are alike or different.

2 PRACTICE AND ASSESS

Read the paragraphs below. Have children decide which words from above belong in each blank. Then have children tell which paragraph tells about things that are different and which paragraph tells about things that are the same.

Many people think my best friend and I are twins. That's because we look _____ and enjoy doing the _____ things. _____ of us have the _____ taste in books and movies. Sometimes we even finish each other's sentences!

My sisters are _____ in every way. _____ one sister likes to swim, the other one doesn't. The older one likes to read, _____ the other one likes math. One sister keeps her room spotless. _____, the other one can't be bothered.

Have children write two sentences about how two things are alike and two sentences that tell how two things are different. Tell them to use at least one clue word in each sentence. Ask children to share their sentences.

Red, White, and Blue
Inflected Endings

1 TEACH

Write the following words on the board:

cries   cried   crying
lucky   luckier   luckiest

Read the words aloud. Explain that each word has a base word and an ending. Point to *cries* and ask children to name the base word. *(cry)* Write *cry* on the board. Ask how *cry* is changed before adding the ending. (*y* is changed to *i* before adding *es*) Continue the routine with the rest of the words.

Remind children that some words have other spelling changes. Review doubling the final consonant, as in *hopped* and *hopping*, or dropping the final *e*, as in *races, raced,* and *racing.*

Review with children how to decode words with endings. Tell them to cover the ending, read the base word, and then blend the base word and ending to read the whole word. Point out that sometimes you have to break the base word into smaller parts to decode it.

2 PRACTICE AND ASSESS

Write the words and endings below on the board. Have pairs of children copy the words and endings on a sheet of paper. Tell one child to write a word with the base word and one of the endings shown. Then have him or her pass the paper to a partner who will add a word with another ending. Tell them to continue until they have written all the new words.

carry (–s, –ed, –ing)   fast (–er, –est)
try (–s, –ed, –ing)   big (–er, –est)
hope (–s, –ed, –ing)   wide (–er, –est)
stop (–s, –ed, –ing)

Have children share their answers. Point out which words had spelling changes.

Red, White, and Blue
Fact and Opinion

1 TEACH

Remind children that a fact is something that can be proved true or false. An opinion cannot be proved true or false. It is what someone thinks or feels.

Tell children you will read some facts and opinions. Tell them to stand up for a fact and to sit down for an opinion.

Say the following aloud:

July Fourth is a holiday in the United States.
Computers are the world's best invention.
The U.S. flag is red, white, and blue.
Pizza is better than popcorn.
Soccer is the most fun sport.
Exercise is good for you.
Everyone should learn another language.

Have children tell why each is fact or opinion.

2 PRACTICE AND ASSESS

Read the following story aloud.

Fish make better pets than dogs. Fish are easier to care for. They don't have to be walked or taken outside. All you need to do is feed them and clean their tank. Fish won't chew your homework or hide your slippers! Fish are prettier than dogs too.

Have children identify facts and opinions. Record responses on a chart like the one below. Encourage children to explain their thinking.

Facts	Opinions

Have children work in pairs and choose a familiar book or selection in the reader. Have them jot down the title and one statement of fact and one statement of opinion from the selection.

A Birthday Basket for Tía

Syllables *-tion,* *-ture*

1 TEACH

Say *go* as you clap one time. Explain that *go* is a word with only one part. Then say *ba-by,* as you clap twice. Explain that *baby* is a word that has two parts. Tell children that each word part is called a *syllable.*

Demonstrate with the word *hip/po/pot/a/mus.* Say: When you see a long word that you don't know, you can break the word up into syllables to make reading the word easier.

Write the words *lotion* and *future* on the board. Read the words aloud and ask children how many syllables they hear. Tell children that *-tion* stands for /shən/ and *-ture* stands for /chər/.

2 PRACTICE AND ASSESS

Read these words together:

adventure	action	furniture
vacationer	section	creature
position	lecture	pictures

Make a three-column chart. As a class, decide under which number each word goes. Show the word written under the number and divided into syllables.

2	3	4 or more
ac tion pic tures	ad ven ture	va ca tion er

A Birthday Basket for Tía

Draw Conclusions

1 TEACH

Remind children that when they read a story, sometimes they must use details from the story and things they know from their own lives to figure out more about the characters or what is happening. Say: If you were reading a story about a boy who was moving to a new place, how would you know how the boy felt if the text didn't tell you? Guide children to understand that they could look for clues in the story that tell what the boy did, thought, or said. They could also put themselves in the boy's place and think about how they would feel.

2 PRACTICE AND ASSESS

Make a chart like the one below. Have children recall *A Birthday Basket for Tía.*

About the Story	How You Know
The family loves Tía. Tía loves Cecelia. Tía is kind and thoughtful. Tía likes her party.	

Encourage children to use clues from the story as well as what they already know to complete the chart.

Cowboys

Suffixes -*ness*, -*less*

1 TEACH

Write -*ness* and -*less* on the board. Say: You know that suffixes are word parts that are added to the end of a word. The word parts -*ness* and -*less* are suffixes.

Write the words *dark* and *bottom.* Have children tell which suffix, -*ness* or -*less,* can be added to each word. Write the new word. Volunteers can tell how many syllables the new word has. (*darkness* – 2, *bottomless* – 3) Repeat with *happy.* Point out that the *y* is changed to *i* before adding -*ness.*

Guide children to understand that each suffix adds a syllable to the base word.

2 PRACTICE AND ASSESS

Have children form new words by adding -*ness* or -*less* to these base words. Remind children of any spelling changes that need to be made. Children should write the number of syllables in each new word they make, such as *thoughtless* – 2, *gentleness* – 3.

thought	quick	sad
cord	friendly	fear
spot	ill	sudden
sick	point	use
bright	gentle	pain

Ask children to tell what each new word means.

Cowboys

Cause and Effect

1 TEACH

Write the following question on the board:

Why did ranchers brand their cattle?

Read the question aloud and say: To answer this question, I might say "Ranchers branded their cattle because they wanted people to know the cattle belonged to them." Remind children that things that happen are often caused by other things. Have children tell what happened (ranchers branded their cattle) and why it happened (because they wanted people to know the cattle belonged to them).

Tell children that *so, if, then,* and *since* are other clue words that help them understand what happened and why.

2 PRACTICE AND ASSESS

Display in two columns the following on strips of paper with double-sided tape on the back of each:

Grandmama couldn't play baseball
The United States flag has fifty stars
It was Tía's 90th birthday
There were no tables or chairs
because our country has fifty states.
so the family had a party for her.
so cowboys sat on the ground.
because she was a girl.

Tell students that they will put together sentences that tell about selections in *Traditions.* Each sentence will tell something that happened and why it happened.

Ask volunteers to put together the two strips that tell a cause-and-effect situation and read the sentence aloud. Have children tell what happened and why it happened.

Jingle Dancer

Prefixes *mis-, mid-*

① TEACH

Write *place* and *week* on the board and *misplace* and *midweek* below them. Read the words aloud and ask children to tell what is the same and what is different about the word pairs. Say: The word *misplace* has a word part at the beginning. That word part is called a prefix. The prefix changes the meaning of the base word, *place*. What does *place* mean? What does *misplace* mean?

Repeat the routine with *week* and *midweek*. To help students with the meanings of *misplace* and *midweek,* explain that the prefix *mis-* means "bad or wrong" and the prefix *mid-* means "middle."

② PRACTICE AND ASSESS

Write these words on the board.

type   stream   read   day   size   spoke

Give these clues and have volunteers add *mis-* or *mid-* to the words above to form a word that tells the answer.

This is the middle of the day. (midday)
If you read something wrong, you do this. (misread)
This is a car that isn't little or big. (midsize)
If you make a mistake while typing, you do this. (mistype)
If you said something wrong, you did this. (misspoke)
This is where you are if you are halfway down the stream. (midstream)

Have children tell why they chose the word they did.

Jingle Dancer

Character, Setting, and Plot

① TEACH

Remind children that stories include characters, setting, and plot. Explain that authors tell where and when a story takes place (setting), what the characters think, feel, say, and do, and what happens at the beginning, middle, and end (plot). Review the fairy tale *Cinderella* with children. Then ask: What is the setting of Cinderella? Who are the characters? What is the plot?

Point out that the setting changes throughout the tale. It begins at the stepmother's home, moves to the palace, and goes back to the stepmother's home.

② PRACTICE AND ASSESS

Write the following on the board:

Story Title: _____
Characters: _____
Setting: _____
Plot:
    Beginning: _____
    Middle: _____
    End: _____

Have children work in pairs to identify the characters, setting, and plot of a favorite story. Children may use a selection in *Traditions* or another book or tale of their choice.

Suggest that children use the format above to record information. Encourage children to list words the author uses to help them understand the characters, setting, and plot. Have children share their answers.

Providing children with reading materials they can and want to read is an important step toward developing fluent readers. A running record allows you to determine each child's instructional and independent reading level. Information on how to take a running record is provided on pp. DI•71–DI•72.

Instructional Reading Level

Only approximately 1 in 10 words will be difficult when reading a selection from the Student Edition for children who are at grade level. (A typical second-grader reads approximately 90–100 words correct per minute.)

- Children reading at grade level should read regularly from the Student Edition and On-Level Leveled Readers, with teacher support as suggested in the Teacher's Editions.
- Children reading below grade level can read the Strategic Intervention Leveled Readers and the Decodable Readers. Instructional plans can be found in the Teacher's Edition and the Leveled Reader Teaching Guide.
- Children who are reading above grade level can use the Advanced Leveled Readers and the Advanced Selection in the Teacher's Edition. Instructional plans can be found in the Teacher's Edition and the Leveled Reader Teaching Guide.

Independent Reading Level

Children should read regularly in independent-level texts in which no more than approximately 1 in 20 words is difficult for the reader. Other factors that make a book easy to read include the child's interest in the topic, the amount of text on a page, how well illustrations support meaning, and the complexity and familiarity of the concepts. Suggested books for self-selected reading are provided with each lesson on p. TR18 in this Teacher's Edition.

Guide children in learning how to self-select books at their independent reading level. As you talk about a book with children, discuss the challenging concepts in it, list new words children find in sampling the book, and ask children about their familiarity with the topic. A blackline master to help children evaluate books for independent reading is provided on p. DI•70.

Self-Selected/Independent Reading

While oral reading allows you to assess children's reading level and fluency, independent reading is of crucial importance to children's futures as readers and learners. Children need to develop their ability to read independently for increasing amounts of time.

- Schedule a regular time for sustained independent reading in your classroom. During the year, gradually increase the amount of time devoted to independent reading.
- More fluent readers may choose to read silently during independent reading time. Other children might read to a partner, to a stuffed animal, or to an adult volunteer.
- Help children track the amount of time they read independently and the number of pages they read in a given amount of time. Tracking will help motivate them to gradually increase their duration and speed. Blackline masters for tracking independent reading are provided on pp. DI•70 and TR19.

Choosing a Book to Read by Yourself

These questions can help you pick a book to read.

_____ 1. Is this book about something that I like?

_____ 2. This book may be about a real person, about facts, or a made-up story. Do I like reading this kind of book?

_____ 3. Have I read other things by this author? Do I like the author?

If you say "yes" to question 1, 2, or 3, go on.

_____ 4. Were there fewer than 5 hard words on the first page?

_____ 5. Does the number of words on a page look about right to me?

If you say "yes" to questions 4 and 5, the book is right for you.

Silent Reading

Write the date, the title of the book, and the number of minutes you read.

Date	Title	Minutes

Taking a Running Record

A running record is an assessment of a child's oral reading accuracy and oral reading fluency. Reading accuracy is based on the number of words read correctly. Reading fluency is based on the reading rate (the number of words correct per minute) and the degree to which a child reads with a "natural flow."

How to Measure Reading Accuracy

1. Choose a grade-level text of about 80 to 120 words that is unfamiliar to the child.
2. Make a copy of the text for yourself. Make a copy for the child or have the child read aloud from a book.
3. Give the child the text and have the child read aloud. (You may wish to record the child's reading for later evaluation.)
4. On your copy of the text, mark any miscues or errors the child makes while reading. See the running record sample on page DI•72, which shows how to identify and mark miscues.
5. Count the total number of words in the text and the total number of errors made by the child. Note: If a child makes the same error more than once, such as mispronouncing the same word multiple times, count it as one error. Self-corrections do not count as actual errors. Use the following formula to calculate the percentage score, or accuracy rate:

$$\frac{\text{Total Number of Words} - \text{Total Number of Errors}}{\text{Total Number of Words}} \times 100 = \text{percentage score}$$

Interpreting the Results

- A child who reads **95–100%** of the words correctly is reading at an **independent level** and may need more challenging text.
- A child who reads **90–94%** of the words correctly is reading at an **instructional level** and will likely benefit from guided instruction.
- A child who reads **89%** or fewer of the words correctly is reading at a **frustrational level** and may benefit most from targeted instruction with lower-level texts and intervention.

How to Measure Reading Rate (WCPM)

1. Follow Steps 1–3 above.
2. Note the exact times when the child begins and finishes reading.
3. Use the following formula to calculate the number of words correct per minute (WCPM):

$$\frac{\text{Total Number of Words Read Correctly}}{\text{Total Number of Seconds}} \times 60 = \text{words correct per minute}$$

Interpreting the Results

An appropriate reading rate for a second-grader is 90–100 (WCPM).

Running Record Sample

Running Record Sample

Just then a fly crawled near Fred.
Fred's long, *^and* sticky tongue shot out in a
flash and caught the tiny insect. */ti nel/*

H
"Delicious! I'm full now," he said
loudly. He had already eaten three other
insects and a worm in the past hour.

sc
Frankie overheard Fred and climbed
down a few branches. He moved quickly
and easily without falling.

"What are you doing, Fred?" he
asked in a friendly voice.

"I was just finishing up my lunch,"
there
Fred answered. "How is life up ~~high~~
today, my friend?"

—From *Frog Friends*
On-Level Reader 2.4.3

Miscues

Insertion
The student inserts words or parts of words that are not in the text.

Mispronunciation/Misreading
The student pronounces or reads a word incorrectly.

Hesitation
The student hesitates over a word, and the teacher provides the word. Wait several seconds before telling the student what the word is.

Self-Correction
The student reads a word incorrectly but then corrects the error. Do not count self-corrections as actual errors. However, noting self-corrections will help you identify words the student finds difficult.

Omission
The student omits words or word parts.

Substitution
The student substitutes words or parts of words for the words in the text.

Running Record Results ▶	**Reading Accuracy** ▶	**Reading Rate**—WCPM
Total Number of Words: **86**	$\dfrac{86 - 5}{86} = \dfrac{81}{86} = .9418 = 94\%$	$\dfrac{81}{64} \times 60 = 75.9 = 76$ words correct per minute
Number of Errors: **5**		
Reading Time: **64 seconds**	Accuracy Percentage Score: **94%**	Reading Rate: **76** WCPM

Teacher Resources

Table of Contents

Bookmarks

Fiction

- Who are the characters?

- Where does the story take place?

- When does the story take place?

- What happens . . .
  at the beginning?
  in the middle?
  at the end?

Nonfiction

- What did I learn?

- What is this mainly about?

Iris and Walter

Short Vowels; Short *e*: ea

add	pan	red	quick	lock	just
ask	pat	sled	rib	lots	luck
back	plan	speck	ring	pond	lump
band	rang	step	rip	rock	mug
bang	sack	tell	sick	shock	must
bank	sad	them	sing	slop	run
black	sang	well	sink	sock	rust
bland	sank	went	six	sod	sung
brand	sat	when	slim	stock	truck
camp	slap	yell	sling	stop	trunk
cap	stack	big	slip	tock	tub
cat	tag	bring	still	top	tuck
crack	tank	cling	swing	bunk	tug
drank	track	crib	think	but	bread
fast	van	fill	thing	chunk	breath
grab	bed	fist	this	cup	dead
grand	bell	fit	tip	cut	dread
grass	bend	fix	will	drum	feather
hand	best	hill	win	duck	head
hat	check	his	wing	dunk	leather
lack	deck	hit	box	dust	meadow
land	desk	kid	clock	fun	read
last	dress	king	dock	gum	ready
man	end	lick	frog	hug	spread
map	get	list	got	hum	sweater
mask	less	mist	honk	hung	thread
mat	let	pick	jog	jump	weather
pack	peck	pink	knock	junk	

Spelling Words

chop
desk
drum
dust
job
list
mess
pack
rib
rock
sack
sad
tag

High-Frequency/ Tested Words

beautiful
country
friend*
front
someone
somewhere

Selection Words

amazing
ladder
meadow
roller-skate

Exploring Space with an Astronaut

Long Vowels CVCe; c/s/, g/j/, s/z/

age	pace	exercise	ride	lone	tube
airplane	page	file	ripe	nose	tune
ate	place	fine	shines	note	use
bake	plane	hike	size	poke	
brave	plate	ice	slice	pose	
cage	race	inside	spice	rode	
cake	rage	kite	time	rose	
cape	rake	lice	twice	telescope	
date	safe	life	white	those	
drape	sage	like	wide	tone	
erase	shake	lime	wise	vote	
face	space	mice	bone	confuse	
game	spaceship	miles	broke	cube	
gape	stage	mime	chose	cute	
lace	take	mine	close	fuse	
lake	tame	nice	code	huge	
lane	wage	outside	dose	mule	
late	bite	pile	home	mute	
made	bride	price	hope	plume	
make	dice	quite	hose	rude	
mane	dime	rice	joke	rule	

Spelling Words

blaze
cube
fine
home
late
mice
nose
page
size
space
tune
vote

High-Frequency/ Tested Words

everywhere
live*
machines
move
woman
work*
world

Selection Words

astronaut
experiment
gravity
shuttle
telescope

* = reviewed high-frequen[cy]
word from Grade 1

Henry and Mudge and the Starry Night

Consonant Blends

act	bride	croak	flock	land	pride	small	stars	tent
ant	bring	crows	flop	last	prop	smelly	state	trace
ask	brisk	crust	flute	long	raft	smile	step	track
band	broke	drank	fly	lost	scrape	snack	stick	tree
best	brush	dread	frame	mask	screech	snake	stink	tribe
black	bust	dreams	frog	milk	scrub	snap	stone	trip
blades	camp	drink	front	must	send	snuck	strand	trunk
blame	clam	drool	glad	nest	skate	snuggle	strap	trust
blank	clamp	drop	glide	next	skills	sound	stream	tusk
blast	clank	drove	grace	past	skit	space	stress	twice
blew	clap	dump	grand	pest	sky	splat	stretch	twigs
blond	clean	dusk	grass	place	slat	splint	strict	twin
bluebird	close	dust	gray	plan	sleep	split	stride	went
branch	crackers	dwell	grind	plank	slept	spread	strike	west
brake	craft	fast	groan	plant	slide	spring	string	wind
brand	cramp	felt	hand	plate	slippery	spruce	stripe	
brave	crate	flake	help	plug	slope	stage	strong	
bread	crept	flat	jump	plump	slow	stamp	stump	
breeze	crest	flex	just	pond	slump	stand	stung	

Spelling Words

ask
brave
breeze
clip
hand
mask
nest
state
stop
strap
stream
twin

High-Frequency/Tested Words

bear
build
couldn't
father
love*
mother
straight

Selection Words

drooled
lanterns
shivered
snuggled

A Walk in the Desert

Base Words and Endings -s, -ed, -ing

-s		dragged	peeled	-ing	playing
amazes	pecks	dropped	petted	amazing	racing
asks	pretends	filled	placed	asking	riding
bakes	protects	gagged	raced	bugging	rubbing
calls	races	gobbled	rested	carving	running
chips	rubs	grabbed	rubbed	confusing	scaring
cools	runs	grinned	saved	dining	shaking
drags	seems	happened	smiled	dragging	sleeping
eats	smiles	hiked	snapped	hiding	sliding
gets	uses	hopped	tagged	hiking	smiling
grows	wags	hugged	traded	hopping	soaring
hikes	walks	jogged	wagged	jumping	sunning
howls	wipes	jumped	walked	lifting	trading
jumps		lifted	watched	looking	wagging
lies	-ed	looked	wiped	making	walking
lives	added	nodded	yelled	opening	winning
makes	amazed	patted		patting	
	asked				

Spelling Words

dropped
dropping
excited
exciting
hugged
hugging
lifted
lifting
smiled
smiling
talked
talking

High-Frequency/Tested Words

animals
early*
eyes*
full
water*
warm

Selection Words

cactus
climate
coyote
desert
harsh

The Strongest One

Consonant Digraphs

ch		fresh	shrimp	teeth	together	stretch
arch	each	fish	shrubs	than		watch
bench	lunch	hush	shut	thank	tch	
branches	much	mash	shy	that	batch	wh
bunch	pinch	mush	splash	them	catch	elsewhere
chalk	such	shack	trash	then	clutch	whale
chase	teach	shake	wash	there	crutch	when
chat	watch	shape	wish	they	ditch	where
check	which	shell		thick	fetch	which
chest		shin	th	thin	hatch	while
chick	sh	shine	bath	think	hutch	whim
chicken	bash	ship	everything	things	itch	whip
chimp	blush	shirt	forth	third	latch	whirl
chin	brush	shone	fourth	thirsty	match	whisk
chip	bushes	shop	math	those	patch	whistle
chop	crush	shore	mouth	thud	pitch	white
chose	dash	shot	path	thumb	scratched	
church	dish	show	something	thump	stitch	

Spelling Words

bunch
chase
itch
match
patch
shape
that
them
whale
what
when
wish

High-Frequency/Tested Words

gone
learn*
often
pieces
though
together*
very*

Selection Words

dangerous
gnaws
narrator
relatives

* = reviewed high-frequency
word from Grade 1

Tara and Tiree, Fearless Friends

r-Controlled ar, or, ore; Syllables VCCV

ar	dark	shark	fork	**ore**	belly	packet
alarm	darling	smart	form	adore	bucket	panda
armies	far	star	fort	before	carpet	pepper
armor	farm	start	horse	bore	chicken	picnic
art	garden	target	morning	chore	corner	pocket
artist	hard	yard	north	more	correct	pompom
barber	harm		orbit	score	darling	problem
bark	harp	**or**	order	shore	distant	puppet
barn	jars	border	porch	sore	enlist	rabbits
car	lark	born	short	store	forget	ribbon
carp	mark	corn	sport	stories	gimmick	socket
carpet	market	corner	stork	therefore	insect	target
cart	parched	correct	storm		kitten	until
cartoon	part	forget	stormy	**VCCV**	mitten	winter
charm	party	forgot	thorn	basket	muffin	

Spelling Words

before
born
chore
corn
farm
hard
horse
more
part
porch
score
smart

High-Frequency/ Tested Words

break
family*
heard
listen
once*
pull*

Selection Words

brave
collar
slipped

Ronald Morgan Goes to Bat

Contractions

aren't	don't	how's	it's	that's	who's
can't	hadn't	I'll	let's	there's	won't
couldn't	haven't	I'm	she's	they'll	you'll
didn't	he's	isn't	she'll	wasn't	
doesn't	he'll	it'll	shouldn't	we'll	

Spelling Words

didn't
hadn't
hasn't
he's
I'll
I'm
isn't
it's
she's
wasn't
we'll
who'll

High-Frequency/ Tested Words

certainly
either
great*
laugh*
second
worst
you're

Selection Words

clutched
spirit
terrific

Turtle's Race with Beaver

r-Controlled er, ir, ur; Syllables VCCV

er	swerve	flirt	curl	turtle	corner	surface
certain	term	shirk	curler	urge	curler	survive
clerk	verse	shirt	disturb	urn	dirty	tender
fern		skirt	fur		disturb	thirty
germ	**ir**	squirrel	furry	**VCCV**	enter	turkey
her	birch	stir	hurry	after	gotten	under
herd	bird	third	hurt	almost	happens	until
herself	birdbath	thirsty	murmur	arrive	happy	winter
jerk	birth	thirty	nurse	batter	hurry	wonder
kernel	birthday	twirl	purple	better	kernel	
nerve	chirp		purse	border	murmur	
perch	circus	**ur**	return	bottom	perfect	
perfect	confirm	blurt	spurt	burger	plenty	
perk	dirt	burden	surf	butter	rabbit	
person	dirty	burger	surface	certain	sherbet	
pert	girl	burn	survive	challenge	sister	
serve	girth	burst	Thursday	chipmunk	splendid	
sherbet	firm	church	turkey	circus	squirrel	
stern	first	curb	turn	confirm	summer	

Spelling Words

birth
curb
curl
dirt
her
nurse
person
purse
serve
skirt
turn
turtle

High-Frequency/ Tested Words

above*
ago
enough*
toward*
whole
word

Selection Words

buried
challenge
dam
embarrassed
halfway
lodge

* = reviewed high-frequency
word from Grade 1

WORD LIST

The Bremen Town Musicians

Plurals -s, -es, -ies

-s
animals
bags
bases
baskets
bikes
bins
books
boys
cages
cards
centers
cents
chores
classmates
corners
crafts
crops
cups
dancers
desks
dimes
dogs

drinks
ducklings
ducks
experts
farms
forests
friends
gerbils
germs
girls
globes
grapes
hands
heels
holes
homes
hoses
hours
houses
jobs
kittens
lamps
lots

monsters
nails
nickels
notes
orders
papers
pencils
piles
places
planes
plates
pockets
purses
races
robbers
rocks
roses
spices
stamps
stands
stars
stores
things

towns
toys
tunes
twigs
vases
years

-es
ashes
batches
beaches
benches
boxes
branches
brushes
bunches
buses
bushes
churches
classes
circuses
crashes
crutches

dishes
ditches
dresses
foxes
glasses
kisses
lashes
leashes
lunches
matches
messes
mixes
patches
peaches
perches
ranches
scratches
switches
watches
wishes

-ies
armies
babies
berries
buddies
bunnies
candies
cherries
cities
daddies
families
flies
jellies
ladies
lilies
mommies
nannies
parties
pennies
ponies
puppies
stories
supplies

Spelling Words
babies
baby
lunch
lunches
note
notes
stories
story
switch
switches
tune
tunes

High-Frequency/Tested Words
bought
people*
pleasant
probably
scared
shall
sign*

Selection Words
excitement
mill
monsters
musicians
robbers

A Turkey for Thanksgiving

Long a: a, ai, ay; Syllables VCV

a
acorns
agent
apron
baby
famous
lady
lazy
paper
table

ai
aim
braid
brain

claim
explain
fail
faint
frail
gain
grain
hail
laid
maid
mail
main
nail
paid
pail

pain
paint
quail
rail
rain
raised
sail
snail
stain
tail
train
waist
wait

ay
away
bay
day
dismay
gray
fray
hay
holiday
lay
may
okay
pay
play
pray

ray
say
spray
stay
stray
sway
today
stay
way

VCV
acorn
agent
baby
began

ever
famous
holiday
lady
lazy
paper
visit

Spelling Words
away
brain
main
paint
play
raise
say
stay
tail
today
tray
wait

High-Frequency/Tested Words
behind*
brought
door*
everybody
minute
promise
sorry

Selection Words
hooves
lumbered
riverbank
Thanksgiving

* = reviewed high-frequency word from Grade 1

Unit 2 Word Lists **TR5**

WORD LIST

Pearl and Wagner: Two Good Friends

Long e: e, ee, ea, y; Syllables VCV

e
be
detail
equal
even
he
maybe
me
meter
recess
secret
she
we

ee
agree
bee
beet
breeze
creep
deep
feed
feel
feet
fifteen
green

greet
jeep
keep
meet
need
screech
seed
seek
seems
sleep
sleet
speech
steep
street
succeed
sweeping
sweet
teeth
three
tree
weed
week
wheel

ea
beach

beam
bean
beat
bleach
cheap
clean
cream
crease
dreamed
each
ease
easel
easy
eating
feast
heal
heap
leafy
leaping
leave
mean
meat
neat
pea
peach
peak

please
read
readers
seal
seat
squeak
stream
teach
teacher
team
tease
treat

y
any
anything
baby
bunny
city
cozy
dirty
everyone
everywhere
funny
happy
jolly

lady
lazy
leafy
lucky
only
party
pony
pretty
ready
really
shaky
silly
story
windy

VCV
city
detail
electric
even
meter
recess
remember
robins

Spelling Words
deep
easy
feel
leave
party
read
seat
sleep
team
teeth
wheel
windy

High-Frequency/ Tested Words
guess
pretty
science*
shoe*
village
watch
won

Selection Words
electricity
robot
trash
wad

Dear Juno

Long o: o, oa, ow; Syllables VCV

o
almost
bold
cold
colt
donate
fold
gold
hello
hero
hold
host
locate
mold
moment
most
noticed
notion
ocean
old

open
over
photograph
post
postcard
rotate
scold
so
soda
sold
strolled
told
unfolded

oa
boast
boat
coach
coast
coat

croak
float
foamy
goal
goat
loaf
loan
moat
oat
oath
road
roam
roast
throat
toad
toast

ow
below
blow

blown
bowl
flow
flown
follow
glow
grow
grown
growth
know
mow
mower
own
owner
row
show
shown
slow
snow
throw

thrown
window
yellow

VCV
donate
favor
hero
locate
moment
noticed
open
photograph
robot
soda

Spelling Words
ago
bowl
float
goat
hold
most
open
show
slow
toad
toast
told

High-Frequency/ Tested Words
answer*
company
faraway
parents
picture*
school*
wash

Selection Words
envelope
persimmons
photograph
smudged

* = reviewed high-frequenc
word from Grade 1

Anansi Goes Fishing

Compound Words

afternoon	carpool	grandpa	mailman	railroad	sunrise	
airline	catfish	grandparents	maybe	raindrop	sunscreen	
airplane	cowboy	grandson	myself	rainstorm	sunshine	
airport	cupcake	grasshoppers	nearby	rainbow	suntan	
anything	daylight	haircut	netmaker	riverbank	supermarket	
babysit	daytime	halfway	network	riverboat	teacup	
backpack	dishpan	haystack	nobody	rowboat	teammates	
backyard	driveway	himself	nothing	sailboat	teardrop	
baseball	drugstore	homemade	nowhere	sandpaper	thunderstorm	
bathtub	everybody	homework	nutshell	schoolyard	treehouse	
bedroom	everyone	inside	oatmeal	seashore	watermelon	
bedtime	everything	landlord	outside	seaweed	weekend	
beehive	everywhere	laptop	pancake	shortstop	whatever	
birthday	faraway	ladybug	paycheck	snowflake	wherever	
blackbird	fireplace	lipstick	peanuts	snowstorm	wildflower	
brainstorm	flashlight	lookout	pinecone	someone	worksheet	
breakfast	forever	lunchbox	pitchfork	something	yourself	
buttermilk	goldfish	lunchtime	playmate	starfish		
cannot	granddad	mailbag	playoff	streetcar		
carefree	grandma	mailbox	popcorn	sunflowers		

Spelling Words

backyard
basketball
bathtub
bedtime
birthday
driveway
mailbox
raindrop
riverbank
someone
something
weekend

High-Frequency/ Tested Words

been
believe
caught
finally
today*
tomorrow
whatever

Selection Words

delicious
justice
lazy
weave

Rosa and Blanca

Long i: i, ie, igh, y

i		lied	nightlight	fly
behind	spider	pie	right	hydrant
bind	wild	tie	sigh	July
blind	tiger	tried	sight	myself
child	tiny		slight	nylon
cider	title	*igh*	thigh	shy
climb		bright	tight	sky
find	*ie*	flight		sly
kind	cried	fright	*y*	try
lilac	cries	high	by	why
mild	die	knight	cry	
mind	dried	light	cycle	
pilot	flies	might	cyclone	
sign	fries	night	dry	
	lie			

Spelling Words

blind
bright
child
cry
find
flight
fly
myself
right
sky
spider
wild

High-Frequency/ Tested Words

alone
buy
daughters
half
many*
their*
youngest

Selection Words

chiles
luckiest
tortillas

A Weed Is a Flower

Comparative Endings

-er	harsher	softer	**-est**	happiest	saddest
bigger	heavier	sooner	biggest	heaviest	silliest
brighter	hotter	stranger	bravest	highest	slowest
colder	higher	taller	brightest	hottest	smallest
fairer	lazier	thicker	busiest	latest	smartest
fancier	littler	thinner	closest	laziest	softest
faster	longer	tighter	coldest	lightest	sweetest
finer	nicer	tinier	cutest	littlest	tallest
friendlier	prettier	uglier	fairest	longest	thinnest
greener	redder	weaker	fastest	nicest	tiniest
happier	sillier	wider	finest	prettiest	ugliest
harder	slower		friendliest	reddest	weakest
			fullest	ripest	widest

Spelling Words

busier
busiest
fatter
fattest
happier
happiest
hotter
hottest
smaller
smallest
sooner
soonest

High-Frequency/ Tested Words

clothes
hours
money
neighbor
only*
question
taught

Selection Words

agriculture
college
greenhouse
laboratory

* = reviewed high-frequency word from Grade 1

The Quilt Story

Syllables: Consonant +le

able	cradle	maple	rattle	stable	twinkle
ankle	cuddle	middle	riddle	staple	uncle
apple	dimple	mumble	rifle	startle	whistle
bottle	fable	nibble	ripple	struggle	wiggle
bubble	giggle	noble	sample	stumble	wobble
bugle	gobble	paddle	scribble	table	
bundle	handle	pickle	simple	tickle	
cable	jumble	puddle	snuggle	title	
candle	ladle	purple	sparkle	trouble	
cattle	little	puzzle	sprinkle	tumble	

Spelling Words

able, ankle, apple, bubble, bugle, bundle, cable, giggle, purple, sparkle, tickle, title

Vocabulary/Tested Words

blankets, pretended, quilt, stuffing, trunks, unpacked, wrapped

High-Frequency Words

beautiful, country, friend, front, someone, somewhere

Life Cycle of a Pumpkin

Vowels oo, u

oo	foot	nook	took	**u**	bushy
book	football	notebook	understood	bull	full
bookbag	footstep	overlook	wood	bulldog	fully
brook	good	root	wooden	bullet	pudding
cook	hood	shook	woodpile	bullfrog	pull
cookbook	hoof	soot	wool	bully	pulley
cookie	hook	stood		bush	push
crook	look	textbook		bushel	put

Spelling Words

brook, cook, full, hood, hook, July, pull, push, put, shook, stood, wood

Vocabulary/Tested Words

bumpy, fruit, harvest, root, smooth, soil, vine

High-Frequency Words

everywhere, live, machines, move, woman, work, world

Frogs

Vowel Diphthongs ou, ow/ou/

ou	house	proud	**ow**	flower	towel
about	loud	round	allow	frown	towers
aloud	mouse	scout	bow	gown	town
amounts	mouth	shout	brown	growl	vow
around	ouch	sound	clown	how	vowel
bounce	ounce	south	cow	howl	
bound	our	sprout	cowboy	now	
cloud	out	stout	crowd	owl	
count	outside	trout	crown	plow	
crouch	pouch	voucher	down	powder	
found	pounce	without	downtown	powerful	
grouch	pound		drown	rowdy	
ground	pout		drowsy	shower	

Spelling Words

about, around, crown, downtown, flower, gown, ground, howl, mouse, pound, south

Vocabulary/Tested Words

crawls, insects, pond, powerful, shed, skin, wonderful

High-Frequency Words

bear, build, couldn't, father, love, mother, straight

I Like Where I Am

Vowel Diphthongs *oi, oy/oi/*

oi	joint	point	**oy**	joy
avoid	joist	poise	annoy	loyal
boil	hoist	poison	boy	oyster
broil	loiter	rejoice	boyhood	ploy
choice	moist	sirloin	cowboy	royal
coil	noise	soil	coy	soy
coin	noisy	spoil	destroy	toy
foil	oily	toil	employ	voyage
join	ointment	voice	enjoy	

Spelling Words

broil
cowboy
destroy
enjoy
foil
joint
joy
loyal
moist
noise
royal
spoil

Vocabulary/ Tested Words

block
chuckle
fair
giant
strong
tears
trouble

High-Frequency Words

animals
early
eyes
full
water

Helen Keller and the Big Storm

Vowels *oo, ew, ue, ui*

oo	moo	spool	**ew**	**ue**	**ui**
bathroom	mood	spoon	blew	blue	bruise
bloom	moon	stoop	brew	clue	cruise
boot	noon	too	chew	cue	fruit
broom	pool	tool	crew	due	juice
classroom	proof	tooth	drew	glue	nuisance
cool	raccoon	troop	few	hue	recruit
food	room	zoo	flew	true	suit
goose	school	zoom	grew		
hoop	scoop		knew		
hoot	smooth		new		
loop	snoop		stew		
loose	soon		threw		

Spelling Words

blue
clue
cool
drew
flew
fruit
juice
new
spoon
suit
too
true

Vocabulary/ Tested Words

angry
branches
clung
fingers
picnic
pressing
special

High-Frequency Words

gone
learn
often
pieces
though
together
very

Firefighter!

Suffixes -ly, -ful, -er, -or

-ly
boldly
bravely
brightly
carefully
clearly
closely
finally
firmly
fondly
gently
gladly
hardly
harshly
kindly

lightly
loudly
lovely
proudly
quickly
quietly
slowly
smoothly
softly
suddenly
sweetly
tenderly
tightly
weekly

-ful
boastful
careful
cheerful
colorful
eventful
graceful
harmful
helpful
hopeful
joyful
peaceful
playful
powerful
restful

skillful
thankful
wonderful

-er
computer
dancer
driver
farmer
fighter
firefighter
gardener
helper
hiker
leader

painter
player
rancher
reader
singer
storyteller
teacher
vacationer
waiter
writer

-or
actor
calculator
conductor

creditor
director
editor
inventor
refrigerator
sailor
supervisor
visitor

Spelling Words
cheerful
fighter
graceful
hardly
helper
quickly
sailor
slowly
teacher
visitor
weekly
yearly

Vocabulary/ Tested Words
building
burning
masks
quickly
roar
station
tightly

High-Frequency Words
break   listen
family   once
heard   pull

One Dark Night

Prefixes un-, re-, pre-, dis-

un-
unable
unclasp
undisturbed
uneasy
uneven
unfair
unfinished
unfold
unfrozen
unglue
unhappy
unhook
unkind
unlatch
unload
unlock

unmasks
unpack
unplug
unroll
unsafe
unseen
untie
untrue

re-
react
reclose
redrew
refilled
refold
reheated
relight

remake
repack
repaint
repave
replace
replaced
replay
rerun
resize
rethink
reuse
rewind
rewire
rework
rewrite

pre-
precooked
predate
preflight
preheat
preorder
prepaid
preread
preschool
preteen
pretest
pretreat
preview
prewash

dis-
disagree
disappear
disappointed
disapprove
disconnect
discount
disinfect
disjoint
dislike
dislocate
displace
displease
disprove
distrust

Spelling Words
disagree
disappear
preheat
preschool
regroup
rerun
retie
rewind
unlock
unpack
unplug
unsafe

Vocabulary/ Tested Words
flashes
lightning
pounds
pours
rolling
storm
thunder

High-Frequency Words
certainly   worst
either   you're
great
laugh
second

Bad Dog, Dodger!

Silent Consonants: kn, wr, gn, mb

kn
knee
kneecap
kneel
knew
knickers
knife
knight
knit
knob
knock

knot
know
knuckle

wr
wrap
wreath
wreck
wren
wrench
wrestle

wriggle
wringing
wrinkle
wrist
write
wrong
wrote

gn
design
gnat
gnaw
gnome
gnu
resign
sign

mb
climb
comb
crumb
dumb
lamb
limb
numb
plumber
thumb
tomb

Spelling Words
climb
comb
gnat
knee
knob
knock
lamb
sign
wrap
wren
write
wrong

Vocabulary/ Tested Words
chased
chewing
dripping
grabbed
practice
treat
wagged

High-Frequency Words
above
ago
enough
toward
whole
word

Horace and Morris but mostly Dolores

ph, gh/f/

ph
alphabet
dolphin
elephant
gopher
graph
nephew
orphan

phantom
phase
pheasant
phone
phony
phooey
photo
phrase

sphere
telegraph
trophy

gh
autograph
cough
enough

laugh
rough
roughly
tough

Spelling Words

cliff
cough
enough
giraffe
graph
laugh
phone
photo
puff
rough
stuff
tough

Vocabulary/ Tested Words

adventure
climbed
clubhouse
exploring
greatest
truest
wondered

High-Frequency Words

bought   scared
people   shall
pleasant   sign
probably

The Signmaker's Assistant

Vowels aw, au, augh, al

aw
awful
bawl
brawny
claw
crawl
draw
drawn
fawn
gnaw
hawk
jaw
law
lawn
paw

raw
saw
scrawl
shawl
squawk
straw
thaw
yawn

au
applaud
August
author
auto
because

cause
fault
haul
haunt
jaunt
launch
laundry
pause
sauce
sausage
vault

augh
caught
daughter

haughty
naughty
slaughter
taught

al
all
also
always
bald
ball
baseball
call
chalk
fall

false
malt
salt
small
talk
taller
walk
wall
walnut
waltz

Spelling Words

August
auto
because
caught
chalk
draw
fault
launch
talk
taught
thaw
walk

Vocabulary/ Tested Words

afternoon
blame
idea
important
signmaker
townspeople

High-Frequency Words

behind   minute
brought   promise
door   sorry
everybody

Just Like Josh Gibson

Contractions

could've	she'd	we're	you'd
don't	should've	we've	you're
he'd	they'd	where'd	you've
I'd	they're	won't	
I've	they've	would've	

Spelling Words

can't
don't
he'd
I'd
I've
she'd
they'd
they're
we're
we've
won't
you're

Vocabulary/ Tested Words

bases
cheers
field
plate
sailed
threw

High-Frequency Words

guess	village
pretty	watch
science	won
shoe	

Red, White, and Blue: The Story of the American Flag

Base Words and Endings

added	cries	having	pinches	spotted
baking	crossed	heading	places	started
beginning	crying	helped	planning	stepped
belonged	danced	hiking	plans	stepping
bigger	dancing	hoped	pointed	steps
biggest	decided	hopes	pouncing	stopped
bombed	discovered	hoping	pounds	stopping
bounced	dropped	hopped	prepays	stops
bounces	drops	hopping	prettiest	streets
bouncing	drumming	hugged	propping	stripes
braver	ended	hurried	purred	talking
burned	erupted	jogging	reapplied	thanks
called	excited	joking	replied	thinking
carried	faster	judging	returns	thornier
carries	fastest	knows	richest	tied
carrying	fighting	landed	rides	tried
changes	fitted	loneliest	rolling	tries
chokes	flies	longest	rubbed	trying
cleaned	floated	luckier	rubbing	unhappier
cleaning	floating	luckiest	rushed	unluckiest
cleared	floats	making	sadder	used
clearer	flying	marched	sailed	visits
clearest	fried	minded	scampered	wanted
clearing	friendlier	moved	scared	watched
clears	funnier	named	sewing	waved
climbed	funniest	needed	shouted	waving
closed	glued	nicer	showed	wider
coming	going	nicest	singing	widest
continued	hammered	nodded	skipping	wishes
cooking	happened	opened	sleepiest	
crazier	happier	owned	smarter	
craziest	happiest	peeking	smiles	
cried	hardest	picked	spiciest	

Spelling Words

cried
crying
hiked
hiking
liked
liking
planned
planning
skipped
skipping
tried
trying

Vocabulary/ Tested Words

America
birthday
flag
freedom
nicknames
stars
stripes

High-Frequency Words

answer	picture
company	school
faraway	wash
parents	

A Birthday Basket for Tía

Syllables *tion, ture*

tion
action
addition
affection
caption
caution
celebration
creation
edition
fiction

fraction
location
lotion
mention
motion
nation
portion
position
potion
recreation

section
station
suction
tuitions
vacation

ture
adventure
capture
creature
culture
feature
fixture
fracture
furniture
future

lecturing
mixture
moisture
nature
picture
puncture
sculpture
vulture

Spelling Words
action
caution
feature
fixture
future
mixture
motion
nation
nature
picture
section
station

Vocabulary/Tested Words
aunt
bank
basket
collects
favorite
present

High-Frequency Words
been
believe
caught
finally
today
tomorrow
whatever

Cowboys

Suffixes *-ness, -less*

-ness
awareness
cheerfulness
brightness
darkness
emptiness
fairness
fitness
fondness
friendliness
fullness
gentleness
goodness
greatness
happiness

illness
kindness
lateness
laziness
loneliness
loudness
madness
quickness
redness
rudeness
sadness
sickness
soreness
stillness
suddenness

sweetness
tenderness
usefulness
watchfulness
weakness
weariness

-less
ageless
bottomless
careless
cloudless
colorless
cordless
countless

fearless
flightless
friendless
harmless
heartless
helpless
hopeless
hopelessly
jobless
joyless
meatless
mindless
painless
penniless
pointless

restless
shameless
shapeless
sleepless
speechless
spotless
thankless
thoughtless
tireless
toothless
useless
worthless

Spelling Words
careless
darkness
fearless
fitness
goodness
helpless
kindness
sadness
sickness
thankless
useless
weakness

Vocabulary/Tested Words
campfire
cattle
cowboy
galloped
herd
railroad
trails

High-Frequency Words
alone
buy
daughters
half
many
their
youngest

Jingle Dancer

Prefixes *mis-, mid-*

mis-
misbehave
misbehavior
miscompute
misconduct
miscopy
misdeed
misdirect
misfile
misfit

misguided
misinform
misjudge
mislabel
mislaid
mislead
misleading
mismatch
misplace
misprint

misquote
misread
misreport
misshape
misspoke
misstep
mistreat
mistype
misunderstood

mid-
midafternoon
midair
midcircle
midday
midlife
midline
midnight
midpoint
midsentence

midship
midsize
midstream
midsummer
midtown
midway
midweek
midyear

Spelling Words
midair
midday
midway
midweek
midyear
misbehave
misdeed
mislead
mismatch
misplace
misprint
mistake

Vocabulary/Tested Words
borrow
clattering
drum
jingles
silver
voice

High-Frequency Words
clothes
hours
money
neighbor
only
question
taught

Position for Writing

Left-handed and right-handed writers slant their papers differently from one another, but they sit and hold their pencils the same way.

Body Position

• Children should sit tall, with both feet flat on the floor and arms relaxed on a table or desk.

• Children should hold their papers with their non-writing hand.

Paper Slant

• Paper should be positioned at a slant that is approximately parallel to the writing arm.

• For left-handed children, the paper should slant from the right at the top to the left at the bottom.

• Right-handed children should slant the paper from the left at the top to the right at the bottom.

Pencil Grip

• Children should grasp the pencil lightly between the thumb and index finger, usually about an inch above the pencil point.

• For a child who grasps the pencil too close to the point, a simple remedy is to wrap a rubber band around the pencil about an inch above the point. Have the child hold the pencil above the rubber band.

Legibility

Legibility should be the goal of handwriting instruction. Children should be praised for writing legibly, even though their writing may deviate from a perfect model. Legibility is based on flexible but standard criteria for letter form, size, and slant, and for letter and word spacing.

Letter Form

• Standards for letter form enable each letter to be distinguished clearly from other letters.

• In the letter *a*, for example, the round part of the letter must be open, and the letter must be closed at the top. The letter *a* must not be confused with *u, d,* or *o.*

• The letters *t* and *f* must be crossed; the letters *i* and *j* dotted.

Letter Size

• Small letters sit on the bottom line and touch the middle line.

• Tall letters sit on the bottom line and touch the top line.

• Letters with descenders have tails that go down under the bottom line and touch the line below.

Letter Slant

• Letter slant should be consistent.

• All letters may slant to the right, to the left, or be straight up and down.

Letter and Word Spacing

• Letters in a word should be evenly spaced. They should not be written too close together or too far apart.

• There should be more space between words in a sentence than between letters in a word. This allows each word to stand out.

D'Nealian™ Alphabet

a b c d e f g h i
j k l m n o p q r s t
u v w x y z

A B C D E F G
H I J K L M N O
P Q R S T U V
W X Y Z . , ' ?

1 2 3 4 5 6
7 8 9 10

Manuscript Alphabet

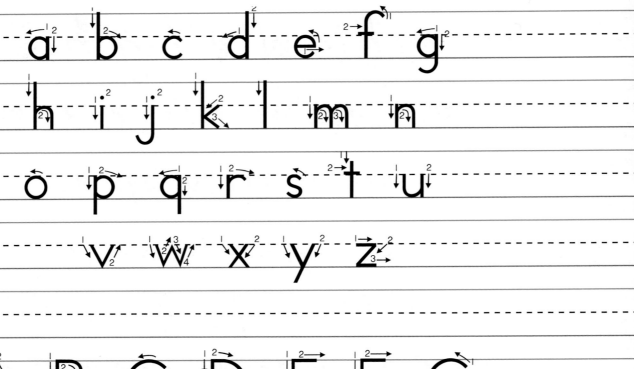

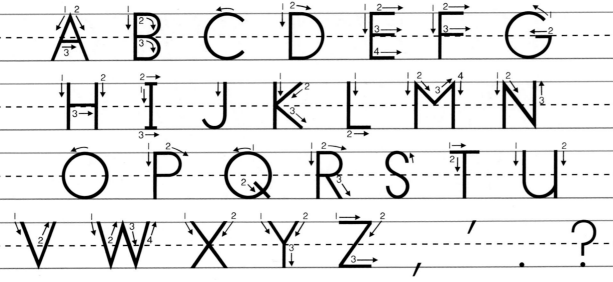

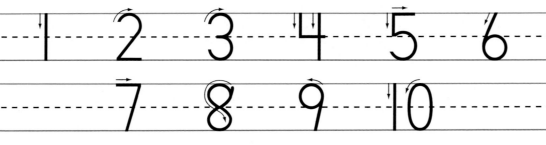

D'Nealian™ Cursive Alphabet

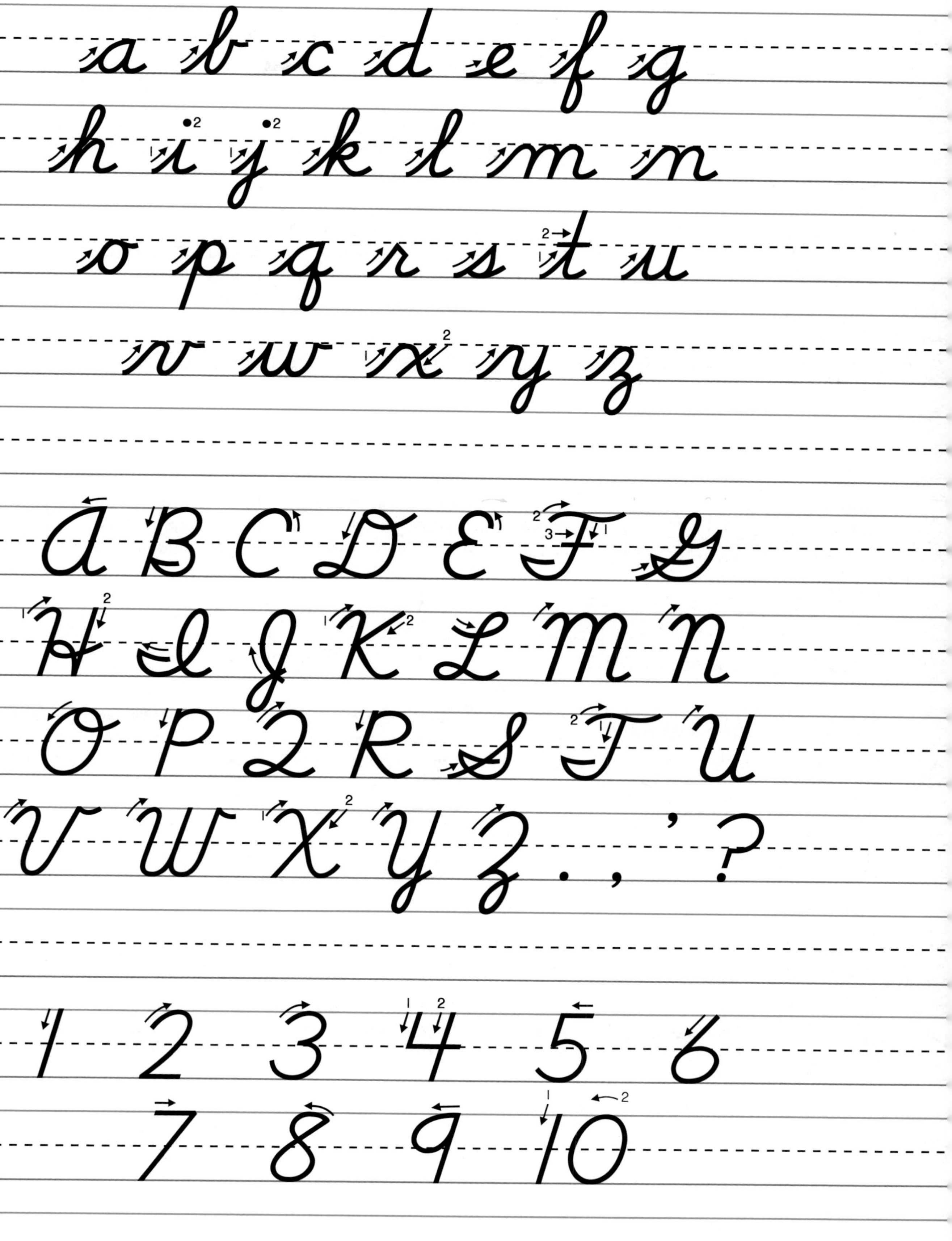

a b c d e f g

h i j k l m n

o p q r s t u

v w x y z

A B C D E F G

H I J K L M N

O P Q R S T U

V W X Y Z . , ' ?

1 2 3 4 5 6

7 8 9 10

Unit 6 *Traditions*

	Below-Level	On-Level	Advanced

Just Like Josh Gibson

To Read Aloud!
The Girl Who Struck Out Babe Ruth
by Jean L. S. Patrick (Carolrhoda Books, 2000) This book profiles one-time professional baseball player Jackie Mitchell, a woman, who, at 17, struck out Babe Ruth and Lou Gehrig back to back.

H is for Home Run
by Brad Herzog (Gale Group, 2004) This book provides a baseball-related term for each letter of the alphabet along with beautiful illustrations to catch the eye.

Negro Leagues: All-Black Baseball
by Laura Driscoll (Grosset and Dunlap, 2002) A little girl writes a report on her recent trip to the Baseball Hall of Fame where she saw an entire room devoted to the Negro Leagues.

Jackie and Me
by Dan Gutman (HarperCollins Children's Books, 2000) A young boy who can travel through time with his baseball cards meets Jackie Robinson.

Red, White, and Blue

To Read Aloud!
America, My New Home
by Monica Gunning (Boyds Mills Press, 2004) This book of short narrative poems capture the feelings of a young girl as she moves from Jamaica to America.

Looking at Liberty
by Harvey Stevenson (Katherine Tegen Books, 2003) This is a poetic look at one of our nation's greatest symbols, the Statue of Liberty.

America Is...
by Louise Borden (Margaret K. McElderry Books, 2002) This book is a beautiful tribute to all of the people, places, and things that make America great.

The American Flag
by Deborah Hess (Benchmark Books, 2004) This well-written book presents basic facts and little-known trivia about our country's flag.

A Birthday Basket for Tía

To Read Aloud!
Birthdays Around the World
by Mary D. Lankford (HarperCollins Publishers, 2002) This book takes a look at how birthdays in other countries, such as Finland, Malaysia, Mexico, the Netherlands, and New Zealand, are celebrated.

Chestnut
by Constance W. McGeorge (Peachtree Publishers, 2004) When his owner falls asleep, it is up to Chestnut the horse to make all of the deliveries for a little girl's birthday party.

Lionel's Birthday
by Stephen Krensky (Dial, 2003) Four brief but funny vignettes make up this book about a little boy's impending birthday.

Polly's Absolutely Worst Birthday Ever
by Frances Thomas (Delacorte, 2003) When Polly gets the chicken pox and her hamster dies, she is convinced that this will be the most terrible birthday ever.

Cowboys

To Read Aloud!
The Amazing World of the Wild West: Discover the Trailblazing History of Cowboys, Outlaws and Native Americans
by Peter Harrison (Lorenz Books, 2004) This book takes a fascinating look at the facts behind the fantasy.

Jess and the Stinky Cowboys
by Janice Lee Smith (Dial Books, 2004) Everything is going fine for Deputy Jess while the Sheriff is away, until a gang of smelly cowboys rides into town.

The Dirty Cowboy
by Amy Timberlake (Farrar Straus Giroux, 2003) This humorous book is about a cowboy trying his best to get rid of the dirt and stench he has gathered on his trip through the West.

Buffalo
by Beverly Brodsky (Marshall Cavendish Corporation, 2003) A beautiful look at the history and demise of the Western buffalo and the animal's strong connection with Native American traditions.

Jingle Dancer

To Read Aloud!
Earth Always Endures: Native American Poems
by Edward S. Curtis (Viking Books, 1996) More than sixty poems written by Native Americans give the reader an eloquent look into Native American life.

The Girl Who Loved Wild Horses
by Paul Goble (Aladdin Paperbacks, 1993) The story of a young Native American girl who takes care of her tribe's horses.

We Are the Many: A Picture Book of American Indians
by Doreen Rappaport (HarperCollins, 2002) In this book, sixteen people are profiled along with one incident from each of their lives, giving the reader a sense of what each person contributed to the world.

Flying with the Eagle, Racing the Great Bear: Stories from Native North America
by Joseph Bruchac (Bridgewater, 1993) Geographically arranged, this collection features sixteen coming-of-age stories centered on male protagonists.

Unit 6 Reading Log

Name _____

Dates Read	Title and Author	What is it about?	How would you rate it?	Explain your rating.
From _____ to _____			Great 5 4 3 2 1 Awful	
From _____ to _____			Great 5 4 3 2 1 Awful	
From _____ to _____			Great 5 4 3 2 1 Awful	
From _____ to _____			Great 5 4 3 2 1 Awful	
From _____ to _____			Great 5 4 3 2 1 Awful	

Unit 6 Narrative Retelling Chart

Selection Title ——————   Name ——————   Date ——————

Retelling Criteria/*Teacher Prompt*	Teacher-Aided Response	Student-Generated Response	Rubric Score (Circle one.)
Connections Does this story remind you of anything else?			4 3 2 1
Author's Purpose Why do you think the author wrote this story? What was the author trying to tell us?			4 3 2 1
Characters What can you tell me about —— (use character's name)?			4 3 2 1
Setting Where and when did the story happen?			4 3 2 1
Plot What happened in the story?			4 3 2 1

Summative Retelling Score   4   3   2   1

Comments ——————

Unit 6 Expository Retelling Chart

Name ——————————————— **Date** —————

Selection Title ———————————————————————

Retelling Criteria/Teacher Prompt	Teacher-Aided Response	Student-Generated Response	Rubric Score (Circle one.)
Connections Did this selection make you think about something else you have read? What did you learn about as you read this selection?			4 3 2 1
Author's Purpose Why do you think the author wrote this selection?			4 3 2 1
Topic What was the selection mostly about?			4 3 2 1
Important Ideas What is important for me to know about ——— (topic)?			4 3 2 1
Conclusions What did you learn from reading this selection?			4 3 2 1

Summative Retelling Score 4 3 2 1

Comments ———————————————————————

———————————————————————

Reading

Concepts of Print and Print Awareness

Concepts of Print and Print Awareness	Pre-K	K	1	2	3	4	5
Develop awareness that print represents spoken language and conveys and preserves meaning	•	•	•				
Recognize familiar books by their covers; hold book right side up	•	•					
Identify parts of a book and their functions (front cover, title page/title, back cover, page numbers)	•	•	•				
Understand the concepts of letter, word, sentence, paragraph, and story	•	•	•				
Track print (front to back of book, top to bottom of page, left to right on line, sweep back left for next line)	•	•	•				
Match spoken to printed words	•	•	•				
Know capital and lowercase letter names and match them	•	• T	•				
Know the order of the alphabet	•	•	•				
Recognize first name in print	•	•	•				
Recognize the uses of capitalization and punctuation			•	•			
Value print as a means of gaining information	•	•	•				

Phonological and Phonemic Awareness

Phonological Awareness

Phonological Awareness	Pre-K	K	1	2	3	4	5
Recognize and produce rhyming words		•	•				
Track and count each word in a spoken sentence and each syllable in a spoken word	•	•	•				
Segment and blend syllables in spoken words			•				
Segment and blend onset and rime in one-syllable words		•	•				
Recognize and produce words beginning with the same sound	•	•	•				
Identify beginning, middle, and/or ending sounds that are the same or different	•	•	•				
Understand that spoken words are made of sequences of sounds	•	•	•				

Phonemic Awareness

Phonemic Awareness	Pre-K	K	1	2	3	4	5
Identify the position of sounds in words		•	•				
Identify and isolate initial, final, and medial sounds in spoken words	•	•	•				
Blend sounds orally to make words or syllables		•	•				
Segment a word or syllable into sounds; count phonemes in spoken words or syllables		•	•				
Manipulate sounds in words (add, delete, and/or substitute phonemes)	•	•	•				

Phonics and Decoding

Phonics

Phonics	Pre-K	K	1	2	3	4	5
Understand and apply the **alphabetic principle** that spoken words are composed of sounds that are represented by letters	•	•	•				
Know letter-sound relationships	•	• T	• T	• T			
Blend sounds of letters to decode		•	• T	• T	• T		
Consonants, consonant blends, and consonant digraphs		•	• T	• T	• T		
Short, long, and r-controlled vowels; vowel digraphs; diphthongs; common vowel patterns			• T	• T	• T		
Phonograms/word families		•	•	•	•		

Word Structure

Word Structure	Pre-K	K	1	2	3	4	5
Decode words with common word parts		•	• T	• T	• T	•	•
Base words and inflected endings			• T	• T	•	•	•
Contractions and compound words			• T	• T	• T	•	•
Suffixes and prefixes			• T	• T	• T	•	•
Greek and Latin roots						•	•
Blend syllables to decode words			• T	• T	• T	•	•

Decoding Strategies

Decoding Strategies	Pre-K	K	1	2	3	4	5
Blending strategy: Apply knowledge of letter-sound relationships to decode unfamiliar words		•	•	•	•		
Apply knowledge of word structure to decode unfamiliar words		•	•	•	•	•	•
Use context and syntax along with letter-sound relationships and word structure to decode		•	•	•	•	•	•
Self-correct			•	•	•	•	•

Fluency

Fluency	Pre-K	K	1	2	3	4	5
Read aloud fluently with accuracy, comprehension, appropriate pace/rate; with expression/intonation (prosody); with attention to punctuation and appropriate phrasing			• T	• T	• T	• T	• T
Practice fluency in a variety of ways, including choral reading, partner/paired reading, Readers' Theater, repeated oral reading, and tape-assisted reading		•	•	•	•	•	•

• instructional opportunity **T** tested in standardized test

	Pre-K	K	1	2	3	4	5	6
ward appropriate fluency goals by the end of each grade			•T	•T	•T	•T	•T	•T
gularly in independent-level material			•	•	•	•	•	•
ently for increasing periods of time			•	•	•	•	•	•

bulary (Oral and Written)

Recognition

	Pre-K	K	1	2	3	4	5	6
ize regular and irregular high-frequency words	•	•	•T	•T				
ize and understand selection vocabulary		•	•	•T	•	•	•	•
and content-area vocabulary and specialized, technical, or topical words			•	•	•	•	•	•

Learning Strategies

	Pre-K	K	1	2	3	4	5	6
vocabulary through direct instruction, concrete experiences, reading, listening to text read aloud	•	•	•	•	•	•	•	•
owledge of word structure to figure out meanings of words			•	•T	•T	•T	•T	•T
ntext clues for meanings of unfamiliar words, multiple-meaning words, homonyms, homographs			•	•T	•T	•T	•T	•T
de-appropriate reference sources to learn word meanings	•	•	•	•	•T	•T	•T	•T
ture clues to help determine word meanings	•	•	•	•	•			
w words in a variety of contexts	•	•	•	•	•	•	•	•
e word usage and effectiveness		•	•	•	•	•	•	•
and use graphic organizers to group, study, and retain vocabulary		•	•	•	•	•	•	•

d Concepts and Word Knowledge

	Pre-K	K	1	2	3	4	5	6
nic language	•	•	•	•	•	•	•	•
w and categorize	•	•	•	•	•	•	•	•
ms and synonyms			•T	•T	•T	•T	•T	•T
raphs, homonyms, and homophones				•	•T	•T	•T	•T
e-meaning words			•	•	•T	•T	•T	•T
words and derivations					•	•	•	•
es						•	•	
ation/denotation						•	•	•
ve language and idioms			•	•	•	•	•	•
tive words (location, size, color, shape, number, ideas, feelings)	•	•	•	•	•	•	•	•
lity words (shapes, colors, question words, position/directional words, and so on)	•	•	•					
nd order words	•	•	•	•	•	•	•	•
on words						•	•	•
rigins: Etymologies/word histories; words from other languages, regions, or cultures					•	•	•	•
ned forms: abbreviations, acronyms, clipped words			•	•	•	•	•T	

Comprehension

	Pre-K	K	1	2	3	4	5	6

rehension Strategies

	Pre-K	K	1	2	3	4	5	6
the text and formulate questions	•	•	•	•	•	•	•	•
monitor purpose for reading and listening	•	•	•	•	•	•	•	•
e and use prior knowledge	•	•	•	•	•	•	•	•
redictions	•	•	•	•	•	•	•	•
comprehension and use fix-up strategies to resolve difficulties in meaning: adjust reading rate, and read on, seek help from reference sources and/or other people, skim and scan, summarize, t features				•	•	•	•	•
and use graphic and semantic organizers		•	•	•	•	•	•	•
questions (text explicit, text implicit, scriptal), including who, what, when, where, why, what if, how	•	•	•	•	•	•	•	•
back in text for answers			•	•	•	•	•	•
er test-like questions			•	•	•	•	•	•
te clarifying questions, including who, what, where, when, how, why, and what if	•	•	•	•	•	•	•	•
ize text structure: story and informational (cause/effect, chronological, compare/contrast, tion, problem/solution, propostion/support)	•	•	•	•	•	•	•	•
arize text		•	•	•	•	•	•	•
ll and retell stories	•	•	•	•	•	•	•	•
ify and retell important/main ideas (nonfiction)	•	•	•	•	•	•	•	•
ify and retell new information				•	•	•	•	•
ze; use mental imagery		•	•T	•T	•T	•T	•T	•T
rategies flexibly and in combination			•	•	•	•	•	•

Scope and Sequence **TR23**

Comprehension Skills

	Pre-K	K	1	2	3	4	5
Author's purpose			• T	• T	• T	• T	• T
Author's viewpoint/bias/perspective					•	•	•
Categorize and classify	•	•	•	•			
Cause and effect		•	• T	• T	• T	• T	• T
Compare and contrast		•	• T	• T	• T	• T	• T
Details and facts		•	•	•	•	•	•
Draw conclusions		•	• T	• T	• T	• T	• T
Fact and opinion				• T	• T	• T	• T
Follow directions/steps in a process	•	•	•	•	•	•	•
Generalize					• T	• T	• T
Graphic sources		•	•	•	•	• T	• T
Main idea and supporting details		• T	• T	• T	• T	• T	• T
Paraphrase			•	•	•	•	•
Persuasive devices and propaganda				•	•	•	•
Realism/fantasy		•	• T	• T	• T	•	
Sequence of events		• T	• T	• T	• T	• T	• T

Higher Order Thinking Skills

	Pre-K	K	1	2	3	4	5
Analyze					•	•	•
Describe and connect the essential ideas, arguments, and perspectives of a text			•	•	•	•	•
Draw inferences, conclusions, or generalizations, support them with textual evidence and prior knowledge	•		•	•	•	•	•
Evaluate and critique ideas and text			•	•	•	•	•
Hypothesize						•	•
Make judgments about ideas and text			•	•	•	•	•
Organize and synthesize ideas and information			•			•	•

Literary Analysis, Response, & Appreciation

	Pre-K	K	1	2	3	4	5
Genre and Its Characteristics							
Recognize characteristics of a variety of genre	•	•	•	•	•	•	•
Distinguish fiction from nonfiction		•	•	•	•	•	•
Identify characteristics of literary texts, including drama, fantasy, traditional tales		•	•	•	•	•	•
Identify characteristics of nonfiction texts, including biography, interviews, newspaper articles		•	•	•	•	•	•
Identify characteristics of poetry and song, including nursery rhymes, limericks, blank verse	•	•	•	•	•	•	•
Literary Elements and Story Structure							
Character	•	• T	• T	• T	• T	• T	• T
Recognize and describe traits, actions, feelings, and motives of characters		•	•	•	•	•	•
Analyze characters' relationships, changes, and points of view		•	•	•	•	•	•
Analyze characters' conflicts				•		•	•
Plot and plot structure	•	• T	• T	• T	• T	• T	• T
Beginning, middle, end	•	•	•	•	•		
Goal and outcome or problem and solution/resolution		•	•	•	•	•	•
Rising action, climax, and falling action/denouement; setbacks						•	•
Setting	•	• T	• T	• T	• T	• T	
Relate setting to problem/solution						•	•
Explain ways setting contributes to mood						•	•
Theme		•	• T	• T	•	•	•
Use Literary Elements and Story Structure	•	•	•	•	•	•	•
Analyze and evaluate author's use of setting, plot, character					•	•	•
Identify similarities and differences of characters, events, and settings within or across selections/cultures		•	•	•	•	•	•
Literary Devices							
Allusion							
Dialect						•	
Dialogue and narration	•	•	•	•	•	•	•
Exaggeration/hyperbole					•	•	•
Figurative language: idiom, jargon, metaphor, simile, slang			•	•	•	•	•

• instructional opportunity   **T** tested in standardized te[st]

	Pre-K	K	1	2	3	4	5	6
...ck						•	•	•
...dowing							•	•
...and informal language				•	•	•	•	•
					•	•	•	•
...and sensory words			•	•	•	•	•	•
				•	•	•	•	•
...ication				•	•	•		
...view (first person, third person, omniscient)					•	•	•	•
...d word play				•	•	•	•	•
...evices and poetic elements	•	•	•	•	•	•	•	•
...ation, assonance, onomatopoeia	•	•	•	•	•	•	•	•
...e, rhythm, repetition, and cadence	•	•	•	•	•	•	•	•
...choice					•	•	•	•
...sm					•	•	•	•
							•	•

...r's and Illustrator's Craft

	Pre-K	K	1	2	3	4	5	6
...ish the roles of author and illustrator		•	•	•				
...ze/analyze author's and illustrator's craft or style			•	•	•	•	•	•

...ry Response

	Pre-K	K	1	2	3	4	5	6
...t, talk, and write about books	•	•	•	•	•	•	•	•
...on reading and respond (through talk, movement, art, and so on)	•	•	•	•	•	•	•	•
...nd answer questions about text	•	•	•	•	•	•	•	•
...about what is read	•	•	•	•	•	•	•	•
...vidence from the text to support opinions, interpretations, or conclusions				•	•	•	•	•
...rt ideas through reference to other texts and personal knowledge				•	•	•	•	•
...e materials on related topic, theme, or idea				•	•	•	•	•
...ate alternative endings to plots and identify the reason for, and the impact of, the alternatives	•	•	•	•	•	•	•	•
...ize and extend the literary experience through creative responses	•	•	•	•	•	•	•	•
...onnections: text to self, text to text, text to world	•	•	•	•	•	•	•	•
...e and critique the quality of the literary experience				•	•	•	•	•
...servations, react, speculate in response to text				•	•	•	•	•

...ry Appreciation/Motivation

	Pre-K	K	1	2	3	4	5	6
...interest in books and reading; engage voluntarily in social interaction about books	•	•	•	•	•	•	•	•
...text by drawing on personal interests, relying on knowledge of authors and genres, estimating text ...y, and using recommendations of others				•	•	•	•	•
...variety of grade-level appropriate narrative and expository texts		•	•	•	•	•	•	•
...om a wide variety of genres for a variety of purposes	•	•	•	•	•	•	•	•
...dependently				•	•	•	•	•
...h familiarity with a topic			•	•	•	•	•	•

...al Awareness

	Pre-K	K	1	2	3	4	5	6
...attitudes and abilities to interact with diverse groups and cultures	•	•	•	•	•	•	•	•
...experiences and ideas with those from a variety of languages, cultures, customs, perspectives	•	•	•	•	•	•	•	•
...and how attitudes and values in a culture or during a period in time affect the writing from that ...or time period						•	•	•
...e language and oral traditions (family stories) that reflect customs, regions, and cultures		•	•		•		•	•
...ze themes that cross cultures and bind them together in their common humanness						•	•	•

guage Arts

...ng	Pre-K	K	1	2	3	4	5	6
...epts of Print for Writing								
...gross and fine motor skills and hand/eye coordination	•	•	•					
...n name and other important words	•	•	•					
...sing pictures, some letters, and transitional spelling to convey meaning	•	•	•					
...messages or stories for others to write	•	•	•					

	Pre-K	K	1	2	3	4	5
Create own written texts for others to read; write left to right on a line and top to bottom on a page	•	•	•				
Participate in shared and interactive writing	•	•	•				

Traits of Writing

Focus/Ideas

	Pre-K	K	1	2	3	4	5
Maintain focus and sharpen ideas		•	•	•	•	•	•
Use sensory details and concrete examples; elaborate		•	•	•	•	•	•
Delete extraneous information			•	•	•	•	•
Rearrange words and sentences to improve meaning and focus				•	•	•	•
Use strategies, such as tone, style, consistent point of view, to achieve a sense of completeness						•	•

Organization/Paragraphs

	Pre-K	K	1	2	3	4	5
Use graphic organizers to group ideas		•	•	•	•	•	•
Write coherent paragraphs that develop a central idea			•	•	•	•	•
Use transitions to connect sentences and paragraphs			•	•	•	•	•
Select an organizational structure based on purpose, audience, length						•	•
Organize ideas in a logical progression, such as chronological order or by order of importance		•	•	•	•	•	•
Write introductory, supporting, and concluding paragraphs					•	•	•
Write a multi-paragraph paper				•	•	•	•

Voice

	Pre-K	K	1	2	3	4	5
Develop personal, identifiable voice and an individual tone/style			•	•	•	•	•
Maintain consistent voice and point of view						•	•
Use voice appropriate to audience, message, and purpose						•	•

Word Choice

	Pre-K	K	1	2	3	4	5
Use clear, precise, appropriate language		•	•	•	•	•	•
Use figurative language and vivid words				•	•	•	•
Select effective vocabulary using word walls, dictionary, or thesaurus		•	•	•	•	•	•

Sentences

	Pre-K	K	1	2	3	4	5
Combine, elaborate, and vary sentences		•	•	•	•	•	•
Write topic sentence, supporting sentences with facts and details, and concluding sentence			•	•	•	•	•
Use correct word order				•	•	•	•
Use parallel structure in a sentence							•

Conventions

	Pre-K	K	1	2	3	4	5
Use correct spelling and grammar; capitalize and punctuate correctly		•	•	•	•	•	•
Correct sentence fragments and run-ons					•	•	•
Use correct paragraph indention				•	•	•	•

The Writing Process

	Pre-K	K	1	2	3	4	5
Prewrite using various strategies	•	•	•	•	•	•	•
Develop first drafts of single- and multiple-paragraph compositions		•	•	•	•	•	•
Revise drafts for varied purposes, including to clarify and to achieve purpose, sense of audience, precise word choice, vivid images, and elaboration		•	•	•	•	•	•
Edit and proofread for correct spelling, grammar, usage, and mechanics		•	•	•	•	•	•
Publish own work	•	•	•	•	•	•	•

Types of Writing

	Pre-K	K	1	2	3	4	5
Narrative writing (such as personal narratives, stories, biographies, autobiographies)	•	•	• T	• T	• T	• T	• T
Expository writing (such as essays, directions, explanations, news stories, research reports, summaries)		•	• T	• T	• T	• T	• T
Descriptive writing (such as labels, captions, lists, plays, poems, response logs, songs)	•	•	• T	• T	• T	• T	• T
Persuasive writing (such as ads, editorials, essays, letters to the editor, opinions, posters)		•	• T	• T	• T	• T	• T

Writing Habits and Practices

	Pre-K	K	1	2	3	4	5
Write on a daily basis	•	•	•	•	•	•	•
Use writing as a tool for learning and self-discovery				•	•	•	•
Write independently for extended periods of time			•	•	•	•	•

ENGLISH LANGUAGE CONVENTIONS in WRITING and SPEAKING

	Pre-K	K	1	2	3	4	5

Grammar and Usage in Speaking and Writing

Sentences

	Pre-K	K	1	2	3	4	5
Types (declarative, interrogative, exclamatory, imperative)	•	•	• T	• T	• T	• T	• T
Structure (simple, compound, complex, compound-complex)	•	•	•	•	•	• T	• T

• instructional opportunity   **T** tested in standardized te

	Pre-K	K	1	2	3	4	5	6
(subjects/predicates: complete, simple, compound; phrases; clauses)				•T	•	•T	•T	•T
ments and run-on sentences		•	•	•	•	•	•	•
oine sentences, elaborate			•	•	•	•	•	•
of speech: nouns, verbs and verb tenses, adjectives, adverbs, pronouns and antecedents, ctions, prepositions, interjections		•	•T	•T	•T	•T	•T	•T
ect-verb agreement		•	•T	•	•	•T	•T	•T
oun agreement/referents			•T	•	•	•T	•T	•T
laced modifiers						•	•T	•T
sed words					•	•	•	•T
tives; avoid double negatives					•	•	•	•

anics in Writing

	Pre-K	K	1	2	3	4	5	6
lization (first word in sentence, proper nouns and adjectives, pronoun *I*, titles, and so on)	•	•	•T	•T	•T	•T	•T	•T
ation (apostrophe, comma, period, question mark, exclamation mark, quotation marks, and so on)		•	•T	•T	•T	•T	•T	•T

lling

	Pre-K	K	1	2	3	4	5	6
ndependently by using pre-phonetic knowledge, knowledge of letter names, sound-letter knowledge	•	•	•	•	•	•	•	•
und-letter knowledge to spell	•	•	•	•	•	•	•	•
sonants: single, double, blends, digraphs, silent letters, and unusual consonant spellings			•	•	•	•	•	•
els: short, long, *r*-controlled, digraphs, diphthongs, less common vowel patterns, schwa			•	•	•	•	•	•
owledge of word structure to spell				•	•	•	•	•
e words and affixes (inflections, prefixes, suffixes), possessives, contractions and compound words				•	•	•	•	•
k and Latin roots, syllable patterns, multisyllabic words				•	•	•	•	•
igh-frequency, irregular words		•	•	•	•	•	•	•
requently misspelled words correctly, including homophones or homonyms				•	•	•	•	•
eaning relationships to spell					•	•	•	•

dwriting

	Pre-K	K	1	2	3	4	5	6
creasing control of penmanship, including pencil grip, paper position, posture, stroke	•	•	•	•				
egibly, with control over letter size and form; letter slant; and letter, word, and sentence spacing		•	•	•	•	•	•	•
owercase and capital letters	•	•	•	•				
uscript	•	•	•	•	•	•		•
ive				•	•	•	•	•
numerals	•	•	•					

ening and Speaking

	Pre-K	K	1	2	3	4	5	6
ning Skills and Strategies								
to a variety of presentations attentively and politely	•	•	•	•	•	•	•	•
onitor comprehension while listening, using a variety of skills and strategies	•	•	•	•	•	•	•	•
for a purpose								
enjoyment and appreciation	•	•	•					•
xpand vocabulary and concepts	•	•	•	•	•	•		•
otain information and ideas	•	•	•	•	•	•	•	•
llow oral directions	•	•	•	•	•	•	•	•
nswer questions and solve problems	•	•	•	•	•			•
articipate in group discussions	•	•	•	•	•	•	•	•
entify and analyze the musical elements of literary language	•	•	•	•	•	•	•	•
ain knowledge of one's own culture, the culture of others, and the common elements of cultures	•	•	•	•	•	•	•	•
nize formal and informal language				•	•	•	•	•
critically to distinguish fact from opinion and to analyze and evaluate ideas, information, experiences		•		•	•	•	•	•
te a speaker's delivery				•	•	•	•	•
ret a speaker's purpose, perspective, persuasive techniques, verbal and nonverbal messages, and rhetorical devices						•	•	•
king Skills and Strategies								
clearly, accurately, and fluently, using appropriate delivery for a variety of audiences, and purposes	•	•	•	•	•			•
roper intonation, volume, pitch, modulation, and phrasing		•	•	•	•	•	•	•
with a command of standard English conventions	•	•	•	•	•	•		•
propriate language for formal and informal settings	•	•	•	•	•	•	•	•

Speak for a purpose	Pre-K	K	1	2	3	4	5
To ask and answer questions	•	•	•	•	•	•	•
To give directions and instructions	•	•	•	•	•	•	•
To retell, paraphrase, or explain information			•	•	•	•	•
To communicate needs and share ideas and experiences	•	•	•	•	•	•	•
To participate in conversations and discussions	•	•	•	•	•	•	•
To express an opinion	•	•	•	•	•	•	•
To deliver dramatic recitations, interpretations, or performances	•	•	•	•	•	•	•
To deliver presentations or oral reports (narrative, descriptive, persuasive, and informational)	•	•	•	•	•	•	•
Stay on topic	•	•	•	•	•	•	
Use appropriate verbal and nonverbal elements (such as facial expression, gestures, eye contact, posture)	•	•	•	•	•	•	•
Identify and/or demonstrate methods to manage or overcome communication anxiety						•	•

Viewing/Media	Pre-K	K	1	2	3	4	5
Interact with and respond to a variety of print and non-print media for a range of purposes	•	•	•	•	•	•	•
Compare and contrast print, visual, and electronic media					•	•	•
Analyze and evaluate media			•	•	•	•	•
Recognize purpose, bias, propaganda, and persuasive techniques in media messages			•	•	•	•	•

Research and Study Skills

Understand and Use Graphic Sources	Pre-K	K	1	2	3	4	5
Advertisement			•	•	•	•	•
Chart/table	•	•	•	•	•	•	•
Diagram/scale drawing			•	•	•	•	•
Graph (bar, circle, line, picture)		•	•	•	•	•	•
Illustration, photograph, caption, label	•	•	•	•	•	•	•
Map/globe	•	•	•	•	•	•	•
Order form/application						•	•
Poster/announcement	•	•	•	•	•	•	•
Schedule						•	•
Sign	•	•	•	•		•	
Time line				•	•	•	•

Understand and Use Reference Sources	Pre-K	K	1	2	3	4	5
Know and use parts of a book to locate information	•	•	•	•	•	•	•
Use alphabetical order			•	•	•	•	
Understand purpose, structure, and organization of reference sources (print, electronic, media, Internet)	•	•	•	•	•	•	•
Almanac						•	•
Atlas		•		•	•	•	•
Card catalog/library database				•	•	•	•
Dictionary/glossary		•	•	•	• T	• T	• T
Encyclopedia			•	•	•	•	•
Magazine/periodical				•	•	•	•
Newspaper and Newsletter			•	•	•	•	•
Readers' Guide to Periodical Literature						•	•
Technology (computer and non-computer electronic media)		•		•	•	•	•
Thesaurus				•	•	•	•

Study Skills and Strategies	Pre-K	K	1	2	3	4	5
Adjust reading rate			•	•	•	•	•
Clarify directions	•	•	•	•	•	•	•
Outline				•	•	•	•
Skim and scan			•	•	•	•	•
SQP3R						•	•
Summarize		•		•	•	•	•
Take notes, paraphrase, and synthesize			•	•	•	•	•
Use graphic and semantic organizers to organize information		•	•	•	•	•	•

• instructional opportunity   **T** tested in standardized tes

Taking Skills and Strategies	Pre-K	K	1	2	3	4	5	6
tand the question, the vocabulary of tests, and key words			•	•	•	•	•	•
the question; use information from the text (stated or inferred)		•	•	•	•	•	•	•
cross texts				•	•	•	•	•
ete the sentence				•	•	•	•	•

nology/New Literacies	Pre-K	K	1	2	3	4	5	6
Computer Electronic Media								
apes/CDs, video tapes/DVDs	•	•	•	•	•	•	•	•
elevision, and radio		•	•	•	•	•	•	•
uter Programs and Services: Basic Operations and Concepts								
curate computer terminology	•	•	•	•	•	•	•	•
name, locate, open, save, delete, and organize files			•	•	•	•	•	•
ut and output devices (such as mouse, keyboard, monitor, printer, touch screen)	•	•	•	•	•	•	•	•
sic keyboarding skills		•	•	•	•	•	•	•
nsible Use of Technology Systems and Software								
ooperatively and collaboratively with others; follow acceptable use policies	•	•	•	•	•	•	•	•
nize hazards of Internet searches			•	•	•	•	•	•
ct intellectual property					•	•	•	•
mation and Communication Technologies: Information Acquisition								
ectronic web (non-linear) navigation, online resources, databases, keyword searches			•	•	•	•	•	•
sual and non-textual features of online resources	•	•	•	•	•	•	•	•
t inquiry			•	•	•	•	•	•
ify questions			•	•	•	•	•	•
te, select, and collect information			•	•	•	•	•	•
ze information			•	•	•	•	•	•
luate electronic information sources for accuracy, relevance, bias				•	•	•	•	•
derstand bias/subjectivity of electronic content (about this site, author search, date created)					•	•	•	•
hesize information				•	•	•	•	•
municate findings				•	•	•	•	•
up strategies (such as clicking *Back, Forward,* or *Undo;* redoing a search; trimming the URL)			•	•	•	•	•	•
unication								
orate, publish, present, and interact with others		•	•	•	•	•	•	•
line resources (e-mail, bulletin boards, newsgroups)			•	•	•	•	•	•
variety of multimedia formats			•	•	•	•	•	•
em Solving								
the appropriate software for the task	•	•	•	•	•	•	•	•
chnology resources for solving problems and making informed decisions			•	•	•	•	•	•
ine when technology is useful					•	•	•	•

Research Process	Pre-K	K	1	2	3	4	5	6
e and narrow the topic; frame and revise questions for inquiry		•	•	•	•	•	•	•
e and evaluate appropriate reference sources			•	•	•	•	•	•
and collect information	•	•	•	•	•	•	•	•
otes/record findings				•	•	•	•	•
ne and compare information				•	•	•	•	•
te, interpret, and draw conclusions about key information			•	•	•	•	•	•
arize information			•	•	•	•	•	•
an outline					•	•	•	•
ze content systematically			•	•	•	•	•	•
unicate information			•	•	•	•	•	•
e and present a report				•	•	•	•	•
lude citations						•	•	•
spect intellectual property/plagiarism						•	•	•
ct and organize visual aids		•	•	•	•	•	•	•

Teacher's Edition

Text

KWL Strategy: The KWL Interactive Reading Strategy was developed and is used by permission of Donna Ogle, National-Louis University, Evanston, Illinois, co-author of *Reading Today and Tomorrow*, Holt, Rinehart & Winston Publishers, 1988. (See also *The Reading Teacher*, February 1986, pp. 564–570.)

Artists

Scott Gustafson: cover, page i

Photographs

Every effort has been made to secure permission and provide appropriate credit for photographic material. The publisher deeply regrets any omission and pledges to correct errors called to its attention in subsequent editions.

Unless otherwise acknowledged, all photographs are the property of Scott Foresman, a division of Pearson Education.

Photo locators denoted as follows: Top (T), Center (C), Bottom (B), Left (L), Right (R), Background (Bkgd).

Page 322K: Hemera Technologies